TEXTBOOK

Obligations:
THE LAW OF TORT

FIFTH EDITION

D G CRACKNELL
LLB, of the Middle Temple, Barrister

OLD BAILEY PRESS

OLD BAILEY PRESS
at Holborn College, Woolwich Road,
Charlton, London, SE7 8LN

First published 1997
Fifth edition 2005

© Holborn College Ltd 2005

ISBN 1 85836 606 2

British Library Cataloguing-in-Publication.
A CIP Catalogue record for this book is
available from the British Library.

Acknowledgement
The publishers and author would
like to thank the Incorporated
Council of Law Reporting for
England and Wales for kind
permission to reproduce extracts
from the Weekly Law Reports, and
Butterworths for their kind
permission to reproduce extracts
from the All England Law Reports.

Printed and bound in Great Britain

Contents

8 The Duty of Care and 'Protected Parties'   *111*

Introduction – The character of the claimant – Judges and legal representatives – Police – Fire brigade – Ambulance service – Negligence in the exercise of a statutory power

9 Negligence: Breach of the Duty   *138*

Introduction – The reasonable man – Foreseeability – Magnitude of the risk – Utility of the defendant's activity – The practicality of precautions – Common practice – Children – Sport – Emergencies – Professionals – Proof of the breach – Res ipsa loquitur

10 Negligence: Causation   *160*

Introduction – But for test – Pre-existing condition – Omissions – Multiple causes – Proof of causation – Loss of a chance – Successive causes

11 Negligence: Remoteness of Damage   *171*

Introduction – *Polemis* and the directness test – *Wagon Mound* and foreseeability – Damage to the person – Damage to property – Cases where the reasonable foresight test does not apply – Intervening acts (novus actus interveniens)

12 Contributory Negligence   *185*

Introduction – The 1945 Act - the general rule – Fault – The standard of care – Children – Workmen – Rescuers – Emergencies – Causation – Apportionment

13 Volenti Non Fit Injuria   *195*

Introduction – The intentional infliction of harm – The negligent infliction of harm – Voluntariness – Agreement – Knowledge – Volenti and exclusion clauses

14 Breach of Statutory Duty   *203*

Introduction – Does the breach confer a right of action in tort? – The remedy provided in the Act – Statutes for the benefit of a class – Public right and special damage – Ambit of the statute – Defences

15 Employers' Liability   *212*

Introduction – Competent staff – Proper plant and equipment – Safe place of work – Safe system of work – The economic welfare of employees – Defences

16 Product Liability   *222*

Introduction – Historical development – Defects in the common law – The Consumer Protection Act 1987

17 Occupiers' Liability   *231*

Introduction – The scope of the 1957 Act – Who is an occupier? – Visitors – Premises – The common duty of care – Children – Common calling – Warning of danger – Independent contractors – Volenti – Contributory negligence – Contractors – Damage to property – Trespassers – Exclusion of the occupier's duty – Liability of independent contractors who are not occupiers – Liability of vendors and lessors – Liability of builders

Preface

Old Bailey Press textbooks are written specifically for students. Whatever their course they will find our books clear and concise, providing comprehensive and up-to-date coverage. Written by specialists in their field, our textbooks are reviewed and updated on a regular basis. A companion 150 Leading Cases, Revision WorkBook and Cracknell's Statutes are also published.

This *Obligations: The Law of Tort* textbook is designed for use by any undergraduates who have Tort within their syllabus. It will be equally useful for all CPE/LLDip students who must study Tort Law as one of their 'core' subjects.

In this edition, many recent cases are covered. They include a number of important decisions of the House of Lords such as *Rees* v *Darlington Memorial Hospital NHS Trust* [2003] 4 All ER 987 (damages where healthy child born after negligent sterilisation operation), *Moy* v *Pettman Smith* [2005] 1 All ER 903 (counsel's 'door-of-the-court' advice not negligent), *D* v *East Berkshire Community Health NHS Trust* (2005) The Times 22 April (child care professionals owe no duty of care to parents against whom they make unfounded allegations of child abuse) and *Mirvahedy* v *Henley* [2003] 2 All ER 401 (interpretation of provisions of Animals Act 1971).

Note is also made of relevant provisions of the Countryside and Rights of Way Act 2000 (which came into force on 19 September 2004), the Children Act 2004 and the Civil Partnership Act 2004 (which comes into force on 5 December 2005).

In preparing this edition, account has been taken of materials available at 22 April 2005.

Table of Cases

Table of Statutes and Other Materials

1

Introduction

1.1 Introduction

The law of tort is an exciting and fascinating subject. It is also a subject of some considerable difficulty and one which demands considerable legal skills. It is customary to commence a book on the law of tort by attempting to frame a definition of tort, but such an approach will not be adopted here because these attempts are either so vague as to be meaningless or they are too restrictive and only apply to certain torts with the result that they are downright misleading. All that will be said at this stage is that the word tort (or the Latin equivalent 'tortum') is derived from the concept of a wrong.

Instead this Chapter will commence by highlighting some of the difficult issues current in tort law, then it will proceed to identify some of the interests protected by the law of tort and it will conclude by distinguishing between tort and other related legal subjects.

1.2 Current difficulties in the law of tort

There are three current difficulties in the law of tort which are worthy of some discussion. The first difficulty lies in finding acceptable control devices for the tort of negligence. This is an issue which has taxed both the judiciary and academics alike. The test laid down by the House of Lords in the case of *Anns* v *Merton London Borough Council* [1978] AC 728 (discussed further in Chapter 6) seemed to herald the prospect of a considerable widening of the ambit of liability in negligence. In retrospect the late 1970s and the early 1980s was a period of considerable expansion for the tort of negligence. By contrast the latter half of the 1980s and the early part of the 1990s has been a period of restriction when the judiciary have refused to extend the tort of negligence in the way that was done towards the end of the 1970s. This process of restriction reached its height in *Murphy* v *Brentwood District Council* [1991] 1 AC 398 when the House of Lords overruled its own decision in *Anns*.

This difficulty of drawing the line between situations where a duty of care is owed and situations where no duty is owed is an issue with which all students of the law of tort must grapple. Nor is the issue a mere academic quibble. The expansion of the law of tort in cases such as *Ross* v *Caunters* [1980] Ch 297 and *Junior Books Ltd* v *The Veitchi Co Ltd* [1983] 1 AC 520 (discussed further in Chapter 7) took tort into areas which were traditionally the domain of the law of contract and these cases posed fundamental questions about the relationship between tort and contract. In particular, these cases seemed to constitute a fundamental attack upon the doctrine of privity of contract. Indeed, in *Junior Books* Lord Roskill opined that

> 'Today the proper control lies not in asking whether the proper remedy should lie in contract ... or tort ... but in the first instance in establishing the relevant principles and then in deciding whether the particular case falls within or without those principles.'

Yet the House of Lords today has chosen to re-emphasise the distinction between contract and tort. Thus, in *D & F Estates* v *Church Commissioners for England* [1989] AC 177 Lord Bridge held that a claim for the cost of repairing a defect in the product itself lay, if at all, in contract and not in tort. For him, the division between contract and tort was fundamental; it was no mere label to be applied after identifying the relevant, underlying principle. This issue of the relationship between tort and contract is one to which we shall return at various stages of the book.

The second current difficulty in the law of tort lies in ascertaining the function which lies behind the corpus of rules that make up the law of tort. Two principal functions may be discerned. The first is to compensate the victims of civil wrongs. Here the emphasis is upon compensation rather than upon punishment. A clear expression of this policy can be seen in the judgment of Lord Reid in *Cassell* v *Broome* [1972] AC 1027. In this case the claimant sought, inter alia, exemplary damages in respect of a defamatory statement published about him by the defendants. The function of exemplary damages is to punish the defendant for the wrong which he has done rather than to compensate the claimant for the damage done to him. The House of Lords took the opportunity to make some general observations about the availability of exemplary damages in tort. Lord Reid said that tort damages have a compensatory aim and that to grant a claimant an award of exemplary damages against the defendants was to confuse the function of the civil law, which was to 'compensate', with that of the criminal law, which was to 'inflict deterrent and punitive penalties'. He said that to allow the punishment of defendants in tort was to 'contravene almost every principle which has been evolved for the protection of offenders'. For example, there was no definition of the offence except that the defendant's conduct must be oppressive, the punishment was left to the jury rather than to an experienced judge, there was no limit on the punishment which could be handed out except that it must not be unreasonable and there was no effective appeal against sentence. On the other hand Lord Wilberforce took the view that it 'cannot lightly be taken for granted ... that the purpose of the law of tort is compensation' or that there is something anomalous about including within an award of damages at civil law a punitive element. He also noted that, at a practical level, the majority conceded that aggravated damages were available in a wider range of circumstances than exemplary damages and he argued that it was not clear exactly where the boundary line between exemplary and aggravated damages lay, so, he claimed, it was better to concede that exemplary damages were available rather than confuse juries by telling them they could award aggravated damages but not exemplary damages (see further Chapter 30, section 30.2).

The second principal function of the law of tort, it is said, is to deter people from committing wrongs which inflict damage upon other people or their property. In essence it teaches people that wrongful acts do not pay and, as a consequence, people will act more carefully. Certainly there are cases where the law of tort can be said to have a deterrent effect. For example the tort of defamation has an impact upon publishers and upon the conduct of the national press. The expansion of the tort of negligence has encouraged governing bodies of professions, such as the accountancy profession, to draw up codes of practice or statements of standard practice to guide their members as to what is expected of them by the tort of negligence and by the public at large. Despite these developments there are a number of criticisms which have been levelled against the idea that tort has a deterrent function.

The first such criticism is that a very general instruction, such as the duty to take reasonable care, is so vague that it has little impact upon people's standard of behaviour. The second criticism is that, in practice, the damages are usually paid by an insurer, which significantly reduces the deterrent effect on the tortfeasor (that is the person who commits the tort) because he passes on the bill to his insurer. It is true that the passing on of the bill may lead to some increased cost to the tortfeasor, in the form of higher premiums (for example, losing a no-claims bonus) but the link between higher premiums and accident prevention is rather tenuous. Thirdly, as we shall see in Chapter 9, the standard of care demanded of a particular defendant may be so high that it is impossible for him to attain it. Where this is the case the law of tort does not have a deterrent effect because the tortfeasor cannot aspire to the standards required of him.

Nevertheless it is true to say that there has been renewed interest in the idea that deterrence is a function of the law of tort. This interest has largely come from American scholars, some of whom are economists, who have argued that tort law aims, or should aim, to reduce accident costs and the costs of accident prevention (see, in particular, Calabresi *The Cost of Accidents* (1970)). This theory is known as general deterrence. The essence of this argument is that the cost of accidents should be imposed on those who take part in the accident-causing activity and so that activity must bear the cost to society of carrying out that activity (for a critique of this theory see Atiyah *Accidents, Compensation and the Law* Chapter 24).

Yet this dichotomy between compensation and punishment (or deterrence) may be said to be a false one because it ignores a third purpose of the law of tort, which is to prevent unjust enrichment. There are a group of cases where the remedy which has been granted to the claimant has sought to strip the defendant of the gain that he has made at the expense of the claimant as a result of the commission of a wrong or a tort. One case which is useful to consider here is *Reading* v *Attorney-General* [1951] AC 507. Sergeant Reading was in the habit of travelling on lorries in Egypt while wearing his army uniform. The reason for his doing so was to enable smugglers to get their lorries carrying illicit goods past army checkpoints. He was paid a considerable sum of money for his participation in the smuggling. After he had been caught the question arose as to who was entitled to the gains which Sergeant Reading had made; was it himself or the Crown? The House of Lords held that the Crown were entitled to the proceeds of Sergeant Reading's wrongdoing. The aim of the award of damages was therefore to deprive the defendant of his unjust enrichment and was measured, not by reference to the *loss* to the claimant, but by reference to the *gain* to the defendant. These damages may be called restitutionary damages. There is a clear difference here between the sum awarded and the sum which would have been awarded had the Crown sued for compensation for its loss because it is clear that the Crown had suffered no loss. It could be argued that the aim of the award of damages was to deter such conduct in the future but it is suggested that deterrence can be distinguished from the prevention of unjust enrichment. Where the aim of an award of damages is to strip the defendant of his unjust enrichment, the sum recoverable is measured definitively by the gain which the defendant has made. But, when the aim of the award of damages is to deter, the amount of the gain made by the defendant is only one factor to which the court will have regard; the amount awarded may therefore exceed the gain which the defendant has made as a result of his tort. There are a number of cases where restitutionary damages have been awarded (see generally Birks *An Introduction to the Law of Restitution* Chapter X). It is beyond the scope of our present discussion to consider when restitutionary damages may be awarded by a court. But it should not be forgotten that tort is not definitively about compensation for loss; it may also be about the reversal of unjust enrichments.

The third difficulty relates to the scope of the law of tort. For example, is breach of confidence a tort? What about other equitable wrongs? One problem which we have here is an historical one; namely that our present law of tort is almost completely derived from actions at law, not actions in equity. Wrongdoing in equity is often discussed in a course on the law of trusts under the heading of constructive trusts. Yet if we say, as we do, that 'tort' simply means 'a wrong' then it is very difficult to explain why these equitable wrongs are excluded from our tort syllabus. If our subject were to be called the law of wrongs, we would be compelled to consider these equity cases. Can we continue to allow the historical division between equity and law to play tricks on us to the extent that it has fooled us into locating equitable wrongs in a course which has nothing to do with wrongs but with the institution of a trust? It is suggested that this will become a matter of hot debate in years to come. Certainly an act carried out with the intent of assisting a tort is not itself a free-standing tort: see the decision of the House of Lords in *Credit Lyonnais Bank Nederland NV* v *Export Credits Guarantee Department* [1999] 1 All ER 929.

The fourth, and final, issue of difficulty in tort law concerns the future of the law of tort. Approximately 75 per cent of cases which are set down for a hearing in the Queen's Bench Division are personal injury cases. However, of these cases, only about 1 per cent actually come to a hearing. The rest are settled out of court or are withdrawn. Of course in all these cases the claimant must prove that the defendant was negligent before he can recover. This raises the extremely important question of why it is necessary for the claimant to prove that the defendant was at fault before he can recover. The following example may help us to consider the issue.

Patrick, aged 42 and a father of four children, suffered a major heart attack in 1986 which left him an invalid who would be unable to work for the rest of his life. Patrick was a professor earning £45,000 per year. He is unable to look after himself and his wife has had to give up work to look after him.

Glanville, aged 45 and also a father of four children, was severely injured in a car crash caused by Brian, whose consciousness had been impaired by a stroke as he was driving. Glanville was so seriously injured that he will never return to work as an executive with a company which publishes law books. He is also unable to look after himself and his wife has had to give up work to look after him. Glanville's employers continue to pay his salary on an ex gratia basis. He is also in receipt of £250 per month under a personal insurance policy during the remaining period of his disability.

You should try to work out the remedies available to Glanville when you have read the Chapter on damages at the end of this book. Only then will you realise the extent to which the victims of torts are placed in a privileged position in comparison with other victims of misfortune in society. In many ways the needs of Patrick and Glanville are identical, but Patrick and his family are condemned to reliance upon social security and whatever personal provision they have made for such an eventuality, whereas Glanville and his family are cushioned by the damages obtainable from a tort action. What is the justification for such a disparity of treatment?

One justification is that in tort cases the accident has been caused by the negligence of the defendant and he is under a moral and legal obligation to compensate the victim. But in our example it cannot be said that Brian was morally at fault for the injuries suffered by Glanville. Nor does the tort action have a deterrent effect upon Brian because he was in no position to prevent the accident from occurring (although it may make him more careful about resuming driving).

On the other hand it should not be thought that the tort system is ideal for Glanville. The system is expensive to operate. The Pearson Commission (*Royal*

Commission on Civil Liability and Compensation for Personal Injury, Cmnd 7054, 1978) found that the cost of operating the tort system accounted for some 85 per cent of the sums paid to accident victims. The legal system is also extremely slow and cumbrous. Damages are also usually paid by means of a lump sum, which requires the courts to engage in what is no more than educated guesswork as to the future needs of the claimant. This can lead in some cases to significant under-compensation where the court's 'guess' is erroneous.

Dissatisfaction with the operation of the tort system in cases of personal injury reached such a height in New Zealand that the tort action was abolished in such cases and replaced by a comprehensive no-fault accident compensation scheme. This scheme covers all accidental injury, but it does not cover diseases, with the exception of occupational diseases; (on the subject of diseases see Stapleton *Disease and the Compensation Debate*). The scheme replaces the victim's financial loss at the rate of 80 per cent of his earnings before the accident. These payments are made weekly and are subject to a maximum amount. In respect of permanent injury or disability a lump sum may be payable, assessed objectively by reference to a schedule of tariffs, but these sums are low in comparison to what can be obtained in a tort action in this country. The scheme is funded by levies on motor vehicles, employers and employees and by funding out of general taxation.

The Pearson Commission did not recommend the abolition of the tort action in this way because their terms of reference did not permit them to do so. The Commission did recommend a small extension of strict liability in certain areas and proposed an extension of the existing industrial injuries scheme to motor accident victims to be funded by a tax on petrol. However there seems to be little political interest at the moment in the reform of the tort system in Britain. But with the anomalies inherent in the present system and the enormous disparities between the treatment of tort victims and other victims of misfortune in society it cannot be long before further consideration is given to the future of the tort action in Britain.

1.3 The interests protected

The law of tort provides protection for a wide range of interests. Such protection may be obtained in one or more of three ways. The first, and most common, way is through an action for damages to compensate the victim for the loss which he has incurred. The second way in which protection may be obtained is through an application to court for injunctive relief. An injunction generally has the effect of prohibiting the defendant from doing certain acts. For example, an employer who knows that a trade union is about to engage in industrial action which will involve the commission of economic torts against him, which will result in the shut down of his factory, is likely to seek injunctive relief to prevent the strike from taking place rather than wait until the damage is done and then seek to recover damages at a later date. The third way in which a victim of a tort may obtain protection is through self help. The law of tort is, however, extremely reluctant to allow people to take the law into their own hands and so this option is only available within extremely narrow bounds. For example, the person who is the victim of the tort of battery may take reasonable steps to defend himself and a person may, in certain circumstances, take steps to abate a nuisance. The following will provide a brief account of some of the interests protected by the law of tort. These issues will be amplified in subsequent Chapters of the book.

The law of tort provides protection for a person's personal security. Thus, where a person is assaulted by another then the victim may have an action in the tort of battery. Similarly where a person is injured as the result of the negligence of another the victim may have an action in the tort of negligence and recover damages in respect of his injuries. The law of tort also provides protection for a person's reputation. A person whose character is damaged by the writings or speeches of another person may have a claim against that person in defamation for libel or slander.

The law of tort provides protection for a person's property. Thus a person who interferes with another's chattel, such as his motor car, may commit one of the torts of interference with chattels, such as conversion. The torts of trespass to land and nuisance provide protection for a person in the use and enjoyment of his land.

The law of tort may also provide protection for a person's interest in the life of another. Thus where the 'breadwinner' in a family is killed due to the negligence of another, then the dependants of the victim may seek compensation in respect of the losses which they have incurred through the loss of the 'breadwinner'. Finally the law of tort provides protection for interests of a purely economic nature. As we shall see the law of tort has traditionally been reluctant to impose liability for negligently inflicted 'pure' economic loss, but the same restraint has not been shown where that loss has been inflicted intentionally. Thus employers who suffer loss as a result of the commission of economic torts during the course of industrial action may have a cause of action against those responsible for the commission of these torts.

1.4 Tort and other legal subjects

Tort and crime

Crimes are those acts and, on rare occasions, omissions which society as a whole prescribes as being completely unacceptable. Crimes are normally prosecuted by the state through the criminal courts, whereas a tort is a civil action which an individual prosecutes in a civil court at his discretion.

There are, however, torts, such as assault and battery, which may also be actionable as crimes and a civil remedy may be obtained after the completion of the criminal proceedings. The result of the criminal proceedings may be used as evidence in the civil claim and so it is often advisable for the victim to wait for the outcome of the criminal proceedings before launching his civil action. Where the person who committed the tort is acquitted in the criminal proceedings, this is not conclusive evidence in the civil action because the standard of proof in the criminal action is beyond reasonable doubt, whereas it is on the balance of probabilities in the civil action. So the fact of acquittal does not mean that the victim will not be able to prove his civil case on the balance of probabilities. The person who is the victim of a criminal offence may also seek compensation through the Criminal Injuries Compensation Scheme.

Tort and contract

Tort and contract are both matters of civil law and there is a much closer relationship between tort and contract than there is between tort and crime. The exact relationship between them is a matter of some controversy and, indeed, the distinction between the two has been denied by some who have sought to argue that English law now has a law of obligations which encompasses both tort and contract. The traditional distinction drawn between tort and contract is that obligations are imposed in tort, whereas in contract obligations are consensually assumed. This dichotomy cannot be completely accepted because some contractual terms are imposed by law (such as the implied conditions relating to title, fitness for purpose etc. in the Sale of Goods Act 1979) and the standard of care in the tort of negligence can be regulated by a contract between the tortfeasor and the victim of the tort.

It is sometimes argued that contract and tort exist to protect different interests. The law of contract is supposed to protect the expectation interest, that is, an award of damages in contract is supposed to put the claimant in the position he would have been in had the contract been performed. On the other hand an award of damages in tort is supposed to protect the reliance interest, that is, it is supposed to put the victim of the tort in the position he would have been in had the tort never been committed. This can be seen in personal injuries cases where the object of an award of damages is to put the claimant in the position he would have been in, so far as this can be done by a monetary award, had the tort not been committed. But this division is not wholly acceptable either. Contract law is not committed to the wholehearted protection of the expectation interest, as doctrines such as mitigation and remoteness show. There have also been cases such as *Ross* v *Caunters* (above) and *Junior Books Ltd* v *The Veitchi Co Ltd* (above) where the effect of the tort action was to protect the expectation interest because the claimant was put in the position he would have been in had the defendant carried out his obligation properly. These cases are, however, a source of some controversy and they will be discussed in greater detail in Chapters 6 and 7 when further consideration will be given to the relationship between contract and tort.

2

Parties to an Action in Tort

2.1 Introduction

2.2 Liability

2.3 Immunity

2.1 Introduction

As a general rule anyone may bring an action in tort. Minors may sue in tort through their 'next friend'. In *McKay* v *Essex Area Health Authority* [1982] QB 1166 the Court of Appeal held that, although no action lay in respect of negligently bringing a child into the world, a child may bring an action in tort in respect of damage done to it between conception and birth as the result of the negligence of those who are looking after its mother's health. In *Burton* v *Islington Health Authority* [1993] QB 204 the Court of Appeal affirmed that, where a child was born suffering from disabilities caused as a result of medical negligence, the child could bring a negligence claim even though the child was not a person in the eyes of the law at the time when the damage was negligently inflicted. Dillon LJ rejected the argument that the passing of the Congential Disabilities (Civil Liability) Act 1976 precluded the courts from recognising the existence of a duty of care in respect of damage suffered prior to the coming into force of the Act. But he did leave open the question whether the estate of a still-born child could recover damages in respect of damage inflicted prior to its birth.

Both *McKay* and *Burton* concerned claimants who suffered damage prior to the coming into force of the Congenital Disabilities (Civil Liability) Act 1976. Now a child is given a cause of action under the 1976 Act where it is born disabled as the result of an occurrence which either affected the ability of either parent to have a normal, healthy child, or affected the mother during the pregnancy, or affected the child in the course of its birth, so that the child is born with disabilities which it would not otherwise have had. Section 1(3) further provides that the defendant is answerable to the child 'if he was liable in tort to the parent or would, if sued in due time, have been so' liable and that it is no answer to the child's claim that there could not have been such liability because the parent suffered no actionable injury. So the child's action is rather unusual in that it is derived from the defendant's tortious duty to the parents. Furthermore s4(5) provides that in respect of a birth occurring after the Act came into force the Act 'replaces any law in force before its passing, whereby a person could be liable to a child in respect of disabilities with which it might be born'.

The Law Reform (Husband and Wife) Act 1962 removed the anomaly which prohibited a husband and wife from suing each other in tort. But under s1(2) of the Act the action will be stayed if no substantial benefit would accrue to either party from it or if the action would be more appropriately dealt with under s17 of the Married Women's Property Act 1882.

A civil partnership is a relationship between two people of the same sex (civil partners) which is formed when they register as civil partners of each other: s1(1) of the Civil Partnership Act 2004. The commencement date for this Act is 5 December 2005. Section 69 provides that where an action in tort is brought by one civil partner against the other during the subsistence of the civil partnership, the court may stay the proceedings if it appears:

> '(a) that no substantial benefit would accrue to either civil partner from the continuation of the proceedings, or
> (b) that the question or questions in issue could more conveniently be disposed of on an application under section 66.'

Section 66 stipulates that 'in any question between the civil partners in a civil partnership as to title to or possession of property, either civil partner may apply to ... the High Court or ... such county court as may be prescribed by rules of court [and that, on] such an application, the court may make such order with respect to the property as it thinks fit (including an order for the sale of the property).'

2.2 Liability

Subject to rules relating to immunity from tortious liability anybody may be sued in tort. The following parties are worthy of further comment.

The Crown

At common law the Crown could not be sued in tort (see *Tobin* v *R* (1864) 16 CBNS 310). However this immunity was removed by the Crown Proceedings Act 1947, which rendered the Crown liable in tort, as if it were a private person of full age and capacity, in respect of torts committed by its servants or agents. The appropriate minister of the Crown is made the nominal defendant and, where there is no appropriate minister, the Attorney-General is made the defendant.

Section 40(1) of the Act provides that the Queen herself may not be sued in tort. Section 2(5) provides a further exception in relation to anything done or omitted to be done by any person while discharging any responsibilities of a judicial nature (although the immunity does not extend to acts which are of an administrative nature: see *Welsh* v *Chief Constable of the Merseyside Police* [1993] 1 All ER 692).

Finally, s10 of the 1974 Act provided that the Crown and members of the armed forces are immune from actions by other members of the armed forces for death or personal injury while on duty or on military premises. This provision was repealed by the Crown Proceedings (Armed Forces) Act 1987, but only prospectively, although its effect can be revived by the Secretary of State 'by reason of any imminent national danger or of any great emergency'. In *Matthews* v *Ministry of Defence* [2003] 1 All ER 689; (2003) The Times 14 February the claimant alleged that, in the course of his service in the Royal Navy from 1955 to 1968, in various boiler rooms he had been exposed to asbestos fibres and, as a result, that he had developed asbestos-related injuries. Taking a preliminary point, the defendant contended that it was immune from liability by virtue of s10 Crown Proceedings Act 1947. The claimant argued that this provision is incompatible with art 6(1) of the European Convention for the Protection of Human Rights and Fundamental Freedoms. The House of Lords agreed with the Court of Appeal that the defendant's preliminary point was valid. In exempting the Crown from liability in tort in respect of the Armed Services, s10 of the 1947 Act had substituted a no-fault system of compensation for claims for damages. That was a matter of substantive domestic law which gave rise to no civil right to which the fair trial requirements of art 6 of the European Convention, as scheduled to the Human Rights Act 1998, might apply.

As to the extent of the immunity of the Ministry of Defence: see *Multiple Claimants* v *Ministry of Defence* (2003) The Times 21 May (no duty to maintain safe system of work for service personnel engaged with enemy in course of combat). In the absence of any imminent attack or threat of attack, no defence of combat immunity is available where the British Army has negligently caused injury while peace-keeping: *Bici* v *Ministry of Defence* (2004) The Times 11 June.

Corporations

It is clearly established that a corporation, which is a legal entity separate and distinct from its members, may commit torts and have torts committed against it. However, there are certain torts which, by their very nature, cannot be committed against a corporation, such as assault or false imprisonment. Corporations are vicariously liable for the torts committed by their employees in the course of their employment. A corporation may also be personally liable where the person who commits the tort is so much in command of the company that his acts are treated as if they were the acts of the company (see *Lennard's Carrying Co* v *Asiatic Petroleum Co Ltd* [1915] AC 705). In the latter case the mere fact that the person in charge of the company has committed a tort or has committed a tort in the course of an ultra vires act will not have the effect of making the tort ultra vires the company (*Campbell* v *Paddington Corporation* [1911] 1 KB 869 and see also s35 of the

Companies Act 1985 (as amended by the Companies Act 1989). Where, however, the employee has committed a tort during the course of an ultra vires act then the corporation may be able to show that the employee was acting outside the scope of his employment and so escape the imposition of liability.

Unincorporated associations

Unlike corporations, unincorporated associations have no legal personality of their own which is separate from that of their membership. Thus clubs and similar unincorporated associations cannot sue or be sued in their own right – see, eg, *R v Darlington Borough Council, ex parte The Association of Darlington Taxi Owners* (1994) The Independent 13 January. The members are themselves jointly and severally liable for their torts but only for their own torts and not for the torts of other members. In some cases a representative action may be brought against an unincorporated association where all the members have a common interest to defend (for example, where a claim is made against a club for damages under the Occupiers' Liability Act 1957 but see *Robertson v Ridley* [1989] 2 All ER 474).

Such an action will be brought against a representative of the club, such as the secretary or chairman: see, eg, *Jones v Northampton Borough Council* (1990) The Independent 25 May. The claimant slipped while playing football at the defendant council's sports centre. The cause of his slip was that water had leaked through a hole in the roof and was lying on the playing surface. Prior to the commencement of the competition in which the claimant was playing, the council informed the chairman of the claimant's sports club that there was water on the pitch. The chairman nevertheless decided to commence the competition. The council settled the claimant's claim and then sought a full indemnity from the club chairman under the Civil Liability (Contribution) Act 1978 (see Chapter 3, section 3.5). The chairman argued that, as a matter of law, no relevant duty of care was owed by one club member to another. The Court of Appeal rejected this argument and held that the council was entitled to a full indemnity from the chairman on the ground that he was in breach of his duty of care to the claimant. Ralph Gibson LJ stated that:

> '... [w]here a club officer or committee member, while performing some task for other club members, learned of circumstances giving rise to risk of injury to club members acting as he knew they would if not told of the danger, then it was open to the court to find that he owed them a duty of care and, if he gave no warning, that he was in breach of it.'

The chairman therefore enjoyed no immunity from suit in tort and was liable to the claimant. See also Chapter 28, section 28.4.

Trade unions

In the famous case of *Taff Vale Railway Co v Amalgamated Society of Railway*

Servants [1901] AC 426 it was held that registered trade unions had the capacity to sue and be sued in their own name, but much of the relevant law is now to be found in the Trade Union and Labour Relations (Consolidation) Act 1992, as amended. For example, specific provision is made for liability in certain proceedings in tort (s20) and as to the limit on the amount that may be awarded against them by way of damages: s22. Again, protection is given for tort liabilities in respect of certain acts done in contemplation or furtherance of a trade dispute (s219) and picketing is covered by special rules: s220.

In *Electrical, Electronic, Telecommunications and Plumbing Union* v *Times Newspapers Ltd* [1980] QB 585 it was held that trade unions, as unincorporated bodies, lacked the necessary legal personality to bring an action in defamation.

Minors

There is no minimum age for the existence of tortious responsibility. Minors are judged by ordinary tort principles. However a minor cannot be sued in tort where that action would have the effect of enforcing a contract which is not binding upon him. There is no general principle in English law that a parent is vicariously responsible for the torts of his children. But a parent may be liable in negligence for giving the child the opportunity to cause damage.

Thus in *Newton* v *Edgerley* [1959] 1 WLR 1031 a father was found to be liable in negligence when he gave his 12-year-old son a .410 rifle without proper training and the son caused damage to the claimant through his use of the gun.

Insanity

The exact effect of insanity upon a defendant's liability in tort is uncertain. It is, however, clear that insanity is not recognised as a defence in tort actions. In *Morris* v *Marsden* [1952] 1 All ER 925 the defendant attacked the claimant and caused him serious injury. The defendant was found unfit to plead in the resulting criminal proceedings for assault and battery but the claimant sued the defendant in tort. It was held that the defendant was liable because he intended to commit the attack even though he had no power to appreciate that it was wrong. What has to be ascertained is whether the defendant possessed the necessary state of mind for the tort for which he is being sued. In Morriss the tort was battery and it was sufficient that the defendant intended to strike the claimant. However if the defendant's act had been involuntary he would not have been liable (for example, if the defendant had been suffering from insane automatism which had caused him to strike the claimant). It is unclear whether an insane person can commit the tort of negligence.

2.3 Immunity

In certain circumstances a defendant enjoys immunity from liability in tort. The most important of these immunities are considered below.

Statutory authority

If a statute makes what was formerly a tort at common law a lawful act then that act is no longer a tortious act. Similarly a statute may give immunity to a particular body or category of persons. For example, under s90 of the Postal Services Act 2000 normally excludes liability in tort for anything done or omitted to be done in relation to any postal packet in the course of transmission by post. On the other hand, the Immigration Act 1971 does not confer upon immigration officers immunity from suit for unlawful acts causing loss of liberty: *D* v *Secretary of State for the Home Department* (2005) The Times 10 February.

Judicial immunity

Judges enjoy an immunity from action in negligence: *Anderson* v *Gorrie* [1895] 1 QB 668 and see, too, s69 of the Courts and Legal Services Act 1990 (exemption of Secretary of State and designated judges from liability). A judge of an inferior court also enjoys such an immunity provided that he honestly believes that he is acting within his jurisdiction: *Sirros* v *Moore* [1975] QB 118, but see *McC* v *Mullan* [1984] 3 All ER 908 and *R* v *Manchester City Magistrates' Court, ex parte Davies* [1989] 1 All ER 90; and see, too, ss51 and 52 of the Justices of the Peace Act 1997 (immunity for acts within, and certain acts beyond, jurisdiction). Witnesses in legal proceedings also enjoy such an immunity (*Evans* v *London Hospital Medical College* [1981] 1 All ER 715; cf *Palmer* v *Durnford Ford (A Firm)* [1992] 1 QB 483), as do potential witnesses and persons invesitgating a crime (*Taylor* v *Serious Fraud Office* [1998] 4 All ER 801; cf *Darker* v *Chief Constable of the West Midlands Police* [2000] 4 All ER 193 (House of Lords acknowledged possibility that things done by police while investigating crime and preparing case for trial not covered by immunity) and those, such as arbitrators, who act in a quasi-judicial manner in resolving disputes between parties: *Sutcliffe* v *Thackrah* [1974] AC 727. The last immunity has, however, been confined within narrow bounds: see *Arenson* v *Casson Beckman Rutley and Co* [1977] AC 405 and *Palacath Ltd* v *Flanagan* [1985] 2 All ER 161.

In *Karling* v *Purdue* (2004) The Times 15 October the Court of Session, Outer House, held that where a pathologist had been engaged by the defence in a murder trial to provide an expert report and the accused was wrongly convicted on the basis of flawed Crown pathology which, as a result of advice given in the expert report, was not challenged at trial, the defence pathologist was immune from suit at the instance of the former accused. In the judge's opinion, the link in time and function with the criminal proceedings was more than sufficiently close to give rise to immunity.

Acts of State

Foreigners normally enjoy the same rights and incur the same liabilities in tort as British nationals. However, where an Act of State is involved then the foreigner may find that he has no cause of action where he otherwise would have had one. But an Act of State is no defence against a wrong done to a British national anywhere: see *Walker* v *Baird* [1892] AC 491.

An Act of State may be defined as 'an act of the executive as a matter of policy performed in the course of its relations with another State including its relations with the subjects of that State unless they are temporarily within the allegiance of the Crown.'

In *Buron* v *Denman* (1848) 2 Exch 167 the claimant, a Spaniard, was a slave trader in Africa. The defendant, a British naval officer, intervened in the claimant's activities and set some slaves free. The defendant's action was subsequently ratified by the Admiralty. The claimant sued the defendant for trespass. It was held that the Admiralty's approval was a defence since it meant that the defendant's act was an Act of State.

Trade unions

This is not the place to embark upon an analysis of the extent of the immunities enjoyed by trade unions and reference should be made to any of the standard works on employment law. See, however, section 2.2, *Trade unions*, above.

3

Joint and Several Tortfeasors

3.1 Introduction

Where two or more breaches of duty by different defendants cause the claimant injury, the liability of the tortfeasors (that is the persons who have committed the torts) may be: independent; several; or joint. In cases where the claimant has available to him the option of suing more than one tortfeasor, special rules have been laid down to deal with the possibility of successive actions by the claimant, and to deal with claims for contribution between defendants. We shall proceed by examining independent, several and joint liability in more detail and then conclude by examining the rules relating to contribution.

3.2 Independent liability

The claimant may suffer damage as the result of two entirely separate torts. In such a case the claimant has two completely separate causes of action against the two tortfeasors. Thus in *Baker* v *Willoughby* [1970] AC 467 (considered further at Chapter 10, section 10.7) the claimant suffered injury to his left leg as a result of the defendant's negligence. At a later date the claimant had to have the same leg amputated after he had been shot in the leg during the course of an armed robbery. It was held that each tortfeasor was liable for the injury which he caused and that the latter injury did not obliterate the liability of the first defendant. Thus the claimant is only entitled to sue each tortfeasor in respect of damage caused by that tortfeasor.

3.3 Several liability

Where tortfeasors act independently to cause the same damage to the claimant, then these tortfeasors are several (or concurrent) tortfeasors. The vital features of this form of liability are that the tortfeasors act independently and that their actions cause the same damage to the claimant. Each tortfeasor is separately liable in respect of the damage, but the claimant can only recover damages once. In *The Koursk* [1924] P 140 two ships by separate and independent negligence collided with each other. One of these ships, without further negligence, went on to collide with the claimant's ship. It was held that the defendants were separate tortfeasors, whose acts combined to produce a single injury and thus both were independently liable to the claimant.

3.4 Joint liability

Joint liability exists where two tortfeasors inflict damage on the claimant in furtherance of the common design of the tortfeasors. Thus in *Brooke* v *Bool* [1928] 2 KB 578 the defendant, a landlord, let premises to the claimant for use as a shop. The defendant remained entitled to enter the premises in the claimant's absence to check that the premises were secure. A lodger in the premises informed the defendant that he could smell gas coming from the shop. Both men investigated the shop. The lodger, with the consent and encouragement of the defendant, lit a match. This caused an explosion in which the claimant's property was damaged. It was held that the defendant was jointly liable for the damage caused by the negligence of the lodger. In such a case there is only one tort committed and so the cause of action against the tortfeasors is the same and is supported by the same evidence. Each tortfeasor is liable for the full amount, but the claimant can only recover once.

Joint liability does not only exist in the case of a tort committed in the course of a common design. It also exists in the case where an employer is held to be vicariously liable for the tort committed by his employee (see further Chapter 4). Both the employer and the employee are, therefore, joint tortfeasors. Joint liability can also arise between a principal and an agent and between an employer and his independent contractor (where the former is under a 'non-delegable' duty – see further Chapter 5).

Two principal consequences followed at common law from the finding that the parties were joint tortfeasors. The first was that judgment against one of the tortfeasors, even if it remained unsatisfied, had the effect of barring any subsequent action against the other joint tortfeasors. Judgment against one also had the effect of denying to the claimant the ability to continue the same action against the other tortfeasors. This rule was, however, reversed by s6 of the Law Reform (Married Women and Tortfeasors) Act 1935, 'the 1935 Act', which is now contained in s3 of the Civil Liability (Contribution) Act 1978, 'the 1978 Act'. Section 3 provides that:

'... judgment recovered against any person liable in respect of any ... damage shall not be a bar to an action, or to the continuance of an action, against any other person who is (apart from any such bar) jointly liable with him in respect of the same ... damage.'

But where the claimant brings an action subsequent to the first action in respect of the same damage against a joint or several (or concurrent) tortfeasor, the claimant will be refused his costs in the subsequent action or actions unless he satisfies the court that there was reasonable ground for bringing the subsequent action or actions (s4 of the 1978 Act).

The second principal consequence at common law of finding that liability was joint was that release of one joint tortfeasor, whether by accord and satisfaction or under seal, had the effect of releasing the other tortfeasors. The reasoning behind this rule was straightforward. In cases of joint liability only one tort was committed, so release of one tortfeasor must automatically result in the release of all (this rule never applied to several (concurrent) tortfeasors because the obligations of several tortfeasors are independent and so release of one tortfeasor leaves the others unaffected). This rule in cases of joint liability has never been reversed by statute, but its effect has been mitigated by the judiciary. What the courts have done is to draw a distinction between a release and an agreement not to sue and hold that the latter does not extinguish the obligation. It simply renders the obligation unenforceable against the tortfeasor released and so the cause of action against the other joint tortfeasors is preserved. The courts are reluctant to interpret an agreement with one joint tortfeasor as a release rather than an agreement not to sue (*Cutler* v *McPhail* [1962] 2 QB 292 and *Watts* v *Aldington* (1993) The Times 16 December) and this refinement makes it easier to avoid the conclusion that the action against the other tortfeasors is barred.

3.5 Contribution between tortfeasors

The general rule at common law was that neither joint nor several tortfeasors could recover contribution or an indemnity from other tortfeasors, in the absence of an express or implied agreement between them to the contrary. This was known as the rule in *Merryweather* v *Nixon* (1799) 8 TR 186. This rule was particularly unfortunate in its operation because it was a matter of chance, or solvency, which tortfeasor was sued and once judgment was entered against one of the tortfeasors he could not look to his fellow joint or several tortfeasors for contribution. This rule was reversed by s6(1)(c) of the 1935 Act, which is now contained in ss1 and 2 of the 1978 Act. These sections will be dealt with separately. Section 1 deals with entitlement to contribution and s2 with assessment of contribution.

Entitlement to contribution

Section 1(1) of the Act provides that '... any person liable in respect of any damage suffered by another person may recover contribution from any other person liable in respect of the same damage (whether jointly with him or otherwise)'. In *Birse Construction Ltd v Haisle Ltd* [1996] 2 All ER 1 it was held that s1(1) should be construed simply and directly as it stood, and that for there to be a contribution under s1(1) two parties had to be liable in respect of the same damage suffered by a third party. In *Royal Brompton Hospital NHS Trust v Hammond* [2002] 2 All ER 801 the House of Lords heard that, under a building contract in standard form an NHS Trust (the employer) employed a main contractor (the contractor) for phase one of the construction of a hospital. Architects (the architect) were engaged under the contract. The work was not completed on time. The contractor and the employer settled their dispute following arbitration and the employer now sued the architect, alleging negligence. The architect sought contribution from the contractor and the contractor applied to strike out this claim. The contractor succeeded at first instance and the Court of Appeal upheld this decision. The architect contended that the words 'the same damage' in s1(1) Civil Liability (Contribution) Act 1978 should be given a broad and purposive interpretation and therefore that the claim should not have been struck out. Their Lordships agreed that this was not the case: the words should be given their natural and ordinary meaning and, on the facts, the claim had been rightly struck out. Lord Bingham of Cornhill said:

> 'It would seem to me clear that any liability the employer might prove against the contractor and the architect would be independent and not common. The employer's claim against the contractor would be based on the contractor's delay in performing the contract and the disruption caused by the delay, and the employer's damage would be the increased cost it incurred, the sums it overpaid and the liquidated damages to which it was entitled. Its claim against the architect, based on negligent advice and certification, would not lead to the same damage because it could not be suggested that the architect's negligence had led to any delay in performing the contract.'

It should also be noted that their Lordships rejected the contention (see, eg. *Friends' Provident Life Office v Hillier Parker May & Rowden* [1995] 4 All ER 260) that the 1978 Act should be given a wide interpretation. See also Chapter 4, section 4.8.

It is further provided in s1(6) that:

> 'references ... to a person's liability in respect of any damage are references to such liability which has been or could be established in an action brought against him in England or Wales by or on behalf of the person who suffered the damage.'

The rationale behind this subsection is that a tortfeasor can only recover a contribution from someone who is, actually or hypothetically, liable to the claimant. The proper interpretation of s1(6) was considered by Hobhouse J in *R A Lister Ltd v Thomson (Shipping) Ltd* [1987] 1 WLR 1614. The defendant charterers argued that they were not 'liable' to the claimant cargo owners under s1(6) because the Court of Appeal had ordered the claimants' action against them to be stayed because the bills of lading contained an Indonesian law and jurisdiction clause. Thus the charterers could only be sued to judgment in Indonesia and not in England. When the shipowners subsequently issued a notice declaring their intention to claim a contribution from the charterers, the charterers applied to strike out the notice. But Hobhouse J refused to strike out the notice. He held that the fact that the charterers could not be sued to judgment in England was not conclusive evidence that they were not liable to the claimants because s1(6) was only concerned with whether the defendants were liable, as a matter of substantive law, to the claimants. He held that it was not concerned with 'any merely procedural considerations as to how [liability] may be enforced'. All that was required was that at the time at which the claimants suffered the damage there was a current and subsisting liability on the part of the charterers relating to the damage. Where the respondent is in fact outside the jurisdiction of the English courts that problem will be resolved by an application of the rules of procedure and not by adopting the charterers' interpretation of s1(6).

Section 1(2) provides that a defendant is entitled to recover contribution despite the fact that he has ceased to be liable to the claimant since the time when the damage occurred, provided that he was so liable immediately before the judgment or settlement in the claimant's favour. So if a tortfeasor settles with the claimant at a time when he has ceased to be liable to the claimant, he cannot recover contribution from the others. But if at the time of the settlement or judgment he was liable to the claimant then his right to contribution is subject to a two year limitation period running from the date of judgment or of the compromise.

Section 1(3) of the Act states that a party from whom contribution is sought is liable to make contribution even though he has ceased to be liable to the original claimant, 'unless he ceased to be liable by virtue of the expiry of a period of limitation or prescription which extinguished the right on which the claim against him in respect of the damage was based'. Thus far the clear purport of this subsection is to reverse the decision of the House of Lords in *George Wimpey and Co Ltd* v *British Overseas Aircraft Corporation* [1955] AC 169. In that case it was held that one tortfeasor could not recover from the other tortfeasor because the claimant's claim against the latter had been held to be time barred. The claim against the tortfeasor having been dismissed in this manner he was not 'liable' to make contribution to the other tortfeasor. Section 1(3) would appear to reverse this decision so that contribution could be recovered.

A difficulty is, however, introduced by s1(5) of the Act which states that 'judgment given in any action' brought by the original claimant 'against any party from whom contribution is sought under this section shall be conclusive in the proceedings for contribution as to any issue determined by that judgment in favour of the person from whom the contribution is sought'. If the phrase 'any issue' in s1(5) is interpreted so as to encompass the issue of limitation, the Act will have failed in its aim of reversing *Wimpey*, because if, in the action by the original claimant, the limitation issue was decided in favour of the defendants, that finding would be 'conclusive' if another defendant then sought to obtain contribution from these defendants and would prevent that other defendant from obtaining contribution.

However, it has been argued (see, for example, *Dias and Markesinis Tort Law*, 2nd ed, p580) that the phrase 'any issue' in s1(5) should be read as if it provided 'any issue as to the merits' of the original claim by the claimant (a similar insertion would then have to be made in s1(3) so that it read 'ceased to be liable on the merits' to the original claimant). The purpose behind this interpretation is to uphold the intention of the Act in reversing *Wimpey* and to hold that the issue of limitation is not a determination on the merits and therefore not 'conclusive' (except where limitation extinguishes not only the remedy, but the claim, on which see Dias and Markesinis loc cit). This interpretation was, however, approved obiter by Balcombe LJ in *Nottingham Health Authority* v *The City of Nottingham* [1988] 1 WLR 903. He held that the effect of s1(3) is to reverse *Wimpey* so that a defendant remains liable to contribute where the effect of the limitation defence is to bar the remedy but does not extinguish the right.

Section 1(5) of the 1978 Act does not bar a defendant, against whom judgment has been given, from appealing against the dismissal of proceedings against a co-defendant: *Moy* v *Pettman Smith* [2005] 1 All ER 903.

Lastly, s1(4) provides that a party who has made a payment under a bona fide settlement or compromise may claim contribution:

> '... without regard to whether or not he himself is or ever was liable in respect of the damage, provided, however, that he would have been liable assuming that the factual basis of the claim against him could be established.'

Apportionment

Section 2(1) of the Act provides that the amount recoverable from any person 'shall be such as may be found by the court to be just and equitable having regard to the extent of that person's responsibility for the damage in question.' There is no suggestion in the Act that the division must be on the basis of equality. Instead the court is required to take into account all the relevant circumstances, such as the degree of blameworthiness and the parties' role in bringing about the damage, and apportion the damages payable in the light of these circumstances.

Section 2(2) empowers the court either to exempt a party from having to pay contribution or to order him to make a complete indemnity. The amount which the tortfeasor can recover by way of contribution is limited to the amount which the claimant could have recovered from that particular defendant had the claimant sued him. So if the defendant from whom contribution is sought has a contract with the claimant which validly restricts that defendant's liability to £25, the defendant seeking contribution from that other defendant cannot recover more than £25 (s2(3)).

4

Vicarious Liability

4.1 Introduction

Before embarking upon an analysis of the rationale behind the doctrine of vicarious liability, it is necessary to give a brief explanation of the essence of the doctrine. The effect of the doctrine of vicarious liability is to render X liable to Z for the damage done to Z by the tort of Y. The commonest example of this is the case where an employer is rendered liable for the tort committed by his employee in the course of the employee's employment. There are two essential elements to vicarious liability. The first is that there must be a relationship, such as the employment relationship, between X and Y which is sufficient to justify the imposition of liability upon X for the tort of Y. The second element is that the tort committed by Y must be referable in some particular way to the relationship between X and Y.

It is essential to note that vicarious liability is concerned with the situation where one person is rendered liable for the tort of another, not with the situation where one person is rendered liable for his own tort. Although this distinction appears to be an obvious one, it can be difficult to draw the line in practice. For example, a National Health Service patient who suffers loss as a result of a negligently performed operation may decide to sue the Area Health Authority directly for its failure to provide adequate levels of staffing in the hospital or he may elect to sue

22

the Area Health Authority as being vicariously liable for the negligence of one of its doctors. While it may be difficult to draw the line in some cases, that line must be drawn if the distinction between primary and vicarious liability is to be preserved.

4.2 The rationale of vicarious liability

One of the unusual features of the doctrine of vicarious liability is that, whilst there is general agreement as to the utility of the doctrine, the doctrine has no clear rationale. A number of possible rationales have been put forward, but none are wholly convincing. These rationales are as follows:

1. The employer has control over his employee therefore he is responsible for the acts of his employee. This, however, is a demonstrable fallacy because in many cases the employee is more skilled than the employer (for example doctors and pilots) and so it cannot be said in any meaningful sense that the employer has control over his employee.
2. The employer was careless in selecting an employee who was negligent and he must accept responsibility because, by selecting a negligent employee, he set in motion the train of events which led to the negligent act of his employee. But no employee is immune from being negligent at some stage in his employment and to insist that an employer only employ non-negligent employees is to place an unreasonable and unjustified burden on the employer.
3. The employer derives benefit from the service of his employee, so it is only right that he takes the burdens as well. This justification purports to give some economic and moral basis to the imposition of liability upon the employer. It may be thought, however, that, in a society which accepts the existence of the division of labour, we often benefit from the works of others without contributing to the cost of that work and the mere fact of receipt of a benefit is not, of itself, sufficient to justify the imposition of an obligation to pay for it.
4. The employer is in a better position than the employee to compensate the victim of the tort. The employee will generally not have the funds available to meet the damages claim nor will he have an insurance policy to meet the claim, whereas an employer will normally have the latter if not the former. The employer is often in the best position to spread the loss because he can take account of the loss as a cost of the production process and thus pass the cost on as part of the cost of his product.
5. By imposing liability on the employer, the employer is thereby given an incentive to ensure that the event does not occur again and that none of his other employees do the same thing.

It is probably true to say that there is no one justification for the imposition of vicarious liability. The best conclusion may be that of Professor Williams when he said in his article Vicarious Liability and the Master's Indemnity ((1957) 20 MLR 220, 232):

> ' ... that vicarious liability owes its explanation, if not its justification, to the search for a solvent defendant. It is commonly felt that when a person is injured ... he ought to be able to obtain recompense from someone; and if the immediate tortfeasor cannot afford to pay, then he is justified in looking around for the nearest person of substance who can plausibly be identified with the disaster. Where there is no immediate tortfeasor at all, the same sentiment works itself out through rules of strict liability.'

So the rationale of vicarious liability may be said to lie closest to category 4. This lack of a coherent rationale for the doctrine does not appear to have troubled the judiciary. Lord Pearce in *Imperial Chemical Industries Ltd* v *Shatwell* [1965] AC 656, 685 said:

> 'The doctrine of vicarious liability has not grown from any very clear, logical or legal principle but from social convenience and rough justice.'

Despite this apparent lack of concern on the part of the judiciary, we shall note at various stages of this Chapter that the issue is an important one and that its resolution would help to stabilise the law and give it greater coherence.

In the next three sections of this Chapter we shall consider the application of the doctrine of vicarious liability to the employment relationship. We shall do so in three stages. First by considering who is an employee (section 4.3). Secondly by demonstrating that the employee must commit a tort (section 4.4) and thirdly by showing that the tort must be committed during the course of the employee's employment (section 4.5).

4.3 Who is an employee?

As vicarious liability arises from the employment relationship and not from the relationship of employer and independent contractor it is important to distinguish between an employee and an independent contractor. This distinction may seem an obvious one, but it has caused the courts great difficulties. These difficulties are likely to increase today because of the growth of what is called 'atypical' forms of employment, where it is difficult to tell whether the worker is an employee or not. These 'atypical' forms of employment include homeworkers, casual workers (for example, those workers who have no fixed hours of work but are called in by their employer as and when required) and those who are told by their employers when they are hired that they are self-employed so that the employer can evade the employment protection legislation. All these categories of workers are likely to present the courts with considerable problems in determining their employment status.

The original test for distinguishing between an employee and an independent contractor was the control test. This test had its origin in the judgment of Bramwell LJ in *Yewens* v *Noakes* (1880) 6 QBD 530 where he said that an employee was anyone 'who was subject to the command of the master as to the manner in which he shall do the work'. This test never meant that the employer in fact controlled the employee for every second of his working day, but that he had the right to do so. However, as we have already noted, this test became impossible to apply as many employees became more skilful, to the extent of being more skilful than their employers.

These difficulties with the 'control' test led to dissatisfaction with the test on the part of the judiciary and an attempt to find an alternative test for distinguishing between employees and independent contractors. So in *Stevenson, Jordan and Harrison Ltd* v *MacDonald* [1952] 1 TLR 101 Denning LJ formulated the 'business integration' test or the 'organisation' test. By this he meant that a worker who is an employee does his work as an 'integral part of the business' whereas an independent contractor is not 'integrated' into the business but is merely 'accessory' to it. While sounding neat in theory it was impossibly vague to apply in practice and was quickly abandoned.

The next attempt at formulating a test for distinguishing between an employee and an independent contractor occurred in *Market Investigations Ltd* v *Minister of Social Security* [1969] 2 QB 173. In this case an interviewer was hired by a research company. She was free to set her own hours of work, although the pattern of her work was set by the research company. She received no sick pay or holiday pay and she was free to work for others. It was held that she was an employee because she was not 'in business on her own account'. Although this test avoids the excesses of the 'business integration' test it is still vague. However, in *Andrews* v *King* (1991) The Times 5 July it was referred to by Browne-Wilkinson VC as 'a fundamental test', and in *Lee Ting Sang* v *Chung Chi-Keung* [1990] 2 AC 374 the Privy Council stated that the test of whether a person is an employee or an independent contractor had never been better put than it was in *Market Investigations*.

Another factor which has been given some weight by the courts is the parties' labelling of their own relationship. This approach reached its height in *Massey* v *Crown Life Insurance* [1978] 1 WLR 676 where a man who had agreed to be self-employed so that he could enjoy certain tax advantages sought to argue that he was an employee so that he could claim the benefits of the employment protection legislation. The Court of Appeal dismissed his claim, Lord Denning saying that 'having made his bed as being self-employed, he must lie on it'. But this approach has not been uniformly accepted. In *Young and Woods* v *West* [1980] IRLR 201 a skilled metal worker, who chose when he was hired to be treated as 'self-employed' so that he could obtain a tax saving of some £500 per year, was nevertheless held to be an employee when he presented a claim that he had been unfairly dismissed. The court held that the parties' labelling of their relationship was only one factor to be taken into account and that employees had to be protected from contracting out of their statutory employment rights. Lest it be thought that Mr West thereby made a considerable tax saving while not losing his statutory employment rights, the court undertook to inform the Inland Revenue of his true employment status, making it a somewhat hollow victory!

The approach which the courts now adopt is to abandon the search for any one factor which will be conclusive in all cases and to examine all the facts of the particular case. An early example of this is the case of *Ready Mixed Concrete (South East) Ltd* v *Minister of Pensions* [1968] 2 QB 497. MacKenna J laid down three conditions for the existence of a contract of employment:

1. the employee agrees to provide his work and skill to the employer in return for a wage or other remuneration;
2. the employee agrees, expressly or impliedly, to be directed as to the mode of performance to such a degree as to make the other his employer; and
3. the other terms of the contract are consistent with there being a contract of employment.

It should not be thought, however, that the courts confine themselves to these three factors. The courts will, in fact, consider a wide range of factors including the degree of control over the worker's work, his connection with the business, the parties' agreement, the regularity and nature of the work and methods of payment etc. In *Lane* v *Shire Roofing Co (Oxford)* (1995) The Times 25 February the Court of Appeal held that the overall employment background today was very different from that when *Ready Mixed Concrete* and *Market Investigations* were decided. The court held that when the control test was not decisive, eg, because the employee was skilled with discretion to decide how the work should be done, the question broadened to 'whose business was it? Was the workman carrying on his own business or, was he carrying on his employer's business?'

Winfield and Jolowicz argue (*Winfield and Jolowicz on Tort*, 14th ed, p595) that the distinction between an employee and an independent contractor has to be drawn for a number of different purposes and that it appears that the same answer will be given regardless of the context in which the question is posed. It is submitted that this is incorrect and that great care will have to be taken in the future in using authorities in this area. Take the case of *O'Kelly* v *Trusthouse Forte plc* [1983] ICR 728 as an example. There the Court of Appeal held that wine butlers at the Grosvenor House Hotel, who were called 'regular' casual workers and worked in a system whereby they were called in to work when required by their employers (although they were free to refuse such work), were not employees for the purposes of the employment protection legislation. What would have been the position if one of the wine butlers had negligently spilt wine over a guest at the hotel? Surely, in such a case a court would conclude that the wine butler was an employee and that his employer was vicariously liable for his employee's negligence. (Some support for paying greater attention to the context in which it is sought to draw the distinction between an employee and an independent contractor can be found in *R* v *Callender* [1993] QB 303, 309.)

One final difficulty, which calls for comment at this stage, arises where an employer lends his employee to another employer. If that employee then commits a tort which employer is vicariously liable? The answer was provided by the House of Lords in *Mersey Docks and Harbour Board* v *Coggins and Griffith (Liverpool) Ltd* [1947] AC 1. They held that the proper test to apply was whether the hirer did or did not have the authority to control the manner in which the employee did his work and that the stipulations of the parties as to who was to be regarded as the employer were not conclusive. They held that the burden of proof was on the general employer (ie the one who hired out the employee) to show that he was not the employer and that the burden was a heavy one to discharge, and which according to Viscount Simon would only be discharged in quite exceptional cases. On the facts the general employers failed to discharge the burden on them because, although the hirers directed the employees as to what parcels they should lift with the crane, they had no authority to tell the employees how to use the crane. Other factors which may be of importance include who pays the wages, who can dismiss the employee, how long the employee is hired out for and whether machinery is also hired out. The latter factor may be important because where it is only labour which is hired out it is much easier to infer that the hirer is the employer, although even here the courts are reluctant to accept that the hirer has control (*Bhoomidas* v *Port of Singapore* [1978] 1 All ER 956). Where, however, it is the employee rather than a third party who suffers injury then the general employer remains liable on the basis that he owes a non-delegable duty of care to his employee and he cannot avoid liability for breach of that duty by delegating it to the hiring employer (see *Morris* v *Breaveglen Ltd* [1993] ICR 766 and *Johnson* v *Coventry Churchill International Ltd* [1992] 3 All ER 14, discussed in more detail at Chapter 15, section 15.5).

Further restrictions may be placed on the ability of the general employer to transfer liability to the hiring employer by the Unfair Contract Terms Act 1977 (UCTA). In *Phillips Products Ltd* v *Hyland* [1987] 2 All ER 620 the defendants hired a JCB excavator and driver to the claimants. Condition 8 of the contract stated that the driver was to be regarded as the employee of the claimants and that the claimants alone should be responsible for all claims arising in connection with the driver's operation of the excavator. Due to the negligence of the driver, the JCB excavator crashed into the claimants' factory wall. The claimants sued for damages and the defendants relied upon condition 8. The claimants argued that condition 8 was caught by s2(2) of UCTA and that it failed to satisfy the requirement of reasonableness. The defendants argued that it was not caught by s2(2) on the ground that there was no negligence within the meaning of s1(1)(b) of UCTA because there had been no breach of their obligations as they had never accepted any liability for the acts of the driver. This argument was rejected by the Court of Appeal. Slade LJ asserted that in considering whether there had been a breach of duty under s1 the court must leave out of account the clause which is relied on by the defendants as defeating the claimants' claim. He found support for his construction of s1(1)(b) in s13 which states that s2 also applies to terms and notices 'which exclude or restrict the relevant obligation or duty'. Having found that condition 8 was caught by s2(2) the Court of Appeal held that it failed to satisfy the reasonableness test.

An apparently conflicting conclusion was, however, reached by a differently constituted Court of Appeal in *Thompson* v *T Lohan (Plant Hire) Ltd* [1987] 2 All ER 631. Once again the case concerned the hiring of an employee and a JCB excavator and a claim arising out of the negligence of the driver. The contract term which was the subject of dispute was a new version of condition 8 (the variation is of no significance for present purposes). But this time it was held that condition 8 was not caught by s2 of UCTA. In *Thompson* the driver's negligence led to the death of Mr Thompson. Mr Thompson's widow recovered damages from the general employers and they in turn sought an indemnity from the hiring employers under condition 8. The hiring employers argued that condition 8 was caught by s2(1) of UCTA and was therefore ineffective. However it was held that condition 8 was not caught by s2(1) and therefore condition 8 was effective to transfer liability to the hiring employer. The distinction between the two cases appears to be that in Thompson condition 8 did not attempt to exclude liability towards Mr Thompson because he had recovered from the general employers and the issue was whether that liability could be transferred (as opposed to excluded) to the hiring employers. On the other hand condition 8 in the *Phillips* case was relied upon in an effort to exclude (rather than transfer) liability towards the hiring employers and therefore was caught by s2(2) of UCTA (for critical anlaysis of these two cases see Adams and Brownsword [1988] JBL 146).

4.4 The employee must commit a tort

This point may be said to be labouring the obvious, but it is inserted because in *Twine* v *Bean's Express Ltd* [1946] 1 All ER 202 Uthwatt J suggested that an employer could be vicariously liable even though the employee has not committed a tort. This error was, however, corrected by the House of Lords in *Imperial Chemical Industries Ltd* v *Shatwell* [1965] AC 656 where the crucial distinction between primary and vicarious liability was reaffirmed. Vicarious liability only arises where the employee commits a tort. See also *Credit Lyonnais Bank Nederland NV* v *Export Credits Guarantee Department* [1999] 1 All ER 929 where the House of Lords stressed that, before an employer could be vicariously liable, all of the features necessary to make the employee liable in tort must have occurred in the course of his employment. As to the vicarious liability of an employer for the tort of harassment, see Chapter 24, section 24.6.

4.5 Course of employment

This is the most difficult issue in vicarious liability. There has been an enormous deluge of cases on this point and many of these cases are irreconcilable. All that can be said is that the courts have provided guidelines which they will use in considering whether the employee was acting within the course of his employment. The employee must, of course, have been acting within the course of his employment before the employer will be held vicariously liable for his employee's tort.

Perhaps the most famous definition of 'course of employment' is provided in the following terms by Salmond and Heuston in *The Law of Torts* (19th ed), pp521–522:

'A master is not responsible for a wrongful act done by his servant unless it is done in the course of his employment. It is deemed to be so done if it is either (i) a wrongful act authorised by the master, or (ii) a wrongful and unauthorised mode of doing some act authorised by the master ... On the other hand, if the unauthorised and wrongful act of the servant is not so connected with the authorised act as to be a mode of doing it, but is an independent act, the master is not responsible: for in such a case the servant is not acting in the course of his employment, but has gone outside of it.'

This statement can be used as a basis for an analysis of the law, although it must be emphasised that it should not be taken as an exclusive statement of the law, but merely as being illustrative of the approach of the courts. It can be discussed under the following headings.

Negligent and careless acts

The fact that the mode of doing a job is wrongful and unauthorised will not prevent the employer being vicariously liable for it provided that at the time the employee was doing some act authorised by the employer. This has the effect of denying to employers the argument that the mere fact that the employee was going about his work in a negligent or mistaken manner takes the employee outside the course of his employment because the employer would not have sanctioned the commission of a negligent or mistaken act.

This can be demonstrated in its application to negligent acts by the case of *Century Insurance Co Ltd* v *Northern Ireland Road Transport Board* [1942] AC 509. The defendants employed Davison as a petrol tanker driver. While discharging petrol at a garage, Davison lit a cigarette. He threw away the lighted match, which caused a fire and an explosion in which the claimant's property was damaged. The House of Lords held that the defendants were vicariously liable for the tort of their employee. Although it was true that the driver had lit a cigarette for his own personal benefit and not for the benefit of his employers, this act of lighting a cigarette could not be viewed in isolation from the job he was doing at that time. At the time of the accident the driver was doing his job of discharging petrol from the tanker, albeit that he was doing his job in an unauthorised and negligent fashion.

Similar reasoning has been deployed in the case of a mistaken act on the part of an employee. Thus in *Bayley* v *Manchester, Sheffield and Lincolnshire Railway Co*

(1873) LR 8 CP 148 a rather over-zealous railway porter forcibly removed the claimant from a train, erroneously believing that the claimant had got onto the wrong train. Part of the porter's job included ensuring that people got onto the correct train and so his employers were held to be vicariously liable for his tort. He was simply doing, in a mistaken manner, what he was employed to do.

A related issue concerns the situation where an employee takes steps to save his employer's property under the mistaken belief that his employer's property is threatened. In *Poland* v *John Parr and Sons* [1927] 1 KB 236 the Court of Appeal held that, as a general rule, an employee is authorised to do acts which are for the protection of his employer's property, although he is not legally 'bound' so to do. However, if the act in question had been excessive in the situation (for example, had he fired a shot at the person whom he believed to be taking his employer's property) then that would have taken the employee out of the course of his employment (see too *Warren* v *Henley's Ltd* [1948] 2 All ER 935, discussed further below).

Express prohibition

It follows from the definition provided by Salmond and Heuston that the mere fact that an employer has placed prohibitions upon the conduct of the employee will not, of itself, operate to restrict the course of employment (see to similar effect the judgment of Lord Dunedin in *Plumb* v *Cobden Flour Mills Co* [1914] AC 62, 67). It may be objected that there is no good reason why an employer should be liable where he has expressly placed prohibitions upon the employee. But such an approach would make it too easy for employers to evade the impact of the vicarious liability doctrine by prohibiting their employees from committing torts. So the law has to strike a balance between denying to employers the ability to exempt themselves from the impact of this doctrine, while avoiding the imposition of liability for acts which are wholly unconnected with the work of the employee. The approach which the law has adopted is to permit employers to limit the acts which the employee may do within the course of his employment, but to deny them the ability to restrict the mode of doing the particular act in question. Thus stated, the crucial distinction is between the mode of doing the act and the act itself. Two cases may help us to understand this distinction.

The first case is *Limpus* v *London General Omnibus Co* (1862) 1 H & C 526. Here the defendants expressly prohibited their drivers from racing with, or obstructing, other buses. Their driver, however, obstructed the claimant's bus to pick up two passengers and, in so doing, caused a collision in which several passengers were injured. It was held that the defendants were vicariously liable for the tort of their driver because at the time of the accident he was simply doing an authorised act (driving a bus) in an unauthorised manner or mode.

On the other side of the line is the case of *Conway* v *George Wimpey & Co Ltd* [1951] 2 KB 266. In this case the defendants provided transport for their employees on a construction site. The drivers were specifically told not to give lifts to employees of other companies. However, one of their drivers gave a lift to the claimant, who was employed by another company (although the driver was unaware of this fact). The claimant was injured as a result of the negligence of the driver and he sued the defendants. The Court of Appeal held that the defendants were not vicariously liable for the tort of the driver because at the time of the accident the driver was doing an unauthorised act (driving his van with an unauthorised passenger on board) and that it was not simply a case of him doing an authorised act in an unauthorised mode.

This sounds fine in theory, but it leaves us with a difficult practical problem. The problem is how do the courts define the 'act' which the employee is employed to do? For example, we could reverse the results in *Limpus* and *Conway* by redefining the act which the employee was employed to do. If in *Limpus* we said that the act which the employee was employed to do was drive buses and that at the time of the accident he was 'racing or obstructing other buses' then the driver would have been doing an unauthorised act. On the other hand, if in *Conway* we defined the act which the driver was doing at the time of the accident as driving the bus, then he would have been doing an authorised act, albeit in an unauthorised manner. It can be argued that the courts have so much discretion in defining the scope of the act that they can decide the case the way they want it to go and then select the appropriate label to justify their decision.

Further evidence of the confusion which currently exists can be discovered by comparing the decisions in *Twine* v *Bean's Express Ltd* (1946) 62 TLR 458 and *Rose* v *Plenty* [1976] 1 WLR 141. In the former case the claimant's husband was given a lift in a van driven by an employee of the defendants. The claimant's husband was killed as a result of the negligence of the driver. The driver had been told that he could only give lifts to certain passengers and the claimant was not one of these passengers. Furthermore there was a notice restricting the class of authorised passengers inside the van. The Court of Appeal held that the defendants were not liable for the tort of their employee. There were two grounds to the decision of the court. The first was that the deceased was a trespasser and as such was not owed a duty of care by the defendants. The second point was that the driver was not acting within the course of his employment because at the time of the accident he was doing an unauthorised act, namely giving a lift to an unauthorised person.

This case was reconsidered by the Court of Appeal in the controversial case of *Rose* v *Plenty* (above). The defendants expressly prohibited their milkmen from permitting boys to ride on their milk floats. Notices were also posted at the depot informing milkmen of this prohibition. In contravention of this order an employee allowed the claimant, a boy aged 13, to ride on his milk float while helping him with his deliveries and collections. As he was riding on the milk float the claimant was injured due to the negligence of the driver. The Court of Appeal held that the defendants were liable for the tort of their employee. Their prohibition had not affected the course of the employee's employment, it had simply affected the mode by which he could do his job. Lawton LJ dissented on the ground that he could not distinguish the present case from *Twine* and he was not prepared to say that the latter decision was wrong.

The majority, Lord Denning MR and Scarman LJ, distinguished *Twine* on two grounds. The first ground was that the deceased in *Twine* was a trespasser and was therefore owed no duty of care by the defendants. It was held that this ground of the decision could no longer stand because, since the decision of the House of Lords in *British Railways Board* v *Herrington* [1972] AC 877, it was clear that a limited duty of care is owed to trespassers (see further Chapter 17, section 17.15).

The second ground on which the majority distinguished *Twine* related to the course of employment point. Lord Denning distinguished *Twine* on the ground that there the lift was not given for any purpose beneficial to the employer (presumably because the lift was given to an employee of another company), whereas in *Rose* the claimant's presence on the milk float was to further the employer's business. This latter point must be regarded as doubtful because, as was pointed out by Lawton LJ, the claimant was not furthering the employer's business but was doing the driver's job for him and making his life an easier one. Scarman LJ dealt more fully with the case law and vainly sought to show that the case law was reconcilable. He said that in *Twine* the employer's prohibition limited the scope of the employee's employment, whereas here the employer's prohibition did not alter the scope of the employee's employment but only affected the mode by which the job was to be done. However, this reconciliation is only effective at the formal level because it does not explain how the courts define the act which the employee is employed to do, as against the mode in which he is to do the job. The more important aspect of the judgment may be that Scarman LJ argued that a broad approach should be taken to the question of the course of employment. Thus, in the recent case of *Racz* v *Home Office* [1994] 2 WLR 23 the House of Lords took a wide approach to this question and held where a prisoner sued the Home Office, alleging misfeasance in public office on the part of prison officers, that the Home Office as employers could be vicariously liable for the torts of its employee prison officers. Dicta in the speech of Lord Bridge in *R* v *Deputy Governor of Parkhurst Prison, ex parte Hague* [1992] 1 AC 58, which suggested that such actions by prison officers took them outside the course of their employment, were not followed in *Racz*.

'Frolics and detours'

Considerable difficulty has arisen with vehicle drivers who depart from authorised routes. One could argue that as soon as an employee departs from his authorised route he goes outside the course of his employment. But that would be a draconian measure for, as LP Emslie said in *Angus* v *Glasgow Corporation* 1977 SLT 206, unauthorised deviations from an authorised route are only to be expected as an incident of modern industrial life. So once again we are faced with the difficulty of devising a test to determine the extent to which an employer is responsible for the unauthorised deviations of his employee. The generally accepted test was laid down by Parke B in *Joel* v *Morrison* (1834) 6 C & P 501 in the following terms:

> 'If [the driver] was going out of his way, against his master's implied commands, when driving on his master's business, he will make his master liable; but if he was going on a frolic of his own, without being at all on his master's business, the master will not be liable.'

It is now necessary to give consideration to what constitutes a 'frolic of his own'. In *Whatman* v *Pearson* (1868) LR 3 CP 422 an employee who went home for his lunch on his horse and cart, contrary to his employer's instructions, was held to remain within the course of his employment so that his employers were liable for the damage done by the horse when, having been left unattended outside the employee's home, it ran off and damaged the claimant's property. On the other hand, in *Storey* v *Ashton* (1869) LR 4 QB 476, the defendant employers were held not liable when their employee, after completing his deliveries, went on a detour to visit his brother-in-law. It was held that this was a new and independent journey which had nothing to do with his employment and so was outside the course of his employment.

In *Williams* v *A & W Hemphill Ltd* 1966 SLT 259, a Scottish case which went on appeal to the House of Lords, some interesting comments were made on this area of law. The case concerned a driver who had gone on a considerable detour when driving boys home, because the boys wanted to follow some girl guides who had been camping in a nearby field. While on this detour the bus was involved in an accident and some of the boys were injured. The driver was held to be within the course of his employment. Lord Pearce said that it was a question of fact in each case whether the employee had gone on a 'frolic of his own'. He considered *Storey* and said that had the driver been carrying, at the time of the accident, some important cargo belonging to the employer then the result might have been different. In *Williams* the continued presence of the boys on the bus made it impossible to say that this was a frolic of the driver's own. This latter case suggests that it is only a new and independent journey, which is solely undertaken for the selfish purposes of the employee, that will constitute a 'frolic of his own'.

A related problem concerns the situation where the employee is travelling to or from work or between two places of work. In *Smith* v *Stages* [1989] AC 928 the claimant was seriously injured in a car accident which was caused by the negligence of a fellow employee, the first defendant. The two employees, who were based in Staffordshire, were sent to work in Pembroke. They worked most of the day on Sunday and worked all night. As the employees had worked all night the employers, the second defendants, agreed to pay the employees eight hours sleeping time and eight hours travelling time to enable them to return home. But they did not direct the employees as to when they should return home or even what method of travel they should adopt. Despite their exertions, the employees decided to travel home immediately after their Sunday night shift and it was on the way home that the accident occurred. The cause of the accident was the negligence of the first defendant. The House of Lords held that the first defendant was in the course of his employment when the accident occurred and that therefore the second defendants were vicariously liable. The first defendant was being paid wages to travel back to Staffordshire and so he was acting within the course of his employment when travelling home.

Lord Lowry, after engaging in a survey of the relevant case law, deduced the following prima facie propositions. The first is that an employee who is travelling from his home to his regular place of work or from his regular place of work to his home is not within the course of his employment. But, if the employee is required by his contract of employment to use the employer's transport, then he will normally be regarded as being within the course of his employment when travelling to work. Secondly, an employee who is travelling between workplaces or in the course of a peripatetic occupation is within the course of his employment. Thirdly, receipt of wages, but not a travelling allowance, suggests that the journey is for the benefit of the employer and that the journey is within the course of employment. Fourthly, an employee is within the course of his employment if he travels in his employer's time from his home to a workplace which is not his regular workplace or to the scene of an emergency. Finally, a deviation from a journey undertaken in the course of employment, unless that deviation is merely incidental to the journey, will take the employee outside the course of his employment for the duration of the deviation. These propositions are, however, subject to two principal qualifications. The first is that they are subject to any agreement to the contrary between an employer and his employee. The second is that these propositions are not intended to define the position of salaried employees, 'with regard to whom the touchstone of payment made in the employer's time is not generally significant'.

Intentional wrongful acts

In cases involving intentional wrongful acts the courts have adopted a much more restrictive approach to the course of employment issue. This can be seen in the following three recent cases. The first is *Heasmans* v *Clarity Cleaning Co Ltd* [1987] IRLR 286. One of the defendants' employees, who was employed to clean the claimant's offices, used the claimant's telephone to make unauthorised international calls costing £1,411. The Court of Appeal held that the defendants were not vicariously liable for the acts of their employee. Nourse LJ stated that the employee was employed to clean the telephones and not to use them. In using them he had not cleaned the telephones in an unauthorised manner, but had done an unauthorised act and so had gone outside the course of his employment. This extremely narrow approach to the course of employment issue is clearly at variance with the much broader approach found in *Rose* v *Plenty* (above). The second case is *Irving* v *The Post Office* [1987] IRLR 289. The claimants claimed that the defendants had unlawfully discriminated against them on the grounds of their race. The claimants lived next door to an employee of the defendants, called Mr Edwards, and they were not on speaking terms. Mr Edwards, during the course of his work sorting mail, saw an envelope addressed to the claimants and wrote on the back of the envelope 'Go back to Jamaica Sambo' and drew a picture of a black smiling face. Mr Edwards was authorised to write on letters which he was sorting but only for the purpose of ensuring that the mail was properly dealt with. The claimants argued that the defendants were vicariously liable for the racial abuse of Mr Edwards but it was held that, in writing racial abuse on the envelope, the employee was doing an unauthorised act and that therefore the defendants were not vicariously liable. The Court of Appeal placed strong reliance upon *Heasmans* v *Clarity Cleaning* (above) and held that the writing of the racial abuse was an act of personal malevolence by Mr Edwards, and they affirmed that it could not be assumed that, merely because the employment had provided the opportunity for the wrong, the employers were therefore liable. Fox LJ stated that 'out of fairness to employers' limits have to be set to the doctrine of vicarious liability, particularly where, as here, it was sought to make the defendants liable for the 'wilful wrongdoing' of their employee which they had in no way authorised. The third case is *General Engineering Services Ltd* v *Kingston and Saint Andrew Corp* [1989] 1 WLR 69. The claimants' property was completely destroyed by fire and the damage was increased by the fact that the firemen who answered the claimants' emergency call were involved in a go-slow in support of a pay claim and deliberately drove slowly to the scene of the fire, taking 17 minutes rather than the normal three and a half minutes to reach the claimants' property. The claimants alleged that the defendants, who were the employers of the firemen, were vicariously liable for the acts of the firemen. The Privy Council held that the defendants were not liable because the firemen were not within the course of their employment in travelling to the claimants' property at such a slow speed. They were employed to travel to the scene of a fire as quickly as reasonably possible and, in travelling as slowly as possible, it could not be said that they were doing an authorised act in an unauthorised manner; they were doing an unauthorised act. Bearing in mind the restrictive tenor of the approach of the courts, we shall discuss this category under three separate headings.

Assault

Some employees, such as 'bouncers' at a discotheque, may be expected to exercise some degree of violence in the course of their employment. We have also noted that employees have some, albeit limited, authority to protect their employers' interests in an emergency (*Poland* v *John Parr* [1927] 1 KB 236). But outside these limited categories the courts have been extremely reluctant to impose liability upon employers for an assault committed by an employee. Thus in *Warren* v *Henley's Ltd* [1948] 2 All ER 935 the defendants were held not to be vicariously liable for the assault of their employee. The assault took place after the employee, who was a petrol pump attendant, had accused a customer of having tried to drive away without paying for his petrol. The customer paid his bill and said he would call the police and that he would also inform the defendants. The employee was so angry at this that he assaulted the customer. The defendants were held not to be liable because this was an act of personal vengeance and so was outside the course of his employment (see to similar effect *Deaton's Property Ltd* v *Flew* (1949) 79 CLR 370).

However, in *Mattis* v *Pollock (t/a Flamingo's Nightclub)* [2004] 4 All ER 85 an altercation occurred in the defendant's nightclub: Cranston, a bouncer employed by the defendant, was chased out of the club and ran to his home, some 500 metres away. Some 20 minutes later, having armed himself with a knife, Cranston set off back towards the club. While still almost 100 metres away from it, Cranston came across a group of people, including the claimant, some of whom had been involved in the earlier incident (the claimant had been on the periphery of it). Most ran off, but Cranston grabbed the claimant and stabbed him in the back, causing him severe injuries. The Court of Appeal held that the defendant was vicariously liable for Cranston's assault on the claimant since the stabbing represented the culmination of the incident which had started within the club. It could not fairly and justly be treated in isolation from earlier events. Even allowing that Cranston's behaviour included an important element of personal revenge, approaching the matter broadly, at the moment when the claimant was stabbed, the defendant's responsibility for Cranston's actions was not extinguished.

See, too, *Ramsay Elshafey* v *Kings School of Macclesfield* which was noted in *Solicitors Journal* 28 November 2003. A player injured in a school rugby match successfully sued his opponent's school for around £100,000, after sustaining injuries to his neck and ligaments. The court found the school vicariously liable for its pupil's actions.

In *Lister* v *Hesley Hall Ltd* [2001] 2 All ER 769 (which was applied in *Mattis*), when aged between 12 and 15, the appellants were residents in the boarding house of the respondents' school. While there, they were sexually abused by the warden of the boarding house, an employee of the respondents. In the appellants' actions for personal injury, the question arose as to whether the respondents were vicariously liable for the torts of their employee. The House of Lords concluded that the respondents were so liable.

Lord Millett said:

> '... the warden's duties provided him with the opportunity to commit indecent assaults on the boys for his own sexual gratification, but that in itself is not enough to make the school liable. The same would be true of the groundsman or the school porter. But there was far more to it than that. The school was responsible for the care and welfare of the boys. It entrusted that responsibility to the warden. He was employed to discharge the school's responsibility to the boys. For this purpose the school entrusted them to his care. He did not merely take advantage of the opportunity which employment at a residential school gave him. He abused the special position in which the school had placed him to enable it to discharge its own responsibilities, with the result that the assaults were committed by the very employee to whom the school had entrusted the care of the boys. ... I would hold the school liable.'

In reaching this conclusion, their Lordships applied *Ilkiw* v *Samuels* [1963] 2 All ER

879, *Morris* v *C W Martin & Sons Ltd* [1965] 2 All ER 725 and *Rose* v *Plenty* [1976] 1 All ER 97, and overruled *Trotman* v *North Yorkshire County Council* [1999] LGR 584.

Theft

In *Cheshire* v *Bailey* [1905] 1 KB 237 it was held that theft necessarily took the employee outside the course of his employment. But this is no longer the position today. In *Morris* v *C W Martin and Sons Ltd* [1966] 1 QB 716 the claimant took her fur coat to a furrier to be cleaned. With her consent, the furrier sent the coat to the defendants for cleaning, but one of the defendants' employees stole the coat. The defendants were held liable for the loss on the ground that they were in breach of their duties as bailees for reward. But the case could have been argued as one of vicarious liability and this fact was referred to by two members of the Court of Appeal. However in *Port Swettenham Authority* v *T W Wu* [1979] AC 580 Lord Salmon rejected the 'heresy' in *Cheshire* that theft necessarily takes the employee outside the course of his employment and approved of *Morris*.

Fraud

In *Lloyd* v *Grace, Smith and Co* [1912] AC 716 the court rejected the proposition adopted in *Barwick* v *English Joint Stock Bank* (1867) LR 2 Ex 259 that the employer is only vicariously liable for the fraud of his employee when the fraud was committed for his (the employer's) own benefit. For the employer to be liable the fraudulent act must have been committed within the scope of the employee's actual or ostensible authority. This test was satisfied on the facts of *Lloyd* because the fraud arose out of a conveyancing transaction and the clerk had authority to enter into such a transaction. The test was not, however, satisfied in the case of *Armagas* v *Mundogas SA, The Ocean Frost* [1986] AC 717. An employee of the defendants entered into a contract for the charter of a ship, into which he had no authority, either actual or ostensible, to enter. The employee did represent that he had authority to enter into such a transaction but such a representation did not fall within the class of representations which a person in the position of the employee was usually authorised to perform. So the claimants could not recover against the defendants because they had placed their reliance upon the employee.

The conclusion which must be drawn is that the 'course of employment' requirement has been interpreted erratically and that the category of assaults committed by employees is out of step with the other categories. This merely serves to illustrate the lack of a clear theoretical basis to the doctrine of vicarious liability.

4.6 The employer's indemnity

There is no doubt that employers and employees are joint tortfeasors, with the result that when the employer is held liable for the tort of his employee, the employer has the right to recover an indemnity under s1(1) of the Civil Liability (Contribution) Act 1978. In the typical vicarious liability case this would mean that the employer could recover a complete indemnity.

In addition to this statutory right the employer may be entitled to recover an indemnity at common law, as in *Lister v Romford Ice and Cold Storage Co* [1957] AC 555. Here a father and son were fellow employees. The father was injured as a result of the negligence of his son. The father sued the employers in negligence and recovered from them. However the employers' insurers successfully recovered from the son as the son was in breach of his implied undertaking to take reasonable care and so they recovered the sum which had been paid to his father.

It must be doubted whether this indemnity should be permitted to continue in present circumstances. The employer is usually in the best position to bear such a loss. In most cases he is insured and it is even more undesirable to allow an insurance company, which has been paid to accept the risk, to recover from the employee when the risk, in fact, materialises. However, it is unlikely that such a case would occur again, as employers' insurers have entered into a gentleman's agreement not to take advantage of the indemnity principle unless there is evidence of collusion or wilful misconduct.

4.7 Principal and agent

A principal may be vicariously liable for torts committed by his agent in the course of his agent's employment (cf *Winfield and Jolowicz on Tort* (14th ed) pp612–15). The main difficulty here arises with what may be called 'ad hoc' agency. These cases are really concerned with liability arising out of road traffic accidents, where the legal response is shaped by the insurance background.

The first case of significance is *Ormrod v Crossville Motor Services* [1953] 1 WLR 1120. The owner of a motor car asked a friend to drive the car from Birkenhead to Monte Carlo, where the owner planned to compete in the car rally. After the rally was over both parties planned to go on holiday together in the car. In the course of the journey the friend was in an accident caused by his negligence. The claimant's bus was damaged in the accident. It was held that the owner was liable for his friend's negligence, even though the friend was going on the journey partly for his own purposes.

However, a different result was reached in *Morgans v Launchbury* [1973] AC 127 where the House of Lords placed a limit on the extent to which a claimant can search for a defendant who has an insurance policy, irrespective of the fault of the defendant. A husband used his wife's car to go to work and when he went out drinking. The wife expressed concern about her husband's drinking habits and told him to get a friend to drive him if he had had too much to drink. One evening the husband got drunk and duly got a friend to drive him home. The friend drove off at 90 mph in the wrong direction and collided with a bus, killing the friend and the husband and injuring passengers on the bus. The passengers sued the wife, claiming that she was vicariously liable. This argument was rejected by the House of Lords on the ground that the husband could not be regarded as the wife's agent, even when he took the car to his work. Lord Wilberforce said that 'in order to fix vicarious liability on the owner of a car in such a case as the present, it must be shown that the driver was using it for the owner's purposes, under delegation of a task or duty'. If, however, the owner has permitted an uninsured driver to drive his car then he will be liable for breach of statutory duty if the driver is unable to satisfy judgment (*Monk* v *Warbey* [1935] 1 KB 175) and if the driver is uninsured then the Motor Insurers' Bureau may meet an unsatisfied judgment in respect of personal injuries.

4.8 Partnership

The vicarious liability of partners is governed by s10 of the Partnership Act 1890 which states that:

> 'Where, by any wrongful act or omission of any partner acting in the ordinary course of the business of the firm, or with the authority of his co-partners, loss or injury is caused to any person not being a partner in his firm, or any penalty is incurred, the firm is liable therefore to the same extent as the partner so acting or omitting to act.'

It is further provided in s12 that the liability of partners is joint and several.

In *Dubai Aluminium Co Ltd* v *Salaam* [2003] 1 All ER 97 it was alleged (but never proved) that Mr Amhurst, a partner in a firm of solicitors (the firm), had assisted in an elaborate fraud by drafting certain agreements. The defrauded claimant's claim against the firm and Mr Amhurst was settled by a payment of $US10 million. The firm now made contribution claims, based on s1(1) Civil Liability (Contribution) Act 1978, against two of the fraudsters. In order to succeed, the firm had to show that it was liable in respect of the claimant's loss. The House of Lords held that the firm's claim would be successful. Mr Amhurst's alleged wrongdoing (a fault-based equitable wrong) had been a 'wrongful act or omission' which he had carried out while 'acting in the ordinary course of the business of the firm', within s10 Partnership Act 1890. As Lord Nicholls of Birkenhead explained, there was nothing in the language of s10 to suggest that the wrongful act or omission was intended to be confined to common law torts as opposed to the equitable wrong of dishonest participation in a breach of trust. Drafting agreements of such a nature for a proper purpose would be within the ordinary course of the firm's business. Drafting those particular agreements was to be regarded as an act done within the ordinary course of the firm's business, even though they were drafted for a dishonest purpose. Those acts were so closely connected with the acts Mr Amhurst was authorised to do that for the purpose of the firm's liability they could fairly and properly be regarded as done by him while acting in the ordinary course of the firm's business and the firm was accordingly liable. In deciding contribution the personal innocence of the other partners was not a relevant matter to be taken into account. For all relevant purposes the firm stood in the shoes of Mr Amhurst. As to s1(1) of the 1978 Act, see Chapter 3, section 3.5.

A limited partnership consists of general partners, who are liable for all debts and obligations of the firm, and limited partners who are not liable beyond their initial contribution. However, if a limited partner takes part in the management of the partnership business, he is liable for all debts and obligations of the firm incurred while he does so as though he were a general partner: ss4(2) and 6(1) of the Limited Partnerships Act 1907. In the case of limited liability partnerships, where a member is liable to any person (other than another member of the limited liability partnership) as a result of a wrongful act or omission of his in the course of the business of the limited liability partnership or with its authority, the limited liability partnership is liable to the same extent as the member: s6(4) of the Limited Liability Partnerships Act 2000.

4.9 Police

The chief officer of police for a police area is liable in respect of torts committed by constables under his direction and control in the performance or purported performance of their functions in like manner as a master is liable in respect of torts committed by his servants in the course of their employment, and accordingly in respect of any such tort is treated for all purposes as a joint tortfeasor: Police Act 1996, s88(1). Any damages or costs awarded against the chief officer, or any moneys required for the settlement of any claim, are payable out of the police fund: s88(2).

5

Liability for Independent Contractors

5.1 Introduction and the general rule

5.2 Exceptions to the general rule

5.3 Conclusion

5.1 Introduction and the general rule

In addition to being liable for the torts of their employees committed in the course of their employment, employers may also, in certain circumstances, be held liable for torts committed by independent contractors which they have employed. It must be stated that none of these cases of liability for the tort of an independent contractor are examples of vicarious liability. They are all examples of primary liability of the employer. The general rule, however, is that an employer is not liable for the tort of his independent contractor. The traditional justification for this is that the employer does not control the independent contractor and so there is no justification for imposing liability upon the employer for the tort of the independent contractor. One example of this general rule is the case of *Morgan* v *Incorporated Central Council of the Girls Friendly Society* [1936] 1 All ER 404. The claimant suffered injury when he fell down a lift shaft on the defendants' premises. The reason for the accident was that the lift shaft had been negligently left unguarded by a firm of independent contractors. It was held that the defendants were not liable for the negligence of the independent contractors.

An interesting challenge to this rule was launched in *D and F Estates Ltd* v *The Church Commissioners for England* [1989] AC 177. The defendants were the main contractors involved in the building of a block of flats and the claimants took a lease of one of the flats. After they had moved in the claimants discovered that the plastering work, which had been done by a firm of independent contractors employed by the defendants, had been done defectively. So they sued the defendants for the cost of the repair and other economic loss on the ground, inter alia, that the defendants owed a duty to the claimants to supervise the work of the subcontractors and that they had failed to discharge this duty properly. The House of Lords rejected the argument that the defendants owed a duty of care to the claimants. The House of Lords also held that the defendants were not liable for the negligence of the subcontractors who failed to carry out the plaster work properly. Lord Bridge affirmed that 'it is trite law that the employer of an independent contractor is, in general, not liable for the negligence or other torts committed by the contractor in the course of the execution of the work'. However, Lord Bridge did acknowledge that, if the main contractor, in the course of the supervision of the subcontractor, comes to know that the subcontractor is carrying out his work in a defective and foreseeably dangerous way and if he condones the negligence on the part of the subcontractor, the main contractor would 'no doubt make himself potentially liable for the consequences as joint tortfeasor'. In the present case there was no evidence that the main contractors actually knew of the defective plastering work and, since the case did not fall within any of the exceptional cases when an employer may be liable for the tort of an independent contractor (on which see section 5.2), the defendants were not liable for the negligence of the plasterers.

5.2 Exceptions to the general rule

There are a number of exceptions to the general rule that an employer is not liable for the tort of an independent contractor. These exceptions may be classified as follows.

Firstly, the employer is liable where he has authorised the independent contractor to commit a tort (*Ellis* v *Sheffield Gas Consumers Co* (1853) 2 E & B 767). In such a case the employer is liable as a joint tortfeasor with the independent contractor.

Secondly, the employer is liable if he is negligent in choosing an independent contractor who is not competent to carry out the job or if the employer fails to instruct him properly or fails to check the work where he is competent to do so (*Pinn* v *Rew* (1916) 32 TLR 451).

Thirdly, statute law may impose upon the employer a duty of care which cannot be discharged by delegating performance to an independent contractor. Whether a statute does impose such an 'absolute' obligation upon the employer is, of course, a question of construction of the particular statute. One example of a statute which imposes such an absolute obligation upon employers is the Factories Act 1961.

Fourthly, at common law certain non-delegable duties are imposed upon employers. 'Non-delegable' duty does not mean that the employer cannot, in fact, delegate performance to an independent contractor. What it means is that the employer cannot delegate responsibility for the performance of the task. There are a number of non-delegable duties which exist at common law, but there is no coherent policy behind the existence of these duties. There are six such common law duties which are worthy of consideration.

The first category consists of cases of (so called) strict liability at common law, such as the rule in *Rylands* v *Fletcher* (see Chapter 20) and nuisance (Chapter 18), where the employer is liable for the tort of the independent contractor. The second, and to some extent analogous, category consists of cases where the employer has employed an independent contractor to do work which is classified as being 'extra hazardous'. The operation of this principle can be illustrated by reference to the case of *Honeywill and Stein Ltd* v *Larkin Brothers Ltd* [1934] 1 KB 191. The claimants were engaged to do acoustics work and employed the defendants, as independent contractors, to take photographs of the cinema as part of their work. The defendants used flash photography which, at that time, required a tray of magnesium to be ignited above the camera lens. In doing this the defendants set fire to the cinema curtains. The claimants paid the damages and then sought to recover from the defendants. It was held that the claimants were liable to the owners of the theatre for the damage caused by the negligence of the defendants and that they were, in turn, entitled to recover damages from the defendants for breach of contract. The operation was a hazardous one and the claimants had assumed an obligation to ensure that reasonable precautions were taken so that no damage would result and this obligation could not be delegated to an independent contractor (it should be noted that the High Court of Australia in *Stevens* v *Brodribb Sawmilling Co Pty Ltd* (1986) 160 CLR 16 has refused to follow *Honeywill* on the ground that this exception cannot be justified in policy terms). This rule does not apply where the activity is not extra hazardous (*Salsbury* v *Woodland* [1970] 1 QB 342). It is not easy to say what constitutes an extra hazardous activity, but it must be something which involves the risk of special danger to others. The fact that a task is difficult does not mean that it is extra hazardous; work is only extra hazardous when, by its very nature, it involves a risk of danger to others unless done with extreme care (*Alcock* v *Wraith* (1992) 59 Build LR 16).

The third category of non-delegable duties at common law relates to liability for the escape of fire (*Balfour* v *Barty-King* [1957] 1 QB 496). *Balfour* was applied in *Johnson* v *BJW Property Developments Ltd* [2002] 3 All ER 574. The claimant and the defendant owned and occupied adjoining properties, separated by a party wall. In the defendant's premises, a fireplace was built into the party wall: a domestic fire lit there spread into, and caused extensive damage to, the claimant's premises. An independent contractor, employed by the defendant, had been negligent in installing a new fire surround: he had removed fire protection from the fireplace and not replaced it. The claimant maintained that the defendant was strictly liable for the escape of fire from its premises, a view supported, by implication, by s86 Fires Prevention (Metropolis) Act 1774 (the fire which spread into its premises had been lit deliberately, it had not 'accidentally' begun). The defendant also relied on s86 of the 1774 Act, contending that 'accidentally' covered fires started in domestic grates. The claimant was successful. The 1774 Act was of no relevance to the fire in the grate since that fire had been started deliberately. It was the escape of the fire which gave rise to liability and the possible defence of accidental escape. Here the escape had not been accidental: it had resulted from negligence for which the defendant was responsible. Judge Thornton QC said:

'... all the requirements that need to be shown to give rise to an occupier's vicarious liability for the negligence of his independent contractor have been made out. The relevant work was undertaken negligently on and adjacent to a party wall. It involved a special risk to, and by its very nature endangered, the claimant's adjoining premises. I conclude that the claimant is entitled to judgment against the defendant for liability with damages to be assessed. That liability is in both negligence and nuisance, being both a primary liability for the fire damage and also vicarious liability for the negligence of its independent contractor in causing that damage.'

The fourth category consists of cases where the work of the independent contractor is done on or over the highway, or some other place to which the public has access. Thus in *Tarry* v *Ashton* (1876) 1 QBD 314 an employer was held liable when a lamp which projected over the highway fell on the claimant. The employer was held liable even though he had contracted with an independent contractor for the repair of the lamp. He remained liable for the negligence of the contractor. Similarly in *Holliday* v *National Telephone Co* [1899] 2 QB 392 the contractor, a plumber, was soldering joints in telephone wires when he immersed a blowlamp in a pot of solder on the highway and it exploded, injuring the claimant. It was held that the defendants, who had employed the plumber, were liable because they had a duty to see that the work was carried out with due care for the protection of those who passed along the highway (in this case the defendants' duty was derived from statute).

The fifth category consists of the employer's non-delegable duty in respect of the safety of his employees (*Wilsons and Clyde Coal Co* v *English* [1938] AC 57). The sixth and final category consists of the rule that a bailee for reward, who entrusts the goods he is supposed to be looking after to an independent contractor, remains liable for any loss or damage to the goods, in the absence of any contractual provision to the contrary (see *Morris* v *CW Martin & Sons Ltd* [1966] 1 QB 716 and *British Road Services* v *Arthur Crutchley* [1967] 1 WLR 835).

Finally, the employer is not liable for the collateral or casual negligence of the independent contractor. In many cases it is difficult to discern what is meant by 'collateral negligence'. In general it can be said to mean that the negligence of the independent contractor must arise out of the very task which is delegated to him and if it is not then his negligence is collateral. Thus in *Padbury* v *Holliday and Greenwood* (1912) 28 TLR 492 the defendants employed a subcontractor to do some work on a house which the defendants were building. One of the subcontractor's employees put a tool on a window sill while he was working. A strong gust of wind blew in the window and the tool fell off the sill and hit the claimant, who was walking along the highway. It was held that the employee's negligence was incidental to the performance of his task and so the defendants were not liable to the claimant.

5.3 Conclusion

Recent years have witnessed a large increase in the number of self-employed workers in this country. This increase threatens to undermine the social purposes served by the doctrine of vicarious liability because, as the law presently stands, employers are not vicariously liable for the torts of independent contractors. As yet the courts have not formed a coherent response to this problem (see generally McKendrick 'Vicarious Liability and Independent Contractors – A Re-Examination' (1990) 53 MLR 770). In some cases they have sought to extend the exceptions to the general rule of no liability (see, for example, *McDermid* v *Nash Dredging and Reclamation Co Ltd* [1987] AC 906), while in other cases they have sought to impose new forms of primary liability upon employers, such as a duty to co-ordinate third parties (see, for example, the decision of the High Court of Australia in *Stevens* v *Brodribb Sawmilling Co Pty Ltd* (1986) 160 CLR 16). One further approach which could be adopted is to abandon the generalist approach of the common law to the question of whether or not a particular worker is an employee (an example of which can be found in the judgment of Wright J in *R* v *Callender* [1993] QB 303, 309). If it was recognised that the question of whether or not a worker is an employee depends upon the context in which the question arises, then there would be room for a more flexible approach in vicarious liability cases. This is because, in such cases, the policies of loss distribution and finding a solvent defendant favour classification of a worker as an employee. One possible line of development would be for the courts to conclude that, once a person is found to be part of an organisation, in the sense that his work is an 'integral part of the business' rather than being merely 'accessory' to it, the organisation is vicariously liable for all the wrongs of that person committed within the scope of his responsibilities, whether he is an employee or an independent contractor. It must, however, be said that English law has presently set its face against the conclusion that an employer can be vicariously liable for the wrongdoing of an independent contractor (see *McDermid* (above)) but, if English law is to meet the challenge presented to it by the increase in the numbers of self-employed workers then it is suggested that it will have to reconsider its position on this issue.

6

Negligence: The Duty of Care – Some General Considerations

6.1 Introduction

In the study of the law of tort the centre stage is occupied by the tort of negligence. The tort of negligence has been defined by *Winfield and Jolowicz on Tort* (14th ed) p78 in the following terms: '... negligence as a tort is the breach of a legal duty to take care which results in damage, undesired by the defendant, to the [claimant]'. Thus stated the tort consists of three distinct elements.

The first element is that the defendant must owe to the claimant a duty of care. The circumstances in which a defendant may owe a duty of care to the claimant will be discussed in this Chapter. The second element is that the defendant must breach the duty of care which he owes to the claimant. This issue will be discussed in Chapter 9. The third element is that the claimant must suffer damage as a result of the defendant's breach of his duty of care. The two main principles here are that the defendant's negligence must have caused the damage to the claimant (discussed in Chapter 10) and the damage which the claimant suffered must not be too remote a consequence of the defendant's negligence (discussed in Chapter 11).

This Chapter will therefore discuss the principles upon which the courts decide whether or not the defendant owes to the claimant a duty of care. The modern source of the duty of care requirement can be found in the celebrated judgment of Lord Atkin in *Donoghue* v *Stevenson* [1932] AC 562. It is of vital significance in English law because it is via the duty of care concept that the courts have sought to limit and control the circumstances in which liability may be imposed upon a defendant for the consequences of his negligence.

As is often the case in studying the law of tort we must commence our study by briefly examining the history of this issue because it is necessary to understand the history if we are to comprehend the present state of the law. We can divide the development of the duty of care into three broad stages; the first being 'the emergence of a general principle', the second being 'the development of the general principle' and the third being 'resiling from the general principle'. It must, however, be said that this tripartite division is a broad one. Cases can always be found within a particular period which appear to defy this analysis. The purpose of this division is simply to enable us to identify the broad thrust of the development of the tort of negligence.

6.2 The emergence of a general principle

A person is not liable for every negligent act which he or she commits. There has always been some control device which has identified and limited the situations in which a person may be held legally liable for the consequences of his negligence. As we have already noted, the principal control device in English law is the requirement that the defendant owe to the claimant a duty of care. This requirement was not articulated as a general principle until the judgment of Brett MR in the case of *Heaven* v *Pender* (1883) 11 QBD 503. At that stage in our legal development, the tort of negligence was applicable to damage caused in certain particular circumstances, such as road accidents, but was not a principle of general application. The innovation in the judgment of Brett MR was that he sought to formulate a general principle for identifying whether or not a duty of care existed, which principle could be applied to new situations as well as to the traditional categories.

But it was not until the famous case of *Donoghue* v *Stevenson* [1932] AC 562 that a general principle was firmly established for determining the existence of a duty of care. The defendants were manufacturers of ginger beer. A friend of the claimant purchased a bottle of ginger beer for the claimant. The claimant drank some of the ginger beer but when she poured out the remainder of the contents of the bottle a decomposed snail floated out of the bottle. The claimant claimed that she suffered severe shock and became very ill as a result of this incident. She was unable to proceed against the manufacturers in contract because there was no contract between the parties. So she brought an action in tort against the manufacturers. The House of Lords held that the defendants, being the manufacturers of the ginger beer, owed a duty of care to the claimant, as the ultimate consumer or purchaser of the ginger beer, to take reasonable care to ensure that the bottle did not contain some substance which was likely to cause injury to health. The decision of the House of Lords is important for two particular reasons.

The first reason is the judgment of Lord Atkin. His statement of principle still forms the basis of the modern law and its importance lies in its attempt to provide a general principle which could be applied in all negligence cases and, thus, could unify what had, hitherto, been a series of discrete rules. He said:

> 'In English law there must be, and is, some general conception of relations giving rise to a duty of care, of which the particular cases found in the books are but instances ... The rule that you are to love your neighbour becomes, in law, you must not injure your neighbour; and the lawyer's question, Who is my neighbour? receives a restricted reply. You must take reasonable care to avoid acts or omissions which you can reasonably foresee would be likely to injure your neighbour. Who, then, in law is my neighbour? The answer seems to be – persons who are so closely and directly affected by my act that I ought reasonably to have them in contemplation as being so affected when I am directing my mind to the acts or omissions which are called in question.'

This dicta is the general principle which has assumed enormous significance in the development of the tort of negligence.

The second point of significance was that their Lordships freed the tort of negligence from what was known as the 'contract fallacy'. According to this contract fallacy, where a manufacturer had entered into a contractual relationship with another, he could not owe a duty of care in tort to a third party who was not privy to that contract. The most oft-quoted example of this contract fallacy is the case of *Winterbottom* v *Wright* (1842) 10 M & W 109. The defendants were coachbuilders. They had a contract with the Postmaster-General to deliver a coach for the delivery of mail. The claimant was the driver of the coach and he was seriously injured when he fell off the coach due to a latent defect in the construction of the coach. It was held that the claimant could not recover from the defendants because he was not privy to the contract for the delivery of the coach. But this fallacy was exploded by the House of Lords in *Donoghue*. It was held that it was irrelevant to the claimant's action in tort that she was not privy to a contract with the defendants for the sale of the ginger beer. The existence of a contractual relationship with the purchaser of the ginger beer did not preclude the existence of liability in tort to the claimant, who was not a party to the contract. Although this contract fallacy was duly disposed of, the issue of the relationship between contract and tort has been a persistent source of difficulty.

6.3 The development of the general principle

Lord Atkin's statement of principle has come to be known as the neighbour or neighbourhood principle. As we have noted, its importance lies in providing a unifying framework for the tort of negligence and a general principle which can be applied to new situations, not falling within the traditional categories. However, some of the judiciary were reluctant to accept that this statement of principle had the effect of constituting a general principle which was applicable to new situations. As late as 1951 in the case of *Candler v Crane Christmas and Co* [1951] 2 KB 164 we find that the majority of the Court of Appeal were unwilling to extend liability for negligent misstatement causing economic loss. Lord Denning argued that the old authorities had to be re-examined in the light of *Donoghue* but this argument was rejected by the majority who slavishly followed the old precedents, which pre-dated *Donoghue*, and refused to subject them to fresh analysis in the light of *Donoghue*. Eventually in the landmark case of *Hedley Byrne & Co Ltd v Heller & Partners Ltd* [1964] AC 465 the House of Lords did extend liability for negligent misstatement, although it is crucial to note that they did not apply ordinary *Donoghue* principles for fear that it would lead to too great an ambit of liability. Instead they preferred to apply a more restrictive test. But *Hedley Byrne* is a significant decision because it demonstrated that the House of Lords were prepared to expand the ambit of liability in negligence in appropriate cases.

However in 1970 Lord Atkin's statement of principle was given explicit recognition by the House of Lords as being a statement of general principle which could be applied to all cases of negligence. In *Home Office v Dorset Yacht Co* [1970] AC 1004 Lord Reid said that:

> '*Donoghue v Stevenson* ... may be regarded as a milestone, and the well-known passage in Lord Atkin's speech should, I think, be regarded as a statement of principle. It is not to be treated as if it were a statutory definition. It will require qualification in new circumstances. But I think that the time has come when we can and should say that it ought to apply unless there is some justification or valid explanation for its exclusion.'

Lord Reid's judgment was an important one because it gave the courts significant freedom to develop the tort of negligence and to apply it to new situations.

This development of a general principle which could be applied to all cases was taken a stage further in the judgment of Lord Wilberforce in *Anns v Merton London Borough Council* [1978] AC 728. Lord Wilberforce said:

> 'Through the trilogy of cases in this House, *Donoghue v Stevenson*, *Hedley Byrne & Co Ltd v Heller & Partners Ltd* and *Home Office v Dorset Yacht Co Ltd* the position has now been reached that in order to establish that a duty of care arises in a particular situation, it is not necessary to bring the facts of that situation within those of previous situations in which a duty of care has been held to exist. Rather the question has to be approached in two stages. First one has to ask whether, as between the alleged wrongdoer and the person who has suffered damage there is a sufficient relationship of proximity or neighbourhood such that, in the reasonable contemplation of the former, carelessness on his part may be

likely to cause damage to the latter, in which case a prima facie duty of care arises. Secondly, if the first question is answered affirmatively, it is necessary to consider whether there are any considerations which ought to negative, or to reduce or limit the scope of the duty or the class of persons to whom it is owed or the damages to which a breach of it may give rise.'

This two-tier approach was in many ways the high-water mark in the development of the tort of negligence. It has been frequently used in the courts. It provided a principle which could be applied to all cases and the effect of its application in some cases was to expand considerably the boundaries of the tort of negligence.

6.4 Resiling from the general principle

The broad general principle established by Lord Wilberforce in *Anns* has since come under heavy fire, both from the judiciary and from many academics. The principal judicial critics have been Lord Keith, Lord Bridge and, albeit to a lesser extent, Lord Oliver. With the benefit of hindsight, the first major judicial criticism of the two tier approach of Lord Wilberforce can be found in the judgment of Lord Keith in *Governors of the Peabody Donation Fund* v *Sir Lindsay Parkinson & Co Ltd* [1985] AC 210. Lord Keith noted the tendency to treat the passage which we have considered in Lord Wilberforce's judgment as if it was of 'a definitive character'. He went on to say that:

> 'This is a temptation which should be resisted. The true question in each case is whether the particular defendant owed to the particular [claimant] a duty of care having the scope which is contended for, and whether he was in breach of that duty with consequent loss to the [claimant]. A relationship of proximity in Lord Atkin's sense must exist before any duty of care can arise, but the scope of the duty must depend on all the circumstances of the case ... So in determining whether or not a duty of care of particular scope was incumbent upon a defendant it is material to take into consideration whether it is just and reasonable that it should be so.'

Although Lord Keith criticised Lord Wilberforce's two-tier approach, his approach, based upon what is 'just and reasonable', does not appear to be any more certain than that adopted by Lord Wilberforce, nor does it appear to be significantly different. However, it has assumed considerable significance in subsequent cases. The most important aspect of this judgment is the emphasis on the need to have regard to all the circumstances of the case in deciding whether or not a duty of care is owed.

Further criticism was levelled against Lord Wilberforce's two-tier approach in the case of *Leigh and Sillivan Ltd* v *Aliakmon Shipping Co Ltd* [1985] 1 QB 350 (CA) and [1986] AC 785 (HL). In the Court of Appeal Oliver LJ stated that it was not correct:

> ' ... to regard *Anns* as establishing some new and revolutionary test of the duty of care,

the logical application of which is going to enable the court in every case to say whether or not a duty of care exists. Nor, as it seems to me, can it properly be treated either as establishing some new approach to what the policy of the law should be or as conferring upon the court a free hand to determine for itself in each case what limits are to be set.'

This judgment adopts a much more conservative approach than did Lord Wilberforce in *Anns*. The fear which is expressed in this judgment is that the first tier of Lord Wilberforce's approach, that of proximity, is too broad and that it leaves too much to the second stage based upon policy. In particular Oliver LJ said that the courts were not free to evolve their own conception of policy without regard to established lines of authority. This reference to the need to have regard to established authorities where no duty of care has been recognised, constitutes an attack on the generality of the principle adopted in *Anns* and seems to take us back to the pre-*Donoghue* situation where a duty of care only existed in certain well-defined situations and was not to be extended. A similar approach was adopted by Lord Brandon in the House of Lords. He said that Lord Wilberforce's judgment did not provide a 'universally applicable test of the existence and scope of a duty of care'. He also said that Lord Wilberforce's judgment was given in the context of a novel factual situation and not in the context of a factual situation in which such a duty had repeatedly been held not to exist. In the latter context *Anns* was not applicable and no duty of care was owed. As Professor Hepple has noted: 'Lord Brandon's rule-orientated approach … is reminiscent of the pre-1932 categorisations of negligence rules and of the shackled judicial reasoning before Wilberforce's emancipation' (All ER Rev 1986 p311).

A more fundamental assault was launched on the approach adopted in *Anns* in *Curran* v *Northern Ireland Co-ownership Housing Association Ltd* [1987] AC 718. Lord Bridge stated that Lord Wilberforce's judgment in *Anns*:

' … may be said to represent the high-water mark of a trend in the development of the law of negligence by your Lordships' House towards the elevation of the "neighbourhood" principle derived from the speech of Lord Atkin in *Donoghue* v *Stevenson* into one of general application from which a duty of care may always be derived unless there are clear countervailing considerations to exclude it.'

To similar effect is the judgment of Lord Keith in *Yuen Kun Yeu* v *Attorney-General of Hong Kong* [1988] AC 175 when he said that Lord Wilberforce's approach 'had been elevated to a degree of importance greater than it merits, and greater perhaps than its author intended'. He added that:

'In view of the direction in which the law has since been developing, their Lordships consider that for the future it should be recognised that the two-stage test … is not to be regarded as in all circumstances a suitable guide to the existence of a duty of care.'

Finally, in *Murphy* v *Brentwood District Council* [1991] 1 AC 398, 461 Lord Keith stated that he considered that the incremental approach adopted by Brennan J in the High Court of Australia in *Council of the Shire of Sutherland* v *Heyman* (1985) 157

CLR 424 (on which see below) was preferable to the two-stage test adopted by Lord Wilberforce in *Anns*.

6.5 A general principle or reasoning by analogy?

In understanding the reasons behind this gradual abandonment of the two-stage test in *Anns* it is very important to have regard to the judgment of Lord Bridge in *Caparo Industries plc* v *Dickman* [1990] 2 AC 605. Lord Bridge there drew a distinction between two different approaches which can be adopted when seeking to identify the existence of a duty of care. The first approach he called the traditional approach where the 'law finds the existence of the duty [of care] in different specific situations each exhibiting its own particular characteristics'. This is the approach which we noted was the predominant one prior to the judgment of Lord Atkin in *Donoghue* (see section 6.2). The second approach identified by Lord Bridge, he called 'the more modern approach of seeking a single general principle which may be applied in all circumstances to determine the existence of a duty of care'. This approach found its classic expression in the judgment of Lord Reid in *Home Office* v *Dorset Yacht* (above) and in the two-stage test of Lord Wilberforce in *Anns*. But Lord Bridge noted that in a series of cases, particularly in the judgments of Lord Keith which we have already noted, the House of Lords had 'emphasised the inability of any single general principle to provide a practical test which can be applied to every situation to determine whether a duty of care is owed and, if so, what is its scope'. He continued:

> 'While recognising ... the importance of the underlying general principles common to the whole field of negligence, I think the law has now moved in the direction of attaching greater significance to the more traditional categorisation of distinct and recognisable situations as guides to the existence, the scope and the limits of the varied duties of care which the law imposes.'

In the light of this judgment it is now extremely difficult, if not impossible, for us to say that we have a general principle for determining the existence of a duty of care which is applicable to all cases. The courts have abandoned the attempt to frame a single general principle and have chosen instead to 'reason by analogy' with 'distinct and identifiable situations' where the law already imposes a duty of care. The difficulty with this approach is that it can easily lead to the conclusion that the categories of negligence are closed because a court may reason that, simply because the precedents are against the recognition of a duty of care, it must necessarily come to the conclusion that on the facts of the case before it no duty is owed. Yet such an approach would be contrary to the famous dictum of Lord Macmillan in *Donoghue* v *Stevenson* when he said that 'the categories of negligence are never closed'. This danger may be avoided if we rename the 'analogy' approach the 'incremental' approach. In his judgment in *Caparo* Lord Bridge said that the House of Lords had to recognise the wisdom contained in the judgment of Brennan J in the High Court of Australia in *Council of the Shire of Sutherland* v *Heyman* when he said that it is:

'... preferable ... that the law should develop novel categories of negligence incrementally and by analogy with established categories, rather than by a massive extension of a prima facie duty of care restrained only by indefinable considerations which ought to negative, or to reduce or limit the scope of the duty or the class of persons to whom it is owed.'

The point to note from this quotation is the contrast between 'incrementally' and 'massive extension'. The fear which Brennan J expresses (and which is now apparently shared by the House of Lords) is that the first tier of the Wilberforce test, namely proximity, was too easily satisfied by a claimant and that the consequence was therefore a 'massive extension of a prima facie duty of care'. On this view the vital control device therefore became the second stage, the policy stage or, as Brennan J preferred to call it, 'indefinable considerations'. Most judges, Lord Denning apart, are reluctant to become embroiled in policy disputes, preferring to leave policy to Parliament. The 'incremental' approach has the advantage of enabling the judiciary to avoid express reliance upon broad considerations of policy by hiding their policy choices behind the finding that there was no 'proximity' between the parties or the conclusion that the existing authorities preclude the finding of a duty of care. The wisdom which lies behind this change of approach is debatable but it is incontestable that such a change has in fact taken place.

In *Law Society* v *KPMG Peat Marwick* [2000] 4 All ER 540 the Court of Appeal heard that the defendant accountants had been engaged by a firm of solicitors to prepare their annual reports to the Law Society, indicating whether the firm had complied with the rules regarding client funds. It subsequently appeared that many of the firm's clients had been defrauded and payments of some £8.5 million were made to them out of the compensation fund. As trustees of the fund, the Society sued the defendants for negligence: had the defendants owed the Society a duty of care in preparing the relevant reports? This preliminary question was answered in the affirmative and Lord Woolf CJ said:

'I will summarise the detailed and careful reasoning of Sir Richard Scott V-C [at first instance]. He applied the three criteria which must be met for there to be a duty of care identified by Lord Bridge of Harwich in *Caparo Industries plc* v *Dickman* [1990] 1 All ER 568, namely: (a) reasonable foreseeability of damage; (b) a relationship of sufficient "proximity" between the party owing the duty and the party to whom it is owed; and (c) the imposition of the duty of care contended for would be just and reasonable in all the circumstances. ... I agree with Sir Richard Scott V-C that the correct approach is to examine the question of whether the accountants owe a duty of care to the Law Society in relation to its responsibilities to protect the compensation fund against the well-established test laid down in the *Caparo Industries* case. ... The threefold approach identified by Lord Bridge can ... be readily applied to the present situation and when it is applied, it can be readily seen that the requirements are fulfilled.'

The decision of the House of Lords in *Waters* v *Commissioner of Police of the*

Metropolis [2000] 4 All ER 934 is also significant in this context. The appellant female police officer alleged that she had been raped and buggered in her police residential accommodation by a fellow officer when they were both off duty. In those proceedings she alleged that her complaint had not been dealt with properly by her superiors, that they had allowed other officers to harass, victimise 'and otherwise oppress her' and that she had suffered psychiatric injury as a result. Their Lordships decided that her claim ought not to have been struck out since it was not plain and obvious that it had to fail.

In the course of his speech, Lord Slynn of Hadley said that, at that stage, he was not prepared to say:

1. in the light of *Caparo Industries*, that it would not be 'fair, just and reasonable' to recognise a duty of care in these circumstances;
2. that the decisions of the House in *Hill* v *Chief Constable of West Yorkshire* [1988] 2 All ER 238 and *Calveley* v *Chief Constable of the Merseyside Police* [1989] 1 All ER 1025 (see Chapter 8, section 8.4) were conclusive against the appellant;
3. it having been said many times that the law of negligence develops incrementally, that the fact that there was no reported case succeeding against the police similar to this one was necessarily a sufficient reason for striking out.

6.6 The incremental approach

How then do the courts decide whether or not to impose a duty of care upon the defendant in a particular case? A crucial factor is obviously earlier authorities. Where a duty of care has been imposed in an earlier analogous case a court will be more inclined to impose a duty on the facts of the case before it unless it is satisfied that the analogy is not properly drawn. Conversely, where the precedents are against the recognition of a duty of care a court will be reluctant to impose a duty unless it considers that the earlier cases are not directly in point or it is convinced that, reasoning incrementally and by reference to the precedents, an extension of the scope of liability is justified.

But what of the novel case, the case where there are no precedents to guide the court? What will a court do then? There are three factors which are employed by the courts in deciding whether or not to impose a duty of care in a novel case: the first is that the loss must be reasonably foreseeable, the second is that there must be a 'proximate relationship' between the claimant and the defendant and the third is that it must be 'fair, just and reasonable that the law should impose a duty of a given scope upon the one party for the benefit of the other' (see, for example, the judgment of Lord Bridge in *Caparo* v *Dickman* [1990] 2 AC 605, 617–618 and *Marc Rich & Co AG* v *Bishop Rock Marine Co Ltd, The Nicholas H* [1995] 3 All ER 307 where the House of Lords followed this approach). These three factors require further comment.

The first factor does not require much by way of comment except to say that reasonable foresight of harm is a necessary requirement but that it is not of itself sufficient. It should, however, be noted that it is the foresight of the reasonable man which is used in determining liability. Thus it is not the foresight of the particular defendant which is in issue but the foresight of the reasonable man standing in the shoes of the defendant. If the claimant cannot show that it was reasonably foreseeable that he would suffer loss as a result of the negligence of the defendant then he cannot succeed in an action in negligence against the defendant. English law does not recognise that negligence exists 'in the air'. This can be demonstrated by reference to the case of *Bourhill* v *Young* [1943] AC 92 where the House of Lords held that no duty of care was owed to the claimant because injury to her was not reasonably foreseeable. The claimant had witnessed a motor accident caused by the negligence of the defendant and in which the defendant was killed. She claimed that she heard the accident and saw the aftermath of it and that this had caused her baby to be born stillborn. It was held that the claimant was so far away from the accident that she was not owed a duty of care by the defendant because it was not reasonably foreseeable that she would suffer nervous shock as a result of the accident. The fact that it was foreseeable that other people might suffer injury as a result of the defendant's negligence was irrelevant because the claimant could not base her case on a wrong which was done, or could have been done, to someone else.

The second element, a 'proximate relationship', does call for further comment because the meaning of this phrase is not at all clear. It will be remembered that in the first stage of his two stage test in *Anns* Lord Wilberforce spoke of a 'relationship of proximity'. The meaning of this phrase became a matter of some controversy until it was authoritatively considered by Lord Keith in his judgment in *Yuen Kun Yeu* (above). Lord Keith there identified two different interpretations of proximity. The first was that it meant simply foreseeability of harm. But Lord Keith stated that, although foreseeability of harm is 'a necessary ingredient' of liability (see above), it is not sufficient of itself automatically to give rise to a duty of care, otherwise 'there would be liability in negligence on the part of one who sees another about to walk over a cliff with his head in the air, and forbears to shout a warning'. Instead Lord Keith held that the second interpretation was the correct one, namely that proximity is a 'composite' test, 'importing the whole concept of necessary relationship between claimant and defendant'. In *Hill* v *Chief Constable of West Yorkshire* [1989] AC 53 Lord Keith repeated the view that 'foreseeability of likely harm is not in itself a sufficient test of liability in negligence' and added that:

'... some further ingredient is invariably needed to establish the requisite proximity of relationship between [claimant] and defendant, and all the circumstances of the case must be carefully considered and analysed in order to ascertain whether such an ingredient is present.'

The necessary ingredient may vary from case to case but it is now clear that what the courts are looking for is a *relationship* of proximity. One caveat must, however, be entered here, which is that in cases where a claimant sustains physical injury the courts do not appear to insist upon a pre-existing relationship of proximity between the claimant and defendant. Take an example. Suppose that I drive my car negligently and I knock you down, causing you severe injury. In such a case a court would not inquire into the nature of our relationship before the accident occurred; rather, it is the negligent infliction of physical injury which of itself *creates* the required degree of proximity. But where the loss which the claimant suffers is economic in character then the fact that the defendant has, through his negligence caused the loss is not, of itself, sufficient to create a relationship of proximity; the court will, in such a case, inquire into the relationship between the parties prior to the occasioning of the loss. This suggests that the requirement that there be a *relationship* of proximity between the claimant and defendant may not be a universal one but that it is confined to particular contexts; for example, where the claimant suffers economic loss or alleges that the defendant is liable for failing to prevent damage being occasioned by a third party to the claimant. This confinement of the proximity requirement to particular contexts suggests that considerations of policy enter into the decisions as to whether or not a relationship of proximity exists in a given case and this point was recently confirmed by Lord Oliver in *Alcock* v *Chief Constable of South Yorkshire* [1992] 1 AC 310, 410 when he said that 'no doubt "policy", if that is the right word, or perhaps more properly, the impracticability or unreasonableness of entertaining claims to the ultimate limits of the consequences of human activity, necessarily plays a part in the court's perception of what is sufficiently proximate'. He concluded: 'in the end, it has to be accepted that the concept of "proximity" is an artificial one which depends more upon the court's perception of what is the reasonable area for the imposition of liability than upon any logical process of analogical deduction.' The consequences of this approach have yet to be worked through (and they may not be shared by the other members of the House of Lords) but they do seem to call into question the division between the second and third stage of the inquiry because considerations of policy would now appear to enter into the second stage as well as the third.

The third factor is that it must be 'just and reasonable' to impose a duty of care. We have already noted the origin of this requirement in the judgment of Lord Keith in *Governors of the Peabody Donation Fund* v *Sir Lindsay Parkinson* (see section 6.4) and argued that it is hard to see any difference between this test and the second of Lord Wilberforce's two stages. But it must be conceded that the courts today tend to use the 'just and reasonable' test in preference to the second stage in *Anns*. However, it must be said that one of the welcome features of the approach adopted by Lord Wilberforce in *Anns* was that it explicitly recognised that considerations of policy play a significant role in determining whether or not a duty of care is held to exist. Lord Wilberforce was by no means the first judge to recognise that the courts were dealing with issues of policy in deciding whether or not a duty of care is owed. In *Spartan Steel and Alloys Ltd* v *Martin & Co (Contractors) Ltd* [1973] 1 QB 27 Lord Denning said that:

'Whenever the courts draw a line to mark out the bounds of duty, they do it as a matter of policy so as to limit the responsibility of the defendant.'

But judges since *Anns* seem to be more reluctant to give explicit consideration to issues of policy. In *McLoughlin* v *O'Brian* [1983] AC 410 Lord Scarman said that:

'The policy issue where to draw the line is not justiciable. The problem is one of social, economic and financial policy. The considerations relevant to a decision are not such as to be capable of being handled within the limits of the forensic process.'

This view was countered by Lord Edmund-Davies in *McLoughlin*, who described Lord Scarman's judgment as being 'as novel as it is startling'. It is probably true to say that the approach of Lord Edmund-Davies is the widely accepted approach. Nevertheless it is true to say that judges appear to be less willing to take considerations of policy explicitly into account. Oliver LJ in *The Aliakmon* (above) stated that a court did not have 'a free hand to determine for itself in each case where the limits are to be set' and in *Yuen Kun Yeu* Lord Keith said that Lord Wilberforce's second stage would rarely be used. In *Hill* v *Chief Constable of West Yorkshire* (above) Lord Keith repeated this view but he also affirmed that the second stage is capable of constituting a 'separate and independent ground' for holding that a duty of care is not owed. Therefore the just and reasonable/policy requirement has not been abolished but its role has been considerably circumscribed. However, it should not be thought that considerations of policy or of what is 'fair, just and reasonable' will cease to play an important role in determining the limits of the duty of care. As we shall see, one of the most important considerations of policy is the need to keep liability within acceptable bounds (the 'floodgates' argument) and the insistence upon the need for a *relationship* of proximity at the second stage of our inquiry reflects these policy considerations because a defendant is likely to have a relationship of proximity with a relatively small group of people. The policy issue of keeping liability within acceptable bounds is therefore addressed at the second stage without requiring a court to give explicit consideration to what is just and reasonable. Therefore what is more likely to happen is that policy choices will continue to be made but will be hidden behind a finding that there was no 'relationship of proximity' between the parties.

Sir Richard Scott V-C found, as a preliminary issue, that the three liability criteria had been satisfied in *Law Society* v *KPMG Peat Marwick* (1999) The Times 3 November. As a result, his Lordship held that if a reporting accountant negligently prepared a report intended to assist the Law Society in deciding whether and when to exercise its powers of intervention in order, among other things, to protect the compensation fund, the reporting accountant should be held responsible for loss to the fund caused by that negligence. See now section 6.5, above.

6.7 Factors inhibiting the imposition of a duty of care

It should now be clear that we are presently in an era in which the courts are narrowing down the scope of liability in negligence. We must now make an attempt to explain why this is so. It must be said at the outset that there is no one factor which explains the current policy of restriction; it is due to a combination of factors. In the remainder of this Chapter and in Chapters 7 and 8 we shall consider the various factors which together explain the reasons behind the abandonment of *Anns* and the current restrictive attitude of the appellate courts.

6.8 The distinction between misfeasance and non-feasance

One major factor which helps to explain the judicial abandonment of the two-stage test in *Anns* is the emphasis which has been placed in a number of recent cases on the distinction between misfeasance and non-feasance, a distinction which was either obscured or ignored in *Anns* itself. The argument that the *Anns* two-stage test was defective in so far as it obscured the misfeasance/non-feasance dichotomy was first accepted by the House of Lords in *Curran v Northern Ireland Co-ownership Housing Association* [1987] AC 718. Lord Bridge, in giving the judgment of the House, referred to an article written by Professors Smith and Burns ('*Donoghue v Stevenson* – The Not so Golden Anniversary' (1983) 46 Modern Law Review 147) and to the 'cogent criticisms' there levelled against the *Anns* two-stage test on the ground that it obscured the important distinction between misfeasance and non-feasance. The importance of this distinction lies in the fact that it is argued by critics, such as Professors Smith and Burns, that the principle enunciated in *Donoghue* applies to cases of causing damage through an act or an action (misfeasance) but that it does not apply to a failure to prevent harm from arising (non-feasance), in the absence of a positive duty to prevent harm from arising. The argument runs that a duty to prevent harm from arising is typically created by a contract between the parties (where one party promises to make the other party's position better) and that it is only exceptionally created in tort.

The distinction between misfeasance and non-feasance can be illustrated by reference to the facts of *Curran* itself. The claimants bought a house, the predecessor in title of which had built an extension with the aid of an improvement grant provided by the defendants. Under the terms of the statutory regulations the defendants had to be satisfied that the property in respect of which an improvement grant was made met certain standards of habitation and the work had to be 'executed to the satisfaction' of the defendants. After purchasing the property the claimants discovered that the extension had been defectively constructed. Indeed, the extent of its defects were such that the extension had to be completely rebuilt at considerable expense. In these circumstances the claimants brought an action against, inter alia, the defendants, alleging that they had been negligent in the exercise of their statutory powers and that their negligence had caused the claimants loss. The House of Lords held that the defendants did not owe the claimants a duty of care because they held that the purpose behind the statutory regulations was to ensure that public funds were properly spent and not to protect the interest of the owner-occupier in the beneficial enjoyment of his dwelling-house. So, the statutory regulations not being enacted for the benefit of the claimants, the defendants did not owe them a duty of care. The important point to note for present purposes is that *Curran* appears to be a case of non-feasance. It was the builders of the extension who were the true cause of the loss because it was their negligence which resulted in the construction of a defective building. The argument against the defendants was that they were negligent because, by virtue of their failure to carry out with reasonable care and skill their supervision of the builders' work, they had *failed to prevent* the builders from building an inadequate extension.

A similar point can be made about the decision of the Privy Council in *Yuen Kun Yeu* v *Attorney-General of Hong Kong* [1988] AC 175. There the claimants invested money with a deposit-taking company and they lost the money which they had invested because the company had been trading fraudulently. Deposit-taking companies had to be registered and licensed under an ordinance of 1976 and the Commissioner of Deposit-taking Companies had various regulatory powers over such companies, including the power to refuse to register or to revoke the registration of a company which he considered to be not a fit and proper body to take deposits. The claimants brought an action in negligence against the Attorney-General (as representing the Commissioner) alleging that the Commissioner had been negligent in the discharge of his regulatory functions on the ground that he had reason to suspect that the company was trading fraudulently and had failed to revoke its registration. However, it was held that the defendant did not owe to the claimants a duty of care. Although it was reasonably foreseeable that damage would be done to persons in the position of the claimants if the defendant did not carry out his duty with proper care and skill, foreseeability of harm was not sufficient of itself to justify the imposition of a duty of care. In the absence of a special relationship between the Commissioner and the claimant investors (the Commissioner did not oversee the day-to-day administration of these companies and it was not reasonable for the claimants to rely on the defendant), it was held that there was no basis for the imposition of a duty of care. Once again this was a case in which it was argued that the Commissioner had *failed to prevent* the infliction of harm upon the claimants. It was the directors of the deposit-taking company who had, by their fraudulent trading, inflicted the loss upon the claimants.

The importance of the misfeasance/non-feasance dichotomy can also be seen in the general rule in English law that, in the absence of a special relationship between the parties, there is no liability in negligence for a failure to rescue another (for criticism of this general rule see Linden (1971) 34 Modern Law Review 241). Indeed, in *Yuen Kun Yeu* Lord Keith regarded it is axiomatic that there is no 'liability in negligence on the part of one who sees another about to walk over a cliff with his head in the air, and forbears to shout a warning'. It should be noted that this is a classic example of non-feasance, a failure to rescue. This explains why Lord Keith insisted that liability in negligence could not be based upon mere foreseeability of harm because the application of such a test to his cliff-top example would have led to the imposition of liability in negligence. Thus it is only where there is a relationship of proximity between the parties, that is a relationship which imposes upon the defendant a duty to take reasonable care for the safety of the claimant, that the defendant is under any obligation to shout a warning to the claimant.

Although the distinction between misfeasance and non-feasance is an important one, it is not the case that liability can never be imposed in negligence in cases of non-feasance. The point was well made by Lord Goff in his important judgment in *Smith* v *Littlewoods Organisation Ltd* [1987] AC 241. While he recognised the existence of a 'general duty to take reasonable care not to cause damage to premises in the neighbourhood', Lord Goff also held 'it is well recognised that there is no general duty of care to prevent third parties from causing such damage'. The 'fundamental reason' for this refusal to impose a general duty of care to prevent others from suffering loss or damage was, he held, that 'the common law does not impose liability for what are called pure omissions'. Thus in *Home Office* v *Dorset Yacht Co Ltd* [1970] AC 1004 Lord Diplock said that:

> 'The very parable of the good Samaritan (Luke 10:30) which was evoked by Lord Atkin in *Donoghue* v *Stevenson* ... illustrates, in the conduct of the priest and of the Levite who passed by on the other side, an omission which was likely to have as its reasonable and probable consequence damage to the health of the victim of the thieves, but for which the priest and Levite would have incurred no civil liability in English law.'

Lord Goff was prepared to concede that the refusal of English law to impose a general duty for pure omissions might 'require one day to be reconsidered especially as it is said to provoke an "invidious comparison with affirmative duties of good-neighbourliness in most countries outside the Common law orbit" ' (see Fleming *The Law of Torts* (6th ed, 1983) p138).

But, rather than seek to impose a general duty to prevent third parties from causing damage to the claimant, Lord Goff held that the task which lay ahead for the courts was to map out the particular circumstances in which such a liability may be imposed. He himself began this task in his judgment in *Smith* v *Littlewoods*, the facts of which neatly illustrate the distinction between misfeasance and non-feasance. The defendants purchased a disused cinema with the intention of turning it into a supermarket. They took possession of the premises on 31 May 1976 and by early July of that year it was reported that the building was no longer lockfast. Vagrants were regularly reported to be in the building and on two occasions attempts had been made to start a fire using the debris lying outside the building. These incidents were not, however, reported to the defendants or to the police. On 5 July the cinema was set on fire and as a result of the fire the claimants' property was extensively damaged. They sought to recover their loss from the defendants in negligence. This was therefore a case in which it was the vandals who by their actions had caused the damage to the claimants. The claimants' argument was that the defendants were liable because they had *failed to prevent* the vandals from inflicting damage upon them. But it was held by the House of Lords that the defendants did not owe a duty of care to the claimants of the type contended for. It was conceded by their Lordships that the defendants were under a duty to ensure that their property was not a source of danger to the neighbouring properties. But they held that this general duty could only extend to prevent damage being done by vandals where a reasonable person would foresee that, if steps were not taken to ensure that the premises were lockfast, damage would be done to neighbouring properties. On the facts, because the defendants had not known of the previous fires, it was not reasonably foreseeable that damage would be done to neighbouring properties.

Smith is an important case because the Court of Appeal had earlier experienced great difficulty in identifying the circumstances in which a defendant could be liable to a claimant in negligence as a result of a deliberate wrong committed by a third party (see, for example, *Lamb* v *Camden London Borough Council* [1981] QB 625, *P Perl (Exporters) Ltd* v *Camden London Borough Council* [1984] QB 342 and *King* v *Liverpool City Council* [1986] 3 All ER 544). In one case (*Lamb*) it was held that the intervention of the third party was too remote a consequence of the defendants' negligence. In another case (*Perl*) it was held that, there being no relationship of control between the defendants and the third party who inflicted the loss upon the claimants, the defendants did not owe a duty of care to the claimants to prevent a third party from gaining entry to their premises, thereby enabling the third party to inflict damage upon the claimants. And, in a third case (*King*) it was held that the defendants were not in breach of their duty of care because it was not possible for them to take effective steps to prevent the third parties from inflicting loss upon the claimants. Although the result in each of the Court of Appeal cases was the same, namely that the defendants were not liable, the justifications offered to support such a conclusion differed in each case, with duty, breach and remoteness all being invoked by the Court of Appeal. There was therefore a great need for the House of Lords in *Smith* to introduce some conceptual stability into this area.

Lord Goff sought to provide such stability by stating that, while there is a general duty to take reasonable care not to cause damage to premises in the neighbourhood, there is no general duty at common law to prevent one person deliberately inflicting damage upon another person's property. In drawing this distinction between misfeasance and non-feasance at the outset of his judgment, it is suggested that Lord Goff identified the correct starting point in seeking to enumerate the situations in which liability can be imposed upon a defendant for loss caused to a claimant as a result of the deliberate act of a third party.

Lord Goff therefore embarked upon the task of identifying the exceptional circumstances in which such liability could be imposed. He identified four such situations (although he conceded that there may be others). The first arose where there was a special relationship between the claimant and the defendant. Such was the case in *Stansbie* v *Troman* [1948] 2 KB 48. The defendant was a decorator who was held liable to the claimants, who were the owners of the premises which he was decorating, because he left the premises unsecured when he went out and a thief got in and stole some of the claimants' property. It was held that the contractual relationship between the claimants and the defendant was sufficient to impose liability upon the defendant for the consequences of the theft committed by the third party. Whether a non-contractual relationship, such as the relationship between an occupier and a licensee, will suffice to justify the imposition of liability remains an open question. In a slightly wider context, the relationship between a claimant and defendant may also justify the imposition of a duty to rescue so that, for example, a parent would be liable in negligence if he stood by and let his child drown in a foot of water (an example that was given in *Carmarthenshire County Council* v *Lewis* [1955] AC 549).

The second situation which Lord Goff identified arises where there is a special relationship between the defendants and the third parties who inflicted damage. Thus in *Home Office* v *Dorset Yacht Co Ltd* (above) the defendants were held liable because the boys who damaged the claimants' property had escaped from the borstal institution where they were under the control of the defendants (see also *Partington* v *Wandsworth Borough Council* (1989) The Independent 8 November).

The third situation arises 'where the defender negligently causes or permits to be created a source of danger, and it is reasonably foreseeable that third parties may interfere with it and, sparking off the danger, thereby cause damage to persons in the position of the pursuer'. Such a case was *Haynes* v *Harwood* [1935] 1 KB 146, where the defendants left horses unattended in a street and a boy threw a stone at the horses, which caused them to bolt, and the claimant was injured trying to save others from being injured by the horses. It was held that the defendants were liable. They had created the danger and so they were liable for the damage caused by the act of the boy.

The final exception arises where the defendant knows or has the means of knowledge that a third party is creating a danger on his property and he fails to take reasonable steps to abate the danger. But Lord Goff held that these exceptional cases did not constitute a justification for a general rule of liability in such cases because:

> 'To impose a general duty on occupiers to take reasonable care to prevent others from entering their property would impose an unreasonable burden on ordinary householders and an unreasonable curb on the ordinary enjoyment of their property.'

Unfortunately, it is not at all clear whether the judgment of Lord Goff constitutes the ratio of *Smith*, though it was applied by the Court of Appeal in *Topp* v *London County Bus (South West) Ltd* [1993] 3 All ER 448. The difficulty here stems principally from the judgment of Lord Mackay (with whom Lord Brandon agreed; Lord Griffiths took his own line, which appears to be closer to Lord Goff than to

Lord Mackay, while Lord Keith managed to concur both with Lord Goff and Lord Mackay). Lord Mackay appeared either to ignore the distinction between misfeasance and non-feasance or to regard the distinction as an irrelevant one. Lord Mackay stated that 'no undue burdens are put on property occupiers' by the application of ordinary *Donoghue* principles and he held that the question to be asked in such cases was whether the damage caused was reasonably foreseeable. However, he added that:

> 'What the reasonable man is bound to foresee in a case involving injury or damage by independent human agency ... is the probable consequences of his own act or omission, but that ... a clear basis will be required on which to assert that the injury or damage is more than a mere possibility.'

In particular, where the intervening act of the third party takes the form of a burglary, Lord Mackay thought that it would be very difficult to establish that such an act was reasonably foreseeable because, by definition, the burglar will enter the premises at a time which is unannounced and unexpected. In choosing to base liability expressly upon ordinary *Donoghue* principles Lord Mackay's judgment must be taken as authority for the proposition that the distinction between misfeasance and non-feasance is here an irrelevant one and that in both cases liability can be based upon the reasonable foresight of harm.

In support of Lord Mackay it must be said that an argument can be made out to the effect that the distinction between misfeasance and non-feasance is an irrelevant one. There are two principal arguments here. The first is that, as Lord Goff noted (above), a refusal to impose a general duty in cases of non-feasance does not encourage co-operation between fellow human beings and it may be said to provoke an 'invidious comparison with affirmative duties of good-neighbourliness' in other jurisdictions. But the House of Lords, as then constituted, was not committed to such an expansive conception of good neighbourliness. Instead a more rugged approach was adopted and a new emphasis placed upon individual responsibility; claimants should take care of their own affairs and not rely upon third parties to exercise reasonable care in looking after them. This new emphasis was best expressed in the judgment of Lord Templeman in *CBS Songs* v *Amstrad Consumer Electronics plc* [1988] AC 1013, 1059 when he said that:

> 'Since *Anns* v *Merton London Borough* put the floodgates on the jar, a fashionable [claimant] alleges negligence. The pleading assumes that we are all neighbours now, Pharisees and Samaritans alike, that foreseeability is a reflection of hindsight and that for every mischance in an accident-prone world someone solvent must be liable in damages. In *Governors of the Peabody Donation Fund* v *Sir Lindsay Parkinson Ltd* the [claimants] were *the authors of their own misfortune* but sought to make the local authority liable for the consequences. In *Yuen Kun Yeu* v *Attorney-General of Hong Kong* the [claimant] *chose* to invest in a deposit-taking company which went into liquidation; the [claimant] sought to recover his deposit from the commissioner charged with the public duty of registering deposit-taking companies ... ' (Emphasis added.)

The second argument in favour of the approach advocated by Lord Mackay is that the line between an act and an omission simply cannot be drawn. For example, a driver who causes an accident through negligently failing to brake cannot argue that he is not liable under ordinary *Donoghue* principles because his negligence took the form of an omission. This is because the omission to brake cannot be viewed in isolation from his positive act of driving the car. But in other cases the line is more difficult to draw. For example, are *Curran* and *Yuen Kun Yeu* cases of misfeasance or non-feasance? Did the defendants cause the damage to the claimants through their own negligent actions (their inadequate supervision) or was it the case that they simply failed to prevent third parties from inflicting loss upon the claimants? It is conceded that these are difficult borderline examples. But it is also suggested that there is a clear distinction between the case where I punch you in the face and the case where your next door neighbour punches you in the face. In the first case I am responsible but in the second case the initial assumption must be that I am not responsible unless some particular ground can be put forward to suggest that I am under an obligation to prevent your neighbour from punching you. And so it is with the tort of negligence. I am under a general duty to take reasonable care not to cause you damage (although, even here, the existence of a 'general' duty must be in doubt, see section 6.5) but I am not under a general duty to prevent third parties from causing you harm. In so far as Lord Mackay can be understood as suggesting that the distinction between misfeasance and non-feasance is an irrelevant one, it is submitted that he is incorrect. The better approach, it is submitted, is the one adopted by Lord Goff in *Smith* and Lord Bridge in *Curran*, which acknowledges the distinction between the two and begins the task of identifying the particular situations in which liability can be imposed for non-feasance.

6.9 The role of Parliament

A second factor which underpins the present restrictive approach adopted by the courts is their perception of their relationship with Parliament. We have already noted that in *McLoughlin* v *O'Brian* [1983] 1 AC 410 Lord Scarman said that 'the policy issue where to draw the line is not justiciable'. Policy is for Parliament not the courts. Although many judges would disagree with the absolute nature of Lord Scarman's statement, it is nevertheless the case that, where Parliament has intervened to regulate a particular issue, the courts are now very unwilling to impose liability at common law where, to do so, would be to go further than Parliament had been prepared to go. This conservative approach was classically demonstrated by Lord Bridge in his judgment in *D & F Estates Ltd* v *Church Commissioners for England* [1989] AC 177. He stated that he was happy to reach the conclusion that no duty was owed on the facts of the case because, had he concluded that a duty was owed, it would have resulted in the common law going further than 'the legislature were prepared to go in [the Defective Premises Act] 1972, after comprehensive examination of the subject by the Law Commission'. This judicial conservatism was also displayed in *Murphy* v *Brentwood District Council* [1991] 1 AC 398. Thus Lord Mackay stated (at p457) that:

> 'It is relevant to take into account that Parliament has made provisions in the Defective Premises Act 1972 imposing on builders and others undertaking work in the provision of dwellings obligations relating to the quality of their work and the fitness for habitation of the dwelling. For this House in its judicial capacity to create a large new area of responsibility on local authorities in respect of defective buildings would in my opinion not be a proper exercise of judicial power.'

And Lord Oliver stated (at p491):

> 'There may be very sound social and political reasons for imposing upon local authorities the burden of acting, in effect, as insurers that buildings erected in their areas have been properly constructed in accordance with the relevant building regulations. Statute may so provide. It has not done so and I do not, for my part, think that it is right for the courts not simply to expand existing principles but to create at large new principles in order to fulfil a social need in an area of consumer protection which has already been perceived by the legislature but for which, presumably advisedly, it has not thought it necessary to provide.'

Other examples can be found of such judicial conservatism (see *McNerny* v *London Borough of Lambeth* (1988) 21 HLR 188; *West Wiltshire District Council* v *Garland* [1995] 2 WLR 439; *X* v *Bedfordshire County Council; M* v *Newham London Borough Council* [1995] 3 WLR 152; and *Reid* v *Rush & Tompkins Group plc* [1990] 1 WLR 212, 222–223) and, indeed, this judicial conservation seems to be spreading to other areas of tort – see the judgment of Lord Goff in *Cambridge Water Co* v *Eastern Counties Leather plc* [1994] 2 WLR 53 at p80, but contrast *Burton* v *Islington Health Authority* [1993] QB 204 where Dillon LJ rejected the argument that the passing of the Congenital Disabilities (Civil Liability) Act 1976 prevented the courts from recognising the existence of a duty of care in respect of damage suffered prior to the coming into force of the Act). There are a number of problems with this approach (see Cane (1989) 52 MLR 200 at pp210–11). The first is that it is not at all clear that consumer protection is better left to Parliament and that the intervention of Parliament should inevitably leave the common law sterile. And the House of Lords is open to the charge of inconsistency on this point because, as we shall see, their decision in *Smith* v *Eric S Bush* [1990] 1 AC 831 (discussed below at Chapter 7, section 7.6) appears to be a classic example of a court engaging in consumer protection in a negligence action.

6.10 The availability of an alternative remedy

The third factor which underpins the present policy of restriction is that the courts are now less willing to impose a duty of care upon a defendant where the claimant has an alternative remedy available to him. Thus, the availability to a claimant of an action on the contract against a third party contractor has been used as a justification for a refusal to impose upon the defendant a duty of care owed to the claimant. A neat example of this is provided by the case of *Simaan General Contracting Co* v *Pilkington Glass Ltd (No 2)* [1988] QB 758. The claimants were main contractors for the construction of a new building in Abu Dhabi. The building owner (who was not a party to the proceedings) required that units of green glass be incorporated in the curtain walling of the building. The choice of colour was significant because green is regarded as the colour of peace in Islam. The claimants subcontracted the supply and erection of the curtain walling to independent contractors, called Feal, who were in turn required by their contract with the claimants to subcontract the manufacture of the glass units to the defendants. The glass units supplied by the defendants were not of a uniform colour of green and the claimants alleged that this had caused them economic loss because performance of the building contract was disrupted. The claimants elected not to bring an action in contract against Feal but to jump down the chain of contracts and bring an action in tort against the defendants. But it was held by the Court of Appeal that the claimants could not bring a direct action against the defendants in the absence of a contract between them. The claimants' remedy, if any, was therefore against Feal in contract and Feal's remedy, if any, was a contractual action against the defendants. The Court of Appeal could see no justification for departing from the chain of contractual claims. In the words of Bingham LJ:

> 'There is no reason why claims beginning with the [building owner] should not be pursued down the contractual chain, subject to any short cut which may be agreed on, ending up with a contractual claim against [the defendants]. That is the usual procedure. It must be what the parties contemplated when they made their contracts. I see no reason for departing from it.'

As Dillon LJ pointed out a number of very difficult practical problems would arise if such a direct action was to be permitted, which problems can be avoided by confining the parties to their ordinary contractual remedies. Yet it must be conceded that this approach has not been adopted consistently by the courts. For example, in *Junior Books Ltd* v *Veitchi Co Ltd* [1983] 1 AC 520 the availability of an action against the main contractor did not shut out the building owner's claim in tort against the subcontractor. But *Junior Books* is a problematic case (discussed in more detail at Chapter 7, section 7.7) and it belongs to the *Anns* era when the courts were prepared to expand the horizons of the tort of negligence. Now that we are in an era of restriction the courts are unlikely to follow *Junior Books* and are more likely to follow the *Simaan* line, thus preserving the structural integrity of a chain of contracts, eg *Gaisford* v *Ministry of Agriculture, Fisheries and Food* (1996) The Times 19 July. However, in exceptional circumstances, the courts are willing to find that a duty of care can co-exist with a contractual duty: *Arbuthnott* v *Feltrim* (1993) The Times 20 October.

In addition to the situation where there is a chain of contracts, the law has been wary of applying a duty of care where the parties are in a contractual relationship. In *Tai Hing Cotton Mill* v *Liu Chong Hing Bank* [1986] AC 800 Lord Scarman stated:

> 'Their Lordships do not believe that there is anything to the advantage of the law's development in searching for a liability in tort where the parties are in a contractual relationship. This is particularly so in a commercial relationship. Though it is possible as a matter of legal semantics to conduct an analysis of the rights and duties inherent in some contractual relationships ... either as a matter of contract law when the question will be what, if any, terms are to be implied or as a matter of tort law when the task will be to identify a duty arising from the proximity and character of the relationship between the parties, their Lordships believe it to be correct in principle and necessary for the avoidance of confusion in the law to adhere to the contractual analysis: on principle because it is a relationship in which the parties have, subject to a few exceptions, the right to determine their obligations to each other, and for the avoidance of confusion because different consequences do follow according to whether liability arises from contract or tort, eg in the limitation of an action.'

In *Henderson* v *Merrett Syndicates Ltd* [1994] 3 WLR 761 Lord Goff, in whose judgment all the other Law Lords concurred, analysed this doctrine. In *Midland Bank Trust Co Ltd* v *Hett, Stubbs and Kemp* [1979] Ch 384, Oliver J had, after a careful consideration of the authorities, concluded that a solicitor could be liable to his client either in contract or in tort. The House of Lords upheld this decision, subject only to the qualification that a concurrent liability in tort will not be allowed if its effect would be to circumvent a contractual limitation or exclusion clause for the act that would otherwise constitute the tort. Thus in *Lancashire & Cheshire Association of Baptist Churches* v *Howard & Seddon Partnership* [1993] 3 All ER 467 it was held that a duty of care could exist where the parties were in a contractual professional relationship, and that the claimants could rely on the limitation period prescribed for tort rather than the contractual limitation period. Indeed, in *Holt* v *Payne Skillington* (1995) The Times 22 December the Court of Appeal held that where a duty of care in tort arose between the parties to a contract, wider obligations could be imposed in tort than in contract. The Court of Appeal based their reasoning on the fact that a *Hedley Byrne* type of duty might arise in an overall set of circumstances and the parties, by reference to certain limited aspects of those circumstances, entered into a contract involving more limited obligations than those imposed by the duty of care in tort.

However it should not be thought that this line of reasoning is confined to contractual claims. Thus the availability of judicial review (*Jones* v *Department of Employment* [1989] QB 1) and the availability of an alternative statutory remedy (*Mills* v *Winchester Diocesan Board of Finance* [1989] Ch 428) have been used as justifications for a refusal to impose upon a defendant a duty of care.

6.11 No undermining of established principles of the common law or equity

Fourthly, the courts are reluctant to impose a duty of care when to do so would be to run counter to established principles of the common law or equity. Thus a duty of care will not be imposed where to do so would be to bypass or undermine the defences which exist to other torts, although in *Joyce* v *Sengupta* [1993] 1 WLR 337 the Court of Appeal emphasised that English law allows a claimant to take full advantage of the various remedies which the law allows for the tort which he alleges has been committed. An example of the refusal to allow the law of tort to undermine established principles of the common law is provided by *Banque Keyser Ullmann SA* v *Skandia (UK) Insurance Co Ltd* [1990] 1 QB 665 where the Court of Appeal noted that 'our law of contract is founded' on 'the general principle of caveat emptor' so that the law of contract does not recognise the existence of a general duty to disclose information to the other party to the contract. The court held that, to recognise the existence of a general duty of disclosure in tort, would be 'to run counter' to established principles of contract law and that the law of tort would not take such a step. As Slade LJ stated: 'it should be no part of the general function of the law of tort to fill in contractual gaps'. Once again this approach has not been adopted consistently by the courts and in both *Ross* v *Caunters* [1980] Ch 297 and *Junior Books* v *Veitchi Co Ltd* [1983] 1 AC 520 the imposition of a duty of care appeared to undermine the doctrines of privity and consideration. But *Ross* and *Junior Books* both belong to the *Anns* era and must be seen in that light. One would not expect a modern court to initiate such an approach (see, for example, *Reid* v *Rush & Tompkins Group plc* [1990] 1 WLR 212), although it must be conceded that examples can still be found of a court recognising a duty of care notwithstanding the fact that in doing so it ran counter to, or even remedied gaps in, established rules of the law of contract (the most important example being *White* v *Jones* [1995] 2 WLR 187).

The refusal to undermine principles of equity was classically illustrated by the Privy Council in *China and South Sea Bank Ltd* v *Tan* [1990] 1 AC 536. The appellant bank lent $HK30 million to a debtor. The defendant guaranteed the loan as surety. The debtor defaulted. At the time of his default the mortgaged shares would have covered the loan, but the bank did not exercise its power of sale at that moment in time. The shares subsequently became worthless. The bank sought payment from the defendant under the guarantee. The defendant refused to pay, arguing that the bank was in breach of its duty of care owed to him in failing to exercise its power of sale before the shares became worthless. The Privy Council rejected the defendant's argument. Lord Templeman stated that:

> 'The tort of negligence has not yet subsumed all torts and does not supplant the principles of equity or contradict promises or complement the remedy of judicial review or supplement statutory rights.'

It was held that it was the domain of equity to protect the surety. The creditor was not obliged to do anything to protect the surety's interest and, in particular, it was not under an obligation to exercise its power of sale at any one time. The bank had not done any act which was injurious to the defendant, nor had it acted inconsistently with the defendant's rights. So the defence that the claimant bank could not recover because they were in breach of a duty of care owed to the defendant failed (see also to the same effect *Downsview Nominees Ltd* v *First City Corporation Ltd* [1993] AC 295, 315–317).

6.12 No duty recognised before

The courts are also extremely reluctant to impose a duty of care where they have refused to impose a duty of care in the past. An interesting case study in this respect is provided by *Leigh and Sillivan Ltd* v *Aliakmon Shipping Co Ltd* [1986] AC 785. The claimants were the consignees of goods carried by sea. They were liable to pay the price to the sellers, irrespective of the condition of the goods. But the claimants were not the owners of the goods. Due to the negligence of the defendants when stowing the goods, the goods were damaged. The claimant buyers were bound to pay the sellers for the damaged goods and the sellers, having been paid in full for the goods, had no interest in suing the defendants for the damage to the goods. So the buyers were left to try to recover their loss from the defendants. There being no contract between the parties, the claimants had to sue in tort.

The difficulty for the claimants was, as Lord Brandon acknowledged, that:

'There is a long line of authority for a principle of law that, in order to enable a person to claim in negligence for loss caused to him by reason of loss or damage to property, he must have had either the legal ownership of or a possessory title to the property concerned at the time when the loss or damage occurred, and it is not enough for him to have only had contractual rights in relation to such property which have been adversely affected by the loss or damage to it.'

Cases in this 'long line of authority' include *Cattle* v *Stockton Waterworks Co* (1875) LR 10 QB 453 and *The Wear Breeze* [1969] 1 QB 219 and they posed a severe problem for the claimants in the *Aliakmon* because, at the time of the damage, they had no possessory or proprietary interest in the goods. But in *The Irene's Success* [1982] QB 481 Lloyd J held, applying the two-stage test in *Anns*, that a person who was not the legal owner of the cargo at the time when the damage was done, could bring an action in tort, notwithstanding the line of authority which we have noted. He held that there was a relationship of proximity between the parties and that there were no reasons of policy to preclude the imposition of a duty of care. This approach was, however, rejected by the House of Lords in *The Aliakmon* and *The Irene's Success* was overruled. Lord Brandon stated that in *Anns*:

'Lord Wilberforce was dealing ... with the approach to the questions of the existence and scope of a duty of care in a novel type of factual situation which was not analogous to any factual situation in which the existence of such a duty had already been held to exist. He was not, as I understand the passage, suggesting that the same approach should be adopted to the existence of a duty of care in a factual situation in which the existence of such a duty had repeatedly been held not to exist.'

Thus the House of Lords affirmed the general rule that a person who, at the time of the damage, is neither an owner of the goods nor in possession of them cannot maintain an action in negligence in respect of any damage to the goods and they dismissed the claimants' claim.

Another example of this type of reasoning is provided by the case of *Stephens* v *Anglian Water Authority* [1987] 1 WLR 1381. There the claimant alleged that the defendants had extracted water from their land or from land of a neighbouring owner with his permission and the result was that part of the claimant's land began to subside. The claimant alleged that the defendants had been negligent in that they had been warned that the consequence of their work would be that the claimant's land would subside. The defendants applied to have the claimant's action struck out on the ground that it disclosed no reasonable cause of action. The Court of Appeal agreed with the defendants and struck out the claimant's claim on the ground that the defendants owed no duty of care to the claimant. For present purposes our interest lies in the court's treatment of the decision of Plowman J in *Langbrook Properties Ltd* v *Surrey County Council* [1969] 1 WLR 167. Plowman J had held that the defendants were entitled to extract the water percolating in undefined channels under their land even though by doing so they caused damage to the property of the claimant. Counsel for the claimant in *Stephens* argued that the authorities relied upon by Plowman J in support of his decision had been decided before the development of the tort of negligence in cases such as *Home Office* v *Dorset Yacht Co Ltd* (above) and therefore had to be subjected to fresh examination. However the Court of Appeal held that the claimant could only succeed if she could distinguish the decision of the House of Lords in *Bradford Corporation* v *Pickles* [1895] AC 587. In the latter case it was held that the defendant, who deliberately drained his land in order to stop water supply reaching the claimant's land, was not liable to the claimant because the claimant had no right to the supply of water and so no right of his had been infringed. The Court of Appeal held that *Pickles* could not be distinguished because 'if a landowner has the right to abstract water from beneath his land, whatever be his motive or intention ... it cannot, in our judgment, be said that he owes a duty to his neighbour to take care in doing it'. It was irrelevant for this purpose that the claimant in *Stephens* suffered physical damage. The Court of Appeal was not without sympathy for the argument put forward by the claimant but they held that they were bound by *Pickles* and concluded that 'whether or not this state of the law is satisfactory is not for us to say'. The Appeal Committee of the House of Lords refused leave to appeal ([1988] 2 WLR 333) and so the decision of the Court of Appeal clearly represents the current state of English law.

Stephens therefore underlines the present unwillingness of the appellate courts to extend the frontiers of the tort of negligence. And it is this refusal to re-examine authorities which led Professor Hepple to argue that the approach of the House of Lords in *The Aliakmon* 'is reminiscent of the pre-1932 categorisations of negligence rules and of the shackled judicial reasoning before Wilberforce's emancipation' ([1986] All ER Rev 311). It is this very 'emancipation' to which the present House of Lords objects, preferring to reason 'incrementally' and by analogy to the existing authorities.

Thus in *Wood* v *The Law Society* (1993) Times 30 July the claimant sought to establish a novel duty of care, namely that a body vested with a power and duty to investigate complaints against its members owed a duty of care to a complainant, the breach of which entitled the complainant to damages. The High Court refused to recognise the existence of such a duty of care on the grounds that there was insufficient proximity between the claimant and the defendant, that the claimant was a member of an unascertained class, that the relevant function of the defendant was to prevent conduct unbecoming to a solicitor not to prevent loss to individuals and that the defendant had no power to control the day-to-day activities of the solicitors who had actually caused loss to the claimant. Similarly, in *Philcox* v *Civil Aviation Authority* (1995) The Times 8 June the Court of Appeal held that the defendants' role was to protect the public against an aircraft owner's failures and not to protect the owner from his own failures.

However, in appropriate situations the courts are willing to find a duty of care in novel fact situations, eg *Kirkham* v *Chief Constable of Greater Manchester* [1990] 3 All ER 246 (police owed a duty of care to a person of unsound mind to pass on to a prison information relating to that person's suicidal tendencies); *Smoldon* v *Whitworth* (1996) The Times 18 December (referee in a colts rugby match owed a duty of care to ensure that scrummages did not collapse dangerously).

6.13 The cost and availability of insurance?

Given that most tort litigation is in fact between insurance companies, it would not be surprising if the incidence and cost of insurance were relevant factors in deciding whether or not to impose upon the defendant a duty of care. Yet judges rarely make explicit reference to the incidence of insurance. Lord Denning was one of the few judges who did so (see, for example, *Spartan Steel and Alloys Ltd* v *Martin & Co (Contractors) Ltd* [1973] 1 QB 27). However the judiciary today may be more inclined to place reliance upon the incidence of insurance. Thus in *Smith* v *Eric S Bush* [1990] 1 AC 831 Lord Griffiths stated that:

> 'There was once a time when it was considered improper even to mention the possible existence of insurance cover in a lawsuit. But those days are long past ...'

Although the courts have not, at least until now, placed express reliance upon the availability and cost of insurance, it is arguable that they have placed implicit reliance upon these factors. Davies has recently argued ('The End of the Affair: Duty of Care and Liability Insurance' (1989) 9 Legal Studies 67) that the availability of liability insurance has been a critical factor in the development of the tort of negligence. He points out that such insurance was not widely available until towards the end of the nineteenth century and he argues that it can be no coincidence that Brett LJ, who was influential in procuring the passing of the Employers' Liability Act 1880 which helped create a market for liability insurance, was the same Brett MR who three years later framed the general duty of care test in *Heaven* v *Pender* (1863) 11 QBD 503 (see further section 6.2), which was to prove so influential in *Donoghue* v *Stevenson*. Aware that defendants could now pay damages, the courts were more prepared to impose a duty and liability. The tort of negligence was thus able to expand its horizons, secure in the knowledge that liability insurance was readily available at reasonable cost. But the late 1980s and early 1990s has been a period in which liability insurance has not been readily available or, particularly in the case of professionals, only available at prohibitive expense. Surely it is no coincidence that the restricted availability of insurance cover is matched by a general restriction in the scope of the tort of negligence?

Although there must be a link between the development of the tort of negligence and the availability of insurance, the court is often not aware of the insurance position as between the parties. This is classically illustrated by the judgment of Lord Denning in *Lamb* v *Camden London Borough Council* [1981] QB 625. The defendants, as a result of their negligence, damaged a water main outside the claimant's house. This resulted in major subsidence of the house. In consequence the tenant moved out and shortly afterwards squatters moved in and inflicted substantial damage on the property. The Court of Appeal held that the claimant could not recover her loss from the defendants. The majority held that the loss was too remote a consequence of the defendants' negligence. But Lord Denning decided as a matter of policy that the claimant was responsible for the insurance of her property and that she should look to her insurers for recompense and not the defendants. The difficulty with this argument is that, as Lee and Merkin have pointed out ((1981) NLJ 965), 'most householders' policies on contents expressly exclude coverage or loss and damage caused to a residence unoccupied for 30 consecutive days'. The claimant was therefore, in all likelihood, uninsured. This case demonstrates that, if the courts are to take the incidence of insurance expressly into account in reaching their decisions, it is vitally important that they be informed of the actual insurance position and not be left to make an educated guess as to the insurance position of the parties before them.

6.14 Conclusion

Thus far we have considered general factors which have been relied upon by the courts when restricting the scope of the tort of negligence. In the next two Chapters we shall look at the development of the tort of negligence in particular areas. We shall do so under two headings. In Chapter 7 we shall consider particular interests (such as economic loss), in relation to which the courts have been reluctant to impose a duty of care. And in Chapter 8 we shall consider particular claimants and defendants in relation to whom the courts have been unwilling to impose a duty of care or have only been prepared to impose a limited duty of care.

7

The Duty of Care and 'Protected Interests'

7.1 Introduction

7.2 Economic loss: introduction

7.3 Economic loss: a definition

7.4 Economic loss: the problem

7.5 Consequential economic loss

7.6 *Hedley Byrne*

7.7 Defective product economic loss

7.8 *Hedley Byrne* re-examined

7.9 '*Ross* v *Caunters* economic loss'

7.10 Solicitors' liability: further cases

7.11 Psychiatric injury or 'nervous shock'

7.1 Introduction

Donoghue v *Stevenson* [1932] AC 562 was a case in which it was alleged that the claimant had suffered personal injury. The law of tort has never had any great difficulty in recognising that a person can recover damages for personal injury suffered as a result of the negligence of the defendant. Thus, in most road accident cases we have no problem in recognising that one road user owes another road user a duty of care. But where the loss which the claimant suffers is not physical injury or damage to property then difficulties can emerge in establishing the existence of a duty of care. This is particularly so where the loss which the claimant suffers is economic (or financial) loss. The problem can also arise where other losses are suffered, for example, where the claimant suffers psychiatric injury as a result of the negligence of the defendant. In this chapter we shall be concerned with economic loss and psychiatric injury because they are both interests in relation to which the courts have had difficulty in recognising the existence and scope of a duty of care.

7.2 Economic loss: introduction

There have been a number of dicta in recent cases which suggest that the courts do not attach as much importance to the protection of a claimant's economic well-being as they do to his physical well-being. For example in *Murphy* v *Brentwood District Council* [1991] 1 AC 398, 487 Lord Oliver stated that:

'The infliction of physical injury to the person or property of another universally requires to be justified. The causing of economic loss does not.'

In *Caparo Industries plc* v *Dickman* [1990] 2 AC 605, 618 Lord Bridge said that:

'One of the most important distinctions always to be observed lies in the law's essentially different approach to the different kinds of damage which one party may have suffered in consequence of the acts or omissions of another. It is one thing to owe a duty of care to avoid causing injury to the person or property of others. It is quite another to avoid causing others to suffer purely economic loss.'

Other dicta can be found to the same effect in recent cases (see *Reid* v *Rush & Tomkins Group plc* [1990] 1 WLR 212, 231 and *Mariola Marine Corp* v *Lloyd's Register of Shipping, The Morning Watch* [1990] 1 Lloyd's Rep 547). The courts seem to be of the view that, while liability can be based upon reasonable foresight of harm in cases where the claimant suffers physical injury (such as a road accident), such a test is manifestly inappropriate in cases of economic loss, where a more restrictive test is required. If this is the case and the law of tort accords less protection to a person's economic well-being than to his physical well-being two questions must be asked. The first is: what is economic loss? And the second is: why is it more difficult to recover damages for economic loss than it is for physical damage?

7.3 Economic loss: a definition

Economic loss could be defined simply as financial loss. But such a definition is too wide. An example will illustrate the point. Suppose that I drive my car negligently and run you down. As a result of the injuries which you receive you have to give up work for a period of time and, consequently, are not paid any wages. This loss is undoubtedly financial loss but we do not experience any great difficulties in allowing such a claim to succeed. It succeeds every day in the courts. This is because it is consequential economic loss; economic loss which is a consequence of your physical injury. Where the law of tort encounters its most severe difficulties is where the claimant only suffers economic (or financial) loss, called 'pure' economic loss by tort lawyers.

A good example of a claimant suffering 'pure' economic loss is provided by the case of *Ross* v *Caunters* [1980] Ch 297. The defendant, who was a solicitor, failed to tell the testator that attestation of the will by the spouse of a beneficiary would invalidate the gift to the beneficiary. The claimant, whose husband had signed the will, sued the defendant in negligence for the loss of her gift under the will. This was not a case in which the claimant suffered physical injury or damage to her property. The only 'loss' which she suffered was that she did not receive the gift promised to her in the will. Her loss was therefore classified by Megarry VC as 'pure' economic loss which, he held, was recoverable (see further section 7.9 below).

Great difficulties have, however, emerged in some cases in distinguishing between economic loss and property damage. Much of the difficulty in this respect has been caused by the decision of the House of Lords in *Anns* v *Merton London Borough Council* [1978] AC 728. In *Anns* the claimants were lessees under long leases of maisonettes built by the first defendants. The second defendants were the local authority who passed the building plans for the maisonettes in 1962. In 1970 structural movements began to occur, cracks appeared in the walls and the floors began to slope. The claimants issued a writ in 1972, alleging that the foundations were inadequate, being two feet six inches in depth rather than the three feet or more shown in the plans. The House of Lords held that the second defendants owed to the claimants a duty of care but, for present purposes, our interest lies in the classification of the loss which the claimants suffered. Lord Wilberforce stated that, if classification of the loss was required, it was 'material, physical damage'. At first sight this classification seems correct because there was physical damage to the maisonettes. But when tort lawyers talk of 'physical damage' they generally mean damage which is inflicted upon a person or upon property other than the defective product itself. A simple illustration will help us to understand the point. Let us suppose that I buy a toy for a child. The toy is defective. It explodes, injuring the child, damaging my settee and destroying the toy. The injury to the child and the damage to my settee are examples of personal injury and property damage respectively. But the damage to the toy is an example of pure economic loss. This is because, as we have noted, when tort lawyers talk about property damage, they are really talking about damage to 'other property', that is, damage to property other than the toy itself. When the toy is damaged my claim is on the contract with the vendor and the nature of my claim is that the toy did not live up to my expectations; and that is a claim in contract, not tort. It is pure economic loss because my argument is that a damaged toy is not as valuable as a toy which complies with the contractual specifications. Another example can be provided by reference to *Donoghue* v *Stevenson*. Suppose that the ginger beer had been flat. Could the claimant have sued in tort? The answer is 'no'. Yet, ginger beer which is flat is damaged, in the sense that it does not live up to the expectations created; but, once again, that is a claim in contract, not tort.

Now let us apply this reasoning to the facts of *Anns*. In *Anns* the only 'damage' was in the building itself but yet the House of Lords concluded that the loss was 'physical', not economic. This is difficult to understand because, in the words of Deane J in the High Court of Australia in *Council of the Shire of Sutherland* v *Heyman* (1985) 157 CLR 424, 504 '[t]he building itself could not be said to have been subjected to "material, physical damage" by reason merely of the inadequacy of its foundations since the building had never existed otherwise than with its foundations in that state'.

So the classification of the loss in *Anns* as physical damage seemed to be contrary to fundamental principle. But it was not until *Murphy* v *Brentwood District Council* [1991] 1 AC 398 that the House of Lords acknowledged that the classification of the loss in *Anns* as physical damage was erroneous. In *Murphy* the claimant purchased a house in 1970 from builders who had constructed it in 1969. The house was built upon a single concrete raft foundation because the site had been filled in and levelled. The foundation raft was designed by a firm of civil engineers but its design was inadequate and differential settlement of the ground beneath the raft caused it to distort and caused cracks to appear in the building. When the claimant discovered the extent of the damage to the house he decided that it was impractical to have the necessary remedial work carried out himself and so he sold it, at a price considerably below the market price of a house which was sound, to a builder who knew the cause of the damage. The claimant then brought an action against the local authority alleging that they had been negligent in passing plans which were inadequate. Our interest in *Murphy* for the moment is confined to the classification of the loss which the claimant had suffered. It was held that his loss was economic and, in many ways, this was obvious because he had realised his loss and his claim was for the diminution in value of his property; all cases in which a claimant seeks to recover the cost of repairing the defect in the product itself are cases of 'economic loss'. This point was accepted by the House of Lords in *Murphy* and it declared that the loss in *Anns* was truly economic loss, not physical damage.

7.4 Economic loss: the problem

Having identified what 'pure' economic loss is, we must now turn to the question of why it is that the courts are reluctant to compensate claimants who suffer such loss. The traditional reason is the fear of the 'floodgates'; that the defendant would be exposed to indeterminate liability for an indeterminate amount to an indeterminate class. This fear of opening the floodgates could be a reference either to the exposure of the defendant to too many claims or to too much liability, or, in fact, it could be a reference to a combination of the two. The courts do not make clear exactly what they mean by the 'floodgates'. This fear of opening the floodgates does not tend to manifest itself in cases of physical injury, although in major tragedies the liability of the defendant can be enormous. But the size of the claim or the number of claimants does not, of itself, provide the defendant with a defence.

However, the 'floodgates' is frequently invoked in economic loss cases. An example will illustrate the point. Suppose that an accountant appears on national television and states that shares in a certain company are bound to be a good investment. Thousands of people go out and buy shares in the company in reliance upon the advice. Unfortunately, the accountant was careless in making his statement. Far from being a good investment, the company goes into liquidation and the investors lose all their money. The investors have all suffered pure economic loss but to allow them all to recover from the accountant would be to expose him to an indeterminate liability for an indeterminate amount to an indeterminate class. This fear of opening the floodgates was reflected in the old rule that damages are not available to compensate a claimant who has suffered pure economic loss as a result of the negligence of the defendant. In *Cattle* v *Stockton Waterworks Co* (1875) LR 10 QB 453 the claimant entered into a contract to build a tunnel under a road. The defendants negligently burst a water pipe which made it more expensive for the claimant to complete the contract. The claimant sought to recover the additional expense from the defendants in tort. It was held that the claimant could not recover in respect of the pure economic loss because, if liability was admitted, where would the courts draw the line? Would the workmen be able to recover for any loss of wages as a result of the defendants' negligence? This fear of opening the floodgates convinced the courts of the need to deny liability in the case of negligently inflicted pure economic loss. Although English law no longer adopts this view, the fear of opening the 'floodgates' can still be seen behind many of the present rules.

There is, however, a second objection to permitting economic loss to be recovered in a tort action. The basis of this objection is that, to do so, would be to undermine established rules and principles of the law of contract. This objection surfaced most clearly in the decision of the House of Lords in *D & F Estates Ltd* v *Church Commissioners for England* [1989] AC 177. The third defendants, Wates Ltd (referred to as 'the defendants'), were main contractors engaged in building a block of flats on land owned by the first defendants. The first claimants, D & F Estates, took a lease of one of the flats and they let into occupation a Mr and Mrs Tillman (the second and third claimants), the controllers of D & F. After they had moved in, the claimants discovered that the plaster work, which had been done by a firm of independent contractors employed by the defendants, had been done defectively. So they sued the defendants for the cost of the remedial work, the cost of cleaning the carpets, loss of rent while the remedial work was being carried out and damages for the disturbance to the second and third claimants. One of the issues argued before the House of Lords was whether the loss sustained by the first claimants in renewing the plaster work was recoverable as damages in tort. The claimants' claim was that the plaster itself was defective and not that the defective plaster had caused damage to other property of the claimants or had caused personal injury. The claim was therefore one to recover damages for pure economic loss. After engaging in an extensive survey of British, American and Commonwealth authorities Lord Bridge concluded that damages in tort do not generally extend to the cost of repairing the defective product itself. Damages were recoverable in tort where the defective product caused personal injury or damaged other property of the claimant but damages were not recoverable in tort in respect of a defect in the product itself; such a claim lay, if at all, in contract. He summed up the general principle by using an illustration concerning a defect in a chattel supplied complete by a manufacturer:

> '... [if] the hidden defect in the chattel is the cause of personal injury or of damage to property other than the chattel itself, the manufacturer is liable. But if the hidden defect is discovered before any such damage is caused, there is no longer any room for the application of the *Donoghue* v *Stevenson* ... principle. The chattel is now defective in quality, but it is no longer dangerous. It may be valueless or it may be capable of economic repair. In either case the economic loss is recoverable in contract by a buyer or hirer of the chattel entitled to the benefit of a relevant warranty of quality, but is not recoverable in tort by a remote buyer or hirer of the chattel.'

It can be seen that this objection has nothing to do with the floodgates argument. It is an argument from first principle, namely that a claim for damages for the cost of repairing a defect in the product itself is a claim in contract and not tort and that, to allow such a claim to lie in tort, is to undermine fundamental contractual principles. Thus *D & F Estates* has been applied in *Preston* v *Torfaen Borough Council* (1993) The Times 21 July and *Lancashire & Cheshire Association of Baptist Churches* v *Howard & Seddon Partnership* [1993] 3 All ER 467, although in the latter case the court recognised that a duty of care could exist where the parties were in a contractual professional relationship. Yet it must be conceded that the courts have not been altogether consistent on this point. Cases, such as *Ross* v *Caunters* [1980] Ch 297 and *Junior Books Ltd* v *Veitchi Co Ltd* [1983] 1 AC 520, can be found in which the courts have permitted an action in tort to lie despite the fact that it appeared to undermine established principles of contract law, such as privity and consideration. However, the dominant attitude in the appellate courts today is to draw a clear, bright line between contract and tort and thus to deny claims in tort which seek to recover as damages the cost of repairing the defect in the product itself (although contrast the much more liberal approach adopted by the Supreme Court of Canada in *Canadian National Railway Co* v *Norsk Pacific Steamship Co Ltd* (1992) 91 DLR (4th) 289, discussed by Markesinis (1993) 109 LQR 5).

With these objections to permitting the recovery of economic loss in mind, let us now turn to examine the cases in more detail. We shall commence our analysis with situations in which such loss is recoverable and then move out into areas where it is more doubtful whether such a claim can be brought successfully.

7.5 Consequential economic loss

The first example of a situation in which a claimant can bring a claim for economic loss is where the claimant suffers 'consequential economic loss', that is, economic loss which is consequential upon physical injury or property damage. It may be objected that this is not an example of 'pure' economic loss and, of course, this is true. But it is nevertheless an area in which the courts do permit economic loss to be recovered and it is therefore worthy of note.

The general rule is that a claimant can recover in respect of economic loss which is consequential upon physical injury or property damage. The most obvious example in this category is a claim for loss of earnings consequential upon negligently inflicted personal injury. In the case of economic loss consequential upon property damage, the leading authority is *Spartan Steel and Alloys Ltd* v *Martin & Co (Contractors) Ltd* [1973] QB 27. In this case the defendants negligently cut through the power cable leading to the claimants' factory. The power was cut off for some 14 hours. The claimants had molten metal in a furnace at the time of the power cut. This molten metal suffered damage assessed at £368 and the claimants lost £400 profit on the melt. They also sought to recover £1,767 in respect of profits which could have been earned on further melts which would have been made had it not been for the power cut. It was held that the claimants could recover in respect of the damage to the molten metal and the £400 consequential loss of profits but that they could not recover in respect of the £1,767 loss of profits. Lord Denning reaffirmed that only 'truly consequential loss' was recoverable and that, apart from that, economic loss was irrecoverable. He said that a power cut of this nature was the type of thing which we must put up with and either insure against such loss or use a stand-by system.

7.6 *Hedley Byrne*

The second situation in which a claimant can recover damages for economic loss which he has suffered is where he can bring himself within the scope of the decision of the House of Lords in *Hedley Byrne & Co Ltd* v *Heller & Partners Ltd* [1964] AC 465. Prior to *Hedley Byrne* such economic loss was only recoverable where there was a pre-existing contractual relationship between the parties or where there was a relationship between the parties, such as solicitor and client or doctor and patient, which equity regarded as being of a 'fiduciary' nature (see *Nocton* v *Lord Ashburton* [1914] AC 932). Beyond these narrow cases, economic loss suffered as a result of reliance upon a negligent misstatement was not recoverable (*Candler* v *Crane Christmas & Co* [1951] 2 KB 164, although contrast the dissenting judgment of Denning LJ). But *Hedley Byrne* considerably expanded the scope of liability for negligent misstatement.

The facts of *Hedley Byrne* were straightforward. The claimants were advertising agents and, under one of their contracts, were personally liable if their clients failed to pay the bill. So they asked their bank to find out about the financial standing of their clients. The bank obtained a reference from the defendants which stated that the clients were good for ordinary business transactions. In fact the clients were in a bad way financially and they went into liquidation shortly afterwards. The claimants sued the defendants in respect of the losses which they had suffered because they were personally liable under the contracts which they had negotiated on behalf of the clients. On the facts of the case it was held that the defendants were not liable because they had provided the reference 'without responsibility'. But, had a disclaimer not been issued by the defendants, it is clear that they would have owed a duty of care to the claimants and been in breach of it.

Although the House of Lords held that, absent a disclaimer, a duty of care would have been owed by the defendants, they were not prepared to apply ordinary *Donoghue* principles because of their fear that to have done so would have been to impose too great a burden upon the makers of statements. Lord Reid stated that the law must treat negligent statements differently from negligent acts for two reasons. The first was that even careful people are likely to make statements on social occasions which may influence others, without taking the care which they would normally take in a business transaction, whereas it was highly unlikely that a person would casually put into circulation a negligently made product. The second, and more compelling, justification for treating negligent statements differently from negligent acts is that words have a greater propensity to spread (for example through newspapers and the television) than acts and so liability for statements must be confined within narrower bounds.

In *Spring* v *Guardian Assurance plc* [1994] 3 WLR 355 Lord Goff, in analysing *Hedley Byrne*, stated (at p367) that its principle was 'an assumption of responsibility ... to the claimant'. Later he quoted from the speeches of Lords Morris and Devlin and said:

> 'The wide scope of the principle recognised in *Hedley Byrne* is reflected in the broad statements of principle which I have quoted. All the members of the Appellate Committee in this case spoke in terms of the principle resting on an assumption or undertaking of responsibility by the defendant to the [claimant], coupled with reliance by the [claimant] on the exercise by the defendant of due care and skill.'

Lord Lowry agreed with Lord Goff's interpretation of *Hedley Byrne*.

Lord Goff also referred to *Hedley Byrne* in *Henderson* v *Merrett Syndicates* [1994] 3 WLR 761 where he again quoted from the speeches of Lords Morris and Devlin and stated:

> 'From these statements, and from their application in *Hedley Byrne*, we can derive some understanding of the breadth of the principle underlying the case ... All their Lordships spoke in terms of one party having assumed or undertaken a responsibility towards the other ...
>
> In subsequent cases concerned with liability under the *Hedley Byrne* principle in respect of negligent misstatements, the question has frequently arisen whether the claimant falls within the category of persons to whom the maker of the statement owes a duty of care. In seeking to contain that category of persons within reasonable bounds, there has been some tendency on the part of the courts to criticise the concept of "assumption of responsibility" as being "unlikely to be a helpful or realistic test in most cases" (see *Smith* v *Eric S Bush* [1990] 1 AC 831, 864–865, *per* Lord Griffiths; and see also *Caparo Industries plc* v *Dickman* [1990] 2 AC 605, 628, *per* Lord Roskill). However, at least in cases such as the present, in which the same problem does not arise, there seems

to be no reason why recourse should not had to the concept, which appears after all to have been adopted, in one form or another, by all of their Lordships in *Hedley Byrne* [1964] AC 465 (see eg Lord Reid, at pp483, 486 and 487; Lord Morris (with whom Lord Hodson agreed), at p494: Lord Devlin, at pp529 and 531; and Lord Pearce at p538). Furthermore, especially in a context concerned with a liability which may arise under a contract or in a situation "equivalent to contract," it must be expected that an objective test will be applied when asking the question whether, in a particular case, responsibility should be held to have been assumed by the defendant to the [claimant]: see *Caparo Industries plc v Dickman* [1990] 2 AC 605, 637, *per* Lord Oliver of Aylmerton. In addition, the concept provides its own explanation why there is no problem in cases of this kind about liability for pure economic loss; for if a person assumes responsibility to another in respect of certain services, there is no reason why he should not be liable in damages for that other in respect of economic loss which flows from the negligent performance of those services. It follows that, once the case is identified as falling within the *Hedley Byrne* principle, there should be no need to embark upon any further enquiry whether it is "fair, just and reasonable" to impose liability for economic loss – a point which is, I consider, of some importance in the present case. The concept indicates too that in some circumstances, for example where the undertaking to furnish the relevant service is given on an informal occasion, there may be no assumption of responsibility: and likewise that an assumption of responsibility may be negatived by an appropriate disclaimer. I wish to add in parenthesis that, as Oliver J recognised in *Midland Bank Trust Co Ltd v Hett, Stubbs & Kemp* [1979] Ch 384, 416F–G, (a case concerned with concurrent liability of solicitors in tort and contract, to which I will have to refer in a moment) an assumption of responsibility by, for example, a professional man may give rise to liability in respect of negligent omissions as much as negligent acts of commission, as for example, when a solicitor assumes responsibility for business on behalf of his client and omits to take a certain step, such as the service of a document, which falls within the responsibility so assumed by him.'

All the other Law Lords in *Merrett* agreed with Lord Goff's speech. In *White v Jones* [1995] 2 WLR 187 Lord Goff and Lord Browne-Wilkinson based their decision on the voluntary assumption of responsibility ground where the existence of the duty itself was to be decided.

The question of assumption of responsibility also arose in *Williams v Natural Life Health Foods Ltd* [1998] 2 All ER 577. Mr Mistlin, the second defendant, formed the defendant company, of which he was managing director and the principal shareholder, in order to franchise the concept of retail health food shops. The claimants entered into a franchise agreement, but their business failed. They were awarded damages for negligent advice. The defendant company having been dissolved, the question was whether Mr Mistlin was personally liable. The House of Lords decided that this was not the case since Mr Mistlin had not assumed personal responsibility for the advice given to the claimants and the claimants had not relied on such an assumption of responsibility. This decision was distinguished by the House of Lords in *Standard Chartered Bank v Pakistan National Shipping Corp (No 2)* [2003] 1 All ER 173 where it was held that a director of a company could not escape liability for deceit (see Chapter 26) on the ground that his act had been committed on behalf of the company.

In *Lennon* v *Metropolitan Police Commissioner* [2004] 2 All ER 266 the claimant member of the Metropolitan Police Service (MPS) was in a non-contractual relationship, akin to employment, with the commissioner. He applied successfully to join the Royal Ulster Constabulary (RUC) and an MPS personnel executive officer (Mrs Bewley) told the claimant to leave everything to her. In particular, she told the claimant that his MPS allowances would not be affected if he took time off before starting with the RUC – which he did, believing that he was on unpaid leave. As it turned out, this three-week period was treated as a break in the claimant's continuity of service and, as a result, he lost his housing allowance, which he would have retained had the matter been handled differently. The Court of Appeal held that the claimant's action for damages in negligence would be successful. Mummery LJ said:

> 'In my judgment, Mrs Bewley expressly assumed responsibility in a particular transaction, namely the transfer of [the claimant] from the MPS to the RUC, for giving advice to [the claimant] in relation to a particular type of loss, namely the loss of the housing allowance, which he had expressly raised with her. Although she was not a professional person or a professional adviser, she occupied a managerial position in the MPS. She had, or had access to, special complex knowledge concerning the effect of transfers on service allowances of that kind. ... [The claimant] does not invoke a general non-contractual duty of care positively to give advice to protect him from economic loss. The striking feature of this case is that the duty of care arises from an express assumption of responsibility for a particular matter, on which [the claimant] relied. Responsibility was undertaken by the commissioner, acting through Mrs Bewley, for the handling of the transfer arrangements. If not carefully handled, the transfer could have an adverse impact on the housing allowance, to which [the claimant] was entitled while he had continuity of service. In my judgment, there is nothing in this case to prevent the *Hedley Byrne & Co Ltd* v *Heller & Partners Ltd* [1963] 2 All ER 575 principle from applying to an omission to give advice in such circumstances, even where the parties are in the relationship of employer and employee or in a situation akin to employment or equivalent to another kind of contract ...'

His Lordship also said: 'It is now well established that liability in tort for pure economic loss can arise from the negligent carrying out of a task undertaken pursuant to an express voluntary assumption of responsibility, on which the claimant has relied. In those circumstances it is unnecessary for the court to consider specifically whether it would be fair, just or reasonable to impose a duty of care.' In reaching their conclusion, their Lordships applied *Spring* v *Guardian Assurance plc* [1994] 3 All ER 129 and *Henderson* v *Merrett Syndicates Ltd* [1994] 3 All ER 506.

See, too, *Crossley* v *Faithful and Gould Holdings Ltd* [2004] 4 All ER 447 where Dyson LJ explained that while it was one thing to say that, if an employer assumed the responsibility of giving financial advice to his employee, he was under a duty to take reasonable care in the giving of that advice, it was quite a different matter to impose on an employer a duty to give his employee financial advice in relation to benefits accruing from his employment, or generally to safeguard the employee's economic well-being.

In *Precis (521) plc* v *William M Mercer Ltd* (2005) The Times 24 February

Arden LJ said that the precise limits of the concept of assumption of responsibility were still in a state of development: there is no comprehensive list of guiding principles to help the courts determine when an assumption of responsibility could be said to arise. The courts, therefore, have to look at all the relevant circumstances and determine whether the circumstances fell within the situations in which circumstances were closely analogous to and consistent with the situations in which liability had been imposed in previous cases. Adopting this approach, the Court of Appeal concluded that the defendant maker of a negligent actuarial valuation report relating to pension funds of a company was not liable for negligent misrepresentation to the claimant which, in reliance on the report, had purchased the shares of the company to which the report related. In all the circumstances, the defendant could not be taken to have assumed responsibility to the claimant and it would not be fair, just or reasonable to impose liability on the defendant.

The courts today seem to place reliance upon a number of factors in deciding whether or not to impose a duty of care. For example, in *Caparo* Lord Bridge identified the following salient features of cases in which liability has been imposed upon the defendant:

> 'The defendant giving advice or information was fully aware of the nature of the transaction which the [claimant] had in contemplation, knew that the advice or information would be communicated to him directly or indirectly and knew that it was very likely that the [claimant] would rely on that advice or information in deciding whether or not to engage in the transaction in contemplation.'

Thus in *Welton* v *North Cornwall District Council* [1997] 1 WLR 570, where an environmental health officer employed by the defendant required the claimants to undertake certain unnecessary works, and threatened to close down the business if these requirements were not met, the Court of Appeal held that a duty of care had arisen. The claimants undertook the work as a result of the officer's pressure; he knew that what he said would be relied on by the claimants without independent inquiry and he inspected and approved the works while they were being carried out. The court held that a duty arose under *Hedley Byrne*, as modified by the later cases including *Henderson*, as the officer had made an assumption of responsibility.

However, *Welton* was distinguished in *Harris* v *Evans* [1998] 3 All ER 522 where the Court of Appeal decided that an enforcing authority (the Health and Safety Executive), in giving advice that led to the issue by local authorities of improvement or prohibition notices, did not owe a duty of care to the owner of the business in question unless, possibly, that advice introduced a risk or danger not previously present.

In *Possfund Custodian Trustee Ltd* v *Diamond* [1996] 2 All ER 774 the thorny problem of whether the subsequent purchasers of shares on the stock market, in addition to the original allottees, could sue the issuers of a misleading prospectus was considered. The court held that if subsequent purchasers could establish that at the date of preparation and circulation of the original prospectus the defendants intended to encourage after-market purchasers in addition to original allottees, then it was arguable that the defendants had assumed a duty of care to the later purchasers.

Reference has already been made to *Smith* v *Eric S Bush* [1990] 1 AC 829 and *Caparo Industries plc* v *Dickman* [1990] 2 AC 605. In *Smith* the claimant applied to a building society for a mortgage to enable her to purchase a house and the building society in turn instructed the defendant surveyor to survey the property. The claimant paid a fee for the survey to be carried out but the surveyor was employed by the building society, not the claimant. The surveyor carried out the survey negligently, failing to note that the removal of the chimney breasts had left the chimney inadequately supported. After the claimant had purchased the house in reliance upon the survey the chimney collapsed causing considerable damage to the house. It was held by the House of Lords that the defendant owed to the claimant a duty of care and that the attempt to exclude that duty by the use of a disclaimer was invalidated by s2(2) of the Unfair Contract Terms Act 1977. Lord Templeman held that the relationship between the defendant and the claimant was 'akin to contract' because 'the valuer knows that the consideration which he receives derives from the purchaser and is passed on by the mortgagee, and the valuer also knows that the valuation will determine whether or not the purchaser buys the home'. The claimant was held to be entitled to rely upon the valuer's report even though the disclaimer said that the survey was prepared for the benefit of the building society and not the claimant.

In *Caparo* the claimants took over a company (Fidelity), allegedly in reliance upon accounts prepared by the defendants. The claimants alleged that the accounts had been negligently prepared with the consequence that they had suffered financial loss. It was held that the defendants did not owe a duty of care to individual shareholders in Fidelity, nor to potential investors in Fidelity. Lord Bridge stated that the crucial factors in cases such as *Hedley Byrne* v *Heller* (above) and *Smith* v *Eric S Bush* (above) were that the defendants were:

'... fully aware of the nature of the transaction which the [claimant] had in contemplation, knew that the advice would be communicated to him directly or indirectly and knew that it was very likely that the [claimant] would rely on that advice or information in deciding whether or not to engage in the transaction in contemplation.'

But he said that the situation was entirely different in a case such as *Caparo* where the:

'... statement [the accounts] was put into more or less general circulation and may foreseeably be relied on by strangers to the maker of the statement for any one of a variety of different purposes which the maker of the statement had no specific reason to anticipate.'

So in *Caparo* the essential element of 'proximity' was missing. The statutory duties placed upon auditors for the benefit of shareholders did not extend to the imposition a duty of care upon auditors in favour of investors (see also *Al Saudi Banque* v *Clarke Pixley (A Firm)* [1990] 2 WLR 344, where Millett J held that no duty of care was owed by the defendant auditors to banks which had advanced money to a company in reliance upon accounts prepared by the defendants), whether these investors were existing shareholders or simply members of the public who had no previous connection with the company. However, Lord Bridge did suggest that a duty of care could be owed to a shareholder who sold shares in reliance upon the auditor's report, on the ground that the loss would be the 'loss of part of the shareholder's existing holding, which, assuming a duty of care owed to individual shareholders, it might sensibly lie within the scope of the auditor's duty to protect'. But no duty was owed to an individual shareholder who purchased new shares in reliance upon the auditor's report. The duty which the auditors owed to shareholders was generally a duty which was owed to the shareholders as a class but not to shareholders as individuals.

In *Morgan Crucible plc* v *Hill Samuel Bank Ltd* [1991] Ch 295 Hoffmann J, at first instance, noted the similarities between the fact situation in *Caparo* and in *Smith* v *Eric S Bush* but that in one case no duty was owed while in the other a duty was owed. He noted the following differences between the two cases. The first was that the claimant in *Smith* paid for the survey while the claimants in *Caparo* did not pay for the audit. The second was that the claimant in *Smith* was a person of modest means making the most expensive purchase of her life, whereas the typical takeover bidder is an entrepreneur taking high risks for high rewards. This factor was also relevant in the case of *James McNaughten Paper Group plc* v *Hicks Anderson* (above) where it was held that the defendant accountants of a company which was the subject of a takeover bid owed no duty of care to a company which made its bid in reliance upon the draft accounts of the company. The chairman of the target company had asked the defendants to prepare draft accounts as quickly as possible so that they could be used in the negotiations for the takeover. One of the factors which persuaded the Court of Appeal to hold that no duty was owed was that the parties were experienced businessmen and that the claimants had their own independent advisers. The third factor identified by Hoffmann J was that the imposition of liability upon surveyors would not be likely to result in a great increase in the insurance costs of surveyors or in the cost of surveys, whereas the same could not be said in relation to the insurance costs of accountants had *Caparo* gone the other way. Thus, on Hoffmann J's analysis, it is the economic implications and the economic environment which justify the different results in *Smith* and *Caparo*. But in the Court of Appeal in *Morgan Crucible* (see above) Slade LJ was rather sceptical about the economic analysis employed by Hoffmann J on the ground that a trial judge will generally not be in a position to form more than a very broad view of the economic consequences of his decision. Despite these doubts expressed by the Court of Appeal it is suggested that there is much to be said for the view of Hoffmann J.

It is suggested that, although there are a number of factors which will be relied upon by the courts in deciding whether or not to impose a duty of care, there are in fact three principal factors to which the courts will have regard. The first is the purpose for which the statement was made. In *Smith* the court concluded that the purpose behind the survey was to enable the claimant to rely upon it in deciding whether or not to purchase the house, while in *Caparo* the House of Lords concluded, after examining the relevant statutes in some detail, that the purpose behind the requirement that an audit report be prepared was not to enable shareholders to sue upon it. And in *Mariola Marine Corporation* v *Lloyd's Register of Shipping, The Morning Watch* [1990] 1 Lloyd's Rep 547 it was held that a surveyor employed by Lloyds did not owe a duty of care to the purchaser of a ship which had been surveyed by the surveyor on the ground that the function of the survey was to protect life and property at sea and not to protect the economic interests of those involved in the sale and purchase of ships. This case demonstrates the importance of the court's perception of the purpose behind the statement because otherwise it is very difficult to distinguish this case from *Smith*.

The second factor of importance is the state of the defendant's knowledge. The greater the knowledge the defendant has of the claimant and the purpose for which he is likely to rely on his statement, the more likely it is that he will owe to the claimant a duty of care (contrast in this respect *Caparo* and *Smith*). The duty is not necessarily confined to the person to whom the statement is made but, as *Smith* demonstrates, can, within narrow limits, extend to the person whom the maker of the statement knew was intended as the ultimate recipient of the report (see also *Punjab National Bank* v *de Boinville* [1992] 1 WLR 1138 where it was held that the defendant insurance brokers owed a duty of care, not to their clients, but to the claimant bank who, to the brokers' knowledge, had actively participated in giving instructions for the insurance and who intended to become an assignee of the insurance policy which the brokers had been instructed to place).

The third factor is the reasonableness of the claimant's reliance upon the defendant's statement. *Harrison* v *Surrey County Council* (1994) The Times 27 January is an interesting novel fact situation in which a duty was imposed upon the defendant Council when it informed a mother that not only was a person a registered child–minder, but also that it would be happy for the child to be in that person's care. But there are a number of circumstances in which it may not be reasonable for a claimant to rely on the defendant's statement. The first is where the claimant has his own independent advisers upon whom he can rely (see *McNaughten* (above)). The second is that it is not generally reasonable to rely upon a representation which is made on a social occasion (*Hedley Byrne* v *Heller*, per Lord Reid). But care must be taken in establishing the existence of a 'social occasion'. This point arose in the case of *Chaudhry* v *Prabhakar* [1989] 1 WLR 29. The defendant, who was a friend of the claimant, offered to help her to find and purchase a suitable motor car. The defendant was not a motor mechanic but he did profess to have some knowledge of cars. The claimant's specification was that the car must not have been involved in an accident. The defendant found a car which had low mileage but which he knew had had its bonnet repaired or replaced. The claimant bought the car in reliance upon the representation of the defendant that it was suitable but it subsequently transpired that the car was unroadworthy, having been inadequately repaired after an accident. The claimant successfully brought an action for damages against the defendant. One of the issues discussed by the Court of Appeal was whether the defendant owed the claimant a duty of care on *Hedley Byrne* principles (counsel for the defendant had conceded the point but the issue was nevertheless discussed by the court). The court held that this was not a purely social relationship because of the claimant's reliance upon the defendant's skill and judgment and the defendant's knowledge of that reliance; indeed, he even informed the claimant that there was no need to have the car inspected by a mechanic. A duty of care was therefore owed on *Hedley Byrne* principles despite the fact that the claimant and the defendant were friends (contrast the dissenting opinion of May LJ who stated that he did not find 'the conclusion that one must impose on a family friend looking out for a first car for a girl of 26 a *Donoghue* v *Stevenson* duty of care in and about his quest, enforceable with all the formalities of the law of tort, entirely attractive' and argued that the decision 'will make social regulations and responsibilities between friends unnecessarily complex').

Thirdly, it may be the case that, in considering whether it is reasonable to rely upon a representation, the courts will draw a distinction between the passing on of information and the giving of advice; holding that it is more reasonable to rely on the latter than the former. A hint of such an approach may be gleaned from the case of *Royal Bank Trust Co (Trinidad) Ltd* v *Pampellonne* [1987] 1 Lloyd's Rep 218. The Pampellonnes alleged that the defendant bank had on two occasions given them negligent advice in relation to certain investments with the result that they lost most of the money which they had invested. The bank denied that they owed the Pampellonnes a duty of care in respect of the advice which they had given. At first instance the trial judge held that no duty of care was owed by the bank but this finding in relation to the second piece of advice was reversed on appeal to the Court of Appeal of Trinidad and Tobago. The Privy Council held that the bank was entitled to succeed in its appeal on the narrow ground that the Court of Appeal was not entitled to conclude that the trial judge had erred in finding that the Pampellonnes were not owed a duty of care by the defendants. Lord Goff pointed out the following relevant factors: (1) that the Pampellonnes' visit to the bank was without prior warnings; (2) that no fee was charged by the bank; (3) that the Pampellonnes did not inform the bank of the monies which they had available for investment; (4) that Mr Pampellonne did not sign any document relating to his alleged request for advice. Lord Goff also stated that:

> '... once it was held ... that at a brief meeting the bank was prepared to do no more than provide such information as was available to them, the Judge was entitled to form the opinion on the evidence before him that no duty of care arose, other than (no doubt) to pass such information accurately to Mr Pampellonne.'

Thus the relative informality of the meeting appeared to negative the assumption of responsibility by the bank.

The minority judgment held that the defendants were experts and that Mr Pampellonne was a naive layman who, in the words of Lord Reid in *Hedley Byrne*, was 'trusting [the bank] to exercise such a degree of care as the circumstances required' and this factor was crucial to their finding that a duty of care was owed. The minority judgment certainly appears to accord more closely with the spirit of the judgments in *Hedley Byrne*. It is, however, unclear what impact the majority judgment will have on the development of the law because Lord Goff was emphatic that the 'appeal does not raise any question of law' but was confined to the question of whether or not the Court of Appeal was entitled to overturn the finding of the trial judge. Nevertheless the refusal of the majority to find the existence of a duty of care on account of the relative informality of the meeting suggests that liability will not easily attach to the passing on of information as opposed to the giving of advice (see further Clements (1987) PN 145).

In *Merrett* v *Babb* (2001) The Times 2 March the Court of Appeal held (Aldous LJ dissenting) that the defendant, a professionally qualified surveyor and valuer employed by a firm of surveyors and valuers, became personally liable in negligence to purchasers whom he knew would rely on his mortgage valuation report, which he had prepared negligently, in buying a property when his firm went out of business and its professional indemnity insurance was cancelled without run-off cover. May LJ explained that the essence of the House of Lords' decision in *Smith* v *Eric S Bush* [1989] 2 All ER 514 was that the professional person who carried out the inspection and made the valuation was the person on whom the purchaser relied to exercise proper skill and judgment, Subsequent House of Lords' decisions had regarded *Smith* v *Bush* as exemplifying its special facts, but had not modified the basis of principle on which it was decided. The defendant, Mr Babb, had not escaped a *Smith* v *Bush* duty of care. The facts were barely distinguishable from *Harris* v *Wyre Forest District Council* (which was decided and reported along with *Smith* v *Bush*) where Mr Lee was an employee of the local authority but was held to owe a duty of care. A submission that his duty lay towards his employer, the council, and not to the claimant mortgagors failed. There was no relevant distinction between Mr Lee and Mr Babb. The relevant relationship was that between the purchaser and the employed professional valuer and the nature of the valuer's employment was not relevant to that relationship. Mr Babb signed the valuation report in his personal capacity and he thus assumed personal responsibility for it. Since he knew that his report would be relied on by the claimant, the responsibility which he assumed included a responsibility to her.

7.7 Defective product economic loss

We have already seen from our discussion of *D & F Estates Ltd* v *Church*

Commissioners for England [1989] AC 177 (see section 7.4) that the general rule is that damages are not recoverable in tort in respect of the cost of repairing a defect in a negligently made product. Defective product economic loss is therefore recoverable in contract, not tort. Although this rule has been firmly established as a *general* rule by cases such as *D & F Estates* and *Murphy* v *Brentwood District Council* [1991] 1 AC 398, it does admit of a number of exceptions. We will now consider three of these exceptions.

The first exception arises out of the infamous decision of the House of Lords in *Junior Books Ltd* v *Veitchi Co Ltd* [1983] 1 AC 520. The defendants were contractors who specialised in laying floors. The claimants had entered into a contract with another firm of contractors for the construction of a factory. The claimants nominated the defendants to lay the floor in the factory. The work of laying the floor was in fact subcontracted by the main contractors to the defendants. So there was a contract between the claimants and the main contractors and between the main contractors and the defendants but there was no contract between the claimants and the defendants. The claimants' statement of claim alleged that the floor had been laid defectively and that they had suffered loss of in excess of £200,000 in repairing the floor and in the consequent disruption of their business. It was not alleged that the floor constituted a danger to health; it was simply a claim to recover pure economic loss (for an explanation of why this was not an economic loss case see section 7.3 above).

It was held that there was such a relationship of proximity between the parties that the defendants owed a duty of care, not simply to prevent the infliction of harm upon the claimants, but to avoid faults being present in the work which they had done. A number of factors were emphasised by the court as giving rise to a sufficient degree of proximity between the parties. The first was that the claimants had nominated the defendants to lay the floor and so they relied upon the defendants to do the work properly. The second was that the defendants knew that the claimants were relying upon their skill in laying the floor and the third factor was that the damage was a direct and foreseeable result of the negligence of the defendants.

Subsequent cases have, however, adopted an extremely restrictive interpretation of *Junior Books* (see, for example, *Tate & Lyle Industries Ltd* v *Greater London Council* [1983] 1 All ER 1159, *Muirhead* v *Industrial Tank Specialities Ltd* [1986] QB 507, *Aswan Engineering Establishment Ltd* v *Lupdine Ltd* [1987] 1 All ER 135, *Simaan General Contracting Co* v *Pilkington Glass Ltd (No 2)* [1988] QB 758 and *Greater Nottingham Co-operative Society Ltd* v *Cementation Piling and Foundations Ltd* [1989] QB 71). In *D & F Estates* Lord Bridge did not engage in a further analysis of *Junior Books* but he did state that:

'The consensus of judicial opinion, with which I concur, seems to be that the decision of the majority is so far dependent upon the unique, albeit non-contractual relationship between the pursuer and the defender in that case and the unique scope of the duty of care owed by the defender to the pursuer arising from that relationship that the decision cannot be regarded as laying down any principle of general application in the law of tort or delict.'

Indeed, in *D & F Estates* Lord Bridge stated that the dissenting opinion of Lord Brandon in *Junior Books* enunciated 'with cogency and clarity principles of fundamental importance'. Lord Brandon had dissented on the ground that the effect of *Junior Books* was to create, as between two parties who were not in a contractual relationship, obligations which were really only appropriate as between contracting parties. He noted that there was no question of any danger to the claimants or to their property and argued that there was nothing to bring the case within the principles laid down in *Donoghue*. This demonstrates that we have come a long way from *Junior Books* in that, not only has the decision of the majority been largely confined to its facts, but the dissenting opinion of Lord Brandon has subsequently gained the approval of the House of Lords.

So, what are the limits of *Junior Books*? The case is dependent upon the finding of a 'unique, albeit non-contractual relationship' between the parties. What are the essential ingredients of this relationship? It is suggested that there are two such ingredients. The first is reasonable reliance upon the defendant by the claimant. This was easily satisfied on the facts of *Junior Books* because Junior Books nominated Veitchi to lay the floor and so they relied upon the skill of Veitchi. In many cases it will be possible to establish that the claimant has relied upon the defendant manufacturer. But it must be remembered that in *Junior Books* Lord Roskill distinguished the facts of *Junior Books* from the 'ordinary everyday transaction of purchasing chattels when it is obvious that in truth the real reliance was on the immediate vendor and not on the manufacturer'. But in many cases when we buy goods we decide the particular brand which we want and we place the real reliance upon the manufacturer of that brand and not upon the vendor. The House of Lords is therefore interpreting reliance, not as a matter of fact, but in the light of policy considerations, these considerations being a desire to exclude the 'ordinary everyday transaction' from the scope of *Junior Books*.

The second element in this unique, albeit non-contractual relationship is an assumption of responsibility by the defendant towards the claimant. It is this aspect of *Junior Books* which is particularly difficult to comprehend. In *Muirhead* v *Industrial Tank Specialities Ltd* [1986] QB 507 Robert Goff LJ clearly had difficulty in understanding the ratio of *Junior Books*. He said that the majority assumed that the defendants had accepted direct responsibility towards the claimants. But, as Robert Goff LJ pointed out, this is difficult to square with the facts of the case where the parties had deliberately structured their relationships in such a way that the defendants were not legally responsible to the claimants. The parties could have structured their relationships in such a way that the defendants were legally responsible to the claimants. But the relationships were structured in such a way that the defendants assumed a legal responsibility towards the main contractors and the main contractors assumed a legal responsibility towards the claimants. In the light of this structure, it is difficult to accept the argument that the defendants did assume a legal responsibility towards the claimants.

It is this latter factor which has assumed importance in subsequent cases as claimants have floundered in their attempt to establish that the defendants have assumed a responsibility towards them. It is clear from cases such as *Simaan General Contracting Co v Pilkington Glass Ltd (No 2)* [1988] QB 758 (discussed in more detail at Chapter 6, section 6.10) that the courts are now unwilling to allow one party to short circuit the contractual chain of actions by a direct action in tort and that, cases of physical damage apart, the assumption of a contractual responsibility by the supplier to the subcontractor will, in most cases, prevent the main contractor showing that the supplier has assumed a responsibility towards him in tort. The significance of the contractual assumption of responsibility can also be seen in the case of *Greater Nottingham Co-operative Society Ltd v Cementation Piling and Foundations Ltd* [1989] QB 71. The claimants employed contractors to extend premises of theirs in Skegness. The defendants were nominated subcontractors who were responsible for the pile-driving. They carried out this task negligently with the result that the claimants suffered economic loss which included the consequence of delay in completion of the building. There was a contract between the claimants and the defendants but the contract only related to the supply of the materials and it did not extend to the manner in which the work was done. The claimants originally brought an action against the defendants in both contract and tort but later abandoned the contractual action and proceeded only in tort. However, the Court of Appeal held that the defendants did not owe a duty of care to the claimants because the contractual relationship between the parties precluded the existence of a duty of care in tort. The contract between the parties contained the sum total of the obligations which the defendants had accepted towards the claimants. Woolf J stated that:

> 'Where, as here, the subcontractor has entered into a direct contract and expressly undertaken a direct but limited contractual responsibility to the building owner, I regard the direct contract as being inconsistent with any assumption of responsibility beyond that which has been expressly undertaken. This does not affect the subcontractor's normal liability in tort but does negative the existence of the exceptional circumstances needed for liability for economic loss.'

So it is clear from *Simaan* and the *Greater Nottingham* case that the assumption of a contractual responsibility by a subcontractor either to the main contractor or to the building owner will make it very difficult to show that the subcontractor has accepted an additional obligation in tort to the building owner. *Junior Books* has therefore received an extremely narrow interpretation in the appellate courts and it must now be regarded as a case decided 'on its own facts' which is only applicable where the relationship between the parties is equivalent to contract (for a different interpretation of *Junior Books* as a *Hedley Byrne* case, see section 7.8 below).

The second exception is an uneasy one because it finds its origins in an explanation of the now discredited and overruled decision of the House of Lords in *Anns* v *Merton London Borough Council* [1978] AC 728 where, it will be recalled, it was held that the claimants could, in principle, recover from the defendants the cost of repairing the defective foundations. In *D & F Estates* both Lord Bridge and Lord Oliver hinted that *Anns* could be justified on the basis of what they called the 'complex structure theory'. On this view, if the constituent parts of a building were viewed as separate items of property which were separate and distinct from the premises as a whole, then the conflict with Lord Bridge's general principle in *D & F Estates* disappeared. We could then say that the defective foundations in *Anns* were separate and distinct from the rest of the building. There would therefore be no objection in principle to awarding damages for the repair of the cracked walls and, of course, to repair the cracked walls properly one must repair or replace the defective foundations themselves. But in *Murphy* v *Brentwood District Council* (above) the House of Lords rejected the complex structure theory as an explanation for *Anns*. For example, Lord Keith stated (at p470) that it would be 'unrealistic' to adopt the complex structure theory 'as regards a building the whole of which had been erected and equipped by the same contractor'. The significance of the 'complex structure' theory has not, however, been completely eliminated because Lords Keith, Bridge and Jauncey all clearly envisaged that a restricted role remained for the theory. Thus Lord Bridge (at p478) sought to draw a distinction between:

'... some part of a complex structure which is said to be a "danger" only because it does not perform its proper function in sustaining other parts and some distinct item incorporated in the structure which positively malfunctions so as to inflict positive damage on the structure in which it is incorporated.'

Examples which he gave in the latter category were a defective central heating boiler which explodes and damages a house or a defective electrical installation which malfunctions and sets the house on fire. In such cases Lord Bridge did not doubt that the owner of the house could recover damages on ordinary *Donoghue* principles from the manufacturer of the boiler or the electrical contractor. Lord Jauncey agreed that the complex structure theory could apply to the boiler and electrical installation examples given by Lord Bridge but he was also of the opinion (at p497) that there would be room for the operation of the theory in the case where:

'... one integral component of the structure was built by a separate contractor and where a defect in such a component had caused damage to other parts of the structure, eg a steel frame erected by a specialist contractor which failed to give adequate support to floors or walls.'

In this example it would appear, rather unusually, to be the presence of a 'separate' contractor which triggers the application of the theory.

The 'complex structure' theory therefore remains alive and well, and indeed has been recently applied in *Jacobs* v *Morton* (1994) 43 Con LR 124, and it should not be thought that it is only of significance in building cases. It is of general significance as can be seen from the case of *Aswan Engineering Establishment Co* v *Lupdine Ltd* [1987] 1 All ER 135. The claimants bought a quantity of liquid proofing compound from the first defendants. This compound was stored in pails supplied by the second defendants. While stacked at a quayside awaiting shipment, the pails, which had been stacked some five or six high, burst and the compound was lost. The first defendants having gone into liquidation, the claim proceeded against the second defendants on two grounds. The first, with which we are not concerned, was that the pails were not of merchantable quality and the second was that the second defendants owed a duty of care in tort to provide pails which were suitable for the journey and which would preserve the compound. The claim was dismissed on both grounds. It was held that the damage to the claimant was not reasonably foreseeable and so the defendants were not liable. The interesting point for present purposes relates to what counts as 'other property'. The answer to this question was not entirely clear in *Aswan*. The compound was damaged by the bursting of the pails. But was the compound 'other property' of the claimants? One would think not, because the claimants bought the compound in the pails and property in the two passed simultaneously. But the 'provisional view' of Lloyd LJ was that there was damage to 'other property'. Lloyd LJ gave another example to illustrate his point: suppose that 'I buy a bottle of wine and find that the wine is undrinkable owing to a defect in the cork'. Once again, Lloyd LJ was of the 'provisional view' that this was a case of damage to 'other property'. These cases demonstrate that difficult issues are likely to arise in the future. But the point is an important one because, if the courts are willing to divide up 'property' in this manner then a remedy will be available to a claimant in a much wider range of circumstances than would be the case if the courts adopted a restrictive approach.

A third exception, of uncertain scope was recognised by Lord Bridge in *Murphy*. He stated (at p475) that:

> 'If a building stands so close to the boundary of the building owner's land that after discovery of the dangerous defect it remains a potential source of injury to persons or property on neighbouring land or on the highway, the building owner ought, in principle, to be entitled to recover in tort from the negligent builder the cost of obviating the danger, whether by repair or by demolition, so far as that cost is necessarily incurred in order to protect himself from potential liability to third parties.'

Lord Oliver was more cautious. He noted (at p489) that:

> 'Whether ... [the builder] could be held responsible for the cost necessarily incurred by a building owner in protecting himself from potential liability to third parties is a question upon which I prefer to reserve my opinion until the case arises, although I am not at the moment convinced of the basis for making such a distinction.'

In support of Lord Bridge's proposition it could be argued that the law of tort has been particularly concerned to protect users of the highway from dangers on or above the highway (see, for example, *Tarry* v *Ashton* (1876) 1 QBD 314 and *Wringe* v *Cohen* [1940] 1 KB 229, discussed further at Chapter 19, section 19.3). On the other hand, it should be noted that the possible exception identified by Lord Bridge is not confined to the highway but extends to damage to 'persons or property on neighbouring land' and, indeed, Lord Oliver talks simply of 'potential liability to third parties'. The limits or indeed the rationale of this exception remain unclear. For example, how would it apply to a case such as *Portsea Island Mutual Co-operative Society Ltd* v *Michael Brashier Associates* (1990) 6 Professional Negligence 43. There the defendant architects were employed by developers to design and supervise the construction of a supermarket. The developers were contractually obliged to repair any defects which were brought to their attention by the claimants within 12 months of practical completion of the building. More than 12 months after practical completion, the claimants alleged that the building was defective because some brickslips had fallen from the walls and others had had to be removed by the claimants to prevent injury being inflicted upon people shopping or working in the store. The claimants incurred expenditure in removing the brickslips and replacing them. The defendants denied that they had been negligent and contended, as a preliminary point, that they did not owe a duty of care to the claimants. They argued that this was a *D & F Estates* pure economic loss claim because the only defect was in the product itself. But His Honour Judge Newey QC held that the claimants could recover as damages the cost of removing the brickslips from the wall and any other expenditure incurred in making the property safe but he held that they could not recover the sums which they had expended in replacing the brickslips because that would be to give them the benefit of a relevant contractual warranty of quality when they were not privy to any contract with the defendants.

Could *Portsea* now be interpreted as a case falling within Lord Bridge's exception? If not, what is the difference between the position of a third party on the highway and a person entering a supermarket? Does the fact that the third party is on the land of the building owner or tenant rather than upon the highway or his own land really matter? If this exception does extend to *Portsea*, what are its limits? Does it extend to any lawful visitor entering the premises of another? Further, what would the measure of damages be? Both Lord Bridge and Lord Oliver in *Murphy* refer to the cost 'necessarily incurred in order to protect [the claimant] from potential liability to third parties'. Is this implicit approval of the approach adopted by His Honour Judge Newey in *Portsea*? Although there may be a public policy justification for this exception in that it is in the public interest to give building owners every incentive to ensure that buildings are repaired and not left in a state whereby they might be a danger to the safety of the public, it is difficult to square this exception with the general principle for which *Murphy* stands as authority and with the refusal of the House of Lords to protect the interest of the occupier himself in his own health and safety.

7.8 *Hedley Byrne* re-examined

It is clear that in the post-*Murphy* world *Hedley Byrne* v *Heller* (above) assumes enormous significance as the one secure species of pure economic loss. But its survival appears to throw up an anomaly. Suppose that a house is built by a builder upon inadequate foundations and some years later the house is sold to a buyer who purchases the property after having the property surveyed for the purposes of obtaining a mortgage. The surveyor fails to notice the cracks in the building and a few years later defects manifest themselves in the building. *Murphy* stands as authority for the proposition that the purchaser has no cause of action at common law against either the builder or the local authority. So why does *Smith* v *Eric S Bush* tell us that the purchaser may have a cause of action against the surveyor, especially as the surveyor has no right after *Murphy* to claim a contribution from the builder, whose primary fault it was? Further, what is the difference between a local authority inspector and a surveyor so that the latter is liable whereas the former is not? These are difficult questions which the courts must answer in the future.

A further question which arises is: how far does the net of *Hedley Byrne* extend? We have already noted that the case can be subjected to different interpretations (see section 7.6). One interpretation was that the case was confined to negligent *statements*; the other view was that it was not so confined. In this connection it is interesting to note that Lord Oliver in *D & F Estates* and Lord Keith in *Murphy* classified *Junior Books* as an example of *Hedley Byrne* type liability yet *Junior Books* cannot reasonably be interpreted as a 'statements' case. This strongly suggests that *Hedley Byrne* can no longer be seen only as a statements case and in *Henderson* v *Merrett Syndicates* (above) Lord Goff seemed to consider *Hedley Byrne* as having a wide ambit. Thus he stated:

> '... though *Hedley Byrne* was concerned with the provision of information and advice, the example given by Lord Devlin ... and his and Lord Morris's statement of principle show that the principle extends beyond the provision of information and advice to include the performance of other services.'

Similarly in *White* v *Jones* [1995] 2 WLR 187 Lord Goff and Lord Browne-Wilkinson applied *Hedley Byrne* to impose liability upon a solicitor who had negligently failed to carry out instructions in preparing a new will resulting in financial loss to the intended beneficiaries. It thus seems that *Hedley Byrne* extends beyond negligent misstatements to cover negligent acts or omissions where the special relationship exists: *Henderson*; *White*.

Another important case in this connection is *Pirelli* v *Oscar Faber & Partners* [1983] 2 AC 1 (discussed in more detail by McKendrick (1991) 11 Legal Studies 326). There the defendants, a firm of consulting engineers, were employed by the claimants to advise them in relation to the building of a new block at their factory, which included a new chimney. The defendants accepted responsibility for the design of the chimney but the concrete used for the refractory inner lining was unsuitable for its purpose and cracks began to appear in the chimney which resulted eventually in the partial demolition and replacement of the chimney itself. It was assumed in the House of Lords that the defendants owed a duty of care to the claimants but this assumption appeared suspect after *D & F Estates*. The only 'damage' in *Pirelli* was damage to the chimney itself; there was no threat of damage to other property and the damages claimed were simply the cost of repairing the defect in the chimney itself which, as we have noted, is not generally recoverable in tort. But in *Murphy* Lord Keith held that *Pirelli* was a *Hedley Byrne* case and approved of it on that basis. Does this mean that there is now one principle for those who give advice but another for those who build, with the liability of the former being more extensive than the latter? How many other cases will be subjected to a process of re-interpretation and 'justified' as examples of *Hedley Byrne* type economic loss? These questions remain to be answered by the courts (the relationship between *Murphy* and *Pirelli* was considered by May J in *Nitrigin Eireann Teoranta* v *Inco Alloys Ltd* [1992] 1 All ER 854 and he stated (at p859) that *Pirelli* could not 'be read as a wide general authority that cracking damage to a chimney itself affords a cause of action against anyone concerned with its supply, manufacture or construction' because to do so 'would be plainly inconsistent with *D & F Estates* and *Murphy*').

7.9 '*Ross* v *Caunters* economic loss'

There remain certain cases in which economic loss has been held to be recoverable and these cases have not been overruled by the House of Lords in *Murphy*. One such case is *Ross* v *Caunters* [1980] Ch 297. The defendant, who was a solicitor, failed to tell the testator that attestation of the will by the spouse of a beneficiary would invalidate the gift to the beneficiary. The claimant, whose husband had signed the will, sued the defendant in negligence for the loss of her gift under the will. Megarry VC held that the claimant was entitled to recover but not on *Hedley Byrne* principles because the claimant had not relied upon the skill of the defendant. In finding for the claimant Megarry VC relied upon the judgments of Mason and Gibbs JJ in *Caltex Oil (Australia) Pty Ltd* v *The Dredge 'Willemstad'* (1976) 11 ALR 227. The test which they proposed was that the defendant should be held liable for economic loss caused by his negligent conduct when he can reasonably foresee that the specific claimant, as opposed to a general class of persons, will suffer financial loss as a result of his negligence. In Ross the claimant was a member of a limited class and therefore loss to the claimant as an individual could actually be foreseen by the defendant. The attraction of this test is that its adoption would not lead to indeterminate liability because a duty would only arise where the claimant could be foreseen as an individual.

Doubts have, however, been cast upon the utility of this test. In *Junior Books Ltd* v *The Veitchi Co Ltd* [1983] 1 AC 520 Lord Fraser doubted whether such an approach was the correct one to adopt. A similar criticism was levelled against this test by Robert Goff LJ in the Court of Appeal in *Leigh and Sillivan* v *The Aliakmon Shipping Co* [1985] 1 QB 350. He said that he did not see why a single employer should be able to recover because he was foreseeable as an individual, but that his employees should be left without a remedy because they were only foreseeable as a class and he said that he would not apply a test which led to such a conclusion.

We are therefore in the rather unusual position that the test which was used to justify the decision in *Ross* has subsequently been rejected, but the decision in *Ross* itself has not been overruled (see *Clarke* v *Bruce Lance and Co (A Firm)* [1988] 1 All ER 364) and indeed in *Murphy* Lord Oliver (at p486) referred to it without disapproval Despite the doubts about the correctness of *Ross*, it was affirmed by the House of Lords in *White* v *Jones* [1995] 2 WLR 187. There a testator had quarrelled with his two daughters and so had instructed his solicitors, the defendants, to prepare a will cutting his daughters out of his estate. This was done and the will was duly executed. The testator was subsequently reconciled with his daughters and so he instructed the defendants to prepare a fresh will, in which he wished to leave £9,000 to both daughters. The defendants, however, did nothing for one month and then began the task of preparing the new will. They then made an arrangement to visit the testator one month later but, unfortunately, the testator died three days before the meeting. The distribution of his estate was covered by the old will and so the daughters were deprived of their bequests of £9,000. They brought a claim against the defendants, alleging that they had been negligent in the preparation of the new will and claimed £9,000 each by way of damages. The trial judge dismissed the claimants' claim but the Court of Appeal allowed their appeal and entered judgment for £9,000. On appeal, the House of Lords dismissed the appeal by a bare majority. Lord Goff applied *Hedley Byrne*, holding that the solicitor had assumed responsibility to his client and that as a matter of law this should be held to extend to an intended beneficiary who could be reasonably foreseen, as a result of the solicitor's negligence, to be deprived of his legacy. Lord Goff expressly refused to proceed on the lines of *Ross* v *Caunters*, stating that it was inappropriate because it did not meet any of the conceptual problems which had been raised. Lord Browne-Wilkinson also followed the assumption of responsibility route, while Lord Nolan considered that the claimants, as daughters of the testator, had relied on the defendants who were acting as family solicitors. Lord Mustill dissented on the ground that *Hedley Byrne* was inapplicable and Lord Keith also dissented.

In *Hooper* v *Fynmores* (2001) The Times 19 July the defendant solicitors postponed a visit to their client in hospital when he was to execute a new will. The client died before his new will could be executed: as a result, the claimant beneficiary failed to receive an additional share in the client's estate. Pumfrey J held that the claimant's action in negligence would be successful. As he explained, when dealing with an elderly client who was in hospital, an appointment for the execution of a will ought to be kept unless it was clear that the client was content for the appointment to be missed.

Note should also be made of *Dean* v *Allin & Watts* (2001) The Times 28 June where the Court of Appeal decided that, on being satisfied that it was fair, just and reasonable to do so, the law would impose a duty of care on a solicitor to a third party, when the solicitor was instructed by his client in relation to a loan transaction and he knew, or ought to have known, that the third party, as the lender, was not obtaining independent legal advice but was relying on him (the solicitor) to set in place an effective security for the loan.

In *Gorham* v *British Telecommunications plc* [2000] 4 All ER 867 it appeared that the late Mr Gorham, when an employee of BT, sought advice on provision for his family from a representative of the defendant insurance company. The representative having negligently failed to advise him that the BT pension scheme might be better for him, he joined one of the defendant's personal pension schemes. After Mr Gorham's death his widow sought damages for herself and her children in respect of the benefit that they would have received had her late husband been properly advised by the defendant's representative. Her action was successful and Schiemann LJ said:

> 'The position of an investor who goes to a financial adviser seeking investment or pensions advice in relation to making provision for his family after his death is analogous to that of a person who goes to a solicitor seeking advice in relation to making provision by will for his family after his death. ... in each of these cases, following the phraseology of Lord Goff of Chieveley in *White* v *Jones*, the adviser's assumption of responsibility towards the investor extends to the intended beneficiaries who (as the financial adviser can reasonably foresee) may, as a result of the adviser's negligence, be deprived of an intended benefit and who, in a very real sense, are dependent upon the dealings between the adviser and the person seeking advice to safeguard their position.'

While an intended beneficiary may have an action against negligent solicitors even though the testator's estate might also have a remedy for breach of duty (*Carr-Glynn* v *Frearsons* [1998] 4 All ER 225), before bringing such an action the disappointed beneficiary is expected to mitigate his loss by seeking rectification of the will under s20(1) of the Administration of Justice Act 1982 (*Walker* v *Geo H Medlicott & Son* [1999] 1 All ER 685) unless there is no prospect of the rectification proceedings resulting in any material recovery of the funds lost: *Horsfall* v *Haywards* (1999) The Times 11 March. Of course, in order to be successful, a disappointed beneficiary would have to adduce convincing evidence that the will had not properly recorded the testator's intentions: *Walker* v *Geo H Medlicott*, above.

In *Hemmens* v *Wilson Browne* [1993] 4 All ER 826 *White* (in the Court of Appeal) was distinguished. In *Hemmens* a client instructed his solicitors to draft a document giving the claimant the right to call on P to pay her the sum of £110,000. The document drafted did not confer any enforceable rights on the claimant, although the defendant explained to the claimant that its effect was 'akin to a trust'. Shortly afterwards the claimant asked the client to fulfil his promise and he refused. The claimant sued the defendant in negligence and negligent misrepresentation. The High Court refused to impose a duty of care in negligence as, although damage to the claimant was reasonably foreseeable and there was a sufficient degree of proximity between the claimant and the defendant, it would not be fair, just or reasonable to impose a duty as the client was still alive and could rectify the situation, and the client had a remedy in breach of contract against the solicitor. Thus the situation differed from *Ross* and *White* where if no duty had been imposed the only person suffering loss would have had no remedy and the only person with a remedy would have suffered no loss. No duty was imposed as regards the negligent misrepresentation by the defendant as it would not be fair, just or reasonable to do so as the defendant had made it clear that he was acting for the client and not for the claimant and that she should not rely on the defendant's opinion regarding the legal effect of the document but should seek independent legal advice.

7.10 Solicitors' liability: further cases

Note should be made of three further cases which shed helpful light on the extent of a solicitor's duty of care to his or her clients. In the first, *Humblestone* v *Martin Tolhurst Partnership* (2004) The Times 27 February, Mann J held that the defendant solicitors who had drafted a will but had not supervised its execution had a duty to check that it had been properly executed when it was returned to them for safekeeping. The second case, *Pickersgill* v *Riley* (2004) The Times 2 March, was an appeal to the Privy Council from the Court of Appeal of Jersey. Giving judgment, Lord Scott of Foscote said that it was plain that when a solicitor was instructed by a client to act in a transaction, a duty of care arose. But the scope of that duty of care was variable. It depended, first and foremost, on the instructions given to the solicitor by the client, but it also depended on the particular circumstances of the case and on the characteristics of the client, in so far as they were apparent to the solicitor. A youthful client, unversed in business affairs, might need explanation and advice from his solicitor before entering into a commercial transaction that it would be pointless, or even sometimes an impertinence, for the solicitor to offer to an obviously experienced businessman.

Lastly, in *Chappell* v *Somers & Blake* [2003] 3 All ER 1076 by will the claimant was appointed executrix and the residuary estate was left to a single beneficiary. The residue included two properties which, according to the executrix, were unlet at the time of the testatrix's death. In January 1996 the executrix instructed the defendant solicitors to act for her in the administration of the estate. According to the executrix, by April 2001 the defendants had done 'absolutely nothing'. At that stage she terminated the defendants' retainer and in these proceedings she alleged that they had been in breach of contractual and tortious duties which they owed to her. In particular, she claimed that she was entitled, as executrix, to sue for the loss of income on the properties, which remained unlet, accounting to the beneficiary for any damages recovered.

Neuberger held that while an executor cannot be held liable for any loss accruing to an estate, or to a beneficiary under a will, as a result of prolonged delay in proving the will, in principle there was no reason why the executrix's claim could not succeed. His Lordship added:

> 'If to hold otherwise would involve the solicitors escaping any liability in damages, then it seems to me that the result would be inconsistent with the reasoning of the majority of the House of Lords in *White* v *Jones* [1995] 1 All ER 691 and of the Court of Appeal in *Carr-Glynn* v *Frearsons* [1998] 4 All ER 225. Furthermore, to hold that the executrix could recover in such circumstances does not seem to me even to fall foul of the reasoning or conclusions of Lord Keith or Lord Mustill, who dissented, in *White*'s case.'

7.11 Psychiatric injury or 'nervous shock'

Another type of loss or interest in respect of which the courts have been reluctant to recognise a duty of care is psychiatric injury or 'nervous shock'. This is an area of the law which classically illustrates the 'incremental' approach currently favoured by the House of Lords because, beginning with a rule of no recovery, the courts have gradually expanded the situations in which damages can be recovered in tort in respect of negligently inflicted psychiatric injury. Until the recent decision of the House of Lords in *Alcock* v *Chief Constable of South Yorkshire* [1992] 1 AC 310 (discussed by Teff (1992) 12 OJLS 440) the picture has been one of a gradual willingness on the part of the courts to allow damages to be recovered for such loss, while at the same time the courts have struggled to find an appropriate test to keep liability within acceptable bounds.

Before analysing the historical development of the law, it is necessary to say a word about what lawyers mean by the phrase 'nervous shock'. To the lawyer nervous shock means a mental injury or psychiatric illness and not simply grief and sorrow (*Brice* v *Brown* [1984] 1 All ER 997). However, where a claimant does suffer nervous shock, he can recover for all the consequences of nervous shock, and that element of his suffering which is due to grief and sorrow is not to be separated and discounted: *Vernon* v *Bosley (No 1)* [1997] 1 All ER 577. But in recent years the courts have begun to move away from this terminology and have begun to talk about 'psychiatric illness' rather than nervous shock (see, for example, *Attia* v *British Gas plc* [1988] QB 304). It should also be noted that the psychiatric injury must be induced by the shock so that a parent who is made distraught by the wayward conduct of a brain damaged child and who suffers psychiatric injury as a consequence has no claim against the tortfeasor who caused the brain damage to the child. As Lord Ackner noted in *Alcock* v *Chief Constable of South Yorkshire Police* (above) the 'shock' must involve a sudden appreciation by sight or sound of a horrifying event and has not yet been extended to psychiatric injury caused by a process of accumulation of gradual assaults on the nervous system.

The original test applied in *Victorian Railway Commissioners* v *Coultas* (1888) 13 App Cas 222 was that no duty of care was owed in respect of psychiatric injury suffered as a result of the negligence of the defendant because it was not the type of injury which, in the ordinary course of things, would result from the negligence of another. The fear behind this approach was that, once it was admitted that a duty of care was owed, the floodgates would be opened and claimants would be encouraged to make unmeritorious claims and an undue burden would be imposed upon defendants. This rigid approach was not, however, adopted for long. In *Dulieu* v *White* [1901] 2 KB 669 it was held that recovery could be granted in respect of psychiatric injury where the claimant was put in fear of her own safety. The claimant, who was pregnant, suffered psychiatric injury, which resulted in the premature birth of her baby, when an employee of the defendants negligently drove his van into a public house where the claimant was serving behind the bar. The claimant, being put in fear of her own safety, was held to be able to recover damages from the defendants.

This test did not, however, last for very long, as it was disapproved of by the Court of Appeal in *Hambrook* v *Stokes Bros* [1925] 1 KB 141. The defendant left his lorry at the top of a hill. The brakes of the lorry were not properly on. The engine was also left running with the result that the lorry started itself off and ran violently down the road. The claimant suffered psychiatric injury on seeing the lorry running down the hill because she had just left her children in the direction in which the lorry was travelling. It was held that the defendant was liable for the psychiatric injury suffered by the claimant, although the grounds of the decision are not entirely clear. Bankes LJ contented himself with saying that the injuries suffered by the mother were the normal consequences which any mother would suffer in such a situation. Sargant LJ dissented and followed the reasoning in *Dulieu*. Atkin LJ placed some emphasis on the fact that the mother was in some physical danger herself and that she perceived the accident with her own senses and not as the result of being told about it by a third party.

The next case of significance in trying to devise an appropriate test is the decision of the House of Lords in *Bourhill* v *Young* (above), the facts of which we have already considered (see Chapter 6, section 6.6). The House was not entirely clear as to which test it thought was applicable. Lords Thankerton, Russell and MacMillan held that the claimant was so far away from the scene of the accident that it was not reasonably foreseeable that she would suffer physical injury. This approach gave rise to the theory that what mattered for the recoverability in respect of psychiatric injury was that the claimant be within the area of physical danger. This theory was not, however, adopted by Lords Wright and Porter who argued that what was determinative of liability was the foreseeability of emotional injury and not the foreseeability of physical injury. It has been argued that this latter approach is the true ratio of *Bourhill* (see Goodhart (1953) 16 MLR 14). However, the case was so uncertain that by no means did it resolve the conflict as to which test was applicable.

Another case of significance is *King* v *Phillips* [1953] 1 QB 429 (on which see Goodhart (1953) 69 LQR 347). The defendant negligently backed his taxi cab over a small boy who had been riding on his bicycle close to the taxi cab. The boy was slightly injured as a result of the accident. The boy's mother, who was standing at her window some 70 yards away, heard her son's scream and saw her son's bicycle under the taxi cab but she could not see her son at all. In these circumstances she suffered psychiatric injury. It was held that the defendant was not liable for the psychiatric injury suffered by the claimant because it was held that it was not a reasonably foreseeable consequence of his negligence. The case is an important one because both Denning LJ and Singleton LJ held that the claimant need not be in the area of physical impact to be able to recover in respect of psychiatric injury and they held that the claimant need not be put in fear of her own safety to be able to recover for psychiatric injury. They held that the appropriate test to apply was that the psychiatric injury must be reasonably foreseeable, but they adopted a rather narrow test of reasonable foreseeability so as to find that the defendant was not liable to the claimant. It is unlikely that such a narrow approach would be adopted today (see Lord Bridge in *McLoughlin* v *O'Brian* [1983] 1 AC 410 and Lord Oliver in *Alcock* v *Chief Constable of South Yorkshire* [1991] 3 WLR 1057, 1114). Later cases such as *Schneider* v *Eisovitch* [1960] 2 QB 430 and *Boardman* v *Sanderson* [1964] 1 WLR 1317 suggested that the courts were beginning to adopt a broader approach based upon the reasonable foreseeability of the claimant suffering psychiatric injury.

The case which finally established the proper test for the recoverability of damages for psychiatric injury was *McLoughlin* v *O'Brian* [1983] 1 AC 410 (discussed by Teff (1983) 99 LQR 100), which was, for a number of years, the leading authority on the recoverability of damages for negligently inflicted psychiatric injury. The House of Lords held that the appropriate test to apply was whether or not it was reasonably foreseeable that the claimant would suffer psychiatric injury as a result of the negligence of the defendant. Although the House agreed on the general test to be applied, they did not agree on the exact ingredients of the test. In the case the claimant's husband and her four children were involved in a car accident which was caused by the negligence of the defendant. One of the claimant's children was killed in the accident and the others were severely injured. The claimant was informed an hour later that an accident had occurred and she went to the hospital where she saw her family and the extent of their injuries, in what were described as circumstances which were 'distressing in the extreme'. As a result of this experience the claimant suffered psychiatric injury. It was held that the claimant's psychiatric injury was a reasonably foreseeable consequence of the defendant's negligence and so she was entitled to recover damages. Two different approaches are discernible in the judgments given.

The first approach was adopted by Lord Wilberforce who held that, because shock was capable of affecting so many people, the law must place a limit upon the situations in which a claimant could recover in respect of psychiatric injury. Lord Wilberforce held that there were three 'elements inherent in any claim' for psychiatric injury. The first was the class of persons whose claims should be recognised. He held that, subject to the special case of a rescuer, 'so far ... the cases do not extend beyond the spouse or children of the [claimant] … including foster children'. But at a later point in his judgment he said:

> 'Other cases involving less close relationships must be very carefully scrutinised. I cannot say that they should never be admitted. The closer the tie (not merely in relationship, but in care), the greater the claim for consideration.'

This latter dicta would appear to suggest that recovery will generally be allowed in respect of injury to close members of the family but not to ordinary bystanders. An exception to the general rule relating to bystanders is that a person who suffers psychiatric injury as a result of seeking to rescue those involved in a terrible accident may be permitted to recover in respect of the injury which he suffers (see *Chadwick* v *British Transport Commission* [1967] 1 WLR 912, as explained in *White* v *Chief Constable of the South Yorkshire Police* [1999] 1 All ER 1).

The second element which Lord Wilberforce identified was that of the proximity of the claimant to the accident. He said that the claimant must be both close in time and space. Such would obviously include someone who saw or heard the accident but Lord Wilberforce said that this category should not be confined to such cases. He said it should also apply to someone who came on the 'aftermath' of the accident, by which he meant 'direct perception of some of the events that go to make up the accident as an entire event'.

The third requirement related to the means by which the injury was caused. He pointed out that the injury must be caused by sight or hearing of the accident or its immediate aftermath, although he did proceed to point out that 'whether some equivalent to sight or hearing, eg through simultaneous television, would suffice may have to be considered'. He also added that there was no case in which compensation had been awarded in which the claimant was only told about the accident by a third party. So for Lord Wilberforce, unless these three requirements were met, there was no liability for psychiatric injury because, if it were otherwise, the floodgates would be opened to unmeritorious claims.

Lord Bridge, however, adopted a different approach. He stated that the vital question was whether or not psychiatric damage was a reasonably foreseeable consequence of the defendant's breach of duty.

It is extremely unfortunate that the House of Lords did not speak with one voice because, until the decision of the House of Lords in *Alcock* v *Chief Constable of South Yorkshire* [1992] 1 AC 310, first instance judges and the Court of Appeal were unsure whether to follow the reasoning of Lord Wilberforce or Lord Bridge. In *Alcock* the House of Lords followed the approach of Lord Wilberforce and held that, to the extent that Lord Bridge had suggested that reasonable foresight of psychiatric injury was sufficient, of itself, to found a duty of care, his approach was not to be followed. A claimant must show, not only that psychiatric injury was reasonably foreseeable, but also that there existed a relationship of proximity between the claimant and the defendant. The three elements relied upon by Lord Wilberforce in

McLoughlin will obviously play a critical role in future cases and, indeed, all three were of significance on the facts of *Alcock*.

Alcock was a case which arose out of the Hillsborough disaster, where 95 football fans died as a result of overcrowding caused by the admitted negligence of the defendant, who was responsible for the policing at the stadium. Claims for damages for psychiatric injury were brought by claimants who had relatives and friends at the match and who had suffered psychiatric injury as a result of the tragedy. In *Alcock* the House of Lords held that a person could only recover for nervous shock which caused psychiatric injury where (i) it was reasonably foreseeable that he would suffer nervous shock as his relationship of love and affection with the primary victim was sufficiently close, (ii) his proximity to the accident or its immediate aftermath was sufficiently close in both time and space, and (iii) he suffered nervous shock through seeing or hearing the accident or its immediate aftermath. Although many of the discussions on nervous shock emphasise strongly these three criteria of relationship, proximity and seeing or hearing the accident, it should not be forgotten that the primary requirement is that nervous shock be reasonably foreseeable in the case of secondary victims. In the case of primary victims there is no need for these control mechanisms to limit the number of potential claimants. Thus in *Page* v *Smith* [1995] 2 WLR 644 the House of Lords held that where an especially sensitive plantiff was involved in an accident, but suffered no physical injury, it was sufficient to ask whether the defendant should have reasonably foreseen that the claimant might suffer personal injury and that it was unnecessary for the defendant to reasonably foresee injury by shock.

Returning now to the three requirements in *Alcock*, the first element concerns the class of persons eligible to claim. The claimants in *Alcock* consisted of a broad range of relatives of people present, injured or killed in the tragedy, including a wife, parents, brothers, sisters, uncles, a grandfather, a brother-in-law, a fiancee and a friend. As we have noted, Lord Wilberforce in *McLoughlin* stated that 'so far ... the cases do not extend beyond the spouse or children of the claimant ... including foster children' and the Court of Appeal in *Alcock* had held that the class of claimants was so restricted. But the House of Lords adopted a rather more expansive approach and held that the category of claimants eligible to claim was not confined to spouses and parents but extended to all relationships which were based upon ties of love and affection and where it could be demonstrated that the love and affection for the victim was comparable to that of the normal parent, spouse or child of the victim. Remoter relationships were therefore not ruled out completely but the House held that, in the case of such relationships, the claimant must prove the closeness of the relationship and the court will scrutinise such claims with care. Indeed, Lord Keith, Lord Ackner and Lord Oliver went so far as to say that the claim of a bystander was not 'entirely excluded' and they suggested that a claim may be brought by a bystander where a catastrophe occurs very close to him which is particularly horrific. However, this expansive approach to the class of claimants has not been followed in the Court of Appeal. In *McFarlane* v *Caledonia Ltd* [1994] 2

All ER 1 it was held that a bystander to a horrific event could not recover on the grounds that the basis of the decision in *Alcock* was that the test of proximity was not simply reasonable foreseeability but that there must be a sufficiently close tie of love and affection between the claimant and the victim. To extend that duty to those who have no such connection would be to base the test on foreseeability alone. Returning to the facts of *Alcock* it was held that only the parents who had lost a son and the fiancee were within the category of claimants eligible to bring a claim. In relation to the brothers and brothers-in-law it was held that they were excluded because there was no evidence of any particularly close ties of love and affection between themselves and their brothers or brothers-in-law. The fact of a sibling relationship is not sufficient of itself; evidence must be brought to establish that the relationship was a close and affectionate one.

Two further points must be made in relation to the class of claimants eligible to claim. The first relates to the category of cases typified by *Dooley* v *Cammell Laird & Co Ltd* [1951] 1 Lloyd's Rep 271. In *Dooley* the claimant was a crane driver who suffered psychiatric injury after his load, without any fault on his part, fell into the hold of a ship where his colleagues were working. He thought that he must have killed or injured some of the men, although in the event no-one was hurt. His claim succeeded. Cases such as *Dooley* could have been used by the House of Lords in *Alcock* to widen the category of claimants eligible to claim but Lord Oliver (and also, it would appear, Lord Jauncey) relied upon them to draw a distinction between cases in which the injured claimant was involved, either mediately or immediately, as a participant and those in which the claimant was no more than the passive and unwilling witness of injury caused to others. In the former category were cases such as *Dulieu* v *White* (above), *Dooley* and *Wigg* v *British Railways Board* (1986) The Times 4 February where the courts are more willing to recognise the existence of a claim, because the fact that the defendant's negligence has resulted in the claimant being an active participant in the accident of itself establishes the existence of a proximate relationship between the claimant and the defendant. In the latter category are cases like *Robertson* v *Forth Bridge Joint Board* (1995) The Times 13 April where recovery was denied to a fellow employee on the ground that he was a mere bystander or witness to the accident rather than an active participant.

The second point which must be noted in relation to the class of claimants eligible to claim is that the relationship can be with the claimant's property. That this is so can be demonstrated by reference to the case of *Attia* v *British Gas plc* [1988] QB 304. There the defendants entered into a contract to instal central heating in the claimant's house. The claimant returned to her home to find that it was on fire as a result of the negligence of the defendants. She telephoned the fire brigade but it took them four hours to bring the fire under control. The claimant claimed that she had suffered psychiatric injury as a result of witnessing the extensive damage to her house. The defendants admitted that they were liable for the damage to the claimant's house and its contents but they denied that they owed a duty of care in respect of the claimant's psychiatric injury. They argued that, as a matter of law and public policy, damages could only be recovered for psychiatric injury where it was suffered as a result of fear of death or personal injury to a person closely related to the claimant. The argument was rejected because the court was not prepared to lay down as a rule of law that in no circumstances could damages be recovered for psychiatric injury suffered as a result of witnessing damage to property. Bingham LJ said 'suppose, for example, that a scholar's life work of research or composition were destroyed before his eyes as a result of the defendant's careless conduct, causing the scholar to suffer reasonably foreseeable psychiatric damage … I do not think that a legal principle which forbade recovery in these circumstances could be supported'. The Court of Appeal did not say what factors would be considered in deciding whether the psychiatric injury was reasonably foreseeable but presumably they would be similar to those considered in *McLoughlin*; namely the closeness of the relationship between the claimant and the 'thing' damaged, the proximity of the claimant to the accident and the means by which the injury was caused.

The second element is the proximity of the claimant to the accident and on the facts of *Alcock* the point in issue related to the scope of the 'immediate aftermath' doctrine. Some of the claimants who identified the bodies of loved ones in mortuaries sought unsuccessfully to bring themselves within the scope of this doctrine. But it was held that these cases did not fall within its scope because the earliest identification of a victim occurred eight or nine hours after the tragedy and this could not be said to be the *immediate* aftermath. Lord Jauncey also had regard to the purpose of the visit to the mortuary, which was simply the identification of the body, and stated that that was very different from the case of a relative who goes within a short time of the accident to rescue or comfort the victim. So it is now clear that the 'immediate aftermath' operates within very narrow confines and the appellate courts will be reluctant to extend it beyond the fact situation in *McLoughlin* itself.

The third element concerned the means by which the shock was caused and this was of vital significance on the facts of *Alcock*. Some of the claimants had watched the events unfold on television but the House of Lords held that viewing the scenes of the tragedy on television was not sufficient because it could not be equated with sight or hearing of the event or its immediate aftermath. This was because viewers on television did not see recognisable individuals (such pictures being excluded by the broadcasting code of ethics). The effect of this conclusion on the facts of the case was that all the claims of the claimants failed because the claimants who satisfied the 'relationship' test did not satisfy this test and those who satisfied this test did not satisfy the relationship test.

Two further points should be noted about the approach of the House of Lords to the third stage. The first is that it is not necessarily the case that television viewers are excluded in all cases. Both Lord Ackner and Lord Oliver stated that they agreed with the judgment of Nolan LJ in the Court of Appeal to the effect that simultaneous broadcasts of a disaster cannot in all cases be ruled out as providing the equivalent of actual sight or hearing of the event or its immediate aftermath. Nolan LJ had given an example of a case in which television cameras 'whilst filming and transmitting pictures of a special event of children travelling in a balloon, in which there was media interest, particularly amongst the parents, showed the balloon suddenly bursting into flames'. In such a case a claim may well lie. On the other hand, Lord Jauncey refrained from making any comment on Nolan LJ's example, so it cannot be assumed that a claim will necessarily lie.

The second point is that it would appear that being told about the accident does not suffice. This can be deduced from the fact that Lord Keith, Lord Ackner and Lord Oliver stated that it must be open to serious doubt whether the first instance decisions *Hevican* v *Ruane* [1991] 3 All ER 65 and *Ravenscroft* v *Rederiaktiebogalet Transatlantic* [1991] 3 All ER 73 were correctly decided. The Court of Appeal has since heard the defendant's appeal in *Ravenscroft* and concluded that in the light of criticisms of their Lordships, the decision could not stand and so allowed the appeal ([1992] 2 All ER 470). No appeal has been heard in *Hevican* and so we shall use that case to illustrate the issues. The claimant was told that the minibus in which his favourite son was travelling had been involved in an accident. He was taken to a police station where he was told that his son had died. He then proceeded to the mortuary where he saw his son's body. The claimant was subsequently diagnosed as suffering from continuing reactive depression which rendered him unable to cope with his work. He was consequently made redundant and his illness prevented his return to the labour market. As Mantell J pointed out this case was clearly further removed from the scene of the accident than was the case in *McLoughlin* where the claimant came upon the 'immediate aftermath' of the accident. This was a case in which the claimant's trauma was the 'realisation coming to him in stages that his son was dead, in other words this was shock brought about from communication by others'. Mantell J noted that there were dicta in cases such as *McLoughlin* to the effect that there was no case in English law in which a claimant had recovered damages for psychiatric injury suffered as a result of being told about an accident. But he asked himself the following rhetorical question: 'can anyone doubt that it was reasonably foreseeable as a likely consequence of passengers in the minibus being killed through careless driving that the news would be communicated to their near relatives and that such news would come as a great shock ...?' However it would now appear that, in the light of *Alcock*, this approach is wrong and that such a claim should now fail. It is suggested that this conclusion will lead to ridiculous results. Suppose that in *McLoughlin* v *O'Brian* Mrs McLoughlin, after having been told that her family had been involved in a serious road accident, had collapsed and consequently suffered from some psychiatric illness. Would a court really deny her claim simply because she had not seen the injured bodies of her children and husband? It would be absurd if she could only recover damages if she was picked up, taken to the hospital, shown her children and then told 'now you can suffer your psychiatric illness'. As Deane J stated in the High Court in Australia in *Jaensch* v *Coffey* (1984) 54 ALR 417, 463:

'It is somewhat difficult to discern an acceptable reason why a rule based on public policy should preclude recovery from psychiatric injury sustained by a wife and mother who is so devastated by being told on the telephone that her husband and children have all just been killed that she is unable to attend at the scene while permitting recovery for the reasonably, but perhaps less readily, foreseeable psychiatric injury sustained by a wife who attends at the scene of the accident or at its aftermath at the hospital when her husband has suffered serious but not fatal injuries.'

If, as would appear to be the case, that such a claim would now fail in the English courts, it is hard to disagree with the view of Lord Oliver in *Alcock* that the present state of the law is neither 'entirely satisfactory' nor 'logically defensible' and one can only join in his appeal for legislative intervention to put the law in this area on a sounder basis.

Nevertheless, the whole matter received further consideration by the House of Lords in *White v Chief Constable of the South Yorkshire Police* [1999] 1 All ER 1, another case arising out of the Hillsborough disaster. The claimant police officers were on duty there and it was found that the immediate cause of the disaster was a senior police officer's decision to open an outer gate to the stadium, a negligent act. The claimants helped to carry the dead and injured or tried (unsuccessfully) to resuscitate spectators, and it was subsequently established that they were suffering from post-traumatic stress disorder as a result of these experiences. They sought to recover damages either as employees of the first defendant or as professional rescuers.

Their Lordships decided that the claimants' actions could not succeed. As to the argument based on the relationship of employer and employee, their Lordships concluded (Lord Goff dissenting) that the assumed existence of this relationship did not of itself convert the claimants from secondary to primary victims. The ordinary rules of the law of tort applied and these contain restrictions on the recovery of compensation for psychiatric harm. The professional rescuer argument failed because (Lords Griffiths and Goff dissenting) the claimants had not shown that they had objectively exposed themselves to danger, or reasonably believed that they were doing so.

In thus reversing the decision of the Court of Appeal (sub nom *Frost v Chief Constable of the South Yorkshire Police* [1997] 1 All ER 540), their Lordships applied *Alcock v Chief Constable of the South Yorkshire Police* [1991] 4 All ER 907 and *Page v Smith* [1995] 2 All ER 736 and considered and explained *Chadwick v British Transport Commission* [1967] 2 All ER 945. Lord Steyn said that Waller J's decision in *Chadwick* had been correct since there had clearly been a risk that a railway carriage might collapse on the claimant rescuer. See also *Hunter v British Coal Corp* [1998] 2 All ER 97 where the Court of Appeal decided that a person not present at the scene of an accident could not recover damages for psychiatric injury suffered because, when news of the accident was broken to him fifteen minutes later, he felt responsible for it.

White and *Alcock* were considered by the House of Lords in making its decision in *W* v *Essex County Council* [2000] 2 All ER 237. In *W* the claimant parents, who had been approved by the defendant council as specialist adolescent foster carers, told the council that they were not willing to accept any child who was known or suspected of being a sexual abuser. Despite this stipulation, the council placed with the parents a 15-year-old boy who had admitted and had been cautioned by the police for an indecent assault on his own sister and who was being investigated for an alleged rape. These facts were not communicated to the parents, although they were recorded on the council's files. Serious acts of sexual abuse against the parents' own children were alleged to have been committed after the boy had arrived at the parents' home. As a result, it was alleged that, because of the abuse, both parents and children suffered psychiatric illness and damage. Parents and children sought damages for personal injury caused by the council's negligence and their Lordships concluded that the parents' claims should not have been struck out (the trial judge and the Court of Appeal had refused to strike out the childrens' claims and there was no further appeal against those decisions). Lord Slynn of Hadley said:

> 'On a strike out application it is not necessary to decide whether the parents' claim must or should succeed if the facts they allege are proved. On the contrary, it would be wrong to express any view on that matter. The question is whether if the facts are proved they must fail. It is not enough to recognise, as I do recognise at this stage, that the parents may have difficulties in establishing their claim.
>
> On the other hand, it seems to me impossible to say that the psychiatric injury they claim is outside the range of psychiatric injury which the law recognises.'

8

The Duty of Care and 'Protected Parties'

8.1 Introduction

8.2 The character of the claimant

8.3 Judges and legal representatives

8.4 Police

8.5 Fire brigade

8.6 Ambulance service

8.7 Negligence in the exercise of a statutory power

8.1 Introduction

In some cases the difficulty in recognising the existence of a duty of care lies not in the interest which is sought to be protected but in the character of the claimant or defendant. For example, the claimant may have been an unborn child at the time at which the damage was inflicted and the defendant may argue that no duty can be owed to a claimant who was not born at the time at which the damage was suffered. On the other hand, the defendant may have been a barrister who maintained that he owed no duty of care to his client because of the undesirable consequences which would have followed, it was believed, from the imposition of a duty of care. In both cases it is the character of the claimant or defendant which is, or was, crucial in deciding whether or not a duty of care is, or was, owed. In this Chapter we shall focus upon particular examples where the character of the claimant or the defendant is the vital issue.

8.2 The character of the claimant

There are now very few claimants who are not granted a cause of action in negligence as the trend in the development of the tort of negligence has been to reduce the types of claimants who are not given a cause of action.

Although the law has become more liberal with the passage of time, there remain certain classes of claimant where the courts remain reluctant, or have had difficulty in recognising, the existence of a duty of care. One case in point is the claimant who suffers injury while participating in a criminal act, as a result of the negligence of the defendant. Such was the case in *Ashton* v *Turner* [1981] QB 137. The claimant suffered injury as a result of the negligence of the defendant who, at the time at which the claimant suffered injury, was driving a getaway car from the scene of a burglary in which they had both participated. Ewbank J held that, on grounds of public policy, the defendant did not owe to the claimant a duty of care. It is not, however, the case that participation in criminal activity will inevitably deprive a claimant of the protection of the law of tort; it is only where it is of sufficient gravity to invoke the maxim ex turpi causa non oritur actio that it will do so (on which see Chapter 31, section 31.3).

A second situation in which the courts have had difficulty in recognising that a duty of care is owed arises where the claimant was an unborn child at the time at which the damage was inflicted. We have already seen (at Chapter 2, section 2.1) that, at common law, a child who was born disabled as the result of the negligence of the defendant during the pregnancy or during birth had a cause of action (*Burton* v *Islington Health Authority* [1993] QB 204) and that right of action is now contained in s1 of the Congenital Disabilities (Civil Liability) Act 1976 (see s4(5) of the Act). But what of the claimant whose claim is that his deformities are such that he should not have been born at all? This question was put to the courts in the case of *McKay* v *Essex Area Health Authority* [1982] QB 1166. The infant claimant was born disabled as a result of her mother suffering an infection of rubella during pregnancy. The claimant claimed that, but for the negligence of the defendants in failing to treat the rubella, her mother would have had an abortion. It was held that the claimant's claim in effect was that she should not have been born at all and that such a claim was contrary to public policy on the ground that it was a violation of the sanctity of life. The other problem was that the court had no means of assessing damages for breach of such a duty, were it to exist, because damages would have to be assessed on the basis of the difference between life and the termination of life, and that the court could not calculate. *McKay* was a case decided at common law but the same position would prevail under the Congenital Disabilities (Civil Liability) Act 1976.

However, although a child cannot be heard to claim damages on the ground that he should not have been born at all, his parents may bring an action for the pain and suffering of giving birth to an 'unwanted' child and for the consequent disruption to family finances. In *Emeh* v *Kensington and Chelsea and Westminster AHA* [1985] QB 1012 the claimant had an abortion followed by a sterilisation operation to prevent her from becoming pregnant again (she had had three children prior to the operation). The operation was, however, performed negligently by the defendants and the claimant became pregnant once again and did not discover this fact until she was 20 weeks pregnant. She refused to have another abortion and she gave birth to a child which was congenitally abnormal. She claimed damages for the pain and suffering of giving birth, her loss of future earnings and the cost of maintenance of the child. It was held that the claimant's failure to have an abortion did not break the chain of causation and that the defendants were liable to the claimant. Prior to *Emeh* there had been a conflict of authority as to whether damages were recoverable for the cost of maintaining the child in the future. In *Udale* v *Bloomsbury Area Health Authority* [1983] 1 WLR 1098 Jupp J held that there were public policy objections to awarding damages for the cost of upkeep of the child because in law the birth of a child was a beneficial and not a detrimental event and there was a risk of the child finding out that he was unwanted. However, in *Thake* v *Maurice* [1984] 2 All ER 513 Peter Pain J held that there were no such public policy objections. He dismissed the idea that the birth of a child was always a blessing and equally he dismissed the argument that the fact that child might find out that he was unwanted should negate the existence of a duty of care. In *Emeh* the Court of Appeal preferred the reasoning of Peter Pain J and held that the parents could recover for all reasonable loss flowing from the tort or breach of contract, including the cost of bringing up the child (the principles to be applied in assessing the damages payable were considered by Brooke J in *Allen* v *Bloomsbury Health Authority* [1993] 1 All ER 651). This approach was adopted in *Nunnerly* v *Warrington Health Authority* (1999) The Times 26 November (where child born disabled, damages could include cost of care after age 18), but Morison J made this decision a month before that in *McFarlane* v *Tayside Health Board*: see below.

In certain circumstances public policy may operate to defeat the parents' claim. Such was the case in *Rance* v *Mid-Downs Health Authority* [1991] 1 QB 587. The claimants' son was born with severe spina bifida and hydrocephalus. The claimants alleged that the defendants had, through their negligence, failed to detect the handicap when the foetus was about 26–27 weeks and that, had it been detected, the mother would have had an abortion. One of the many points which was raised in the case was whether the defendants owed the claimants a duty of care. Brook J held that they did not because the claimants could only have avoided their loss (which was the birth of their son) had the pregnancy been terminated. Such a termination, Brook J held, would have been unlawful under s1 of the Infant Life (Preservation) Act 1929. Using the Act as his primary reference point he held that, in enacting the 1929 Act, Parliament had made a policy decision that the sanctity of the lives of children capable of being born alive be respected and that the duty of the court was to uphold that policy and therefore to dismiss the claimants' claim.

The principles to be applied in unwanted pregnancy cases were authoritatively laid down by the House of Lords in *McFarlane* v *Tayside Health Board* [1999] 4 All ER 961. Following the husband's vasectomy and advice that the operation had achieved its purpose, the wife conceived and gave birth to a healthy daughter. In an action for damages for negligence, the couple sought damages for the costs of rearing the child and for the pain and distress suffered by the wife in carrying and giving birth to her. The first claim failed but the second (including financial loss associated with the pregnancy) was successful. After reviewing relevant decisions in England and Scotland, other European states, the United States of America and the Commonwealth, Lord Slynn of Hadley stated the underlying principles as follows:

1. the wife is entitled by way of general damages to be compensated for the pain and discomfort and inconvenience of the unwanted pregnancy and birth, special damages associated with both (extra medical expenses, clothes for herself and equipment on the birth of the baby) and compensation for any loss of earnings due to the pregnancy and birth;
2. a failure to arrange adoption (or an abortion) is not a new act which breaks the chain of causation or makes the damage necessarily too remote;
3. it is not fair, just or reasonable to impose on the doctor or his employer liability for the consequential responsibilities, imposed on or accepted by the parents to bring up the child, and the doctor or his employer could not be said to have assumed responsibility for such economic losses.

McFarlane was applied by the Court of Appeal in *Greenfield* v *Irwin* (2001) The Times 6 February where the Court of Appeal decided that a woman who would have aborted her baby in order to continue in work had she known she was pregnant had no claim for loss of employment against the medical practice whose nurse had, on the assumed facts, negligently failed to discover her pregnancy. Additionally, their Lordships said:

1. the Human Rights Act 1998 did not require that the law provide the woman with an adequate remedy;
2. it was no longer the law that 'advice' cases of the type of *Hedley Byrne and Co Ltd* [1964] AC 465 (see Chapter 7, section 7.6) fell into a different category from cases involving physical damage.

In *Rees* v *Darlington Memorial Hospital NHS Trust* [2003] 4 All ER 987 the severely visually handicapped claimant had been adamant that she did not want a child: her disability would make difficult its care and upbringing. A sterilisation operation was performed negligently by the defendants: subsequently, she gave birth to a son who was healthy, although there was a low risk that he had inherited the claimant's genetic condition. Could the claimant recover any, and if so which, of the costs of bringing up her child? The Court of Appeal held (Waller LJ dissenting) that the claimant could recover any extra costs which were attributable to her disability, but the House of Lords allowed an apeal against this decision holding, by a four to three decision, that a disabled mother who gave birth to a normal, healthy child after a failed sterilisation operation could not recover by way of damages the extra costs of rearing him which were referable to her disability.

However, their Lordships also concluded that the mother was a victim of a legal wrong which it was appropriate to recognise by the award of a conventional sum. As Lord Bingham of Cornhill explained, an award immediately relating to the unwanted pregnancy and birth did not give adequate recognition of or do justice to that loss.

He would accordingly support the suggestion favoured by Lord Millett in *McFarlane* that in all such cases there be a conventional award to mark the injury and loss. The conventional award would not be, and would not be intended to be, compensatory. It would not be the product of calculation. But it would not be a nominal, let alone a derisory, award. It would afford some measure of recognition of the wrong done and it would afford a more ample measure of justice than the pure *McFarlane* rule. He would apply that rule, without differentiation, to cases in which either the child or the parent was or claimed to be disabled. In the event, their Lordships awarded £15,000 under this head.

In *AD* v *East Kent Community NHS Trust* [2003] 3 All ER 1167, while a patient detained under the Mental Health Act 1983, the claimant was placed by the defendant in a mixed psychiatric ward. Following intercourse with an unknown patient, she gave birth to a healthy daughter for whom she was unable to care. The child's grandmother was granted a residence order and assumed full responsibility for looking after the child. The claimant alleged that her pregnancy and the resultant birth had resulted from the defendant's negligence in caring for her and she sought damages, inter alia, for the cost of the child's upbringing, maintenance and education. These claims were dismissed and the Court of Appeal dismissed her appeal. Judge LJ said:

> '... even if the birth of the child resulted from medical negligence, damages are not recoverable to compensate for the cost of rearing a healthy child, notwithstanding that identifiable expense can be established. The cost of rearing [the child] is not "additional" or "extra" in the sense envisaged in *Parkinson* v *St James and Seacroft University Hospital NHS Trust* [2001] 3 All ER 97 and *Rees* v *Darlington Memorial Hospital NHS Trust* [2002] 2 All ER 177. For all practical purposes, they are the same costs, now being borne by someone other than the mother, [the grandmother], gratuitously providing for her granddaughter in the same way as the child's mother would have done, if she had been fit. As a head of damages, on the authorities, these costs are not recoverable as part of the mother's claim.'

As to the inability of the grandmother to claim, Judge LJ recalled that in *Hunt* v *Severs* [1994] 2 All ER 385 Lord Bridge of Harwich, giving the judgment with which the other members of the House of Lords had agreed, made clear that the person providing the voluntary services had no cause of action of her own.

In *Parkinson*, the Court of Appeal held that, after a sterilisation operation performed negligently, the claimant mother of four children gave birth to a boy. During this pregnancy the claimant was advised that the child might be born with a disability, but she chose not to have an abortion. In the light of behavioural problems, the defendant accepted that the boy should not be regarded as a 'healthy' child. The trial judge concluded that the claimant could recover damages for the costs of providing for her son's special needs and care relating to his disability, but that she could not recover damages for the basic costs of his maintenance. Both sides appealed against these decisions: both appeals were dismissed. Brooke LJ explained his approach as follows:

'I can see nothing in any majority reasoning in *McFarlane* v *Tayside Health Board* [1999] 4 All ER 961 to deflect this court from adopting this course, which in my judgment both logic and justice demands. Although [counsel for the claimant] had a cross-appeal in which he sought full recovery for his client, and not the limited recovery ordered by the judge, he did not press his cross-appeal very vigorously, and in my judgment it would not be fair, just and reasonable to award compensation which went further than the extra expenses associated with bringing up a child with a significant disability. What constitutes a significant disability for this purpose will have to be decided by judges, if necessary, on a case by case basis. The expression would certainly stretch to include disabilities of the mind (including severe behavioural disabilities), as well as physical disabilities. It would not include minor defects or inconveniences, such as are the lot of many children who do not suffer from significant disabilities. ... A negligent surgeon should not, without more, be held liable for the economic consequences of the birth of a child with significant disabilities if the child's disabilities were brought about between conception and birth by some ultroneous cause (for which see Lord Wright in *Lord* v *Pacific Steam Navigation Co Ltd, The Oropesa* [1943] 1 All ER 211 at 215). Similarly, the ordinary rules relating to contributory negligence will be applied in an appropriate case to limit recovery.'

It is interesting that Hale LJ added a word about fathers. Acknowledging that there are cases where the care and up-bringing of the child are shared, more or less equally, or where the primary carer is the father, it was her tenantive view that if there is a sufficient relationship of proximity between the tortfeasor and the father who not only has but meets his parental responsibility to care for the child, then the father too should have a claim. However, the issue did not arise here so it was unnecessary for her to express a concluded opinion.

Note should also be made of Morland J's decision in *Enright* v *Kwun* (2003) The Times 20 May (woman aged 37 at time of conception and birth: defendant doctor and hospital did not counsel her as to increased risk of Down's syndrome child: child born with Down's syndrome: woman entitled to damages).

8.3 Judges and legal representatives

Before Arthur J S Hall & Co *v* Simons

Having considered the position of claimants in relation to whom there is a difficulty in establishing the existence of a duty of care, we must now turn to the position of defendants. There are a number of defendants who owe a limited duty of care or even enjoy an absolute immunity from suit in negligence. One such group which enjoys some form of immunity in tort is judges and, to a lesser extent, immunity was enjoyed by legal representatives. As we noted in Chapter 2 of this book (section 2.3), judges enjoy immunity from suit in negligence and this immunity has been extended to witnesses in legal proceedings and arbitrators who act in a quasi-judicial capacity. A preliminary point must, however, be noted: a negligence action cannot be used as a vehicle to challenge the decision of a court of competent jurisdiction. The proper method of challenge is to appeal against the decision (see *Hunter* v *Chief*

Constable of West Midlands [1982] AC 529). Thus, an action cannot be brought against a barrister or a solicitor where the effect of such an action would be directly or indirectly to challenge the decision of a court of competent jurisdiction (*Somasundaram* v *M Julius Melchior* [1989] 1 All ER 129; *Smith* v *Linskills* [1996] 2 All ER 353). However, this rule will only apply where the claimant had a full opportunity to contest the decision of the court. Where the claimant alleges that his legal adviser had failed to advance a point of law which might have caused a decision adverse to the claimant to be set aside, such an action does not amount to relitigation of a decided issue and the claimant may then sue his legal adviser: *Walpole* v *Partridge & Wilson* [1993] 3 WLR 1093.

While barristers and solicitors did not enjoy the same immunity from suit as do judges, they did enjoy some immunity. In *Rondel* v *Worsley* [1969] 1 AC 191 the House of Lords held that a barrister has an immunity from suit at the instance of his client in respect of his conduct and management of a court case and in respect of the preliminary work connected with the case, such as the preparation of pleadings. In *Saif Ali* v *Sydney Mitchell and Co Ltd* [1980] AC 198 it was held by the House of Lords that the immunity declared in *Rondel* was not confined to court work but that it extended to pre-trial work provided that the pre-trial work was intimately connected with the conduct of the case before the court and that it affected the way in which the case was to be handled. See also *Atwell* v *Michael Perry & Co* [1998] 4 All ER 65 (barrister's immunity extends to pre-trial deliberations as to his case plan but not to advice as to prospects of an appeal).

The immunity accorded to those who act qua advocates was confirmed by s62 of the Courts and Legal Services Act 1990 (a person who is not a barrister but who lawfully provides any legal services in relation to any proceedings shall have the same immunity from liability for negligence in respect of acts or omissions as he would have if he were a barrister lawfully providing these services), but this provision has now been repealed.

A barrister did not, however, have total immunity in his or her conduct of a case. If time has been wasted by counsel during the conduct of proceedings and the court is satisfied that counsel had acted negligently, unreasonably or improperly, the court can make an order for wasted costs against the barrister: see s51(6) Supreme Court Act 1981 and *Ridehalgh* v *Horsefield* [1994] 3 WLR 463.

The immunity of barristers and solicitors was not founded upon the lack of foreseeability of harm but on considerations of public policy: a barrister must be able to carry out his duty to the court fearlessly, negligence actions against barristers would make a retrial of the original action inevitable and so lengthen proceedings and a barrister has to accept any client, however difficult he may be.

The reluctance of the courts to impose a duty of care arising out of the conduct of litigation was not confined to cases involving barristers and solicitors, as can be seen from the case of *Business Computers International Ltd* v *Registrar of Companies* [1988] Ch 229. The defendant served a winding-up petition on the claimants at the wrong address. The result was that the winding-up petition was made before the claimants were aware of its existence. The claimants alleged that the defendant owed them a duty of care to ensure that the winding-up order was correctly served at the claimants' registered office and that that duty had been breached. They claimed damages of £8,000 in respect of having the winding-up order set aside and £90,000 in respect of the loss of goodwill caused as a result of the winding-up order. Scott J held that the defendant did not owe to the claimants a duty of care in respect of the conduct of litigation. He held that it was not 'just and reasonable' to impose a duty of care in a case such as the present where the parties were antagonists in an adversarial system of litigation and where the safeguards against impropriety were to be found in the rules and procedures that control litigation and not in any remedy in tort. See, however, *Al-Kandari*, below, and *Customs and Excise Commissioners* v *Barclays Bank plc* (2004) The Independent 2 December (claimant obtained freezing injunction over account held at defendant bank: defendant allowed withdrawals from account: defendant liable for breach of duty of care).

Where, however, there are no rules which act as a safeguard against impropriety a court may be more inclined to hold that it is just and reasonable to conclude that a duty of care should be owed. In *Welsh* v *Chief Constable of the Merseyside Police* [1993] 1 All ER 692 the Crown Prosecution Service (CPS) agreed to notify the magistrates' court that the claimant accused's offences had been taken into consideration by the Crown Court. Unfortunately, it failed to so inform the magistrates and, when the claimant did not appear before the magistrates' court to answer the charges which he thought had been dealt with, they issued a warrant for his arrest. The claimant was subsequently arrested and kept in custody for a period of time. He brought a claim for damages and the CPS applied to strike out the claim against them as an abuse of process of the court. Tudor Evans J refused to strike out the claim. He held that there was no authority which unambiguously stated that proof of malice was an integral part in an action which touched upon the judicial process and the factors which had troubled Scott J in *Business Computers* were not present on the facts of this case. Although the parties were antagonists in adversarial litigation, Tudor Evans J thought that it was highly arguable that the CPS were not in the same position as solicitors acting at arm's length in civil litigation. For example, prosecutors are under a duty to make available to the defence witnesses who can give material evidence. So the fact that the parties were antagonists in the litigation was not a conclusive bar to the existence of a duty of care. In the later case of *Elguzouli-Daf* v *Metropolitan Police Commissioner* [1995] 2 WLR 173 (which was applied in *Olotu* v *Home Office* [1997] 1 All ER 385) the Court of Appeal held that as a general rule the CPS does not owe a duty of care to persons it prosecutes unless by its conduct it assumes responsibility to a particular defendant, and that this had been done in *Welsh*. The Court of Appeal stated that *Welsh* had been correctly decided, but the scope of *Welsh* has been limited by *Elguzouli-Daf*. See, too, *Cullen* v *Chief Constable of the Royal Ulster Constabulary* [2004] 2 All ER 237 (claimant detained by police denied statutory right to consult solicitor privately: denial did not cause or prolong unlawful detention: claimant's remedy judicial review, not action for damages).

Even within the context of civil litigation, there may be exceptional cases in which a court may be prepared to conclude that a duty of care is owed in the context of hostile litigation. That this is so can be illustrated by the case of *Al-Kandari v JR Brown & Co* [1988] QB 665. The defendant solicitors were acting for their client in custody proceedings involving their client and the claimant, who was the former wife of their client. The defendants' client was granted access to the children after the defendants gave an undertaking to the court that they would retain their client's passport (the passport covered the children as well as the defendants' client). Their client had previously taken the children to Kuwait and refused to return them, so the undertaking was given in circumstances where there was a real risk that if their client obtained his passport he would abduct the children and flee the country. The defendants' client then informed the defendants that he wished to have the names of the children removed from his passport. To achieve this it was necessary to return the passport to the Kuwaiti embassy. The defendants arranged for the passport to be taken to the embassy but they had to leave it there while the necessary amendments were being made. The defendants told the embassy that they were not to give the passport to their client, but they did not inform the claimant that the passport was out of their control. Their client obtained his passport from the embassy by deception, he beat up the claimant, kidnapped the children and fled with them to Kuwait. The claimant sued the defendants for the injuries which she suffered and for the fact that she had not seen her children since they had been abducted. The defendants denied that they owed a duty of care to the claimant.

The Court of Appeal affirmed that in a 'hostile litigation' public policy would usually require, for the reasons given in *Rondel v Worsley* (above), that a solicitor be protected from a claim in negligence by his client's opponent. But in the present case the defendants had 'stepped outside their role as solicitors' and had accepted a responsibility towards the claimant and her children. In particular they had accepted a responsibility to keep their client's passport in safe custody. They were held to be in breach of this duty and were liable in damages to the claimant.

Where the considerations of policy discussed in *Rondel* were not present, in other words where the negligence did not relate to the conduct of the case in court, then a solicitor or barrister may have owed – and would still owe – a duty of care to the claimant (see *Ross v Caunters* [1980] Ch 297, the facts of which are discussed in Chapter 7, section 7.9). However, where there is a conflict between the interest of the client and the interest of the claimant, it is unlikely that the solicitor will be held to owe a duty of care to the claimant (see to the same effect *Gran Gelato Ltd v Richcliff (Group) Ltd* [1992] Ch 560 where Sir Donald Nichols VC stated that in 'normal conveyancing transactions solicitors who are acting for a seller do not in general owe the would-be buyer a duty of care when answering enquiries before contract or the like'; cf *Edwards v Lee* (1991) 141 NLJ 1517).

Arthur J S Hall & Co *v* Simons

Arthur J S Hall & Co v *Simons*, *Barratt* v *Ansell* and *Harris* v *Scholfield Roberts & Hill* [2000] 3 All ER 673 were three appeals to the House of Lords which gave rise, in the words of Lord Steyn, to the same two fundamental general questions, namely:

1. Ought the current immunity of an advocate in respect of and relating to conduct of legal proceedings as enunciated by the House in *Rondel* v *Worsley* [1967] 3 All ER 993, and explained in *Saif Ali* v *Sydney Mitchell & Co Ltd* [1978] 3 All ER 1033, to be maintained in England?
2. What is or ought to be the proper scope in England of the general principle barring a collateral attack in a civil action on the decision of a criminal court as enunciated in *Hunter* v *Chief Constable of West Midlands* [1981] 3 All ER 727?

Their Lordships' answers to these questions may be summarised as follows:

1. Although they were far from saying that *Rondel* v *Worsley* had been wrongly decided at the time, in today's world the decision did not correctly reflect public policy. Advocates' immunity in civil and (Lords Hope, Hutton and Hobhouse dissenting) criminal proceedings would therefore be abolished.
2. If a convicted person succeeded in having his conviction set aside, an action against his original advocate in negligence would no longer be barred by the policy identified in *Hunter*, but the Civil Procedure Rules make provision for unsustainable actions to be struck out.

In the course of his speech, Lord Steyn said:

> '... the ending of immunity ... will bring to an end an anomalous exception to the basic premise that there should be a remedy for a wrong. There is no reason to fear a flood of negligence suits against barristers. The mere doing of his duty to the court by the advocate to the detriment of his client could never be called negligent. Indeed if the advocate's conduct was bona fide dictated by his perception of his duty to the court there would be no possibility of the court holding him to be negligent. Moreover, when such claims are made courts will take into account the difficult decisions faced daily by barristers working in demanding situations to tight timetables. ... The courts can be trusted to differentiate between errors of judgment and true negligence. In any event, a [claimant] who claims that poor advocacy resulted in an unfavourable outcome will face the very great obstacle of showing that a better standard of advocacy would have resulted in a more favourable outcome. Unmeritorious claims against barristers will be struck out. ... The basis of the immunity of barristers has gone. And exactly the same reasoning applies to solicitor advocates. There are differences between the two branches of the profession but not of a character to differentiate materially between them in respect of the issue before the House. I would treat them in the same way.'

In *Moy* v *Pettman Smith* [2005] 1 All ER 903 Lord Hope of Craighead recalled that in *Arthur J S Hall* v *Simons*, above, Lord Hobhouse of Woodborough had explained that one of the protections of the advocate was that the standard of care to be applied in any negligence action was the same as that applicable to any other skilled professional who has to work in an environment where decisions and exercises of judgment have to be made in often difficult and time-constraining circumstances. In the same case he (Lord Hope) had said that the measure of the advocate's duty to his client is that which applies in every case where a departure from ordinary professional practice is alleged, and that it could not be stressed too strongly that a mere error of judgment on his part will not expose him to liability for negligence.

In *Moy*, at the door of the court, counsel had advised the claimant to proceed with his action rather than accept an offer of £150,000. The Court of Appeal found that counsel had been negligent in failing to give the claimant sufficiently detailed advice. The House of Lords allowed counsel's appeal against this decision. The advice given had fallen within the range of that to be expected of reasonably competent counsel of her seniority and experience and her failure, in those circumstances, to spell out the considerations which led her to give her advice did not amount to negligence.

8.4 Police

A number of interesting recent negligence cases have been reported in which the defendants have been members of the police force. However, it must be said at the outset of our discussion that the police do not enjoy a general exemption from the ordinary law of the land (see *Marshall* v *Osmond* [1983] QB 1034). Thus the police have been held liable in negligence when they have negligently inflicted damage in the course of their work (see *Rigby* v *Chief Constable of Northamptonshire* [1985] 1 WLR 1242 and *Kirkham* v *Chief Constable of Greater Manchester Police* [1990] 2 QB 283, discussed in more detail at Chapter 13, section 13.4) or negligently allowed damage to arise: see, eg, *Reeves* v *Commissioner of Police of the Metropolis* [1999] 3 All ER 897 (person of sound mind and a known suicide risk committed suicide in custody). Two particular problems have, however, arisen in relation to actions brought against members of the police force; the first is the role of public policy in denying the existence of a duty of care and the second is whether, and if so when, the police can be held liable for the deliberate wrongdoing of third parties.

The role of public policy can be illustrated by reference to two recent cases. The first is *Calveley* v *Chief Constable of the Merseyside Police* [1989] AC 1228. Three police officers alleged that the defendant chief constable was vicariously liable for the negligence of investigating officers who were responsible for carrying out investigations into complaints made by members of the public who had been arrested by the claimant officers. The claimants alleged that the investigating officers had been negligent in failing to proceed expeditiously with their investigations and in failing to provide them with written notice of the complaints which had been made against them as soon as possible. The House of Lords dismissed the claimants' claim, holding that no duty of care was owed by the investigating officers to the claimants. The anxiety, ill-health and loss of reputation allegedly suffered by the claimants were not a reasonably foreseeable consequence of the alleged negligence. Nor had the claimants suffered any reasonably foreseeable economic loss because they had been suspended on full pay during the investigations. The House of Lords also held that it would be contrary to public policy to recognise the existence of such a duty because there was a public interest in the full and free investigation of such complaints and the imposition of a duty of care might impede such investigations. Lord Bridge also held that no duty is owed to a civilian suspect by a police officer who is investigating a suspected crime. But see *Waters* v *Commissioner of Police of the Metropolis* [2000] 4 All ER 934 in Chapter 6, section 6.5.

The second case is *Hughes* v *National Union of Mineworkers* [1991] 4 All ER 278. The claimant police officer suffered injury while seeking to maintain order at a colliery during the bitter mineworkers' dispute in the early part of the 1980s. At one point a vast number of pickets surged forward and struggled with the police; the claimant was knocked over and eight to ten pickets fell on him, occasioning him injury. The claimant brought an action against the Chief Constable of North Yorkshire, alleging that he had deployed his forces negligently, leaving the claimant in an unsupported and unprotected position. May J struck out the claim on the ground that the proceedings disclosed no reasonable cause of action. It was held that it was not in the public interest that a senior police officer, who was charged with the task of deploying police officers to control a serious public disorder, should have to make critical decisions in the knowledge that they might be the basis for a claim in negligence (although May J did acknowledge that there may be exceptions to this general rule, for example *Knightley* v *Johns* [1982] 1 WLR 349, discussed at Chapter 11, section 11.7). A similar public policy rule states that a serviceman owes no duty of care to his fellow servicemen in battle conditions: *Mulcahy* v *Ministry of Defence* [1996] 2 WLR 474.

The second issue is whether the police can be liable to a claimant for loss suffered as a result of the deliberate wrongdoing of a third party. This raises the misfeasance/non-feasance issue (discussed in more detail in Chapter 6, section 6.8). The leading case is *Hill* v *Chief Constable of West Yorkshire* [1989] AC 53. The claim arose out of one of the murders committed by the 'Yorkshire Ripper'. The claimant was the mother of Jacqueline Hill, who was the last victim of the 'Yorkshire Ripper'. The claimant argued that the defendant had failed to exercise all reasonable care and skill in seeking to apprehend the perpetrator of these murders and that, had he exercised proper care and skill, the perpetrator would have been apprehended earlier and her daughter would not have been murdered. The defendant applied to have the action struck out on the ground that it disclosed no reasonable cause of action. The House of Lords held that the claim disclosed no cause of action and it was struck out. The House of Lords held that it was foreseeable that if a violent criminal was not apprehended a citizen could suffer injury, but it was also held that foreseeability of harm did not of itself establish the existence of a duty of care. But see *Waters* v *Commissioner of Police of the Metropolis* [2000] 4 All ER 934 in Chapter 6, section 6.5.

While at common law police officers owe to the general public a duty to enforce the criminal law which is enforceable, in an appropriate case, by mandamus (*R v Commissioner of Police of the Metropolis, ex parte Blackburn* [1968] 2 QB 118 that duty could not be translated into a general duty of care to identify and apprehend an unknown criminal. Even in the case where a criminal escapes (as in *Home Office v Dorset Yacht* [1970] AC 1004) it was held that the duty of care only extends to those who are at special risk in the course of the escape (as was the case with the yacht owners in *Dorset Yacht*) and that it does not extend to members of the public who suffer injury when the criminal resumes his general criminal career. In the present case it could not be said that Miss Hill was at a special risk and so no duty of care was owed. Lord Keith also added that public policy negated the existence of a duty of care because the imposition of a duty of care could lead to police discretion being exercised in a 'detrimentally defensive frame of mind' and because any investigation by the court would be a 'significant diversion of police manpower and attention from their most important function, that of the suppression of crime' (contrast the wider view of Lord Templeman).

Hill has been applied in a number of recent cases. In *Clough v Bussan (West Yorkshire Police Authority, third party)* [1990] 1 All ER 431 the claimant was injured in a road accident, which occurred at a road junction where the traffic lights were malfunctioning (the lights showing green in both directions). The police were informed of the malfunction some 35 minutes before the accident occurred but took no steps to alert motorists. The claimant brought an action in negligence against the driver of the other car who, in turn, issued a third party notice against the police authority. The police authority applied to strike out the third party notice on the ground that it disclosed no reasonable cause of action. It was held that the police did not owe a duty of care to the claimant. Although the police were under a general duty to preserve law and order and to protect life and property, there was nothing to show that they owed a particular duty of care to this particular claimant. The fact that the police had been informed of the malfunction was not sufficient, of itself, to justify the imposition of a duty of care 'to every motorist who might thereafter use the junction'. In *Alexandrou v Oxford* [1993] 4 All ER 328 the claimant owned a shop and installed a burglar alarm which, when activated, raised an alarm to a local police station. One evening the alarm was activated and the police checked the front of the premises. They failed to check the rear of the shop where the burglars had forced entry and were hiding. The burglars later, when the police had left, removed a large amount of goods from the shop. The Court of Appeal held that the defendants owed no duty of care to the claimant. If such a duty were held to exist it would be owed to all 999 callers. There was no special relationship between the parties, as in *Home Office v Dorset Yacht* (above), and, following *Hill*, it was held not to be just and reasonable to impose upon the defendants a duty of care. See also *Hussain v Lancaster City Council* [1999] 4 All ER 125 (it would not be fair, just and reasonable for council to be liable for racial and other harassment by its tenants).

Similar reasoning was applied by the Court of Appeal in *Osman v Ferguson*

[1993] 4 All ER 344, where a schoolteacher formed an unhealthy attachment to a 15-year-old male pupil and harassed the boy by making a series of untrue sexual allegations. The teacher changed his surname to that of the boy and damaged property belonging to the boy's family. He was dismissed from his job but continued the harassment. The police were aware of these facts and the teacher even told a police officer that he feared that he would do something criminally insane. Later the teacher deliberately rammed a vehicle in which the boy was a passenger. The police, as a result, laid an information alleging driving without due care and attention but it was not served. Finally, the teacher shot and severely injured the boy and killed his father. An action was brought against the police alleging negligence in that although the police had been aware of the teacher's activities for nearly a year they had failed to apprehend him or interview him or charge him with a more serious offence before the shooting. The court held that it was arguable that a very close degree of proximity amounting to a special relationship existed between the boy's family and the police, but it was against public policy to impose a duty of care, following *Hill* and *Alexandrou*.

However, the police do not enjoy a blanket immunity in this area. In *Swinney* v *Chief Constable of Northumbria Police* [1996] 3 All ER 449 the claimant passed on to the police certain information concerning the unlawful killing of a police officer. The person implicated was known by the police to be violent. The informant requested total confidentiality as she did not want the information to be traced back to her. A document containing the information supplied, together with the informant's name, was left in an unattended police car in an area where vehicle crime was common. The car was broken into, and the person implicated in the killing obtained the document. Thereafter, the informant and her husband were threatened with violence and arson and both suffered psychiatric damage. The claimant sued in negligence and the police applied to have the action struck out, but the Court of Appeal refused to do this. The Court held that a sufficient relationship of proximity existed between the claimant and the police. As regards public policy, the court refused to accept that the police have a blanket immunity, and indeed stated that some considerations of public policy, such as the need to protect and encourage informers, acted against the police in this case. The Court also considered that it was at least arguable that the police had assumed a responsibility of confidentiality to the claimant.

In *Costello* v *Chief Constable of the Northumbria Police* [1999] 1 All ER 550 the Court of Appeal heard that the claimant woman police constable was attacked and injured by a woman prisoner in a police cell. A police inspector standing nearby had done nothing to help. The claimant contended that the inspector had owed her a duty of care, that he had been in breach of it and that the defendant was vicariously liable. The claimant's contention was upheld and Hirst LJ stated his position as follows:

> 'At the conclusion of the hearing I felt considerable anxiety whether, in the light of the authorities relied on by [counsel for the defendant] and in particular *Hill v Chief Constable*

of West Yorkshire [1988] 2 All ER 238, it was just and reasonable to impose liability on the defendant in the present case, seeing that the events occurred in an operational context, and involved an omission to act on [the inspector's] part, not, as in *Knightley* v *Johns* [1982] 1 All ER 851, a positive act of giving a negligent order to a subordinate officer.

Moreover, *Swinney* v *Chief Constable of the Northumbria Police* [1996] 3 All ER 449, on which [counsel for the claimant] strongly relied, was a striking out case, and not conclusively decisive that the defendant was liable.

However, I have been persuaded by May LJ's judgment that in the quite exceptional circumstances of the present case ... a duty of care did arise.

I ... would only add that, as I said in *Swinney*'s case, our decision should not be interpreted in any shape or form as undermining the general principle laid down in *Hill*'s case.'

Distinguishing *Costello*, in *Cowan* v *Chief Constable of Avon and Somerset Constabulary* (2001) The Times 11 December the Court of Appeal held that police officers called to an incident where a member of the public had been threatened with violence if he did not leave his rented property and who was then evicted in their presence, did not owe a duty of care to prevent an offence being committed against him under the Protection from Eviction Act 1977. Keene LJ said that the mere presence of the officers at the scene was not in the circumstances sufficient to give rise to the necessary special relationship between police and tenant. The judge found that the officers attended in order to prevent a breach of the peace. While the issue of whether there was a special relationship was to be determined objectively, nothing said or done by the officers indicated that they were assuming a responsibility to prevent the tenant being evicted. Unlike in *Costello*, the purpose for which the officers were present was one which they fulfilled. His Lordship found it impossible to discern any sufficiently weighty countervailing public interest which would make a duty of care appropriate or render it just or reasonable to impose such a duty.

In *Leach* v *Chief Constable of Gloucestershire Constabulary* [1999] 1 All ER 215 the Court of Appeal decided that the police had not assumed responsibility to an independent voluntary worker whom they had asked to be an 'appropriate adult' at the interview of Frederick West, a multiple murder suspect, although their Lordships allowed to proceed to trial the allegation that they had a duty to offer her counselling during or within a short time after her harrowing experience.

Vellino v *Chief Constable of Greater Manchester Police* [2002] 3 All ER 78 should also be noted. Often before when the police had come to arrest the claimant in his second-floor flat he had sought to evade arrest by jumping from a window. On this occasion, after he had been arrested, he broke away from the arresting officer, jumped from the window and fractured his skull. He claimed damages for personal injury, but the Court of Appeal (Sedley J dissenting) held that his action could not succeed. The maxim ex turpi causa non oritur actio, which prevented a claimant sustaining an action in law which arose from his own crime, made the claim untenable because the claimant had to rely on his criminal conduct in escaping lawful custody to found his claim. While Schiemann LJ was content to assume, without so deciding, that when a police officer arrested a citizen, the police officer put himself in a relationship with that prisoner which could involve the police officer in having some duties for the breach of which the prisoner could sue, when a man broke away from the arresting officer – and therefore committed a crime – the position was manifestly different.

As to the vicarious liability of a chief officer of police for the torts committed by his constables: see s88 of the Police Act 1996, as amended. A chief officer is vicariously liable for an intentional tort committed by one of his officers if the officer, although off duty, was apparently acting in his capacity as a constable: *Weir* v *Chief Constable of Merseyside Police* (2003) The Times 4 February.

8.5 Fire brigade

A trio of appeals (*Capital and Counties plc* v *Hampshire County Council* and *Digital Equipment Co Ltd* v *Hampshire County Council; John Munroe (Acrylics) Ltd* v *London Fire and Civil Defence Authority; Church of Jesus Christ of Latter Day Saints (Great Britain)* v *West Yorkshire Fire and Civil Defence Authority* [1997] 2 All ER 865), concerning the liability of the fire brigade in negligence, was heard and decided by the Court of Appeal together.

In *Church of Jesus Christ of Latter Day Saints (Great Britain)* a fire broke out in a classroom attached to the claimants' chapel. The fire brigade was called and of the seven fire hydrants round the premises, four failed to work and the other three were found so late as to be of little use. As a result water had to be obtained from half a mile away and the claimants claimed that a fire which should have been contained to the classroom destroyed the entire chapel as well. The claimants alleged breach of duty in failing to inspect regularly the hydrants, failing to observe or repair the defects and allowing one hydrant to become hidden by vegetation. The High Court held that it was not fair, just and reasonable to impose a duty of care at common law and employed the same arguments that mitigated against imposing a duty of care on the police in their operations. The court also failed to find sufficient proximity between the parties.

In *John Munroe (Acrylics) Ltd* the claimants' premises were showered with flaming debris following an explosion on adjoining land. The fire brigade was called to the scene of the explosion and decided that the fire there had been extinguished, but its officers did not inspect the claimants' premises. Had they done so, they would have seen smouldering debris and combustible materials which later caused the premises to be seriously damaged by fire. The claimants sued the defendants in negligence and the High Court decided, as a preliminary issue of law, that no duty of care was owed. The court held that there was no sufficient proximity, nor did a special relationship exist between the fire brigade and the owner of any property on fire so as to impose a duty of care, and that there were many considerations of public policy that mitigated against imposing such a duty. The court went on to hold that by responding to a call, the fire brigade did not assume a responsibility to those in danger so as to cause a duty of care to arise. To establish the necessary proximity it had to be shown that the fire brigade had undertaken a personal responsibility to an individual over and above performance of its public duty.

However, in *Capital and Counties plc* a different decision was reached. Here a fire broke out in the roof space of the claimants' premises. The premises, including the roof space, were fitted with a sprinkler system. The fire officer in charge mistakenly believed that there were no sprinklers in the roof, and thus that the sprinkler system was not assisting in fighting the fire, but was instead hampering the firemen. He therefore ordered the whole sprinkler system to be turned off. Following this the fire spread rapidly and the whole building was destroyed. The claimants sued in negligence and the High Court held that the fire brigade owed a duty of care not to commit positive acts of negligence, and in relation to such acts there were no public policy reasons why the fire brigade should be immune from a suit in negligence.

All three appeals were dismissed and Stuart Smith LJ explained the position as follows:

> 'Although the [Fire Services Act 1947] does not in express terms confer on the fire authority the power to fight fires, it is implicit in the powers conferred in s30(1), (2) and (3) and indeed the whole tenor of the 1947 Act that they do have such a power. The style of drafting adopted may be no more than the recognition that any citizen is entitled to fight fires, although in doing so he will not enjoy the immunity from suit for trespass afforded to fire officers and constables by s30(1). ... The question whether, in the absence of a statutory duty, a statutory power to act can be converted into a common law duty to exercise the power has been extensively considered by the House of Lords in *Stovin v Wise (Norfolk County Council, third party)* [1996] 3 All ER 801 ... In our judgment the fire brigade are not under a common law duty to answer the call for help and are not under a duty to take care to do so. If therefore they fail to turn up or fail to turn up in time because they have carelessly misunderstood the message, got lost on the way or run into a tree, they are not liable. [See, eg, *Hill v Chief Constable of West Yorkshire* [1988] 2 All ER 238.] ... But where the rescue/protective service itself by negligence creates the danger which caused the [claimant's] injury there is no doubt in our judgment the [claimant] can recover. ... it seems to us that there is no difference in principle if, by some positive negligent act, the rescuer/protective service substantially increases the risk; he is thereby creating a fresh danger, albeit of the same kind or of the same nature, namely fire. [See, eg, *Knightley v Johns* [1982] 1 All ER 851.] ... In our judgment there is no doubt on which side of the line a case such as the *Capital and Counties plc* case falls. It is one where the defendants, by their action in turning off the sprinklers, created or increased the danger. There is no ground for giving immunity in such a case. ... Although the powers are very wide, there is nothing in s30 which permits them to be exercised negligently. If it had been intended to exclude liability for negligence express provision could readily have been made. None was ...'

Stovin v Wise was distinguished in *Kane v New Forest District Council* [2001] 3 All ER 914: see Chapter 19, section 19.3.

8.6 Ambulance service

An ambulance service may owe a duty of care to a particular patient once it accepts a request to provide an ambulance for that person: *Kent* v *Griffiths* [2000] 2 WLR 1158.

In that case the claimant, who was pregnant and an asthmatic, telephoned for an ambulance, explaining her condition. The ambulance took 38 minutes to arrive and the claimant suffered a respiratory arrest with catastrophic consequences, including a miscarriage. The trial judge found that there had been no reasonable excuse for the ambulance's delayed arrival and that, had it not been delayed, it was highly probable that the claimant would not have had a respiratory arrest.

Upholding the trial judge's conclusion that the ambulance service was liable in negligence, the Court of Appeal distinguished *Alexandrou* (police: see section 8.4) and *Capital and Counties* (fire brigade: see section 8.5), believing that the position of an ambulance service was more akin to that of a hospital making provision for individual patients. Commenting on all three cases in *Watson* v *British Boxing Board of Control Ltd* (2001) The Times 2 February, Lord Phillips of Worth Matravers MR said that the cases on the assumption of responsibility to exercise reasonable care to safeguard a victim from the consequences of an existing personal injury or illness supported the proposition that the act of undertaking to cater for the medical needs of a victim generally carried with it the duty to exercise reasonable care in addressing those needs.

8.7 Negligence in the exercise of a statutory power

The final type of defendant who may owe a limited duty of care is a defendant who commits a tort in the course of the exercise of a statutory power. Where the defendant fails to exercise a statutory duty, that failure may of itself give rise to an action in tort (see further Chapter 14). Different considerations arise where the negligence lies in the exercise or non-exercise of a statutory *power*. The difficulty which arises in the latter type of case is that the courts must reconcile the principles of the tort of negligence with public law doctrines relating to the control by the courts of the exercise of statutory powers and the exercise of discretion conferred by Parliament.

The problem can be illustrated by reference to the case of *Sheppard* v *Glossop Corporation* [1921] 3 KB 132 (the whole issue is fully discussed by Craig (1978) 94 LQR 428. The defendants were empowered to install street lighting but, in the exercise of their discretion, they decided to turn the lamps off at 9 pm. The claimant was injured when he fell in the street in the dark. He brought an action in negligence against the defendants. The Court of Appeal held that the defendants could not be held liable in negligence when they had decided, in the exercise of their discretion, not to light the streets or only to light them for a certain time. To allow such an action would be to second guess the defendants in the exercise of their discretion and have the effect of exercising for the defendants the discretion which Parliament had conferred upon the defendants (see too *East Suffolk Rivers Catchment Board* v *Kent* [1940] 1 KB 319 (CA) and [1941] AC 74 (HL).

The issue was further considered by the House of Lords in *Home Office* v *Dorset Yacht Co* [1970] AC 1004. The claimant's yacht was damaged when it was rammed by some boys, who had escaped from a borstal training camp and boarded a yacht. The boys had escaped because the men in charge of them had gone to sleep and left the boys unsupervised. The defendants, who were the employers of the officers who let the boys escape, argued that they owed no duty of care to the claimant because they were acting in pursuance of a discretion which had been conferred on them by Parliament. They argued that, in the exercise of their discretion as to the control to be exercised over the boys, they had decided to institute a system of open borstals, where emphasis was placed upon the training of the boys. A finding for the claimant would result in stricter discipline and the operation of a closed borstal system rather than an open one and thus an undermining of the discretion which had been conferred upon the defendants. The preliminary point which was argued in the House of Lords was whether the defendants owed any duty of care to the claimant.

It was held that the defendants could owe a duty of care to the claimant but that in considering the duty of care owed by the defendants to the claimant account had to be taken of the statutory powers. Lord Diplock held that where the defendants made a decision of policy in the exercise of their discretion it must be shown that the public body had acted ultra vires before a claim in negligence could succeed. However where the negligence was at the level of the implementation of these policies, referred to as the operational level, then the defendants would not enjoy an immunity from suit because there the imposition of liability in tort would not conflict with the exercise of the defendants' discretion.

In *X* v *Bedfordshire County Council* [1995] 3 WLR 152 the House of Lords rejected the concept that negligence in the performance of a statutory power could only be actionable if the person concerned had acted ultra vires, while upholding the policy/operational dichotomy. Their Lordships stated that where Parliament has conferred a statutory discretion on a public authority it is for that authority, and not the courts, to exercise the discretion. Hence nothing within the ambit of that discretion is actionable at common law. However, if the decision falls outside the statutory discretion, it can (but not necessarily will) be actionable at common law. In *X* (which was applied in *Harris* v *Evans* [1998] 3 All ER 522: see Chapter 7, section 7.6), the question before the House of Lords related to a local authority's decision whether or not to take a child into care: such a decision could not be reviewed by way of an action for damages in negligence. The question in *Barrett* v *Enfield London Borough Council* [1999] 3 All ER 193 was different; the child had already been taken into care.

The claimant in *Barrett* had been in the care of the defendant authority, subject to a care order, between the ages of ten months and 17 years. He alleged that the defendants had owed him a common law (as opposed to a statutory) duty of care and that he had suffered personal injury because they had been in breach of such a duty, eg, by negligently making foster home placements and failing to arrange for his adoption. The Court of Appeal upheld the judge's decision to strike out the claim, holding that it would be contrary to the public interest to impose a duty of care on the defendant authority. This decision was reversed by the House of Lords, their Lordships concluding that it would be for the trial judge to decide, on the facts, in relation to which issues, if any, a duty of care arose and whether the defendants had been in breach of any such duty. Lord Browne-Wilkinson explained:

'I find it impossible to say that all careless acts or omissions of a local authority in a relation to a child in its care are not actionable: indeed I do not read the Court of Appeal so to have held. If certain careless conduct (operational) of a local authority is actionable and certain conduct (policy) is not, it becomes necessary to divide the decisions of the local authority between those which are "policy" and those which are "operational". It is far from clear what the expressions "operational" and "policy" connote. Therefore unless it can be said (as did the Court of Appeal) that operational carelessness could not have caused the damage alleged in the present case it would be impossible to strike out any part of the claim.'

Similar points arose in appeals to the House of Lords ([2000] 4 All ER 504) in *Phelps* v *Hillingdon London Borough Council*, *Jarvis* v *Hampshire County Council* and two unreported Court of Appeal decisions. All four appeals, which were heard together, raised questions as to the liability of a local education authority for what was said to have been a failure, either by the local authority or by employees for whom the local authority was vicariously liable, in the provision of appropriate educational services for children at school.

The facts and decision in *Phelps* are taken here to illustrate the approach of the House of Lords in answering these questions. With a history of 'lack of educational progress', assessment and help of various kinds dating back to 1980, in 1985 the claimant, then aged 11, was seen by Miss Melling, an educational psychologist employed by the defendants who were responsible for the claimant's education. Miss Melling failed to identify the claimant as dyslexic, but such a finding was made in 1990 by a clinical and educational psychologist to whom the claimant was referred by her parents. The claimant sought damages for breach of statutory duty or in negligence. Their Lordships concluded that the claim for breach of statutory duty could not succeed: there were alternative remedies (appeal procedures and judicial review) and it could be assumed that Parliament had not intended to create a statutory remedy by way of damages. However, Miss Melling had owed the claimant a duty of care to diagnose her condition and take appropriate action and for the breach of this duty the defendants were vicariously liable. Lord Slynn of Hadley said:

'I do not think that in this case it is any answer to the claim that a duty of care existed that others had been involved in psychological advice at an earlier stage, or that [Miss

Melling] was said to be part of the multi-disciplinary team, including the teaching staff. … she was the professional person brought in to this case and her role, difficult though it was, was pivotal. I see no reason why in this situation she did not have a duty of care to [the claimant]. Her relationship with the child and what she was doing created the necessary nexus and duty. The learned [trial] judge was both entitled and right to find that she owed a duty of care. He was equally entitled and might hold that, if she was in breach of her duty, Hillingdon was vicariously liable.'

Applying *Barrett* and *Phelps*, in *Carty* v *Croydon London Borough Council* (2005) The Times 3 February the Court of Appeal said that where an education officer in the performance of his statutory administrative functions entered into a relationship with, or assumed responsibilities toward a child, he might owe a duty of care to that child. Whether such a duty was in fact owed would require consideration of the substance of the act or omission in question and, if the matter was justiciable, would depend on the application of the classic three stages enunciated in *Caparo Industries plc* v *Dickman* [1990] 1 All ER 568: foreseeability of damage, proximity, and whether the situation was one in which it was fair, just and reasonable that the law should impose such a duty. In the event, their Lordships concluded that the judge had been right to hold that no breach of duty had occurred when the education officer failed to reassess the claimant's educational needs and to amend a statement of needs after the breakdown of a placement.

In *D* v *East Berkshire Community Health NHS Trust* [2003] 4 All ER 796 the Court of Appeal heard that, from birth, child M presented allergic symptoms. He received treatment over the next few years, but the doctors concluded (incorrectly) that M's mother, the claimant, might be exaggerating or fabricating the illness. Social services were called upon to assist and, for a time, M was placed on the At Risk Register. The mother claimed in respect of acute anxiety and distress and she alleged she had suffered as a result of this incorrect accusation, alleging that the defendant was vicariously liable for the negligence of its doctors. The trial judge concluded that the doctors had owed no duty of care to the mother and accordingly dismissed her claim, a decision upheld by the Court of Appeal.

The House of Lords (Lord Bingham of Cornhill dissenting) ((2005) The Times 22 April) dismissed the mother's appeal against this decision, holding that healthcare and other child care professionals do not owe a common law duty of care to parents against whom they make unfounded allegations of child abuse and who, as a result, suffer psychiatric injury.

As Lord Nicholls of Birkenhead explained, it was difficult to see why, if no duty was owed to a suspected childminder or teacher, it should be owed to a parent. He accepted, however, that there was one major difference: in the case of a parent suspicion might disrupt his family life; that would not be so with the childminder or teacher. The crucial question was therefore whether that potential disruption tilted the balance in favour of imposing liability in negligence where abuse by a parent was erroneously suspected.

Until recently the duty contended for would have been unthinkable, health professionals did not owe a duty even to the child. But the law had moved on since *X (Minors)* v *Bedfordshire County Council*. Later authority showed that common law duties might be owed to children in the exercise of child protection duties. Ultimately, it was the factor conveniently labelled 'conflict of interest', which persuaded his Lordship that at common law interference with family life did not justify according a suspected parent a higher level of protection that other suspected perpetrators. A doctor was obliged to act in the best interests of his patient, here that was the child. He was charged with the protection of the child, not of the parent. The best interests of parent and child normally marched hand in hand. But when considering whether something aroused suspicion a doctor had to be able to act single-mindedly in the child's interests. He ought not to have at the back of his mind an awareness that if his doubts proved unfounded he might be exposed to claims by a distressed parent.

His Lordship rejected the claimants' contention that the content of the duty to the parent was the same as that owed to the child. The time when the presence or absence of a conflict of interest mattered was when the doctor carried out his investigation. He did not then know whether there had been abuse by the parent but he did know that when considering that possibility the interests of parent and child were diametrically opposed. The child's interests were that the doctor should report his suspicions and further investigate in consultation with other child care professionals. The parent's interests favoured neither step. That difference of interest in the outcome was an unsatisfactory basis for imposing a duty of care on a doctor in favour of a parent.

Lord Nicholls concluded that common law should not recognise the duty sought. In principle, the appropriate level of protection for a suspected parent was that the investigations had to be conducted in good faith. That afforded him a similar level of protection to that afforded generally to persons suspected of committing crimes. That should be the general rule where the relationship between doctor and parent was confined to that of father or mother of the doctor's patient. Exceptionally, there might be circumstances where that was not so. Different considerations might apply then. There was nothing of that sort here.

Phelps and *Caparo Industries plc* v *Dickman* [1990] 1 All ER 568 (see Chapter 6, section 6.5) were applied by Garland J in *Bradford-Smart* v *West Sussex County Council* (2000) The Times 5 December where it appeared that the claimant had been bullied between the ages of nine and 12 while a pupil at a maintained primary school for which the defendant council was responsible. The bullying had occurred on the estate where the claimant lived and on the bus going to and from school. She now sought damages for psychiatric injury caused by the bullying. Her claim failed. His Lordship said that even if a school knew that a pupil was being bullied at home or on the way to and from school, it would not be practical, let alone fair, just and reasonable, to impose upon it a greater duty than to take reasonable steps to prevent that bullying spilling over into the school. The school's duty went no further than to prevent the bullying actually happening inside the school.

In *S* v *Gloucestershire County Council, L* v *Tower Hamlets London Borough Council* [2000] 3 All ER 346 the Court of Appeal heard that, when the claimants were children, they were in the care of their defendant local authority, living with foster parents. They claimed that their foster father abused them sexually and that in consequence they suffered physical and long-term psychological damage. They alleged that the damage was caused by the negligence of the local authority which was responsible for placing them with their foster parents and for subsequently monitoring their placement. Each of the foster fathers was later convicted of sexual offences with children. The defendant local authorities successfully applied for the claims to be struck out on the ground that they disclosed no reasonable cause of action. When the claimants appealed, the defendants contended that child abuse cases were bound to fail as a class. Their Lordships rejected this contention. On the facts, S's appeal was allowed since the Court was not persuaded that his claim had no real prospect of success, but L's appeal was dismissed.

In *Gower* v *Bromley London Borough Council* (1999) The Times 28 October the Court of Appeal accepted that, in principle, the teaching staff of a special school for disabled pupils could owe a duty of care to educate a pupil according to his needs and that the local education authority, as their employer, could be vicariously liable for their failure to do so. As Auld LJ there explained, the true ratio in *Phelps* (in the Court of Appeal) was that the education authority was not liable for failure of its psychology service to diagnose the claimant's dyslexia because the service's function was to advise the authority, not those for whom it provided education. The issue there was therefore one of proximity. That was unlikely to be an issue in the present case, where the claimant might be able to prove at trial that the head teacher and staff at the school owed him a duty properly to teach him and otherwise provide for his educational needs.

The extent of the duty of care owed by adoption agencies and their staff to prospective adopters was considered by the Court of Appeal in *A* v *Essex County Council* (2004) The Times 22 January. Social workers employed by the defendant local authority placed a child for adoption with the claimant husband and wife. Although the social workers were aware of the child's condition, they did not inform the claimants that he was hyperactive, impossible to control and liable to damage their home, health and family life. The claimants sought damages in negligence. Applying *Phelps*, Buckley J held that the defendant was liable to the claimants for failing to take reasonable steps to provide them with all relevant information about the children they were to adopt or to take such steps to ensure that it was provided. However, such liability extended only to injury, loss and damage sustained between the time the child was placed with the claimants as prospective adopters and the date he was adopted by them. Both sides appealed, both appeals were dismissed.

Hale LJ said it was not fair, just and reasonable to impose upon the professionals involved in compiling reports for adoption agencies a duty of care towards the prospective adopters and that there is in general no duty of care owed by an adoption agency or the staff which it employed in relation to deciding what information should be conveyed to prospective adopters. Only if they took a decision which no reasonable agency could take could there be liability. However, once the agency had decided, either in general or in particular, what information should be given, then there was a duty to take reasonable care to ensure that such information was both given and received. Here, there had been a breach of that restricted duty which had caused harm which, applying *Page* v *Smith* [1995] 2 All ER 736 (see Chapter 7, section 7.11), included psychiatric damage. In looking to the extent of liability, Buckley J had rightly found there to be a cut-off at the time when the adoption orders were made; by this time enough had happened to enable the claimants to make a decision for themselves.

In *Anns* v *Merton London Borough Council* [1978] AC 728 further consideration was given to the approach adopted by Lord Diplock in *Dorset Yacht*. Before entering into a discussion of this aspect of *Anns* it must be recalled that *Anns* has since been overruled by the House of Lords in *Murphy* v *Brentwood District Council* [1991] 1 AC 398 (discussed further at Chapter 7, section 7.3). In *Murphy* it was held that the loss which the claimants suffered in *Anns* was truly economic loss and that the local authority owed no duty of care to the claimants in respect of that pure economic loss. However it remains unclear whether local authorities owe any duty of care to house purchasers arising out of their exercise of their statutory powers to secure compliance with the building by-laws. In *Murphy* the defendant council did not seek to argue that they owed no duty of care at all to persons who might suffer injury through their failure to take reasonable care to secure compliance with the relevant building by-laws; they were content to accept that such a duty existed but argued that it did not extend to pure economic loss. But Lords Mackay, Bridge, Keith and Jauncey all expressly reserved their opinion on the correctness of the defendants' assumption. So the point must be regarded as an open one. Although the House of Lords in *Murphy* held that *Anns* was incorrect in relation to the particular by-laws at issue, *Murphy* itself does not cast doubt on the policy/operational dichotomy with which we are here concerned.

Returning to the facts of *Anns*, the claimant bought a flat in a two storey block of maisonettes. By 1970 cracks had appeared in the walls and the floors had begun to slope. The reason for this damage occurring was that the houses were built on an inadequate foundation. So the claimants brought an action in negligence against the builders and the local authority. The action against the latter alleged that they had been negligent in approving the foundations of the property because the foundations were only made to a depth of 2 feet 6 inches and not the 3 feet which was required under the by-laws. The defendants had a statutory discretion to decide whether or not to inspect the premises and they argued that the existence of this statutory discretion precluded the existence of a duty of care towards the claimant. Lord Wilberforce had no difficulty in concluding that there was a sufficient degree of proximity between the parties to found a duty of care; the problem was as to the effect of the statutory discretion on the existence of a duty of care.

Lord Wilberforce adopted the distinction we have noted between a policy decision and an operational decision. He said that, in making a decision as to which buildings to inspect, the defendants were making a decision of policy but that they 'are under duty to give proper consideration to the question whether they should inspect or not. Their immunity from attack, in the event of failure to inspect ... though great is not absolute'. However he did not make it clear whether the action which he envisaged would be available was a public law action seeking judicial review or an action in the tort of negligence. On the other hand Lord Salmon was of the opinion that, were such a cause of action to exist, it could take the form of an action in negligence. Lord Wilberforce said that, where the negligence existed at the operational level, then it would be easier to superimpose a common law duty of care than in the case of negligence at the policy level. Even at the operational level it must be remembered that the case must be interpreted against the statutory background and that it must be shown that the defendants did not act within the limits of their discretion, bona fide exercised.

The policy/operational dichotomy has, however, come under criticism from the Privy Council in *Rowling* v *Takaro Properties Ltd* [1988] AC 473 (see Craig (1988) 104 LQR 185). In giving judgment Lord Keith noted the academic criticism which had been levelled against the dichotomy (see Craig *Administrative Law* pp534–538 and Bowman and Bailey [1986] CLJ 430) and stated that the distinction did not provide a 'touchstone of liability'. Instead he said that the dichotomy expressed a need to exclude discretionary decisions as to the allocation of scarce resources from the scope of a negligence action. Thus Lord Keith appears to be saying that the crucial question is whether or not the issue is justiciable in the sense that it is unsuitable for judicial resolution because, for example, it concerns the exercise of a discretion which Parliament has entrusted to the local authority. But he said that a conclusion that the decision was not within the 'policy' category did not mean that a duty of care will necessarily exist. All the facts had to be examined carefully before such a conclusion was to be reached.

The negligence in *Rowling* was alleged to consist of a negligent interpretation by the Minister of Finance of his statutory powers. The claimant had earlier been granted judicial review of the minister's decision and the decision was quashed on the ground that it was based upon an irrelevant consideration. By the time that the defendants' appeal against the grant of judicial review was dismissed, the claimant had suffered extensive and irremediable financial loss and he sought to recover these losses from the defendants.

The Privy Council was prepared to assume for the purposes of argument that the minister owed a duty of care to the claimant but found that, on the facts, there had been no breach of duty. But the Privy Council also pointed to the existence of a number of factors which militated against the imposition of a duty of care in a case such as the present. These factors are likely to be of considerable importance in future cases where it is alleged that a duty of care is owed in the exercise of a statutory power. The first is that in many cases the claimant will be able to obtain judicial review within a short space of time and so the only damage which will be suffered is the cost of delay, which is unlikely to be large. The second is that it will be very difficult to establish that an error in interpreting a statute is negligent, because a misconstruction of a statute can be severely criticised without it being held to be negligent. Thirdly the court must bear in mind the danger of overkill in that the imposition of liability may result in the cautious civil servant going to extreme lengths before making a decision in order to escape liability in negligence (see, for example, the judgment of the Court of Appeal in *Martine* v *South East Kent Health Authority* (1993) The Times 8 March where this criterion was invoked). Finally it will be very difficult to establish a case in which the minister is under an obligation to seek legal advice as to the extent of his statutory powers. Of particular importance is the third factor and a regard to the consequences of the finding that a duty of care is owed may lead courts to conclude that no duty of care is owed in the exercise of a statutory power (see too *Jones* v *Department of Employment* [1989] QB 1, where it was held that an adjudication officer did not owe a duty of care to a claimant for unemployment benefit unless it could be shown that the officer was guilty of misfeasance and that the remedy, if any, for a claimant was by way of judicial review).

Although the courts are now undoubtedly more reluctant to conclude that a defendant owes a common law duty of care when exercising a statutory power, this does not mean that a negligence claim can never lie in such circumstances. That this is so can be demonstrated by reference to the case of *Lonrho plc* v *Tebbit* [1992] 4 All ER 280. The case arose out of the long-running dispute between Lonrho and the Al-Fayed brothers over the takeover of the House of Fraser group. In 1981 the claimants, Lonrho, gave an undertaking to the Secretary of State for Trade and Industry that they would not acquire more than 30 per cent of House of Fraser's share capital (when they gave the undertaking they owned 29.9 per cent of the shares) while a reference was made to the Monopolies and Mergers Commission (MMC). In November 1984 the claimants sold the vast majority of their shares in House of Fraser to a company controlled by the Al-Fayed brothers. On 14 February 1985 the MMC reported that the proposed merger between the claimants and House of Fraser would not be contrary to the public interest. On 4 March the company controlled by the Al-Fayed brothers made a public offer for the remaining shares in House of Fraser which enabled them to acquire more than 50 per cent of its shares. On 14 March the Secretary of State released the claimants from their undertaking, but it was then too late for the claimants to make a successful bid for House of Fraser. So the claimants brought an action against the Secretary of State, Mr Tebbit, alleging that he had been negligent in the exercise of his statutory power because of his delay in releasing the claimants from their undertaking. At first instance, Sir Nicolas Browne-Wilkinson V-C refused to strike out the claimants' claim and the defendants appealed to the Court of Appeal.

The defendants argued that they did not owe a duty of care in private law to the claimants and that the issues which arose on the facts of the case all belonged within the domain of public law. Both arguments were rejected by the Court of Appeal. A central plank in the defendants' argument was that there was no precedent for holding that a minister owed a duty of care sounding in private law as a result of his exercise of public law powers, and that there was no precedent for holding a minister liable in damages (particularly for economic loss) because in good faith he had misconstrued his legal position. But Dillon LJ rejected this argument on the basis that the public interest in the *release* of the undertaking was considerably smaller than in its imposition. In light of the factors set out by Lord Keith in his speech in *Rowling* (above), the court acknowledged that the claimants' case faced a number of difficulties but concluded that these were not sufficient to warrant striking out the claim. Dillon LJ stated that it did not appal him that it should be suggested that the Secretary of State should assume a private law duty to the claimants to release the undertaking when it was no longer needed and the restriction on the claimants' freedom to conduct their business no longer had a rationale.

9

Negligence: Breach of the Duty

9.1 Introduction

Having established that the defendant owes to the claimant a duty of care, the second thing which must be established is that the defendant breached that duty of care. Professor Fleming has said of negligence that it is 'conduct falling below the standard demanded for the protection of others against unreasonable risk of harm' (*The Law of Torts* (7th ed) p96). The important point to note is that the standard required of the defendant is an objective one, that is it depends on the standard of care which would have been adopted by the reasonable man in the circumstances. The most famous description of this objective standard was provided by Alderson B in *Blyth* v *Birmingham Waterworks Co* (1856) 11 Ex 781, 784 when he said:

'Negligence is the omission to do something which a reasonable man, guided upon those considerations which ordinarily regulate the conduct of human affairs, would do, or doing something which a prudent and reasonable man would not do.'

Although the standard is an objective one, the question whether a particular defendant has breached the standard of care is largely a question of fact. There are, however, certain principles which the court will apply in considering whether the defendant has breached the standard of care. We shall consider these principles in this Chapter. We shall commence by giving further consideration to the reasonable man standard, then we shall consider the various factors which the courts balance in deciding whether the defendant has breached his duty of care. We shall then consider various situations in which difficulties have arisen in identifying the requisite standard of care. Finally we shall examine the issues which arise in attempting to prove that the defendant was negligent.

9.2 The reasonable man

As we have already noted the standard which is applied in considering whether the defendant has been negligent is the standard of the reasonable man. The requirements of the reasonable man standard were clearly articulated by the House of Lords in *Glasgow Corporation* v *Muir* [1943] 2 AC 448. The manageress of the defendants' tearoom gave a church party permission to use the tearoom when rain prevented them from eating their food outside. Two of the leaders of the church party were carrying a tea urn down a narrow passage when one of them, for some unexplained reason, let go of one of the handles of the urn, with the result that tea poured out and some children were badly scalded. The claimants sought to recover damages from the defendants on the ground that the manageress was negligent in giving permission for the tea urn to be brought down the narrow passage. One of the issues argued before the House of Lords concerned the standard of care owed by the defendants. Lord MacMillan provided the following analysis of the reasonable man standard:

'The standard of foresight of the reasonable man is in one sense an impersonal test. It eliminates the personal equation and is independent of the idiosyncrasies of the particular person whose conduct is in question. Some persons are by nature unduly timorous and imagine every path beset with lions; others, of more robust temperament, fail to foresee or nonchalantly disregard even the most obvious dangers. The reasonable man is presumed to be free both from over-apprehension and from over-confidence.'

However Lord MacMillan did concede that the test did contain a subjective element because the standard of the reasonable man had to be applied to the facts of the case and to what the reasonable man, in the position of the particular defendant, ought to have foreseen. It was held on the facts that the defendants were not negligent because they could not have foreseen that such an accident would occur.

The application of this objective reasonable man test can be seen in the case of *The Lady Gwendolen* [1965] P 294. Two ships were involved in a collision in foggy conditions. The accident was caused by the negligence of the defendants, who were a firm of brewers who used the ship to carry stout from Dublin to Liverpool. The defendants argued that they should be judged by the standard of the reasonable brewers who happened to hire a ship and not according to the standards of the reasonable shipowner. This argument was rejected by the court. The standard of care which was owed by the defendants was the same as the standard of care owed by every other shipowner. Winn LJ stated that 'the law must apply a standard which is not relaxed to cater for [the defendants'] factual ignorance of all activities outside brewing: having become owners of ships, they must behave as reasonable shipowners'.

A well known example of the objective standard of care is provided by cases involving car drivers. The most well known case is *Nettleship* v *Weston* [1971] 2 QB 691. The claimant, who was an experienced driver, agreed to give driving lessons to the wife of one of his friends. On her third lesson, with the claimant moving the gear lever and the defendant steering the car, the defendant panicked and the car, moving at walking pace, mounted the pavement and struck a lamp-post. The claimant suffered a broken knee cap and sought to recover from the defendant. The defendant denied that she had been negligent. The Court of Appeal held that the defendant was negligent. They held that the standard of care required of a learner driver was the same as the standard required of an experienced driver; that standard being the standard of the reasonably competent and experienced driver. Lord Denning said that, while the defendant was not morally at fault, she was legally required to be insured and therefore the risk should fall on her. Megaw LJ stated that, if it was accepted that the standard of care was a variable one, it could not logically be confined to car drivers and would have to be a principle of universal application. The adoption of a variable standard, he said, would lead to unpredictability, uncertainty and the impossibility of arriving at fair and consistent decisions. So he concluded that a general standard was preferable to 'the vagaries of a fluctuating standard'.

A similar approach was adopted in the case of *Roberts* v *Ramsbottom* [1980] 1 All ER 7. The defendant argued that he was not liable to the claimant, whom he had knocked down, because he had suffered a stroke 20 minutes before the accident occurred and that his driving had been impaired by the stroke. It was accepted by the court that, after the stroke, the defendant was, through no fault of his own, unable to control the car properly. However it was held that this was not sufficient to free the defendant from liability unless the facts established a defence of automatism, that his actions were wholly beyond his control. On the facts it was held that the defendant retained some control over his actions, although that control was admittedly imperfect, and therefore the standard of the reasonably competent driver was applicable and the defendant was in breach of it. These two decisions were obviously influenced by the fact that the defendants were insured and so were in a better position to bear the loss, but it would be a mistake to dismiss them solely on that ground. As Megaw LJ stated, if it was accepted that the standard required was a variable one, then this would lead to enormous uncertainty and difficulty in practice. It is for this reason that the courts have set their face against a variable standard of care.

Having considered what the objective standard of the reasonable man involves, consideration will now be focused upon the different factors to which the courts have regard in considering whether or not the defendant was negligent.

9.3 Foreseeability

The standard of care is based upon what the reasonable man would have foreseen in the circumstances. The defendant may not be liable because the harm to the claimant was not foreseeable. Such was the case in *Roe* v *Minister of Health* [1954] 2 QB 66. In 1947 the claimant went into hospital for a minor operation. He was paralysed because a spinal anaesthetic which he was given became tainted with phenol when it was in a syringe which was stored in phenol. At the time it was not known that the phenol could seep into the syringe through invisible cracks in the syringe. It was held that the defendants were not negligent. Denning LJ said that the court could not look at the accident which occurred in 1947 'with 1954 spectacles'. In 1947 it was not known that harm to the claimant could occur in this way and so the defendants were not liable.

When a supplier of petrol unlawfully sold some to a person under the age of 16 (in fact, to the claimant and his friend who were both aged 13), and the claimant later suffered serious burns when petrol which had spilled onto his trousers was ignited by a match or lighter thrown down by his friend, the court found that the supplier had owed the claimant a common law duty of care to prevent him from having control over the petrol and that the claimant's action would be successful: *Evans* v *Souls Garages Ltd* (2001) The Times 23 January.

As John Leighton Williams QC explained, mishandling, misuse and the resulting spillage and ignition of the petrol were the very types of conduct which the defendants ought to have foreseen, and were easily foreseen. Solvent sniffing was established misconduct by 1988 and was something which those selling petrol ought to have been guarding against. In reaching his conclusion his Lordship rejected the defences of ex turpi causa non oritur actio (see Chapter 31, section 31.3) and volenti non fit injuria (see section 9.13), but he found that the claimant had been contributorily negligent (see Chapter 12) to the extent of one-third and he reduced the amount awarded by way of damages accordingly.

In *Maguire* v *Harland and Wolff plc* (2005) The Times 27 January the Court of Appeal heard that the claimant's husband had worked in the defendant's shipyard from 1961 until 1965 and, in the course of his work, he had been exposed to asbestos dust. The claimant wife had contracted mesothelioma and she sought damages for secondary exposure to asbestos dust brought home by her husband. Morland J had allowed her claim, but this decision was reversed on appeal. As Judge LJ explained, until late 1965 there had been nothing in the literature about the risks of familial or secondary exposure to asbestos dust. In view of this, it could not be accepted that, ahead of contemporary understanding, the defendant should have appreciated the risk to the claimant and that its failure to do so and take appropriate precautions for her safety was negligent.

9.4 Magnitude of the risk

Although harm to someone may be foreseeable, the risk of that harm being inflicted may be so unlikely that the defendant will not be required to take precautions against it happening. Such was the case in *Bolton* v *Stone* [1951] AC 850. The claimant, who was standing on the road close to a cricket ground, was hit by a cricket ball which had been hit for six straight out of the ground. There was a fence around the ground which was seven feet high and, due to the slope of the ground, the top of the fence was some 17 feet above the level of the pitch. The fence was located some 80 yards from where the batsman stood, so it was an exceptional hit. There was evidence that cricket balls had been hit out of the ground on about six occasions in the previous 30 years. It was held that the likelihood of a person outside the ground suffering injury in this way was so slight that the defendants were not negligent in continuing to play cricket there without taking additional precautions. Lord Oaksey said that the standard of the reasonable man did not require a man to take precautions against 'every foreseeable risk' and that 'life would be almost intolerable if [the ordinarily careful man] were to attempt to take precautions against every risk which he can foresee'.

Bolton v *Stone* was distinguished in the case of *Hilder* v *Associated Portland Cement Manufacturers Ltd* [1961] 1 WLR 1434. The defendants were the occupiers of land and they permitted some small boys to play football on their land. The land was close to a road and one of the boys kicked the ball on to the road and caused the claimant's husband to have an accident, in which he was killed. It was held that the defendants were negligent. The risk of injury to a road user was much greater than the risk in *Bolton*. The land was only some 15 yards from the road and the risk of injury was not one which the reasonable man would have disregarded.

In *Haley* v *London Electricity Board* [1965] AC 778 the House of Lords was impressed by the statistical evidence of the likelihood of an accident occurring. The defendants dug a hole in the pavement. They took sufficient steps to warn a sighted person of the hole but they took insufficient steps to warn a blind person. The claimant, who was blind, fell into the hole, through no fault of his own. As a result of the fall he became deaf. The House was provided with evidence of the number of blind people in London and of the proportion of the population who were blind and concluded that the likelihood of a blind person falling into the hole was not so small that the defendants could ignore it and that therefore the defendants were negligent. It should not be thought, however, that statistical evidence is a regular feature of negligence cases. Even where it is adduced and the court has regard to it, it will only be one factor among many to be weighed in the balance.

Where the harm which is likely to be done if the risk materialises is serious, then more will be required of the defendant. This requirement can be demonstrated by reference to the case of *Paris* v *Stepney Borough Council* [1951] AC 367. The claimant, who only had one eye, was employed by the defendants in a job which involved some risk of injury to his eye. Had the claimant had two eyes the risk of injury would not have required the defendants to supply the claimant with goggles. But the fact that the claimant only had one eye meant that the consequences of an injury to his eye were so serious that the reasonable man would have supplied the claimant with goggles. When the claimant suffered injury to his eye at work, which rendered him blind, the defendants were held to have been negligent in not supplying the claimant with goggles.

On the other hand a different result was reached by the court in *Withers* v *Perry Chain Co* [1961] 1 WLR 1314. The claimant was particularly susceptible to dermatitis on coming into contact with grease. The defendants, who were her employers, put her on the most 'grease-free' job they could find, but the claimant still contracted dermatitis. It was held that the defendants were not liable for the dermatitis which the claimant contracted. The defendants had done all they could to avoid the claimant contracting dermatitis and the only thing which they could have done to ensure that the claimant did not contract it was to dismiss her. It was held that the defendants were not negligent in failing to dismiss the claimant, as such a step would not have been in the interest of any of the parties.

The Court of Appeal reached the opposite conclusion in *Coxall* v *Goodyear Great Britain Ltd* (2002) The Times 5 August. Although the defendant employer's manufacturing process was safe and satisfactory, as both the defendant and the claimant employee were aware, exposure to the fumes involved placed the claimant asthma sufferer at risk of exacerbation of his condition. His condition having deteriorated, he sought damages from the defendant. His action was successful. Simon Brown LJ said that counsel for the defendant's central contention had been that an employer was not under a duty to remove an employee from safe work, still less dismiss him, because he was not suited to the work. Rather, he submitted, it was for the employee to decide whether or not to take the risk of continuing in his job. He had relied on *Withers* v *Perry Chain Co Ltd* [1961] 1 WLR 1314. His Lordship thought that this argument went too far. The principal consideration in determining whether any particular case fell within the *Withers* principle was the actual nature and extent of the known risk. Cases would undoubtedly arise when, despite the employee's desire to remain at work notwithstanding his recognition of the risk he ran, the employer would nevertheless be under a duty in law to dismiss him for his own good so as to protect him against physical danger. That duty arose in this case.

Stress at work

The Health and Safety Executive defines stress as 'the adverse reaction people have to excessive pressures or other types of demand placed on them'. The ordinary principles of employer's liability apply to claims for psychiatric or physical injury or illness arising from the stress of work: *Hatton* v *Sutherland* (2002) The Times 12 February. In her judgment in that case, Hale LJ identified four categories of claims for psychiatric injury and enunciated 16 propositions in relation to aspects of liability arising from stress at work.

In *Hartman* v *South Essex Mental Health and Community Care NHS Trust* (2005) The Times 21 January the Court of Appeal affirmed that liability for psychiatric injury caused by stress at work is in general no different in principle from liability for physical injury: the practical propositions set out by Hale LJ in *Hatton* remained helpful signposts for judges faced with the sometimes complex facts of stress at work cases, although care should be taken in their application since they were not intended to cover all the infinitely variable facts that were likely to arise. Scott Baker LJ said that in *Hartman* the critical issue was whether the defendant trust should have appreciated that the claimant, who was employed by the defendant at a children's home as a nursing auxiliary, was at risk of succumbing to psychiatric injury. In all the circumstances, the trial judge should have rejected Mrs Hartman's claim on the ground that it was not reasonably foreseeable to the defendant that she would suffer psychiatric injury and therefore it was not in breach of duty to her.

However, in *Barber* v *Somerset County Council* [2004] 2 All ER 385 the House of Lords heard that a restructuring of staffing at the defendant's school led to the claimant, a dedicated and conscientious teacher there, being appointed project manager for public and media relations. In that capacity he worked long, stressful hours and, after a year, he suffered a mental breakdown. His action for damages for personal injuries was successful, the judge taking the view that the failure of the school's senior management team to support the claimant was a continuing breach of their mutual employer's duty of care and that this breach had caused the claimant's breakdown. The Court of Appeal said that the defendant employer had not been in breach of its duty of care, but the House of Lords allowed the claimant's appeal and restored the trial judge's decision as to liability. Lord Rodger of Earlsferry said:

> 'I am satisfied that there was material on which the judge was entitled to take [his] view. Counsel for [defendant] did not suggest that he had applied the wrong test. In these circumstances I am unable to say that the judge, who had enjoyed the advantages, "sometimes broad and sometimes subtle", of seeing and hearing the witnesses, was "plainly wrong" (see *Clarke* v *Edinburgh and District Tramways Co Ltd* 1919 SC (HL) 35 per Lord Shaw of Dunfermline, quoted with approval by Lord Thankerton in *Watt (or Thomas)* v *Thomas* [1947] 1 All ER 582). It follows that the Court of Appeal should not have disturbed the judge's conclusion that the school authorities ought to have foreseen that Mr Barber's mental health would be impaired if he continued to work the same hours.'

See also Chapter 15, section 15.5 (*Safe system of work*).

9.5 Utility of the defendant's activity

The social utility of the defendant's conduct is a relevant factor in considering whether the defendant was negligent. The greater the social utility of the defendant's conduct, the less likely it is that the defendant will be held to be negligent. As Asquith LJ stated in *Daborn* v *Bath Tramways* [1946] 2 All ER 333:

> 'If all the trains in this country were restricted to a speed of five miles an hour, there would be fewer accidents, but our national life would be intolerably slowed down. The purpose to be served, if sufficiently important, justifies the assumption of abnormal risk.'

A similar result was reached in the case of *Watt* v *Hertfordshire County Council* [1954] 1 WLR 835. The claimant, who was a fireman, was injured when travelling to rescue a woman who had been reported to have been trapped under a heavy lorry. Two of the claimant's colleagues threw a jack, in haste, into the lorry in which they were travelling. The jack was needed to save the woman's life. The lorry was not equipped for carrying the jack and the claimant was injured when the driver of the lorry braked suddenly and the jack fell on him. It was held that the defendant employers were not negligent because the need to act speedily in an attempt to save the woman's life outweighed the risk to the claimant. But Denning LJ said that if the accident had occurred in a commercial enterprise the claimant would have recovered. He said that 'the commercial end to make profit is very different from the human end to save life or limb'. However it should not be thought that drivers of fire engines have carte blanche in their rush to get to the scene of a fire. In *Ward* v *London County Council* [1938] 2 All ER 341 a driver of a fire engine was held to have been negligent in driving through a traffic light which was at red.

9.6 The practicality of precautions

If the cost of eliminating the risk is exorbitant or out of all proportion to the benefit obtained by its elimination, then it will not generally be negligent to fail to eliminate the risk. An example of this principle at work is the case of *Latimer* v *AEC Ltd* [1953] AC 643. The floor of the defendants' factory was flooded by an exceptionally heavy rainstorm. One of the consequences of the flooding was that oil which was normally kept in troughs was washed out on to the floor. The defendants put sawdust on the floor in an effort to prevent their employees from falling but there was not enough sawdust to cover the whole factory floor. Despite these efforts the claimant fell and broke his ankle. It was held that the defendants were not liable for the injury suffered by the claimant. They had done all they could, short of closing the factory, to prevent injury arising to their employees. Although this case illustrates the principle that the practicability of precautions is one factor to be taken into account, the decision has been criticised on the ground that commercial profitability was given so much prominence over the employees' interest in their personal security and the fact that no consideration was given to the practicability of other precautions such as roping off the area where no sawdust had been put down.

Although the facts were very different, *Latimer* may be compared with *Kearn-Price* v *Kent County Council* (2002) Solicitors Journal 8 November. Before school one morning, children were playing in the playground with a full size leather football, an activity which was banned because it was known to be dangerous, The ball struck the 14-year-old claimant in the eye and caused him serious injury. The Court of Appeal was satisfied that, as a matter of law, a school could owe a duty to supervise pupils who were on school premises before or after school hours.. That conclusion was not inconsistent with *Ward* v *Hertfordshire County Council* [1970] 1 WLR 356. A school owed to all pupils who were lawfully on the premises the general duty to take such measures to care for their health and safety as were reasonable in all the circumstances. The governing principle was that the school was required to do what was reasonable in all the circumstances (*Geyer* v *Downs* [1977] 17 ALR 408). The judge had been entitled to hold that the scope of the duty of care owed by the school encompassed a duty to take reasonable steps to enforce the ban on full size leather footballs during the pre-school period and that no such steps were taken. The ban was not being enforced by the school staff and, significantly in this context, the required steps to enforce the ban would not have imposed an undue burden on the school. It had also been open to the judge to find, as a matter of causation, that attempts to enforce the ban would have prevented the accident. Accordingly, the Court of Appeal upheld the judge's conclusion that the boy's claim would be successful.

Another very different case is *Bottomley* v *Secretary and Members of Todmorden Cricket Club* (2003) The Times 13 November. The defendant cricket club engaged an independent contractor to present a fireworks display on its land. During the display the claimant, who had been engaged by the contractors to help them in the display, suffered injuries. The club failed to take reasonable care in the selection of a suitable contractor: the contractor did not have public liability insurance or written safety plans. The Court of Appeal concluded that the club was liable in respect of the claimant's injuries. As Brooke LJ explained, occupiers would usually escape liability in cases such as this because they are able to show that they had taken reasonable care to select competent and safe contractors. In those cases an injured employee or agent could look no further than his own employer or principal for redress. There might be circumstance, though, in which the occupier of land who wished something dangerous to be done on his land for his benefit might be liable, too, and this was one of those cases. The injuries suffered by the claimant were foreseeable because there was no proper safety plan. There was the requisite proximity between the club and the claimant, who was lawfully on its premises that evening. It was fair, just and reasonable to impose liability on the club because it did not do what it ought to have done before it allowed a dangerous event to take place on its land.

However, in *Payling* v *Naylor (t/a Mainstreet)* (2004) The Times 2 June it appeared that the claimant had suffered serious head injuries after being ejected from the defendant's nightclub by a door attendant employed by a firm engaged to provide security. The claimant alleged that the defendant was in breach of his duty of care to him, a visitor to the club, since he had failed to ensure that the firm had public liability insurance cover. Here, the Court of Appeal held that the claim in negligence would fail. Latham LJ said that the question arose as to whether in the circumstances the defendant was obliged to check the contractor's insurance position as a necessary or at least prudent means of assessing his competence. There were clear distinctions between the present case and *Bottomley* where checks on the insurance position might have had a bearing on the assessment of competence. Here, the contractor had provided employees who were licensed and approved by a scheme operated by the local council and police authority.

9.7 Common practice

Where there is a common practice in the activity with regard to which the defendant is alleged to have been negligent, conformity with that common practice by the defendant is very good evidence that the defendant has not been negligent. It is not, however, conclusive evidence that the defendant has not been negligent because the common practice itself may be negligent (*Lloyd's Bank Ltd* v *E B Savory & Co* [1933] AC 201).

On the other hand failure to conform to the common practice, without good reason, is good evidence that the defendant has been negligent. Once again, however, a failure to conform with common practice is not conclusive evidence that the defendant has been negligent. In *Brown* v *Rolls Royce Ltd* [1960] 1 WLR 210 the claimant contracted dermatitis at work and she claimed that this was caused by the negligence of the defendants, her employers. Although the defendants provided adequate washing facilities at the work place they did not supply a barrier cream which was commonly supplied by other employers who were engaged in the same type of work. But, while this cream was in common use in the type of work in which the claimant was involved, there was conflicting evidence about its efficacy and it was not proved that, had the defendants supplied the cream, the claimant would not have contracted dermatitis. It was held that the defendants were not negligent in failing to supply the cream because it was not proved that it would have prevented the claimant from contracting dermatitis.

The role of common practice is likely to assume greater importance in negligence cases involving professionals. Some professional bodies have issued guidelines or statements of standard practice in an effort to provide guidance for their members who are concerned about being sued in negligence. For example, the governing bodies of the accountancy profession have drawn up some 'Statements of Standard Accountancy Practice' (SSAP) in an effort to provide some guidance to their members as to the standards expected of them. How much weight will be accorded to such statements by the courts in considering whether a defendant has been negligent? Some indication of the answer to this question may be gleaned from the case of *Lloyd Cheyham & Co Ltd* v *Littlejohn & Co* QBD 30 September 1985 (Unreported). The case turned upon whether the defendants had complied with the requisite standard of care. The claimants argued that the defendants were negligent because they had failed to comply with the standards laid down in SSAP 2. Woolf J rejected the claimant's argument and held that the defendants had not been negligent. During the course of his judgment he said that the SSAPs were:

> '... not conclusive, so that a departure from their terms necessarily involves a breach of the duty of care and they are not ... rigid rules. They are very strong evidence as to what is the proper standard which should be adopted and unless there is some justification a departure from this will be regarded as constituting a breach of duty.'

It is clear that these and other standards laid down by the professions will assume growing significance in negligence actions. In considering whether a professional has been negligent the courts make allowance for the existence of differing views within the profession and will not choose between the different schools of thought, holding one to be negligent and the other not (*Maynard* v *West Midlands Health Authority* [1984] 1 WLR 634 (discussed at section 9.11) and *Luxmoore-May* v *Messenger May Baverstock* [1990] 1 All ER 1067).

These factors which we have discussed at sections 9.2–9.7 are the principal factors to which the courts will have regard in deciding whether a defendant was or was not negligent. No one factor predominates to the exclusion of the others. In each case a court will balance the different factors and come to a conclusion on the facts. There are, however, certain particular cases to which special rules are applicable. We shall now consider these special cases.

9.8 Children

Where it is alleged that a child has been negligent the question arises as to the standard of care required of the child. In *McHale* v *Watson* [1966] ALR 513 the High Court of Australia rejected the application of the reasonable man standard to cases involving children. The claimant, who was a nine-year-old girl, was injured when she was struck in the eye by a steel rod thrown by the defendant, a twelve-year-old boy. The defendant was throwing the rod at a post, but it glanced off the post and struck the claimant who was standing nearby. Kitto J said it was 'absurd ... to speak of normality in relation to persons of all ages taken together'. The standard to be applied was the standard of a child of a corresponding age. The test remained an objective one, however, and so it was 'no answer for him ... to say that the harm he caused was due to his being abnormally slow-witted, quick-tempered, absent-minded or inexperienced'. Applying that standard it was held that the boy was not negligent. In England, the courts, in contributory negligence cases, have been prepared to take account of the special position of children (see Chapter 12, section 12.5) and in *Mullin* v *Richards* [1998] 1 All ER 920 the Court of Appeal adopted the *McHale* approach. However, on the facts, their Lordships concluded that an accident arising from a 'sword fight', using plastic rulers, between two 15-year-old schoolgirls had not been foreseeable.

9.9 Sport

The courts have had occasion to consider the standard of care owed by sportsmen to each other and to spectators. The most famous of these cases is *Wooldridge* v *Sumner* [1963] 2 QB 43. The defendant was an experienced horseman taking part in a competition. He galloped his horse so fast round a corner that his horse went out of control after completing the turn and plunged out of the arena and the claimant, who was a photographer, was injured in the ensuing chaos. It was held by the Court of Appeal that the defendant's failure to control his horse was not negligence but was simply an error of judgment. It was further held that the relationship between a competitor and a spectator was a special one and that a spectator took the risk of any damage done to him during the course of the game, even though his injury resulted from an 'error of judgment' on the part of a competitor. It was only where the competitor deliberately intended to injure the spectator or demonstrated a reckless disregard for the safety of the spectator that the spectator would have a cause of action in respect of the damage done.

In *Wilks* v *Cheltenham Cycle Club* [1971] 1 WLR 668 the approach in *Wooldridge* was followed rather reluctantly. However, Phillimore LJ did affirm that the test remained simply one based upon 'negligence' and Edmund-Davies LJ referred to *Wooldridge* as a 'puzzling case'. Further, in the more recent case of *Condon* v *Basi* [1985] 2 All ER 453 the Court of Appeal had to consider the standard of care owed by one sportsman to another. The claimant was injured during a football match when the defendant, who was playing for the opposing side, tackled him and broke his leg. The defendant was held to be negligent. The finding of fact that the tackle was made in a 'reckless and dangerous manner' meant that the court did not have to resolve the conflict over the status and interpretation of *Wooldridge*. However it was held that the standard required was an objective one and that a higher standard would be required of a First Division footballer than would be required of a footballer in a local league. This latter statement suggests that the court would have applied the standard based upon the reasonable sportsman rather than the approach based upon recklessness and that this will be the approach adopted in the future.

Wooldridge was also applied in *Blake* v *Galloway* [2004] 3 All ER 315 where the Court of Appeal heard that during a practice break, a group of 15-year-old, or thereabouts, jazz musicians went outside and, for the fun of it, threw twigs and pieces of bark chipping at each other. The claimant (a member of the jazz quintet) joined in and threw a piece of bark approximately 4 cms in diameter towards the lower part of the defendant's body. The defendant returned it, striking the claimant in his right eye and causing a significant injury. The claimant contended that the injury was caused by the defendant's battery and/or negligence. The claimant's action did not succeed. Dyson LJ said:

> 'I would ... apply the guidance given by Diplock LJ in *Wooldridge* v *Sumner* [1962] 2 All ER 978, although in a slightly expanded form, and hold that in a case such as the present there is a breach of the duty of care owed by participant A to participant B only where A's conduct amounts to recklessness or a very high degree of carelessness. ... This was an unfortunate accident, and no more. There was no breach of the duty to take reasonable care. ... It is difficult to envisage circumstances in which a participant in a contact sport or game would be taken to have impliedly consented to an act which would otherwise amount to a battery, where that act was negligent in the sense previously explained. As we have seen, a breach of the duty of care in such circumstances will only be established where there has been recklessness or a very high degree of carelessness. So how should these principles be applied in the present case? It was conceded on behalf of the defendant before the judge that, but for the issue of consent, he would be liable in the tort of battery. ... By participating in this game, the claimant must be taken to have impliedly consented to the risk of a blow on any part of his body, provided that the offending missile was thrown more or less in accordance with the tacit understandings or conventions of the game. As I have already explained, this is indeed what happened.'

In passing, for the Court of Appeal's conclusions as to when it would be appropriate for criminal proceedings to be instituted after an injury has been caused to one player by another in the course of a sporting event, the bases for the application of the defence of consent and the level of the criminal threshold, see *R* v *Barnes* [2005] 2 All ER 113.

Boxing

Boxing is in a special position in relation to the duty of care in so far as the object of the exercise could be said to be to cause physical injury to one's opponent. However, as *Watson* v *British Boxing Board of Control Ltd* (2001) The Times 2 February has shown, circumstances can arise in which an injured boxer is able to recover damages in negligence.

The claimant professional boxer was injured during a contest: he had a brain haemorrhage and lost consciousness. After seven minutes a doctor in attendance examined the claimant and he was taken by ambulance to a nearby hospital. He received treatment there and was then transferred to a neurosurgical unit where he had surgery. By then he had sustained serious brain damage that left him with other physical and mental disabilities. Had ringside resuscitation been available the outcome would have been significantly better.

The defendant was the sole controlling body regulating professional boxing in the United Kingdom and the claimant contended that the defendant had been under a duty of care to see that all reasonable steps were taken to ensure that he received immediate and effective medical attention and treatment should he sustain injury in the fight. The Court of Appeal shared the view of the trial judge that the defendant had owed the claimant such a duty of care and that it was liable in negligence because it had been in breach of it.

Referees

In *Vowles* v *Evans* (2002) The Times 31 December (affirmed (2003) The Times 13 March) it appeared that the claimant had been playing as hooker for Llanharan second fifteen, an amateur rugby team. He had been injured during the match with resultant permanent incomplete tetraplegia and he now brought a negligence claim against, inter alia, the defendant amateur referee who had been refereeing the game. His claim was successful. Morland J explained that, as a matter of policy, it was just and reasonable that the law should impose upon an amateur referee of an amateur rugby match a duty of care towards the safety of the players. Such a duty would be breached if the claimant established that the referee failed to take reasonable care for the safety of the players by a sensible and appropriate application of the laws of rugby having regard to the context and circumstances of the game. The proceedings had also be brought against Welsh Rugby Union Ltd – who, presumably, had appointed the referee to take charge of the game – and they accepted vicarious liability for the referee's breach of his duty of care.

In the Court of Appeal, the The Master of the Rolls, Lord Phillips of Worth Matravers, said that the parties had rightly proceeded on the premise that the test of duty applied by the House of Lords in *Caparo Industries plc* v *Dickman* [1990] 2 AC 605 had to be applied. Counsel for the defendants had conceded that: (1) the relationship between the claimant and the first defendant was sufficiently proximate to satisfy that element of the test; and (2) that it was reasonably foreseeable that, if the first defendant failed to exercise reasonable care in refereeing the match, injury to the claimant might result. The debate centred on the question of whether it was fair, just and reasonable to impose on an amateur referee a duty of care towards the players in the game refereed.

His Lordship emphasised that rugby football was an inherently dangerous sport and that some of the rules, including the rule in question, were specifically designed to minimise the inherent dangers. Players were dependent for their safety on the due enforcement of the rules and the role of the referee was to enforce the rules. Where a referee undertook to perform that role, it was manifestly fair, just and reasonable that the players should be entitled to rely upon the referee to exercise reasonable care in so doing. The law rarely, if ever, absolved from any obligation of care a person whose acts or omissions were manifestly capable of causing physical harm to others in a structured relationship into which they had entered. Further points made by Lord Phillips of Worth Matravers MR should be noted as follows:

1. The decision of the referee which had given rise to liability had been made while play was stopped and there was time to give considerable thought to it. Very

different considerations would be likely to apply where it was alleged that the referee was negligent because of a decision made during play.
2. The referee's qualifications had been appropriate for the game that he was refereeing. He could reasonably be expected to be conversant with the laws of the game and competent to enforce them. The allegations of breach of duty made against him did not involve any higher standard of skill than that of basic competence.

9.10 Emergencies

Where the defendant acts in an emergency or in the heat of the moment, the standard of care is adjusted to take account of the dilemma in which the defendant is placed (*Ng Chun Pui* v *Lee Chuen Tat* [1988] RTR 298, see further 9.13). Provided that the decision which the defendant makes is a reasonable decision in the circumstances, he will not be held to have been negligent, even though with hindsight he would have adopted another course of action (see *Jones* v *Boyce* (1816) 1 Stark 493, discussed further at Chapter 12, section 12.8).

9.11 Professionals

A person who claims to have a special skill is judged, not according to the standard of the reasonable man in the street, but according to the standard of the reasonable person enjoying the skill which he claims to possess. We have already seen that compliance with common practice is good, but not conclusive, evidence that the defendant has not been negligent (see section 9.7). Generally the same rule applies in cases of alleged professional negligence (*Edward Wong Finance* v *Johnson, Stokes & Master* [1984] AC 296), although practically it is extremely difficult to show that standard professional practice is negligent. This is especially so in cases of alleged medical negligence where the medical profession appears to have been allowed to set its own standard of care (see Grubb [1988] CLJ 12, contrast Jones *Textbook on Torts* (3rd ed) pp113–114). The ground rules were laid down by McNair J in *Bolam* v *Friern Hospital Management Committee* [1957] 1 WLR 582 in the following terms:

> 'Where you get a situation which involves the use of some special skill or competence, then the test as to whether there has been negligence or not is not the test of the man on the top of the Clapham omnibus, because he has not got this special skill. The test is the standard of the ordinary skilled man exercising and professing to have that special skill ... he is not guilty of negligence if he has acted in accordance with a practice accepted as proper by a responsible body of medical men skilled in that particular art.'

The importance of common practice in cases of medical negligence can be seen by contrasting the following two cases. In *Clark* v *MacLennan* [1983] 1 All ER 416 the defendant was held to have been negligent when he failed to conform to the general practice. On the other hand in *Maynard* v *West Midlands Health Authority* [1984] 1 WLR 634 the defendant was able to show that he had followed one school of thought in preference to another. The House of Lords held that the court was not required to choose as between the schools of thought. As long as the defendant could show that he acted in accordance with a standard which was accepted as proper by professional and competent people within his profession then the defendant would not be negligent. See also *Penny* v *East Kent Health Authority* (1999) The Times 25 November (standard to be applied to work of cervical screener that of reasonably competent screener exercising reasonable care at time screening took place).

So it is clear that the *Bolam* standard applies in the context of diagnosis and treatment, but does it apply to the risks involved in a course of treatment which a doctor should be required to disclose to a patient? An argument could be made out to the effect that it should not, because each individual is entitled to decide for himself whether or not to undergo an operation or course of treatment, and that sufficient information must be disclosed to enable the patient to give his 'informed consent' to the operation (for discussion of the issue of 'informed consent' see Robertson (1981) 97 LQR 102, Teff (1985) 101 LQR 432 and Brazier (1987) 7 Legal Studies 169). The issue was considered by the House of Lords in *Sidaway* v *Bethlem Royal Hospital Governors* [1985] AC 871. The claimant was advised by her surgeon to have an operation on her spinal column because of the pain which she was experiencing in her neck and shoulders. The surgeon did not warn the claimant that there was a risk, assessed at less than 1 per cent, of damage being done to her spinal cord due to the fact that he would be operating within less than three millimetres of her spinal cord. The claimant consented to the operation which was carried out by the surgeon with all due care and skill. But the risk of damage to her spinal cord materialised and the claimant was left severely disabled. She alleged that the surgeon had been negligent in failing to disclose to her the risk of damage to her spinal cord. The House of Lords dismissed the claimant's claim. They held, Lord Scarman dissenting, that English law did not require a doctor to disclose sufficient information to enable the claimant to give an informed consent to the operation. But there the unanimity ends and it is not altogether clear what is the ratio of *Sidaway*. Two principal speeches were given. The first was given by Lord Diplock and he held that the proper test to apply was the *Bolam* test, that is to say, the test in all cases was whether a reasonable doctor would have acted as the defendant had done. Thus it was for the medical profession to set the appropriate standards of disclosure. He held that a distinction should not be drawn between, on the one hand, diagnosis and treatment and, on the other hand, the disclosure of risks to patients; all cases were to be governed by the *Bolam* test. But Lord Bridge, with whom Lord Keith agreed, was prepared to override the *Bolam* test in certain cases. He said that the judge 'might in certain circumstances come to the conclusion that the disclosure of a particular risk was so obviously necessary to an informed choice on the part of the patient that no reasonable prudent medical man would fail to make it'. The type of case which he had in mind was an operation involving 'a substantial risk of grave adverse consequences, as for example the 10 per cent risk of a stroke from the operation'.

Further consideration was given to *Sidaway* by the Court of Appeal in *Gold* v *Haringey Health Authority* [1988] QB 481. The claimant underwent a sterilisation operation but was not told of the risk of the operation failing; nor was she told that the failure rate for sterilisation was higher than the failure rate for a vasectomy. The sterilisation was not a success and the claimant subsequently became pregnant. She brought a negligence action against the defendant health authority. The trial judge found for the claimant ([1987] 1 FLR 125), holding that *Bolam* only applied to advice given in a therapeutic context and that it did not apply in a non-therapeutic context.

The Court of Appeal rejected this argument and held that *Bolam* applied in both contexts. Applying *Bolam* they held that the defendants were not liable because there was a substantial body of medical opinion which in 1979 would not have warned the claimant of the risk of failure. Both Lloyd LJ and Stephen Brown LJ relied on the judgment of Lord Diplock in *Sidaway* and, although the court was not asked to choose between the approaches adopted by Lord Diplock and Lord Bridge in *Sidaway*, it would seem that the former approach has gained the approval of the Court of Appeal. However, it is unfortunate that the Court of Appeal did not consider the conflicting opinions delivered in *Sidaway*, and its uncritical reliance upon the judgment of Lord Diplock is likely to be subjected to some re-examination in the future (see Grubb [1988] CLJ 12 and Lee (1987) 103 LQR 513).

These decisions should be compared with *Chester* v *Afshar* [2004] 4 All ER 587, a decision of the House of Lords. For some years the claimant had suffered severe back pain. As the defendant surgeon was aware, she was anxious to avoid surgery. Nevertheless, he advised her to have an operation, but failed to warn her of the risk of paralysis. The operation was performed without negligence but paralysis ensued. The claimant alleged that, had she been warned, she would have sought further opinions as to her options: she did not contend that she would never, at any time or under any circumstances, have consented to surgery. On appeal against the decision that he was liable in respect of the claimant's injury, the claimant contended that, in order to establish causation in the case of a surgeon's failure to warn a patient of a significant risk of injury, the patient had to prove not only that she would not have consented to run the relevant risk then and there, but also that she would not at any time have consented to run the relevant risk. By a majority, their Lordships dismissed the appeal. Lord Steyn said:

> 'It is true that there is no direct English authority permitting a modification of the approach to the proof of causation in a case such as the present. On the other hand, there is the analogy of *Fairchild* v *Glenhaven Funeral Services Ltd* [2002] 3 All ER 305 which reveals a principled approach to such a problem. ... the House of Lords held that a modified approach to proof of causation was justified. ... *Fairchild's* case is, of course,

very different from the facts of the present case. A modification of causation principles as was made in *Fairchild*'s case will always be exceptional. But it cannot be restricted to the particular facts of *Fairchild*'s case. Lord Bingham of Cornhill observed in *Fairchild*'s case: "It would be unrealistic to suppose that the principle here affirmed will not over time be the subject of incremental and analogical development." At the very least *Fairchild*'s case shows that where justice and policy *demand* it a modification of causation principles is not beyond the wit of a modern court. Standing back from the detailed arguments, I have come to the conclusion that, as a result of the surgeon's failure to warn the patient, she cannot be said to have given informed consent to the surgery in the full legal sense. Her right of autonomy and dignity can and ought to be vindicated by a narrow and modest departure from traditional causation principles.'

A practitioner of traditional Chinese herbal medicine (TCHM) is not liable for harm suffered by a patient as a result of taking one of his remedies if it is shown that the practitioner acted in accordance with the standard of care appropriate to TCHM as property practised in accordance with the standards required in this country: *Shakoor v Situ* [2000] 4 All ER 181.

It is not unlawful to withhold medical treatment, including artificial feeding and the administration of antibiotic drugs, from an insensate patient with no hope of recovery when it is known that the result will be that the patient will shortly thereafter die, provided responsible and competent medical opinion is of the view that it will be in the patient's best interests not to prolong his life by continuing that form of treatment because such continuance is futile and would not confer any benefit on him: *Airedale NHS Trust v Bland* [1993] 1 All ER 821. The *Airedale* approach does not contravene the Human Rights Act 1998: *NHS Trust A v M, NHS Trust B v H* [2001] 1 All ER 801.

In *Simms v Simms* [2003] 1 All ER 669 Dame Elizabeth Butler-Sloss P said that where no alternative treatment is available and the disease is progressive and fatal, it is reasonable to consider experimental treatment with unknown benefits and risks, but without significant risks of increased suffering to the patient, in cases where there was some chance of benefit to the patient. A patient who is not able to consent to pioneering treatment ought not to be deprived of the chance in circumstances where he would have been likely to consent if he had been competent. Since it could not be said that, in principle, the treatment in question was clearly futile or that it would not, in suitable cases, be proper to give it, treatment complied with the requirement for a doctor to act at all times in accordance with a responsible and competent body of relevant professional opinion. Her Ladyship concluded that the treatment proposed should be carried out.

9.12 Proof of the breach

The claimant bears the burden of proof of showing that the defendant was negligent. He must prove his case on the balance of probabilities (the problems of proof which arise where there are difficulties in showing that the defendant's negligence was the cause of the damage to the claimant will be discussed at Chapter 10, section 10.6).

There are certain cases where the legal burden of proof can be switched to the defendant. Section 11(1) of the Civil Evidence Act 1968 permits a claimant to lead evidence that the defendant was convicted of a criminal offence arising out of the act which is the subject of the civil action. So where the defendant has been convicted of careless driving and that careless driving caused the accident in which the claimant was injured, the claimant may succeed in an action in negligence simply by proving that the defendant was convicted of the offence of careless driving, unless the defendant can discharge the onus of proving that he was not negligent. In *Wauchope* v *Mordecai* [1970] 1 WLR 317 the claimant, who was riding his bicycle, was injured when the defendant suddenly opened the door of his parked car and hit the claimant. The defendant was convicted of an offence arising out of this incident and it was held that the effect of s11 of the 1968 Act was to shift the burden of proof to the defendant in the negligence action to show that he was not negligent.

Where there is conflicting expert evidence as to issues of fact, the trial judge may have the unenviable task of deciding, as a matter of fact, which of the experts were correct: see, eg, *Penny* v *East Kent Health Authority* (1999) The Times 25 November. The Court of Appeal should be slow to interfere with the trial judge's primary findings of fact on 'mundane matters': *Pickford* v *Imperial Chemical Industries plc* [1998] 3 All ER 462.

9.13 Res ipsa loquitur

The phrase res ipsa loquitur means that the thing speaks for itself. Where the maxim applies the court is prepared to draw the inference that the defendant was negligent without hearing detailed evidence of what the defendant did or did not do. The application of the maxim can be illustrated by reference to the case of *Scott* v *London and St Katherine Docks Co* (1865) 3 H & C 596. The claimant was passing the defendant's warehouse when six bags of sugar, which were being hoisted by the defendant's crane, fell on the claimant and caused him injury. The only thing which the claimant could prove was that the bags fell on him and caused him injury. It was held that the facts were sufficient to give rise to an inference of negligence on the part of the defendant and so the maxim was applicable. There are three conditions which must be satisfied before res ipsa loquitur is applicable.

The first condition which must be satisfied is that the defendant must be in control of the thing which caused the injury to the claimant. Here two cases are customarily contrasted. The first case is *Gee* v *Metropolitan Railway* (1873) LR 8 QB 161. The claimant leaned against the door of an underground train shortly after it left the station. The door flew open and the claimant fell out of the train, suffering serious injury. It was held that the door had recently been in the control of the defendants because the train had just left the station and so there was evidence of negligence on the part of the defendants. On the other hand a different result was reached in the case of *Easson* v *LNE Railway* [1944] 2 KB 421. In this case the claimant, who was a four year old boy, fell through the door of a corridor train and was severely injured. At the time of the accident the train was seven miles from its last stopping place. It was held that res ipsa loquitur did not apply because the door was not under the control of the defendants. The train was sufficiently far away from the station for the door to have been opened by a passenger rather than by one of the defendants' employees.

The second condition which must be satisfied for res ipsa loquitur to apply is that the accident must be of such a nature that it would not have occurred in the ordinary course of events without negligence. This requirement can be demonstrated by reference to the facts of *Scott* v *London and St Katherine Docks* (above) because bags do not normally fall from a height from cranes without negligence on the part of somebody. Similarly in *Byrne* v *Boadle* (1863) 2 H & C 722 the claimant was able to invoke the maxim when a barrel of flour fell on him as he was passing underneath the defendant's upstairs window. Similarly the maxim was invoked in *Mahon* v *Osborne* [1939] 2 KB 14. The claimant went into hospital for an abdominal operation. He died and on examination it was discovered that the surgeon had left a swab in his body. It was held that the claimant was entitled to call expert evidence to demonstrate that the accident would not have occurred without negligence. If it were otherwise the claimant would be severely handicapped in his attempt to invoke the maxim.

The third condition which must be satisfied is that there must be no explanation for the accident. This requirement is not of any great practical significance because all that it means is that, where the facts are sufficiently known, there is no need to invoke the maxim because the claimant can prove what actually happened (see *Barkway* v *South Wales Transport Co Ltd* [1950] 1 All ER 392).

Once these three conditions for the application of the maxim are satisfied, the question arises as to what effect the maxim has on the case. This question has given rise to some controversy (on which see Atiyah (1972) 35 MLR 337). There are basically two schools of thought relating to the effect of res ipsa loquitur. The first is that, while the maxim raises an inference that the defendant was negligent, if the defendant rebuts that inference then the claimant has to prove that the defendant was negligent. In other words the legal burden of proof rests on the claimant throughout. The second school of thought takes a broader view of the effect of the maxim. According to them, the maxim reverses the burden of proof so that the legal burden of proof passes to the defendant so that, once the claimant has made out a prima facie case of negligence, the defendant then bears the burden of proving on the balance of probabilities that he was not negligent.

The first view appeared to be adopted by the House of Lords in *Colvilles Ltd* v *Devine* [1969] 1 WLR 475 where Lord Donovan said that the maxim had no effect on the legal burden of proof. However a year later the House of Lords took a different approach in the case of *Henderson* v *Henry E Jenkins & Sons* [1970] AC

282. An employee of the defendants was driving one of the defendants' lorries down a hill when the brakes suddenly failed. As a result of the brake failure the lorry careered into a van, killing the claimant's husband. The brake failure was caused by the corrosion of the pipe carrying brake fluid. The defendants had had the lorry maintained but the pipe which had corroded could only be seen by dismantling the pipe and this was not recommended by the manufacturers until the lorry had done a certain mileage. The claimant raised a prima facie case of negligence on the part of the defendants. The defendants then showed that the vehicle had been properly maintained, that the corrosion could only be seen by removing the pipe and that such a practice was not recommended by the manufacturers. Despite these arguments the House of Lords held that the defendants had failed to rebut the inference of negligence. It was held that they should have gone on to show that there was nothing in the history of the vehicle that would have caused abnormal corrosion or required special treatment or inspection. They had therefore failed to displace the inference that their negligence had been the cause of the accident. Although the language of the judgments was not entirely clear, their effect appeared to be to apply the view of the second school of thought, namely that the effect of res ipsa loquitur is to switch the legal burden of proof to the defendant (see also *Ward* v *Tesco Stores Ltd* [1976] 1 WLR 810).

But the issue has been reconsidered by the Privy Council in *Ng Chun Pui* v *Lee Chuen Tat* [1988] RTR 298. A coach skidded across the central reservation of a dual carriageway and collided with a bus which was travelling on the opposite carriageway, injuring the claimants who were passengers on the bus. The claimants alleged that the accident was caused by the negligence of the first defendant, who was the driver of the coach. At the trial of the action the claimants called no oral evidence but invoked the doctrine of res ipsa loquitur. The first defendant led evidence to the effect that a car had cut out in front of the coach, which had forced him to swerve to avoid that car, and, in doing so, the coach had skidded across the central reservation. The trial judge found for the claimants, on the ground that the defendants had failed to discharge the burden of disproving negligence. The trial judge was reversed by the Court of Appeal of Hong Kong and the claimants appealed to the Privy Council. The Privy Council dismissed the appeal.

Lord Griffiths, giving the judgment of the Privy Council, stated that res ipsa loquitur is no more than a maxim 'to describe a state of the evidence from which it is proper to draw an inference of negligence'. Crucially he stated that:

'It is misleading to talk of the burden of proof shifting to the defendant in a res ipsa loquitur situation. The burden of proving negligence rests throughout the case on the [claimant].'

Where, as in a case such as *Scott* v *London and St Katherine Docks* (above), the claimant suffers injury as a result of an accident which should not have occurred if the defendant had taken due care, it is possible for a court to draw the inference from the facts of the case that, on a balance of probabilities, the defendant failed to exercise reasonable care. In such a case, where the defendant adduces no evidence, he will have failed to rebut the inference of negligence and the claimant will have proved his case. On the other hand, the defendant can lead evidence in an effort to rebut the inference of negligence. Lord Griffiths stated that:

> 'Loosely speaking this may be referred to as a burden on the defendant to show that he was not negligent, but that only means that faced with a prima facie case of negligence the defendant will be found negligent unless he produces evidence that is capable of rebutting the prima facie case. Resort to the burden of proof is a poor way to decide a case; it is the duty of the judge to examine all the evidence at the end of the case and decide whether on the facts he finds to have been proved and on the inferences he is prepared to draw he is satisfied that negligence has been established. In so far as resort is had to the burden of proof, the burden remains at the end of the case as it was at the beginning upon the [claimant] to prove that his injury was caused by the negligence of the defendants.'

Applying this approach to the facts of the case, it was held that the evidence of the defendants displaced any inference of negligence by the driver of the coach. Although a decision of the Privy Council is not technically binding, it is suggested that future English courts will follow *Ng Chun Pui* and conclude that res ipsa loquitur does not reverse the burden of proof; the burden remains upon the claimant throughout.

10

Negligence: Causation

10.1 Introduction

A defendant is not liable in negligence unless the claimant's loss has been caused by the negligence of the defendant. Sometimes when discussing causation a distinction is drawn between causation in fact and causation in law. The former is concerned with whether, as a matter of fact, the defendant's negligence was a cause of the claimant's loss. The test which has been adopted here is whether the claimant's loss would have occurred 'but for' the defendant's negligence. The latter concept of causation, causation in law, is concerned with whether, as a matter of law, the defendant is to be held liable for the damage which he has, in fact, caused. Thus causation in law is concerned with the situation where the defendant's negligence has in fact caused loss to the claimant and the question which arises is whether the law will attribute the damage which has arisen to the negligence of the defendant. This latter form of causation is really concerned with remoteness of damage and will be dealt with in Chapter 11. Here we will concentrate upon causation in fact.

10.2 But for test

In considering whether the defendant's act or omission was a cause of the claimant's loss the test which is generally adopted is called the 'but for' test. In *Cork* v *Kirby MacLean Ltd* [1952] 2 All ER 402 Lord Denning said that 'if the damage would not have happened but for a particular fault, then that fault is the cause of the damage; if it would have happened just the same, fault or no fault, the fault is not the cause of the damage.'

The application of the 'but for' test can be seen in the case of *Barnett* v *Chelsea and Kensington Hospital Management Committee* [1969] 1 QB 428. The claimant's husband went to a casualty department of a hospital complaining that he had been vomiting. The doctor refused to examine him and he was told to go home and consult his own doctor in the morning. The claimant's husband was, in fact, suffering from arsenical poisoning and he died some five hours later. The claimant sued the hospital alleging that they had been negligent in the treatment given to her husband and that as a result of their negligence her husband had died. It was held, however, that the defendants were not liable to the claimant as their negligence had not caused her husband's death. Even if the doctor had examined her husband and treated him her husband would still have died from the poisoning and so the doctor's negligence was not a cause of the husband's death.

In the vast majority of cases the 'but for' test gives rise to no legal problems but, in the following cases, it has given rise to considerable difficulty.

10.3 Pre-existing condition

If the damage is attributable to a pre-existing condition rather than to the negligence of the defendant then the defendant will not be liable for the full extent of the damage. In *Cutler* v *Vauxhall Motors Ltd* [1971] 1 QB 418 the claimant suffered a graze to his right ankle in an accident caused by the negligence of the defendants. Shortly after the accident it was discovered that the claimant had a pre-accident condition of varicosity in the veins of both of his legs. Because an ulcer had formed on the site of the graze it was decided to operate immediately to cure the varicose condition of his legs. As a result of the operation the claimant suffered pain and discomfort and a loss of earnings of £173. He sought to recover this sum from the defendants. It was held that the claimant was entitled to damages for the graze but that he could not claim for the losses due to the operation. The condition of varicosity was not connected with the negligence of the defendants and it would have required treatment at some time in the future. So the claimant would have suffered such a loss at some time in the future and the defendants' negligence was not a cause of the claimant's loss.

Russell LJ stated that the maxim, that the tortfeasor must take his victim as he finds him, can work to the advantage of the tortfeasor when the victim suffers from a pre-existing condition. He found support for this argument in the case of *Performance Cars* v *Abraham* [1962] 1 QB 33. The defendant negligently crashed into the claimant's Rolls-Royce and caused damage to the wing and bumper of the Rolls-

Royce. The damage would normally have required a respray but the Rolls-Royce had previously been involved in another accident caused by the negligence of a third party and the damages which had been awarded as a result of the latter accident included the cost of a respray. So it was held that the claimant could not recover the cost of the respray from the defendant as well because the defendant had 'damaged' an already damaged car and so had not caused any loss to the claimant. Had the claimant been allowed to recover the cost of the respray from the defendant it would have resulted in the claimant being compensated twice for the same loss.

10.4 Omissions

It is extremely difficult to apply the 'but for' test where the negligence of the defendant takes the form of an omission to act. This difficulty can be demonstrated by reference to the case of *McWilliams* v *Sir William Arrol & Co Ltd* [1962] 1 WLR 295. The claimant, who was a steel erector, fell to his death at work. At the time of the accident the claimant was not wearing a safety belt. The defendants were in breach of their statutory duty in failing to supply safety belts but there was evidence that the claimant had rarely, if ever, worn such a safety belt in the past and so the defendants argued that he would not have worn a safety belt even if one had been made available. A crucial point to note here is that the onus of proof is on the claimant to show, on a balance of probabilities, that the defendant's negligence is a cause of the damage which he has suffered. It was held that the defendants were not liable because it was probable that the claimant would not have worn a safety belt and so would have fallen to his death even if the defendants had provided safety belts. In this type of case the court is engaged upon a hypothetical inquiry and has to speculate, in the light of all the evidence, as to what would have happened on a given state of facts. Lord Reid in *McWilliams* said that the 'natural' and 'almost inevitable' inference was that the claimant would not have worn a safety belt and that 'that inference is strengthened by the general practice of other men not to wear belts'. While the principle underlying this decisiion remains sound, the actual situation would have to be considered in the light of today's extensive and detailed health and safety at work legislation. Compare, however, *Spencer* v *Boots The Chemist Ltd* (2002) Solicitors Journal 8 November (little doubt claimant pharmacist's shoulder injury due to repetitive lifting of bottles onto high shelf: claim against employer failed since injury could not have been foreseen: employer had not been in breach of statutory health and safety regulations since, even if a risk assessment had been carried out, this risk would not have been foreseen by a reasonable employer). For the legal consequences of a doctor's omission to give advice to his patient, see Chapter 9, section 9.11.

10.5 Multiple causes

Where there is more than one cause of the damage to the claimant the 'but for' test can run into difficulties. An example given by Professor Atiyah illustrates the point (*Accidents, Compensation and the Law* (4th ed) p99). Two fires started independently by A and B unite and spread to C's house which is destroyed. The 'but for' test would appear to acquit both parties because if the question is asked 'would the damage have occurred but for the negligence of A?' the answer would be 'yes' and the same answer would be given if the question is asked 'would the damage have occurred but for the negligence of B?' This absurd result would not, however, be reached by the courts. Judges in such cases decide issues of causation upon ideas of common sense rather than metaphysics. As Lord Wright said in *Yorkshire Dale Steamship Co Ltd* v *Minister of War Transport* [1942] AC 691 'causation is to be understood as the man in the street, and not as either the scientist or the metaphysician, would understand it.' In *Galoo* v *Bright Grahame Murray* [1994] 1 WLR 1360 the Court of Appeal held that in tort cases which were analogous to a breach of contract the court had to decide whether the breach was the cause of the loss or merely the occasion of the loss on the basis of the application of common sense.

A similar problem arises where it is not apparent which of two parties has caused the loss to the claimant. It was sometimes thought that there was no clear English authority on this point, but the issue arose in the Canadian case of *Cook* v *Lewis* [1952] 1 DLR 1. The claimant was injured by a gun shot. It was unclear which of the two defendants had caused injury to the claimant as they had both fired shots simultaneously. It was held that both defendants were liable because the burden of proof lay on them to show that they had not been negligent and they failed to discharge the burden. However, in *Fairchild* v *Glenhaven Funeral Services Ltd* [2002] 3 All ER 305 the House of Lords established that, in certain special circumstances, the court could depart from the usual 'but for' test of causal connection and treat a lesser degree of causal connection as sufficient, namely that the defendant's breach of duty had materially contributed to causing the claimant's disease by materially increasing the risk of the disease being contracted. Lord Bingham of Cornhill stated the essential question which had arisen for their Lordships' decision as follows:

'If (1) C was employed at different times and for differing periods by both A and B, and (2) A and B were both subject to a duty to take reasonable care or to take all practicable measures to prevent C inhaling asbestos dust because of the known risk that asbestos dust (if inhaled) might cause a mesothelioma, and (3) both A and B were in breach of that duty in relation to C during the periods of C's employment by each of them with the result that during both periods C inhaled excessive quantities of asbestos dust, and (4) C is found to be suffering from a mesothelioma, and (5) any cause of C's mesothelioma other than the inhalation of asbestos dust at work can be effectively discounted, but (6) C cannot (because of the current limits of human science) prove, on the balance of probabilities, that his mesothelioma was the result of his inhaling asbestos dust during his employment by A or during his employment by B or during his employment by A and B taken together, is C entitled to recover damages against either A or B or against both A and B?'

In the Court of Appeal ([2002] 1 WLR 1052) C failed against both A and B. However, the House of Lords decided that C could recover damages against both A and B. Lord Bingham of Cornhill explained the position as follows:

'I would answer that where conditions (1)–(6) are satisfied C is entitled to recover against both A and B. That conclusion is in my opinion consistent with principle, and also with authority (properly understood). Where those conditions are satisfied, it seems to me just and in accordance with common sense to treat the conduct of A and B in exposing C to a risk to which he should not have been exposed as making a material contribution to the contracting by C of a condition against which it was the duty of A and B to protect him. I consider that this conclusion is fortified by the wider jurisprudence reviewed above. Policy considerations weigh in favour of such a conclusion. It is a conclusion which follows even if either A or B is not before the court. It was not suggested in argument that C's entitlement against either A or B should be for any sum less than the full compensation to which C is entitled, although A and B could of course seek contribution against each other or any other employer liable in respect of the same damage in the ordinary way. No argument on apportionment was addressed to the House. I would in conclusion emphasise that my opinion is directed to cases in which each of the conditions specified in (1)–(6) … above is satisfied and to no other case. It would be unrealistic to suppose that the principle here affirmed will not over time be the subject of incremental and analogical development. Cases seeking to develop the principle must be decided when and as they arise.'

Where a claimant suffers injury as a result of exposure to a noxious substance by two or more persons, but claims against one person only, that person is liable only to the extent that he had contributed towards the disability: *Holtby* v *Brigham & Cowan (Hull) Ltd* [2000] 3 All ER 421.

10.6 Proof of causation

Considerable difficulty arises where it is unclear whether or not the damage to the claimant has been caused by the negligence of the defendant. In such a case the standard of proof of causation assumes enormous significance. This area of law has, for many years now, been dominated by the case of *McGhee* v *National Coal Board* [1973] 1 WLR 1.

In *McGhee* the pursuer worked in brick kilns, where the working conditions were extremely hot and dirty. Despite this fact the pursuer had to cycle home in his dirty clothes because there were no washing facilities at his place of work. He contracted the skin disease dermatitis. The defenders admitted that they had been negligent but they argued that their negligence was not the cause of the pursuer contracting dermatitis. The pursuer pleaded that, had the defenders provided washing facilities, he would not have contracted the disease. The House of Lords held that the medical evidence did not prove that the pursuer would not have contracted the disease had the defenders provided the washing facilities, but that the pursuer was entitled to recover damages on the ground that the defenders had materially increased the risk of the pursuer contracting the disease. Their Lordships held that it did not expect the pursuer to show on a balance of probabilities that the defenders' breach was actually the cause of his disease, but merely that it materially increased the risk of his contracting the disease. The unusual feature of this case is that, in effect, the pursuer succeeded without ever showing that the defenders' negligence caused him any damage. All that he did show was that the defenders had increased the risk of him suffering damage. Lord Wilberforce justified the conclusion which he reached on the ground that the defenders, by their negligence, had created the risk of a particular damage occurring and when that risk became reality they were not allowed, on grounds of policy, to hide behind the evidential difficulty of showing what had caused the damage to the pursuer. As between the two parties it was the defenders who had to shoulder the evidential difficulty.

This decision was applied by the House of Lords in *Fairchild* v *Glenhaven Funeral Services Ltd* [2002] 3 All ER 305: see section 10.5, above. In relation to *McGhee* Lord Nicholls of Birkenhead said:

'Given the medical evidence in *McGhee's* case, it was not open to the House, however robustly inclined, to draw an inference that the employer's negligence had in fact caused or materially contributed to the onset of the dermatitis in the sense that, but for that negligence, the dermatitis would not have occurred. Instead, a less stringent causal connection was regarded as sufficient. It was enough that the employer had materially increased the risk of harm to the employee … In an area of the law already afflicted with linguistic ambiguity I myself would not describe this process of legal reasoning as a "legal inference" or an "inference of causation". This phraseology tends to obscure the fact that when applying the principle described above the court is not, by a process of inference, concluding that the ordinary "but for" standard of causation is satisfied. Instead, the court is applying a different and less stringent test. It were best if this were recognised openly.'

See also *Chester* v *Afshar* [2004] 4 All ER 587, Chapter 9, section 9.11.

McGhee was distinguished by the House of Lords in *Kay* v *Ayrshire and Arran Health Board* [1987] 2 All ER 417. Here the claimant's son, who at the time was suffering from pneumococcal meningitis, was given an overdose of penicillin as a result of the negligence of one of the doctors employed by the defendants. After recovering from the meningitis the claimant's son was found to be deaf. Deafness is a common consequence of meningitis, but the claimant argued that the deafness was caused by the defendants' negligence in giving him an overdose of penicillin. There was no established medical evidence that an overdose of penicillin could lead to deafness, and the deafness was held to have been caused by the meningitis and the claim against the defendants was dismissed. It was held that, had there been medical evidence that an overdose of penicillin was known to create an increased risk that the meningitis would result in deafness, then *McGhee* would have been applicable. However the law could not presume that the defendant's negligence was responsible for the claimant's injury, in the absence of evidence to show that the defendant's negligence was capable of causing damage to the claimant. In this case the issue was relatively clear; there was no medical evidence of a link between the negligence of the defendants and the damage to the claimant and so the claimant's case was dismissed.

Reference should also be made to *Hotson* v *East Berkshire Area Health Authority* [1987] AC 50. The claimant injured his hip when he fell out of a tree. He was taken to a hospital run by the defendants but the injury to his hip was not diagnosed and it was not until some five days later that the injury to his hip was discovered. The effect of the hip injury was to leave the claimant with a severe and permanent disability by the time that he was 20. Had the hospital discovered the damage to his hip when he was first admitted then the claimant would have had a 25 per cent chance of recovery, but the effect of the delay in diagnosis was that the claimant lost his 25 per cent chance of a recovery. The trial judge awarded the claimant a sum by way of damages which equalled 25 per cent of the full damages awardable. That decision was affirmed by the Court of Appeal but was reversed by the House of Lords. The crucial principle which was relied upon by their Lordships was that the claimant must prove his case on a balance of probabilities. It was held that the claimant failed to prove his case on a balance of probabilities. On a balance of probabilities the injury was caused when the claimant fell out of the tree. Neither party placed reliance upon *McGhee* and Lord Mackay recognised that '*McGhee* [was] far removed on its facts from the circumstances of the present appeal'.

In *Wilsher* v *Essex Area Health Authority* [1988] AC 1074 the House of Lords affirmed that in all cases the claimant bears the burden of proving on a balance of probabilities that the damage was caused by the negligence of the defendants. When the infant claimant was born prematurely he was suffering from various illnesses. In the defendants' baby unit he was given excess oxygen and it was later discovered that he had an incurable condition of the retina. This condition could have been caused by excess oxygen; it also occurred in premature babies suffering from the claimant's illnesses. At the trial of the claimant's action for negligence the medical evidence was inconclusive as to the cause of the claimant's condition. Their Lordships concluded that there should be a new trial as (contrary to the view of the courts below) the claimant had not discharged the burden of proving the causitive link between the defendants' negligence and his injury.

In *Fairchild*, Lord Rodger of Earlsferry suggested that in *McGhee*'s case the members of the House could have proclaimed more clearly and more openly that they were stating a new principle. In *Wilsher*'s case the House had examined *McGhee*'s case and come to the conclusion – mistakenly in his Lordship's view – that the decision rested not on any legal principle but on nothing more than 'a robust and pragmatic approach' to the facts of the case. In *Wilsher*, adopting the reasoning of Browne-Wilkinson V-C in the court below, the House had correctly reversed the decision of the Court of Appeal. In particular, there had been nothing to show that the risk which the defendants' staff had created – that the claimant would develop retrolental fibroplasia because of an unduly highly level of oxygen – had eventuated. That being so, there was no proper basis for applying the principle in *McGhee*'s case. As Browne-Wilkinson decisively observed, a failure to take preventive measures against one of five possible causes was no evidence as to which of those five had caused the injury. The reasoning of Browne-Wilkinson V-C, which the House adopted, provided a sound and satisfactory basis for distinguishing *McGhee*'s case and for allowing the appeal. The year before indeed, in *Kay*'s case, the House had distinguished *McGhee*'s case on the basis that a pursuer had not proved that the junior house officer's mistake had materially increased the risk of the particular kind of neurological damage suffered by his son. In Lord Rodger's view, *McGhee* undoubtedly involved a development of the law relating to causation.

By way of a summary of the present position, it is helpful to note another passage from Lord Nicholls' speech in *Fairchild*:

'In the normal way, in order to recover damages for negligence, a [claimant] must prove that but for the defendant's wrongful conduct he would not have sustained the harm or loss in question. He must establish at least this degree of causal connection between his damage and the defendant's conduct before the defendant will be held responsible for the damage. Exceptionally this is not so. In some circumstances a lesser degree of causal connection may suffice. This sometimes occurs where the damage flowed from one or other of two alternative causes. Take the well-known example [of *Cook* v *Lewis*, above] ... As I understand it, the decision of your Lordships' House [in *McGhee*] is an example of the application of [this] approach ... In the circumstances of that case the House departed from the usual threshold "but for" test of causal connection and treated a lesser degree of causal connection as sufficient. The novelty in the decision lay in the adoption of this approach in this country and, further, in the type of claim to which this approach was applied: there, as with the present appeals, the field of industrial diesase.'

In *Pickford* v *Imperial Chemical Industries plc* [1998] 3 All ER 462 a claim in negligence for damages for repetitive strain injury, the House of Lords said that it was for the claimant to prove that her condition had been caused by repetitive movements while typing and, on the facts, this she had been unable to do.

10.7 Loss of a chance

A question that has appeared with a remarkable lack of frequency in the law reports is whether a claimant can recover in tort for the loss of a chance. At first glance the decision of the House of Lords in *Hotson* v *East Berkshire Area Health Authority* (supra) would appear to be authority for the proposition that such loss is irrecoverable. Indeed, in *Gregg* v *Scott* (2005) The Times 28 January, applying *Hotson* – and *Wilsher* and *Fairchild* – the House of Lords held that where a doctor negligently failed to refer for investigation a patient with possible symptoms of cancer, with the result that there was a nine-month delay in treatment for the condition, the patient, whose chances of survival during that delayed period had fallen from 42 per cent to 25 per cent, could not recover damages for that loss of a chance. The delay had not deprived the patient of the prospect of a cure because, on a balance of probability, he would probably not have been cured anyway, and loss of a chance is not in itself a recoverable head of damage for clinical negligence.

However, it is important to distinguish between an act that has occurred and a possible future event. In *Allied Maples Group Ltd* v *Simmons & Simmons* [1995] 1 WLR 1602 this whole topic was considered by the Court of Appeal who held that where the negligent act had occurred then the claimant had to establish on the balance of probabilities a causal link betwen the defendant's act and the claimant's loss. Once this had been done the claimant was entitled to recover his damages in full. However, where the amount of the claimant's loss depended upon future uncertain events, the court had to assess the likelihood of this occurrence. Where the plantiffs' loss depended on the hypothetical action of a third party, the claimant would succeed if he could show that there was a real or substantial chance, rather than a speculative chance, of the third party so acting. If the claimant succeeds in so doing then the evaluation of the chance is part of the assessment of the quantum of damage, and the range would lie between something that just qualifies as real or substantial and near certainty. The court expressly declined to lay down in percentage terms what the lower and upper ends of the bracket should be. *Allied Maples* has been followed in the Court of Appeal in *Stovold* v *Barlows* [1995] NLJ 1649 and *Maden* v *Clifford Coppock & Carter* [2005] 2 All ER 43 (damages discounted by 20 per cent for loss of a chance).

The situation in tort thus resembles the position in contract, as laid down in the famous case of *Chaplin* v *Hicks* [1911] 2 KB 786.

When assessing the value of a claim where a claimant lost the opportunity to pursue an action because of the negligence of his solicitor, the court may take into account the possibility that, had the action been pursued, it would have settled: *Harrison* v *Bloom Camillin* (1999) The Times 12 November. As Neuberger J there explained, the great majority of professional negligence claims are settled out of court.

In *Sharif* v *Garrett & Co* [2002] 3 All ER 195 the Court of Appeal heard that the appellants' cash and carry warehouse had been partially destroyed by fire. Insurance cover had been arranged by brokers (PBL) but the insurers refused to meet the claim. The appellants engaged the respondent solicitors to sue PBL but the claim was struck out for want of prosecution. The respondents admitted that they had been negligent and accepted that, if the claim against PBL had been successful, the appellants would have recovered at least £842,000 plus interest. In their claim against the respondents the appellants were awarded only the premium paid to the insurers (about £12,000) and the costs paid to the respondents (about £11,000) plus interest, the judge having concluded that their prospects of recovering their losses from PBL were negligible. On appeal, the appellants contended that their prospects had been good: the judge should have awarded them substantial damages for loss of a chance. The appeal was allowed and, in all the circumstances, the appellants were awarded £250,000 by way of damages. Their claim against PBL had not been entirely straightforward. Indeed, there had been a substantial risk that they would lose altogether and, if they had won, it was most unlikely that they would recover the full value of their claim. For a statement of the principles to be applied to the assessment of damages in cases such as this, see the judgment of Simon Brown LJ in *Mount* v *Baker Austin* [1998] PNLR 493 at 510–511.

10.8 Successive causes

Where the claimant suffers successive injuries, one of these injuries being caused by the negligence of the defendant, then difficulty arises because of the relationship between two decisions of the House of Lords.

The first decision is *Baker* v *Willoughby* [1970] AC 467. The claimant was knocked down by the defendant while he was crossing the road. As a result of the accident the claimant suffered injuries to his left leg, which caused him some pain and discomfort and also detrimentally affected his earning power. The claimant took up a new job after the accident, but while he was at work he was shot in the same leg during an armed robbery. As a result of this second incident the claimant's left leg had to be amputated. The defendant argued that his liability to the claimant in respect of the injury to his left leg had to be reduced in the light of the robbery because the claimant's left leg had to be amputated as a result of the shot fired during the robbery and so the effect of his negligence had been obliterated.

This argument was rejected by the House of Lords. They rejected the argument that the claimant's loss had been diminished as a result of the shooting. Lord Reid said that the claimant is not compensated for the physical injury itself but for 'the loss he suffers as a result of that injury'. The shooting incident had not diminished the claimant's pain and suffering, nor had it diminished the claimant's loss of his earning capacity. The second reason for rejecting the defendant's argument was that, had the claimant sued the robbers, the robbers would have been able to take advantage of the rule that a tortfeasor takes his victim as he finds him and so would only have been liable for the damage which they had caused to an already damaged leg. So to refuse the claimant a remedy in respect of the damage done by the defendant would be to leave the claimant under-compensated because he would not be able to recover in respect of that damage from the robbers. So, to do justice on the facts of the case, the defendant was held liable to the claimant.

A different result was, however, reached by the House of Lords in the case of *Jobling* v *Associated Dairies* [1982] AC 794. The claimant suffered injury to his back at work in 1973. This injury was caused by the defendants' breach of statutory duty and the effect of the injury was to compel the claimant to take a less strenuous job, with the result that his earning capacity was reduced by 50 per cent. Before the action against the defendants was tried in 1979 it was discovered in 1976 that the claimant was suffering from a crippling back disease called myelopathy. The effect of the latter disease was to render him totally unfit for work by the end of 1976. There was no connection between the myelopathy and the defendants' negligence. It was held that the defendants were not liable for any loss of earnings suffered by the claimant after 1976 when the myelopathy rendered the claimant totally unfit for work.

The House of Lords in *Jobling* were critical of the judgments handed down in *Baker*. Lord Edmund-Davies criticised *Baker* on the ground that it failed to take account of the fact that the claimant could have received some compensation from the Criminal Injuries Compensation Scheme. So a finding that the defendant was not liable would not necessarily have left the claimant under-compensated. This criticism is not, however, entirely accurate. The Criminal Injuries Compensation Board, in assessing the sum payable, proceeds upon a similar basis to a court and so would have taken account of the existing disability and there would have been no double compensation.

Baker was also criticised on the ground that it took no account of the vicissitudes of life. Lord Wilberforce stated that in assessing damages payable the court took account of the vicissitudes of life and reduced the damages payable accordingly. It was then argued that if a court reduced damages on account of the possibility that the claimant might suffer some misfortune which was not attributable to the negligence of another, then surely it should also reduce damages when that possibility became a reality. Thus the House appeared to suggest that the contraction of another independent disease would count as a vicissitude and would have the effect of reducing the damages payable, but that the commission of another tort was not a vicissitude of life and so would not reduce the damages payable. But, as has been pointed out, 'it is just as much a contingency of life that one might get knocked down by a negligently driven car as it is that one might suffer some disabling illness' (Evans (1982) 45 MLR 329, 332). So this distinction is hardly a satisfactory one.

There is also a conflict of policy between *Baker* and *Jobling*. The policy behind *Baker* is to prevent the claimant from being left under-compensated. But the policy behind *Jobling* is the oppposite one of preventing the claimant from being over-compensated. In fact it increases the possibility of the claimant being under-compensated because no inquiry was made as to whether or not the claimant was entitled to receive state benefits in respect of the injury to his back. Of the two decisions, *Jobling* seems to be preferred by the courts. Thus in *Beoco Ltd* v *Alfa Laval Co Ltd* [1994] 3 WLR 1179 where defective property was destroyed by the intervening act of another before it could be repaired, the person responsible for the destruction was not liable in damages in tort for the losses which the claimant would have incurred during the period which would have been necessary to repair the property if it had not been subsequently destroyed. The Court of Appeal followed *Jobling* in the instant case.

11

Negligence: Remoteness of Damage

11.1 Introduction

11.2 *Polemis* and the directness test

11.3 *Wagon Mound* and foreseeability

11.4 Damage to the person

11.5 Damage to property

11.6 Cases where the reasonable foresight test does not apply

11.7 Intervening acts (novus actus interveniens)

11.1 Introduction

Having established that the defendant owes the claimant a duty of care, and that duty was breached causing loss to the claimant, it must now be considered whether the loss which the claimant has sustained is one which is recoverable in negligence. The defendant is not liable for all the loss which flows from his breach of his duty of care. The law places limits upon the extent to which a claimant can recover in negligence. We have already noted in Chapter 10 that the claimant must show that the defendant's negligence was the cause of his loss. Here we shall consider the limits placed upon the damages recoverable by the rules relating to remoteness of damage. We shall also note that there is a degree of overlap between the rules relating to remoteness and the rules relating to causation.

The legal position in relation to remoteness of damage has been dominated by two different cases and the rules laid down in these cases. These two cases are *Re Polemis and Furness, Withy & Co* [1921] 3 KB 560 and *Overseas Tankship (UK) Ltd v Morts Dock & Engineering Co (The Wagon Mound (No 1))* [1961] AC 388. We shall consider the tests laid down in these cases before proceeding to examine the present state of the law.

11.2 *Polemis* and the directness test

The first case of importance is the case of *Re Polemis* (above) and the test laid down in this case held sway for a considerable period of time before it was displaced in 1961.

In *Re Polemis* the charterers of a ship loaded a quantity of benzine on board the ship. The benzine leaked, causing the hold of the ship to fill with vapour. A stevedore, employed by the charterers, negligently dropped a wooden plank into the hold of the ship. This dropping of the plank caused a spark, which ignited the vapour, and the ship exploded. The owners of the ship sued the charterers in negligence in respect of the damage done by their servant. The charterers defended the action on the ground that the loss caused to the owners by the negligence of their servant was too remote to be recovered in a negligence action. The Court of Appeal held that the charterers were liable for the negligence of the stevedores and that the loss was not too remote.

Although the ratio of the decision is not entirely free from doubt (for consideration of the different interpretations see Clerk and Lindsell on *Torts* (16th ed) para 10–151), the generally accepted view is that as long as some damage to the claimant is foreseeable, the defendant is liable for all the damage that directly results from the negligence. It was once thought that *Polemis* stood for the proposition that a defendant was liable for all the damage directly resulting from his negligent behaviour and even to a claimant who was not within the reasonable foresight of the defendant. Such a proposition is, however, clearly in conflict with the neighbour principle laid down in *Donoghue* v *Stevenson* and has been properly rejected. So the crucial determinant of liability in *Polemis* has been perceived to be the issue of directness, as compared with the standard of reasonable foresight which was employed in *The Wagon Mound (No 1)* (above).

Although the decision in *Polemis* is said to rest on the proposition that the damage to the claimant must arise 'directly' from the negligence of the defendant, the unusual feature of the case is that nobody seems to know what was meant by the word 'directly' in *Polemis*. All that was said in *Polemis* was that 'indirect' meant damage due to the 'operation of independent causes having no connection with the negligent act, except that they could not avoid its results' (per Scrutton LJ).

So it is submitted that the crucial element in determining the scope of *Polemis* lies not in the element of directness but in the meaning of the requirement that 'some damage to the claimant must be foreseeable'. In considering whether damage to the claimant is foreseeable, one could say that the fact that any sort of damage to the claimant is foreseeable is sufficient. But the law has not adopted such an approach. Instead *Polemis* may be said to draw a distinction between damage to property, damage to the person and economic damage. What *Polemis* seems to suggest is that once a defendant can foresee some damage to the claimant within one of these categories then damage is foreseeable and the defendant is liable. Thus in *Polemis* it did not matter that the type of property damage which in fact occurred was different in kind from what was reasonably foreseeable. In other words, it did not matter that the damage caused by the dropping of the wood was an explosion rather than a dent in some part of the ship.

This proposition is subject to the qualification that economic damage seemed to be treated differently from damage to the person or damage to property. This can be seen from the case of *Liesbosch Dredger* v *SS Edison* [1933] AC 449. In this case the 'Edison' negligently struck the dredger 'Liesbosch' in a harbour and as a result the 'Liesbosch' sank. At the time of the accident the 'Liesbosch' was under contract and the owners, as a result of the delay caused by the accident, had insufficient time to complete the work under the contract. Being short of money, they did not have the cash to purchase a new dredger to complete the work and so they hired a dredger, at an exorbitant price, to complete the work under the contract. The claimants sought to recover the money they had expended on the hire of the dredger from the defendants. It was held that the claimants were only entitled to the cost of the new dredger which, but for their own impecuniosity, they would have been able to purchase at the earlier date. It was held that the claimants' impecuniosity was an extraneous factor for which the defendants were not liable. Lord Wright specifically distinguished *Polemis* on the ground that the losses suffered there were the 'immediate physical consequences of the negligent act'. Had the House of Lords applied *Polemis* the owners would surely have recovered damages because economic damage was foreseeable and the fact that the economic damage was of a greater size than was anticipated would not have mattered. However, in *Mattocks* v *Mann* (1992) The Times 19 June the Court of Appeal noted that the law of damages had not stood still since 1933, and that in *Perry* v *Sidney Phillips & Son* [1982] 1 WLR 1297 Kerr LJ had stated that the authority of what Lord Wright said in *Liesbosch* was consistently being attenuated in more recent decisions. In *Mattocks* the court stated that 'in the varied web of affairs after an accident, only in exceptional circumstances was it possible or correct to isolate impecuniosity of a claimant as a separate cause and as terminating the consequences of a defendant's wrong'.

In *Lagden* v *O'Connor* [2004] 1 All ER 277; (2003) The Times 5 December the House of Lords learned that the claimant's car had been damaged as a result of the defendant's negligent driving. While his car was being repaired, since he could not afford the cost of hiring a replacement car from a car-hire company, he obtained a replacement by using the services of a credit-hire company, at additional cost. Would his damages include this additional amount? Their Lordships (Lords Scott of Foscote and Walker of Gestingthorpe dissenting) answered this question in the affirmative since in measuring the loss suffered by an impecunious claimant by loss of use of his own car the law would recognise that, because of his lack of financial means, the timely provision of a replacement vehicle for him cost more than it did in the case of his more affluent neighbour. The defendant had relied upon the rule in *Liesbosch Dredger* that the damages for which a defendant was liable could not be increased by reason of the claimant's impecuniosity. However, as Lord Hope of Craighead observed, that case had been decided in a climate when directness of causation was the test for remoteness of damage in tort. While it was not necessary for the House now to say that it was wrongly decided, it was clear that the law had moved on, and that the correct test of remoteness today was whether the loss was reasonably foreseeable. The wrongdoer had to take his victim as he found him: that applied to the economic state of the victim in the same way as it applied to his physical and mental vulnerability.

11.3 *Wagon Mound* and foreseeability

A different approach was, however, adopted by the Privy Council in *The Wagon Mound (No 1)* (above). This decision was heralded as introducing a new approach to the issue of remoteness in English law. Due to the negligence of the defendants' employees, furnace oil leaked from the defendants' ship, the 'Wagon Mound', and into Sydney harbour. The furnace oil floated across the harbour to the claimants' wharf where welding was taking place. The claimants had sought scientific advice as to the likelihood of the oil igniting during their welding operations and they were assured that there was no danger of the oil igniting. So they resumed their welding. Two days later, however, the oil did in fact ignite and the claimants' wharf and the ships on which the claimants were working were damaged in the blaze. The claimants sought to recover from the defendants in respect of their losses. The Privy Council held that the defendants were not liable for the destruction of the wharf because they could not have foreseen the risk of damage by fire. The expert opinion of that time was that it was impossible to set furnace oil alight while it was on water. Therefore the defendants could not have foreseen that the oil which they negligently discharged was likely to go on fire. It should be noted, however, that the defendants could have foreseen the risk of damage to the property of the claimants. They could have foreseen that the furnace oil would cause damage to the claimants' wharf through pollution. But the Privy Council held that damage by fire was different in kind from damage by pollution and that therefore the damage which occurred was not reasonably foreseeable. The vital factor emphasised by the Privy Council was that the kind of damage must be reasonably foreseeable, although neither the extent of the damage nor the precise manner of its occurrence need be reasonably foreseeable.

The essential difference between the test laid down in *The Wagon Mound (No 1)* and the test laid down in *Polemis* is said to be that *Polemis* only requires that the damage be a direct consequence of the defendant's negligence, whereas under *Wagon Mound* the kind of damage must have been a reasonably foreseeable consequence. But how does 'foreseeability' differ from 'directness'? In *The Wagon Mound* Lord Simonds said that it was the foresight of the reasonable man which alone can determine responsibility. However, as was the case with directness in *Polemis*, there does not appear to be any definition of exactly what constitutes reasonable foresight and how it differs from directness. In *The Wagon Mound* the Privy Council did say that a reasonably foreseeable risk was a real risk and was one which would occur to the mind of the reasonable man. It did not, however, extend to a risk which the reasonable man would dismiss as being far-fetched. Nevertheless it is a noticeable feature of the case that there was no extended analysis of what constitutes reasonable foresight.

It will be remembered that in discussing *Polemis* we noted that there was a three-fold division of the kind of damage employed; damage to property, damage to the person and economic damage. We noted that under the rule in *Polemis* it was sufficient that damage to the claimant's person or property be foreseeable and that these interests were not sub-divided. We shall examine the categories of damage to the person and damage to property to see how, if at all, the standard adopted in *The Wagon Mound (No 1)* differs from the standard adopted in *Polemis*.

11.4 Damage to the person

A strong argument can be made that the law does not divide up damage to the person as a category and that as long as damage to the person is foreseeable it does not matter that the consequences of the damage are unforeseeable. This can be seen in what has come to be known as the 'egg-shell skull' rule. In *Dulieu* v *White & Sons* [1901] 2 KB 669, 679 Kennedy J stated that 'if a man is negligently run over or injured in his body, it is no answer to the sufferer's claim for damages that he would have suffered less injury, or no injury at all, if he had not had an unusually thin skull or an unusually weak heart.'

The impact of the egg-shell skull rule can be demonstrated by reference to the case of *Smith* v *Leech, Brain & Co* [1962] 2 QB 405. Here the defendants failed to provide adequate protection for the claimant's husband as he was working with molten metal in their factory. Some of the molten metal splashed out of the tank at which he was working and burnt him on the lip. This burn induced cancer, which developed at the site of the burn. It was not known at the time of the accident that the claimant's husband had any form of pre-malignant cancer. The claimant's husband died from the cancer three years after the accident. He might never have developed the cancer had it not been for the burn. The defendants argued that they were not responsible for the death of the claimant's husband because his death was not a reasonably foreseeable consequence of their negligence. This argument was rejected by the court. It was held that a tortfeasor must take his victim as he finds him. Lord Parker CJ stated that the test was not whether the defendants could have foreseen that the burn would induce cancer which in its turn would kill the claimant's husband, but whether the defendants could have reasonably foreseen that the claimant's husband would be burnt. The answer to this question was 'yes' and so the defendants were liable.

Three further cases illustrate the operation of the egg-shell skull rule. The first is the case of *Bradford* v *Robinson Rentals* [1967] 1 WLR 337. The claimant was required to drive a van for his employers from Bedford to Exeter on one exceptionally cold day in winter. There was no heater in the van and the claimant was held up on his journey on several occasions on account of the weather. As a result of the journey the claimant suffered frostbite, which was virtually unknown in Britain. It was held that the defendants were liable for the frostbite suffered by the claimant. It did not matter whether or not the claimant was abnormally susceptible to frostbite because the defendant had to take his victim as he found him.

The second case which illustrates the operation of the egg-shell skull rule is *Robinson* v *Post Office* [1974] 1 WLR 1176. Here the claimant, who was employed by the Post Office, fell down a ladder in the course of his employment. The cause of his fall was some oil which had been left on one of the steps. As a result of the fall the claimant cut his leg and when he visited the doctor some eight hours later he was given an anti-tetanus injection. The doctor did not test for any allergy to such an injection but, even if he had, there would have been no indication of any allergy. As a consequence of the injection the claimant contracted encephalitis, which is an inflammation of the brain. The defendants argued that they were only liable for the injury to the claimant's shin and not for the encephalitis. This argument was rejected by the court on the ground that the defendant must take his victim as he finds him and that the need for an anti-tetanus injection was a reasonably foreseeable consequence of the claimant's fall. Professor Atiyah (*Accidents, Compensation and the Law* (4th ed) p115) has used this case in an effort to demonstrate how 'generous' the law of tort is prepared to be to tort victims. He argues that a case such as *Robinson* is 'in a sense, a bridgehead between liability for fault and strict liability. While initial negligence must be proved, the claimant recovers damages for what most people would regard as nothing but an accident.'

The third, and most important, case is the decision of the House of Lords in *Hughes* v *Lord Advocate* [1963] AC 837. Some employees of the Post Office left a manhole in Edinburgh uncovered, with only an erected tent and some paraffin lamps surrounding the manhole. While the employees were away on their tea-break, the claimant, a ten year old boy, climbed down the manhole. He took one of the paraffin lamps with him. When he was climbing back up out of the manhole, the paraffin lamp fell back into the hole. Due to an extremely rare combination of circumstances, there was a violent explosion in which the claimant was badly burned. He brought an action against the defendants in respect of the injuries which he had suffered. The defendants disputed liability on the ground that the explosion was too remote to be foreseen by them, so they argued that they were not liable for the injuries suffered by the claimant as a result of the explosion. This argument was rejected by the House of Lords on the ground that as long as injury by burning was foreseeable it did not matter that the method by which the burning occurred was unforeseeable. Lord Reid stated that:

> 'A defender is liable, although the damage may be a good deal greater in extent than was foreseeable. He can only escape liability if the damage can be regarded as differing in kind from what was foreseeable.'

So the mere fact that the damage is greater in extent than could have been foreseen will not act as a defence. It must be shown that the damage which occurred was of a different kind to the damage which was foreseeable. In *Hughes* it was held that damage caused by the explosion was not different in kind from the damage which was foreseeable, as it was foreseeable that a child might be burned by one of the paraffin lamps.

In *Jolley* v *Sutton London Borough Council* [2000] 3 All ER 409 the House of Lords heard that the defendant council left lying (for at least two years) a boat on their land outside some flats. The 14-year-old claimant and his friend decided to repair it. The jacked it up but, while they were at work, the boat fell on the claimant and caused him serious injuries. The defendants accepted that they had been negligent in failing to remove the boat but contended that the accident was not one that they could have reasonably foreseen. In allowing the defendant's appeal the Court of Appeal accepted this contention, but the House of Lords saw things differently. In their Lordships' view, the accident had been reasonably foreseeable. Lord Hoffmann explained his approach as follows:

> 'The short point in the present appeal is … whether the [trial] judge was right in saying in general terms that the risk was that children would "meddle with the boat at the risk of some physical injury" or whether the Court of Appeal were right in saying that the only foreseeable risk was of "children who were drawn to the boat climbing upon it and being injured by the rotten planking giving way beneath them" … Was the wider risk, which would include within its description the accident which actually happened, reasonably foreseeable? … I think that the judge's broad description of the risk as being that children would "meddle with the boat at the risk of some physical injury" was the correct one to adopt on the facts of this case. The actual injury fell within that description and I would therefore allow the appeal.'

These cases suggest that a broad approach is taken by the law to the issue of injury to the person and that as long as injury to the claimant is foreseeable it does not matter that the extent or precise manner by which the injury was inflicted is unforeseeable. Such a position is consistent with the aim of tort law which is to protect a claimant's interest in his personal safety and to uphold the principle of full compensation for tort victims.

11.5 Damage to property

This category of damage is more difficult to deal with than damage to the person. It is clear that it is not sufficient that some damage to the claimant's property be foreseeable because in *The Wagon Mound (No 1)* damage to the claimant's property through fouling was foreseeable but this was not sufficient to ground liability. Thus the Privy Council clearly envisaged a narrower definition of foreseeability in cases of damage to property than the simple requirement that some damage to the claimant's property must be reasonably foreseeable. It was held that damage to property by fire was different in kind from damage to property by fouling or pollution. But how was it different? In answering this question it is necessary to consider the decision of the Privy Council in *The Wagon Mound (No 2)* [1967] 1 AC 617. In this case the owners of the two ships which were being repaired at the wharf of the claimants in *The Wagon Mound (No 1)* sued the owners of the 'Wagon Mound' in respect of the damage done to their ships. This time the defendants were held to be liable to the claimants. The vital difference between the two *Wagon Mound* cases concerns a finding of fact at first instance. In *The Wagon Mound (No 2)* the trial judge found that there was a bare possibility of fire as a result of the oil spillage. The trial judge held that the likelihood of fire was so remote that the defendants were entitled to ignore it. The trial judge was, however, reversed by the Privy Council on this point and it was held that as long as the fire was foreseeable as a kind of damage by the defendants they were liable in respect of it, even though the possibility of a fire occurring was remote.

So it appears that kind of damage is divided into a narrower category than damage to property simpliciter. It is submitted that there are two major policy reasons behind this narrower approach in the case of damage to property. The first policy reason is that the claimant whose property is damaged is much more likely to be insured against such damage than is the person who is injured as the result of the defendant's negligence. So the claimant, in the case of property damage, is often in a better position to bear the loss. The second policy reason is that the measure of damage in a case of property damage can be far greater than in a case of personal injury, for example where, as in *The Wagon Mound*, the negligence leads to extensive damage to a ship. Where this is the case there is a reluctance on the part of the court to find the defendant liable for the whole of the loss, especially when, as we have already noted, the claimant is likely to be insured against such a loss.

So it is submitted that there are good reasons behind the courts' narrower approach to damage to property. The difficult question which remains is how we divide up property damage. We could say that the vital question is whether the events which have occurred are within the 'risk' which has been created by the defendant. This does not take us very far unless a definition is provided of the risk which was created by the defendant. For example what was the risk created by the defendants in the *Wagon Mound* cases? Another approach is to say that the distinction depends on the nature of the impact of the damage. This approach can explain *The Wagon Mound (No 1)* because it can be said that the damage was done by the impact of fire whereas the foreseeable impact was damage by fouling. But it is doubtful whether or not it is applicable to all cases and again much depends on how impact is defined.

However it is submitted that the courts are correct in taking a narrower approach in the case of damage to property because tort law is generally less assiduous of interests in property than it is in a person's interest in his personal security and because of the availability of insurance in cases of damage to property.

11.6 Cases where the reasonable foresight test does not apply

There are a number of situations where the reasonable foresight test does not apply. The test does not apply where the defendant intended to inflict harm upon the claimant. In *Quinn* v *Leatham* [1901] AC 495 Lord Lindley stated that 'the intention to injure the claimant ... disposes of any question of remoteness of damage' (see too *Doyle* v *Olby (Ironmongers) Ltd* [1969] 2 QB 158).

The reasonable foresight test also does not apply in cases of breach of statutory duty because, since by virtue of the nature of the action the Act must have been passed for the benefit of the claimant, it is difficult to conceive of his loss being too remote.

11.7 Intervening acts (novus actus interveniens)

Novus actus interveniens simply means that an act or event has intervened to break the chain of causation which was set in motion by the defendant's negligence. It is at this stage that the close link between the rules relating to remoteness and the rules relating to causation becomes apparent. Some commentators include novus actus interveniens within the section of their book on causation; others include it in the section on remoteness of damage. We are considering novus actus interveniens at this stage because, having considered the rules relating to both causation and remoteness, we are now in a position to assess whether these rules are properly part of the rules relating to remoteness of damage or whether they are part of the rules relating to causation. The argument that will be put forward at the end of this section will be that they are best regarded as part of the rules relating to causation. The cases on novus actus interveniens can be split into the following three categories.

Intervening act of the claimant

The defendant will not be liable where the conduct of the claimant has amounted to a novus actus interveniens. The claimant's conduct may amount to a novus actus interveniens when his conduct has been so careless that his injury can no longer be attributed to the negligence of the defendant. But it is not every act of carelessness on the part of the claimant which amounts to a novus actus interveniens. Sometimes it is held to be simply contributory negligence on the part of the claimant, which has the effect of reducing the damages payable to the claimant, rather than an event which completely breaks the link between the defendant's negligence and the damage to the claimant: see, eg, *Reeves* v *Commissioner of Police of the Metropolis* [1999] 3 All ER 897 (due to police negligence, person in custody committed suicide, but damages awarded against police reduced by one-half). The distinction between these two types of case is illustrated by reference to the following two cases.

The first case is the decision of the House of Lords in *McKew* v *Holland &
Hannen & Cubitts (Scotland) Ltd* [1969] 3 All ER 1621. The pursuer was injured as
a result of the negligence of the defenders. His injury was only a slight one but it
caused him occasionally to lose control of his left leg. Despite this weakness in his
left leg the pursuer went down a steep flight of stairs which had no handrail. On his
way down the stairs his left leg gave way and he fell and broke his ankle. It was held
that the pursuer's act of going down a steep flight of stairs which had no handrail
was unreasonable and that its effect was to break the chain of causation. So the
defenders were not liable in damages for the injury caused by the claimant falling
down the stairs. Lord Reid stated that 'if the injured man acts unreasonably he
cannot hold the defender liable for injury caused by his own unreasonable conduct.'

On the other hand a different conclusion was reached in the case of *Wieland* v
Cyril Lord Carpets [1969] 3 All ER 1006. The claimant suffered injury as a result of
the negligence of the defendants. As a consequence of the injury a surgical collar
was fitted to her neck, which restricted her ability to move her head, and she was
unable to use her bi-focal spectacles with her customary skill. While in this
condition the claimant fell down a flight of stairs. It was held by Eveleigh J that the
defendants were liable for the injury which the claimant sustained when she fell
down the stairs. Eveleigh J said that this was not a case where the claimant had been
unreasonable in continuing to wear bi-focals. This was a case where the claimant had
been left, as a result of the accident, unable to cope with the vicissitudes of life and
the defendants were liable for the further injury which she received while in this
condition.

The distinction between *McKew* and *Wieland* lies in the fact that the conduct of
the pursuer in *McKew* was unreasonable, whereas the conduct of the claimant in
Wieland was held to be reasonable. It is not altogether clear why *McKew* was not
treated as a contributory negligence case. It seems that the pursuer's conduct was
held to be so unreasonable that it was more than being contributorily negligent and
that it broke the chain of causation. It is largely a matter of conjecture as to when a
claimant's conduct will be held to transcend the boundaries of contributory
negligence and constitute a novus actus interveniens.

Intervening act of nature

If the damage suffered by the claimant is the result of an act of nature which is
independent of the negligence of the defendant, the defendant is not liable. The
operation of this rule can be demonstrated by reference to the decision of the House
of Lords in *Carslogie Steamship Co* v *Royal Norwegian Government* [1952] AC 292.
The claimants' ship was damaged in a collision caused by the negligence of the
defendants. Temporary repairs were done to the ship which restored her to a
seaworthy condition. She then set out on a voyage to America. She would not have
made this trip had it not been for the negligence of the defendants. During the
voyage the ship suffered extensive damage in a storm. The claimants sought to

recover, inter alia, the cost of repairing the damage done by the storm. It was held that the defendants were not liable for the cost of the repairs because, although the ship would not have been caught in the storm but for the negligence of the defendants, this 'was not in any sense a consequence of the collision, and must be treated as a supervening event occurring in the course of a normal voyage'. It should be noted that this was not a case where the negligence of the defendants left the ship unseaworthy. Had this been the case then different principles would have come into play.

Intervening act of a third party

If it is the act of a third party which is the true cause of the damage to the claimant then the general rule is that the defendant is not liable to the claimant. This is, in many ways, one of the most interesting areas of the law of tort, partly because there are a number of different conceptual devices, such as the existence of a duty of care, causation and remoteness, which can all be used in an attempt to resolve these problems.

A case which illustrates the problems which can arise here is *The Oropesa* [1943] P 32. Two ships were in a collision as a result of the negligent navigation of the defendants' ship, the 'Oropesa'. The captain of the other ship involved in the collision, the 'Manchester Regiment', in an effort to save his ship, set out in rough seas in a lifeboat with 16 of his crew. The lifeboat overturned in the rough seas and some of the crew were drowned. It was held that the defendants were liable for the deaths of the members of the crew and that the captain's decision to take out the lifeboat was a reasonable action taken in an attempt to save the ship and so did not break the chain of causation. Lord Wright said that:

> 'To break the chain of causation it must be shown that there is something which I will call ultroneous, something unwarrantable, a new cause which disturbs the sequence of events, something which can be described as either unreasonable or extraneous or extrinsic.'

So the defendant remains liable where the act of the third party is not truly independent of the defendant's negligence, as was the case in *The Oropesa*. The defendant will also remain liable where the act of the third party was an involuntary one. Thus in *Scott v Shepherd* (1733) 2 Wm Bl 892 the defendant threw a lighted squib into a market place. The stall holders, to avoid injury, threw the squib from stall to stall until eventually it exploded, blinding the claimant. It was held that the defendant was liable and that the actions of the stall holders in ridding themselves of the squib did not break the chain of causation because their actions were instinctive in an effort to save themselves from injury. It should finally be noted in this context that the defendant remains liable where he intentionally procures the third party to do the intervening act.

Difficulty has also arisen in relation to the negligent intervention of third parties.

The difficulties which arise here can be seen by contrasting the following two cases. In *Knightley* v *Johns* [1982] 1 WLR 349 the defendant's negligent driving caused an accident which had the effect of blocking a busy tunnel. The second defendant, a police officer, forgot to seal off the tunnel and, in breach of police standing orders, sent the claimant, a police motor cyclist, back into the tunnel against the flow of traffic. While travelling through the tunnel the claimant was injured when he was involved in a collision with another driver. It was held that the second defendant was negligent in not closing the tunnel when the initial accident occurred and so the first defendant was not liable for the injuries sustained by the claimant. The court held that 'negligent conduct is more likely to break the chain of causation than conduct which is not' and that there were so many errors and 'departures from the common sense procedure' that the chain of causation was broken.

On the other hand a different result was reached in the case of *Rouse* v *Squires* [1973] QB 889. The first defendant, through his negligent driving, caused an accident, in which his lorry jack-knifed across the road. A few minutes later the second defendant negligently collided with the vehicles involved in the first accident and killed the claimant. It was held that the first defendant's negligence was an operative cause of the claimant's death and so he was held to be 25 per cent responsible for the claimant's death. Here the second accident was a natural and probable consequence of the first accident and was foreseeable, therefore it did not amount to a break in the chain of causation.

Where the intervention of the third party takes the form of a reckless act, then it is more likely to break the chain of causation. That this is so can be demonstrated by reference to the case of *Wright* v *Lodge and Shepherd* [1993] 4 All ER 299. The second defendant's car broke down in the nearside lane of an unlit dual carriageway one foggy night. While she was attempting to start the car a lorry driven by the first defendant crashed into the back of her car and seriously injured, one of the claimants who was sitting in the back of the car. The lorry then veered out of control across the central reservation and came to rest on its side on the other carriageway, where it was struck by three cars and a lorry. The driver of one of the cars was killed and another was injured, and the latter and the personal representatives of the former brought a claim in damages against the defendants. The trial judge found that the first defendant was driving recklessly and was liable to the claimants. He ordered that the second defendant pay a contribution of 10 per cent in relation to the claim by the passenger in her car but dismissed the contribution claims in relation to the claims of the other claimants. The first defendant appealed to the Court of Appeal, arguing that the second defendant should be ordered to pay a 10 per cent contribution in respect of the other claims. The Court of Appeal dismissed his appeal. The sole cause of the lorry being on the other side of the carriageway was the reckless driving of the first defendant, for which the second defendant could not be responsible. The court held, relying in part upon the judgment of Cairns LJ in *Rouse* v *Squires*, that the trial judge was entitled to distinguish between the consequences of deliberate or reckless driving which causes the obstruction into which other vehicles subsequently collide and the consequences which would have occurred even as a result of negligent driving. The former does break the chain of causation, while the latter does not.

The most difficult issue of all arises where the intervention of the third party takes the form of a wilful wrong towards the claimant. We have already considered these cases in Chapter 6 where we noted that the general principle is that the defendant is not liable to the claimant for the loss wilfully inflicted upon the claimant by a third party over whom the defendant has no control. Reference should be made to the discussion of these cases in Chapter 6, section 6.8, as we shall not go over the same ground here but will confine ourselves to the comments made by the judiciary in these cases on the subject of novus actus interveniens.

The starting point is the judgment of Lord Reid in *Home Office* v *Dorset Yacht Co Ltd* [1970] AC 1004 when he said that:

'Where human action forms one of the links between the original wrongdoing and the loss suffered by the [claimant], that action must at least have been something very likely to occur if it is not to be regarded as a novus actus interveniens.'

Thus Lord Reid clearly envisaged that a defendant would only be liable for the wilful wrong of a third party in restricted circumstances and that, in the vast majority of cases, the intervention of the third party would break the chain of causation.

However, as we noted in Chapter 6 when discussing the case of *Smith* v *Littlewoods Organisation Ltd* [1987] AC 241, the courts have recently preferred to resolve these cases on the ground that no duty of care exists rather than on the ground of a break in the chain of causation. Nevertheless some interesting comments have been made about remoteness and causation in this context. In *Lamb* v *Camden London Borough Council* [1981] QB 625 Lord Denning said that:

'the truth is that all these three, duty, remoteness and causation, are all devices by which the courts limit the range of liability for negligence and nuisance ... All these devices are useful in their way. But ultimately it is a question of policy for the judges to decide.'

While one may disagree with Lord Denning's heavy reliance upon policy, it is difficult to refute his argument relating to the similarities of these doctrines. Indeed in *P Perl (Exporters) Ltd* v *Camden London Borough Council* [1984] QB 342 Oliver LJ stated that:

'I think that the question of the existence of a duty and that of whether the damage brought about by the act of a third party is too remote are simply two facets of the same problem; for if there be a duty to take reasonable care to prevent damage being caused by a third party then I find it difficult to see how damage caused by the third party consequent on the failure to take such care can be too remote a consequence of the breach of duty.'

As has been pointed out elsewhere (see Jones (1984) 47 MLR 223), the problem really lies in 'the overworked concept of reasonable foreseeability', which can come into the duty issue, remoteness and causation.

So then we have a number of different doctrines competing for a role to play in resolving these problems. In relation to the wilful intervention of third parties the courts have chosen the duty issue as their preferred method of solution. But which doctrine lies at the root of novus actus interveniens? We could say that it is remoteness because where the intervening act is foreseeable it generally will not break the chain of causation and so we are really concerned here with events which are not reasonably foreseeable and therefore too remote. The solution advocated here is, however, to treat novus actus interveniens as part of the rules relating to causation on the ground that, while there are similarities with the rules relating to remoteness, 'it ... seems sensible to maintain a distinction between cases of multiple cause, where the question is which cause is to be treated as having legal significance, and cases where on any view the defendant's negligence was the cause of the harm, but it is thought to be unfair to hold him responsible because it occurred in some unusual or bizarre fashion' (Jones *Textbook on Torts* (3rd ed) p143).

12

Contributory Negligence

12.1 Introduction

Where the damage which the claimant has suffered has been caused partly by his own negligence and partly by the negligence of the defendant then the damages which the claimant can recover from the defendant may well be reduced because of the claimant's contributory negligence. The damages payable to the claimant may fall to be reduced under the Law Reform (Contributory Negligence) Act 1945. This Act was introduced to reverse the rule at common law which was that contributory negligence was a complete defence which precluded the claimant from recovering anything, ie if the claimant was responsible, whether in whole or in part, for the injury which he sustained his claim against the defendant failed and he recovered nothing on the ground that he had been guilty of contributory negligence.

12.2 The 1945 Act – the general rule

The new general rule is now contained in s1(1) of the Law Reform (Contributory Negligence) Act 1945 which provides that:

'Where any person suffers damage as the result partly of his own fault and partly of the fault of any other person or persons, a claim in respect of that damage shall not be defeated by reason of the fault of the person suffering the damage, but the damage recoverable in respect thereof shall be reduced to such extent as the court thinks just and equitable having regard to the claimant's share in the responsibility for the damage.'

This section is now the source of the general rule relating to contributory negligence. Two points should be noted about this section. The first point is that the section only applies to a person who suffers damage. 'Damage' is defined in s4(1) as including 'loss of life and personal injury'. It is generally agreed that the Act also applies to property damage, as such damage was covered by the common law. The second point to note is that a claim only arises out of damage caused partly by the 'fault' of the defendant and partly as the result of the 'fault' of the claimant. 'Fault' is defined in s4(1) as meaning 'negligence, breach of statutory duty or other act or omission which gives rise to liability in tort or would, apart from this Act, give rise to the defence of contributory negligence'. Thus the Act applies to nuisance and cases under the rule in *Rylands* v *Fletcher* as well as negligence actions. It remains unclear whether or not it applies to trespass to the person (see further Chapter 24, section 24.2). But the Act does not apply to cases of intentional interference with chattels, nor does it apply to deceit. The latter point was confirmed by the House of Lords in *Standard Chartered Bank* v *Pakistan National Shipping Corp* [2003] 1 All ER 173. Although the claimant bank had been negligent, in a case of fraudulent misrepresentation (which this was) at common law there is no defence of contributory negligence and it followed that no apportionment under the 1945 Act was possible.

In order to make out the defence of contributory negligence the defendant must prove two things. The first thing he must prove is that the claimant was at fault. This requirement contains two distinct elements which will be considered separately. The first relates to the meaning of the word 'fault' (section 12.3) and the second relates to the standard of care required of the claimant (sections 12.4–12.8). The second thing which the defendant must prove is that the claimant's negligence was a cause of the damage which he suffered (section 12.9).

12.3 Fault

We have already noted the definition of fault in s4(1) of the Act and that the effect of that definition is that the Act only applies to those torts committed by the defendant which come within the meaning of the word 'fault'. Here we are concerned with the meaning of the word 'fault' as it is applied to the claimant. Does it mean that the claimant must be held to owe a duty of care to the defendant? The answer to that question is 'no'. In *Nance* v *British Columbia Electric Railway Co Ltd* [1951] AC 601 Viscount Simon said:

'When contributory negligence is set up as a defence, its existence does not depend on any duty owed by the injured party to the party sued and all that is necessary ... is to prove to the satisfaction of the jury that the injured party did not in his own interest take reasonable care of himself and contributed, by this want of care, to his own injury.'

The fact that the claimant need not owe a duty of care to the defendant means that the claimant's fault may simply consist of failing to look after himself properly. Thus in *Davies* v *Swan Motor Co* [1949] 2 KB 291 the claimant's damages fell to be reduced on the ground of contributory negligence, even though the claimant owed no duty of care to the defendant. The claimant's husband was riding on the offside steps of a dust-cart, knowing of the dangers of such a practice. As the dust-cart was being overtaken by one of the defendants' buses a collision occurred and the claimant was killed. It was held that the driver of the bus, the driver of the dust-cart and the claimant were all negligent: the bus driver because he had overtaken on a bend; the driver of the dust-cart because he had turned across the road without signalling; and the claimant because of the dangerous manner in which he was riding on the dust-cart. It was held that the bus driver was guilty of negligence, but that the claimant was guilty of contributory negligence. The Court of Appeal affirmed that negligence in this context did not mean breach of the duty of care, but simply that the claimant had been careless.

Where it cannot be shown that the claimant was at fault, the claimant is entitled to recover in full. Thus in *Tremayne* v *Hill* [1987] RTR 131 the claimant was able to recover in full because the defendant was unable to show that the claimant had been at fault. The claimant was held to be under no duty to keep a look-out for cars when the traffic lights were at red and the defendant had gone through the lights when they were at red and collided with the claimant. It was held that a pedestrian was not under a duty either to keep a look-out for traffic going through red lights nor was he under a duty to use a pedestrian-controlled crossing. Although the Court of Appeal spoke of the pedestrian not being 'under a duty' it is submitted that they simply meant he was not careless and it should not be read as referring to the duty of care in the *Donoghue* sense.

12.4 The standard of care

In *Jones* v *Livox Quarries Ltd* [1952] 2 QB 608 Lord Denning said that:

'A person is guilty of contributory negligence if he ought reasonably to have foreseen that, if he did not act as a reasonable, prudent man, he might be hurt himself; and in his reckonings he must take into account the possibility of others being careless.'

It can be seen from this statement that, in considering whether the claimant has acted with reasonable care, the courts take account of similar factors to those which they take account of when they consider whether the defendant has acted with reasonable care. Like the standard of care in establishing that the defendant was negligent the test for want of care by the claimant is an objective one and one which varies depending upon the facts of the case. It may, however, be the case that the courts expect less from a claimant in complying with the standard of reasonable care than they do of defendants.

The standard of care may be adjusted to meet changing conditions as in the case of seat-belts. In *Froom* v *Butcher* [1975] 3 WLR 379 the claimant's car was in collision with the defendant's car. The collision was caused by the negligence of the defendant. The claimant was not wearing a seat-belt at the time of the accident because he did not like to do so and he had seen a number of accidents where the driver had been trapped in the car as the result of wearing a seat-belt. The claimant's injuries were worse than they would have been had he been wearing a seat-belt. The Court of Appeal held that the damages which should be awarded to the claimant should be reduced by 25 per cent on account of the contributory negligence of the claimant. The court affirmed that the standard of care demanded of a claimant was to be judged objectively and they held that a prudent man would always wear a seat-belt unless there were exceptional circumstances, for example where the person concerned was a pregnant woman. This case should now be read in the light of subsequent legislation which made the wearing of seat-belts mandatory: see now ss14 (adults) and 15 (children) of the Road Traffic Act 1988 and regulations made thereunder.

Nevertheless, *Froom* v *Butcher* remains significant. In *Jones (A Minor)* v *Wilkins* (2001) The Times 6 February the Court of Appeal said that consequent on a road traffic accident caused by the admitted negligence of the defendant, the apportionment of responsibility for serious injuries to a child passenger not properly secured by suitable seat restraints was to be determined by applying the test laid down in s2(1) of the Civil Liability (Contribution) Act 1978, ie, what was just and equitable: see Chapter 3, section 3.5. Their Lordships added that, in applying that test, the decision in *Froom* v *Butcher* continued to provide valuable guidance. In the event, their Lordships upheld the trial judge's decision that a 75 per cent (the defendant driver) and 25 per cent (the claimant's mother and aunt) distribution of liability was appropriate in all the circumstances.

There are four situations where particular problems arise in establishing the requisite standard of care. We shall now discuss these four situations.

12.5 Children

It is not entirely clear whether or not there is an age below which a child cannot be held to be guilty of contributory negligence. The standard textbooks, such as *Winfield and Jolowicz*, state that 'while it is not possible to specify an age below which, as a matter of law, a child cannot be guilty, of contributory negligence, age of the child is a circumstance which must be considered in deciding whether it has been guilty of contributory negligence' (*Winfield and Jolowicz on Torts* (13th ed) p162). This view was accepted in Scotland in the case of *McKinnell* v *White* 1971 SLT (Notes) 61 where a child of five years of age was held to have been guilty of contributory negligence.

But in the case of *Gough* v *Thorne* [1966] 1 WLR 1387 Lord Denning cast doubt on whether such a proposition represents the current state of English law. Three children, aged 17, 13½ and 10, crossed a road in front of a lorry. The lorry driver indicated to the children that they could cross the road and he put out his hand to warn the traffic which was coming up the road. But a 'bubble' car, which came up too fast from behind, overtook the lorry and seriously injured the 13½ year old claimant. It was held that the child was not guilty of contributory negligence. She had been beckoned to cross the road by the lorry driver and she had done so. She had done everything which could have been expected of a child of her age. During the course of his judgment Lord Denning said that:

'A very young child cannot be guilty of contributory negligence. An older child may be; but it depends on the circumstances. A judge should only find a child guilty of contributory negligence if he or she is of such an age as reasonably to be expected to take precautions for his or her own safety: and then he or she is only to be found guilty if blame should be attached to him or her.'

Hence in *Adams* v *Southern Electricity Board* (1993) The Times 21 October the Court of Appeal found an intelligent 15-year-old boy to be guilty of contributory negligence where he knew that what he did was wrong and dangerous, and in *Morales* v *Eccleston* [1991] RTR 151 an 11-year-old boy was held to be guilty of contributory negligence.

Another example of the more benevolent English approach is the case of *Yachuk* v *Oliver Blais Co Ltd* [1949] AC 386. A nine-year-old boy purchased from the defendants a quantity of petrol, falsely stating that his mother wanted the petrol for her car. In fact he used the petrol to play with and as a result of doing so he was badly burned. It was held that the defendants were negligent in supplying petrol to such a young child. But the boy was not guilty of contributory negligence because he neither knew, nor could be expected to know, of the dangers of petrol. This decision should be compared with *Evans* v *Souls Garages Ltd* (2001) The Times 23 January (child aged 13 unlawfully and negligently supplied with petrol contributorily negligent in suffering serious burns).

So while it may, nominally, be the case that there is no age below which a child cannot be guilty of contributory negligence, in practice it is extremely difficult and, in cases involving very young children, almost impossible, to show that the child was guilty of contributory negligence.

It should also be noted that a child will not be 'identified' with the negligence of his parent or guardian. In *Oliver* v *Birmingham and Midland Omnibus Co* [1933] 1 KB 35 the claimant, a four-year-old boy, was injured when crossing the road with his grandfather. A bus belonging to the defendants approached them without warning. The grandfather was so startled that he let go of the claimant's hand. The boy ran onto the road and was struck and injured by the defendants' bus. It was held that the defendants were liable to the claimant in negligence and that the claimant was not prevented from recovering from the defendants on account of the negligence of his grandfather.

12.6 Workmen

Where a workman sues his employer for breach of statutory duty, or possibly in negligence, the court is more reluctant to find that the employee has been guilty of contributory negligence. The reason for this is that statutes, such as the Factories Acts, have been introduced for the protection of employees and the courts have held that such protection should not be undermined by a finding that the employee cannot recover damages, or that his damages should be reduced, on the ground that he was guilty of contributory negligence.

In considering whether the workman has been guilty of contributory negligence the court will have regard to the fact that the workman's sense of danger has been dulled by factors such as repetition, noise, fatigue and confusion. In *Caswell* v *Powell Duffryn Associated Collieries Ltd* [1940] AC 152 Lord Wright stated that:

> 'What is all important is to adapt the standard of negligence to the facts, and to give due regard to the actual conditions under which men work in a factory or mine, to the long hours and the fatigue, to the slackening of attention which naturally comes from constant repetition of the same operation, to the noise and confusion in which the man works, to his pre-occupation in what he is actually doing at the cost perhaps of some inattention to his own safety.'

It is unclear whether this leniency also applies to cases where the employer is sued for negligence and not for breach of statutory duty. The cases are heavily influenced by the desire to avoid the undermining of the statutory regulations and it is not clear that it will be extended to cases where the courts are not influenced by the statutory background.

It should not be thought that this lenient approach means that a workman cannot be guilty of contributory negligence. In *Jayes* v *IMI (Kynoch) Ltd* [1985] ICR 155 the claimant, who was a very experienced worker, was cleaning a machine of which the safety guard had been removed when his hand was pulled into the moving machinery and he lost the tip of his finger. He claimed that the defendants were in breach of their absolute statutory duty under s14 of the Factories Act 1961. But he admitted that what he had done was very foolish and he was held to have been guilty of 100 per cent contributory negligence (although it should be noted that a reduction of 100 per cent could not now be supported according to the Court of Appeal in *Pitts* v *Hunt* [1991] 1 QB 24, see section 12.10). Similarly, where the workman fails to comply with the statutory regulations placed upon him, he may be found to be guilty of contributory negligence. In *Bux* v *Slough Metals Ltd* [1974] 1

All ER 262 the claimant, who was a die-caster employed in the defendants' iron foundry, was given a pair of goggles which he was told to wear at work. The claimant refused to wear the goggles because he found that they misted up when in use. He did, however, ask if any better goggles were available, but he got no reply. The claimant sued the defendants after molten metal splashed up into his eyes, causing him injury. It was held that the defendants were liable in negligence for failing to ensure that the claimant wore the goggles, but that the claimant was also guilty of contributory negligence in failing to comply with the regulations requiring him to make 'full and proper use' of equipment provided for his protection.

12.7 Rescuers

In *Sayers* v *Harlow UDC* [1958] 1 WLR 623 it was established that damages can be reduced on the ground that a rescuer is guilty of contributory negligence if the rescuer is negligent in carrying out a rescue. The courts are reluctant, however, to hold that a rescuer has been guilty of contributory negligence. This reluctance can be seen in the case of *Harrison* v *British Railways Board* [1981] 3 All ER 679. The claimant, who was a guard on a train, was injured in attempting to pull a passenger onto a moving train. His instructions from his employers were that, in such a case, he was to pull on the brake rather than attempt to pull the passenger onto the train. If the guard had pulled on the brake he may not have been so severely injured or possibly he may not have been injured at all. The claimant was held to be guilty of contributory negligence and his damages were reduced by 20 per cent.

12.8 Emergencies

Where the claimant is placed in a position of imminent danger by the negligence of the defendant, the courts are more sympathetic towards the claimant who makes a wrong decision in the heat of the moment. This can be demonstrated by reference to the case of *Jones* v *Boyce* (1816) 1 Stark 493. The claimant was a passenger on top of the defendants' coach. The coupling ring of the coach broke and the coach was in imminent danger of overturning. Thinking that the coach was about to overturn and, in order to save himself, the claimant jumped from the top deck of the coach and broke his leg. In fact the coach did not overturn and, when the claimant sued the defendants in respect of his injuries, the defendants argued that he had been guilty of contributory negligence. Lord Ellenborough CJ directed the jury that the claimant was not guilty of contributory negligence if he selected the more perilous of the two alternatives with which he was confronted by the defendant's negligence, provided that the claimant had acted as a reasonable and prudent man would have done. The jury found for the claimant.

12.9 Causation

It is not necessary that the claimant's negligence contribute to the accident. What is essential is that the claimant's negligence must contribute to the damage which he has suffered. Thus in *Froom* v *Butcher* (above) the claimant's damages were reduced because his negligence, in not wearing a seat-belt, contributed to the damage which he suffered, even though his negligence in no way contributed to the accident. A claimant's damages may also fall to be reduced where a motorcyclist fails to wear a crash helmet (see *O'Connell* v *Jackson* [1972] 1 QB 270) or fails to fasten the chin strap of a crash helmet (*Capps* v *Miller* [1989] 2 All ER 333). Equally damages may fall to be reduced where a person accepts a lift in a car when he knows that the driver has consumed substantial quantities of alcohol (see *Owens* v *Brimmell* [1977] QB 859).

This principle can also be illustrated by reference to the case of *Jones* v *Livox Quarries Ltd* [1952] 2 QB 608. The claimant was riding on the towbar of a 'traxcavator' in breach of safety instructions which he had been given. The driver of the traxcavator was unaware of the presence of the claimant on the vehicle and he stopped suddenly so that he could change gear. A dumper truck, which was following behind the traxcavator, collided with the back of the traxcavator and injured the claimant. It was found that the claimant was guilty of contributory negligence and his damages were reduced by 20 per cent. It was held that the claimant's position on the vehicle was one of the causes of his damage. It had been argued that the claimant's negligence had not been the cause of damage to himself because it was only foreseeable that the claimant would suffer injury as the result of falling off the traxcavator and not from being run into from behind. This distinction was rejected by the court and it was held that the claimant's negligence had been a cause of the damage which he suffered. Lord Denning did, however, say that 'if the claimant, whilst he was riding on the towbar, had been hit in the eye by a shot from a negligent sportsman, I should have thought that the claimant's negligence would in no way be a cause of his injury'. In other words, Lord Denning is saying that the damage must not be too remote and that the claimant's negligence must have exposed him to the particular risk of the type of damage suffered.

The 1945 Act did not alter the rules for determining whether or not contributory negligence exists, nor did it deal with the issue of whether the claimant's negligence was so overwhelming as to be the sole effective cause of his loss. Some difficult questions relating to causation can still arise as was demonstrated by the case of *Stapley* v *Gypsum Mines Ltd* [1953] AC 663. The claimant's husband worked in the defendants' gypsum mine. He was told that he and another worker were to bring down a roof in the mine which was unsafe before they recommenced their normal work. After making unsuccessful attempts to bring down the roof the claimant's husband and his mate decided to give up and return to their normal work. The roof later collapsed and the claimant's husband was killed. In these circumstances the claimant brought an action against the defendants. The court had to decide whether the damage had been done solely as a result of the negligence of the claimant's husband or whether the negligence of his mate was also a cause of his death. In answering this question the House of Lords had to resort to the common law of causation, as the 1945 Act does not deal with the problem of causation, although, as Lord Porter noted, the 1945 Act does enable the court:

> '... to seek less strenuously to find some ground for holding the claimant free from blame or for reaching the conclusion that his negligence played no part in the ensuing accident in as much as owing to the change in the law the blame can now be apportioned equitably between the two parties.'

Approaching the issue of causation in a 'common sense manner' the House of Lords held that the other workman had been negligent in disobeying orders and that the claimant's husband had not been the sole cause of his own death. However they also held that her husband had been guilty of contributory negligence and her damages were reduced by 80 per cent.

It should also be noted in this context that a distinction must be drawn between contributory negligence and novus actus interveniens. The latter breaks the chain of causation with the result that the defendant ceases to be liable for the damage which occurs after the chain of causation is broken. The former is covered by the 1945 Act and the court has the power to apportion the damages under s1(1) of the Act (see further *McKew* v *Holland & Hannen & Cubitts* [1969] 3 All ER 1621, discussed in greater detail in Chapter 11, section 11.7).

12.10 Apportionment

Under s1(1) of the Act damages awarded to the claimant who has been contributorily negligent are to be reduced 'to such extent as the court thinks just and equitable having regard to the claimant's share in the responsibility for the damage'. The apportionment of damage is regarded by the courts as a matter of fact. In assessing what is 'just and equitable' the courts have regard to the extent to which the claimant's and the defendant's negligence was the cause of the damage which the claimant sustained, but the more important factor is the comparative blameworthiness or culpability of the parties. The Act presupposes that the person suffering the damage will recover at least some damages and so damages cannot be reduced by 100 per cent on the ground that the claimant was guilty of contributory negligence (*Pitts* v *Hunt* [1991] 1 QB 24).

Where there is more than one defendant the position should be considered separately between the claimant and each defendant. Thus, in *Fitzgerald* v *Lane* [1989] AC 328 the claimant and two defendants were held to be equally to blame for the claimant's injuries. As each party was equally at fault the House of Lords held that the claimant could only recover half of his damages from each defendant and so the claimant was entitled to half of the total award of damages, with each defendant being liable to make an equal contribution to the amount recoverable by the claimant (for analysis see Chandler and Holland [1989] LMCLQ 30).

Where the accident is a common one the court may produce guidelines to be used in apportioning damages. Thus in *Froom* v *Butcher* (above) it was suggested that the courts should proceed on the basis that, where the injuries could have been completely prevented by the wearing of a seat-belt, damages should be reduced by 25 per cent, but that, where the wearing of a seat-belt would simply have reduced the severity of the claimant's injuries, then damages should be reduced by 15 per cent. Such an approach has the merit of providing some certainty and consistency, and in *Capps* v *Miller* [1989] 2 All ER 333 Croom-Johnson LJ stated that, 'ordinarily [these guidelines] should be adhered to because it is of the greatest importance that they should be generally kept for the sake of the swift conduct, and it may be settlement, of litigation.'

Where there has been a negligent valuation, the amount of the overvaluation is the amount of damages recoverable by the person who lends money on the strength of the valuation. However, where the lender has been contributorily negligent, the appropriate reduction is made from his overall loss, where such loss exceeds the amount of the overvaluation. As Lord Millett explained in *Platform Home Loans Ltd* v *Oyston Shipways Ltd* [1999] 1 All ER 833, where the lender's negligence has caused or contributed directly to the overvaluation, then it may be appropriate to apply the reduction to the amount of the overvaluation as well as the overall loss. Where, however, the lender's imprudence was partly responsible for the overall loss but did not cause or contribute to the overvaluation, it is the overall loss alone which should be reduced, possibly but not necessarily leading to a consequential reduction in the damages.

13

Volenti Non Fit Injuria

13.1 Introduction

13.2 The intentional infliction of harm

13.3 The negligent infliction of harm

13.4 Voluntariness

13.5 Agreement

13.6 Knowledge

13.7 Volenti and exclusion clauses

13.1 Introduction

Volenti non fit injuria or volenti, as it is more usually called, is a complete defence to the claimant's action. The defence is said to apply when the defendant can prove that the claimant knew of the risk of harm or injury and had voluntarily submitted to that risk.

It should be noted that volenti only comes into play where it has been demonstrated that the defendant has committed a tort. Volenti has a role to play in the case of both the intentional infliction of harm and the negligent infliction of harm. Salmond and Heuston (*The Law of Torts* (20th ed) p485) suggest that a distinction should be drawn between the role of consent in the intentional infliction of harm and the negligent infliction of harm. We shall adopt this suggestion and consider the intentional infliction of harm and the negligent infliction of harm separately.

13.2 The intentional infliction of harm

In relation to the intentional infliction of harm, consent negatives what would otherwise be a tort. Thus consent negatives what would otherwise be a trespass; whether that trespass be trespass to the person (Chapter 24) or trespass to land (Chapter 25). So the doctor who performs an operation after the claimant has signed a consent form consenting to the operation does not commit the tort of battery because the claimant has given him permission to carry out the operation.

13.3 The negligent infliction of harm

It is in relation to the negligent infliction of harm that the defence of volenti has given rise to the greatest difficulty. There are a number of conditions which must be made out for the defence to apply and we shall now give consideration to these conditions (sections 13.4–13.6).

13.4 Voluntariness

The claimant must have voluntarily submitted to the risk of injury. This requirement was clearly articulated by Scott LJ in the case of *Bowater* v *Rowley Regis Corporation* [1944] KB 476 when he said that:

> 'A man cannot be said to be truly "willing" unless he is in a position to choose freely, and freedom of choice predicates, not only full knowledge of the circumstances on which the exercise of choice is conditioned, so that he may be able to choose wisely, but the absence from his mind of any feeling of constraint so that nothing shall interfere with the freedom of his will.'

This element was not always rigidly insisted upon in the nineteenth century when the defence of volenti was at its widest. In many cases concerning the employment relationship it was not recognised that the employee was under pressure from his employer and so was not simply free to refuse to accept a particular practice.

But a more realistic approach was adopted by the House of Lords in the case of *Smith* v *Baker* [1891] AC 325. The claimant was employed by the defendants. He worked in a quarry, drilling in the rock face. While he did this a crane worked overhead and, as both he and his employers knew, there was a risk that a heavy stone would fall from the crane. The claimant was never warned as to when the crane would be operating. A stone fell from the crane and injured the claimant. It was held that, although the claimant knew of the risk of injury and incurred it as part of his job, the defence of volenti was not made out because the claimant was threatened with the loss of his job if he objected to the crane working overhead. So it could not be shown that the claimant had voluntarily consented to the risk of injury. This decision is a welcome one in so far as it recognises the industrial realities of the employment relationship.

Where, however, the employee is not under pressure at his work and he adopts a dangerous method of work which causes damage to himself, the courts are more willing to hold that the defence of volenti is applicable. This can be demonstrated by reference to the case of *Imperial Chemical Industries Ltd* v *Shatwell* [1965] AC 656.

The claimant and his brother, James, were working as shotfirers in the defendants' quarry. Both were employees of the defendants. In breach of the instructions given to them by the defendants and in breach of certain statutory regulations, they decided to test some detonators without standing in a shelter which had been provided for them. While they were testing the detonators without using the shelter the claimant was injured. He sued the defendants on the ground that he claimed that they were vicariously liable for the negligence of his brother, James. It was held that the claimant and his brother were fully aware of the risk of injury and that they were volens as regards the injury because it had been caused by their conduct in deliberately not using the shelter when there was a risk of injury from the explosion.

Where the claimant attempts to rescue another, the courts have not accepted that the claimant has thereby voluntarily accepted the risk of injury. This principle can be traced back to the case of *Haynes* v *Harwood* [1935] 1 KB 146. The claimant, who was a policeman on duty, was injured attempting to prevent some horses, which had bolted, from injuring bystanders. The claimant sought to recover in respect of his injuries from the defendant, who was the owner of the horses and who had negligently left his horses unattended. It was held that the defendant could not rely on the defence of volenti because the claimant, as a policeman, was under a duty to try to stop the horses and therefore had not acted voluntarily.

The principle is not, however, confined to cases where the claimant's job is to try to prevent injury being inflicted on others. It applies to anyone who attempts to rescue another. Thus in *Chadwick* v *British Transport Commission* [1967] 1 WLR 912 the claimant suffered nervous shock as the result of leaving his home, which was near a railway line, to go to help in a rescue operation after a major railway accident. It was held that the defendants were liable for the injury suffered by the claimant because it was their negligence which had caused the accident and the claimant's injury was a reasonably foreseeable consequence of the defendants' negligence. The claimant was not volens. If it had been held that the claimant was volens it would, to a large extent, have undermined the rule that a duty of care is owed to a rescuer (on which see Chapter 8, section 8.2 and, see also, Chapter 7, section 7.11).

Where, however, there is no real danger, the claimant who attempts a rescue may be held to be volens in respect of any injury which he receives. Such was the case in *Cutler* v *United Dairies* [1933] 2 KB 297. The defendant, who was a milkman, carelessly left his horses unattended with the result that they bolted. The claimant was injured when he tried to stop the horses and the milk cart in a meadow. It was held that the horses were not a source of danger to anyone when they were in the meadow and so the claimant could not recover in respect of his injuries as he was held to be volens.

Finally, it is difficult to establish that a claimant was volens when, at the relevant time, he was of unsound mind. In *Kirkham* v *Chief Constable of Greater Manchester Police* [1990] 2 QB 283 the claimant's husband, who was known by the police to have suicidal tendencies, was taken into police custody. The police failed to inform the prison authorities of his suicidal tendencies and he subsequently committed suicide in the remand centre to which he had been sent. The claimant alleged that the defendants were negligent in failing to pass on to the prison authorities the information relating to her husband's suicidal tendencies. The defendants argued, inter alia, that the claimant's claim must fail because her husband was volenti. Lloyd LJ conceded that volenti could be invoked against a person of sound mind who committed suicide (but see *Reeves* v *Commissioner of Police of the Metropolis* [1999] 3 All ER 897 where the House of Lords took the opposite view). But he held that, where the person who committed suicide was of unsound mind, it could not be said that he was volens because his judgment was impaired and he could not be said to have 'waived or abandoned any claim arising out of his suicide'. On the other hand, 'impairment' of mind which is induced by alcohol will not necessarily result in the conclusion that the claimant is not volens. In *Morris* v *Murray* [1991] 2 QB 6 the claimant was a passenger in an aeroplane which crashed because the pilot was drunk. The claimant was an active participant in the whole enterprise. He had been out drinking with the pilot, had driven him to the airport and assisted him in the preparations for the flight. The claimant brought a claim against the estate of the deceased pilot claiming damages for the personal injury which he suffered in the crash. An autopsy on the pilot showed that he had consumed the equivalent of 17 whiskies and the claimant had been drinking on a similar scale. One of the issues which was before the Court of Appeal was whether or not the claimant was volens. The court held that he was volens because he was not so drunk that he was incapable of appreciating the risks involved in the flight and this was evidenced by the fact that he had driven the car to the airport and had assisted in the preparations for the flight.

13.5 Agreement

It is clear that the defence is applicable where the claimant agrees with the defendant that he, the claimant, will accept the risk of injury. Where the parties expressly agree in advance that the defendant shall not be liable to the claimant for any future act of negligence which he commits it is clear that the defence of volenti is applicable. This is subject to the caveat that where the parties agree in advance that the defendant shall not be liable for his breach of duty then that agreement will amount to an exclusion clause which must then satisfy the provisions of the Unfair Contract Terms Act 1977 (see further section 13.7). The courts are also prepared to concede that, in an appropriate case, the parties may have impliedly agreed that the defendant will not be liable to the claimant for future acts of negligence. But the courts are reluctant to spell out an implied agreement that the claimant will accept the risk of injury. This has been particularly evident in cases involving persons who accept a lift in a car from a driver whom they know to be incapable of driving, for example, through intoxication. In such cases the courts have not generally held that the person accepting the lift has impliedly agreed to waive his right to sue in respect of any act of negligence by the driver (see *Dann* v *Hamilton* [1939] 1 KB 509 (discussed further below) and *Nettleship* v *Weston* [1971] 2 QB 691; cf *Ashton* v *Turner* [1981] QB 137). Such an implied agreement was, however, held to exist on the facts of *ICI* v *Shatwell* (above). The two employees had expressly agreed that the dangerous act of testing the detonators be done without using the shelter and from this express agreement it was not difficult to imply an agreement that they accepted the risk of any injury resulting from this dangerous practice.

Although it is clear that the parties may agree expressly or impliedly to forego a claim in respect of a future act of negligence by the defendant, two further problems remain and it is to these problems that we now turn. The first problem relates to whether the defence of volenti can be made out when there is no agreement between the parties. The second problem concerns whether an agreement that the defendant will not be liable can validly be made between the parties after the negligent act has been committed.

The first problem concerns whether agreement is an essential element in the defence of volenti. Professor Williams has stated (*Joint Torts and Contributory Negligence* p308) that:

'To constitute a defence, there must have been an express or implied bargain between the parties whereby the [claimant] gave up his right of action for negligence.'

Support for such a view can be found in the judgment of Lord Denning in *Nettleship* v *Weston* [1971] 2 QB 691 when he said that:

'Nothing will suffice short of an agreement to waive any claim for negligence. The [claimant] must agree, expressly or impliedly, to waive any claim for any injury that may befall him due to the lack of reasonable care by the defendant.'

This view has not, however, been accepted in other cases. One such case is *Dann* v *Hamilton* [1939] 1 KB 509. The defendant, the claimant and two other people went out drinking and the defendant, who was the driver of the car, was rather drunk by the end of the evening. They all nevertheless went home in the defendant's car. One of the three passengers later got out of the car close to his home and he stated to the other two passengers that they had more pluck than he had in staying in the car with the defendant. The claimant replied 'You should be like me. If anything is going to happen, it will happen.' A few minutes later the defendant crashed the car. The defendant was killed and the claimant was injured. The claimant sued the defendant's estate in respect of the injuries which she suffered. It was held that the claimant could recover and that the defence of volenti did not apply in such a case. But Asquith J held that the type of case in which the claimant comes into a situation where the danger has already been created by the negligence of the defendant was the type of case to which the defence of volenti was applicable. It has also been pointed out (Jaffey [1985] CLJ 87, 92–95) that certain statutory provisons appear to assume that the defence can be made out by showing that the claimant encountered an already existing danger created by the defendant's negligence (see, for example, s2(5) of the Occupiers' Liability Act 1957 and s5(2) of the Animals Act 1971).

Although Asquith LJ accepted that volenti could apply to a case in which a claimant came into a situation in which the danger had already been created by the negligence of the defendant, his conclusion that, on the facts of the case, the claimant was not volenti has been subjected to considerable criticism. In defence of Asquith J it should be noted that contributory negligence was not pleaded as a defence in *Dann* (despite the suggestion by Asquith J that the pleadings should be amended to incorporate the defence) and so *Dann* does not prevent a defendant invoking contributory negligence in an analogous case. Nevertheless in relation to the volenti point, *Dann* has been subject both to judicial criticism and a narrow interpretation in recent years. The first case which we can note here is *Pitts* v *Hunt* [1991] 1 QB 24. The claimant was a pillion passenger on a motor cycle and the first defendant was the motor cyclist. The claimant knew that the first defendant did not have a driving licence and that he was uninsured. Immediately prior to the accident, both the claimant and the first defendant had been drinking and the claimant encouraged the first defendant to drive in a reckless manner by weaving in and out of the white lines in the centre of the road. While driving in this reckless manner the motor cycle was in collision with a car driven by the second defendant. The first defendant was killed and the claimant was seriously injured in the accident. It was held that the second defendant had not been negligent and so the claimant's claim against him was dismissed. At first instance and in the Court of Appeal it was held that the claimant's claim against the first defendant must also fail because at the time of the accident they were both involved in the commission of a criminal offence which was of sufficient gravity to bring the maxim ex turpi causa non oritur actio into play (see further Chapter 31, section 31.3). But at first instance ([1989] 3 WLR 795, 805–808) Judge Fallon QC also noted the criticisms which have been levelled against the decision of Asquith J in *Dann* and he stated that it 'has not been approved of universally', thereby suggesting that it may yet be open to re-examination in the appellate courts. However it was not necessary for him to engage in such a re-examination on the facts of *Pitts* because he was able to distinguish *Dann*. He held that volenti was established on the facts of this case because the first defendant was so obviously drunk that the case was distinguishable from *Dann*. However, on the facts of the case, he held that the first defendant could not invoke volenti successfully because s148(3) of the Road Traffic Act 1972 (see now s149(3) of the Road Traffic Act 1988) had the effect of precluding reliance upon volenti in such road accident cases. The Court of Appeal in agreeing with Judge Fallon QC was more circumspect. Although *Dann* was cited to them, they did not discuss it in their judgments. They simply stated (at p556) that, while the claimant had voluntarily accepted the risk of injury by taking part in such a foolhardy, risky and illegal activity, such a voluntary acceptance of risk did not relieve the first defendant of liability because of the operation of s148(3) of the 1972 Act.

A second case which subjected *Dann* to a narrow interpretation is *Morris* v *Murray* (above) where, it will be recalled, the claimant was a passenger in an aeroplane which crashed because the pilot was drunk. The Court of Appeal held that the claimant's claim must fail because he was volens. It was held that *Dann* was distinguishable because in *Morris* the pilot's drunkenness was extreme and glaring and the journey was fraught with danger from its very inception (which was not the case in *Dann* because there the driver did not get drunk until a later stage in the social outing at a time when it might not have been very easy for the claimant 'to extricate herself without giving offence'). Sir George Waller was also of the opinion that there was a fundamental difference between driving a car and piloting an aeroplane, the latter being more risky and requiring greater accuracy of control than the former. Although *Dann* has survived this scrutiny by the Court of Appeal it is now clear that its sphere of application is limited and that it has no application where the driver of the vehicle is obviously and glaringly drunk.

Despite this doubt about the application of the principle laid down in *Dann* to the facts of the case, the majority view appears to be that an agreement is not necessary and that the defence can be established where the claimant encounters a danger which has already been created by the defendant's negligence.

The second problem concerns whether an agreement between the claimant and the defendant, under which the claimant agrees to accept the risk of injury, can be made after the defendant has committed the negligent act which caused the damage to the claimant. Once again there is no clear authority on this point (in *Titchener* v *British Railways Board* [1983] 1 WLR 1427 Lord Fraser appeared to accept that such an agreement could be made but this view was not shared by Diplock LJ in *Wooldridge* v *Sumner* [1963] 2 QB 43), but there is academic support for the argument that such an agreement may be made (Clerk and Lindsell on *Tort* (16th ed) paras 1–161).

13.6 Knowledge

Mere knowledge of the danger is not sufficient, of itself, to establish the defence of volenti. As has frequently been pointed out the maxim is *volenti* non fit injuria not *scienti* non fit injuria (see, for example, *Dann* v *Hamilton* (above) where the claimant had knowledge of the risk of injury but was held not to have accepted the risk of injury). It must be proved that the claimant consented to the risk, not simply that he had knowledge of the risk.

Having said that, knowledge of the risk does play a role within the defence of volenti because for the defence to be applicable it must be known that the claimant had knowledge of the danger. The test of knowledge is a subjective one (see *Smith* v *Austin Lifts Ltd* [1959] 1 WLR 100). Where the claimant was not aware of the danger in a situation where he ought to have been aware of it, the defence of volenti is not made out and the defendant should rely instead on the argument that the claimant was guilty of contributory negligence.

13.7 Volenti and exclusion clauses

Although the claimant may conclude an agreement with the defendant that he (the claimant) will accept the risk of injury, that agreement may constitute an exclusion clause, the validity of which may be affected by the Unfair Contract Terms Act 1977. Here we are concerned with s2 of the Act which regulates attempts to exclude or restrict liability for negligence. Section 2(1) provides that:

> 'A person cannot by reference to any contract term or to a notice given to persons generally or to particular persons exclude or restrict his liability for death or personal injury resulting from negligence.'

A number of points should be noted about this subsection. The first is that it only applies to attempts to exclude or restrict liability and does not apply to clauses which merely define the obligations between the parties (unless such clauses are caught by s13 of the Act). The second point is that the subsection only applies to attempts to exclude or restrict business liability (defined in s1(3) of the Act). The third point to note is that it only applies to 'negligence' (which is defined in s1(1) of the Act).

Section 2(2) of the 1977 Act provides that:

> 'In the case of other loss or damage, a person cannot so exclude or restrict his liability for negligence except in so far as the term or notice satisfies the requirement of reasonableness.'

Once again this subsection only applies to attempts to exclude or restrict liability, business liability and negligence. In considering what constitutes reasonableness regard should be had to the general guidelines provided in s11 of the Act.

In relation to road traffic legislation it is provided in s149(3) of the Road Traffic Act 1988 that a clause in a contract or a notice which purports to exclude liability in circumstances where compulsory insurance is required is of no effect.

Finally the exact wording of s2(3) of the Unfair Contract Terms Act 1977 should be noted. It provides that:

> 'Where a contract term or notice purports to exclude or restrict liability for negligence a person's agreement to or awareness of it is not of itself to be taken as indicating his voluntary acceptance of any risk.'

It has been pointed out by Jaffey ([1985] CLJ 87, 95) that this subsection envisages that the defence of volenti may exist in the absence of an agreement between the parties (see section 13.5). This is because, where there is an agreement between the parties, the case will be covered either by s2(1) or by s2(2), so s2(3) of the Act can only apply where there is no agreement between the parties and it therefore supports the argument of those who maintain that the defence of volenti may be made out in the absence of an agreement between the parties.

14

Breach of Statutory Duty

14.1 Introduction

14.2 Does the breach confer a right of action in tort?

14.3 The remedy provided in the Act

14.4 Statutes for the benefit of a class

14.5 Public right and special damage

14.6 Ambit of the statute

14.7 Defences

14.1 Introduction

A breach by the defendant of his statutory duty may give the claimant a cause of action in tort. The difficulty which arises with breach of statutory duty lies in discerning which statutes, in their breach, give rise to a cause of action in tort. Sometimes this can be clear, as when the statute is enacted for the very purpose of giving the claimant a cause of action in tort in a situation in which he would not have had a cause of action before (see, for example, the Occupiers' Liability Act 1984, discussed at Chapter 17, section 17.15) or where the statute expressly excludes a cause of action in respect of a failure to comply with its provisions (see, for example, s133 of the Medicines Act 1968 or s5 of the Guard Dogs Act 1975). But in the vast majority of cases the statute is completely silent as to whether or not breach gives rise to a cause of action in tort. So we must look to the cases to see the principles which the courts have applied in considering whether breach of statutory duty gives rise to a cause of action in tort.

The standard required of the defendant in a particular case depends on the wording of the statute. The statute may, in effect, impose absolute liability upon the defendant or it may require that the defendant be guilty of negligence before its provisions are breached (see further section 14.6).

14.2 Does the breach confer a right of action in tort?

In deciding whether the breach of statutory duty confers upon the claimant a cause of action in tort the general approach which the courts adopt is one of construction; that is, does the Act, on its true construction, confer upon the claimant a right of action in tort in respect of the breach of the statute (*Cutler* v *Wandsworth Stadium Ltd* [1949] AC 398; *R* v *Deputy Governor of Parkhurst Prison, ex parte Hague* [1992] 1 AC 58). As we have noted the Act is generally silent on this issue and so it is left to the courts to discern the intention of Parliament. In a recent consolidated case the House of Lords held that it was not the intention of Parliament to confer a right of action in tort for breaches of the Children and Young Persons Act 1969, the Child Care Act 1980, the Children Act 1989, the Education Acts 1981 and 1994, or the Nurseries and Child-Minders Regulation Act 1948: *X* v *Bedfordshire County Council* [1995] 3 WLR 152: see also Chapter 8, section 8.6. In *Lonrho Ltd* v *Shell Petroleum Co Ltd (No 2)* [1982] AC 173 Lord Diplock stated that the initial presumption was that, where the statute created an obligation and a means of enforcing that obligation, such as a criminal penalty, then the obligation cannot be enforced in any other way (see the statement of principle by Lord Tenterden CJ in *Doe d Bishop of Rochester* v *Bridges* (1831) 1 B & Ad 847, 849). Lord Diplock held that there were two main exceptions to this initial presumption. The first arose where the statute was enacted for the benefit of a particular class of individuals and the second was where the statute created a 'public right' and the claimant had suffered 'special damage', which was damage over and above the damage suffered by the public at large.

The importance of these presumptions can be seen in the decision of the Court of Appeal in *CBS Songs Ltd* v *Amstrad Consumer Electronics plc* [1988] Ch 61 (affirmed by the House of Lords [1988] AC 1013). The defendants manufactured a twin-deck tape-recording machine which could be used to copy directly from one tape on to another. The claimants, who were three record companies who were also representing other copyright owners in the music industry, alleged that the defendants had advertised the machines in such a way as to incite members of the public to commit the criminal offence of taping copyright material in breach of s21(3) of the Copyright Act 1956. The claimants sought an injunction to restrain the defendants from selling the machines unless they ensured that the claimants' copyright material would not thereby be infringed. The Court of Appeal, by a majority, refused to grant the injunction.

Nicholls LJ held that Lord Diplock's judgment in *Lonrho* was a comprehensive one. He held that in the present case the claimants did not come within either of the two exceptions to the initial presumption so that they could not maintain an action in tort for breach of statutory duty. He rejected the idea that there was a third exception under which a court could in equity grant an injunction to a claimant to restrain a breach of the criminal law. He conceded that the court might grant such an injunction where the defendant's crime infringed a property right of the claimant, but he held that such a jurisdiction arose out of a concern to protect the property rights of the claimant and not out of a desire to ensure that the criminal law was enforced. The remedy open to the claimants was not an action in tort but a private prosecution against the defendants. In *X* v *Bedfordshire County Council* (above) the House of Lords reiterated Lord Diplock's views and stated that a claimant who wished to sue for breach of statutory duty must satisfy Lord Diplock's criteria or had to show that a duty of care would have arisen at common law.

We shall adopt the approach of Lord Diplock in analysing the law. First we shall consider whether the Act itself makes any provision for a remedy for its breach (section 14.3), then we shall consider the two exceptions, relating to statutes enacted for the benefit of a class (section 14.4) and the 'public right' exception (section 14.5).

14.3 The remedy provided in the Act

One of the crucial issues in determining whether breach of the statute gives rise to a cause of action in tort is the remedies provided, or not provided, in the Act for breach of its provisions. Where the Act imposes a duty upon the defendant, but provides no remedy for breach of that duty, then the presumption is that breach does give rise to a cause of action in tort. Thus in *Thornton* v *Kirklees Metropolitan Borough Council* [1979] QB 626 the defendants were in breach of the Housing (Homeless Persons) Act 1977 and the claimant suffered loss thereby. There was no provision in the Act for a remedy for breach of the Act's provisions and so the court held that a cause of action lay in tort in respect of the defendants' failure to comply with their statutory obligations (cf *Cocks* v *Thanet District Council* [1983] 2 AC 286 and Buckley (1984) 100 LQR 204, 217–20).

On the other hand, where the statute itself provides a remedy for breach of its provisions, then it is much harder to show that the breach also gives rise to a cause of action in tort. It is not, however, impossible to show that the claimant still has a cause of action. Thus in *Groves* v *Lord Wimborne* [1898] 2 QB 402 the defendants were subject to a fine of £100 for breach of their statutory duty in failing to put a fence around their machinery. The claimant was injured by the unfenced machinery. But AL Smith LJ pointed out that 'not one penny of a fine imposed under the sections [of the Act] need ever go into the pocket of the person injured'. He held that the object of the fine was to inflict a punishment upon the employer for his breach of duty and that the compensation of the victim of the employer's failure to comply with his obligation was an entirely separate issue. The fine imposed on the offender under the Act could also have been a small one in comparison with the injury to the claimant. It was held that there was no reason why the claimant should be bound by this limitation and this was held to be another reason for not denying to the claimant a cause of action in respect of the breach of the Act.

Again, a different approach was taken in the case of *Atkinson* v *Newcastle Waterworks Co* (1877) 2 Ex D 441 (cf *Read* v *Croydon Corporation* [1938] 4 All ER

631). The defendants, who supplied water to Newcastle, were statutorily required to keep their pipes at a certain pressure level. Failure to do so could result in a fine of £10, no part of which was payable to the person affected by the defendants' failure to comply with their obligations. The claimant's premises caught fire and, due to the pressure in the pipes being insufficient, there was no water to extinguish the fire and the premises were burnt down. It was held that the penalty imposed in the statute was an exclusive one and that it could not have been intended that the defendants would become, in effect, an insurer that sufficient water would be available to put out a fire. The fact that the fine, which was payable in respect of the breach, did not go into the pocket of the individual but was a 'public' penalty was held to be evidence that the Act did not give a cause of action to an individual in respect of a breach of its provisions and that the purpose behind the fine was simply to impose a security for performance of the statutory duty (cf *Groves* v *Lord Wimborne* (above)).

It is not entirely clear how the cases of *Groves* and *Atkinson* are to be reconciled. It may be that the latter case is the one that will be followed today and that *Groves* will be distinguished on the ground that it was a case of a statute enacted for the benefit of a class (see further 14.4 below). Whichever way the cases are eventually reconciled, it is clear that it is difficult to show that a claimant has a cause of action in tort where the statute provides another remedy for its breach (for a recent example see *Wentworth* v *Wiltshire County Council* [1993] 2 WLR 175). These cases also show that it cannot necessarily be assumed that the mere fact that the statutory penalty is inadequate will lead a court to conclude that the claimant has available to him a cause of action in tort in respect of the damage which he has suffered as a result of the breach.

It should also be noted in this context that the fact that the claimant had available to him a remedy at common law may affect the willingness of the court to conclude that the claimant also has available to him a tort action in respect of the breach of statutory duty. In *Phillips* v *Britannia Hygienic Laundry Co Ltd* [1923] 2 KB 832 the defendants were in breach of the Motor Cars (Use and Construction) Order 1904 because their vehicle was in a defective condition. The reason for it being in a defective condition was the negligence of the people to whom they had entrusted the car for repair. While the defendants were using the vehicle in this defective state, it was involved in an accident in which the claimant's van was damaged. The claimant claimed damages in respect of the breach of statutory duty. The regulations made provision for a criminal penalty in respect of their breach but were silent as to a civil remedy. It was held that the duty owed under the regulations was a public one and that it did not give a member of the public, and therefore the claimant, a cause of action in respect of its breach. Atkins LJ stated that:

'The obligations of those who bring vehicles upon highways have already been well provided for and regulated by the common law. It is not likely that the legislature intended by these regulations to impose upon the owners of vehicles an absolute obligation to make them roadworthy in all events, even in the absence of negligence.'

However, it should not be thought that the availability of an alternative remedy makes it impossible to show that the claimant also has a cause of action in respect of the breach of statutory duty. Cases such as *Groves* v *Lord Wimborne* show that it is possible to bring such a cause of action where an alternative remedy is available. Winfield and Jolowicz (*Winfield and Jolowicz on Tort* (13th ed) pp176–7) suggest that:

> 'The courts will, in the absence of clear indications to the contrary, lean against a statutory duty which would contradict the general pattern of liability in a particular area of activity but will find one which will support or supplement it.'

They then use this rationalisation to explain the case of *Monk* v *Warbey* [1935] 1 KB 175, which is a case which has seemed to defy explanation. The defendant, in breach of the Road Traffic Act 1930, gave permission to an uninsured driver to drive his car. The negligence of the latter caused an accident in which the claimant was injured. The claimant was unable to recover from the driver because he was not worth suing. So he sued the defendant and was held to be entitled to recover. The effect of the judgment was to reinforce the commitment of the common law to those injured as the result of the negligence of another because it created another means by which such people could enforce judgment. On the other hand, had the defendants been held liable in *Phillips* v *Britannia Hygienic Laundry* (above), that would have run counter to the development of the common law because it would have had the effect of imposing liability in the absence of fault rather than imposing liability where it could be shown that the defendant was at fault.

In *Todd* v *Adams* (2002) The Times 3 May the Court of Appeal heard that four fishermen had lost their lives when the defendants' fishing vessel capsized and sank while hauling her fishing gear. Claims were made under the Fatal Accidents Act 1976 and the Law Reform (Miscellaneous Provisions) Act 1934 and the claimants alleged that the accident was caused or contributed to by the defendants' breach of statutory duty under r16 of the Fishing Vessel (Safety Provisions) Rules 1975 to satisfy the specified stability criteria applying to the vessel in all its foreseeable operating conditions. Their Lordships concluded that the actions could not succeed. In all the circumstances (eg, by virtue of s121 of the Merchant Shipping Act 1995, a breach of the rules resulted in the owner or master of the vessel being liable to a fine on summary conviction or conviction on indictment), Parliament had not intended the 1995 Act to give the Secretary of State for Trade and Industry authority to confer on individuals private civil law rights as a consequence of a breach of the rules made (in effect) under that Act.

14.4 Statutes for the benefit of a class

The first exception to the initial presumption which was identified by Lord Diplock in *Lonrho* v *Shell Petroleum* (above) concerned statutes which were passed for the benefit of a class. If the Act was intended to protect the claimant himself, or a class of persons to which the claimant belongs, then the claimant has a cause of action in tort. The difficulty with this formulation is to ascertain what exactly constitutes a class of persons. Employees are generally regarded as a class of persons in relation to industrial safety legislation. This can be seen in the case of *Groves* v *Lord Wimborne* (above). The claimant lost an arm when it was caught in some machinery in the defendants' factory. At the time of the accident the machine was unfenced, which was a breach of the regulations passed under the Factory and Workshop Act 1878. That Act imposed criminal sanctions upon the employer for breach of its requirements but it made no mention of any civil remedy. It was held that the Act was 'passed for the benefit of workmen in factories, by compelling the masters to do certain things for their protection'. So the claimant was held to have a cause of action against the defendants.

Employees have been treated generously by the courts in respect of a breach of the industrial safety legislation and the courts have been ready to find that they constitute a class for whose benefit the legislation was enacted. The courts have, however, been much more reluctant to create civil liabilities out of the road traffic legislation and have held that the public using the highway is not a class (*Phillips* v *Britannia Hygienic Laundry Co Ltd* (above) and *Coote* v *Stone* [1971] 1 WLR 279, but contrast *London Passenger Transport Board* v *Upson* [1949] AC 155). A similar reluctance was evident in the case of *McCall* v *Abelesz* [1976] QB 585 where it was rather surprisingly held that a group of residential tenants was not a class of persons for whose benefit the Rent Act 1965 had been passed. In *R* v *Deputy Governor of Parkhurst Prison, ex parte Hague* [1992] 1 AC 58 the House of Lords held that a breach of the Prison Rules 1964 did not give to a prisoner a private law claim for damages. The Prison Rules and the Prison Act 1952 were designed to deal with the administration of prisons and the management and control of prisoners; they were not intended to create private law rights of action. Another example of this more restrictive approach is the case of *Cutler* v *Wandsworth Stadium* [1949] AC 398. The claimant, who was a bookmaker, was unable to find a space where he could carry out his trade at the defendants' dog track. He sued the defendants for breach of statutory duty, alleging that the defendants had caused him loss through their breach of s11(2) of the Betting and Lotteries Act 1934, which provided that the occupier of the track should ensure that there was 'available space for bookmakers on the track'. It was held that the purpose behind the legislation was to regulate the conduct of bookmakers, but that the legislation was not passed for their benefit but for the benefit of the race-going public. As the Act was not passed for the benefit of the claimant it was held that he had no cause of action in tort in respect of the alleged breach of the statute. In *West Wiltshire District Council* v *Garland* [1995] 2 WLR 439 a district auditor employed to audit the accounts of the local authority in accordance with the Local Government Finance Act 1982 owed a statutory duty not to the officers of the authority but to the authority itself, since the purpose of the audit was to protect the authority; and in *Richardson* v *Pitt-Stanley* [1995] 2 WLR 26 the majority of the Court of Appeal refused to apply Lord Diplock's reasoning to allow an employee to recover for a breach of the Employer's Liability (Compulsory Insurance) Act 1969.

These cases demonstrate a rather variable approach to the issue of what constitutes a class of persons for whose benefit the legislation was passed. There does not appear to be any discernible consistency in the approach which the courts have adopted and much depends on the facts of each case.

14.5 Public right and special damage

In *Lonrho* v *Shell Petroleum* (above) Lord Diplock said that the second case in which the initial presumption did not arise was:

> ' ... where the statute creates a public right (ie a right to be enjoyed by all those of Her Majesty's subjects who wish to avail themselves of it) and a particular member of the public suffers what Brett J in *Benjamin* v *Storr* (1874) LR 9 CP 400 at 407 described as "particular, direct and substantial" damage other and different from that which was common to all the rest of the public.'

It was held on the facts of *Lonrho* that the statutory prohibition upon supplying oil to Southern Rhodesia did not create a public right to be enjoyed by all Her Majesty's citizens. It did the opposite, by prohibiting the members of the public from doing what had previously been lawful for them to do. Therefore no cause of action arose in respect of the defendants' breach of their statutory duty. This distinction between statutes which create public rights and statutes which merely prohibit what was previously lawful activity does not seem to be a satisfactory distinction or to be one which is based upon any obvious coherent principle. Nevertheless it must be conceded that, at present, it does represent the current state of English law.

14.6 Ambit of the statute

Since the claimant's action is based upon the defendant's breach of his statutory duty it is obvious that the claimant's action is heavily dependent upon the wording of the particular statute which he claims that the defendant has breached. For example, the claimant must show that the act which he alleges has caused him damage is one which is regulated by the statute and that he is one of the people whom the Act was intended to protect. The claimant must also show that the injury or damage which he has suffered is of a kind which the statute was intended to prevent. The operation of this latter principle can be demonstrated by reference to the case of *Gorris* v *Scott* (1874) LR 9 Exch 125. The defendant shipowner was statutorily required to provide pens for cattle on board his ship. The reason for this was to lessen the risk of cattle catching a contagious disease called murrain. The claimant's sheep were swept overboard because they were not in pens and he brought an action against the defendants in respect of their breach of statutory duty. It was held that the defendants were not liable because the purpose behind the statute was to protect cattle from murrain and not to protect them from being swept overboard.

Since the claimant's action is so heavily dependent upon the wording of the statute, it is the particular statute that is in issue to which we must look to ascertain the standard required of the defendant. Thus the statute may impose an absolute duty upon the defendant or it may require proof that he was negligent. For example some of the provisions contained in the Factories Act 1961 impose absolute standards, such as the duty in s14 'that every dangerous part of any machinery ... shall be securely fenced unless it is in such a position or of such construction as to be as safe to every person employed or working on the premises as it would be if securely fenced'. That breach of this section is not dependent upon the defendant having been negligent can be demonstrated by reference to the case of *John Summers & Sons Ltd* v *Frost* [1955] AC 740. The claimant's thumb was injured when it was in contact with a revolving grinding wheel which belonged to the defendants. The claimant alleged that, in failing to fence the machine, the defendants had breached s14. He alleged that the section had been breached even though the effect of fencing the machine would have been to render the machine useless. It was held that the machine was indeed a dangerous one and that s14 required it to be 'securely fenced' and that, therefore, the machine must be so fenced even though the consequences of doing so would be to render the machine inoperable. On the other hand the statute may impose a standard which is closer to the common law negligence standard in that it only requires the defendant to do that which is practicable or reasonably practicable. In such a case the statutory obligation has little effect upon the obligations owed by the defendant at common law.

Lastly it must be shown that the defendant's breach of his statutory duty was the cause of the claimant's loss. This can give rise to difficult problems of causation where the defendant's breach of statutory duty takes the form of an omission, such as the failure to provide safety belts (see, for example, *McWilliams* v *Sir William Arrol & Co Ltd* [1962] 1 WLR 295 and the discussion of this particular issue at Chapter 10, section 10.4).

14.7 Defences

The defence of volenti is not available where an employer has breached his statutory duty and in consequence one of his employees suffers damage, unless the case falls within the narrow confines of *Imperial Chemical Industries Ltd* v *Shatwell* [1965] AC 656. It is not entirely clear whether the defence is available in all other cases. The majority view among commentators is that the defence is available, although an argument can be made out to the effect that any attempt to contract out of a statutory duty is void (see further Chapter 15).

The defence of contributory negligence is also available in an appropriate case, but the courts tend to be rather reluctant to accept it, especially when an employee is suing his employer and the employer alleges that the employee was guilty of contributory negligence. In *Westwood* v *Post Office* [1974] AC 1 the claimant, who was a Post Office employee, entered the lift room of the telephone exchange. He was, in fact, forbidden to go in there. While there he fell through a defective trap door and was killed. It was alleged that the defendants had breached their statutory duty under the Offices, Shops and Railway Premises Act 1963. The defendants alleged that the claimant had been guilty of contributory negligence. It was held that the claimant was not guilty of contributory negligence. The fact that he was a trespasser did not have the effect of entitling the defendants to act in breach of their statutory duty and the claimant was entitled to assume that the defendants would comply with their statutory obligations (see further Chapter 12).

Finally it should be noted that, as a general rule, a person who is the subject of a statutory duty cannot discharge that duty by entrusting responsibility for its performance to someone else.

15

Employers' Liability

15.1 Introduction

Employers owe certain duties to their employees. These duties are derived from both common law and statutory sources. We have noted that an employer may be vicariously liable for the torts of his employee (see Chapter 4). Here we are concerned, not with the case where the employee negligently causes loss to a third party, but with the liability of an employer for the injury suffered by one of his employees. This area of law was for many years troubled by the doctrine of common employment which had the effect of reducing the liability of an employer towards his employees. According to this doctrine, an employer was not liable where injury was negligently inflicted on one employee by another employee on the ground that the employee had consented to the risks involved in his employment, including the risk that one of his fellow workers would be negligent (see *Bartonshill Coal Co v Reid* (1858) 3 Macq 266 (HL)). This doctrine was finally abolished by sl of the Law Reform (Personal Injuries) Act 1948. However the doctrine of common employment has left its mark on the development of this area of law. This is particularly so in relation to the personal non-delegable duties which are owed by employers to their employees. These personal non-delegable duties were introduced in an effort to mitigate the rigours of the common employment doctrine because, where it could be shown that the employer was in breach of his own duty to his employee, the employer could not rely on the doctrine of common employment because that doctrine only came into play where the cause of the injury was the negligence of a fellow employee. So at common law it was crucial to distinguish between the employer's breach of his own personal duty, for which the employer was liable, and the breach of duty by one of his employees, for which the employer was not vicariously liable.

But now that the doctrine of common employment has been abolished, the employer may be liable either vicariously for the negligence of his employee committed in the course of his employment or for breach of his own personal non-delegable duty. It is still important to keep the two forms of liability separate because one is vicarious liability, whereas the other is primary. The rules applicable may therefore differ depending on whether we are dealing with primary liability or vicarious liability. For example, in vicarious liability, it is necessary to show that the employee committed the tort in the course of his employment, but there is no such limitation in the case of primary liability. Similarly vicarious liability only arises as between an employer and an employee, it does not extend to an independent contractor; whereas an employer may be in breach of his primary duty where he entrusts the work to an independent contractor. So, although the distinction is no longer as crucial as it once was, it is a distinction which still must be drawn because different rules are applicable depending on whether we are dealing with primary or vicarious liability.

In addition to these two common law sources of liability, statute has intervened to impose certain obligations upon employers in relation to the safety of their employees. The principal example of such legislative intervention is the Health and Safety at Work Act 1974, which, in s2, imposes a general duty upon 'every employer to ensure, so far as is reasonably practicable, the health, safety and welfare at work of all his employees'. We shall not, however, be concerned with these statutory obligations in this Chapter but shall confine our attention to the common law duties imposed upon employers. In so far as failure to comply with these statutory obligations gives rise to an action in tort this issue has been considered in Chapter 14 when discussing breach of statutory duty.

Before embarking upon an analysis of these common law duties, it is necessary to give brief mention to the statutory Industrial Injuries Scheme. Today many accidents at work are covered by this scheme. Ever since the first Workmen's Compensation Act in 1897 there has been in existence a statutory scheme which operates upon a no-fault basis and which compensates those injured in an accident 'arising out of and in the course of his employment': see now the Social Security Contributions and Benefits Act 1992, Pt V (Benefits for Industrial Injuries). It is to this scheme that most employees injured at work will look for compensation and the Pearson Commission noted that only 12.5 per cent of those injured at work obtain any compensation through a tort action. It should also be noted that it is compulsory for employers to have insurance for personal injury to their employees under the Employers' Liability (Compulsory Insurance) Act 1969. It is, however, important to note that the Act only applies to liability for bodily injury or disease which is sustained by employees 'arising out of and in the course of their employment in

Great Britain' (s1, see also *Reid* v *Rush & Tompkins Group plc* [1990] 1 WLR 212, discussed below at section 15.6).

We shall now consider the four principal duties which employers owe to their employees. It is important to note that these duties are personal non-delegable duties and so an employer cannot discharge his responsibility simply by entrusting the performance of the work to an employee or to an independent contractor. We shall start by considering the employer's duty to provide competent staff.

15.2 Competent staff

At common law an employer owes a duty to his employees to select competent employees. The operation of this principle was considered in the case of *Hudson* v *Ridge Manufacturing Co Ltd* [1957] 2 QB 348. There it was held that an employer was liable for the foolish prank committed by one employee upon another in the course of his employment. The employer was held to be in breach of his personal duty because the employee's readiness to involve himself in such pranks had been known to them for a considerable period of time and they failed to take proper steps to put an end to these pranks. However, the position may be different where the employer has no cause to know that the employee has violent tendencies. (In such a case it may also be very difficult for the injured employee to argue that the employee who assaulted him was acting in the course of his employment because of the reluctance of the courts to hold an employer vicariously liable for an assault committed by his employee. See further Chapter 4, section 4.5.)

Hudson should be contrasted with the case of *Smith* v *Crossley Brothers Ltd* (1951) 95 Sol Jo 655. The claimant was injured at work when a fellow apprentice approached him from behind and placed a compressed air pipe near his rectum and signalled to another apprentice to turn on the compressed air. As a result the claimant suffered severe internal injuries. The claimant's action against the defendant employers failed because he could not show that they had failed to take reasonable care for his safety; they could not have foreseen that the apprentices would do such a thing.

15.3 Proper plant and equipment

The employer owes a duty to his employees to provide properly maintained plant and equipment. This can be seen in the case of *Smith* v *Baker* [1891] AC 325. There Lord Herschell said that:

> 'The contract between employer and employed involves on the part of the former the duty of taking reasonable care to provide proper appliances, to maintain them in proper condition, and so to carry on his operations as not to subject those employed to unnecessary risk.'

In *Davie* v *New Merton Board Mills Ltd* [1959] AC 604 the House of Lords held that the defendant employers were not liable for the injury to the claimant, one of their employees, which was caused by a defective tool which the defendants had purchased from a third party. It was held that the defendants were not liable because they had purchased the tool from a reputable firm of manufacturers and the defect was not discoverable on a reasonable inspection of the tool. So the defendants had fulfilled their duty to the claimant. This decision was, however, reversed by the Employers' Liability (Defective Equipment) Act 1969 which provided that where the defective equipment is supplied to the employer then the employer may be vicariously liable for the supplier's negligence. Section 1(1) of the 1969 Act states that:

> 'Where … an employee suffers personal injury in the course of his employment in consequence of a defect in equipment provided by his employer for the purposes of the employer's business and the defect is attributable wholly or partly to the fault of a third party (whether identified or not) the injury shall be deemed to be also attributable to negligence on the part of the employer.'

The meaning of the word 'equipment' was considered by the House of Lords in *Coltman* v *Bibby Tankers Ltd* [1988] AC 276. A ship sank in 1980 with the loss of all the crew. The claimant, who represented the estate of one of the crew members, brought an action against the defendants under s1(1) of the 1969 Act. The defendants argued that the 1969 Act was not applicable because a ship was not 'equipment' for the purposes of the Act. 'Equipment' is defined in s1(3) of the Act as including 'any plant and machinery, vehicle, aircraft and clothing'. The Court of Appeal had held that a ship was not equipment because equipment was ancillary to something else and did not encompass the workplace itself. But in the House of Lords Lord Oliver held that there was no warrant for holding that equipment is restricted to parts of a larger whole. Their Lordships conceded that the strongest argument for the defendants was the omission of ships from the definition in s1(3). Lord Oliver said that the omission was 'certainly curious', but it was held that Parliament could not have intended to exclude ships from the ambit of the Act. To adopt such a narrow construction of the Act would require a court to draw a distinction between machinery on a ship which was not part of the ship and machinery which was actually part of the ship itself; an almost impossible task. Lord Oliver held that the purpose behind the Act was to render the employer liable for defective equipment of every type and, adopting a purposive construction of the Act, he held that there was no reason to exclude ships from the ambit of the Act.

The need for a purposive interpretation of 'equipment' was also emphasised by the House of Lords in *Knowles* v *Liverpool City Council* [1993] 4 All ER 321. The claimant suffered personal injury in the course of his employment when the flagstone which he was handling broke. The defendants, his employers, argued that the flagstone was not 'equipment' but was 'material upon which the employee used the equipment'. In rejecting this argument Lord Jauncey stated that it was necessary to adopt a broad approach to the construction of the Act, bearing in mind its broad purpose, rather than engage in a precise construction of its terms.

15.4 Safe place of work

The employer is under a duty to provide a safe place of work for his employees. It should be noted that this obligation is not an absolute one but is one which demands that the employer take reasonable steps to provide a safe place of work. In *Latimer* v *AEC* [1953] AC 643 (discussed further at Chapter 9, section 9.6) it was emphasised that the employer's obligation to provide a safe place of work only required the employer to do what was reasonable to eliminate the risk and that, where the cost of eliminating the risk was exorbitant by comparison with the benefit obtained by the elimination of the risk, then it was not generally negligent to fail to eliminate the risk (see also *Gitsham* v *CH Pearce & Sons plc* [1992] PIQR 57).

15.5 Safe system of work

The employer is also under a duty to provide his employees with a safe system of work. What constitutes a safe system of work depends on the facts of each case. This can be demonstrated by reference to the case of *General Cleaning Contractors* v *Christmas* [1953] AC 180. The claimant, who was a window cleaner, was employed by the defendants to clean windows. He was informed that he should use the 'sill' method of cleaning the upper windows, which involved standing on the window ledge and holding the window sash while cleaning the windows. While he was cleaning the upper windows in this way, a window fell on his fingers and he fell to the ground and suffered various injuries. It was held that the defendants could not have provided the claimant with safety ropes as there was nothing on the building to which they could have been attached. But it was held that they should have told the claimant to test the window sashes to see whether they were loose and that they could have provided him with wedges for the windows. So it was held that in all the circumstances the defendants had failed to supply a safe system of work. In contrast, it was held in *Mulcahy* v *Ministry of Defence* [1996] 2 WLR 474 that the defendants had no duty to maintain a safe system of work in battle conditions in a war zone. In considering all the relevant circumstances regard should also be had to the character and attributes of the claimant. Thus in *Paris* v *Stepney Borough Council* [1951] AC 367 the employers were held to have been negligent in failing to provide their employee with goggles because the employee only had sight in one eye and so the consequence of any eye injury to him was much greater than if he had sight in both eyes (see further Chapter 9, section 9.4). Where the employer has adopted the standard practice in the industry, that is good, but not conclusive, evidence that the employer has provided a safe system of work (see *Thompson* v *Smiths Shiprepairers (North Shields) Ltd* [1984] 1 All ER 881).

In *McDermid* v *Nash Dredging and Reclamation Co Ltd* [1987] AC 906 the defendants employed the claimant, who was an inexperienced 18-year-old, as a deckhand and, while he was working under the control of another company (who were the parent company of the defendants), he was seriously injured and his leg had to be amputated. The claimant brought an action for damages against the defendants. The House of Lords held that the defendants were under a non-delegable duty to ensure that a safe system of work was provided for the claimant and that that system was operated safely. It is important to note that the duty encompasses both the *devising* of a safe system of work and the *operation* of a safe system of work (for criticism of this extension see McKendrick 'Vicarious Liability and Independent Contractors – a Re-examination' (1990) 53 MLR 770, esp pp773–774). Lord Brandon said that the essential feature of a non-delegable duty is that:

'If it is not performed, it is no defence for the employer to show that he delegated performance to a person, whether his servant or not his servant, whom he reasonably believed to be competent to perform it. Despite such delegation the employer is liable for the non-performance of the duty.'

There are two vital factors which limit the scope of *McDermid*. The first is that, in accordance with general principle, the obligation of the employer is not strict but requires only the exercise of reasonable care. This can be illustrated by reference to the case of *Cook* v *Square D Ltd* [1992] ICR 262. The claimant was sent by the defendants, his employers, to work as a computer consultant in Saudi Arabia. While working there he slipped into a small hole in the tiled floor of the control room and suffered injury. The claimant relied upon *McDermid* but the Court of Appeal rejected the analogy and held that there had been no breach of duty by the defendants. The site was some 8,000 miles away and both the site occupiers and the general contractors were reliable companies who were aware of their responsibility for the safety of workers on site. The court did not, however, rule out the possibility that circumstances might require employers in the UK to take steps to satisfy themselves as to the safety of foreign sites, for example, where a number of their employees are going to work on a foreign site or where one or two employees are going to work there for a considerable period of time (but contrast *Johnson* v *Coventry Churchill International Ltd* [1992] 3 All ER 14, discussed below).

The second factor is that the claimant must be an employee of the defendant employers. In *Watts* v *Lowcur Ltd* (Queen's Bench (Commercial Division) 11 February 1988) the claimant had been employed by the first defendants but was hired by them to the second defendants (who worked on the same building site) so that the latter became his employers. The claimant was injured as a result of the second defendants' breach of statutory duty in failing to provide him with a suitable and safe access to his place of work. It was held that the claimant could not recover damages from the first defendants. McDermid was distinguished on the ground that the claimant in Watts was no longer in the employment of the first defendants and so they ceased to be under a duty to provide him with a safe place or a safe system of work.

Watts should, however, be contrasted with the recent decision of the Court of Appeal in *Morris* v *Breaveglen Ltd* [1993] ICR 766. The claimant was employed by the defendants and was sent by them to work at Dartmoor Prison farm pursuant to a labour only sub-contract which the defendants had entered into with the main contractors at the site. Under the terms of the sub-contract, the defendants accepted that they were liable to observe and perform all safety obligations imposed by statute or common law and to maintain employers' liability insurance in respect of their employees. The trial judge found that, while the claimant was working on the site, it was the main contractors who had the right to control what he did and how he did it. The claimant volunteered to drive the main contractors' dumper truck but while doing so he suffered serious injury when the truck went over the edge of the site. The trial judge found that the accident was caused by an unsafe system of work and by the claimant's lack of instruction in the use of the truck and held that the defendants were liable in damages to the claimant. The defendants appealed, arguing that it was the main contractors who were liable to the claimant and not themselves. This argument was rejected by the Court of Appeal. The court held that a vital distinction had to be drawn between two types of claim. The first arises where the sub-contracted employee causes damage to a third party, in which case the employer responsible for the damage is the one who has the right of control over the employee (see *Mersey Docks and Harbour Board* v *Coggins & Griffiths (Liverpool) Ltd* [1947] AC 1, discussed at Chapter 4, section 4.3). The second type of claim arises when it is the subcontracted employee himself who is injured. In such a case it is the general employer who remains liable because he is personally liable for the performance of his duty to the employee and cannot avoid liability by delegating it to a main contractor (see *McDermid* v *Nash Dredging & Reclamation Ltd* (above)). Therefore the Court of Appeal held that, on the present facts, the defendants were liable to the claimant.

However, as was pointed out in *Morris*, if there is negligence on the part of a supervisor to whom the employee had been entrusted, the employers of that supervisor might be vicariously liable, and thus more than one defendant could be found liable. This principle was applied in *Nelhams* v *Sandells Maintenance Ltd* (1995) The Times 15 June where an employee was told by his main employer to work under the instruction of a second employer. The employee was injured and it was found as a fact that the accident was wholly due to the instructions issued by the supervisor of the second employer. The Court of Appeal therefore held that the employee was entitled to recover against both employers, and that the damages should be apportioned under the Civil Liability (Contribution) Act 1978. On the facts the main employer was entitled to a complete indemnity from the second employer.

So, where the general employer remains the employer of the sub-contracted employee, a non-delegable duty of the type recognised in *Morris* will be in play. But where, as in *Watts*, the employment relationship is terminated by the hiring, the original employer's non-delegable duty will also come to an end. It may, however, be no easy task to persuade a court that the employment relationship has been terminated as a result of the hiring of the employee, as can be seen from the recent case of *Johnson* v *Coventry Churchill International Ltd* [1992] 3 All ER 14. The claimant fell while working on a building site in Germany and suffered serious injury. He brought a claim in negligence against the defendants, who were an employment agency recruiting personnel to work abroad, arguing that he was their employee and that they were in breach of their duty to provide him with a safe system of work. The defendants argued that they were not his employers because his contract with them was described as a 'sub-contract', and that his employers were the owners of the site in Germany where he had been sent to work by the defendants. It was held that, having regard to the realities of the relationship between the parties, the claimant was an employee of the defendants and that he had not been transferred to the employment of the German employers. It was held that there would have to be 'clear and cogent evidence' that the claimant had knowingly accepted a transfer before such a conclusion could be reached. The evidence established that the defendants remained his employers: they continued to pay him and generally acted as if they were his employers. The adoption of this approach will make it very difficult for a general employer to argue that the employee is no longer its employee.

The duty owed to an employee does not merely encompass the employee's physical safety but extends to his mental condition. In *Walker* v *Northumberland County Council* [1994] 1 All ER 737 the High Court held that where it is reasonably foreseeable to an employer that an employee might suffer a nervous breakdown because of the stress and pressures of his workload, the employer is under a duty of care, as part of the duty to provide a safe system of work, not to cause the employee psychiatric damage by the volume or character of the work that the employee is required to perform. In *Walker* the claimant was employed as a social services officer managing four teams of field workers in an area which had a high proportion of child-care problems. He suffered a nervous breakdown because of the stress and pressures of work and was off work for three months. Before his return to work his supervisor agreed that assistance would be provided to lessen the burden of the claimant's workload. In the event only very limited assistance was provided, and the claimant also had to deal with the backlog of work that had built up in his absence. Six months later he suffered a second breakdown as a result of which he had to stop work permanently. Colman J held that this breakdown was reasonably foreseeable and was caused by the employer's breach of their duty of care.

On the other hand, in *Barrett* v *Ministry of Defence* [1995] 1 WLR 1217 the Court of Appeal held that the Ministry of Defence was under no duty to take reasonable care to prevent a member of its forces from drinking himself to the point of unconsciousness at one of their duty-free bars. Students should be warned that although they are not employees of their university, a similar decision would certainly be reached regarding an undergraduate and Student Union bars.

See also Chapter 9, section 9.4 (*Stress at work*)

15.6 The economic welfare of employees

The cases which have been discussed thus far are all cases in which a duty had been imposed upon the employer to protect the employee's physical safety or well-being. But does the duty imposed upon employers extend to the economic welfare of the employee? That was the critical question considered by the Court of Appeal in *Reid v Rush & Tompkins Group plc* [1990] 1 WLR 212. The claimant was employed by the defendants and was sent by them to work in Ethiopia, where he suffered serious injury in an accident caused by the negligence of an unidentified driver. There was no equivalent to the Motor Insurers' Bureau in Ethiopia and so the claimant had no effective means of recovering compensation from the other driver. So he alleged that the defendants were negligent either in failing to take out insurance on his behalf or in failing to advise him of the need to take out such insurance. The Court of Appeal held that the defendant employers were not under a duty to take out insurance on his behalf, nor were they under a duty to advise him of the need to take out such insurance. Ralph Gibson LJ held that, while a duty may be imposed upon an employer to warn a prospective employee of the physical risks he would expose himself to if he accepted the job (*White* v *Holbrook Precision Castings Ltd* [1985] IRLR 215), the duty imposed upon employers 'has hitherto not been extended to the taking of reasonable care to protect the servant from economic loss' (see *Deyong* v *Shenburn* [1946] KB 227 and *Edwards* v *West Herts Group Hospital Management Committee* [1957] 1 WLR 415). Although such a duty does not arise out of the general relationship of employer and employee, it may arise on a particular set of facts (for example, it may arise from an express or implied term of the contract of employment or from a voluntary acceptance of responsibility (in the *Hedley Byrne* sense) by the employer for the employee's economic welfare).

15.7 Defences

The defence of volenti (see further Chapter 13) is applicable to employers' liability. In *Smith* v *Baker* [1891] AC 325 the House of Lords recognised the economic realities of the employment relationship in applying the doctrine of volenti to employment situations. It was held that the mere fact that the employee had continued to work in dangerous circumstances did not mean that he was volens because knowledge of the danger is not the same as consenting to the risk of danger. Unless it can be clearly shown that the employee voluntarily accepted the risk of injury the defence will not be applicable (see further Chapter 13, section 13.4).

The damages payable to the employee may fall to be reduced on the ground that the employee was guilty of contributory negligence. In the case of *Bux* v *Slough Metals Ltd* [1974] 1 All ER 262 the damages payable to the claimant employee fell to be reduced by 40 per cent on the ground that the employee was guilty of contributory negligence. However it should be noted that the courts tend to be more lenient in applying the doctrine of contributory negligence to cases concerning the liability of employers towards their employees (see further Chapter 12, section 12.6).

16

Product Liability

16.1 Introduction

16.2 Historical development

16.3 Defects in the common law

16.4 The Consumer Protection Act 1987

16.1 Introduction

The subject of liability in tort for dangerous or defective products has undergone considerable change as the law of tort has developed. This form of liability has now been transformed as a result of the enactment of the Consumer Protection Act 1987. The first part of this Act renders a producer strictly liable to a consumer when a defective product causes personal injury or damage to property of the consumer. Before analysing the provisions of this Act, it is necessary to give consideration to the development of the common law for two reasons. The first is that the Act has not repealed the common law rules and the second is that the deficiencies in the common law were a factor which influenced the pressure for reform of this particular area of law.

16.2 Historical development

Prior to *Donoghue v Stevenson* [1932] AC 562 the ambit of liability was extremely narrow due to the operation of what has become known as the 'contract fallacy' (see further Chapter 6, section 6.2). According to this fallacy there was no duty of care owed by a manufacturer to any person who was not a party to a contract with him and who was injured or otherwise suffered loss as a result of a defect in the manufacturer's goods. As we have noted (see Chapter 6, section 6.2) this contract fallacy was exploded by the decision of the House of Lords in *Donoghue v Stevenson* (above). In *Donoghue* Lord Atkin laid down the following statement of principle:

'A manufacturer of products, which he sells in such a form as to show that he intends them to reach the ultimate consumer in the form in which they left him with no reasonable possibility of intermediate examination, and with the knowledge that the

222

absence of reasonable care in the preparation or putting up of the products will result in an injury to the consumer's life or property, owes a duty to the consumer to take that reasonable care.'

Although this statement of principle constituted a major step forward in the development of the law, it is the subject of a number of restrictions. The first is that the statement, as originally explained by Lord Atkin, was only applicable to manufacturers. It has since, however, been extended to repairers (*Haseldine* v *Daw* [1941] 2 KB 343), erectors (*Brown* v *Cotterill* (1934) 51 TLR 21) and builders (*Sharpe* v *E T Sweeting & Sons Ltd* [1963] 1 WLR 665). This category of persons to whom the principle has been extended are characterised by the fact that they created the danger or were responsible for the creation of the danger. The difficulty which then arises is whether the principle should also be applied to the vendor of the defective goods. Here, of course, the situation is different because the vendor has not created the danger, he has simply sold the product to the consumer. Of course, such a vendor could be liable to the consumer in contract and the consumer would be able to claim the benefit of the protection afforded by the Sale of Goods Act 1979 where the subject matter of the contract between the parties was goods. But can the supplier also be liable in tort? It seems that he may be liable in tort where he fails to inspect the goods and he is under a duty so to inspect the goods. Such a duty to examine the goods does not arise in every case, it only arises where the supplier could reasonably be expected to carry out such an examination. Winfield and Jolowicz (*Winfield and Jolowicz on Tort* (13th ed) p241) put the issue in the following way:

'A second-hand car dealer may be expected to discover a patent defect in the steering mechanism of one of his cars ... but a retail grocer, for example, cannot be expected to institute inspections to discover whether his tinned food is contaminated.'

So the obligation imposed upon suppliers does not arise in every case and, even where it does arise, it is not an onerous obligation and it can even be discharged by selling the goods 'as seen and with all its faults and without warranty' (see *Hurley* v *Dyke* [1979] RTR 265).

The second qualification in Lord Atkin's judgment is that it only applies to 'products'. However the principle, as interpreted, is not confined to items such as food and drink. It has been applied, for example, to tombstones (*Brown* v *Cotterill* (above)) and to cars (*Andrews* v *Hopkinson* [1957] 1 QB 229). Nor is it confined to consumers in the strict sense; it applies to the ultimate user of the product as well as to persons within close proximity of the product.

The third qualification is that the manufacturer must intend the goods to reach the consumer in the form in which they left him. This is not to say that they must be in exactly the same form. For example in *Grant* v *Australian Knitting Mills Ltd* [1936] AC 85 the defendants were held to be liable to the claimant, who contracted dermatitis as a result of wearing underwear which had been manufactured by the defendants and which contained an excess of sulphite. The defendants argued that they were not liable to the claimant because the underwear left their factory in packs of six and only two had been sold to the claimant, so somebody could have tampered with them when they were in the shop being unpacked. This argument was rejected by the Privy Council who held that the mere possibility of someone else tampering with the goods was insufficient to discharge the liability of the defendants. But the Privy Council did concede that, where there was the possibility of someone else tampering with the goods, the difficulties of proof may be greater for the claimant because the claimant must provide sufficient evidence that the defect existed when the product left the possession of the defendants (see *Evans* v *Triplex Safety Glass Co Ltd* [1936] 1 All ER 283).

The fourth qualification is that Lord Atkin's original statement of principle was confined to the case where there was 'no real possibility of intermediate examination' by the consumer. So where the claimant is actually aware of the defect the principle does not apply. In *Kubach* v *Hollands* [1937] 3 All ER 907 some manufacturers sold a chemical to the second defendants, with an express warning that the chemical had to be tested before use. The second defendants then mistakenly sold the chemical to a school teacher but did not supply the warning relating to the need to test before use. The claimant, a schoolgirl, was injured when the chemical exploded in an experiment. The claimant was unsuccessful in her attempt to recover damages from the school (the first defendants), but she did succeed against the second defendants. The second defendants then sought to claim an indemnity from the manufacturers. It was held that they were not entitled to such an indemnity because they had been given adequate warning by the manufacturers of the danger and had chosen to ignore it.

It is not, however, the case that the mere fact that there was a possibility of intermediate examination is sufficient, of itself, to exonerate the defendant (see, for example, *Griffiths* v *Arch Engineering Co* [1968] 3 All ER 217). In *Andrews* v *Hopkinson* (above) the claimant bought a car on hire purchase from the defendant. The car was second-hand and the defendant had taken no steps to ensure that the car was roadworthy, although the car had been in his possession for a week. The car had a defective steering mechanism and, as a result, the claimant was involved in an accident shortly after he took possession of the car. It was held that this was the type of defect of which the claimant should have been warned by the defendant and that it was not the type of defect which the claimant was expected to discover upon a reasonable examination of the car. So the defendant was held to be liable to the claimant.

The fifth qualification contained in Lord Atkin's statement of principle relates to the nature of the loss recoverable. It is clear from his judgment that damages are recoverable in respect of 'injury to the consumer's life or property'. But caution must be exercised in relation to the recovery of damages in respect of property damage. It is submitted that what Lord Atkin had in mind was not a claim in tort on the ground that the goods which the consumer had bought were less valuable than he had anticipated, but a claim in tort on the ground that the goods had damaged other property of the consumer (see the judgment of Lloyd LJ in *Aswan Engineering Establishment Co* v *Lupdine Ltd* [1987] 1 All ER 135, discussed at Chapter 7, section 7.7). Where the claimant's claim is that the defect in the product has simply rendered the goods less valuable then, subject to the principle laid down in *Junior Books Ltd* v *The Veitchi Co Ltd* [1983] 1 AC 520 (see further Chapter 7, section 7.7), his claim lies in contract and not in tort.

The sixth and final qualification in the judgment of Lord Atkin relates to the nature of the defendant's obligation. It is simply an obligation to take reasonable care and the burden is on the claimant to show that the defendant has failed to exercise reasonable care. This can be done by showing that the product was defective and that, on the balance of probabilities, that defect arose during the course of the manufacturing process. In *Mason* v *Williams & Williams Ltd* [1955] 1 WLR 549 the claimant was injured when using a cold chisel which had been manufactured by the defendants. The chisel was too cold for the purpose for which it was intended and it was held that the claimant had established that the defendants were negligent by demonstrating that nothing could have happened to the chisel after it left the defendants' possession which could have caused the excessive hardness of the chisel.

16.3 Defects in the common law

Although Lord Atkin's statement of principle, as subsequently developed, was an improvement on the state of the law pre-1932, it did suffer from certain defects. The first defect was the difficulty which could be experienced in showing that the defect occurred during the manufacturing process. This can be demonstrated by reference to the case of *Evans* v *Triplex Safety Glass Co Ltd* (above). The claimant purchased a new Ford car which was fitted with a 'Triplex Toughened' windscreen. A year after the car was purchased the windscreen suddenly shattered for no apparent reason and injured the occupants of the car. It was held that the defendants were not liable to the claimant for the injuries which he and his family had received because the claimant could not show that the defect existed in the windscreen at the time at which it left the defendants' possession. The defect could have arisen when the windscreen was screwed in place on the assembly line or have been due to some event which occurred during the year in which the claimant used the car.

The second difficulty arises where the damage was purely economic in the sense that the claimant's complaint was that the product was simply less valuable than he had anticipated. It has been argued that such a claim properly lies in contract and not in tort and that, while in many cases the Sale of Goods legislation will provide the claimant with adequate protection, there may be cases where the claimant cannot rely upon the Sale of Goods legislation, for example, because he was given the goods as a gift (see also *Daniels* v *R White & Sons Ltd* [1938] 4 All ER 258; cf *Hill* v *James Crowe (Cases) Ltd* [1978] 1 All ER 812).

The third difficulty is the problem which we have noted of establishing a claim in tort against the suppliers of the goods, although once again, in the majority of cases, the claimant will have available to him a contractual action in respect of the losses which he has suffered.

The final difficulty concerns the practical problem of showing that the manufacturer was at fault. The manufacturer may be able to show that it was not financially reasonable to take the safety precautions advocated by the claimant or be able to show that the state of knowledge at the time of the alleged negligence was not sufficient to enable the manufacturer to avoid injury to the claimant.

These defects led to strong arguments for reform. Advocates of reform included the Pearson Commission (Cmnd 7594) and the Law Commisson (No 82 Liability for Defective Products (1977)). Finally the European Economic Community produced a Directive on product liability (Directive 85/374/EEC) which gave member states three years from 25 July 1985 to introduce national laws which complied with the terms of the Directive. It was this Directive which was one of the main influences behind the Consumer Protection Act 1987 and the Act is intended to bring English law into line with the provisions of the Directive (for consideration of some of these proposals for reform, see Stapleton (1986) 6 OJLS 392): for an example of their application, see *A* v *National Blood Authority* [2001] 3 All ER 289 (producers liable for supplying blood infected with Hepatitis C virus)).

16.4 The Consumer Protection Act 1987

Here we shall simply outline the main provisions of the Act, as a detailed analysis is beyond the scope of this book (for further details see R Merkin *A Guide to the Consumer Protection Act 1987*). The general principle is contained in s2(1) of the Act which provides that:

> 'Where any damage is caused wholly or partly by a defect in a product, every person to whom subsection (2) ... applies shall be liable for the damage.'

This statement of principle can be broken down into a number of separate elements. The first element relates to the persons to whom s2(2) applies. These persons are the producer of the product, any person who holds himself out as being a producer of the product, the importer of the goods into the EEC and, in more limited circumstances, the supplier of the product. The 'producer' of the product is defined in s1(2) as the person who manufactured the product, where the substance is 'won or abstracted' the person who won or abstracted it, or, in the case of a product which has been neither manufactured nor won or abstracted 'but essential characteristics of which are attributable to an industrial or other process having been carried out ... the person who carried out that process'. Where a defective product, such as a defective tyre, is contained in a car, it appears that both the manufacturer of the car and the manufacturer of the tyre may be liable (s1(3)). A person holds himself out as being the producer of the product where he puts his name on the product or uses a trade mark or 'other distinguishing mark in relation to the product' (s2(2)(b)). This definition would catch a supermarket chain which had its own logo upon a product and which held itself out as being the manufacturer of the product. The supplier is only liable where the person who suffered the damage requests the supplier (within a reasonable time of the damage and when it is not practicable for him to identify the producer, the person who has acted as the producer or the importer of the goods into the EEC) to identify one of those persons who may be liable and the supplier fails to comply with the request or to identify the persons who supplied the products to him (s2(3)). Thus the liability of the supplier is a secondary liability which may be discharged by him identifying his producer and it is only where he fails to do this that he will be liable. It should be noted that the supplier can discharge his liability by identifying his supplier, even if that supplier is bankrupt or otherwise unable to satisfy judgment. The liability of these persons is joint and several (s2(5)).

The second element which should be noted is that the principle contained in s2(1) only applies to a 'product'. 'Product' is defined in s1(2) as:

> ' … any goods or electricity and (subject to subsection (3)) includes a product which is comprised in another product, whether by virtue of being a component part or raw material or otherwise.'

Goods is further defined in s45(1) as including:

> ' … substances, growing crops and things comprised in land by virtue of being attached to it and any ship, aircraft or vehicle.'

A number of difficulties are likely to arise in the interpretation of the word 'product', particularly in the context of intellectual products, such as books and computer programmes, where it remains wholly unclear whether such products are caught by the Act (see further Whittaker 'European Product Liability and Intellectual Products' (1989) 105 LQR 125). Although buildings are not expressly excluded from the scope of the Act, it is provided in s46(4) of the Act that references to supplying goods shall not include references to supplying goods comprised in land where the supply is effected by the creation or disposal of an interest in the land. So where the builder sells the building that sale lies outside of the scope of the 1987 Act, although it may be caught under the Defective Premises Act 1972 (see further Chapter 17, section 17.19).

The third point to note about the statement of principle is that the product must suffer from a defect. It should be noted that there are broadly two approaches which could be adopted to the issue of 'defectiveness' (see Clark 'The Conceptual Basis of Product Liability' (1985) 48 MLR 325). On one view it could be said that a product is defective when it does not live up to the expectations of consumers ('the contract standard'). On the other hand, a product could be said to be defective when the product is unreasonably dangerous to people or to their property ('the tort standard').. The 1987 Act adopts the tort standard rather than the contract standard because s3(1) states that a defect is contained in the product where:

'... the *safety* of the product is not such as persons generally are entitled to expect.'

The Act does not require that the product be absolutely safe; it suffices that the product is reasonably safe. The Act does not contain an exhaustive definition of 'safety', but it does provide a list of factors to be taken into account in considering what is meant by 'safety'. The Act provides in s3(2) that 'all the circumstances shall be taken into account' including:

1. the manner in which, and purposes for which, the product has been marketed, its get-up, the use of any mark in relation to the product and any instructions for, or warnings with respect to, doing or refraining from doing anything with or in relation to the product;
2. what might reasonably be expected to be done with or in relation to the product; and
3. the time which the product was supplied by its producer to another.

These then are the specific factors to which the courts are directed to have regard, but they are not the only factors to which the courts can have regard. It is not yet clear whether the courts will have regard to the cost of making the product safe or the cost of the product itself.

In *Abouzaid* v *Mothercare (UK) Ltd* (2001) The Times 20 February the Court of Appeal heard that the claimant had sustained an injury to his eye as a result of the recoil of an elasticated strap attached to one of the defendant's products. His claim under the 1987 Act turned on whether there was in the product a defect as defined in s3 and art 6 of the EEC Directive. It had been established that the defectiveness of the product was to be determined by reference, not to its fitness for use, but to the lack of the safety to which the public at large were entitled to expect: see *Commission* v *United Kingdom (Re Product Liability Directive)* Case C–300/95 [1997] 3 CMLR 923. Although the case was close to the borderline, their Lordships concluded that the product was defective within the meaning of the 1987 Act.

The Act also contains some defences in relation to products which would otherwise be held to be defective. These defences are extremely important in setting the limits of the ambit of liability. These defences are contained in s4 of the Act. It should be noted that in all cases the burden of proof is on the defendant to establish the defence. The defences include a defence that the defect was attributable to 'compliance with any requirement imposed by or under any enactment or with any Community obligation' and that the defect did not exist in the product at the 'relevant time' (defined in s4(2)(a)). The most important and controversial defence is, however, the development risks defence which is contained in s4(1)(e) in the following terms:

'... that the state of scientific and technical knowledge at the relevant time was not such that a producer of products of the same description as the product in question might be expected to have discovered the defect if it had existed in his products while they were under his control.'

This version of the 'development risks' defence differs in significant respects from the wording of art 7 of the EEC Directive which states that a producer shall not be liable if he proves:

' ... that the state of scientific and technical knowledge at the time when he put the product into circulation was not such as to enable the existence of the defect to be discovered.'

The vital difference between the Act and the Directive concerns the scope of the inquiry relating to knowledge. Under the Act the inquiry is limited to producers of 'products of the same description as the product in question' but no such limitation is contained within the Directive. See also *Abouzaid* v *Mothercare (UK) Ltd*, above, where the defendant sought to rely on the absence in the Department of Trade and Industry's database of any record of a comparable accident at the time of supply, as constituting scientific and technical knowledge which was not available in 1990, the year of the claimant's injury. Pill LJ was very doubtful whether a record of accidents came within the category of scientific and technical knowledge and, as has been seen, the claimant won his case.

The inclusion of the 'development risks' defence in both the Directive and the Act has been the subject of considerable criticism. The Directive in fact gave to member states the option whether or not to include the defence within the implementing legislation and the British government elected to incorporate it into the Act. The defence is likely to assume great significance in cases involving drug manufacturers where the manufacturers will, in many cases, argue that the state of scientific knowledge did not enable them to discover that the drug had the particular side effect which has caused the damage which the claimant has suffered (for an excellent analysis of the development risks defence see Newdick 'The Development Risks Defence of the Consumer Protection Act 1987' [1988] CLJ 455). The effect of this defence may well be to bring the law back to a standard which approximates more closely to liability for negligence than to strict liability. This is because this defence, as contained in the 1987 Act, appears to make a defendant manufacturer liable only where other producers of products of the same description had the relevant knowledge but the defendant did not; an inquiry very similar to the one which would be carried out in a negligence action. The only difference is that s4 makes it clear that the burden is upon the defendant to establish the defence, whereas at common law the burden rests on the claimant throughout.

The fourth point to note is that the factor of causation plays a crucial role in determining the ambit of liability. The claimant must show that the damage was caused wholly or partly by the defect in the product. There is no requirement that the loss be a foreseeable one; simply that it was caused by the defect in the product. Nor need the defect be the sole cause of the damage to the claimant. It is sufficient that it was partly responsible for the damage which occurred.

The fifth point to note is that the Act only applies to certain types of losses which are suffered by the claimant. Damage is defined in s5(1) as meaning 'death or personal injury or any loss of or damage to any property (including land)'. Damage to business property is outside the scope of the Act. A claim may only be made under the Act where, at the time of the damage, the property was 'of a description of property ordinarily intended for private use, occupation or consumption' and it was 'intended by the person suffering the loss or damage mainly for his own private use, occupation or consumption' (s5(3)). There is, however, a crucial limitation in s5(2) which provides that a defendant shall not be liable in respect of 'the loss of or damage to the product itself or for the loss of or any damage to the whole or any part of the product which has been supplied with the product in question comprised in it'. So, as at common law, the claimant can recover in respect of damage to other property of his, but not in respect of the defective product itself. There is also a minimum amount of damages which must be payable before the Act can apply. Section 5(4) provides that damages shall not be awarded under the Act in respect of damage to property where the amount which would be awarded, apart from interest, could not exceed £275. The aim of this requirement is clearly to exclude the possibility of the courts and insurers being flooded with masses of small claims. There is no ceiling on the limit of liability imposed in the Act. Finally it is provided in s7 of the Act that liability under s2(1) of the Act 'shall not be limited or excluded by any contract term, by any notice or by any provision'.

The Act constitutes a significant improvement upon the common law and is a real improvement for consumers. In this respect the Act is to be welcomed. However it is by no means the case that the Act has removed all the problems which existed at common law. The Act does not remove the difficulty of recovering in respect of the defect in the product itself. The defence that the defect did not exist in the product at the relevant time may also leave the consumer with considerable problems of proof, but, as compared with the common law, these problems may be alleviated by the fact that the burden is on the defendant to prove the defence rather than the burden being upon the claimant. Finally the inclusion of the state of the art defence may undermine, to a considerable degree, the claim of the Act to have introduced a regime of strict liability which is applicable to defective products. While it must be remembered that an increase in the extent of liability brings with it increased costs, in the form of higher insurance premiums, the cost of which is passed on to the public, the inclusion of this defence in the Act may prove a significant flaw in the legislation and it is likely to lead, at some time in the future, to still further calls for reform of the law relating to product liability.

An element of consumer protection is also provided by the General Product Safety Regulations 1994 (SI 1994/2328) which came into force on 3 October 1994. These regulations are similar in nature to the Consumer Protection Act 1987 but provide only criminal penalties for their breach.

17

Occupiers' Liability

17.1 Introduction

In many ways this area of law is but a specialised aspect of common law negligence. The vital difference, however, is that it is governed by statute, namely the Occupiers' Liability Acts of 1957 and 1984, rather than by purely common law principles. This calls for a different approach in analysing problems concerned with occupiers' liability because very close attention must be paid to the *exact words* used by Parliament as these are the words which set the limits to the ambit of liability.

Before embarking upon an analysis of these Acts it is necessary to make a few points about the pre-1957 law. The common law distinguished between different categories of entrant who came on to the land and held that occupiers owed a different duty to each category. The highest standard of care was owed to a contractor because here the occupier's freedom to use his land as he saw fit had to be balanced against the contractual rights of the contractor. Invitees, who were people invited on to the occupiers' land because they had some mutual interest of a business, or other material nature, with the occupier, were owed the next highest standard of care. The next category of visitors was licensees, who were persons who had permission to enter on to the land for some purpose of their own. They were owed a still lesser standard of care. The last category was trespassers, who were those persons who came on to the land without the consent of the occupier. They were owed the lowest standard of care of all.

Considerable criticism was directed against this classification, especially the narrowness of the distinction between the second and third categories. Criticism was also levelled against the idea that the occupier should be as free as possible in the use of his land and it was argued that greater weight should be given to the interests of those who come on to the land. It was in these circumstances that, in 1957, the Law Reform Committee reported on the urgent need to reform the law and it was their report which formed the basis of the 1957 Act.

The following discussion will concentrate upon the Occupiers' Liability Act 1957 ('the 1957 Act'), and the Occupiers' Liability Act 1984 ('the 1984 Act') will be discussed primarily in section 17.15. Relevant provisions of both statutes have been amended by s13 of the Countryside and Rights of Way Act 2000, as from a day to be appointed.

17.2 The scope of the 1957 Act

Before the enactment of the 1957 Act, a distinction was drawn between damage arising as a result of an activity carried out on the premises (the 'activity duty') and damage occurring due to the state of the premises (the 'occupancy duty'); the former being governed by *Donoghue* v *Stevenson* principles, while the latter was governed by a separate line of authority solely applicable to occupiers' liability. It is unclear whether this distinction has survived the Act. Section 1(1) of the Act states that the Act shall apply 'in respect of dangers due to the state of the premises *or to things done or omitted to be done on them*'. The latter part of the subsection clearly envisages that the Act shall apply to the 'activity duty'. But in s1(2) it is provided that the Act shall 'regulate the nature of the duty imposed by law in consequence of a person's occupation or control of premises'. This subsection does not appear to encompass the 'activity duty'. There is no authoritative decision on the point, but the weight of academic opinion is that the Act only applies to the 'occupancy duty' (see *Winfield and Jolowicz on Tort* (14th ed) p226). In *Ogwo* v *Taylor* [1987] 2 WLR 988 Stephen Brown LJ stated that he did not think that injury suffered by the claimant fireman while fighting a fire on the defendant's premises, which was started by the defendant's negligence, was 'strictly a case for consideration in the context of the Occupiers' Liability Act' because the injury did not result from a defect in the premises. Neither of the other judges commented on this issue and Stephen Brown LJ's dicta was strictly obiter, but it is submitted that, as it is consistent with the majority of academic opinion, it should be taken to represent the law. However, in practice, the issue is not of great importance because there is little, if any, difference between the standard of care owed at common law and the standard of care owed under the 1957 Act.

17.3 Who is an occupier?

Section 1(2) of the Act states that the definition of 'occupier' remains the same as at common law, so it is necessary to go back and consider common law authorities. The original test for identifying an occupier focused on the fact of control over the premises, in the sense of having the power to control entry to the premises (*Cavalier* v *Pope* [1906] AC 428). But the test was rejected by the House of Lords in *Wheat* v *E Lacon and Co Ltd* [1966] AC 522.

In *Wheat* the defendants owned a public house, which was managed by one of their employees, Richardson. Richardson and his wife occupied the first floor of the public house as their private dwelling, but they did not have any interest in the premises. Indeed, under an agreement with the defendants, it was provided that there was not even a tenancy agreement between the parties. Richardson's wife was given permission to take in paying guests in a part of the first floor which they occupied. There was no direct access from the first floor to the public house, but there was an outside staircase which went to the rear of the premises. The handrail of this staircase terminated directly above the third step and the staircase was not lit because someone had stolen the bulb. The claimant and her husband were paying guests of the Richardsons. One night the claimant's husband fell down the stairs and fractured his skull. He died from his injuries. It was held that both the Richardsons and the defendants were occupiers of the staircase, but that the defendants were not in breach of their duty of care because the staircase was normally safe and they were not responsible for the act of a stranger in removing the bulb.

The most influential judgment was given by Lord Denning. He said that:

'Wherever a person has a sufficient degree of control over premises that he ought to realise that any failure on his part to use care may result in injury to a person coming lawfully there, then he is an "occupier" and the person coming lawfully there is his "visitor".'

Lord Denning then divided the law up into four categories, which form a useful basis for analysis. These categories were as follows:

1. Where a landlord lets premises by demise the landlord is regarded as having parted with all control over the premises so that the tenant is the occupier.
2. Where a landlord lets part of a building but retains other parts, such as the common staircase, then the landlord remains liable as an occupier for the parts of the building which he has retained (for an example of this see *Miller* v *Hancock* [1893] 2 QB 177).
3. Where a landowner licenses a person to occupy his premises on terms which do not amount to a demise and the owner still has the right to enter on to the premises to do repairs then the owner remains sufficiently in control to be an occupier (see *Wheat* itself).
4. Where an occupier employs independent contractors to do some work on his premises, the owner is generally still sufficiently in control to be an occupier. The difficulty really lies in determining whether or not the independent contractors are also occupiers. It should be noted that there is no requirement that control be exclusive, so that there can be more than one occupier at the same time, as in *Wheat*. Independent contractors were held to be occupiers in *AMF International Ltd* v *Magnet Bowling Ltd* [1968] 1 WLR 1028. The claimants' timber was damaged by rainwater while it was on the first defendants' premises. The rainwater got in through an unfinished doorway. The claimants only brought the timber on to the land, after the first defendants and the second defendants, who were a firm of independent contractors, had confirmed that the property was ready for installation of the timber. It was held that both defendants were sufficiently in control to be occupiers (see too *Collier* v *Anglian Water Authority* (1983) The Times 26 March).

This four-tier approach is useful but it is not exhaustive, as was confirmed by the Court of Appeal in *Harris* v *Birkenhead Corporation* [1976] 1 WLR 279. The first defendants, in pursuance of a slum clearance policy, issued a compulsory purchase order over a house owned by the second defendant. They then issued her with a notice of entry under the Housing Acts, which entitled them to take over the premises after 14 days. The house was not, however, vacated for another several months. After the house was vacated the first defendants took no steps to have the house boarded up, even though they knew that failure to do so was likely to lead to vandalism. The claimant, a child of four and a half, wandered into the house through an unsecured door and suffered serious injuries when he fell from a second floor window. Megaw LJ analysed the four-fold classification of Lord Denning and concluded that actual physical possession was not a necessary ingredient of control. In this case the fact that the first defendants had, by virtue of their having served a notice of entry, the legal right to control the premises made them the occupiers to the exclusion of the second defendant, even though the first defendants had not, actually or symbolically, taken possession of the premises. In all cases the question of sufficiency of control is one of fact.

17.4 Visitors

The duty owed by an occupier under the 1957 Act is owed to those who are his 'visitors'. Once again resort must be had to the common law because s1(2) states that a lawful visitor is, for the purposes of the Act, either an invitee or a licensee. It should be noted that the Act only applies to persons who come on to the occupier's premises; it has no application to someone who remains outside the premises. In considering who is a visitor it is helpful to divide the issue up into the following categories.

Express permission

This is the easiest category of all and simply depends on proof that the occupier did, in fact, give permission.

Implied permission

The onus of proving the existence of implied permission rests on the person who alleges that it exists. Many of the cases under this category concern policemen seeking entry to a private dwelling house. One such case is *Robson* v *Hallett* [1967] 2 QB 393. There it was laid down that a person who enters upon the premises of the occupier for the purpose of communicating with the occupier is treated as having the occupier's implied permission to be there until the visitor knows or ought to know that his permission has been revoked. Once his permission has been revoked he has a reasonable time to leave the premises before becoming a trespasser.

Another problem which has troubled the courts has arisen where the occupier knows that persons are in the habit of coming on to his land. Does this knowledge, of itself, operate to convert that other person into his visitor? In *Lowery* v *Walker* [1911] AC 10 the public had been in the habit of taking a short cut across the defendant farmer's land for some 35 years. The defendant had never taken legal proceedings to stop them, however, because many of them were his customers. One day he put a wild horse into the field. The claimant, who was taking a short cut, was injured by the horse. It was held that the claimant was not a trespasser but, by virtue of the long use of the short cut to the knowledge of the defendant, was a licensee. Care must be used in relying upon this case as it was decided at a time when the courts were very willing to classify claimants as licensees because the duty which was owed by an occupier to a trespasser was so minimal (see section 17.15). Now that trespassers are covered by the 1984 Act there is no longer the same need to adopt such a benevolent approach.

The issue was, however, reconsidered by the House of Lords in *Edwards* v *Railway Executive* [1952] AC 737. The claimant, a nine-year-old boy, was seriously injured by a train after he had fallen on the railway line. He had got on to the railway line by climbing through the boundary fence in order to retrieve his ball which had gone on to the railway line. The defendants knew that the boundary fence was frequently broken by children who then made their way on to the railway line, but they repaired the fence whenever they discovered that it had been broken. The claimant argued that this step was not sufficient to keep children out and so the claimant was not a trespasser but was a licensee. The House of Lords unanimously rejected this argument. Lord Goddard stated that some of the earlier cases appeared to be decided out of sympathy for the claimant rather than upon sound legal principle. He affirmed that repeated trespass does not, of itself, turn a person into a licensee. There must be evidence of the landowner's express consent or conduct on his part which is such that he cannot be heard to say that he did not give permission. *Lowery* was distinguished on the ground that the defendant was not entitled to let loose a horse which he knew to be dangerous without giving any warning whatsoever. So while knowledge of a person's presence is not sufficient, of itself, to give that person a licence to be present, an occupier who is aware that people are in the habit of coming on to his land should take positive and regular steps to ensure that these people know that they are not welcome.

Public and private rights of way

In *Holden* v *White* [1982] 2 WLR 1030 it was held that persons lawfully exercising a private right of way were not 'visitors' for the purposes of the 1957 Act. Oliver LJ noted that the purpose behind the 1957 Act was to remove the old common law categorisations, but he said that the purpose behind the Act was not to extend the category of persons to whom a duty was owed. As a person lawfully exercising a right of way was not an invitee or licensee at common law he could not be covered by the 1957 Act. This decision has now been reversed by s1(1)(a) of the Occupiers' Liability Act 1984 and such people are now owed a duty of care under that Act but it must be stressed that the duty owed under the 1984 Act is different from the duty owed under the 1957 Act (see section 17.15 below). One problem remains here and it concerns who the occupier is. In the Law Commission Report *Liability for Damage or Injury to Trespassers and Related Questions of Occupiers' Liability* (paras 42–56) it was assumed that it would be the occupier of the servient land and this point was conceded by counsel in *Holden*. But Oliver LJ doubted whether this concession was correct and thought that it was the occupier of the dominant land who was the occupier. So the position is unclear at the moment.

In *Greenhalgh* v *British Railways Board* [1969] 2 QB 286 the Court of Appeal held that persons lawfully exercising a public right of way were not visitors for the purposes of the 1957 Act. Section 1(7) of the 1984 Act states that they are not covered by that Act either. So they are only protected by the common law which states that the occupier is liable for negligent misfeasance but not for negligent nonfeasance. In other words the occupier is not liable for a failure to repair the right of way. This rule was recently upheld by the House of Lords in *McGeown* v *Northern Ireland Housing Executive* [1994] 3 All ER 53, which again held that a person using a public right of way was neither a licensee nor invitee and so was not a visitor within the Occupiers' Liability Act (Northern Ireland) 1957 which is in its material aspects identical to the Occupiers' Liability Act 1957.

By virtue of s13(1) Countryside and Rights of Way Act 2000, which came into force on 19 September 2004 and substituted s1(4) Occupiers' Liability Act 1957, a person entering any premises in exercise of rights conferred by s2(1) Countryside and Rights of Way Act 2000 (access for purposes of open-air recreation) or an access agreement or order under the National Parks and Access to the Countryside Act 1949 is not, for the purposes of the 1957 Act, a visitor of the occupier of the premises. Such a person will become a trespasser on the land if he breaks or damages any wall, fence, hedge, stile or gate or fails to comply with the general restrictions in Sch 2 to the Act of 2000: ibid, s2(4).

Lawful authority

Section 2(6) of the 1957 Act expressly provides that persons who enter premises for any purpose in the exercise of a right conferred by law are to be treated as having permission by the occupier to be there for that purpose, whether they in fact have permission or not.

Limitations on permission

The occupier may give the visitor permission to enter the premises, but may elect to limit that permission in one of three ways.

The first limitation relates to space. An occupier may give a visitor permission to enter some parts of his premises but not others. In *The Calgarth* [1927] P 93 Scrutton LJ said that 'when you invite a person into your house to use the stairs, you do not invite him to slide down the bannisters'. In *Gould* v *McAuliffe* [1941] 2 All ER 527 the claimant got lost looking for the outside lavatory in a public house. She went through an open gate and was attacked by a dog. The defendants argued that the claimant was a trespasser. This was rejected by the court on the ground that the gate was not locked, there was no notice that the yard was private or that a dangerous dog was there. So, if an occupier wishes to place limitations upon the visitor, then he must take steps to bring the limitation to the visitor's attention.

The second limitation relates to the purpose for which the visitor comes on to the land. This was considered in the criminal case of *R* v *Smith and Jones* [1976] 1 WLR 672. In this case a son broke into his father's house and stole a television set. At the son's trial the father said that the son would never be a trespasser in his house. It was held that, for the purposes of the Theft Act 1968, the son was a trespasser because he knew when he entered the house that he was entering in excess of the permission given to him or he was reckless whether his entry was in excess of that permission.

The third limitation relates to the time at which the visitor may come on to the premises. In *Stone* v *Taffe* [1974] 1 WLR 1575 the claimant's husband died when he fell down the stairs outside a public house after attending a party, held by the manager of the public house, which had continued after licensing hours. The widow sued the owners of the public house, who claimed that the deceased was a trespasser. Stephenson LJ held that an occupier who intends to permit a person to enter his premises for a limited period of time only must give that person a clear indication that his permission to be on the premises is subject to a time limit. On the facts the deceased had not been given any indication that his permission to be on the premises was subject to a time limit and so the deceased was not a trespasser. The deceased did not know that the manager of the public house was only entitled to hold a private party out of hours if prior permission had been given by the owners and the police had been notified.

Multiple occupiers

Where there is more than one occupier the possibility arises of a claimant being a visitor in relation to one occupier and a trespasser as regards the other occupier. Such a possibility was considered by the House of Lords in *Ferguson* v *Welsh* [1987] 3 All ER 777. The occupiers of the land were the defendant council. They had accepted a tender from an independent contractor, Spence (S), to demolish a building. It was a condition of the tender that the work was not to be subcontracted without the permission of the council. Notwithstanding this prohibition S subcontracted the work to Welsh Brothers (W) who in turn employed the claimant to demolish the building. The claimant was injured because of an unsafe system of work employed by W. The claimant brought an action against W, S and the council. The difficulty for the claimant was that W were men of straw and S was unlikely to have sufficient funds to meet the claimant's claim, which was for £150,000. So the claim against the council was of crucial significance to the claimant. The council conceded that both they and S were occupiers of the building. The House of Lords held that the council were not liable to the claimant (see sections 17.6 and 17.10). A preliminary point concerned whether or not the claimant was a visitor in relation to the defendant council. Lord Keith, with whom Lord Brandon and Lord Griffiths concurred, held that there was evidence capable of establishing that the claimant was a visitor vis-à-vis the council. Despite the terms of the contract between the council and S, the council had placed S in control of the building for the purpose of its demolition and therefore S had been clothed with ostensible authority to invite W and their employees on to the land. However Lord Goff could not see any difficulty in an appropriate case in holding that the claimant was a lawful visitor as against S but a trespasser as against the council. He said that the answer to the question whether or not the claimant was a visitor as against the council must depend on whether S, as an occupier, had authority from the council (whether that authority be actual (express or implied) or ostensible) to allow a third party on to the land of the council. On the fact he was prepared to assume for the purpose of the appeal that S did have ostensible authority.

17.5 Premises

The 1957 Act applies to an occupier of 'premises'. There is no exhaustive definition of premises in the Act. It obviously includes land, houses and buildings. Some guidance is afforded by s1(3)(a) which states that the Act shall regulate 'the obligations of a person occupying or having control over any fixed or moveable structure, including any vessel, vehicle or aircraft'. In *Wheeler* v *Copas* [1981] 3 All ER 405, the claimant, who was constructing a house on the defendant's land, borrowed a ladder from the defendant, without asking whether the ladder was suitable for his purpose. The ladder was not suitable for his purpose and he fell and was injured. It was held that the defendant was not liable to the claimant under s1(3)(a) because, although the Act might in appropriate circumstances apply to a ladder, it could not be said that in this case the defendant was still the occupier of the ladder once he handed it to the claimant. The defendant was, however, liable to the claimant in negligence.

17.6 The common duty of care

One of the major innovations of the 1957 Act was to enact a common duty of care which is owed to all visitors. Section 2(1) of the Act states that:

> 'An occupier of premises owes the same duty, the 'common duty of care', to all his visitors, except in so far as he is free to and does extend, restrict, modify or exclude his duty to any visitor or visitors by agreement or otherwise.'

This common duty of care is defined in s2(2) in the following terms:

> ' ... a duty to take such care as in all the circumstances of the case is reasonable to see that the visitor will be reasonably safe in using the premises for the purposes for which he is invited or permitted by the occupier to be there.'

A number of points may be made about this definition. The first is that the visitor must be reasonably safe 'in using the premises for the purposes for which he is invited or permitted by the occupier to be there'. In *Ferguson* v *Welsh* (above) Lord Goff held that claimant's action against the defendant council must fail because it could not be said that the claimant was not 'reasonably safe in using the premises for the purposes for which he was invited to be there'. Rather his injuries arose because of the 'manner in which he carried out his work on the premises' and such injuries were not caught by s2(2). However Lord Keith, with whom Lord Brandon and Lord Griffiths agreed, stated that the safety referred to in s2(2) was safety 'not only from dangers due to the state of the premises but also known dangers due to things done or permitted by the occupier to be done on them'. Thus he held that s2(2) was applicable, although he found that there had been no breach of the common duty of care (see section 17.10). The second is that it is the *visitor*, not the premises, which must be reasonably safe. The third is that the duty to take such care as is reasonable in the circumstances involves consideration of issues similar to those involved in a common law negligence action. This can be demonstrated by reference to the case of *Sawyer* v *H and G Simonds Ltd* (1966) 197 EG 877. The claimant was injured when he slipped at the bar of the defendants' hotel and hurt his hand on some broken glass on the floor. Veale J held that it was not proved that the defendants had failed to keep a reasonable look-out for broken glass and so the defendants had discharged the duty which they owed. The court considered the nature of the danger, the length of time that the danger was in existence, the steps necessary to remove the danger and the likelihood of injury resulting. These are the very factors which would be taken into account in a common law negligence action. As in all negligence actions, each case in which it is alleged that the defendant has breached his duty of care depends ultimately on the application of an established principle to the facts of the case. Thus *Sawyer* can be contrasted with the recent case of *Murphy* v *Bradford Metropolitan Council* [1992] PIQR 68. The claimant teacher fell on a path leading to a school run by the council and she suffered injury. The path was notoriously slippery but on the morning of the accident the school caretaker had cleared the path of snow at 6.30 am and treated it with rock salt and done so again at 8 am, on being told that the path was still slippery. Despite these efforts the claimant still slipped on the path half an hour later. The trial judge held that the defendants had not discharged their duty under s2(2) because the path was a likely place for an accident to occur and they had failed to lay grit and cinders on it. This finding was upheld by the Court of Appeal.

It should also be noted that an occupier may be in breach of his duty of care to a visitor as a result of his failure to control the activities of a third party on his land. This was the case in *Cunningham* v *Reading Football Club Ltd* (1991) The Independent 20 March. The claimants were police officers on duty at a league football match played at the defendants' football ground and were injured by missiles thrown by fans attending the match. The defendants had failed to maintain their ground with the result that it was possible to break off pieces of concrete from the structure of the ground and use the pieces of concrete as missiles. The defendants knew both that it was possible to break off lumps of concrete and that fans in the past had used them as missiles. It was held that the defendants were liable because they knew of the condition of their ground, they knew that it was 'very probable' that such missiles would be used (see *Home Office* v *Dorset Yacht* [1970] AC 1004, discussed at Chapter 11, section 11.7) and they had therefore failed to discharge the common duty of care owed to the claimants.

The fourth, and final, point to note about s2(2) is that, where there is more than one occupier of the premises at the one time, it may be that the standard of care required of each occupier is different.

But it must be noted that the Act differs from the common law in that specific provision is made in the Act for particular situations. These provisions will be considered in sections 17.7 to 17.10.

17.7 Children

Section 2(3)(a) of the 1957 Act provides that 'an occupier must be prepared for children to be less careful than adults'. This sentiment was echoed by Hamilton LJ in *Latham* v *R Johnson and Nephew Ltd* [1913] 1 KB 398, 415 when he said:

> 'In the case of an infant, there are moral as well as physical traps. There may accordingly be a duty towards infants not merely not to dig pitfalls for them, but not to lead them into temptation.'

There have been numerous cases reported involving an application of this principle. Two cases will be discussed here to illustrate its application. The first case is *Glasgow Corporation* v *Taylor* [1922] 1 AC 44. A child aged seven died after eating poisonous berries which he had picked off a bush in a public park. The berries resembled blackberries and were very tempting to the child. The bush was not fenced off in any way, nor was there any warning of the dangerous nature of the berries. It was held that the defendants were liable (see too *Moloney* v *Lambeth London Borough Council* (1968) 198 EG 895).

On the other hand in *Liddle* v *Yorks (North Riding) County Council* [1934] 2 KB 101 the defendants were not liable to the child claimant. Here the defendants left a heap of soil close to a wall so that it was possible to climb up the soil and on to the wall. The claimant, a boy aged seven who had previously been warned off by the defendants, climbed up the soil on to the wall and, in trying to show his little friends how bees flew, fell off the wall and was injured. It was held that the defendants were not liable because the danger of falling off the wall was obvious, even to the child claimant.

A particular problem which has emerged concerns particularly young children, as there is hardly anything which is not a danger to such children. The position was authoritatively considered by Devlin J in *Phipps* v *Rochester Corporation* [1955] 1 QB 450. Here a boy aged five fell into a trench and broke his leg. Children were in the habit of using this area as a play area and this fact was known to the defendants, but they took no steps to prevent the children from playing there. It was held that the defendants were not liable to the claimant. Devlin J held that, in cases involving children of 'tender years', account must be taken of the fact that: reasonable parents will not permit children to be sent into danger without protection; guardians of the child and the place of the accident must both act reasonably; and each is entitled to assume that the other will act reasonably.

In *Phipps* the five-year-old claimant was only accompanied by his seven-year-old sister and there was no evidence of any breach of duty by the defendants (see too *Simkiss* v *Rhondda Borough Council* (1983) 81 LGR 460 and *Jolley* v *Sutton London Borough Council* [2000] 3 All ER 409: see Chapter 11, section 11.4).

17.8 Common calling

Section 2(3)(b) provides that 'an occupier may expect that a person, in the exercise of his calling, will appreciate and guard against any special risks ordinarily incident to it, so far as the occupier leaves him free to do so'. This subsection was considered by the Court of Appeal in *Roles* v *Nathan* [1963] 1 WLR 1117. Here two chimney sweeps were killed by carbon monoxide fumes while sealing up a sweep-hole in the vertical chimney shaft of a furnace on the occupier's premises. Lord Denning thought that s2(3)(b) applied here because a householder can reasonably expect a sweep to take care of himself in respect of dangers arising out of the flue. Harman LJ doubted whether s2(3)(b) applied on the facts of the case because it was the occupier who created the danger by lighting the furnace when he had been told not to. Pearson LJ thought that s2(3)(b) was inapplicable because this was not a risk which was 'ordinarily incident' to the sweeps' calling, as was shown by the repeated warnings which the sweeps received.

The fact that the visitor is possessed of a particular skill is not sufficient, of itself, to discharge the duty of care owed to the visitor. Thus, in *Salmon* v *Seafarer Restaurants Ltd* [1983] 3 All ER 729 it was held that an occupier owes the same duty of care to a fireman as to any other visitor and the argument that the duty was limited to protecting the fireman from special risks not associated with normal fires was rejected. *Salmon* was approved by the House of Lords in *Ogwo* v *Taylor* [1988] AC 431. The House of Lords dismissed the argument that a duty of care was owed only in relation to exceptional risks which were greater than the 'ordinary' risks inherent in fire-fighting. In all cases they held that the appropriate question was whether the injury to the fireman was reasonably foreseeable. The person who starts a fire negligently is, however, entitled to expect that the fireman will act in accordance with standard practice in fighting the fire and not expose himself to 'unnecessary' risks in a 'foolhardy' manner.

This phrase 'ordinarily incident' was important in the case of *Bird* v *King Line* [1970] 1 Lloyd's Rep 349. Here a foreman scaler, who tripped over an empty bottle lying on the deck of a ship, was held to be entitled to recover from the defendants because the risk of tripping over an empty bottle was not 'ordinarily incident' to the work of a foreman scaler (see too *Woollins* v *British Celanese Ltd* (1966) 110 SJ 686).

17.9 Warning of danger

It is provided in s2(4)(a) that, in determining whether an occupier has discharged his duty of care, regard is to be had to all the circumstances so that, for example:

> 'Where damage is caused to a visitor by a danger of which he has been warned by the occupier, the warning is not to be treated without more as absolving the occupier from liability, unless in all the circumstances it was enough to enable the visitor to be reasonably safe.'

This subsection was considered by the Court of Appeal in *Roles* v *Nathan* (above). In this case the sweeps were given a warning of the danger of fumes by a heating engineer. The sweeps were repeatedly told not to stay in the flue for too long and that the boiler was not to be turned on until the sweep-hole was sealed. Lord Denning said that this was a clear case for the application of s2(4)(a) as the warnings given were sufficient to enable the sweeps to be reasonably safe and that what happened was entirely the sweeps' own fault. Harman LJ agreed with Lord Denning on this point, but Pearson LJ dissented on the ground that it was the occupier's agents themselves who, in disregard of the warning, did the dangerous act of lighting the fire before the access had been sealed and so the warning did not enable the sweeps to be reasonably safe.

It should be noted that, for the purposes of s2(4)(a), the warning must be given by the occupier. This was satisfied in *Roles* because the heating agent who gave the warning was treated as the agent of the occupier.

If a warning is given then it should be given in clear terms because an inadequate warning may lead to the imposition of liability. This is because the fact that the occupier has gone to the trouble of putting up a warning notice suggests that he is aware of the existence of the danger and his failure to take sufficient steps to bring the danger to the attention of the visitor is a breach of duty on his part (see *Woollins* v *British Celanese Ltd* (above)). It should also be noted that s2(4)(a) states that a warning shall not, without more, absolve the occupier from liability. This suggests that a warning may, in combination with some other factor such as a handrail, be sufficient to discharge the duty upon the occupier.

However, there is no need for an occupier to warn a visitor of an obvious danger. Thus in *Staples* v *West Dorset District Council* (1995) The Times 28 April the Court of Appeal held that there was no need to warn a visitor of the obvious danger of visible algae on a stone surface.

17.10 Independent contractors

It is provided in s2(4)(b) that:

> 'Where damage is caused to a visitor by a danger due to the faulty execution of any work of construction, maintenance or repair by an independent contractor employed by the occupier, the occupier is not to be treated without more as answerable for the danger if in all the circumstances he had acted reasonably in entrusting the work to an independent contractor and had taken such steps (if any) as he reasonably ought in order to satisfy himself that the contractor was competent and that the work had been properly done.'

This subsection was introduced to reverse the decision of the House of Lords in *Thomson* v *Cremin* [1956] 1 WLR 103 that an occupier owes a personal non-delegable duty to his invitees to take reasonable care and that he cannot discharge this duty by entrusting the work to independent contractors.

A number of points may be made about this subsection. The first is that it only applies to the 'faulty execution of any work of construction, maintenance or repair'. This phrase was interpreted liberally by Mocatta J in *AMF International Ltd* v *Magnet Bowling Ltd* [1968] 1 WLR 1028. There it was argued that the independent contractors had simply failed to prevent the flooding arising and that no faulty work had been done. However, Mocatta J managed to find that some very minor work had been done and this was sufficient to make the subsection applicable. He went on to say that, if a builder failed to take adequate steps against flooding in the course of the construction of a building and damage resulted, it would be 'too technical' to hold that this was not within s2(4)(b). So a narrow approach will not be taken to the construction of this subsection. This liberal approach is further evidenced by the judgment of Lord Keith in *Ferguson* v *Welsh* (above). He held that by a 'broad and purposeful construction' of s2(4)(b) works of demolition could be included within 'construction'. With the greatest respect to his Lordship it is difficult to see how construction can encompass demolition; demolition is the very opposite of construction. Where a contractor is employed to demolish a building prior to constructing a new one it is conceded that such demolition work should be caught by s2(4)(b), but the same reasoning should not apply where, as in *Ferguson*, the contractors were employed only for the purpose of demolition.

The second point to note is that it must be reasonable for the occupier to entrust the work to an independent contractor. It is submitted that it is reasonable to do so whenever the work requires special skill or it is commercial practice to engage an independent contractor in the circumstances. The third point to note is that the occupier must take reasonable care to ensure that the contractors, to whom he entrusts the work, are competent to carry the work out.

The fourth, and final, point to note about this subsection is that the occupier must take reasonable care to check, where possible, that the work 'had been properly done'. It should be noted that, although the subsection actually states that 'the work had been properly done', it was held in *Ferguson* v *Welsh* (above) that the subsection did not depend for its application upon the work having been completed but that it could apply where the work was still being done and had not been completed. In general it may be said that the more technical the work, the less reasonable it is to require the occupier to supervise the work. This can be demonstrated by reference to the following cases. In *Haseldine* v *Daw* [1941] 2 KB 343 the claimant was killed, when the lift in which he was travelling fell to the bottom of the shaft. This happened because of the negligence of a firm of contractors employed by the defendants to repair the lift. It was held that, in employing a competent firm of contractors to keep the lift in repair, the defendants had discharged their duty to the claimant. To go further and impose liability upon them would be to make them insurers of the safety of the lift.

On the other hand the defendants were held liable in *Woodward* v *Mayor of Hastings* [1945] KB 174. The claimant, a school pupil, was injured when he slipped on an icy step at the school. The step was in an icy condition because it had been negligently cleaned by a cleaner. Assuming that the cleaner was an independent contractor, it was held that the defendants were still liable under s2(4)(b) because they had failed to take reasonable steps to inspect the cleaner's work. Du Parcq LJ said that the 'craft of the charwoman may have its mysteries, but there is no esoteric quality in the nature of the work which the cleaning of a snow-covered step demands'.

One final problem arises where the employee of an independent contractor is injured on the premises of the occupier as the result of an unsafe system of work used by the independent contractor. In such a case can the injured party bring an action against the occupier? In *Ferguson* v *Welsh* Lord Keith, with whom Lord Brandon and Lord Griffiths concurred, held that it would not ordinarily be reasonable to expect an occupier of premises, who has engaged an independent contractor whom he had reasonable grounds to believe was competent, to supervise the contractor's activities in order to ensure that the independent contractor was discharging his duty to his employees to use a safe system of work. However he did indicate that, in exceptional cases, such as where the occupier knows or has reason to suspect that the independent contractor is using an unsafe system of work, it might well be reasonable to expect the occupier to take reasonable steps to see that the system is made safe. This proposition was, however, doubted by Lord Goff. He thought that the knowledge of an occupier that an independent contractor was using an unsafe system of work was not ordinarily sufficient to impose liability on the occupier in an action under the 1957 Act or in a common law negligence action. He gave the example of a householder who employs an electrician to do some repair work. He held that if the electrician then sends an employee to do the work, and the employee uses an unsafe system of work established by his employer, then 'I cannot see that, in ordinary circumstances, the householder should be held liable under the 1957 Act, or even in negligence, for failing to tell the man how he should be doing his work'. He concluded by saying that there may be exceptional cases where the occupier may be liable for failing to warn the employee, but he held that in such a case the liability of the occupier would be as a joint tortfeasor with the independent contractor. Lord Oliver agreed with Lord Goff that in such a case the liability of the occupier would be as a joint tortfeasor.

17.11 Volenti

It is provided in s2(5) of the 1957 Act that:

'The common duty of care does not impose upon an occupier any obligation in respect of risks willingly accepted as his by the visitor (the question whether a risk was so accepted to be decided on the same principles as in other cases in which one person owes a duty of care to another).'

For an example of the courts' approach in this area see *Simms* v *Leigh Rugby FC* [1969] 2 All ER 923.

17.12 Contributory negligence

In s2(3) of the 1957 Act it is provided that in considering the common duty of care the circumstances relevant include the 'degree of care, and of want of care, which would ordinarily be looked for in such a visitor'. So it is clear that the apportionment provisions of the Law Reform (Contributory Negligence) Act 1945 are applicable. In *Stone* v *Taffe* [1974] 1 WLR 1575, for example, the claimant's damages were reduced by 50 per cent on the ground of contributory negligence (discussed further in Chapter 12).

17.13 Contractors

Specific provision is made in the 1957 Act for those who enter an occupier's premises in pursuance of a contract with the occupier. Section 5 provides that:

'Where persons enter or use, or bring or send goods to, any premises in exercise of a right conferred by contract with a person occupying or having control of the premises, the duty he owes them in respect of dangers due to the state of the premises or to things done or omitted to be done on them, in so far as the duty depends on a term to be implied in the contract by reason of its conferring that right, shall be the common duty of care.'

However, s5 does not apply to:

'... obligations imposed on a person by or by virtue of any contract for the hire of, or for the carriage for reward of persons or goods in, any vehicle, vessel, aircraft or other means of transport, or by virtue of any contract of bailment.'

The position of third parties to the contract is governed by s3 of the Act. That section provides that:

'Where an occupier of premises is bound by contract to permit persons who are strangers to the contract to enter or use the premises, the duty of care which he owes to them as his visitors cannot be restricted or excluded by that contract, but (subject to any provision of the contract to the contrary) shall include the duty to perform his obligations under the contract, whether undertaken for their protection or not, in so far as those obligations go beyond the obligations otherwise involved in that duty.'

The effect of this section is twofold. The first is that the occupier cannot reduce his obligation to a visitor who is a stranger to the contract below that contained in the common duty of care. Secondly, if the contract imposes some higher duty on the occupier, then the visitor shall have the benefit of that provision.

Section 3(2) provides that:

'A contract shall not by virtue of this section have the effect, unless it expressly so provides, of making an occupier who has taken all reasonable care answerable to strangers to the contract for dangers due to the faulty execution of any work of construction, maintenance or repair or other like operation by persons other than himself, his servants and persons acting under his direction and control.'

17.14 Damage to property

Section 1(3)(b) makes it clear that the Act applies to 'damage to property, including the property of persons who are not themselves his visitors'. The Act does not, however, create a liability where none existed at common law (see *Tinsley* v *Dudley* [1951] KB 18).

17.15 Trespassers

The duty owed by an occupier to a trespasser is regulated by the Occupiers' Liability Act 1984. Although we shall commence our analysis with a consideration of the common law, this is done for the sole purpose of giving a background to the development of the law and to shed light on the likely interpretation of the 1984 Act. It is the 1984 Act which now forms the basis of the law.

A trespasser was defined by Lord Dunedin in *Robert Addie and Sons (Collieries) Ltd* v *Dumbreck* [1929] AC 358 in the following terms as:

' ... he who goes on to the land without invitation of any sort and whose presence is either unknown to the proprietor or, if known, is practically objected to.'

But it must be stressed that not every trespasser is a criminal or an immoral person. A person who overstays his welcome could be a trespasser as could a child who wanders innocently on to someone else's land. In truth it covers both the 'wicked' and the 'innocent'.

Background

The duty originally owed to trespassers, which was laid down by the House of Lords in *Addie* v *Dumbreck* (above), was an extremely narrow one. It only arose where the trespasser's injury was due to some wilful act on the part of the occupier, which was done either with the intention of doing harm to the trespasser or was done with reckless disregard of the presence of the trespasser. The decision reflected two particular policy considerations. The first was that the property rights of the occupier were sacrosanct and could only be interfered with in meritorious situations. The second was that trespassers were wrongdoers who were not worthy of such protection.

These policy reasons are no longer so persuasive as they were in 1929 and so some judges sought to escape from this restrictive ruling. They did so in one of two ways. The first was to classify the entrant as an implied licensee rather than a trespasser. This approach can be seen in the case of *Lowery* v *Walker* (above) and in many cases involving children. The second approach was adopted in a case called *Videan* v *British Transport Commission* [1963] 2 QB 650, where an attempt was made to confine *Addie* to breaches of the 'occupancy duty' and hold that it had no application to the 'activity duty'. This approach was, however, rejected by the Privy Council in *Commissioner for Railways* v *Quinlan* [1964] AC 1054.

Surprisingly trespassers were omitted from the coverage of the 1957 Act and they had to wait until 1972 for the judiciary to intervene to alleviate their position. This was done in *British Railways Board* v *Herrington* [1972] AC 877. The claimant, a six- year-old boy, climbed through a gap in a fence beside an electrified railway track run by the defendants and was seriously injured when he was burnt on the live wire. The fence was in a dilapidated condition so that it was relatively easy to get on to the railway line. It had been in this state for some time and it had been reported to the defendants that people were using the gap as a short cut, but the defendants had done nothing about it. The House of Lords held that *Addie* was no longer an exclusive statement of the law and, in particular, they considered that the two policies which we noted underpinned the decision no longer held good. Yet the House was not prepared to impose full *Donoghue* v *Stevenson* liability because it was thought that this would place too onerous a burden upon occupiers. It is not clear exactly what test the House intended to impose because the five judgments given were not a model of clarity. It is sometimes referred to as the duty of 'common humanity' and is a duty in between that imposed in *Addie* and the *Donoghue* standard. There would appear to be two principal differences between the *Herrington* standard and the *Donoghue* standard.

The first difference is that, in most cases, the presence of the trespasser will not be reasonably foreseeable. Lord Reid said that the occupier must have knowledge of a 'substantial probability' of the presence of the trespasser. Lord Diplock was the most extreme in saying that the occupier must actually know that the trespasser is present or have actual knowledge of the facts from which a reasonable person would infer that a trespasser was present on his land. This test is much more subjective than the *Donoghue* standard. The second point of difference is that the standard of care required of an occupier towards a trespasser is less onerous than that required in relation to a lawful visitor. The most controversial aspect here was the dicta of Lords Reid, Wilberforce and Diplock that the resources of the particular occupier were to be taken into account in assessing what it was reasonable for the occupier to do. Once again this is a much more subjective test than that which prevails under *Donoghue*.

In practice, however, there was not much of a difference between the *Herrington* standard and the *Donoghue* standard (see for example *Pannett v McGuinness* [1972] 2 QB 599). The distinction between the two standards became even harder to discern after the decision of the Privy Council in *Southern Portland Cement Ltd v Cooper* [1974] AC 623 (valuably discussed by Spencer [1974] CLJ 202). There the Privy Council appeared to eradicate the two differences noted above between *Herrington* and *Donoghue*. In relation to the need for some subjective knowledge of the presence of the trespasser, Lord Reid rejected the view that 'no duty was owed unless the advent of the trespasser is extremely probable', although he did concede that an occupier could ignore a bare possibility. In relation to the second point, Lord Reid suggested that the duty of common humanity may not be entirely subjective where the occupier creates the danger by his own activity, rather than simply failing to deal with a danger which had arisen from another source. This tendency to synthesise the *Donoghue* and *Herrington* standards can also be seen in *Harris v Birkenhead Corporation* (above).

The uncertainties in the judgments in *Herrington* and the subsequent interpretation of the decision were the subject of much criticism and debate. Yet it should be noted that in *Leakey v National Trust* [1980] QB 485 Megaw LJ saw no difficulty in applying the *Herrington* standard to a nuisance action concerning the liability of a landowner for the natural condition of his land which has caused damage to his neighbour's land (see Chapter 18, section 18.10). Despite this latter point the Law Commission reported on the decision in *Herrington* and their report formed the basis of the 1984 Act.

The 1984 Act

The 1984 Act applies to 'persons other than ... visitors' and so it encompasses not only trespassers, but also persons entering pursuant to a private right of way (see section 17.3) and persons who enter land in the exercise of rights conferred by an access agreement or order under the National Parks and Access to the Countryside Act 1949 s60. The Act determines:

'(a) whether any duty is owed by a person as occupier of premises to persons other than his visitors in respect of any risk of their suffering injury on the premises by reason of any danger due to the state of the premises or to things done or to be done on them; and
(b) if so, what that duty is.'

Thus the Act would appear to apply to the 'activity' duty as well as the 'occupancy' duty. In the remainder of this section we shall apply this Act to trespassers, but it should be borne in mind that the Act applies to the wider category of non-visitors. See also *Open-air recreation*, below.

In considering the duty of care that is owed to trespassers, the 1984 Act adopts a two-stage approach. Section 1(3) of the Act provides that an occupier of premises owes a duty of care to a non-visitor if:

> '(a) he is aware of the danger or has reasonable grounds to believe that it exists;
> (b) he knows or has reasonable grounds to believe that the other is in the vicinity of the danger concerned or that he may come into the vicinity of the danger (in either case, whether the other has lawful authority for being in that vicinity or not); and
> (c) the risk is one against which, in all the circumstances of the case, he may reasonably be expected to offer the other some protection.'

In *White* v *St Albans City and District Council* (1990) The Times 12 March (noted by Mullis [1991] Conveyancer 54) the claimant took a short cut across the defendants' land and fell down a trench which he had not seen. The defendants were aware of the danger and so the claimant could satisfy s1(3)(a) (cf *Rhind* v *Astbury Water Park Ltd* [2004] EWCA Civ 756: occupier of water-filled gravel pit into which trespasser claimant dived to retrieve football not aware of presence there of fibreglass container on which claimant hit his head: occupier not liable since requirement of s1(3)(a) not satisfied). The difficulty arose over the proper interpretation of s1(3)(b). The claimant argued that, once it was demonstrated that the occupier had taken steps to prevent people getting on to his land, it followed that the occupier had reason to believe that someone was likely to come into the vicinity of the danger and so the requirement of s1(3)(b) was satisfied. The court rejected this argument and held that the question had to be answered in the light of the actual state of affairs on the premises when the injury occurred and that the vital question was the simple one of whether the occupier had reasonable grounds to believe that someone would come into the vicinity of the danger. On the facts the Court of Appeal held that the trial judge was justified in reaching the conclusion that the defendant council had no reason to believe that the claimant would be in the vicinity of the danger; the fence which had been put up by the defendants was insufficient to prevent all but the elderly and disabled from entering the land and there was no evidence that people tended to use the land as a short cut.

White was applied by the Court of Appeal in *Donoghue* v *Folkestone Properties Ltd* [2003] 3 All ER 1101. Shortly after midnight on 27 December 1997 the claimant decided to go for a swim in the defendant's harbour. He dived in from a slipway, struck his head on a submerged pile, broke his neck and was rendered tetraplegic. In his action for damages for breach of duty under s1 of the Occupiers' Liability Act 1984, the trial judge found that the claimant had gone onto the slipway as a trespasser and that the defendant, by way of notices and (during the summer) the use of security guards, had tried to prevent swimming in the harbour. The judge found in favour of the claimant, although he concluded that he could only recover 25 per cent of his damages because he had contributed to the accident by his own negligence. The defendant appealed successfully, the Court of Appeal holding that, in all the circumstances, the defendant had owed no duty to the claimant. Lord Phillips of Worth Matravers MR said:

'The observations of members of this court … in *Ratcliff* v *McConnell* [1999] 1 WLR 670 and *White* v *St Albans City and District Council* (1990) The Times 12 March suggest that the test of whether a duty of care exists under the 1984 Act must be determined having regard to the circumstances prevailing at the time that it is alleged that the breach of duty resulted in injury to the claimant. That is my own reading of the relevant provisions of the 1984 Act. At the time that Mr Donoghue sustained his grievous injuries, Folkestone Properties had no reason to believe that he, or anyone else, would be swimming from the slipway. The criterion of s1(3)(b) of the 1984 Act was not satisfied. Folkestone Properties owed no duty to Mr Donoghue …'

In *Ratcliff* v *McConnell* (see above) a student had gained access to a swimming pool by climbing over a locked gate at night and dived into the shallow end, sustaining severe injuries. He claimed that the defendants were liable under the 1984 Act in that they should have taken greater precautions to prevent such an accident. The Court of Appeal held that no duty was owed to him under the 1984 Act because he was aware of the risk involved and willingly accepted it.

In *Tomlinson* v *Congleton Borough Council* [2003] 3 All ER 1122 a disused quarry in the defendant's public park was now a lake and it was extremely popular for yachting and other regulated activities. However, as notices made clear, swimming and diving were prohibited. When he plunged forward from a standing position in the water the claimant struck his head and was paralysed from the neck down, a condition from which he had made only a limited recovery. The defendant had developed a scheme for planting vegetation on the lake's shores which would have made them inaccessible but, for financial reasons, the work had not been carried out. At the trial of the claimant's action for damages, the judge found that the claimant had seen and ignored the notices. Accordingly, he had ceased to be a visitor and had become a trespasser: it followed that he had not been owed the common duty of care under the Occupiers' Liability Act 1957 but the duty contained in s1 of the Occupiers' Liability Act 1984. The trial judge found against the claimant, the Court of Appeal allowed his appeal and the House of Lords allowed the defendant's appeal. Even if swimming had not been prohibited, and the defendant had owed a duty under s2(2) of the 1957 Act, that duty would not have required the defendant to have taken any steps to prevent the claimant from diving or warning him against dangers that were perfectly obvious. It followed that there could have been no duty under the 1984 Act. At the same time, Lord Hutton did not exclude the possibility of there being an exceptional case where a claimant might be able to establish that the risk arising from some natural feature on the land was such that the occupier might reasonably be expected to offer him some protection against it, eg where there was a very narrow and slippery path with a camber beside the edge of a cliff from which a number of persons had fallen.

Gross J followed the *Tomlinson* approach in *Simonds* v *Isle of Wight Council* (2003) The Times 20 September (during primary school sports day, five-year-old claimant took himself off to swings from which he jumped and broke arm: accident, no liability attached).

The second stage of the inquiry is contained in s1(4) which provides that the duty is:

> ' ... to take such care as is reasonable in all the circumstances of the case to see that [the non-visitor] does not suffer injury on the premises by reason of the danger concerned.'

This appears to be the familiar negligence standard and there is no reference to the resources of the particular occupier. In *Revill* v *Newberry* [1996] 2 WLR 239 the question arose as to the duty of care owed to a trespasser engaged in criminal activities. It was held that s1(4) applied, and that the trespasser could claim for injuries suffered from the use of force which exceeded reasonable limits.

One or two other points may be made about the 1984 Act. The first is that s1(5) provides that the occupier can discharge the duty by taking such steps as are reasonable in all the circumstances of the case to give warning of the danger concerned, or to discourage persons from incurring the risk. Section 1(6) preserves the defence of volenti. The final point concerns the situation which arises where the property of the trespasser is damaged. The Law Commission in their report considered whether recovery should be allowed in respect of the clothes which the trespasser was wearing when he entered the premises, but considered that this would be illogical. So the definition of injury in s1(9) is confined to death or personal injury, including disease and any impairment of physical or mental condition and s1(8) provides that the occupier's duty does not extend to any loss of or damage to property. In the absence of statutory protection the trespasser must look to the common law for any available protection. It is unlikely that the *Herrington* standard of 'common humanity' is applicable to property damage because it is a test designed to deal with personal injuries. The only remaining option, if option there be, is the standard laid down in *Addie*.

Open-air recreation

Section 13(2) Countryside and Rights of Way Act 2000 inserted s1(6A)–(6C) of the Occupiers' Liability Act 1984 with effect from 19 September 2004. The new subsection (6A) provides that when the right conferred by s2(1) of the 2000 Act (access for purposes of open-air recreation) is exercisable in relation to land which is access land for the purposes of Pt I of that Act, an occupier of the land owes no duty by virtue of s1 of the 1984 Act to any person in respect of:

1. a risk resulting from the existence of any natural feature of the landscape, or any river, stream, ditch or pond whether or not a natural feature, or

2. a risk of that person suffering injury when passing over, under or through any wall, fence or gate, except by proper use of the gate or of a stile.

For the purposes of subsection (6A), any plant, shrub or tree, of whatever origin, is to be regarded as a natural feature of the landscape: s1(6B).

Subsection (6A) does not prevent an occupier from owing a duty by virtue of s1 of the 1984 Act in respect of any risk where the danger is concerned is due to anything done by the occupier:

1. with the intention of creating that risk, or
2. being reckless as to whether that risk is created: s1(6C).

17.16 Exclusion of the occupier's duty

Separate consideration will be given to the ability of an occupier to exclude liability towards a visitor and to his ability to exclude liability towards a trespasser. Visitors will be considered first.

One of the problems with the 1957 Act is that it has a number of provisions which appear to overlap here. The first is s2(4)(a) which concerns warnings (considered in section 17.9). A warning is, however, different from an exclusion clause. The latter simply seeks to exclude liability on the happening of a specified event, while the former seeks to inform the visitor of a danger so that he can take steps to avoid it (see the approach of Buckley and Roskill LJJ in *White* v *Blackmore* [1972] QB 651). The second provision which overlaps is s2(5) which deals with volenti (discussed in section 17.11). Volenti looks at the issue from the perspective of the visitor and asks whether he has assumed the risk of injury, while an exclusion clause is concerned with the steps taken by the occupier to bring the exclusion clause to the attention of the visitor. So, in some ways, the two look at the same thing from different perspectives.

The provision of the 1957 Act which deals with exclusion clauses is s2(1). So far as material the section states that the occupier owes the common duty of care to all his visitors 'except in so far as he is free to and does extend, restrict, modify or exclude his duty to any visitor or visitors by agreement or otherwise'. The words 'by agreement or otherwise' demonstrate that liability may be excluded by a non-contractual notice. Thus effect was given, in the 1957 Act, to the decision of *Ashdown* v *Samuel Williams and Sons Ltd* [1957] 1 QB 409 (criticised by Gower (1956) 19 MLR 532 and (1957) 20 MLR 181).

But the critical qualification in s2(1) is that the occupier may only exclude or restrict his duty 'in so far as he is free to do so'. There are three restrictions on the occupier's freedom. The first is contained in s3 of the 1957 Act which provides that an occupier cannot by contract with one person exclude or restrict the common duty of care which he owes to third parties (see section 17.13).

The second, and major, restriction upon the freedom of an occupier to exclude or modify his obligations under the 1957 Act is the Unfair Contract Terms Act 1977 (UCTA). Here we are concerned with the controls in UCTA directed at attempts to exclude or restrict liability for negligence. The definition of negligence in s1 of UCTA includes, in s1(1)(c), the common duty of care under the 1957 Act. However, UCTA only places controls upon attempts to exclude or restrict 'business liability'. The latter phrase is defined in s1(3) as liability for breach of an obligation or duty arising:

> '... from things done or to be done by a person in the course of a business (whether his own business or another's) or
> ... from the occupation of premises used for business purposes of the occupier.'

'Business' is defined in s14 as including 'a profession and the activities of any government department or local or public authority'. This rather vague definition led to difficulties in the situation where a fee was charged for entrance on to the land, but the proceeds were devoted to a charitable purpose (see, for example, the fact situation in *White* v *Blackmore* [1972] QB 651). To take account of this point the definition of 'business liability' in s1(3) was amended (by s2 of the 1984 Act) by the addition of the following words:

> ' ... but liability of an occupier of premises for breach of an obligation or duty towards a person obtaining access to the premises for recreational or educational purposes, being liability for loss or damage suffered by reason of the dangerous state of the premises, is not a business liability of the occupier unless granting that person access for the purposes concerned falls within the business purposes of the occupier.'

This addition will relieve some of the uncertainty, but it still does not provide us with a definition of 'business' (for further consideration of this amendment see Bragg and Brazier (1986) 130 SJ 251 and 274).

Section 2(1) of UCTA makes attempts to exclude or restrict liability for death or personal injury resulting from negligence void and in the case of other loss or damage such attempts are subject to a reasonableness test.

The third and final restriction upon the ability of an occupier to exclude or restrict liability exists, or may exist, at common law. Winfield and Jolowicz argue (*Winfield and Jolowicz on Tort* (13th ed) p222) that the *Herrington* standard, based as it is upon 'common humanity', represents a minimum legal standard which cannot be excluded by agreement or by notice. There is, however, no authority for or against such a proposition.

In relation to trespassers there is a logical difficulty in imposing conditions upon the terms of entry of a trespasser because in the vast majority of cases the occupier will be unaware of the trespasser, so he can hardly impose terms on his entry. However UCTA does not apply in the case of a trespasser because the definition of negligence in s1 of UCTA only includes the common duty of care under the 1957 Act; it makes no mention of the duty owed under the 1984 Act.

A number of arguments can be adduced in favour of holding that the duty owed under the 1984 Act is unexcludable. The first is that there is some authority for the proposition that an agreement to contract out of a statutory duty is void. The second point is that s2(1) of the 1957 Act makes provision for contracting out, so the failure to include such a provision in the 1984 Act is surely significant, especially when provision was made in the Law Commission's Draft Bill, which formed the basis of the Act, for contracting out. The third argument is that, since the duty owed to trespassers is the very minimum imposed by law, it should not, as a matter of public policy, be excludable. Lastly, if the argument of Winfield and Jolowicz is accepted, and the *Herrington* standard is held to be unexcludable, then some symmetry is produced with the 1984 Act because the standard adopted by *Herrington* or the 1984 Act becomes a minimum which cannot be excluded in any case. However, the point remains to be resolved (see Jones (1984) 47 MLR 713 and Buckley [1984] Conv 413).

17.17 Liability of independent contractors who are not occupiers

Once again we must distinguish between the duty which is owed to visitors and the duty which is owed to trespassers. In relation to visitors it is clear that it is ordinary *Donoghue* v *Stevenson* principles which are applicable and not the standards applicable under the Occupiers' Liability Act 1957, although it has been noted that there is little difference between the two standards (see *A C Billings and Sons Ltd* v *Riden* [1958] AC 240).

The position in relation to trespassers is more complex. In *Buckland* v *Guildford Gas Light and Coke Co* [1949] 1 KB 410 ordinary *Donoghue* principles were applied by Morris J. However, in *Herrington*, Lords Pearson and Wilberforce suggested that no distinction should be drawn between occupiers and non-occupiers in relation to the duty owed to trespassers and that 'common humanity' be applied in all cases involving trespassers. But it is clear that independent contractors, who are not occupiers, are not caught by the 1984 Act because that Act only applies to occupiers. So it is a straight choice between applying *Herrington* or *Donoghue*. Since the purpose behind the 1984 Act was to replace *Herrington* it would be odd if *Herrington* were to be resurrected in this context and it is submitted that the approach adopted in *Buckland* is the preferable one.

17.18 Liability of vendors and lessors

In this section consideration is given to the liability of vendors and lessors of defective premises. Here we are dealing with the situation where a vendor or a lessor creates a danger or defect in his premises and then sells or lets the property to another person who then suffers injury as a result of the danger or defect. Vendors and lessors do not fall within the ambit of the Occupiers' Liability Acts if they are not occupiers of the premises. So some other action must be used if liability is to be imposed on the vendor or lessor.

One possibility is a contractual action by the purchaser against the vendor or by the lessee against the lessor. The difficulty here is that the implied obligations as to the quality of the premises are much less extensive than in the case of a contract for the sale of goods. The rule in relation to the sale or letting of land is 'caveat emptor' (but see Gleeson and McKendrick in 'The Rotting Away of Caveat Emptor?' [1987] Conv 121). So a contractual action offers little prospect of hope.

An action in tort used to provide little comfort either. The reason was that vendors and lessors enjoyed extensive immunities from suit in tort. In *Cavalier* v *Pope* [1906] AC 428 the immunity of a landlord from suit in tort in respect of dangerous premises was established (cf *Cunard* v *Antifyre* [1933] 1 KB 551). In *Bottomley* v *Bannister* [1932] 1 KB 458 a similar immunity was extended to vendors. So at this stage in our legal development vendors and lessors enjoyed immunity for their own acts or omissions before letting or selling the premises.

An attack was launched upon *Cavalier* v *Pope* in the case of *McNerny* v *London Borough of Lambeth* (1988) 21 HLR 188 (noted by Smith [1989] Conv 216). But the Court of Appeal rejected the argument that *Cavalier* had to be re-examined in the light of the expansion of the tort of negligence which began with *Donoghue* v *Stevenson* [1932] AC 562. So *Cavalier* remains good law. But the Court of Appeal did note that there are two exceptions to the rule in *Cavalier*. The first is that it does not apply to furnished lettings and the second is that it does not apply to cases in which the landowner is the builder of the house and the house has been built negligently (see *Rimmer* v *Liverpool City Council* [1984] 1 All ER 930, recently followed by the Court of Appeal in *Targett* v *Torfaen Borough Council* [1992] 3 All ER 27, who rejected the argument that *Rimmer* could no longer be regarded as good law in the light of the decision of the House of Lords in *Murphy* v *Brentwood District Council* [1991] 1 AC 398).

A more successful attack on the immunity of vendors and lessors was begun in *Dutton* v *Bognor Regis UDC* [1972] 1 QB 373. The Court of Appeal stated, obiter, that the principle of *Donoghue* v *Stevenson* applied to realty as well as to personalty. This statement was approved by the House of Lords in *Anns* v *Merton London Borough Council* [1978] AC 728 and was applied by the Court of Appeal in *Batty* v *Metropolitan Realisations Ltd* [1978] QB 554 (but doubted by the House of Lords in *D & F Estates Ltd* v *The Church Commissioners for England* [1989] AC 177).

The major assault on the immunities of the vendor and lessor are to be found, however, in the Defective Premises Act 1972. Section 3 of that Act provides that:

'Where work of construction, repair, maintenance or demolition or any other work is done on or in relation to premises, any duty of care owed, because of the doing of the work, to persons who might reasonably be expected to be affected by defects in the state of the premises created by the doing of the work shall not be abated by subsequent disposal of the premises by the person who owed the duty.'

This section, which is subject to exceptions in s3(2), virtually restates the position which the courts have reached at common law and in some ways it, or the decisions at common law, could be said to be superfluous.

In relation to landlords, s4 of the 1972 Act is a much more far-reaching provision. It states that:

'(1) Where premises are let under a tenancy which puts on the landlord an obligation to the tenant for the maintenance or repair of the premises, the landlord owes to all persons who might reasonably be expected to be affected by defects in the state of the premises a duty to take such care as is reasonable in all the circumstances to see that they are reasonably safe from personal injury or from damage to their property caused by a relevant defect.

(2) The said duty is owed if the landlord knows (whether as the result of being notified by the tenant or otherwise) or if he ought in all the circumstances to have known of the relevant defect.'

'Relevant defect' is defined in s4(3). These provisions apply to the landlord who has a power, express or implied, to enter and repair the premises as well as to the landlord who is under an obligation to repair (s4(4), the scope of which was discussed by the Court of Appeal in *McAuley* v *Bristol City Council* [1992] 1 QB 134). But no duty is owed in respect of a defect which has arisen out of a failure by the tenant to carry out his express obligations under the tenancy agreement (s4(4)).

To succeed, a claimant under s4 of the 1972 Act merely has to show a failure on the part of the landlord to take such care as was reasonable in all the circumstances to see that the claimant was safe from personal injury: *Sykes* v *Harry* (2001) The Times 27 February (landlord liable for consequences of failure to repair or maintain gas fire).

17.19 Liability of builders

A builder may be liable to his 'employer' (that is the person who has contracted with the builder for the commission of the work) in contract. In many ways the liability of builders here involves the application of ordinary contractual principles, although there are certain terms which are implied into such contracts, but these are beyond the scope of this book. The position in tort is more complex. In *Bottomley* v *Bannister* [1932] AC 458 it was held that the builder on land who owned the land upon which the building was constructed was not liable in negligence for personal injury or damage to property caused by the defective state of the premises. This immunity was not, however, enjoyed by builders who built on someone else's land. Such a builder was subject to *Donoghue* principles.

The immunity of the builder/vendor or builder/lessor was removed by the Court of Appeal in *Dutton* v *Bognor Regis UDC* [1972] 1 QB 373. Lord Denning said that there was no sense behind the distinction which was drawn at common law because:

'... it would mean that a contractor who builds a house on another's land is liable for negligence in constructing it, but that a speculative builder, who buys land and himself builds on it for sale, and is just as negligent as the contractor, is not liable. That cannot be right. Each must be under the same duty of care and to the same persons.'

In *Anns* v *Merton London Borough Council* [1978] AC 728 the House of Lords approved of this dictum of Lord Denning. However, since *Anns* the common law liability of the builder has been considerably circumscribed. In *D & F Estates* v *Church Commissioners for England* [1989] AC 177 it was held that a claim for the cost of repairing a defect in the building itself did not lie against a builder in tort, only in contract, and this approach was affirmed by the House of Lords in *Murphy* v *Brentwood District Council* [1991] 1 AC 398, which itself overruled *Anns*. The effect of this cutting back upon the scope of common law liability is to attach much greater significance to the Defective Premises Act 1972. Indeed, in *D & F Estates* Lord Bridge said that he was happy to reach the conclusion that the cost of repairing the defect in the building itself was not recoverable in tort because, had he decided otherwise, it would have resulted in the common law going further than 'the legislature were prepared to go in 1972, after comprehensive examination of the subject by the Law Commission'. He concluded that 'consumer protection is an area of law where legislation is much better left to the legislators'. The common law is therefore unlikely to be extended beyond the scope of the 1972 Act. Section 1(1) of the Act provides that:

'A person taking on work for or in connection with the provision of a dwelling (whether the dwelling is provided by the erection or by the conversion or enlargement of a building) owes a duty: (a) if the dwelling is provided to the order of any person, to that person; and (b) without prejudice to paragraph (a) above, to every person who acquires an interest (whether legal or equitable) in the dwelling, to see that the work which he takes on is done in a workmanlike or, as the case may be, professional manner, with proper materials and so that as regards that work the dwelling will be fit for habitation when completed.'

The scope of s1(1) was recently considered by the Court of Appeal in *Andrews* v *Schooling* [1991] 1 WLR 783. The third defendants granted the claimant a 199-year lease of a ground floor flat, including a cellar. Extensive work had been done to the flat itself but the only work which had been done in the cellar was the painting of the walls. The claimant later discovered that the flat suffered from penetrating dampness which she alleged emanated from the cellar. She claimed damages from the defendants, alleging that they were in breach of the duty which they owed to her under s1. The defendants argued that they were not liable because they had not done any relevant work on the flat so that it could not be said that they had 'taken on work' in relation to the cellar. Thus they argued that the Act applied only to cases of misfeasance and not non-feasance. This argument was rejected by the Court of Appeal and damages were awarded to the claimant. It was held that a dwelling was unfit for habitation when it was without some essential attribute when the works were completed, even though the problems arising therefrom had not then been patent. The requirement that the dwelling be fit for habitation when completed is not part of the duty itself but is the intended consequence of the proper performance of the duty. So a claimant who cannot show that the dwelling is unfit for habitation cannot bring a claim under s1(1) of the Act (*Thompson* v *Clive Alexander & Partners* (1992) 28 Con LR 49).

A defence is provided for builders in s1(2) which states that:

> 'A person who takes on any such work for another on terms that he is to do it in accordance with instructions given by or on behalf of that other shall, to the extent to which he does it properly in accordance with those instructions, be treated for the purposes of this section as discharging the duty imposed on him by subsection (1) above except where he owes a duty to that other to warn him of any defect in the instructions and fails to discharge that duty.'

The operation of s1 is also limited by the fact that in s2 it is provided that s1 does not apply to dwelling houses covered by an 'approved scheme'. The National House Builders Protection Scheme (NHBPS) is such an approved scheme. Under this scheme the builder warrants that the house is properly constructed and that he will obtain NHBC insurance cover for the dwelling, which will cover any unfulfilled judgment or arbitration award against a builder.

It should be noted that this section only applies to dwellings. The section also suffers from the drawback that the six-year limitation period runs from the date of completion of the dwelling, or, if further work was done on the dwelling after the dwelling was completed, the period begins to run from the date of completion of that work (s2(5)). However, the claimant may be able to enjoy the longer limitation period under the Latent Damage Act 1986 (see Chapter 31, section 31.5).

18

Private Nuisance

18.1 Introduction

A well-known American jurist called Dean Prosser once wrote of nuisance that 'there is perhaps no more impenetrable jungle in the entire law than that which surrounds the word nuisance' (*Prosser on Torts* (4th ed) p571). But the difficulty with nuisance appears to lie more in applying the legal principles to the facts of a particular case. Nuisance cases are so infinite in their variations that it is often difficult to discern any general principles at work. This tort is not difficult in the same way that negligence is difficult, where the complexities are often conceptual (for example, the role of reasonable foreseeability in determining the existence of a duty of care). Ironically the only real conceptual difficulty which arises in the law of nuisance concerns the role of negligence within nuisance.

Nuisance is basically concerned with unreasonable interference with a person's use or enjoyment of his land or some right in connection with his land. Thus in *Crown River Cruises Ltd* v *Kimbolton Fireworks Ltd* (1996) The Times 6 March where a barge was damaged, it was held that the owner could sue in private nuisance as the barge was permanently attached to a mooring on the bed of the river of which the barge owner had exclusive use and occupation pursuant to a licence. As the barge was itself in use as a mooring it was so attached to enjoy the mooring right and sufficient interest to sue in nuisance was present. Nuisance concerns disputes between neighbours relating to their respective uses of their land. But it can also apply to environmental disputes, for example, when large manufacturing concerns pollute the atmosphere. In the latter context statute has intervened to regulate activities which harm the environment (see, for example, the Control of Pollution Act 1974, the Clean Air Acts 1956 and 1968 and the Public Health Act 1936). Within these statutes nuisance sometimes has a role to play in defining the offence but, since these Acts are largely enforced by public bodies, they do not fall within the scope of this book.

Nuisance can be divided into two categories; public and private nuisance. We shall deal with the former in Chapter 19. Here we are only concerned with private nuisance. Private nuisance has been defined by *Winfield and Jolowicz on Tort* (14th ed) p404 as 'an unlawful interference with a person's use or enjoyment of land, or some right over, or in connection with it'. The essence of the tort is said to be found in the maxim sic utere tuo alienum non laedas (that no man is allowed to use his property in such a way as to injure another). But the law of nuisance does in fact allow one person to use his land in such a way as to injure another. What is struck at by the law of nuisance is the unreasonable use of land by one person which causes damage to another. So nuisance really seeks to balance two competing policies. The first is the interest of the landowner in using his land as he sees fit and the second is the interest of the neighbour in the quiet enjoyment of his land. As we shall see throughout this Chapter these two policies are constantly in tension.

18.2 The interests protected

Since we have defined private nuisance in terms of the unlawful interference with a person's use or enjoyment of land, it should follow that only those who have an interest in the land affected can sue in nuisance. Thus in *Malone* v *Laskey* [1907] 2 KB 141 the defendant let a house to a tenant who sublet it to a company. The managing director of the company and his wife then lived in the house. The water cistern fell off the wall while the wife was using the lavatory. The causes of the fall of the cistern were vibrations from adjacent premises caused by machinery belonging to the defendant and the negligent repairs done to the cistern by the defendant's employees or agents. It was held that the wife was unable to sue in private nuisance as she had no proprietary or possessory interest in the land (this case was decided in the days when it was not common for property to be held in joint names). *Malone* therefore stands as authority for the proposition that a claimant must have an interest in the land or a legal right of occupation before he or she can bring an action in private nuisance (see also *Metropolitan Properties Ltd* v *Jones* [1939] 2 All ER 202). Thus guests staying in the family home or children of the owners of the property would appear to be unable to bring an action in nuisance because they lack the necessary interest in land.

A more generous approach was adopted by the Court of Appeal in *Khorasandjian* v *Bush* [1993] 3 WLR 476, but in *Hunter* v *Canary Wharf Ltd; Hunter* v *London Docklands Development Corp* [1997] 2 All ER 426 the House of Lords applied *Malone* and overruled *Khorasandjian*.

In the first action, the claimants sought redress for interference with television reception by Canary Wharf Tower, a building 250 metres high and over 50 metres square, erected on land developed by the defendants. In the second, the claimants claimed damages in respect of damage caused by what they alleged were excessive amounts of dust created by the construction by the defendants of the 1,800 metres long Limehouse Link Road. The claimants lived in areas affected by the interference or dust. Preliminary issues of law to reach the House of Lords in the first action were: (1) whether interference with television reception is capable of constituting an actionable nuisance, and (2) whether it is necessary to have an interest in property to claim in private nuisance and, if so, what interest in property will satisfy this requirement. In the second action, at this stage only question (2) arose. Their Lordships' answers were: (1) in the absence of an easement, more was required than the mere presence of a neighbouring building, and (2) a right to the land, greater than that of a mere licensee or occupier, was an essential element, although in an exceptional case a person in exclusive possession but unable to prove title to the land could sue.

A 'tolerated trespasser', in accordance with the Housing Act 1985, has a sufficient interest in his or her flat to support an action for nuisance: *Pemberton* v *Southwark London Borough Council* [2000] 3 All ER 924. Sir Christopher Slade said:

'... during the period between the termination of the secure tenancy and either its revival or the execution of the order for possession (which I will call the "limbo period"), the occupation of the tenant derives not so much from any agreement between the parties as from the 1985 Act itself. ...

The "tolerated trespasser" thus constitutes a peculiar category ... The inclusion of the word "trespasser" in the description may possibly give rise to misunderstandings since, read by itself, it is ordinarily an inappropriate description of anyone who has the right to assert occupation of the relevant property as against the true owner. ...

Since the "tolerated trespasser" has the right to exclusive possession of the relevant property during the "limbo period", there is in my judgment nothing to prevent his pursuing a cause of action in nuisance against his landlords or anyone else during that period, in accordance with the principles laid down in *Hunter* v *Canary Wharf Ltd, Hunter* v *London Docklands Development Corp* provided that he can establish the other essential ingredients of the tort.'

In *Bridlington Relay Ltd* v *Yorkshire Electricity Board* [1965] Ch 436, which was distinguished on its facts in *Hunter*, the claimants sought an injunction to restrain the defendants from operating a new overhead power line on the ground that it would cause electrical interference which would detrimentally affect the reception on their broadcasting system. The defendants argued that the claimants' use was an extremely sensitive one and that the claimants were seeking a higher degree of interference-free reception than the ordinary man would require. Buckley J refused to grant an injunction and one of his reasons was that, for the purpose of the tort of nuisance, recreational considerations were on a different level from considerations of health and physical comfort. So he held that occasional, if recurrent and severe, electrical interference affecting only one of the available programmes did not constitute a nuisance. In *Bridlington* Buckley J also stated:

> 'For myself, however, I do not think that it can at present be said that the ability to receive television free from occasional, even if recurrent and severe, electrical interference is so important a part of an ordinary householder's enjoyment of his property that such interference should be regarded as a legal nuisance ...'.

The phrase 'at present' has been seized on by later plantiffs and in the Canadian case of *Nor-Video Services Ltd* v *Ontario Hydro* (1978) 84 DLR (3d) 231 the Ontario High Court held that:

> 'Whatever the situation in England at the time of *Bridlington*, in my opinion it is manifest that in Canada today television viewing is an important incident of ordinary enjoyment of property and should be protected as such.'

18.3 Conduct amounting to a private nuisance

This is where the difficulties arise in the application of the law to the many situations which come before the courts. A convenient starting point is the case of *St Helens Smelting Co* v *Tipping* (1865) 11 HL 642. In this case the claimants bought an estate in a manufacturing area of town. The defendant operated a copper smelting works close to the claimants' estate and the vapours from the defendant's factory caused damage to the claimants' trees. The defendant argued that he was not liable to the claimants because his factory was located in an industrial area and so the vapours were acceptable. This argument was rejected by the House of Lords and the claimants recovered damages. In reaching their decision the House of Lords held that there was a distinction between an action in nuisance which alleged that the nuisance caused material damage to property and an action in nuisance which alleged that the nuisance produced personal discomfort in the use or enjoyment of the land. In the former case it is easier to establish nuisance because the locality of the nuisance is only a relevant consideration in the latter case (see further section 18.6).

The normal use of a residential flat cannot be a nuisance to the tenants of adjoining flats even though (due to inadequate soundproofing) all of the neighbours' everyday activities could be heard: *Southwark London Borough Council* v *Mills; Baxter* v *Camden London Borough Council* [1999] 4 All ER 449. Again, the acts of which complaint is made must arise out of the use of the defendant's land: *Hussain* v *Lancaster City Council* [1999] 4 All ER 125 (council not liable in respect of racial and other harassment by its tenants).

In considering what constitutes an unreasonable user of land the courts have to balance a wide range of factors in reaching their decision. The most important of these factors are considered in sections 18.4 to 18.9.

18.4 The duration of the nuisance

The shorter the duration of the interference, the less likely it is that the use will be found to be unreasonable. In *Harrison* v *Southwark and Vauxhall Water Co* [1891] 2 Ch 409 it was held that the actions of the defendants in sinking a shaft in the land adjoining the claimant's land did not constitute a nuisance because of the temporary nature of the work. Professor Fleming has stated that 'the temporary nature of the harm is only one, but by no means a conclusive, factor in deciding whether the injury is too trivial to qualify as a nuisance' (*The Law of Torts* (7th ed) p389). The temporary nature of the harm is more important in a case where the claimant seeks an injunction because courts tend to be reluctant to grant an injunction where the harm is of a temporary nature and is unlikely to continue or to recur. But where the claimant's claim is for damages the mere fact that the harm is temporary will not, where the other factors also point in the direction of the existence of an actionable nuisance, deny to the claimant the ability to claim damages.

A related question concerns whether an isolated or a single escape can constitute a nuisance. There is a conflict of authority on this point. In *Bolton* v *Stone* [1949] 1 All ER 237 Oliver J stated that a nuisance must 'be a state of affairs, however temporary, and not merely an isolated happening'. So the isolated escape of a cricket ball from a cricket ground was held not to constitute a nuisance. But in *Midwood* v *Manchester Corporation* [1905] 2 KB 597, where there was a gas explosion, this was held to be an actionable nuisance on the basis that, although it was an isolated event, it was due to a pre-existing state of affairs (ie the build up of gas in the main). The generally accepted view now is that the event must be attributable to a 'state of affairs' before it will constitute a nuisance. So if a cricket ball is hit out of the ground often enough then there can be said to be a dangerous state of affairs which can ground an action in nuisance (see *British Celanese* v *A H Hunt Ltd* [1969] 1 WLR 959 and *SCM (United Kingdom) Ltd* v *W J Whitall and Son Ltd* [1970] 1 WLR 1017).

18.5 Abnormal sensitivity

A man cannot increase his neighbour's liability merely because he puts his land to some special use. Thus in *Robinson* v *Kilvert* (1889) 41 Ch D 88 the defendant, who was the tenant of a cellar in a house, heated up the cellar to a temperature of 80 degrees fahrenheit. The heat had the effect of causing damage to some sensitive paper which was stored upstairs on the floor of the claimant's premises. It was held that the heat was not of such a character as would ordinarily interfere with the normal use of the rest of the house. A similar result was reached in the case of *Heath* v *Mayor of Brighton* (1908) 98 LT 718 where a church minister sought to obtain an injunction to restrain the noise which emanated from the defendant's electrical power station. There was no evidence that any member of the congregation was upset by the noise, the minister was not prevented from conducting his services and there was no evidence of any decline in the attendance at the church because of the noise, so the court refused to grant an injunction.

18.6 Character of the neighbourhood

We have already noted that the case of *St Helens Smelting Co* v *Tipping* (above) stands as authority for the proposition that the character of the neighbourhood is not a relevant factor in cases of physical damage to property. So here we are only concerned with cases of interference with enjoyment or use of land. The classic statement on this point was given by Thesiger LJ in *Sturges* v *Bridgman* (1879) 11 Ch D 852 when he said that 'what would be a nuisance in Belgravia Square would not necessarily be so in Bermondsey'.

It should not be thought, however, that the character of the neighbourhood is always the decisive factor. It is but one factor to be weighed in the balance. Thus in *Roshmer* v *Polsue and Alfieri Ltd* [1906] 1 Ch 234 a milkman, who had lived and managed a dairy for eighteen years in a neighbourhood in which he was the only resident and which was largely dedicated to printing, sought and obtained an injunction restraining the defendants from using a new machine in their printing press at night because it interfered with the milkman's sleep. It was held that the noise of this machine at night was too great even for an area largely dedicated to printing.

18.7 Utility of the defendant's conduct

As nuisance seeks to identify what is an unreasonable use of land, it is not unnaturally the case that some attention is given to the utility of the defendant's conduct. The more reasonable and useful it is, the more likely it is that the claimant's action will be unsuccessful. For example the construction of houses necessitates the making of a certain amount of noise but the noise is only temporary and it is necessary to achieve the desirable social goal of constructing houses, so it is less likely to constitute a nuisance.

However in the Irish case of *Bellew* v *Cement Co* [1948] Ir R 61 the court granted an injunction for a nuisance which had the effect of closing down Ireland's only cement factory for three months at a time when it was urgently needed. So once again this factor cannot be treated as a conclusive factor.

18.8 Malice

In a sense this category bears a strong resemblance to the issues discussed in section 18.7 because where the defendant's acts are malicious they are devoid of social utility and so are less deserving of protection. Two cases illustrate the approach of the courts here. The first is *Christie* v *Davey* [1893] 1 Ch 316. Here the claimant was a teacher of music whose house was separated from the defendant's house by a party wall. The defendant became so fed up with the constant noise made by the claimant's pupils trying to play the piano that he took to interrupting the lessons by beating on trays, whistling and shrieking. It was held that, in making these noises, the defendant was acting maliciously and so an injunction was granted restraining him from making these noises.

Another example of the approach of the courts is the case of *Hollywood Silver Fox Farm Ltd* v *Emmett* [1936] 2 KB 468. Here the defendant deliberately caused guns to be fired on the boundary of his own land. The boundary was very close to the claimants' land and the purpose behind firing the shots was to scare the claimants' silver foxes during their breeding time. These types of vixens were extremely nervous during breeding time and any loud noise was likely to deter them from breeding, produce miscarriages or cause them to kill and devour their young. It was held that the claimants were entitled to an injunction and damages, even though the shooting took place on the defendant's land, where he was entitled to shoot. This case shows the importance which a malicious motive may have on the outcome of a case because, in the absence of malice, the injunction would probably have been refused on the ground that the claimants were using their land for an abnormally sensitive purpose.

It should also be noted in this context that it must be shown that the defendant maliciously interfered with a right of the claimant. If no such right is interfered with then no cause of action sounds in nuisance. Thus in *Bradford Corporation* v *Pickles* [1895] AC 587 the defendant, who deliberately drained his land in order to stop the water supply reaching the claimants' land, was not liable to the claimants because the claimants had no rights in relation to the supply of water and so no right of theirs had been infringed (see too *Home Brewery plc* v *William Davis and Co (Loughborough) Ltd* [1987] QB 339).

18.9 Fault?

One of the most vexed issues in the law of nuisance is whether or not it is necessary to prove that the defendant was negligent before a claimant can succeed in a nuisance action. In many ways the dominance of the tort of negligence has become such that the common law is reluctant to impose liability in the absence of fault. But if the claimant can show that the defendant was negligent then he can plead negligence and there is no need to rely upon the tort of nuisance. Thus stated the tort of nuisance is in danger of becoming redundant and being swallowed up by the tort of negligence.

Lord Reid contributed to the confusion here in *The Wagon Mound (No 2)* [1967] 1 AC 617, 639 when he said that 'negligence is not an essential element in nuisance. Nuisance is a term used to cover a wide variety of tortious acts or omissions and in many negligence in the narrow sense is not essential'. He then went on to qualify this by saying that 'although negligence may not be necessary, fault of some kind is almost always necessary and fault generally involves foreseeability'. This statement has caused a certain amount of confusion, but in *Cambridge Water Company* v *Eastern Counties Leather plc* [1994] 2 WLR 53 the House of Lords held that foreseeability of damage of the relevant kind was an essential ingredient of nuisance. However, it should be noted that the fact that the defendant has taken all reasonable care will not of itself exonerate him from liability, the relevant control mechanism being the principle of reasonable user – the principle of give and take as between neighbouring occupiers of land: see *Bamford* v *Turnley* (1860) 3 B & S 62.

18.10 Who can be sued in nuisance?

The creator of the nuisance

The person who creates a nuisance by some positive act on his part (misfeasance) rather than by nonfeasance may be sued in respect of the nuisance. The generally accepted view is that the creator may be sued whether or not he is the occupier of the land from which the nuisance came (*Southport Corporation* v *Esso Petroleum Co* [1953] 3 WLR 773 per Devlin J and [1954] QB 182 per Morris LJ, cf Denning LJ).

The occupier of the land

It is clear that the occupier of the land where the nuisance exists is liable when he creates the nuisance. The occupier is also vicariously liable where it is his employee who creates the nuisance in the course of his employment. The occupier may also be liable for the nuisance created by his independent contractor where the occupier is under a non-delegable duty (see further Chapter 5) or where the occupier could reasonably have foreseen, from the instructions which he gave to the independent contractor, that a nuisance was likely to occur. Thus in *Bower* v *Peate* (1876) 1 QBD 321 the claimant and defendant were the owners of adjoining properties. The claimant was entitled to the support for his house of the defendant's soil. The defendant employed an independent contractor to demolish, excavate and rebuild his house. The contractor took the risk under the contract to shore and support the claimant's house during the works. The claimant's house was damaged during the works because of the means used by the contractor to support the claimant's house. It was held that the defendant was liable. The undertaking concerning shoring up and support did not exclude the defendant from liability for nuisance.

The difficulty arises here where the act creating the nuisance is done by a trespasser or it arises as the result of an act of nature. The position in relation to the acts of trespassers was considered by the House of Lords in *Sedleigh-Denfield* v *O'Callaghan* [1940] AC 880. A local authority trespassed on to the defendant's land without the defendant's knowledge or consent and placed a culvert in a ditch on the defendant's land. The culvert was placed in the wrong place with the result that a risk of flooding was created which was likely to spread to the claimant's land. The defendant, through his employees, came to know of the work that had been done by the local authority. He did nothing about it, although he should have realised that it created a risk of flooding on the claimant's land. During a heavy rainstorm the ditch flooded because of the local authority's work and the claimant's land was damaged. The claimant sued to recover damages for his loss. The House of Lords held that the defendant was liable to the claimant because he knew or ought to have known of the risk of flooding and he had done nothing to prevent the claimant's land from becoming flooded. Viscount Maugham rejected the argument that an occupier of land is necessarily free from liability where the nuisance was created by a trespasser. Instead he held the cases held that an occupier was liable where he either 'continued' or 'adopted' the nuisance created by the trespasser. He then went on to say that:

> 'An occupier of land "continues" a nuisance if, with knowledge or presumed knowledge of its existence, he fails to take any reasonable means to bring it to an end, though with ample time to do so. He "adopts" it if he makes use of the erection, building, bank or artificial contrivance which constitutes the nuisance.'

Lord Atkin said that the occupier was not an insurer of the premises and that there must be some element of personal responsibility on his part. This element of personal responsibility existed where the occupier either continued or adopted the nuisance. On the facts in *Sedleigh-Denfield* the defendant was held to have both continued and adopted the nuisance.

So *Sedleigh-Denfield* settled the position at an early date in relation to the liability for the acts of trespassers, but it was not until much later that the position was settled in relation to the liability of occupiers for nuisance arising out of the natural condition of the land. The first major attempt at dealing with this issue can be found in the decision of the Privy Council in *Goldman* v *Hargrave* [1967] 1 AC 645.

A very large redgum tree on the defendant's land was struck by lightning and caught fire. The defendant had the land in the immediate vicinity of the tree cleared and got a tree feller to cut the tree down. The defendant did not take any steps to have the fire put out but chose to let the fire burn itself out. Unfortunately the temperature increased rather than decreased and a strong wind sprang up. This caused the fire to spread extremely rapidly from the defendant's land and on to the claimants' lands, where extensive damage was done. The claimants sued to recover damages for the damage done. The Privy Council held that the risk of the fire spreading was a foreseeable one and that the defendant was liable for failing to take adequate steps to prevent the fire from spreading. Lord Wilberforce recognised that occupiers of land were not simply under a duty to refrain from causing damage to the claimants, but could be under a positive duty to take steps to prevent such harm from arising. However he did not say whether this duty existed in nuisance or negligence.

The issue was further considered by the Court of Appeal in *Leakey* v *National Trust* [1980] QB 485. The defendants owned and occupied land, which included a conical shaped hill called 'Burrow Mump'. This hill had a steep side overlooking the claimants' houses. During a period of drought in the summer of 1976 there appeared large cracks in the hill adjacent to the claimants' property. The hot summer of 1976 was followed by a very wet autumn. In September of 1976 the claimants pointed out to the defendants that a large crack had opened in the side of the hill and that there was a risk of a major collapse. The defendants, however, said that they were not under a duty to do anything because the danger arose from the natural condition of the soil for which they were not responsible. So they did nothing. At a later date the earth duly fell on the claimants' houses. The defendants were prepared to permit the claimants to come on to their land to remove the debris but the defendants were not prepared to contribute anything to the cost of the work. In these circumstances the claimants brought an action against the defendants seeking injunctions requiring the defendants to remove the soil and to take steps to prevent further falls. The defendants were held to be liable to the claimants. The Court of Appeal held that a person on whose land a hazard occurred naturally, whether that hazard was in the soil itself or was in something on or growing on the land, and which encroached or threatened to encroach on another's land thereby causing or threatening to cause damage, was under a duty, if he knew or ought to have known of the risk of encroachment, to do what was reasonable in the particular circumstances to prevent or minimise the risk of known or foreseeable damage to the other person or his property, and was liable in nuisance if he did not take such steps. It has been noted that this decision represents a change of policy in English law because it moves away from the laissez-faire idea that each landowner is autonomous and under no obligation to come to the aid of his neighbour towards the goal of accident prevention under which positive duties may be owed towards one's neighbours (see Markesinis [1980] CLJ 259).

So the Court of Appeal has clearly held that such positive duties are owed under the tort of nuisance and that a claimant will not be prejudiced by his failure to plead negligence. However *Leakey* does not hold out the prospect of us all being under an obligation to go to the aid of our neighbours, regardless of the cost of so doing. This is because of the standard of care which the Court of Appeal held to be appropriate in such a case. The court held that the hypothetical reasonable man standard of *Glasgow Corporation* v *Muir* [1943] 2 AC 448 was not the appropriate standard. The court held that the appropriate standard was a subjective one and that regard was to be had to the abilities and resources of the particular defendant. This standard was directly derived from the decision of the House of Lords in *British Railways Board* v *Herrington* [1972] AC 877. The court, however, deprecated a minute analysis of the financial standing and abilities of the defendant. Megaw LJ said that where substantial expenditure was required to prevent or minimise the risk of damage then the resources of the occupier, assessed upon a broad basis, were a relevant factor in deciding what was reasonably required of the occupier to discharge the duty imposed upon him and that the neighbour's ability to protect himself from damage, also considered on a broad basis, might similarly be a relevant factor to be taken into account depending on the circumstances of the particular case.

The scope of a landowner's duty in nuisance was considered by the Court of Appeal in *Holbeck Hall Hotel Ltd* v *Scarborough Borough Council* [2000] 2 All ER 705. The defendant council owned and occupied the land between the claimants' cliff-top hotel and the sea. Land slips occurred in 1982 and 1986 and there was a massive slip in 1993. The last slip caused the collapse of the hotel's seaward wing and the rest of the hotel had to be demolished for safety reasons. The court decided that the defendant was not liable for the claimants' loss since its duty was to take care to avoid damage which it ought to have foreseen without further geological investigation and the 1993 damage was greater than anything that was foreseen or foreseeable, without further geological investigation. As Stuart-Smith LJ explained:

'The cases of *Goldman* v *Hargrave* and *Leakey* v *National Trust* were decided before the decision of the House of Lords in *Caparo Industries plc* v *Dickman* [1990] 1 All ER 568 [see Chapter 6, section 6.5] in which the three-stage test for the existence of a duty of care was laid down, namely foreseeability, proximity and the need for it to be fair, just and reasonable. ... I do not think it is just and reasonable in a case like the present to impose liability for damage which is greater in extent than anything that was foreseen or foreseeable (without further geological investigation), especially where the defect and danger existed as much on the claimants' land as the defendants.'

Sedleigh-Denfield, Goldman and *Leakey* were all considered by the Court of Appeal in *Bybrook Barn Garden Centre Ltd* v *Kent County Council* (2001) The Times 5 January. The claimants' garden centre was bounded by a stream passing under a road via a culvert built by the defendant's predecessor. When constructed, the culvert was adequate to carry the volume of water passing through it: subsequently, the stream's volume increased as the area developed and the culvert, no longer able to cope with the flow during heavy rain, became an obstruction and aggravated any flooding. The stream flooded the garden centre and the claimants sought damages in nuisance and negligence and an injunction to prevent further flooding.

The action was successful. As Waller LJ explained, a defendant is not entitled simply to say that something was not causing a nuisance when it came on his land or when it was constructed and thus no liability could be imposed on him. A defendant's duty is to do what is reasonable for him to do. In all the circumstances, it had been reasonable to expect the defendant to prevent flooding by enlarging the culvert, which it could have done at some cost but without great difficulty.

In *Rees* v *Skerrett* (2001) The Times 18 June the Court of Appeal learned that numbers 14 and 14A Hastings Street were part of a terrace of houses. The defendant owner of 14A had demolished the building. The owners of 14 sought damages for the harm suffered by their property. Their Lordships decided that their claim would be successful. Lloyd J said that *Phipps* v *Pears* [1965] 1 QB 76 remained authority for the proposition that there was no absolute duty to provide weatherproofing, but where a right of support existed there was an absolute liability for loss caused by the withdrawal of that support. However, in the light of *Leakey* v *National Trust* [1980] QB 485 and cases since, including *Holbeck Hall Hotel Ltd* v *Scarborough Borough Council* [2000] 2 WLR 1396, it seemed right to hold that the defendant was under a duty to take reasonable steps to provide weatherproofing for the wall once it was exposed to the elements as a result of demolition of 14A.

Again, in *Marcic* v *Thames Water Utilities Ltd* [2004] 1 All ER 135 the House of Lords heard that, like many others in the area, the claimant's house was regularly and seriously affected by flooding and back flow of foul water from the defendant statutory water and sewerage undertaker's sewer system. He sought an injunction to prevent the flooding and damages in respect of the damage which it caused to his property. The Water Industry Act 1991 set out the powers and duties of water and sewerage undertakers, subject to supervision and control by the Director-General of Water Services. Reversing the decision of the Court of Appeal, their Lordships concluded that the claimant could not succeed. While Lord Nicholls of Birkenhead accepted that *Goldman* and *Leakey* exemplified the standard of conduct expected today of an occupier of land towards his neighbour, the defendant was not an ordinary occupier of land. The public sewers were vested in the defendant under the 1991 Act and the defendant's obligations regarding those sewers could not sensibly be considered without regard to the elaborate statutory scheme. The common law of nuisance should not impose on the defendant obligations inconsistent with the statutory scheme. To do so would run counter to the intention of Parliament. In his Lordship's view, the cause of action in nuisance asserted by the claimant was inconsistent with the statutory scheme. The claimant's claim under the Human Rights Act 1998 also failed. The scheme set up by the 1991 Act was Convention-compliant: it provided a remedy for persons in the claimant's unhappy position, but he had chosen not to avail himself of it. See, too, *Arscott* v *Coal Authority* [2004] EWCA Civ 892 (defendants built up recreation area, susceptible to flooding, with coal waste: river overflowed causing damage to claimant's properties: accepted building-up of recreation area a material cause: nevertheless, defendants not liable since, at time of building-up, had not been reasonably foreseeable that work might cause flood damage to claimant's properties).

Landlords

The liability of a landlord in nuisance is not altogether easy to state. The general rule is that a landlord who has relinquished possession and control of premises which he has demised is not liable for any nuisance which is committed on the demised premises. There are, however, three situations where a landlord may be liable for a nuisance committed on demised premises.

The first situation where a landlord may be liable arises in relation to a nuisance which existed before the landlord demised the premises. A landlord may be liable for a nuisance which existed before the date of the grant of the tenancy and before the landlord went out of possession if the landlord knew or ought to have known of the nuisance. In this situation, however, the landlord may escape liability to the tenant for such a nuisance by covenanting with the tenant, under the lease, that the tenant will take steps to discontinue or prevent the nuisance (see *Gandy* v *Jubber* (1865) 9 B & S 15). In the case of a third party, the landlord cannot escape liability in respect of a known pre-existing nuisance by contracting with the tenant that the tenant shall bear the responsibility for the repair of the premises because the landlord is not permitted to rid himself of his obligation to the third party in this way.

The second situation in which a landlord may be liable for nuisance which occurs on demised premises arises where a landlord lets premises to a tenant for purposes which are, in themselves, a nuisance. Thus in *Harris* v *James* (1876) 45 LJQB 545 a landlord let land to a tenant for the purpose of carrying out blasting operations and lime-burning. The landlord was held to be liable in nuisance because he knew of and permitted these activities to take place on his land. Similarly in *Tetley* v *Chitty* [1986] 1 All ER 663 it was held that the defendant council were liable in nuisance to the claimants. The defendants had granted permission to a go-kart club to use their land for the purpose of using go-karts. The claimants, who lived close to the go-kart track, complained of the noise made by the go-karts. The defendants argued that they were not liable in nuisance because they had not created the nuisance nor had they permitted the go-kart club to cause a nuisance. This argument was rejected by McNeill J on the ground that the noise made by the go-karts was an 'ordinary and necessary' consequence of the use of go-karts and therefore the defendants were held to have consented, either expressly or impliedly, to the commission of the nuisance.

The third situation in which a landlord may be liable for the commission of the tort of nuisance on demised premises arises where a landlord expressly or impliedly reserves to himself the right to enter and repair the premises. In such a case the landlord will be liable to a third party or, in some cases, the tenant for damage caused by the nuisance. In *Payne* v *Rogers* (1794) 2 H Bl 350 Heath J appeared to suggest that the tenant would not be liable where a third party was injured and that it was the landlord who was liable, but in *St Anne's Well Brewery Co v Roberts* (1928) 140 LT 1 it was held that the tenant could also be liable and that the tenant's obligation to the third party could not be discharged simply because the landlord was under an obligation to repair the premises. In *Wringe v Cohen* [1940] 1 KB 229 the gable end of a house belonging to the defendant fell onto the highway during a heavy fall of rain and caused damage to the claimant's shop. The defendant's premises had been in a state of disrepair for three years. The defendant, who was the landlord of the premises, argued that, although he was under an obligation to repair the premises, he would only be liable if, as a matter of fact, he knew or ought to have known of the disrepair. It was held that the defendant was liable whether or not he knew or ought to have known of the danger because he had accepted an obligation to repair the premises. This obligation to repair gave him the control of the premises and gave him the right to enter the premises to maintain them. The landlord is not, however, liable where the nuisance has been created by a trespasser or by an act of nature, unless the principles established in *Sedleigh-Denfield v O'Callaghan* (above) or *Leakey v National Trust* (above) have been satisfied. It should be noted that in addition to his liability in nuisance a landlord may also be subject to the controls laid down in s4 of the Defective Premises Act 1972 (discussed at Chapter 17, section 17.18).

18.11 Types of harm

It is not possible to classify every type of harm which may be actionable in nuisance. Three broad categories can, however, be identified.

Encroachments

This category includes physical objects which actually interfere with the claimant's land, for example, tree roots which damage the claimant's house (*Davey v Harrow Corporation* [1958] 1 QB 60), trees which overhang a neighbour's land (*Lemon v Webb* [1895] AC 1) and landslides on to the claimant's land (*Leakey v National Trust* [1980] QB 485).

As to the encroachment of tree roots and its consequences, the decision of the House of Lords in *Delaware Mansions Ltd v Westminster City Council* [2001] 4 All ER 737 provides a further example. Delaware Mansions Ltd (Delaware) was the management company owned by the tenants of a block of flats. Flecksun Ltd (Flecksun), a wholly-owned subsidiary of Delaware, purchased the freehold of the flats in June 1990. The defendant highway authority owned a London plane tree growing in the pavement some four metres from the flats. In March 1990 (before the transfer of the freehold) Delaware and the then freeholders were advised that cracking in some of the flats had been caused by the roots of the tree. A more detailed survey was carried out in 1991, but the defendants were not made aware of the problem until nearly two months after the transfer of the freehold. In 1995 Delaware and Flecksun issued a writ claiming damages for nuisance in respect of damage caused to the flats by the roots of the tree. The trial judge found that 'all or almost all' of the structural damage had occurred before the transfer of the freehold as a result of the 1989 drought and that any cracking after the transfer of the freehold was a consequence of it. He decided that the claim could succeed only in respect of fresh damage, if and when it occurred, but the Court of Appeal concluded that it could succeed on the basis that there had been a continuing nuisance. The defendants' appeal against this decision was dismissed since there had been a continuing nuisance of which they knew or ought to have known. As Lord Cooke of Thorndon explained:

> 'I think that there was a continuing nuisance during Flecksun's ownership until at least the completion of the underpinning and the piling in July 1992. It matters not that further cracking of the superstructure may not have occurred after March 1990. The encroachment of the roots was causing continuing damage to the land by dehydrating the soil and inhibiting rehydration. Damage consisting of impairment of the load-bearing qualities of residential land is, in my view, itself a nuisance. ... Cracking in the building was consequential. Having regard to the proximity of the plane tree to Delaware Mansions, a real risk of damage to the land and the foundations was foreseeable on the part of Westminster, as in effect the judge found. It is arguable that the cost of repairs to the cracking could have been recovered as soon as it became manifest. That point need not be decided, although I am disposed to think that a reasonable landowner would notify the controlling local authority or neighbour as soon as tree root damage was suspected. It is agreed that if the plane tree had been removed, the need to underpin [at a cost of £571,000] would have been avoided and the total cost of repair to the building would have been only £14,000. On the other hand the judge has found that, once the council declined to remove the tree, the underpinning and piling costs were reasonably incurred ... Westminster had ample notice and time before the underpinning and piling, and is in my opinion liable.'

Physical damage to the claimant's land

This category includes overflows from blocked drains and culverts (*Sedleigh-Denfield v O'Callaghan* [1940] AC 880), dilapidated buildings falling onto neighbouring property (*Wringe v Cohen* [1940] 1 KB 229), vibrations *(Hoare and Co v McAlpine* [1923] 1 Ch 167) and, probably, damage caused by trespassers encamped on the defendant's land: *Lippiatt v South Gloucestershire Council* [1999] 4 All ER 149.

Acts interfering with a neighbour's enjoyment of his own property

This category mainly consists of non-physical injuries to the enjoyment of property such as noise (*Halsey v Esso Petroleum Co* [1961] 1 WLR 683), smell (*Adams v Ursell* [1913] 1 Ch 269) and fumes, heat and dust (*Matania v National Provincial Bank Ltd*

[1936] 2 All ER 633), harassing telephone calls (*Khorasandjian* v *Bush* [1993] 3 WLR 476) and using premises in a residential area as a sex shop (*Laws* v *Florinplace Ltd* [1981] 1 All ER 659). See also section 18.3.

Personal injury

It is a moot point as to whether damages for personal injury can be recovered in private nuisance. As the tort exists to protect interests in land it might be thought that recovery for personal injury is inappropriate. However, such recovery has been allowed under the rule in *Rylands* v *Fletcher* which also exists to protect property interests (see Chapter 20, section 20.10) which suggests that it should, by analogy, be allowed in nuisance. However, since *Cambridge Water* it is highly arguable whether damages for personal injury are recoverable in either nuisance or under *Rylands* (see Chapter 20, section 20.10).

18.12 Defences

There are a number of defences to a nuisance action. The most important of these defences are dealt with below.

Prescription

Continuance of a nuisance for 20 years will, by prescription, legalise a private nuisance (but not a public one). The crucial point to note is that the time does not begin to run for this purpose until the claimant is aware of the existence of the nuisance. If it were otherwise the claimant might find that he had lost his right of action before he even knew that it existed. But this rule can have rather odd effects in practice. In *Sturges* v *Bridgman* (1879) 11 Ch D 852 the defendant, who was a sweet manufacturer, had for more than 20 years used certain machinery in the manufacture of sweets. The claimant, who was a doctor, bought property nearby in 1865. In 1873 the claimant built his consulting rooms in his garden, adjacent to the defendant's premises. The noise from the defendant's machines disturbed the claimant in the use of his consulting rooms. In the claimant's nuisance action the defendant claimed that he had acquired a right to make the noise by 20 years' prescription. It was held that there was no nuisance until the consulting rooms were built in 1873 and that time did not begin to run until that date and so there had been no 20-year prescription.

Statutory authority

If the act which gave rise to the nuisance was authorised by statute, that statutory authority will afford the defendant a defence only if it can be shown that the interference with the claimant's rights was, either expressly or impliedly, permitted by the wording in the statute. The scope of this defence was recently considered by the House of Lords in *Allen* v *Gulf Oil Refining Ltd* [1981] AC 1001. The defendants were authorised by the Gulf Oil Refining Act 1965 to construct an oil refinery on certain lands at Milford Haven, together with railways, jetties and harbours to serve the refinery. The refinery was built very close to a small village where the claimants lived. The operation of the refinery caused noxious fumes to be emitted over the claimants' village and the claimants brought an action in nuisance in respect of the noxious odours, vibrations, continuous roars, high-pitched noises and flames from burning waste gases. The defendants argued that their activities did not constitute a nuisance because they had statutory authority for their activities. The Act under which they claimed that they had statutory authority empowered the defendants to construct the refinery but it conferred no express authority to use the refinery once built.

The majority of the House of Lords held that Parliament had, by necessary implication, authorised the operation and use of the refinery. Parliament could not have intended the refinery to stand unused as an 'adornment' of the countryside. In adopting this approach the House of Lords approved of the approach adopted by Lord Dunedin in *Corporation of Manchester* v *Farnworth* [1930] AC 171 when he said that:

> 'When Parliament has authorised a certain thing to be made or done in a certain place, there can be no action for nuisance caused by the making or doing of that thing if the nuisance is the inevitable result of the making or doing so authorised. The onus of proving that the result is inevitable is on those who wish to escape liability for nuisance.'

In *Allen* this onus was satisfied by those committing the nuisance and it was held that they had immunity from any non-negligent interferences with the enjoyment of, or damage to, the claimants' property.

Lord Keith dissented and took an extremely literal approach to the interpretation of the statute upon which the defendants purported to rely. He said that the Act only authorised the construction of the refinery. It made no mention of the use of the refinery and so, in using the refinery, the defendants could not claim the authorisation of the statute. The difficulty with this view lies in seeing how the refinery was to operate at all because Parliament surely could not have intended that the refinery, once built, would lie unused.

Lord Denning, in the Court of Appeal in *Allen*, sought to find a solution to this problem by formulating a new principle to be applied in cases where statutory authority was invoked as a defence to a nuisance action. He said that, even where the statutory defence was applicable, the claimant should not be left without a remedy when the use and enjoyment of his property had been interfered with. However, he argued that the claimant should not be granted an injunction because that would be to allow private rights to prevail over valuable public projects. But he did argue that the claimants were entitled to damages in respect of the damage they had suffered as a result of the nuisance. This may produce the fairest result because it would not prevent the operation of the refinery, yet it would not leave the claimants without a remedy in respect of the damage which they had suffered. This approach was, however, rejected by the House of Lords on the ground that it was inconsistent with established authorities.

The situation regarding planning permission has been considered in public nuisance (see Chapter 19, section 19.1) and those considerations would also apply in private nuisance.

Other defences

The Law Reform (Contributory Negligence) Act 1945 is applicable to nuisance and, therefore, is a defence. Agreement to the existence of the nuisance is also a defence. Act of God and act of a stranger may also constitute a defence, unless the defendant has 'adopted' or 'continued' the nuisance. Inevitable accident is a defence in cases where negligence is of the essence of liability. Ignorance of the nuisance may in certain cases amount to a defence. For example, in *Noble* v *Harrison* [1926] 2 KB 332 a branch of a tree overhung a highway. The fact that it overhung did not make it a nuisance. It fell due to a latent defect, not discoverable by any reasonably careful inspection, on to the claimant's car. It was held that the defendant was not liable. The branch fell due to a latent crack caused 'by a secret and unobservable operation of nature' for which the defendant was not liable.

The following are NOT defences to a nuisance action.

Coming to the nuisance

As a general rule it is no defence to show that the claimant came to the nuisance, that is to say the defendant cannot argue that he was making the nuisance before the claimant moved into the area. We have already seen the operation of this rule in *Sturges* v *Bridgman* (above). The doctor built his consulting room after the defendant had been using the offending machinery, but it was held that this fact did not give the defendant a good defence to the doctor's action. This may seem to be unfair to the defendant because the doctor chose to put his consulting rooms close to the defendant's machinery and so he should take the consequences. But if the law did adopt such an approach its effect would be to freeze the use of land and this is undesirable. The rule is also mitigated in its application by the locality principle, under which the claimant must, in relation to interference with the enjoyment of his property, accept the standard of noise, smell etc customary in that particular area.

Although this particular rule is well established in terms of age it was not viewed with great favour by the Court of Appeal in *Miller* v *Jackson* [1977] QB 966. Houses were built on the edge of a cricket ground. Cricket had been played there for some considerable time before the houses were built. Cricket balls kept on landing in the gardens of these houses or even in the houses themselves. The cricket club did what they could. They built a fence around the boundary line and they even asked batsmen to try to hit fours rather than sixes. But still the balls kept on landing in the houses. The claimants, who owned the houses, brought an action against the cricket club in nuisance. Lord Denning, in a robust judgment, upheld the values of playing cricket and said that the damage was due to the building of the houses and not to the playing of cricket. He held that *Sturges* was no longer binding today and so found for the defendants. But long established authority cannot simply be brushed aside in such a manner. The other judges were more circumspect. Geoffrey Lane LJ said that, had the matter been an open one, he would have found for the defendants but he felt constrained by authority to find for the claimants. Having said that, this fact that the houses were built at a time when cricket was already being played on the ground was used to justify refusing to grant an injunction to the claimants and so their claim was relegated to a damages claim. So *Sturges* may yet be open to re-examination in the House of Lords.

Usefulness is not, in itself, a defence

The mere fact that the defendant's activity is socially useful is not, of itself, a defence to a nuisance action. The case most commonly cited in this connection is the case of *Adams* v *Ursell* [1913] 1 Ch 269. Here the defendant opened a fish and chip shop in what had been, hitherto, a rather 'well-to-do' residential part of a street. The argument that the granting of an injunction to stop the nuisance created by the smell would cause hardship to the defendant's business and to the 'less well off' who were his regular customers was rejected. The defendant should have located his shop in the area where his customers resided, presumably because they would not be offended by the smell emanating from the shop.

No defence that it is due to many

It is no defence to an action in nuisance that the nuisance was caused by many people acting together and that the defendant's act, taken alone, would not have amounted to a nuisance. In assessing what is a reasonable user the courts will take account of all the surrounding circumstances, including the conduct of other people.

18.13 Remedies

There are three basic remedies in English law which are available to a claimant in a nuisance action. These three remedies are an injunction, damages and abatement. Since an injunction is the most important remedy, consideration will be given to this remedy first.

Injunctions

An injunction is an extremely powerful weapon because it gives to the court the power to order the defendant to stop the activity which has given rise to the nuisance. The order may require the defendant to halt the activity immediately or it may give him a reasonable time in which to comply with the court order. The court in a nuisance action will generally grant a prohibitory injunction, that is an injunction requiring the defendant to stop the particular activity which is the subject of the action.

An injunction is a discretionary remedy. The general rule in relation to the granting of injunctions is that an injunction may be granted where damages are inadequate. In many cases it is not difficult for a claimant to show that damages are inadequate because, once he can show that the nuisance is a continuing one and that the damage will therefore continue, damages are presumed to be inadequate because the claimant would have to keep coming back to court for more damages as the nuisance continued. Until 1977 it could be said with some confidence that an injunction would be available as a matter of course to restrain a continuing nuisance. This was largely because of the high value placed by the English judiciary upon property rights and their refusal to countenance the interference with these property rights. Thus in *Pride of Derby* v *British Celanese Ltd* [1953] Ch 149 an injunction was granted restraining the defendants from polluting a river with untreated sewage and the claimant club's private interest in fishing in the river was allowed to prevail over the interest of the town in having its sewage cheaply and easily disposed of. But in *Miller* v *Jackson* (above) Lord Denning adopted a different approach. He said that:

> 'There is a contest here between the interest of the public at large and the interest of the private individual. The public interest lies in protecting the environment by preserving our playing fields in the face of mounting development, and by enabling our youth to enjoy all the benefits of outdoor games such as cricket and football. The private interest lies in securing the privacy of [the claimant's] home and garden without intrusion or interference by anyone … As between their conflicting interests I am of the opinion that the public interest should prevail over the private interest.'

However, in the later case of *Kennaway* v *Thompson* [1981] QB 88 the Court of Appeal refused to follow the approach adopted by the court in *Miller*. In *Kennaway*, the claimant, who was an old lady, lived in a house close to a lake. Her enjoyment of her property was spoilt by power boat racing which was held by the defendant club on the lake. Some of these races were very important races (for example national championship races were held there) but the boats were also extremely noisy. The claimant sought an injunction and damages against the defendant club. The Court of Appeal reaffirmed that in cases where there was a continuing actionable nuisance the court's jurisdiction to award damages instead of an injunction was only to be exercised very sparingly and that the public interest did not prevail over the private interest. Lord Denning's judgment in *Miller* was said to be inconsistent with the principles laid down by the House of Lords in *Shelfer* v *City of London Electric Lighting Co Ltd* [1895] 1 Ch 287 and was not followed. So there remains a conflict of authority on this point, but it must be conceded that the approach adopted by the court in *Kennaway* represents the traditional view in English law (the cases are usefully discussed by Tromans (above) and by Tettenborn and Markesinis (1981) 131 NLJ 108).

Abatement

As we noted in Chapter 1 of this book the law of tort is extremely reluctant to allow a claimant to take the law into his own hands. An exception to this can be found in the willingness of the law to permit a claimant to abate a nuisance. This remedy can, however, only be resorted to within narrow confines. In particular, three conditions must be met.

In the first place, before any attempt is made to abate the nuisance, notice should be given to the defendant (that is, the person committing the nuisance) to remedy the nuisance, unless the nuisance can be abated without obtaining entry to the defendant's premises or the security of life or property is at risk and time does not permit the giving of notice (see *Lemon* v *Webb* [1895] AC 1). The nuisance can be abated without going on to the defendant's land where, for example, the branches from the defendant's tree hang over into the abator's land, in which case the abator can simply lop off the offending branches while standing on his own property.

The second condition which must be complied with is that the abator must not do unnecessary damage to the defendant's property when abating the nuisance. The third, and final, condition is that where there is more than one way of abating the nuisance, the method which involves the least cost to the defendant should be employed unless the adoption of that method would have a detrimental effect on the interests of innocent third parties or on the public at large.

Damages

In many ways damages is the residuary remedy in the tort of nuisance because in most cases the claimant will want an injunction to put a stop to the nuisance. But there are cases where a claimant will want damages, for example where the nuisance is not continuous or where the claimant's property has been damaged by the nuisance.

The easiest way for a claimant to show that he has suffered damage is to show that his property has diminished in value as a result of the nuisance: see, for example, *Louis* v *Sadiq* (1996) The Times 22 November. However, it is not necessary to show the existence of damage in all cases. Thus in *Fay* v *Prentice* (1845) 1 CB 828 the claimant was able to recover without showing the existence of damage. The defendant erected a cornice on his house which projected over the claimant's garden, with the result that water dripped from it on to the claimant's garden. It was held that the cornice was a nuisance and that the claimant did not have to show that damage had been caused. So the fact that it had not rained was irrelevant because when it did rain damage of some kind could be presumed.

The approach to the award of damages in cases of interference with the enjoyment of property was demonstrated by the Court of Appeal in *Bone* v *Seale* [1975] 1 All ER 787. The defendants owned a pig farm which was adjacent to the claimant's property. The storage of pig manure and the boiling of pig-swill emitted intolerable smells, both day and night. The claimant sought an injunction and damages in respect of these smells. It was held that, on the facts, there was no pecuniary loss to the claimant, there was no damage to his property and no interference with his health. So the court awarded damages on a basis analogous to that adopted in cases of loss of amenity in personal injuries cases. The court awarded damages of £1,000, being similar to the sum which would have been awarded in a personal injury case for loss of the sense of smell.

There is little explicit authority on the question whether economic loss is recoverable in nuisance. In *British Celanese Ltd* v *A H Hunt Ltd* [1969] 1 WLR 959 Lawton J was prepared to concede that economic loss was recoverable in nuisance, but this is only an obiter remark (although in *Ryeford Homes Ltd* v *Sevenoaks District Council* (1989) 16 Con LR 75 Judge Newey QC said that, on the facts of the case, if economic loss was held to result from the commission of the tort of nuisance, then he thought that such loss was 'probably recoverable'. There is no English authority which expressly affirms or denies the existence of a right to bring an action for damages for personal injury in a nuisance action. Canadian authority can, however, be found to support the proposition that damages for personal injury can be recovered in a nuisance action (*Devon Lumber Co Ltd* v *MacNeill* (1988) 45 DLR (4th) 300, discussed at section 18.2). It can be argued that the claimant in a case such as *Devon Lumber* ought to be able to bring an action for damages because his injury is suffered qua occupier (that is to say, it arises because he or she lives next door to the cedar mill). But, where the injury which is suffered is incidental to the claimant's enjoyment of land (for example, where the vibrations from the defendants' factory cause a heavy object to fall and hit the claimant), it is arguable that such a claim can only be brought in negligence because, given that the injury could equally have been suffered by a visitor to the premises, 'it would be anomalous and unfair if the occupier could plead strict liability in nuisance whilst a visitor, equally affected, could only sue in negligence' (Kodilyne (1989) 9 Legal Studies 284 at 290).

The loss must not be too remote, or else it will be irrecoverable. In *The Wagon Mound (No 2)* [1967] 1 AC 617 the House of Lords held that the test for remoteness of damage was reasonable foreseeability of the kind of damage, as it is in the case of negligence.

Where the court refuses, in the exercise of its discretion, to grant an injunction then the court may award damages in equity in lieu of (in place of) an injunction. But the court uses this power to grant damages in lieu of an injunction very sparingly. The relevant principles were laid down by the Court of Appeal in *Shelfer v City of London Electric Lighting Co Ltd* [1895] 1 Ch 287. The court held that damages should only be awarded where: the injury to the claimant's legal rights is small; the damage is capable of being estimated in money; the damage can be adequately compensated by a small money payment; and the case is one in which it would be oppressive to the defendant to grant an injunction.

This power to award damages in lieu of an injunction is now contained in s50 of the Supreme Court Act 1981.

19

Public Nuisance

19.1 Introduction

19.2 The elements of the tort of public nuisance

19.3 Public nuisance and the highway

19.1 Introduction

Public nuisance is generally given separate consideration from private nuisance on the ground that public nuisance is a crime as well as a tort. Indeed in many ways its primary significance is as a crime rather than as a tort. It is a crime of somewhat uncertain ambit. *Archbold's Criminal Pleading and Practice* ((42nd ed) para 27–44) defines a public nuisance in the following terms:

> 'Every person is guilty of an offence at common law, known as public nuisance, who does an act not warranted by law, or omits to discharge a legal duty, if the effect of the act or omission is to endanger the life, health, property, morals, or comfort of the public, or to obstruct the public in the exercise of enjoyment of rights common to all Her Majesty's subjects.'

Statute has, however, intervened to amend this list: the Public Health Act 1936 has made certain activities a public nuisance, for example to permit insanitary water tanks to be used for domestic purposes. However, cases of public nuisance are still prosecuted: see *R v Shorrock* [1993] 3 WLR 698 and *R v Johnson* (1996) The Times 22 May for modern examples of the use of this action as a crime.

One interesting question concerns the relationship between public nuisance and such modern regulatory legislation. One facet of this issue was discussed by Buckley J in *Gillingham Borough Council* v *Medway (Chatham) Dock Co Ltd* [1993] QB 343 when he was asked to consider the relationship between public nuisance and planning legislation. The defendants were lessees of a port. The claimants alleged that the use of the roads around the port at night by numerous heavy goods vehicles (HGVs) constituted a public nuisance. The evidence established that in 1988 there were approximately 750 HGV 'movements' every night and that the sleep and comfort of the residents in the vicinity of the port were disturbed. The defendants conceded that these conditions constituted a substantial interference with the residents' enjoyment of their property up to June 1990 and that, subject to defences, enough residents were affected to constitute a public nuisance. However, the defendants argued that they had been given planning permission to operate a commercial port, that such a port could operate viably only on a 24-hour basis, that no limits had been placed on the volume of traffic in the vicinity when they had been granted planning permission and that their estimate of the likely throughput of traffic had been remarkably accurate. Buckley J noted that planning legislation had been enacted by Parliament in an effort to balance the interests of the community and the interests of individuals likely to be adversely affected by the plans being put forward. He then asked himself the question whether residents can defeat the planning legislation by bringing an action in nuisance. His conclusion was that 'where planning consent is given for a development or change of use, the question of nuisance will thereafter fall to be decided by reference to a neighbourhood with that development or use and not as it was previously'. So planning permission is not, of itself, a defence to a nuisance action but it is a factor to be taken into account in identifying the character of the neighbourhood. So, on the facts of the present case, account had to be taken of the fact that planning permission had been given to use the dockyard as a commercial port. In the light of this fact, Buckley J held that the disturbance experienced by the residents of the area was not an actionable nuisance. However, in *Wheeler* v *J J Saunders* [1995] 3 WLR 466 the Court of Appeal, in a private nuisance action, refused to accept that there was immunity as regards *any* nuisance that flowed from the granting of planning permission. Such a proposition would have the effect of depriving those persons adversely affected of their common law rights without compensation. In *Wheeler* the distinction was drawn between the power of a planning authority to alter the character of a neighbourhood, which it possesses and which it did in *Gillingham Borough Council*, and the lack of power of a planning authority to authorise a nuisance. The essential difference between *Gillingham* and *Wheeler* was that in the former the character of the neighbourhood was altered by the planning permission, whereas in the latter it was not.

19.2 The elements of the tort of public nuisance

There are two basic elements which must be established in showing that the tort of public nuisance has been committed. The first is that it must be shown that the persons affected by the nuisance constituted the public or a section of the public. The intention behind this requirement is to distinguish a public nuisance from a private nuisance. In *Attorney-General* v *PYA Quarries* [1957] 2 QB 169 the defendants argued that the persons affected by the blasting operations at their quarry were not sufficiently numerous to constitute a section of the public. The only persons affected by their blasting operations, and the dust and vibrations created thereby, were the residents who lived close to the quarry. So they argued that, at worst, they had committed the tort of private nuisance. The Court of Appeal held that a public nuisance was a nuisance which 'materially affects the reasonable comfort and convenience of life of a class of Her Majesty's subjects'. Lord Denning declined to answer the question how many people were needed to constitute a 'class of Her Majesty's subjects'. He indicated that it was not simply a question of numbers but that regard had to be had to the effect of the nuisance. He held that a public nuisance was a nuisance which was so widespread that it was not reasonable to expect one individual to bring an action to put a halt to it, but rather that it was the responsibility of the whole community to bring the action. In *R v Johnson* (1996) The Times 22 May a person made a number of obscene telephone calls, to numerous women, and it was held that although each call was a single isolated act it was both permissible and necessary to look at the cumulative effect of these calls in determining whether the conduct amounted to a public nuisance. If the scale of the nuisance was sufficient it could amount to a public nuisance.

The second element which a claimant must establish in an action in public nuisance is that he suffered special damage. The claimant must establish that he suffered particular damage over and above the annoyance and inconvenience suffered by the public at large. This requirement of special damage prevents a multiplicity of actions arising out of the one event and so it operates as a limitation upon the damages for which the defendant may be liable. In *Rose v Miles* (1815) 4 M & S 101 the defendant moored his barge across a canal in such a way as to block the canal. The claimant was put to considerable extra expense because he had to unload his barge and carry his cargo by land because the blockage of the canal meant that he could not continue down the canal. It was held that the obstruction had caused the claimant special damage because of the extra expense which he had incurred and so the defendant was liable in public nuisance.

Apart from these two particular requirements there is much in common between public and private nuisance and the courts balance roughly similar factors in each case. There are, however, one or two other differences between the torts. Private nuisance is concerned with the protection of interests in land and so it is arguable that the claimant must have an interest in the land affected (see Chapter 18, section 18.2) but there is no such limitation in cases of public nuisance. Prescription is not a defence to a public nuisance, whereas it is a defence to a private nuisance. There are also certain special rules which have grown up in relation to public nuisances and the highway. We will now consider some of these rules.

19.3 Public nuisance and the highway

There has been considerable case law concerned with public nuisance and the highway. It is a public nuisance to obstruct the highway or to create a danger on, or close to, the highway. We shall consider first the law relating to obstruction of the highway.

Obstruction of the highway

The highway does not have to be completely blocked before a public nuisance may be committed. It is sufficient if the highway is unreasonably obstructed. However it is not necessarily a nuisance to leave a vehicle stationary on the road for a period of time. But in *Dymond* v *Pearce* [1972] 1 QB 497 it was held that the defendant had committed a public nuisance in leaving his lorry parked on the highway. It was a large lorry but he had left it with its parking lights on and the lorry was visible from a distance of 200 yards. Despite this the claimant, who was on his motor cycle, collided with the lorry. It was held that the defendant, in leaving the lorry on the public highway for his own convenience, had committed a public nuisance. The defendant was not, however, liable for the injuries to the claimant because they were caused entirely by the negligence of the claimant and not by the defendant leaving his lorry on the highway. However, the case might have been decided differently if the reason for the defendant leaving his lorry on the highway was that it had broken down. It was held that the leaving of the lorry on the highway could be a public nuisance even though there was no foreseeable risk of injury. But as Sachs LJ pointed out, where the leaving of the lorry does not create a foreseeable risk of injury, it is unlikely that it will be the cause of the injury to the claimant, as *Dymond* itself demonstrates. It is submitted, however, that these cases could be more appropriately dealt with as cases of negligence (see Newark (1949) 65 LQR 480). Where stationary vehicles are left where they may foreseeably be a source of danger to others then it could be said that the defendant has been negligent in leaving his vehicle on the highway. Thus liability would only be imposed in respect of the creation of a foreseeable risk of injury and resort would not have to be had to the awkward issues of causation discussed in *Dymond* when the risk of injury is not foreseeable.

While the courts have recognised the right of an occupier of premises adjoining the highway to erect hoardings to a reasonable extent and for a reasonable time in connection with building works being carried out lawfully on those premises, that right does not displace the general rule that interference in substantial measure and over a substantial period of time with the right of the public to make use of the highway constitutes a public nuisance: *Westminster City Council* v *Ocean Leisure Ltd* [2004] EWCA Civ 970 (two hoardings placed on highway to facilitate building works, one there for two years, the other for 13 months: hoardings constituted public nuisance: occupier of shop in proximity entitled to compensation under statutory scheme).

A public nuisance can also be created where the obstruction of the highway is of a temporary nature. Thus in *Barber* v *Penley* [1893] 2 Ch 447 it was held that a queue waiting to get into the defendants' theatre was a public nuisance when it made it difficult for the claimant to gain access to his premises (see too *Lyons* v *Gulliver* [1914] 1 Ch 631).

In *Hubbard* v *Pitt* [1976] QB 142 the defendants were picketing on the highway outside an estate agent's shop. The Court of Appeal held that picketing on the highway may constitute a public nuisance (see too *Thomas* v *NUM (S Wales Area)* [1985] 2 All ER 1, where Scott J invented a tort of unreasonable harassment which, he claimed, was committed by pickets on the highway).

Dangers on the highway

A public nuisance may also be created where a danger is created on the highway. Almost anything which is left on the highway may be a source of danger. A pile of rubble left on the highway may constitute such a danger (see *Clark* v *Chambers* (1878) 3 QBD 327), as may a vehicle which is left on the highway (see *Dymond* v *Pearce* (above)).

In *Wandsworth London Borough Council* v *Railtrack plc* [2002] 2 WLR 512 it was established that feral pigeons had roosted under the defendant's railway bridge over Balham High Road and created a hazard over the pavements. Gibbs J ([2001] 1 WLR 368) decided that the defendant was liable in public nuisance and the Court of Appeal concluded that this decision had been correct. Chadwick LJ said that liability in public nuisance arose where the landowner had knowledge of the existence of a nuisance on or emanating from his land, where there were means reasonably open to him for preventing or abating it, and where he failed to take those means within reasonable time. The three elements of knowledge, means to abate and failure to take those means were all present in this case.

Dangers close to the highway

The danger may not actually be on the highway but be very close to the highway. The occupier of premises close to the highway may thus come under a duty to members of the public using the highway to keep his premises in repair. Thus in *Tarry* v *Ashton* (1876) 1 QBD 314 the defendant was held to be liable in public nuisance when a lamp which overhung his premises fell and injured the claimant, who was a passer-by. The defendant had argued that he was not liable because he had employed an independent contractor to repair the lamp and so he claimed that he had discharged the duty upon him. But it was found that the lamp was insecure because it had not been properly repaired. It was held that the defendant was under a duty to keep the lamp in good repair, that he had been in breach of that duty because the duty was a non-delegable one and so he was liable to the claimant.

In *Wringe* v *Cohen* [1940] 1 KB 229 it was held that the occupier of premises on the highway was under a duty to keep the premises in repair whether he knew of the danger or not. This principle laid down by the Court of Appeal in *Wringe* appears to be a principle of strict liability (see Friedmann (1940) 3 MLR 305). However the court said that the rule would not apply where the damage resulted from the 'secret and unobservable operation of nature' or from the unforeseeable act of a trespasser. These exceptions have been seized upon in subsequent cases to narrow the scope of the principle laid down in *Wringe*. One example of this restrictive interpretation is *British Road Services Ltd* v *Slater* [1964] 1 WLR 498. A large oak tree on the defendant's land overhung the highway. A branch of the tree which overhung the highway caused a package to be knocked off a lorry which was travelling along the highway. The package fell on to the road and the lorry which was travelling behind was damaged when it had to swerve to avoid the package. It was held that the defendant landowners were not responsible for the damage done to the claimant's lorry. The branch was not a foreseeable source of danger and it was only through 'fortuitous circumstances' that the damage had been done to the claimant's lorry.

It seems that the rule in *Wringe* creates a liability in between strict liability and liability for fault. Once the claimant demonstrates that the defendant had control over the premises and that he (the claimant) was injured, then the onus seems to switch to the defendant to show that the accident was an inevitable one which could not have been prevented by taking all reasonable care to keep the premises in good repair. The point was made by Denning LJ in *Mint* v *Good* [1951] 1 KB 517 when he said that 'when structures fall into dangerous disrepair' then 'there must be some fault on the part of someone or other for that to happen' and that it is the defendant who is legally held responsible for the damage which ensues.

The condition of the highway

At common law the highway authorities were only liable for misfeasance and not non-feasance. In other words they were liable for a repair which they had carried out negligently but not for a mere failure to repair. This immunity from suit in respect of negligent non-feasance was removed by the Highways (Miscellaneous Provisions) Act 1961. The law is now stated in the Highways Act 1980.

It is provided in s41 of that Act that the highway authorities are under a duty to maintain the highway. Under s58(1) of the Act the highway authorities are provided with a defence where they have taken reasonable care in all the circumstances to ensure that 'the part of the highway to which the action relates was not dangerous for traffic'. In s58(2) it is provided that in considering what constitutes reasonable care regard is to be had to, amongst other things, the character of the highway, the appropriate standard of maintenance and what constitutes a reasonable standard of repair.

Some controversy has arisen as to what is the correct interpretation of what is now s58 of the 1980 Act. In *Griffiths* v *Liverpool Corporation* [1967] 1 QB 374 Diplock and Salmon LJJ were of the opinion that s58 imposed an absolute liability upon the highway authorities subject to the defence provided in s58(1). Sellers LJ thought that negligence was an essential ingredient in the cause of action, but it appears that where the claimant can show that the highway is not in a proper state of repair the onus is on the highway authority to show that their statutory obligations have been discharged: see too *Littler* v *Liverpool Corporation* [1968] 2 All ER 343 and *Haydon* v *Kent County Council* [1978] QB 343.

The duty of a highway authority in relation to ice on the highway was considered and explained by the House of Lords in *Goodes* v *East Sussex County Council* [2000] 3 All ER 603. At about 7.10 am, when overtaking vehicles on the A267, the claimant's car skidded on ice on the road surface, left the road and he suffered severe injuries. A forecast of frost had been received by the defendant at 11.45 pm the previous evening. Pre-salting had been arranged, starting at 5.30 am, and the stretch of road where the accident occurred would have been treated within 15 minutes after its occurrence. Had the defendant highway authority been in breach of its duty, imposed by s41 of the Highways Act 1980, to maintain the road? The Court of Appeal answered this question in the affirmative. On the highway authority's successful appeal against this decision, the House of Lords said that s41 of the 1980 Act did not oblige the defendant to keep the highway free from ice. Lord Hoffmann said:

'It must be remembered that the duty [under s41 of the 1980 Act] is an absolute one and in this context there seems to me an important difference between a duty to maintain the fabric of the road in good repair and a duty to prevent or remove the formation or accumulation of ice and snow. In the case of the duty to repair, the road either satisfies the objective test formulated by Diplock LJ in *Burnside* v *Emerson* [1968] 3 All ER 741 [ie, to put the road "in such good repair as renders it reasonably passable for the ordinary traffic of the neighbourhood at all seasons of the year without danger caused by its physical condition"] or it does not. The requirements of that objective test may become more exacting with the passing of the years, but the court ... can examine the highway and decide whether it meets the test or not. The highway authority can, by periodic inspection, preventive maintenance and repair, keep the highway in accordance with the necessary standard. If it does not, it can be ordered by the court under s56(2) of the 1980 Act to "put it in proper repair within such reasonable period as may be specified in the order". But an absolute duty to keep the highway free of ice would be an altogether different matter. No highway authority could avoid being from time to time in breach of its duty, which would apply not merely to fast carriage roads but to all highways, including pavements and footpaths. ... There would be no question of ordering the highway authority to comply with its duty.'

For the sake of completeness, it should be noted that the House of Lords disapproved *Haydon* v *Kent County Council* [1978] 2 All ER 97 and *Cross* v *Kirklees Metropolitan Borough Council* [1998] 1 All ER 564.

In *Sandhar* v *Department of Transport, Environment and the Regions* (2004) The Times 15 November the Court of Appeal established that there is no common law duty of care upon highway authorities to remedy the formation of ice on roads. However, s111 Railways and Transport Safety Act 2003 inserted s41(1A) Highways Act 1980 which provides:

'In particular, a highway authority are under a duty to ensure, so far as is reasonably practicable, that safe passage along a highway is not endangered by snow or ice.'

In effect, this new provision reverses the decision of the House of Lords in *Goodes* v *East Sussex County Council*, above, and it came into force on 31 October 2003.

Two further points should be noted. First, s41 does not require the highway authority to carry out work on land which does not form part of the highway, and the authority does not owe a common law duty of care to road users to alleviate known dangers impairing visibility on land adjoining the highway: see *Stovin* v *Wise* [1996] 3 WLR 389. Second, in *Wentworth* v *Wiltshire County Council* [1993] 2 WLR 175 the Court of Appeal held that the right to recover damages from the highway authority for breach of statutory duty is limited to users who suffer damage to property or the person, and does not cover economic loss.

Stovin v *Wise* was distinguished in *Kane* v *New Forest District Council* [2001] 3 All ER 914. An agreement between a developer and the respondent planning authority required the former to construct a footpath before commencing the development. The footpath ended on the inside bend of a road and, although provision had been made for the eventual improvement of the sightlines, at the material time this work had not been carried out. Mr Kane, the appellant, emerged from the footpath and he was struck by a car. His proceedings for negligence against the respondents were dismissed as having no real prospect of success and he appealed against that decision. His appeal was allowed: the appellant's prospects of success were not merely realistic, he had a positively powerful case. Simon Brown LJ said:

> 'It is plain that *Stovin* v *Wise* [1996] 3 All ER 801 proceeded upon the basis "that the complaint against the council was not about anything which it had done to make the highway dangerous, but about its omission to make it safer" per Lord Hoffmann ... Here, by contrast, the starting point must surely be that the respondent council *did* create the source of danger. They it was who required this footpath to be constructed. I cannot accept that in these circumstances they were entitled to wash their hands of that danger and simply leave it to others to cure it by improving the sightlines. It is one thing to say that at the time when the respondents required the construction of this footpath they had every reason to suppose that the improvements ... would ultimately allow it to be safely opened and used: quite another to say that they were later entitled to stand idly by whilst, as they must have known, the footpath lay open to the public in a recognisably dangerous state ... the respondents here could and plainly should have required the opening of this footpath to be delayed until after the sightlines had been improved.'

In *Gorringe* v *Calderdale Metropolitan Borough Council* [2004] 2 All ER 326 the claimant had approached a sharp crest in the road at 50 mph. Just before she reached the top, she saw a bus coming in the opposite direction. She slammed on her brakes and skidded into the bus, suffering severe brain injuries as a result. She claimed damages against the defendant highway authority, alleging that it had caused the accident by failing to give her proper warning of the danger involved in driving fast when it was impossible to see what was coming. More particularly, she contended that the absence of suitable road signage constituted a failure 'to maintain' the road in such a condition as to be safe for use (as required by s41(1) Highways

Act 1980) and, second, that the council's common law duty of care required it to put into effect safety measures that included the positioning of road signs in order to discharge its duty under s39 Road Traffic Act 1988. The House of Lords held that her action could not succeed. As Lord Hoffmann explained, the provision of information, whether by street furniture or painted signs, was quite different from keeping the highway in repair (ie, maintaining it) and s39 of the 1988 Act could not have created a common law duty of care to act (ie, to provide road signs). However, his Lordship did accept the principle that if a highway authority conducts itself so as to create a reasonable expectation about the state of the highway, it will be under a duty to ensure that it does not thereby create a trap for the careful motorist who drives in reliance upon such an expectation.

See, too, *Thompson* v *Hampshire County Council* (2004) The Times 14 October (highway authority not responsible, under its statutory duty to maintain highway, for highway's layout).

20

The Rule in *Rylands* v *Fletcher*

20.1 Introduction

We have noted in earlier chapters the dominant role played by the fault principle in the law of tort in England. Nevertheless, negligence has never succeeded in taking over the whole of the law of tort. There have always been pockets of tort law where the progress of negligence has been resisted. There are some cases where a defendant is held to be strictly liable for the consequence of his activities. A word of explanation is required about the phrase 'strict liability'. It does not necessarily mean that liability is absolute, admitting of no defence whatsoever. As we shall see, 'strict liability' is a somewhat ambiguous phrase and that it can admit of defences to a greater or to a lesser degree.

The classic example of strict liability in English law is the rule in *Rylands* v *Fletcher* (1868) LR 3 HL 330, affirming (1866) LR 1 Ex 265. Until recently it was thought by most lawyers that this rule was anomalous and not to be extended. But strict liability appears to be regaining its popularity. The EEC proposed to extend it to areas such as product liability (for consideration see Finch (1986) 2 PN 53) and these proposals have been put into effect by the Consumer Protection Act 1987. Even within the tort of negligence there have been cases where the standard of care required by the courts has been so high that, in practice, it has really amounted to the imposition of strict liability (see for example *Nettleship* v *Weston* [1971] 2 QB 691) although as we shall see later both negligence and the rule in *Rylands* v *Fletcher* now require the foreseeability of damage, so the term 'strict liability' is rather misleading.

20.2 The rule

It is now time to consider the rule that was actually laid down in the case of *Rylands* v *Fletcher*. First it is necessary to examine the facts of the case. The defendants were mill owners who wished to improve the water supply to their mill. In order to do this they employed some independent contractors, who were apparently competent, to construct a reservoir on their land, which would supply the defendants with water. During the course of their work the independent contractors discovered some underground passages and mines on the land where the reservoir was to be constructed. They did not seal these mines and shafts properly with the result that, when the reservoir was filled with water, the water burst through into the mines and shafts and flooded the claimant's coal mine, causing damage agreed at £937. The defendants were held liable for the damage.

Dias and Markesinis, in their book *Tort Law* (2nd ed) p344, helpfully considered whether the court could have decided the case on the existing law rather than develop a new principle of liability. They concluded that the claimant could not have succeeded in an action in trespass because the damage caused by the flooding was not a direct and immediate consequence of the defendants' activities. Nor could it have amounted to a nuisance since the damage was not continuous or recurring (but see *British Celanese* v *A H Hunt* [1969] 1 WLR 959). Although it was clear that the independent contractors had been at fault it was not clear whether they should have foreseen that their conduct could cause damage to the claimant. Similarly it was unclear whether the defendants would have been held liable for the negligence of the independent contractors. So it was unlikely that the claimant would have succeeded in negligence.

Therefore the traditional view was that the court had to develop a new principle of liability in order to find for the claimant. However, it should be noted that, in the Court of Exchequer Chamber, Blackburn J did not appear to be aware of the fact that he was extending the law in any significant way when he stated:

> 'We think that the true rule of law is, that the person who for his own purposes brings on to his lands and collects and keeps there anything likely to do mischief if it escapes, must keep it in at his peril, and, if he does not do so, he is prima facie answerable for all the damage which is the natural consequence of its escape.'

However, the whole scope of the rule in *Rylands* was reviewed and the rule analysed and restated by the House of Lords in *Cambridge Water Co* v *Eastern Counties Leather plc* [1994] 2 WLR 53. Lord Goff, with whose judgment all the other Law Lords agreed, stated that Blackburn J had not stated any new principle of law but merely extended the law of nuisance to cases of an isolated escape.

Although this is the crucial statement of principle which has emerged from the case it should be noted that it was given by Blackburn J who was a member of the Court of Exchequer Chamber. The case was, in fact, appealed to the House of Lords where Lord Cairns LC gave the leading judgment and explicitly approved of the judgment of Blackburn J. He did, however, add a crucial addition that in *Rylands* the defendants made a 'non-natural' use of their land. This addition has assumed great significance in subsequent cases. The present scope of the rule in *Rylands* can be discussed under the following nine headings (sections 20.3 to 20.11).

20.3 Accumulation

It should be noted that in his judgment Blackburn J referred to 'bringing' things on to the defendant's land. Thus he clearly intended to distinguish between things which are naturally on the land and things which are brought on to the land; only the latter being caught by the rule in *Rylands*. Thus in cases such as *Smith* v *Kenrick* (1849) 7 CB 515, *Pontardawe RDC* v *Moore-Gwyn* [1929] 1 Ch 656 and *Giles* v *Walker* (1890) 24 QBD 656 no liability was imposed under the rule in *Rylands* because the 'thing' which caused the damage either grew naturally on the land (thistle seed in *Giles* v *Walker*) or it accumulated naturally on the land (rain water as in *Smith* v *Kenrick*). It should not be assumed, however, that because the claimant cannot succeed under *Rylands* that he has no cause of action at all. It may be that he has a cause of action in nuisance or negligence (see *Leakey* v *National Trust* [1980] QB 485, discussed at Chapter 18, section 18.10).

20.4 Non-natural user

This requirement has caused many problems. As we have already noted this requirement did not appear in Blackburn J's statement of principle, but was introduced as a gloss by Lord Cairns LC in the House of Lords. In an important article (Non-Natural User and *Rylands* v *Fletcher* (1961) 24 MLR 557) Professor Newark has examined the use of the words 'natural' or 'naturally' in the judgments in *Rylands*. In the judgment of Blackburn J, the words 'natural' or 'naturally' occurred eight times. On six occasions they related to the type of consequence for which the defendants would be liable (ie 'natural and foreseeable consequences'). On one occasion it related to the capacity of the dangerous thing to do damage (ie 'will naturally do damage if it escapes'). On the other occasion it related to the circumstances in which the dangerous thing came to be on the land (ie it had to be brought onto the land, see section 20.3). So for Blackburn J the word 'natural' simply meant something which was naturally there or something which was there by nature. In his examination of the judgment of Lord Cairns LC, Professor Newark demonstrates that Lord Cairns also meant by the use of the word 'natural' something which was naturally on the land.

Professor Newark then demonstrates that, starting with the case of *Farrer* v *Nelson* (1885) 15 QBD 258 and culminating in the famous case of *Rickards* v *Lothian* [1931] AC 263, the courts misconstrued the use of the word 'natural' in *Rylands* so that it came to mean not 'natural' in the sense of according to nature, but came to mean 'ordinary' or 'usual', thus altering the scope of the rule.

In *Rickards* v *Lothian* (above) the claimant leased second-floor offices in premises occupied by the defendants. One morning the claimant discovered that his offices had been flooded and that his stock-in-trade had been damaged by the water. The water had come from a fourth-floor lavatory basin, which had been plugged with nails, soap, pen-holders and string and whose tap had been fully turned on. The jury found that the defendants had been careless in failing to provide an overflow pipe, but that the plugging of the outlet and the turning on of the tap had been the 'malicious act of some person'. The Privy Council held that the defendants were not liable to the claimant. Lord Moulton stated that it was not every use of land which brought the rule in *Rylands* into play; he continued:

> 'It must be some special use bringing with it increased danger to others, and must not merely be the ordinary use of the land or such a use as is proper for the general benefit of the community.'

In *Cambridge Water* Lord Goff agreed that by 'natural' Blackburn J meant something which is there by nature and stated that Lord Moulton's expression 'ordinary use of land' was lacking in precision. Lord Goff particularly criticised the alternative criterion 'or such use as is proper for the general benefit of the community' as introducing doubt and being interpreted in a way that would not keep the exception within reasonable bounds. Lord Goff expressly rejected the finding of the judge at first instance in *Cambridge Water* that the use of the land by the defendants created employment and thus constituted a natural or ordinary use of land.

Lord Goff continued, however, by stating that he did not need in the instant case to redefine natural or ordinary use. Strictly speaking, therefore, his judgment on this criterion could be considered obiter, but in view of the House's root and branch reconsideration of the rule his views must be of great persuasive authority. Lord Goff went on to state that he felt 'that the storage of substantial quantities of chemicals on industrial premises should be regarded as an almost classic case of non-natural use'.

Given the views of Lord Goff on non-natural use, the judgment of Mackenna J in *Mason* v *Levy Auto Parts of England Ltd* [1967] 2 QB 530 can be reconciled. Here the defendants stored on their land crates and a large quantity of combustible materials which ignited in mysterious circumstances. The resulting fire spread to and damaged the claimant's premises. The defendants were held liable under *Rylands*. The factors which persuaded the judge to hold that this was a non-natural user of land were:

1. the quantities of combustible material which the defendants brought on to their land;
2. the way in which the materials were stored; and
3. the character of the neighbourhood.

The later case of *British Celanese* v *A H Hunt* [1969] 1 WLR 959 now seems suspect. In British Celanese the defendants used an industrial estate to manufacture electrical components. Lawton J held that the use was natural because the defendants were using the land for the very purpose for which it was designed and that the goods manufactured were needed for the general benefit of the community. Although the actual decision in *British Celanese* may be correct, the ratio decidendi cannot be justified in the light of *Cambridge Water*.

Further light was shed on this whole question in *Transco plc* v *Stockport Metropolitan Borough Council* [2004] 1 All ER 589; (2003) The Times 20 November. In this case water for domestic use in the defendant council's block of flats was fed first into tanks in the basement. Without negligence on the defendant's part, this main pipe failed at a point within the block and, again without negligence, the failure remained undetected for a prolonged period. Due to the lie of the defendant's land, the water which had escaped from the pipe percolated into an embankment supporting the claimant's gas main, causing the embankment to collapse and create an immediate and serious risk. The claimant took prompt and effective remedial measures: was it entitled to recover the cost involved? The House of Lords held that it was not: since the piping of water to the block of flats was a normal use of land, the rule in *Rylands* v *Fletcher* did not apply. Lord Bingham of Cornhill said that no ingredient of *Rylands* v *Fletcher* liability had provoked more discussion than the requirement of Blackburn J ((1866) LR 1 Ex 265, 280) that the thing brought on to the defendant's land should not be something 'not naturally there', an expression elaborated by Lord Cairns ((1868) LR 3 HL 330, 339) when he referred to the putting of land to a 'non-natural use'. Read literally, those expressions might be thought to exclude nothing which had reached the land otherwise than through operation of the laws of nature. But such an interpretation has been fairly described as 'redolent of a different age': see *Cambridge Water Co* v *Eastern Counties Leather plc* [1994] 2 AC 264 (at p308).

In his Lordship's view, the rule in *Rylands* v *Fletcher* was engaged only where the defendant's use was shown to be extraordinary and unusual. Accordingly, an occupier of land who could show that another occupier of land had brought or kept on his land an exceptionally dangerous or mischievous thing in extraordinary or unusual circumstances was entitled to recover compensation from that occupier for any damage caused to his property interest by the escape of that thing, subject to defences of act of God or of a stranger, without the need to prove negligence. By the end of the hearing, the dispute between the parties had narrowed down to two questions. Had the council brought on to its land something likely to cause danger or mischief if it escaped? Was that an ordinary user of its land? Applying the principles outlined, it was clear that the first question had to be answered negatively, and the second affirmatively. While it was true that water in quantity was almost always capable of causing damage if it escaped, the piping of a water supply from the mains to the storage tanks in the block was a routine function which would not have struck anyone as raising any special hazard.

In truth, the defendant council did not accumulate any water, it merely arranged a supply adequate to meet the residents' needs. The situation could not stand comparison with the making by Mr Rylands of a substantial reservoir. Nor could the use by the council of its land be seen as in any way extraordinary or unusual. It was entirely normal and routine. His Lordship was satisfied that the conditions to be met before strict liability could be imposed on the council were far from being met.

20.5 Dangerous things?

As originally formulated in *Rylands* the rule purported to apply to 'anything likely to do mischief if it escapes'. But there are few, if any, objects which do not give rise to a risk of danger if they escape. But reference can still be seen in the cases to the dangerousness of the thing which has escaped (see *Hale* v *Jennings* [1938] 1 All ER 579 and *Perry* v *Kendrick Transport Ltd* [1956] 1 WLR 85). However, it was not mentioned at all in *British Celanese* v *A H Hunt* (above) and in *Read* v *Lyons Ltd* [1947] AC 156 where Lord MacMillan said that it would be impracticable to devise a legal framework which distinguished between dangerous things and non-dangerous things, attaching liability to the former but not to the latter. The Law Commission in its report entitled *Civil Liability for Dangerous Things and Activities* (1970) (Law Com No 32) came to a similar conclusion. So it is submitted that there is no longer a separate requirement that the thing which escapes be dangerous, but that this requirement has been subsumed within the non-natural user test and that the more dangerous a thing is, the more likely it is that it will be held to constitute a non-natural use.

20.6 Escape

It is clear from the judgment of Blackburn J that the thing must escape from the defendant's land. This requirement was of vital significance in the case of *Read* v *Lyons Ltd* (above). The claimant was employed as an inspector at the defendants' munitions factory during the war. She was injured in the course of her employment at the factory by the explosion of a high explosive shell. She sued the defendants, but made no allegation of negligence. It was held that the defendants were not liable under the rule in *Rylands* because there was no escape of the dangerous thing from their premises; the explosion was confined within their premises.

20.7 Occupation

In his judgment in *Rylands* Blackburn J referred to the defendant bringing the thing on to 'his lands'. Thus he clearly envisaged that the defendant would be in occupation of the land from which the thing escaped. But in the Australian decision of *Benning* v *Wong* (1969) 122 CLR 249 gas escaped from a leaking pipe under a public street. The defendants had no title in the public street, but they were responsible for the maintenance of the pipe. Windeyer J, who dissented, rejected the argument that this took the defendants outside of the rule in *Rylands*. For him the critical question was whether the defendants had control of the place from which the thing escaped. It is unclear whether this approach would be followed in England.

20.8 'His own purposes'

The reference to 'his own purposes' in the judgment of Blackburn J suggests that the rule only applies where the landowner brings the thing on to his land for his own purposes and that whenever the thing is brought on for the purposes of someone else the rule does not apply. The position was considered by the House of Lords in *Rainham Chemical Works* v *Belvedere Fish Guano Co* [1921] 2 AC 465. Two parties, F and P, entered into an agreement for the tenancy of a factory, which they wished to use for the purpose of manufacturing explosives. They covenanted, inter alia, not to assign the premises without the prior consent of the landlords. In fact, at a later date, F and P assigned the benefit of the tenancy, without obtaining the prior consent of the landlords, to a private company which they had formed. An explosion then occurred at the factory and the claimant's property was damaged. The House of Lords held that F and P were liable under *Rylands* because they had not effectively divested themselves of their occupation under the terms of the tenancy agreement. Lord Parmoor, however, was of the opinion that if the private company had become tenants in exclusive occupation of the premises then it, and not F and P, would have been liable.

An owner who is not in occupation of the land at the time when the thing escapes may be liable if he has authorised the accumulation which has escaped (see *Rainham* above).

20.9 Foreseeability of damage

Perhaps the most fundamental change to the rule in *Rylands* v *Fletcher* was made by the House of Lords in *Cambridge Water Co* v *Eastern Counties Leather plc* [1994] 2 WLR 53 when, after an extensive historical survey of the scope of the rule and its application, the House held that, as in nuisance, foreseeability of damage was an ingredient of the cause of action under *Rylands*.

The effect of this aspect of the judgment is that, as mentioned in paragraph 20.2 above, the rule in *Rylands* is in many respects merely the law of nuisance extended to cover the situation of an isolated escape. The House of Lords held that the earlier cases of *West* v *Bristol Tramways Co* [1908] 2 KB 14 and *Rainham Chemical Works Ltd* v *Belvedere Fish Guano Co* [1921] 2 AC 465, which suggested that no foreseeability of damage was required, did not provide a firm enough basis to reject the requirement as stated by Blackburn J in his original judgment, and that the point was open for consideration by the House in the instant case.

20.10 Protected interests

In considering whether a claimant can recover damages under *Rylands* it is important to ascertain what his interest in the land (if any) is and the type of injury in respect of which he is suing. It is important to distinguish between damage to property, physical injury and economic loss, as shown in the following five categories.

An owner of land suffers property damage on his land

This is the clearest category of all because it is clear from *Rylands* itself that an owner may recover in respect of such damage.

The owner of land suffers property damage but at the time of the damage the property was not on his land

This might arise where the land owner's car is damaged while it is parked on a public street. Surprisingly, there is no clear decision on the point. However, in *Halsey* v *Esso Petroleum Ltd* [1961] 1 WLR 683, the claimant was allowed to recover damages under *Rylands* in respect of damage to his car while it was on a public street, although no authorities were considered by Veale J on this point. It is submitted that this approach is the preferable one and that it should be followed.

Personal injury suffered by the owner of land

This point was considered by the Court of Appeal in *Hale* v *Jennings Bros* (above). The defendant had a licence to use certain ground for a fun fair. He erected chair o'planes. While these were in operation one day, a chair, with its occupant, became detached from the chair o'plane and landed in a shooting gallery belonging to the claimant, severely injuring the claimant. The defendant was held liable to the claimant. Scott LJ thought that the point that *Rylands* applied to personal injury to be so obvious that it was not worth arguing. However the position has been complicated by the restrictive decision of the House of Lords in *Read* v *Lyons Ltd* (above). Although the House decided the case on the escape point, they proceeded to consider whether *Rylands* could apply to personal injuries. Viscount Simon and Lord Simonds reserved their opinion on the point and Lord Uthwatt made no mention of the point. Lord Porter considered that any suggestion that *Rylands* applied to personal injuries was an extension of the original principle formulated by Blackburn J and as such would have to be considered carefully. Lord MacMillan adopted the most restrictive approach. He considered that the rule in *Rylands* was confined to conflicts between neighbouring landowners relating to property damage and, because of its anomalous nature, it would not be extended to apply to personal injury. It should be noted here, that in his leading judgment in *Cambridge Water* (above), Lord Goff referred to Professor Newark's 'seminal' article 'The Boundaries of Nuisance' (1949) 65 LQR 480. In particular Lord Goff quoted a passage which reads: 'They [the legal profession] rashly jumped to two conclusions ... and secondly that the Rule could be used to afford a remedy in cases of personal injury'. Professor Newark was of the clear opinion that *Rylands* should not apply to personal injuries, but Lord Goff did not consider this point at all. In view of the House of Lords' acceptance of the basis of Professor Newark's article, however, recovery for personal injuries under *Rylands* must be considered an arguable or questionable point.

Personal injury suffered by persons who are not owners of the land

This is the most difficult category of all because it is here that *Read* is directly in point because the claimant who was injured was merely in the position of an invitee and was not the owner of the land. Prior to *Read* there had been an obiter remark in a case called *Shiffman* v *Order of St John* [1936] 1 All ER 557 to the effect that damages were recoverable in such a situation. The case was in fact decided on the ground of negligence. However it is true to say that *Read* is not a popular decision. Thus in *Perry* v *Kendrick Transport Ltd* [1956] 1 WLR 85 the Court of Appeal held that *Rylands* did apply to personal injury. This view was followed by Veale J in *Halsey* v *Esso Petroleum Ltd* (above) and by the High Court of Australia in *Benning* v *Wong* (above), although it is difficult to reconcile these cases with the general tenor of the judgment of the House of Lords in *Cambridge Water*.

Economic loss

Once again there is no clear authority on the point. In *Weller* v *Foot and Mouth Disease Research Institute* [1966] 1 QB 569 Widgery J held that the defendants could not be liable to the claimants under the rule in *Rylands* because the claimants, who were cattle auctioneers who lost business as a result of an outbreak of foot and mouth disease, had no interest in any land to which the virus had escaped. But in the second and fourth categories above it has already been argued that a proprietary interest is not essential to recovery under *Rylands*, so this reasoning is not convincing. On the other hand, in *Ryeford Homes Ltd* v *Sevenoaks District Council* (1989) 16 Con LR 75 Judge Newey QC stated that whether economic loss could be a 'sufficiently direct result' of an escape 'must I think be a question of fact'. It is submitted that economic loss is, in principle, recoverable under *Rylands*, although it could be argued that it should be no more recoverable under *Rylands* than in negligence itself.

20.11 Defences

The scope of the defences is vitally important in determining the nature of the action in *Rylands* because, if wide defences are admitted, the less likely it is that the action will be one of strict liability. In fact, the defences have been remarkably wide and have stopped only just short of actually admitting absence of negligence as a defence. The defences are as follows:

Act of God

This was defined in *Tennant* v *Earl of Glasgow* (1864) 2 M (HL) 22, 26–7 as:

> ' ... circumstances which no human foresight can provide against, and of which human prudence is not bound to recognise the possibility, and of which when they do occur, therefore, are calamities that do not involve the obligation of paying for the consequences that may result from them.' – per Lord Westbury.

The difficulty lies in determining what constitutes an Act of God. In *Nichols* v *Marsland* (1876) 2 Ex D 1 some artificial lakes had been created by the damming up of a natural stream. An extraordinary rainstorm occurred, the artificial banks burst, and the claimant's property was damaged in the ensuing flood. The defendants were excused after the jury found that the defendants could not reasonably have anticipated such an extraordinary storm. But a different view was taken by the House of Lords in *Greenock Corporation* v *Caledonian Railway Co* [1917] AC 556. The Corporation constructed a paddling pool for children in the bed of a stream, by diverting the natural course of the stream and obstructing the natural flow of water. After an extremely heavy rainstorm, the stream overflowed and in the flood created thereby the claimant's property was damaged. It was held that the Corporation was liable because the rainfall was not an Act of God. The court held that the criterion to be applied in determining whether there has been an Act of God is not, as in *Nichols*, whether the event could reasonably have been anticipated but whether or not human foresight and prudence could reasonably recognise the possibility of such an event. See also *Bybrook Barn Garden Centre Ltd* v *Kent County Council* (2001) The Times 5 January (defendant liable for flooding caused by culvert which had become inadequate since it had been reasonable to expect them to remedy the situation) and Chapter 18, section 18.10.

Default of the claimant

If the damage has been caused by an act or default of the claimant himself then he has no remedy. Thus in *Ponting* v *Noakes* [1894] 2 QB 281 the claimant was unable to recover when his horse reached over his neighbour's boundary fence and ate some poisonous berries, as a result of which the horse died. The damage was due to the intervention of the horse and not to any escape from the defendant's land.

Consent of the claimant

If the claimant consents, expressly or impliedly, to a dangerous thing being brought on to the defendant's land which may cause him damage if it escapes, he cannot recover damages unless he can show that the damage was caused by the negligence of the defendant. In *Kiddle* v *City Business Premises Ltd* [1942] 2 All ER 216 the claimant leased a shop to the defendants in an arcade. A part of the roof of the arcade also formed the roof of part of the defendants' premises and sloped towards the claimant's shop. As a consequence of wartime bombing the gutter became clogged with dust and the claimant's shop was flooded. It was held that the claimant had impliedly consented to the water drainage system and that he was unable to succeed in his action in the absence of proof of negligence.

Common benefit

Where the source of the danger is maintained for the common benefit of both the claimant and the defendant, the defendant is not liable for any escape in the absence of negligence on his part. This defence was also relevant in the case of *Kiddle* (above).

Independent act of a third party

This is the defence which has played the greatest role in enabling a comparison to be made between negligence and the rule in *Rylands*. It is difficult to reconcile this defence with the existence of strict liability because it provides that if the act of the third party was not foreseeable the defendant is not liable and, when we move into the language of foreseeability, we move very close to, if not into, the language of negligence. Thus in *Rickards* v *Lothian* (above) the defendants succeeded in showing that it was third parties, for whom the defendants bore no responsibility, who were responsible for the escape.

In *Perry* v *Kendrick Transport Ltd* (above) two boys ignited the empty fuel tank of a disused bus. The claimant, a boy aged ten, who was near to the bus, was seriously injured by the resulting explosion. The Court of Appeal held, assuming that *Rylands* applied to cases of personal injury, that the claimant had failed to show that the act of a stranger in removing the petrol cap was the type of action which the defendant could have reasonably anticipated and guarded against. The claim therefore failed. The crucial factors here appear to be knowledge of the risk and control over the situation (see too *North Western Utilities* v *London Guarantee and Accident Co* [1936] AC 108). An independent contractor employed by the defendant does not constitute a third party for these purposes (*E Hobbs (Farms) Ltd* v *The Baxenden Chemical Co Ltd* [1992] 1 Lloyd's Rep 54).

Statutory authority

If a dangerous thing is operated or maintained under a statutory authority, liability will not arise under the rule in *Rylands* unless negligence is established. The question whether a statute exempts a defendant from liability is a question of construction in each case. Thus in *Green* v *Chelsea Waterworks* (1894) 70 LT 547 a main, which belonged to a company which was statutorily authorised to lay mains, burst without any negligence on the part of the defendants. It was held that the defendants were not liable since they were authorised by statute to lay mains and since they were under a statutory duty to maintain a continuous supply of water, the statute, by necessary implication, exempted them from liability where there was no negligence on their part. In certain cases, rather than create defences to strict liability actions, Parliament has created absolute liability for the escape of dangerous things, rendering all of these defences useless (see, for example, the Nuclear Installations Act 1965).

21

Fire

21.1 Introduction

We noted at the outset of Chapter 20 that there are pockets of tort law where the progress of negligence has been resisted and liability is imposed in the absence of fault. One such 'pocket', where it has been argued that liability was strict, is liability for damage caused by fire. It has never, however, been clear whether liability was strict or whether it was based on fault. It has also been noted that the extent of liability for fire has undergone considerable change as the law of tort has developed (see Ogus [1969] CLJ 104). We shall commence our analysis by considering liability at common law for the damage done by the escape of fire before considering the various statutory interventions in this area.

21.2 Liability at common law

At common law liability for the escape of fire was probably established originally by an action on the case for negligently permitting a fire to escape (see Winfield (1926) 42 LQR 42). The existence of such liability has been traced back as far as the decision in *Beaulieu v Finglam* (1401) YB Pasch 2 Hen 4 f 18 pl 6). It should be noted that, although this liability may originally have been an example of strict liability, it is a form of liability which pre-dates the rule in *Rylands v Fletcher* and much confusion has arisen in ascertaining the relationship between liability for fire and the rule in *Rylands*.

The relationship between liability at common law for fire and the rule in *Rylands* was considered by MacKenna J in *Mason v Levy Auto Parts of England Ltd* [1967] 2

QB 530 (the facts of which are discussed at Chapter 20, section 20.4). MacKenna J started his analysis by discussing the judgment of Bankes LJ in *Musgrove* v *Pandelis* [1919] 2 KB 43, where Bankes LJ said that there were three alternative heads of liability at common law for damage done by a fire which started on a person's property. The first was liability 'for the mere escape of the fire', the second was an action in negligence in respect of the fire and the third was an action under the rule in *Rylands*. It was argued by MacKenna J that, in making a distinction between the first head of liability and the third head, Bankes LJ was 'making a distinction unknown to the common law'. MacKenna J pointed out that liability for fire cannot be based exactly upon the rule in *Rylands* because the 'thing' has not escaped from the defendant's land (see Chapter 20, section 20.6). So he held that there were two alternatives open to him. The first alternative was to require the claimant to prove:

'(1) that the defendant had brought something onto his land likely to do mischief if it escaped; (2) that he had done so in the course of a non-natural user of the land; and (3) that the thing had ignited and that the fire had spread.'

The alternative was to require the claimant to show that:

'(1) the defendant brought onto his land things likely to catch fire, and kept them there in such conditions that if they did ignite the fire would be likely to spread to the [claimant's] land; (2) he did so in the course of some non-natural use; and (3) the things ignited and the fire spread.'

MacKenna J preferred to adopt the latter approach on the ground that the first alternative was not 'very sensible' because it made 'the likelihood of damage if the thing escapes a criterion of liability, when the thing had not in fact escaped but had caught fire'. So, although involving considerations similar to those in a *Rylands* case, the test to be applied is the slightly different one adopted by MacKenna J in *Mason*.

The claimant who suffers damage as the result of a fire on the defendant's land or a fire which was started by the defendant may also be able to bring an action in either nuisance or negligence. The claimant may be able to bring an action in nuisance where the fire interfered with his use or enjoyment of his property or where it damaged his property (see *Spicer* v *Smee* [1946] 1 All ER 489 and *Goldman* v *Hargrave* [1967] 1 AC 645). Finally the claimant may be able to bring an action in negligence where it can be shown that the defendant failed to take reasonable care to prevent the fire from doing damage to his neighbour (see *Musgrove* v *Pandelis* (above) and see also *Ogwo* v *Taylor* [1987] 3 All ER 961).

21.3 Defences at common law

There are certain defences which exist at common law in relation to liability for fire. In *Mason* v *Levy Auto Parts of England Ltd* (above) MacKenna J said that at common law 'a person from whose land a fire escaped was held liable to his neighbour unless he could prove that it had started or spread by the act of a stranger or of God'. Thus these two defences are clearly established and the principles involved in these defences have already been discussed at Chapter 20, section 20.11 (see too *HN Emanuel Ltd* v *GLC* [1971] 2 All ER 835 on the act of a stranger defence). Other defences which are available at common law include default of the claimant, consent of the claimant and statutory authority (see further the discussion of these defences at Chapter 20, section 20.11).

21.4 The Fires Prevention (Metropolis) Act 1774

One of the principal statutory controls upon liability for fire is the Fires Prevention (Metropolis) Act 1774. Section 86 of that Act provides that:

' ... no action, suit, or process whatever, shall be had, maintained, or prosecuted against any person in whose house, chamber, stable, barn or other building, or on whose estate any such fire shall ... accidentally begin, nor shall any recompense be made by such person for any damage suffered thereby, any law, usage, or custom to the contrary notwithstanding.'

The effect of this section is to place a strict limit on the extent of liability for damage caused by fire by providing that the defendant shall not be liable for a fire which was begun 'accidentally'. This section appears to proceed on the assumption that liability at common law for the escape of fire was strict.

The meaning of the word 'accidentally' was considered by the court in *Filliter* v *Phippard* (1847) 11 QB 347. The defendant lit a fire on his land to burn weeds. He then neglected the fire and the fire spread to the claimant's land, damaging the claimant's hedge. It was held that the defendant could not rely on the Act because the fire did not begin 'accidentally'. It began negligently. It was held that a fire was only begun 'accidentally' where the fire was produced by 'mere chance' or 'was incapable of being traced to any cause'. So the important principle was established that the Act did not apply to a fire which was started negligently (see too *Mulholland* v *Baker* [1939] 3 All ER 166 and *Johnson* v *BJW Property Developments Ltd* [2002] 3 All ER 574: for the facts of the latter case, see Chapter 5, section 5.2).

A similar interpretation has been adopted where the fire started accidentally but was then negligently allowed to spread. This can be demonstrated by reference to the case of *Musgrove* v *Pandelis* (above). The claimant let part of his garage, which was below his flat, to the defendant. The claimant's flat was damaged by a fire which was started when the petrol in the carburettor of the defendant's car suddenly caught fire. Although the fire in the carburettor did indeed begin 'accidentally', the defendant's chauffeur was negligent in failing to prevent the fire from spreading. He could have prevented the fire from spreading to the claimant's flat by taking immediate steps to turn off the tap connecting the petrol tank with the carburettor. It was held that the fire which damaged the claimant's flat was not the fire which began accidentally in the carburettor but the fire which the defendant's chauffeur had negligently permitted to spread. These two fires were thus treated as different fires for the purposes of the Act and so the Act was held to be inapplicable. A similar result was reached in the case of *Goldman* v *Hargrave* (above, the facts are discussed at Chapter 18, section 18.10) where the fire was initially caused by lightning (an Act of God), but was allowed to spread through the negligence of the defendant. It was held that in such a case the 1774 Act was not applicable.

The logical consequence of the ruling in *Musgrove* is that, where the fire is started intentionally but then spreads accidentally and it is the fire which spreads which causes the damage to the claimant, then the defendant should be able to claim the protection of the Act. This is because, according to *Musgrove*, the two fires are separate and the fire which caused the damage to the claimant was one which was begun accidentally and therefore covered by the Act. This was held to be the case in *Sochacki* v *Sas* [1947] 1 All ER 344 where liability was not imposed when damage was caused by a fire which was lit in a grate and then for some unknown reason spread and caused damage to the claimant's property.

The second point which was established in *Musgrove* was that the Act did not apply where the defendant is liable under the rule in *Rylands* v *Fletcher*.

21.5 The railway statutes

Legislation has also been enacted to deal with the liability for fires started by sparks from railway engines. In the nineteenth century railways were constructed and operated under statutory powers and, at that time, railway engines were in the habit of shooting out sparks and fire, which could damage the land adjacent to the railway line and to things growing on that land. As statute had generally authorised the use of the railway line by such engines, liability could not be imposed in respect of such use in the absence of negligence on the part of the railway owners. Thus it was very difficult, if not impossible, for landowners to recover their losses from the railway owners in respect of such fires. This can be illustrated by reference to the case of *Vaughan* v *Taff Vale Railway Co* (1860) 5 H & N 679. Sparks from an engine belonging to the defendants set fire to a wood which belonged to the claimant. Extensive damage was done to the wood. The defendants had been statutorily authorised to use the railway in this manner and it was held that they could not be held liable for so acting, in the absence of negligence on their part. As they had taken all possible steps to avoid such damage occurring they were not negligent and so the claimant was not entitled to succeed.

On the other hand, where the defendant was not able to rely upon statutory authority for the operation of his railway, the task of the claimant was made much easier. This can be seen in the case of *Jones* v *Ffestiniog Railway Co* (1868) LR 3 QB 733 where the defendants were held liable under the rule in *Rylands* v *Fletcher* when a spark from one of their engines set the claimant's haystack alight and destroyed it.

It was held that the defendants were liable because they had no statutory authorisation to use locomotive engines.

However, where the defendants did have such statutory authorisation it remained very difficult for landowners to recover any compensation for the damage done to their land and so, in an effort to restore the balance, the Railway Fires Acts of 1905 and 1923 were enacted. The effect of these Acts is to create liability for the fire damage caused by such sparks but to limit that liability to £200 in respect of damage to the land or crops.

22

Animals

22.1 Introduction

A person may be liable for the damage caused by an animal both at common law and under statute law. The most significant intervention in this area is the Animals Act 1971 and it is upon this Act that most attention will be focused in this Chapter. We shall, however, commence our analysis with an examination of the liability which exists at common law and then the remainder of the Chapter will be devoted to an analysis of the 1971 Act.

22.2 Liability at common law

A person may be liable under ordinary principles of tort law for acts he has done through the agency of an animal which he owns or which is in his possession. A person may commit the tort of nuisance through permitting his animals to block the highway (*Cunningham* v *Whelan* (1917) 52 Ir LT 67), or by allowing the stench created by his pigs (*Aldred's Case* (1610) 9 Co 57b) or the noise created by the crowing of his cockerels (*Leeman* v *Montagu* [1936] 2 All ER 1677) to unreasonably affect his neighbours' enjoyment of their property. A person who sets his dog on to someone else may commit the tort of battery (see Chapter 24) and a person who teaches his parrot to utter defamatory statements commits the tort of defamation.

Similarly the person who permits his animal to trespass on the land of another may commit the tort of trespass (see Chapter 25). Finally it should be noted that a person may be liable under ordinary principles of negligence where he fails to exercise reasonable care over his animal and as a result the claimant suffers damage. Such was the case in *Draper* v *Hodder* [1972] 2 QB 556. The defendant was the owner of some Jack Russell terriers. He failed to take reasonable precautions to prevent them from escaping and when they escaped they mauled the claimant, causing him serious injury. There was no evidence that these terriers had ever attacked a person before, but there was evidence that such terriers were known to be dangerous when they were in a pack and permitted to roam free. It was held that the defendant was negligent in failing to take reasonable precautions to prevent the terriers from escaping because it was foreseeable that they would do such damage if a pack of them escaped and were permitted to roam free.

So far we have been considering the applicability of ordinary tort principles to damage which is caused by an animal. It should, however, be noted that the common law also possessed a form of action which was specifically applicable to damage caused by animals. This was an action on the case for damage done by savage or dangerous animals and was known as the 'scienter' action. In this action the claimant had to show that the defendant, who was the keeper of the animal, knew or ought to have known that the animal was of a dangerous character. He could do this in one of two ways. The first was to show that the animal belonged to a class which was known as ferae naturae (ie was of a dangerous species), in which case the defendant was deemed to know of its dangerous character. The second way was to demonstrate that the animal belonged to a class known as mansuetae naturae (ie they were not of a dangerous species) and liability was established here where it could be shown that the defendant knew of the animal's dangerous or vicious characteristics. Once one of these two hurdles was overcome by the claimant the liability which was imposed on the defendant was strict. This common law action has now, however, been replaced by the provisions of the Animals Act 1971 (see s1(1)(a)).

22.3 Dangerous animals

The Animals Act 1971 (referred to as 'the 1971 Act') follows the common law approach in drawing a distinction between dangerous animals (which were known at common law as ferae naturae) and non-dangerous animals (which were known at common law as mansuetae naturae). In this section we will deal with dangerous animals, while non-dangerous animals will be dealt with at section 22.4.

Section 2(1) of the 1971 Act contains the following statement of general principle:

'Where any damage is caused by an animal which belongs to a dangerous species, any person who is a keeper of the animal is liable for the damage, except as otherwise provided by this Act.'

This section makes the keeper of the animal strictly liable for the damage done by an animal which falls within the ambit of this section. The liability is not, however, absolute (see further section 22.5 on defences). There are two crucial phrases in this section which require further explanation.

The first relates to the meaning of the word 'keeper'. Section 6(3) of the Act states that a person is a keeper of an animal if:

'(a) he owns the animal or has it in his possession; or
(b) he is the head of a household of which a member under the age of sixteen owns the animal or has it in his possession;
and if at any time an animal ceases to be owned by or to be in the possession of a person, any person who immediately before that time was a keeper thereof by virtue of the preceding provisions of this subsection continues to be a keeper of the animal until another person becomes a keeper thereof by virtue of those provisions.'

It is provided in s6(4) that a person is not to be deemed to be a keeper of an animal simply because he has taken possession of the animal for the purpose of preventing it from causing damage or for the purpose of restoring the animal to its owner. There is nothing in the 1971 Act to prevent one keeper of an animal suing another keeper of that animal: *Flack* v *Hudson* (2000) The Times 22 November.

The second, and more important, phrase which requires some explanation is 'dangerous species'. 'Dangerous species' is defined in s6(2) as a species:

'(a) which is not commonly domesticated in the British Islands; and
(b) whose fully grown animals normally have such characteristics that they are likely, unless restrained, to cause severe damage or that any damage that they may cause is likely to be severe.'

This definition of dangerous species is likely to be considerably wider than the category of ferae naturae which existed at common law. A number of points should be noted about the wording of s6(2). The first is that 'species' is defined in s11 as including 'sub-species and variety'. The second is that damage is defined in s11 as including 'the death of, or injury to, any person (including any disease and any impairment of physical or mental condition)'. Thus property damage is not expressly covered by the Act, although it has been argued that, because the definition of damage in s11 does not purport to be exhaustive, then the Act does, in fact, cover damage to property (see *Winfield and Jolowicz on Tort* (13th ed) p458 n26).

The third point to note about this section is that it is the 'species' which must be dangerous and not the particular animal which did the damage. So if the animal which was the cause of the damage was tame, but happened to be a member of a species which is dangerous, it is no defence to show that the animal was not dangerous but was tame. The fourth point to note is that it is probably a question of law and not a question of fact whether or not a particular species is dangerous (see

Behrens v *Bertram Mills Circus Ltd* [1957] 2 QB 1, which, although decided at common law, is presumed to represent the position under the Act).

The fifth point which should be noted is that the requirement in s6(2)(a) is that the animal be of a type which is not commonly domesticated in the British Islands and, for the purpose of this inquiry, it is irrelevant that the animal happens to be one, such as a camel, which is commonly domesticated in another country. Finally it should be noted that s6(2)(b) is worded in the alternative; that is to say it is satisfied *either* by showing that the animal was likely to cause severe damage *or* by showing that, if it were to do damage, that damage was likely to be severe.

22.4 Non-dangerous animals

Non-dangerous animals are covered by s2(2) of the Act which provides that:

'Where damage is caused by an animal which does not belong to a dangerous species, a keeper of the animal is liable for the damage ... if –
(a) the damage is of a kind which the animal, unless restrained, was likely to cause or which, if caused by the animal, was likely to be severe; and
(b) the likelihood of the damage or of its being severe was due to characteristics of the animal which are not normally so found in animals of the same species or are not normally so found except at particular times or in particular circumstances; and
(c) those characteristics were known to that keeper or were at any time known to a person who at that time had charge of the animal as that keeper's servant or, where that keeper is the head of a household, were known to another keeper of the animal who is a member of that household and under the age of sixteen.'

In applying s2(2) to the facts of any given case it is essential that the requirements of paragraphs (a), (b) and (c) be considered separately. However, it must be noted that the drafting of this subsection was subjected to severe criticism by Stuart-Smith and Nourse LJJ in *Curtis* v *Betts* [1990] 1 All ER 769. It is important to note that paragraph (a), like s6(2)(b) (on which see section 22.3), is worded in the alternative; that is to say, it can be satisfied either by showing that the damage was of a kind which the animal was likely to cause unless restrained or by showing that the damage was of a kind which, if caused by the animal, was likely to be severe. The claimant in *Curtis* was attacked by a bull mastiff which was owned by his neighbours, the defendants. The claimant had known the dog since it was a puppy and had been very friendly with it. But, on one occasion, the claimant approached the dog while it was being loaded into a Land Rover owned by the defendants, when the dog leapt at the claimant, biting him on the face. Slade LJ stated that the requirement of paragraph (a) was satisfied because, although the damage was not of a kind which the dog, unless restrained was likely to cause (the dog was lazy and docile), it was damage of a kind which, if caused by the dog, was likely to be severe. The court rejected an argument, based upon Professor North's book (*The Modern Law of Animals* p56), to the effect that the latter requirement was only satisfied where 'the animal had such abnormal characteristics that it was likely that, if it did cause damage, the damage would be severe' because it was pointed out that the abnormal characteristic requirement is contained in paragraph (b), not paragraph (a).

Paragraph (b) gives rise to more difficult problems of interpretation. Nourse LJ stated that the words 'the likelihood of the damage or of its being severe' were 'inept' and were probably attributable to the fact that the draftsman had reproduced the wrong part of s2(2)(a) in paragraph (b). All that was required was the use of the words 'the damage' so that the paragraph read 'the damage was due to characteristics of the animal etc'. Stuart-Smith LJ was equally critical of the drafting of paragraph (b). He was of the opinion that the words 'the likelihood of' suggested that the damage must be foreseeable, whereas paragraph (b) without these words dealt with causation. Although he found it difficult to give a meaning to the words 'the likelihood of' he concluded that paragraph (b) required that there be a causal link between the characteristic and the damage, and this interpretation was also used in *Jaundrill* v *Gillet* (1996) The Times 30 January, where the plantiff failed because he could not establish a causal link between the animal's characteristic under s2 and the damage.

On the facts of *Curtis* it was held that the requirements of paragraph (b) were satisfied because the dog had a characteristic which was not normally found in bull mastiffs except at particular time or at particular places. That characteristic was a tendency to act in a frightening and aggressive manner when protecting its own territory, which, in this case, included the back of the Land Rover.

At common law, under the old scienter action, it was held that, for liability to arise in relation to non-dangerous animals, the claimant must show that the animal had a vicious or mischievous propensity to attack people or other animals (see *Fitzgerald* v *Cooke Bourne (Farms) Ltd* [1964] 1 QB 249). However it was held by Park J in *Wallace* v *Newton* [1982] 1 WLR 375 that this requirement, that the animal have a vicious propensity to attack others, was not incorporated into s2(2) of the 1971 Act. He held that all that need be shown is that the animal was possessed of a characteristic not normally found in an animal of the same species. On the facts in *Wallace* the claimant was held to be entitled to recover damages in respect of her injuries. The claimant, who was a groom employed by the defendants, was seriously injured when a horse, which she was loading into the trailer, suddenly and without any warning became violent and uncontrollable. It was held that, because the horse was known to be unreliable and unpredictable, it was possessed of characteristics which were not normally found in horses and so the requirements of s2(2)(b) were satisfied. Similarly in *Kite* v *Napp* (1982) The Times 1 June it was held that the claimant was entitled to recover damages in respect of his injuries when he was bitten by a dog which had a propensity to attack people carrying bags. It was held that such a propensity constituted a characteristic not normally so found in animals of the same species under s2(2)(b) of the Act. In *Hunt* v *Wallis* (1991) The Times 10 May it was held that, in deciding whether a dog (a border collie) which had caused injury to the claimant had characteristics which were not normally found in 'animals of the same species' the relevant comparison was with other dogs of the same breed (border collies) and not with dogs generally. Pill J held that, given the interpretation of 'species' in s11 of the Act as including 'sub-species and variety', where an identifiable breed existed, such as border collies, the relevant comparison should be made with that breed and not with dogs generally.

The exception in paragraph (b) relating to characteristics which are only found in such species 'at particular times and in particular circumstances' has the effect of making normal behaviour in an animal at a particular stage of its development actionable under s2(2). Thus a female animal which bites to protect her young would appear to be caught under this provision notwithstanding the fact that such behaviour is normal in an animal at that stage. This exception was considered by the Court of Appeal in *Cummings* v *Grainger* [1977] QB 397 in a case in which the claimant was attacked by a guard-dog (it should, however, be noted that since 1975 it has been a criminal offence under s1(1) of the Guard Dogs Act 1975 to use or permit the use of a guard-dog on premises without the guard-dog being at all times under the control of a handler). The claimant, who was a young barmaid, entered a scrapyard next to the bar in which she worked. She knew that the defendant, who was the owner of the yard, kept an untrained Alsatian dog in the yard. She also knew that there were 'Beware of the dog' notices on the gate of the yard. While the claimant was standing in the yard she was attacked and bitten by the dog. She brought an action against the defendant under s2(2) of the 1971 Act claiming that the defendant was liable for the damage done by the dog. It was held that the claimant had made out a prima facie case under s2(2) against the defendant (but see further section 22.5 on defences). It was held that the requirement of s2(2)(a) was satisfied because the damage done by a bite from an Alsatian dog was likely to be severe. It was held that s2(2)(b) was also satisfied because Alsatians were not normally vicious except 'in the particular circumstance' of their being kept as guard-dogs. So, although this dog was acting 'normally' for an Alsatian which had been trained as a guard-dog, it was nevertheless covered by s2(2)(b) because it was not a normal characteristic of dogs as a species, but only an Alsatian dog in the 'particular circumstances' of having been trained as a guard-dog. The requirement of s2(2)(c) was also satisfied because the keeper knew of these characteristics in the Alsatian.

It should also be noted that the liability under s2(2) is qualified by the need to show that the keeper has actual knowledge, as opposed to constructive knowledge, of these characteristics of the animal. It should be noted that the two exceptions contained in s2(2)(c) are tightly drawn. The servant of the keeper must have 'charge' of the animal before his knowledge becomes relevant and the knowledge of the member of the household who is under 16 is only relevant where that person is the keeper, unless that knowledge is communicated to the keeper.

Aspects of s2 of the 1971 Act were considered by the House of Lords in *Mirvahedy* v *Henley* [2003] 2 All ER 401. The facts of this case are as follows. Apparently very badly frightened by some unknown event, shortly after midnight the defendants' three horses stampeded out of their field, pushing over an electric wire fence and a wooden fence. They fled 300 yards up a track and then almost a mile along a minor road and onto a major road where one of them collided with a car driven by the claimant, causing him serious personal injuries. Such behaviour is usual in horses when they are sufficiently alarmed by a threat. A claim in negligence (insufficient fencing of the field) was dismissed, but a claim was also made under s2 of the Animals Act 1971. This claim, too, was dismissed at first instance, but it succeeded on appeal to the Court of Appeal: see [2002] QB 769. On the defendants' appeal to the House of Lords, the only question was: Is the keeper of an animal such as a horse strictly liable for damage caused by the animal when the animal's behaviour in the circumstances was in no way abnormal for an animal of the species in those circumstances? With Lords Slynn of Hadley and Scott of Foscote dissenting, their Lordships said that the answer was in the affirmative and the appeal was dismissed. Lord Nicholls of Birkenhead said:

> 'I agree with the interpretation of s2(2)(b) [of the 1971 Act] adopted in *Cummings* v *Granger (sued as Grainger)* [1977] 1 All ER 104 and *Curtis* v *Betts* [1990] 1 All ER 769 and by the Court of Appeal in the instant case. The fact that an animal's behaviour, although not normal behaviour for animals of that species, was nevertheless normal behaviour for the species in the particular circumstances does not take the case outside s2(2)(b). I also agree with the decision of the Court of Appeal on the facts in the present case. Horses are large and heavy animals. But it was not this innate physical characteristic of the defendants' horses which caused the road accident. The horses escaped because they were terrified. They were still not behaving ordinarily when they careered over the main road, crashing into vehicles rather than the other way about. Hale LJ concluded that it was precisely because they were behaving in this unusual way caused by their panic that the road accident took place ... That conclusion, on the evidence, seems to me irrefutable and to me fatal to the case of [the defendants].'

22.5 Defences

The liability which is imposed on the keeper of the animal by virtue of s2 is strict, but this is not to say that there are no defences to the action. There are a number of defences contained in s5 of the Act. A person is not liable where the damage is due 'wholly to the fault of the person suffering it' (s5(1)). Where the damage is not wholly, but only partly, the fault of the person suffering the damage then reliance cannot be placed on s5(1) but the defendant may be able to argue that the claimant was guilty of contributory negligence (s10). A person is not liable where the person who suffered the damage has voluntarily accepted the risk of such damage (s5(2)). However a person is not treated as having voluntarily accepted the risk where he is employed by the keeper of an animal and incurs a risk incidental to his employment (s6(5))

A person is not liable under s5(3) for any damage caused by an animal:

'... kept on any premises or structure to a person trespassing there, if it is proved either –
(a) that the animal was not kept there for the protection of persons or property; or
(b) (if the animal was kept there for the protection of persons or property) that keeping it there for that purpose was not unreasonable.'

The scope of this defence was considered by the Court of Appeal in *Cummings* v *Grainger* (the facts of which are considered at section 22.4 above). The defendant claimed that he was not liable on the ground that he was entitled to the protection contained in s5(3). As we have already noted the claimant had made out a prima facie case under s2(2), but her case failed because the defendant was able to rely on the defences contained in both s5(2) and s5(3). The claimant was held to have known of the risk created by the dog and to have accepted that risk so as to bring her within the defence in s5(2). The Court of Appeal also held that the defendant could have relied upon the defence contained in s5(3) because the claimant was a trespasser and keeping a guard-dog for the purpose of seeking to protect the defendant's property in the yard was not unreasonable (although see now the Guard Dogs Act 1975). Lord Denning said that the only way of protecting the place was to have a guard-dog since the yard was 'in the East End of London where persons of the roughest type come and go'.

Neither an act of God nor an act of a stranger constitute a defence to any of the liabilities contained in s2 of the 1971 Act.

22.6 Straying livestock

At common law the owner of cattle was strictly liable for the damage done by his cattle when they strayed on to the land of his neighbour. This common law action has now been abolished (s1(1)(c) of the Animals Act 1971) and has been replaced by s4(1) of the 1971 Act which provides that:

'Where livestock belonging to any person strays on to land in the ownership or occupation of another and –
(a) damage is done by the livestock to the land or to any property on it which is in the ownership or possession of the other person; or
(b) any expenses are reasonably incurred by that other person in keeping the livestock while it cannot be restored to the person to whom it belongs or while it is detained in pursuance of section 7 of this Act, or in ascertaining to whom it belongs;
the person to whom the livestock belongs is liable for the damage or expenses, except as otherwise provided by this Act.'

'Livestock' is defined in s11 as 'cattle, horses, asses, mules, hinnies, sheep, pigs, goats and poultry and also deer not in the wild state'. Once again damage is defined in s11 as including 'the death of, or injury to, any person (including any disease and any impairment of physical or mental condition)'. The incorporation of this definition of damage into s4 is rather unusual because it is clear that s4(1)(a) is directed at damage to property and not personal injury. It is submitted that the better view is that, despite the incorporation of s11, damages for personal injury are not recoverable under s4. For the purposes of s4 livestock belongs to the person who has possession of the livestock (s4(2)). The livestock must also 'stray' on to the land of another, so it is necessary to show that there was some degree of entry on to the claimant's land (see *Ellis* v *Loftus Iron Co* (1874) LR 10 CP 10).

Section 7 empowers an occupier of land to detain livestock which has strayed on to his land and to sell the livestock to recover for the damage to his property and expenses he has incurred in detaining the animal. This power can only be exercised, however, within certain rigidly defined constraints (s7(3)). The right to detain the livestock ceases to exist:

1. after 48 hours has elapsed unless both the police and the person to whom the livestock belongs (provided that he knows to whom the livestock belongs) have been informed; or
2. an amount to satisfy his claim under s4 has been tendered; or
3. where there is no claim under s4 and the person entitled to possession of the livestock claims them.

The occupier who detains livestock is liable for any damage caused to the livestock by his failure to exercise 'reasonable care' or by his failure to supply the livestock with 'adequate food and water'. Where the net proceeds of any sale exceed the value of the claim for damages and expenses which the detainer had against the possessor of the livestock, the excess is recoverable from the detainer by the person who would be entitled to the livestock but for their being sold (s7(5)).

It is a defence to show that the damage was due wholly to the fault of the claimant (s5(1)), or to show that the claimant was guilty of contributory negligence (s10). It is also provided in s5(5) of the Act that:

> 'A person is not liable under section 4 of this Act where the livestock strayed from a highway and its presence there was a lawful use of the highway.'

This section was thought to give effect to the rule at common law contained in *Tillet* v *Ward* (1882) 10 QBD 17. The defendant was driving his ox to market when it entered the open door of the claimant's property and did considerable damage to that property before it was finally removed from the property. It was held that the defendant was not liable for the damage because he was not negligent and he was making a reasonable use of the highway. The scope of the defence in s5(5) was recently considered by the Court of Appeal in *Matthews* v *Wicks* (1987) The Times 25 May. The defendants were the owners of sheep and they had a right to let them graze on common land. They also left them free to wander at will on to the highway. One night the sheep got into the claimant's garden where they did extensive damage. The defendants sought to rely upon s5(5) as a defence to the claimant's claim. It was held that permitting livestock to wander at will on to the highway did not constitute a 'lawful use of the highway' and so the defendants were held to be unable to rely on the defence contained in s5(5).

It is also provided in s5(6) that damage shall not be treated as being due to the fault of the person who has suffered the damage on the sole ground that he could have prevented the damage from occurring by fencing the land. However, there is no liability under s4 where it is proved that the straying of the livestock on to the land would not have occurred but for a breach of duty by any other person, being a person having an interest in the land, of a duty to fence.

22.7 Straying on to the highway

Where animals stray on to the highway the person who is responsible for the animals will be liable under s8(1) of the 1971 Act if he did not take reasonable care to prevent them from straying on to the highway. The practical effect of s8(1) is to place an obligation upon keepers to keep their animals fenced in: see, eg, *Donaldson* v *Wilson* (2004) 148 SJ 879 (field gate on much used public right of way in effect last barrier between field and highway: gate left open by walkers, cattle strayed on to highway causing injury to claimant motorist: farmer liable).

However where the damage is caused by animals which have strayed from unfenced land on to the highway, s8(2) provides that the person who placed the animals on that land will not be regarded as having breached his duty of care by placing them there if:

'(a) the land is common land, or is land situated in an area where fencing is not customary, or is a town or village green; and
(b) he had a right to place the animals on that land.'

22.8 Protection of livestock against dogs

Section 3 of the 1971 Act provides that a keeper is strictly liable 'where a dog causes damage by killing or injuring livestock'. This liability does not depend upon it being shown that the defendant was negligent so it is no defence for the defendant to show that he had no reason to believe that his dog would attack livestock. 'Livestock' is defined in s11 of the Act (see section 22.6 above).

In certain circumstances it may be lawful for the owner of livestock to kill or injure a dog to protect his livestock. This right was originally recognised at common law (see *Cresswell* v *Sirl* [1948] 1 KB 241) and is now enshrined in s9 of the 1971 Act. Section 9 provides that it is a defence to any civil proceedings against a person (referred to as the defendant) for killing or causing injury to a dog to prove that: the defendant acted for the protection of his livestock and was entitled so to act; and the officer in charge of a police station was informed of the incident within 48 hours of its occurring.

The defendant is deemed to have been entitled to act for the protection of his livestock only if 'the livestock or the land on which it is belongs to him or to any person under whose express or implied authority he is acting' (s9(2)(a)). A person shall be deemed to be acting for their protection under s9(3) only if:

'(a) the dog is worrying or is about to worry the livestock and there are no other reasonable means of ending or preventing the worrying; or
(b) the dog has been worrying livestock, has not left the vicinity and is not under the control of any person and there are no practicable means of ascertaining to whom it belongs.'

23

Defamation

23.1 Introduction

The tort of defamation seeks to protect the interest of an individual in his reputation. Where a defendant makes an untrue defamatory statement about the claimant, the claimant will have a right of action against the defendant unless the defendant can establish one of the many defences available in a defamation action. The courts here are required to balance the interest of the individual in the protection of his reputation against the freedom of speech of the person who makes the allegedly defamatory statement. We have no constitutionally protected freedom of speech in this country, so the courts do not often expressly consider the freedom of speech implications of a ruling in a defamation case. It may seem at first sight that the maker of a defamatory statement should not be able to claim the benefit of a constitutionally protected freedom of speech because his statement is of little value, but it should be remembered that some statements which are alleged to be defamatory are statements which are critical of the government or public figures or statements on matters of public interest. Thus a person who is in fear of being sued in a defamation action will be discouraged from criticising the government or from making statements on matters of public interest and a fundamental principle of democracy will be undermined. Of course not all defamatory statements are on matters of public interest and so worthy of protection, but it should be remembered that the easier it is for a claimant to succeed in a defamation action, the more likely it is that significant inroads will be made into the protection of freedom of speech.

As a tort, defamation is unusual in that it is one of the few civil actions still tried before a jury: see s69(1) of the Supreme Court Act 1981 and *Safeway Stores plc* v *Tate* [2001] 4 All ER 193 (Civil Procedure Rules did not empower judge to assume role of jury); cf *Alexander* v *Arts Council of Wales* [2001] 4 All ER 205 (judge had correctly withdrawn issue of malice from jury since case unsound and artificial). It is the jury which assesses the damages payable by the defendant and concern has been expressed about the apparently excessive awards made by some juries. There has also been considerable criticism of some of the substantive rules of the tort and in 1996, the Defamation Act 1996, which was intended to modernise the law, received Royal Assent. This Act made major changes to defamation law, although not all of its provisions were brought into force immediately.

23.2 The distinction between libel and slander

Defamation consists of two categories; libel and slander. The difference between the two is historical in origin. Libel evolved from the old Court of Star Chamber in Tudor times as a criminal action and it remains, in certain circumstances, a criminal offence. Slander, on the other hand, developed out of the ecclesiastical courts and the common law courts. The Star Chamber was eventually abolished and its jurisdiction was assumed by the common law courts, who also have jurisdiction in slander cases, but the distinction between libel and slander has never been abolished.

Libel is a defamatory statement which is contained in a permanent form. The commonest way in which libel is committed is by writing. However it may be committed in other ways as long as it is in a permanent form. Thus in *Monson* v *Tussauds Ltd* [1894] 1 QB 671, the defendants were held to have libelled the claimant in displaying a waxwork effigy of him near the 'Chamber of Horrors' in their wax-works. It was held that a waxwork could be a libel as it was in a permanent form. Lopes LJ stated that, although libels:

> ' ... are generally in writing or printing, ... this is not necessary; the defamatory matter may be conveyed in some other permanent form. For instance, a statue, a caricature, an effigy, chalk marks on a wall, signs, or pictures may constitute a libel.'

Slander, on the other hand, is a defamatory statement which is not in a permanent form, such as a spoken statement. Although the distinction between libel and slander is easy to state in the abstract, it can be difficult to apply in practice. Sometimes Parliament has intervened to resolve the problem and, for example, it is provided in ss166 and 201 Broadcasting Act 1990 and s16 Defamation Act 1952 that television and radio broadcasts are treated as a libel and s4 of the Theatres Act 1968 provides, subject to the exceptions contained in s7, that a theatre performance is a libel.

However, Parliament has not resolved all of the problems in distinguishing between libel and slander. For example, if I dictate a defamatory statement to my typist, do I commit libel or slander? The answer appears to be that the dictation of the defamatory statement to the secretary is slander, but that the sending of the letter is libel. However, rather unusually, it appears that a person who reads out defamatory matter from a written document to a third party publishes a libel and not a slander (*Forrester* v *Tyrell* (1893) 9 TLR 257).

There are other cases where it can be difficult to distinguish between libel and slander. Does sky-writing constitute libel? What if I make a record which contains defamatory material, is that libel or slander? In *Youssoupoff* v *Metro-Goldwyn-Mayer* (1934) 50 TLR 581 the claimant claimed damages from the defendants for an alleged libel when, in a sound film, it was alleged that the claimant had been seduced by Rasputin. The Court of Appeal held that a defamatory statement contained in a film was libel. Slesser LJ stated that, because 'the photographic part of the exhibition' was in a permanent form, then it was the proper subject of an action for libel. He said that the speech part of the film was merely 'ancillary' to the film; being 'part of the surroundings explaining that which is to be seen'. However, it is not entirely clear whether Slesser LJ would have regarded the sound alone, without the vision, as being a libel and so it remains uncertain whether a defamatory statement contained on a record is libel or slander.

The difficulty of distinguishing between libel and slander does little credit to the law. But this difficulty of distinguishing between these two categories is only of relevance where there is a difference between the rules relating to libel and slander.

In fact there are some crucial differences between libel and slander. Libel can be a crime as well as a tort. Slander is only a tort, although the spoken words may constitute a crime, for example, blasphemy. Libel is actionable per se but the general rule is that slander is only actionable where the claimant can show that he has suffered special damage. Special damage requires that the claimant suffer loss which is capable of being estimated in money. Loss of friendship is not capable of being estimated in money terms and so does not constitute special damage, but loss of hospitality or loss of marriage prospects may constitute special damage (*Roberts* v *Roberts* (1864) 5 B & S 384).

Although the claimant in a slander action must generally show that he has suffered special damage, there are certain exceptional cases where this is not so. These exceptional cases are as follows.

Imputation of a crime

Where the defendant implies that the claimant has committed a crime which is punishable by imprisonment then the claimant need not show that he has suffered special damage (*Hellwig* v *Mitchell* [1910] 1 KB 609). However where the imputation is that the claimant has committed a crime which is not punishable by imprisonment, but is punishable by a fine, then the claimant must show that he has suffered special damage.

Imputation of unchastity in women

Under the Slander of Women Act 1891 the imputation of unchastity in women is actionable without proof of special damage. Such imputations include an imputation of lesbianism (*Kerr* v *Kennedy* [1942] 1 KB 409) and an imputation that the claimant had been raped (*Youssoupoff* v *Metro-Goldwyn-Mayer* (above)).

Imputation of disease

Where there is an imputation that the claimant suffers from an infectious or contagious disease, such as venereal disease, which is likely to prevent other persons from associating with the claimant, then such a slander is actionable without proof of special damage (*Bloodworth* v *Gray* (1844) 7 Man & G 334).

Imputation of unfitness to one's trade or calling

This is the most important category where it is not necessary for the claimant to show that he has suffered special damage. This exception is now enshrined in s2 of the Defamation Act 1952 which provides that:

> 'In an action for slander in respect of words calculated to disparage the [claimant] in any office, profession, calling, trade or business held or carried on by him at the time of the

publication, it shall not be necessary to allege or prove special damage, whether or not the words are spoken of the claimant by way of his office, profession, calling, trade or business.'

The wording of this section would appear to be wide enough to encompass any slander which is reasonably capable of injuring the claimant in his office and it need not be shown that the slander was referable to the claimant in the capacity of his office (as was the case at common law in *Jones* v *Jones* [1916] 2 AC 481).

These exceptions considerably reduce the distinction between libel and slander, and there are, in fact, many common elements. These are that the statement of the defendant must be defamatory, it must be published to others and it must be understood as being referable to the claimant. We shall discuss these separate elements after discussing who can be defamed.

23.3 Who may be defamed?

It is only a living person who can bring an action in defamation. A dead person cannot be defamed, no matter how distressing the defendant's statement is to the deceased's relatives. Corporations, whether trading or non-trading, have personality for this purpose so that they can sue for defamatory statements made affecting their corporate reputation (*Metropolitan Saloon Omnibus Co* v *Hawkins* (1859) 4 H & N 87, approved by the House of Lords in *Derbyshire County Council* v *Times Newspapers Ltd* [1993] 2 WLR 449). Different considerations have been held to apply to local authorities because of the fact that a local authority is a democratically elected government body which must be open to uninhibited public criticism. Therefore it has been held that a local authority is not entitled to bring a claim in defamation (*Derbyshire County Council* v *Times Newspapers Ltd* (above)). Individual councillors who are defamed may, of course, bring an action in their own name, as may officers (ie paid staff) of a local authority. Indeed, a local authority may fund its officers' libel proceedings or indemnify them against the costs involved: *R (Comninos)* v *Bedford Borough Council* (2000) The Times 11 February.

Trade unions, because they are unincorporated associations, do not to have any personality for this purpose and so cannot maintain an action in defamation (*Electrical, Electronic, Telecommunication & Plumbing Union* v *Times Newspapers Ltd* [1980] QB 585).

23.4 What is defamatory?

The words which are used by the defendant must be words which are defamatory. The definition of defamatory is an issue of considerable difficulty. The difficulty is not only the legal one of framing a satisfactory definition of the word, but it is also a troublesome issue of policy. Lord Atkin in *Sim v Stretch* [1936] 2 All ER 1237 said that defamatory words were 'words which tend to lower the claimant in the estimation of right thinking members of society generally'. The statement may lower the claimant in the estimation of right thinking people by exposing him to 'hatred, contempt or ridicule' (*Parmiter v Coupland and Another* (1840) 6 M & W 105). But the statement need not have that effect. Thus it has been held in *Youssoupoff v Metro-Goldwyn-Mayer* (1934) 50 TLR 581 to be defamatory to impute that the claimant had been raped. The fact that the claimant was said to have been raped would not have exposed her to 'hatred, contempt or ridicule' but it may have caused people to shun her or to avoid or lose confidence in her. However deplorable we feel that this attitude to the victims of rape may be, defamation takes people as they are and not as they ought to be. In *Berkoff v Burchill* [1996] 4 All ER 1008 it was held that although insults which did not diminish a person's standing were not defamatory, a statement could be defamatory if it held up the claimant to contempt, scorn or riducule or tended to exlude him from society, even if the statement did not impute disgraceful conduct or any lack of professional or business skill.

This test, based as it is upon the opinion of 'right thinking members of society', begs a number of questions. For example, who is a 'right thinking' member of society? Would the 'right thinking' person consider it defamatory to call a person who refuses to participate in industrial action a 'scab'? In answering this question regard may be had to the case of *Byrne v Deane* [1937] 1 KB 818: see also section 23.6. The claimant reported to the police that the defendants' club unlawfully kept some automatic gambling machines on their premises. After these machines had been removed by the police, a typewritten message was put on the wall of the club premises which stated that 'he who gave the game away may he burn in hell and rue the day'. It was held that to allege that the claimant had reported a crime to the police was not defamatory because it would not be so regarded by a 'good and worthy subject of the King'. It did not matter for this purpose that the claimant would be less well thought of by his fellow club members. So the fact that the section of the public with which the claimant has the closest contact thinks less of him is not conclusive that the statement is defamatory if the views of that group are not consistent with our right thinking member of society. So it may not be defamatory to allege that a person is a 'scab'. Similarly, where the defendant alleges that the claimant has carried out an act, it is what the claimant was said to have done, and not what the defendant thought of the act that is important. Thus, where that act amounted to cheating it was irrelevant that the defendant did not consider the act to be cheating: *Botham v Khan* (1996) The Times 15 July.

Some guidance as to the approach to be adopted in deciding whether a particular statement was defamatory was provided in the case of *Hartt v Newspaper Publishing plc* (1989) The Times 7 November where it was held that, in deciding whether or not a statement was defamatory, the approach which should be adopted is that of the hypothetical ordinary reader who was neither 'naive' nor 'unduly suspicious' but who 'could read in an implication more readily than a lawyer, and might indulge in a certain amount of loose thinking'. On the other hand, the hypothetical ordinary reader was not someone who was 'avid for scandal' and he was not someone who selected one bad meaning where other, non-defamatory meanings were available. These guidelines were repeated by the Court of Appeal in *Skuse* v *Granada Television Ltd* (unreported 30 March 1993) as reported by the Court of Appeal in *Gillick* v *British Broadcasting Corporation* (1995) The Times 20 October. The publisher of an alleged defamatory document is entitled to have the publication looked at in full and in the proper context. The claimant cannot select part of the statement to justify his claim. Thus in *Charleston* v *News Group Newspapers* [1995] 2 WLR 450, where two well known actors had their faces superimposed in pornographic photographs in a newspaper, and the accompanying text stated that they were innocent and unknowing participants, no action in defamation lay. The Court of Appeal, however, stated that the law might some time be required to consider the impact of photographs on the readers of tabloid newspapers in particular.

In considering whether a statement is defamatory regard must be had to all the circumstances of the case. Words must be interpreted in the context in which they were spoken or written. Thus where a book describes statements made in the 1960s the question as to whether or not they are defamatory must be decided on whether they would have been defamatory in the cultural context and circumstances of the time: see *Mitchell* v *Book Sales Ltd* (1994) The Independent 25 March. Additionally it is sometimes said that vulgar abuse is not defamatory. But this is not entirely accurate. Much depends on the manner in which the words were spoken. Were they slanderous or merely vituperative? In *Fields* v *Davis* [1955] CLY 1543 the defendant called the claimant, who was a married woman, a 'tramp'. It was held that the words were not defamatory because they were uttered by the defendant in a fit of temper and were understood by those around as being mere vulgar abuse. Where the words are written they will not be interpreted as mere vulgar abuse because the defendant has time for consideration of the words before writing them and the reader has no way of knowing that the words were merely vituperative rather than libellous.

It need not be shown that the defendant intended to defame the claimant. In *Cassidy* v *Daily Mirror Newspapers Ltd* [1929] 2 KB 331 the defendants published a picture of the claimant's husband and another woman in their newspaper and under the photograph were the words 'Mr M Corrigan, the race horse owner and Miss X, whose engagement has been announced'. The claimant was, in fact, married to her husband, although they did not live together, except on the rare occasion that he stayed with her. She claimed that she had suffered damage through the imputation that she lived in immoral cohabitation with her husband. The defendants published the article in all good faith, not knowing that it was in any way defamatory and they argued that it would amount to a great hardship if liability was to be imposed upon them. However, it was held that the defendants had libelled the claimant. Russell LJ stated that 'liability for libel does not depend on the intention of the defamer, but on the fact of defamation'.

The fact that the defendant has an innocent motive is not, therefore, a defence to a defamation action, but, by the same token, the fact that the words are, on the face of it, innocent, does not mean that the statement cannot be defamatory. The words may, on a natural and ordinary interpretation, contain nothing of a defamatory nature, but may be defamatory when combined with some extrinsic facts known to readers of the publication. This is called innuendo. An example will help to illustrate what is meant by innuendo. In *Tolley* v *JS Fry & Sons Ltd* [1931] AC 333 the claimant was the English amateur golf champion and he was featured, without giving his consent, on a poster advertising the defendants' chocolate bar. The text of the poster compared the excellence of the chocolate bar with the excellence of the claimant's swing. The claimant alleged that this constituted an innuendo because it implied that he had agreed to feature in the poster for financial gain and that he had flouted the rules relating to his amateur status. It was held that the innuendo was made out and that the claimant was entitled to succeed in his action against the defendants.

However, a distinction must be drawn between a 'false' innuendo and a 'true' innuendo. A 'false' innuendo arises where the claimant alleges that the words, in their ordinary and natural meaning, bear a particular meaning which is discernible without the need for additional evidence. On the other hand, a 'true' innuendo arises where the claimant has to adduce additional evidence to establish the meaning which he alleges that the words should be given. The distinction is an important one because an innuendo must be distinctly pleaded and proved. A case which illustrates this distinction is *Lewis* v *Daily Telegraph Ltd* [1964] AC 234. It was reported by the defendants in their newspaper that the Fraud Squad were investigating the claimant's firm. It was argued that the words 'Fraud Squad Probe City Firm' were defamatory because they indicated that the claimant was guilty of fraud or was, at least, suspected of fraud by the police. It was held that the statement that a person was being investigated for fraud was not the same thing as saying that he was guilty of fraud. It was therefore held that the words were not in their ordinary meaning defamatory and it was only by pleading additional facts, which the claimant did not do, that he could have proved that the statement was defamatory. On the other hand *Tolley* was a case of true innuendo because the claimant had to plead additional evidence of his amateur status to prove that the statement was defamatory.

It is the task of the jury to decide whether or not a given statement is defamatory. However, the judge retains the prior task of deciding whether or not there is a case for the jury to consider and whether, as a matter of law, the defendant's words are capable of bearing a defamatory meaning. This role can be seen in the case of *Capital & Counties Bank Ltd* v *Henty & Sons* (1882) 7 App Cas 741. The defendants quarrelled with the manager of one of the claimants' banks and then sent out a circular letter to their own customers, who in turn showed it to other people, which stated that the defendants would not accept as payment any cheque which was drawn on the claimant bank. The claimant bank alleged that this circular letter was defamatory because it implied that they were insolvent. It was held that the words were not, in their ordinary and natural meaning, defamatory and that a reasonable man would not infer any innuendo that the claimants were insolvent (but see the criticism of the application of this test on the facts in *Slim* v *Daily Telegraph Ltd* [1968] 2 QB 157). So it was held that there was no case to go to the jury and judgment was entered for the defendants.

As from 1 September 1994 under a new Rule of the Supreme Court, O.82 r3A, either party may apply to a judge for an order determining whether or not the words complained of are capable of bearing a meaning attributed to them in the pleadings. With effect from 28 February 2000, see Practice Direction PD 53, para 4.

23.5 Refers to the claimant

The statement uttered by the defendant must be shown to have referred to the claimant. This requirement is easily satisfied where the claimant is referred to by name by the defendant. Where the claimant is expressly referred to by the defendant, the claimant need not show that the defendant intended to refer to him. This can be seen in the case of *Hulton* v *Jones* [1910] AC 20 (cf *Blennerhassett* v *Novelty Sales Services Ltd* (1933) 175 LT 393). The defendants published an article in their newspaper which purported to describe a motor festival in Dieppe. In the article they described the activities of one Artemus Jones, who was a churchwarden in Peckham and who was described as 'the life and soul of a gay little band that haunts the Casino and turns night into day, besides betraying a most unholy delight in the society of female butterflies'. The claimant, who was called Artemus Jones but was a barrister rather than the churchwarden at Peckham, brought a libel action against the defendants. Neither the writer of the article nor the editor of the paper had heard of the claimant and neither intended to refer to him, but the claimant produced witnesses who said that they thought that the article referred to him. It was held by the House of Lords that if reasonable people understood the language of the article as being defamatory of the claimant, it was irrelevant that the defendants did not intend to defame the claimant.

A defendant may also be liable where his statement is true of one person but is, in fact, defamatory of another person of the same name or same description, who was not known to the defendant, and who suffered injury as a result of the publication of the statement. Such was the case in *Newstead* v *London Express Newspapers Ltd* [1940] 1 KB 377. An article in the defendants' newspaper entitled 'Why do people commit bigamy?' referred to a self-confessed bigamist called 'Harold Newstead, a thirty-year-old Camberwell man'. The claimant, who was of the same name and lived in Camberwell, brought a libel action against the defendants. The defendants argued that they had not intended to refer to the claimant but to another Harold Newstead who lived in Camberwell. It was held that the defendants were liable to the claimant because they should have taken greater care to ensure that their article could not have been taken as referring to someone else.

However, there is no requirement that the claimant be expressly referred to by the defendant. It is sufficient if the statement impliedly referred to the claimant (*Le Fanu* v *Malcolmson* (1848) 1 HL Cas 637) and it can also be satisfied where the defendant's statement does not make any obvious reference to the claimant. Such was the case in *Morgan* v *Odhams Press Ltd* [1971] 1 WLR 1239. The claimant claimed that he had been libelled by the defendants in an article concerned with a dog-doping gang which had allegedly kidnapped a certain Miss Murray. At the time Miss Murray was staying in the claimant's flat and the claimant produced six witnesses who testified that they thought that the article was referring to the claimant and that he was involved with this dog-doping gang. It was held by the House of Lords that there was sufficient evidence to go to the jury because the ordinary reader who had special knowledge of the circumstances would conclude that the article referred to the claimant.

In considering whether a defamatory statement referred to the claimant, regard may be had to subsequent statements which shed light on the person to whom the defamatory article referred (*Hayward* v *Thompson* [1982] QB 47).

One important issue is whether a group can sue where it is alleged that the group as a whole has been defamed. This issue was considered by the House of Lords in *Knupffer* v *London Express Newspapers Ltd* [1944] AC 116. The claimant was a Russian refugee and was a member of the 'Young Russian Party', which had 24 members in this country and several thousand members abroad. The article alleged that this group were Nazis. The House of Lords held that the claimant could sue in respect of this statement if he could prove that the statement was capable of referring to him and that it was in fact understood as referring to him. It was held that the claimant could not show that the article was capable of referring to him as it referred mainly to the activities of the group overseas and so his action was dismissed. This ruling makes it extremely difficult for a claimant to sue in respect of a group libel unless the group which is alleged to have been libelled is very limited in size, so that the statement can be understood as referring to the claimant (*Browne* v *DC Thompson* 1912 SC 359). This can have detrimental civil liberties implications where the group which has been defamed is an oppressed minority group with little other hope of obtaining redress (but see s70 of the Race Relations Act 1976 and, in America, *Beauharnais* v *Illinois* 343 US 250 (1952)).

23.6 Publication

The defendant must publish the defamatory statement about the claimant because it is the claimant's reputation in the eyes of others which is protected and not the claimant's pride. For this purpose a communication between the defendant and his spouse does not constitute publication (*Wennhak* v *Morgan* (1888) 20 QBD 635). However a communication to the spouse of the claimant does constitute publication for this purpose (*Wenman* v *Ash* (1853) 13 CB 836). The handing back of a defamatory statement by the printer to the author of the statement does not constitute publication, although, of course, there is a publication where the author hands the defamatory material to the printer for printing (*Eglantine Inn Ltd* v *Smith* [1948] NI 29).

The defendant need not have intended that the defamatory statement be communicated to any particular person. It is sufficient that the publication to that person could have been reasonably anticipated. This can be seen in the case of *Theaker* v *Richardson* [1962] 1 WLR 151. The defendant wrote a defamatory letter to the claimant, accusing her of being a whore and a brothel keeper. The claimant was a married woman and was a fellow local councillor with the defendant. The defendant put the defamatory letter through the claimant's letterbox in a manilla envelope, similar to the type used for election addresses. The claimant's husband picked up the envelope and, believing it to contain an election address, he opened it and read its contents. The jury found that the defendant was liable because it was a reasonable and probable consequence of the defendant's method of delivery of the letter that the claimant's husband would open it and read it and the Court of Appeal upheld this finding. The limits of this rule can, however, be seen in the case of *Huth* v *Huth* [1915] 3 KB 32. The defendant sent a defamatory letter to his wife, from whom he was separated, stating that they were not married and that their children were illegitimate. The letter was opened by a curious butler who read its contents. It was held that there was no publication of the letter because the defendant could not reasonably have anticipated that an inquisitive butler would open his wife's mail.

Whenever a customer of an Internet service provider accesses its newsgroup and sees a posting defamatory of the claimant there is a publication to that customer: *Godfrey* v *Demon Internet Ltd* [1999] 4 All ER 342. Libel has been established where untruthful allegations were made on banners towed by a private aircraft and leaflets dropped indiscriminately from it: *Howlett* v *Holding* (2003) (unreported).

Every time that the defamatory statement is repeated, the tort is committed again and a fresh cause of action arises. In *Cutler* v *McPhail* [1962] 2 QB 292 a defamatory letter was written to a newspaper and the letter was subsequently published by the newspaper. It was held that the writer of the letter was liable for the libel which he had written, but the publishers of the newspaper were also liable for the libel which was published. The maker of a defamatory statement may also find himself liable for the damage caused by the repetition of the defamatory statement by a third party, at least where that repetition was reasonably foreseeable. In *Slipper* v *British Broadcasting Corporation* [1991] 1 QB 283 the claimant alleged that he was libelled by a film which was broadcast by the defendants. The claimant argued that, in assessing general damages, regard should be had to reviews of the film in national newspapers which repeated the sting of the libel because the defendants had invited the press to review the film, they knew that the film would be reviewed by the national press and that people would read the reviews who would not have seen the film. The defendants applied to strike out the claimant's claim in so far as it related to the reviews in the national press on the ground that they could not be liable for the repetition of the libel which was not authorised by them and which was made by an independent third party. The Court of Appeal held that the law relating to republication was an aspect of novus actus interveniens and that the critical question was therefore whether or not there was a break in the chain of causation. Slade LJ was prepared to accept that prima facie a court will regard an unauthorised repetition of a libel by an independent third party as a novus actus interveniens but, on the facts, the court refused to strike out the claim. The court regarded it as 'plainly arguable' that the defendants could reasonably foresee and anticipate as a natural and probable consequence of the film that the sting of the libel would be repeated in the reviews in the national press.

The Court of Appeal took *Slipper* into account when reaching its conclusion in *McManus* v *Beckham* [2002] 4 All ER 497. The claimant proprietors of an autograph shop alleged that the defendant, Victoria Beckham, had said, in the presence of customers, that the autograph on a photograph of her husband David was a fake. The incident received considerable press coverage. Could the claimants rely on the press coverage in establishing the loss they said they had suffered? Their Lordships decided that they could, to the extent that it was just to do so. As Waller LJ explained:

'What the law is striving to achieve in this area is a just and reasonable result by reference to the position of a reasonable person in the position of the defendant. If a defendant is actually aware (1) that what she says or does is likely to be reported, and (2) that if she slanders someone that slander is likely to be repeated in whole or in part, there is no injustice in her being held responsible for the damage that the slander causes via that publication. I would suggest further that if a jury were to conclude that a reasonable person in the position of the defendant should have appreciated that there was a significant risk that what she said would be repeated in whole or in part in the press and that that would increase the damage caused by the slander, it is not unjust that the defendant should be liable for it. Thus I would suggest a direction along the above lines rather than by reference to "foreseeability".'

In *Jameel (Yousef)* v *Dow Jones and Co Inc* (2005) The Times 14 February Lord Phillips of Worth Matravers MR said that English law had been well served by a principle under which liability turned on the objective question of whether the publication was one which tended to injure the claimant's reputation and that it would not be right to abandon that principle in the absence of a convincing case that it was in conflict with art 10 of the European Convention for the Protection of Human Rights and Fundamental Freedoms 1950. However, their Lordships accepted that in the rare case where a claimant brought an action for defamation his reputation had suffered no or minimal actual damage, that might constitute an interference with freedom of expression which was not necessary for the protection of the claimant's reputation. In the case which was then before them, their Lordships concluded that it would be an abuse of process to continue to commit the resources of the court, including substantial judge and possibly jury time, to an action where so little was at stake. To dismiss the claim for abuse of process would not infringe art 6 of the Convention since that article did not require the provision of a fair and public hearing in relation to an alleged infringement of rights when the alleged infringement was shown not to be real and substantial.

Article 10 of the Convention does not require a corporation suing for libel to prove special damage: *Jameel (Mohammed)* v *Wall Street Journal Europe Sprl* (2005) The Times 14 February.

23.7 Summary procedure

Since 28 February 2000, ss8 and 9 of the Defamation Act 1996 have provided a new summary procedure for claims. It provides a 'fast track' procedure for the disposal of straightforward cases, and damages are assessed by a judge not a jury and are limited to £10,000. The procedure can be used by both claimants and defendants seeking a rapid decision before costs escalate. The court may dismiss the claimant's claim if it has no realistic prospect of success: s8(2). By s9, summary relief may include a declaration that the statement was false and defamatory, publication of an apology, an injunction regarding further publication and damages not exceeding £10,000.

23.8 Defences

There are a number of defences to the tort of defamation, including some inserted and modified by the Defamation Act 1996. In many ways these defences are the most important aspect of the law of defamation.

23.9 Responsibility for publication

The defence, which is contained in s1 Defamation Act 1996, replaces the common law defence of innocent dissemination. It provides that a person has a defence if he can show that:

1. he was not the author, editor or publisher of the statement complained of;
2. he took reasonable care in relation to its publication; and
3. he did not know, and had no reason to believe, that what he did caused or contributed to the publication of the defamatory statement.

An Internet service provider publishes a posting on its newsgroup whenever a subscriber accesses the newsgroup and sees the posting. It follows that the defence under s1 of the 1996 Act is not available to the service provider: *Godfrey* v *Demon Internet Ltd* [1999] 4 All ER 342.

23.10 Offer to make amends

This defence, which is contained in s2(4) of the Defamation Act 1996, was brought into force on 28 February 2000. It replaces the defence of unintentional defamation contained in s4 of the Defamation Act 1952.

By s2(4) an offer to make amends must offer to make and publish a suitable correction and apology, and to pay compensation. By s3 if such an offer is accepted then defamation proceedings are ended, and if the parties cannot agree on compensation this amount may be decided by the court.

In *Milne* v *Express Newspapers Ltd* [2005] 1 All ER 1021 May LJ helpfully explained the effect of ss2 and 3 of the 1996 Act. Section 2 provides that a person who has published a statement alleged to be defamatory may offer to make amends under the section. The offer may be in relation to the defamatory statement generally or in relation to a specific defamatory meaning which the person making the offer accepts that the statement conveys. An offer to make amends is an offer to make and publish a suitable correction and a sufficient apology, and to pay such compensation and costs as may be agreed or determined. An offer to make amends may not be made after a person has served a defence in defamation proceedings brought against him in respect of the publication in question.

Section 3 provides that, if an offer to make amends is accepted, the party accepting the offer may not bring or continue defamation proceedings against the person making the offer in respect of the publication, but he is entitled to enforce the offer. The parties can agree the steps to be taken. If they do not agree, the party who made the offer may take such steps as he thinks appropriate. He may make the correction and apology by a statement in open court in terms approved by the court. He may give an undertaking to the courts as to the manner of publication. If the parties do not agree the amount to be paid by way of compensation, it is to be determined by the court on the same principles as damages in defamation proceedings. Proceedings under this section are to be heard and determined without a jury. the court is to take account of any steps taken in fulfilment of the offer, including the suitability of the correction, the sufficiency of the apology and whether the manner of their publication was reasonable in the circumstances: and the court may reduce or increase the amount of compensation accordingly. Thus, if in an ordinary case a claimant in defamation proceedings accepts an offer to make amends, he becomes entitled either by agreement or by determination of the court to full proper compensation for the defamatory publication. The defendant has capitulated at an early stage and before serving a defence on all issues except the amount of damages, if this is not agreed. The claimant can bring or continue the proceedings to determine the compensation. It is to be expected that most sensible claimants will accept unqualified offers to make amends. the main purpose of the statutory provisions is to encourage the sensible compromise of defamation proceedings without the need for an expensive jury trial.

As to the determination of compensation by the court under s3(5) of the 1996

Act, in *Nail* v *News Group Newspapers Ltd* [2005] 1 All ER 1040 the Court of Appeal affirmed that the same principles as to damages in defamation proceedings are to be applied and that those principles included the principle that conduct of the defendant after publication could aggravate or mitigate the damage and therefore the award. While each determination of compensation under s3(5) would depend on its own facts, if an unqualified offer to make amends were made and accepted and an agreed apology published, as in the cases which were then before their Lordships, there was bound to be substantial mitigation.

By s4 of the 1996 Act if an offer to make amends is not accepted the making of the offer is a defence to defamation proceedings. However, there is no such defence if the offeror knew that the statement could refer to the claimant and was both false and defamatory. The burden of proving this lies on the claimant. Parliament intended to exclude from this defence only those who had acted in bad faith, ie, where the defendant knew that what he was alleging was untrue or where he had chosen to ignore or shut his mind to information which should have led him to believe, not merely suspect, that the allegation was false: *Milne* v *Express Newspapers Ltd* [2003] 1 All ER 482; affd [2005] 1 All ER 1021.

23.11 Consent

It is a defence to show that the claimant consented to the publication of the statement which would otherwise be defamatory. In *Chapman* v *Lord Ellesmere* [1932] 2 KB 431 the claimant, who was a trainer of horses at Newmarket, was given a licence by the Jockey Club to train horses and his licence was the subject of a number of conditions. One of these conditions was that the Jockey Club could withdraw his licence and publish this in the *Racing Calendar*. The claimant accepted his licence on these conditions. At a subsequent race a horse was found to have been doped and the claimant, as its trainer, was given a warning which was published in the *Racing Calendar* and in *The Times*. The claimant sued both publications for libel. It was held that the defendant had consented to the publication of the warning in the *Racing Calendar* when he accepted his licence and so he had no cause of action against the *Racing Calendar*. However the claimant was able to succeed against *The Times* on the ground that he had not consented to publication in that paper.

23.12 Justification or truth

Where the defendant can show that his statement was true then no action in defamation lies. It is for the defendant to prove that his statement was true and not for the claimant to show that the statement was false. The fact that the defendant was inspired by malice is irrelevant if the statement is true. The defendant must prove that the statement was actually true. Where a defendant repeats a defamatory statement he must prove that the statement is true and not simply that it is true that such a statement was made to him (*'Truth' (NZ) Ltd* v *Holloway* [1960] 1 WLR 997). It is no defence that he reasonably believed that the statement was true if, in fact, it was false. Similarly, there is authority for saying that hearsay and rumor cannot contitute justification for asserting that the rumor was well founded: *Aspro Travel Ltd* v *Owners Abroad Group plc* [1996] 1 WLR 132, although in *Shah* v *Standard Chartered Bank* [1998] 4 All ER 155 the Court of Appeal felt that *Aspro* should be confined to its own facts and not treated as having laid down a general principle. See also *Piper* v *Stern* [1996] 3 WLR 715.

In *Chase* v *News Group Newspapers Ltd* (2002) The Times 31 December the Court of Appeal held that the coming into force of the Human Rights Act 1998 had no effect on three principles underpinning the English law of defamation in cases where the defendant had pleaded justification based upon reasonable grounds for suspecting that the claimant had committed an offence. Those specific principles were:

1. that in establishing a defence of justification, it was not permitted to rely upon hearsay, a part of the 'repetition' rule;
2. that the defence had to focus upon some conduct of the claimant that in itself gave rise to the suspicion, the 'conduct' rule; and
3. that the grounds post-dating publication could not be pleaded in such a defence.

In relation to these three principles, in the course of his judgment Brooke LJ made important observations as follows:

1. Provided the requirements and safeguards of the Civil Evidence Act 1995 and Part 33 of the Civil Procedure Rules were observed, a defendant could now in theory adduce hearsay evidence of whatever degree in an attempt to prove the truth of the particulars of justification.
2. There could be cases in which, depending on the terms of the publication, a defendant could rely on matters that did not directly focus on conduct of the claimant. A defendant could, for example, rely on strong circumstantial evidence implicating the claimant which could amount, objectively speaking, to the requisite grounds for reasonable suspicion.
3. In cases where there had been allegations that there existed sufficient grounds for investigating whether the claimant had committed an offence, the relevant principle was that the sufficiency of the grounds had to be assessed on the material available at the date of publication. Although there appeared to be no authority directly in point, that principle seemed to be properly applicable to allegations that there were reasonable grounds at the date of publication for suspecting that the claimant had been guilty of an offence. What would be in issue at the eventual trial, therefore, would be whether, at the time of publication, such reasonable grounds existed.

The defendant need not show that his statement is literally true; it is sufficient if the substance of it is true. In *Alexander* v *North Eastern Railway Co* (1865) 6 B & S 340 the defendants stated that the claimant was fined £9, or three months' imprisonment in default of paying the fine, for riding on the railway without a ticket. In fact the claimant had been fined £9 but was only given a sentence of two weeks' imprisonment in default of paying the fine. It was held that this was a sufficiently minor inaccuracy for the defence to succeed. It should also be noted that s5 of the Defamation Act 1952 provides that, where there is more than one distinct charge against the claimant:

> 'A defence of justification shall not fail by reason only that the truth of every charge is not proved if the words not proved to be true do not materially injure the claimant's reputation having regard to the truth of the remaining charges.'

In proving the truth of a statement it should be noted that, under s13 of the Civil Evidence Act 1968 (as modified by s12 Defamation Act 1996), evidence of a conviction in a criminal court is conclusive evidence of guilt of the claimant. Under the Rehabilitation of Offenders Act 1974 a conviction becomes spent after a period of time and cannot be used in judicial proceedings, but this is subject to the caveat that, under s8(3) of the Act, a spent conviction may be proved for the purpose of establishing the defence of justification, fair comment or qualified privilege, unless the publication is proved to have been with malice (s8(5)).

The defendant may wish to argue that the words bear a less defamatory meaning than that alleged by the claimant and that in this less defamatory sense they are true. Conversely, he may wish to argue that the words should be understood as imparting a general charge of dishonesty rather than an allegation of dishonesty confined to a particular event. The latter issue was considered by the Court of Appeal in *Williams* v *Reason* [1988] 1 All ER 262. The claimant, a well-known amateur rugby football player, brought an action against the defendants alleging that they had libelled him in publishing an article claiming that he had breached the rules relating to his amateur status by writing a book for money during his career. The defendants sought leave to bring new evidence to the effect that the claimant had accepted 'boot money' during his career. It was held that the defendants were entitled to lead this evidence. The sting of the libel was that the claimant was guilty of 'shamateurism' and it was held that evidence that the claimant had accepted 'boot money' was relevant to the charge of 'shamateurism'. It was held that the defendants could lead evidence of facts which were capable of justifying the words in a wider sense than that pleaded by the claimant provided that the words which the defendants sought to justify were capable of bearing that meaning. In *Prager* v *Times Newspapers Ltd* [1988] 1 All ER 300 the Court of Appeal affirmed that the defendants were entitled to plead justification of any alternative meaning which the words which had been published were capable of meaning, and that they were not restricted to attempting to justify the meaning which the claimant had pleaded.

The defendant who pleads that his statement was justified must particularise the meaning of the words which he alleges to be justified. In *Lucas-Box* v *News Group*

Newspapers Ltd [1986] 1 WLR 147 the claimant brought a libel action against the defendants in respect of a newspaper article which inferred that she had knowingly associated with Italian terrorists. The defendants' original defence was that the article could not, in its ordinary and natural meaning, be understood as being defamatory of the claimant. Two years after the defences were served the defendants obtained leave to amend their defences so as to plead the defence of justification (for consideration of the principles to be applied in considering an amendment to plead justification at a late stage see *Atkinson* v *Fitzwalter* [1987] 1 All ER 483; see also *McPhilemy* v *Times Newspapers Ltd* [1999] 3 All ER 775 (reamendment allowed to cover potentially important evidence central to a legitimate defence)). The claimant argued that it was not clear in what respect the defendants were seeking to justify their statements. It was held that the defendants were under an obligation to make clear the respect in which they were seeking to rely on the defence of justification and the meaning which they were seeking to justify (but see *Viscount De L'Isle* v *Times Newspapers* [1987] 3 All ER 499). This achieves some degree of parity between the parties because it is settled practice for a claimant to plead the meaning which he alleges that the words which he used mean where the meaning of the words is not clear.

In *Grobbelaar* v *News Group Newspapers Ltd* [2002] 4 All ER 732 in a series of articles in the defendants' newspaper (*The Sun*) it had been alleged that the claimant, a professional footballer, had taken money to fix matches. He brought an action for libel and the defendants' plea of justification was left to the jury. In the event, the jury awarded the claimant damages of £85,000. The defendants appealed and the Court of Appeal concluded that the jury's verdict represented a miscarriage of justice and would be set aside. The claimant having appealed against this decision, the House of Lords held that, while it was safe to infer that the jury was satisfied that the claimant had made corrupt agreements and corruptly accepted money, since the defendants had failed to prove that the claimant had actually fixed matches or attempted to do so, the first instance finding in the claimant's favour would be restored. Lord Steyn dissented from this decision. However, since it would be an affront of justice to award the claimant substantial damages, the jury's award would be quashed and an award of £1 substituted. Lord Millett explained his approach as follows:

> 'In my view an appellate court ought not to find the verdict of a jury on liability to be perverse unless there is no rational explanation for it … If the jury found that the sting of the libel lay in the allegations of match-fixing rather than the allegations of the corrupt agreements, they were entitled to find that this had not been established. This is sufficient to uphold their verdict for the appellant on liability. They should not be taken to have reached a perverse finding, in the teeth of overwhelming evidence to the contrary, that the newspaper had also failed to establish the existence of the corrupt agreements. But a finding that the appellant had been a party to either or both corrupt agreements would be enough to deprive him of any right to substantial damages. It would be an affront to justice if a man who accepts bribes to throw matches should obtain damages for the loss

of his reputation as a professional sportsman merely because he cannot be shown to have
carried out his part of the bargain.'

23.13 Absolute privilege

It is a defence for the defendant to show that his statement was absolutely
privileged. There are certain cases in which English law recognises that a statement
made by the defendant enjoys absolute privilege from suit in defamation. It does not
matter how untrue or how outrageous the statement is, it still enjoys absolute
privilege. The cases where a statement enjoys absolute privilege are as follows.

Statements in Parliament

Any statement made by a member of either of the Houses of Parliament during the
course of parliamentary proceedings enjoys an absolute privilege (Bill of Rights Act
1688). The privilege extends to statements made during debates in the House, to
proceedings in committee, but not to statements made by MPs outside the House.
In *Church of Scientology of California* v *Johnson-Smith* [1972] 1 QB 522 the claimants
alleged that a statement which had been made about them was made maliciously and
to substantiate their claim that the defendant was motivated by malice, they sought
to refer to a statement which the defendant had made in Parliament. It was held that
the claimants could not use statements made by the defendant in the House as
evidence of malice because such statements enjoyed absolute privilege. See also
Allason v *Haines* [1995] NLJ 1576 where a libel action brought by the claimant
Member of Parliament was stayed as parliamentary privilege prevented the
defendants from putting forward their defence. The absolute privilege is extended
by the Parliamentary Papers Act 1840 to cover reports, papers and proceedings
authorised to be published by Parliament.

In *A* v *United Kingdom* (Application No 35373/97) (2002) The Times 28
December the European Court of Human Rights held that the rule of absolute
parliamentary immunity, and the absence of legal aid for defamation proceedings,
did not violate art 6 of the European Convention for the Protection of Human
Rights and Fundamental Freedoms (right of access to court).

However, s13 Defamation Act 1996 allows MPs and peers to waive the
protection of parliamentary privilege in order to pursue a defamation action: see, eg,
Hamilton v *Al Fayed* [2000] 2 All ER 224 where the House of Lords said that, as a
result of such a waiver, any privilege of Parliament as a whole would not be
infringed by virtue of s13(2)(b) of the 1996 Act. Note that by s13(4) absolute
privilege still attaches to MPs and peers for words spoken in Parliament. Thus,
these persons are in the fortunate position of having absolute privilege when it suits
them, but being able to waive it when it suits them.

National Assembly for Wales

For the purposes of the law of defamation, any statement made in, for the purposes of or for purposes incidental to, proceedings of the Assembly (including proceedings of a committee of the Assembly or of a sub-committee of such a committee), and the publication by or under the authority of the Assembly of a report of such proceedings, is absolutely privileged: Government of Wales Act 1998, s77(1). Section 77(4) provides that the Assembly is a legislature for the purposes of Sch 1 to Defamation Act 1996 (qualified privilege for fair and accurate report of public proceedings of legislatures, etc), and is treated as if it were a Minister of the Crown for the purposes of para 11(1)(c) of that Schedule (report of proceedings of person appointed by a Minister, etc for the purpose of an inquiry): see section 23.14, *Privileged reports*.

Judicial proceedings

Statements made during the course of judicial proceedings are also the subject of absolute privilege. The privilege is a wide one and extends to statements made by judges, counsel, parties and witnesses during the court proceedings (*Royal Aquarium and Summer and Winter Garden Society* v *Parkinson* [1892] 1 QB 431; see also *Taylor* v *Serious Fraud Office* [1998] 4 All ER 801 (absolute immunity of potential witnesses and persons investigating a crime), *Mahon* v *Rahn (No 2)* [2000] 4 All ER 41 (response to request for information by the Securities Association (predecessor of the Securities and Futures Authority) published on an occasion of absolute privilege) and *Mond* v *Hyde* [1998] 3 All ER 833 (an official receiver in bankruptcy immune in respect of statements in the course of, or for purposes of, bankruptcy proceedings)). The courts have taken a wide view of what constitutes judicial proceedings for this purpose and it has been held to extend to other hearings, such as a military court of inquiry or a professional disciplinary committee (*Addis* v *Crocker* [1961] 1 QB 11).

In *Gray* v *Avadis* (2003) The Times 19 August Tugendhat J followed guidance of the House of Lords in *Trapp* v *Mackie* [1979] 1 WLR 377 that the principle that absolute privilege attached to words spoken or written in the course of giving evidence in proceedings in a court of justice had long been extended to evidence given before tribunals which acted in a manner similar to that in which courts of justice acted. In the light of its powers and procedures and the consequences of the conclusions of its investigations, the office for the supervision of solicitors was the kind of tribunal to which the principle should be so extended.

However in *Hasselblad (GB) Ltd* v *Orbinson* [1985] 1 All ER 173 it was held that proceedings before the Commission of the European Communities were administrative rather than judicial so that absolute privilege did not apply to documents used as evidence before the Commission in a restrictive practices case under art 85 of the Treaty (now art 81 EC).

Although the privilege applies to statements made during judicial proceedings the statement which is the subject of the defamation action must, in some way, be connected with the case. The defendant cannot use the occasion of judicial proceedings to make defamatory statements totally unconnected with the case and then claim absolute privilege (*More* v *Weaver* [1928] 2 KB 520).

The importance of the context of judicial proceedings is made clear in the decision of the Court of Appeal in *Waple* v *Surrey County Council* [1998] 1 All ER 624. The claimant and her husband were the adoptive parents of a boy and, problems having arisen between the boy and his adopters, the defendant council placed the boy with foster parents. The husband having declined to supply the council with details of his means, the council served on him a contribution notice requiring him to contribute to the boy's maintenance. In response to inquiries made by the adoptive parent's solicitor as to the decision to remove the boy from them, the council's solicitor wrote a letter which allegedly defamed the claimant. In proceedings for defamation the judge decided that the letter had been written on an occasion of absolute privilege. The claimant's appeal against this decision was allowed since the letter did not have an immediate link with possible proceedings. Indeed, it did not follow from the mere service of a contribution notice that proceedings would ever be commenced.

It is unclear whether absolute privilege also extends to statements made between a solicitor and his client. If the communication is made in relation to the judicial proceedings then it is the subject of absolute privilege. The uncertainty relates to communications which are not related to the judicial proceedings. In *More* v *Weaver* (above) the privilege was held to be absolute, but the point was expressly left open by the House of Lords in *Minter* v *Priest* [1930] AC 558. If it is held that these communications are not deserving of absolute privilege, it does not mean that these statements enjoy no privilege at all; they still enjoy qualified privilege (on which see section 23.14).

Absolute privilege is also extended to fair and accurate contemporaneous reports of judicial proceedings in the United Kingdom, the European Court, the European Court of Human Rights and certain international courts by s14 of the Defamation Act 1996. See, too, Chapter 2, section 2.3, *Judicial immunity*.

Official communications

A communication made by one officer of state to another in the course of his official duties is the subject of absolute privilege (*Chatterton* v *Secretary of State for India* [1895] 2 QB 189). The rationale behind this protection is said to be that a minister of state must be free to carry out his duties without fear of being the subject of a defamation action. It is, however, unclear how far this exception extends. The courts have not given altogether consistent signals on this point. In *Szalatnay-Stacho* v *Fink* [1946] 1 All ER 303 it was held that the exception did not extend below the rank of minister and in *Merricks* v *Nott-Bower* [1965] 1 QB 57 it was held that it probably did not extend to a memorandum written by a deputy commissioner of the

Metropolitan Police to the Commissioner. On the other hand in *Dawkins* v *Lord Paulet* (1865) LR 5 QB 94 it was held that the exception did apply to a report about a lieutenant-colonel written by a major-general to the Adjutant-General. The extent of this privilege was recently in issue in *Fayed* v *Al-Tajir* [1987] 2 All ER 396. The claimant was criticised in a memorandum, for which the defendant was responsible, and he claimed that it libelled him. The defendant claimed that the memorandum was the subject of absolute privilege because it was prepared at a time at which he was acting as the ambassador of the United Arab Emirates and the memorandum was of an inter-departmental nature. It was held that the memorandum was protected by absolute privilege because public policy required that the interference with the affairs of a foreign sovereign be kept to a minimum and because art 24 of the Vienna Convention on Diplomatic Relations required embassy documents to be treated as inviolable.

Further examples of the conferring of absolute privilege by statute are to be found in the Health Service Commissioners Act 1993 in so far as reports of the investigation of complaints by the Health Service Commissioner for England (s14(5)) and Wales (s14C(2)) enjoy that status.

23.14 Qualified privilege

There are certain types of statements which, although not qualifying for absolute privilege, nevertheless are entitled to what is known as qualified privilege. This protects the maker of the statement from suit in defamation provided that he acted honestly and without malice. It is for the claimant to prove that the defendant was actuated by malice. Malice simply means that the defendant has no honest belief in the truth of his statement (see *Horrocks* v *Lowe* [1975] AC 135). It is sometimes said that the defendant has acted in excess of privilege. However this seems to mean simply that the privilege is not available on the facts because the case does not fall within one of the categories in which the privilege is available. In *Reynolds* v *Times Newspapers Ltd* [1999] 4 All ER 609 the House of Lords rejected the submission that there should be an incremental development of the common law by the creation of a new category of occasion when privilege derives from the subject matter alone: political information, ie, information, opinion and arguments concerning government and political matters that affect the people of the United Kingdom.

There is no rule of practice that courts should direct issues of qualified privilege to be heard in advance of the main trial of defamation, although in exercise of his discretion the judge could direct this course: *Macintyre* v *Phillips* (2002) The Times 30 August.

Qualified privilege is applicable in cases under the following categories.

Privileged reports

This category encompasses such things as fair and accurate reports of parliamentary proceedings, including extracts of reports, papers etc published by order of Parliament (see s3 of the Parliamentary Papers Act 1840). Other reports which enjoy qualified privilege include fair and accurate reports of judicial proceedings which the public may attend. This qualified privilege applies to any court and, unlike absolute privilege, is not confined to contemporaneous reports or to newspaper reports. This privilege does not extend to such reports of proceedings in foreign courts, unless the public interest requires their publication (*Webb* v *Times Publishing Co* [1960] 2 QB 535).

Qualified privilege also extends to certain fair and accurate reports published in any way. Section 15 of the Defamation Act 1996 provides that certain reports and statements are privileged. The reports are divided into two categories: those contained in Pt I, Sch 1 of the Act which are privileged unless published with malice, and those in Pt II, Sch 1 which are privileged subject to the defendant publishing a statement by way of explanation or contradiction if requested to do so by the claimant.

Statements in Pt I, Sch 1 include fair and accurate reports of proceedings in public of:

1. a legislature anywhere in the world;
2. a court anywhere in the world;
3. a public inquiry anywhere in the world.

Statements in Pt II, Sch 1 include fair and accurate reports of proceedings at a public meeting of:

1. a local authority;
2. a commission or tribunal;
3. a local authority inquiry;
4. any public meeting;
5. a UK public company.

It also includes a fair and accurate report of any finding or decision of a UK association formed for the purpose of encouraging or promoting any art, science, religion, learning, sport or charitable object or trade association. A communication made at a child protection conference is protected by qualified privilege: *W* v *Westminster City Council* (2005) The Times 7 January.

It is for the jury to strike a balance between the rights of the press and the rights of individuals and it is only in the clearest of cases that a judge should withdraw the issue of the fairness and accuracy of the report from the jury (*Kingshott* v *Associated Kent Newspapers Ltd* [1991] 1 QB 88). A newspaper article regarding a matter of public concern, but shorn of an important element of the story, is not information which the public has 'a right to know': see *Reynolds* v *Times Newspapers Ltd* [1999] 4

All ER 609 (defence of qualified privilege not available since no mention made of claimant's considered explanation of his position).

In *Loutchansky* v *Times Newspapers Ltd* [2001] 4 All ER 115 in an action for libel the defendants sought permission to amend their defence of qualified privilege by adding matters which were not known to them at the time of publication of the newspaper articles which had given rise to the proceedings. They asserted that they were entitled to rely on facts of which they had been unaware at the material time in support of their contention that they were under a duty, in the public interest, to publish the matters of which complaint was made. Gray J refused permission to make the amendments and the defendants appealed against this decision. The Court of Appeal decided that the appeal would be dismissed. Brooke LJ said:

> 'The House of Lords has ruled in *Reynolds* v *Times Newspapers Ltd* [1999] 4 All ER 609 ... that the media do not have an unfettered right to publish what they believe to be in the public interest. Some discipline has to be introduced, in order to give appropriate effect to the interests recognised as legitimate by art 10(2) [of the European Convention for the Protection of Human Rights and Fundamental Freedoms]. This discipline involves the court examining the occasion of a publication, and not the circumstances as they might have appeared to the publishers weeks or months later if they had waited to make further inquiries, or waited to see if further facts came to light. If they were to be taken to have that additional opportunity, they would by the same token have more time to seek out the complainant and obtain his version of events. It would then be likely that what they then published would be different from what they in fact published, and it is what they in fact published which is the subject of Mr Loutchansky's complaint.'

Two further points regarding press publication should be noted. In *Loutchansky* v *Times Newspapers Ltd (No 2)* [2002] 1 All ER 652 the Court of Appeal said that when deciding whether there was a duty to publish defamatory words to the world at large, the relevant interest was that of the public in a modern democracy in free expression and, more particularly, in the promotion of a free and vigorous press to keep the public informed. The corresponding duty on the journalist and his editor was to act responsibly. In *Baldwin* v *Rusbridger* (2001) The Times 23 July the Court of Appeal concluded that there are powerful considerations of public policy against extending the law to give journalists qualified privilege for attacks in their newspapers upon those who had criticised them in court.

Statements made in furtherance of a duty

Where the defendant was under a legal, moral or social duty to communicate the information to the recipient of the information, the statement enjoys a qualified privilege. In *Watt* v *Longsden* [1930] 1 KB 130 an overseas manager of a company wrote to the defendant, who was one of the company directors, informing him that the claimant, the overseas managing director, was dishonest and was leading an immoral and drunken life. The defendant showed the report to the company chairman and to the claimant's wife. The report proved to be false and the claimant brought a libel action against the defendant. It was held that the statements made between the company officers were all privileged because they all had a common interest in the running of the company and they were all entitled to discuss the claimant's behaviour. However, it was held that the communication to the claimant's wife was not protected by privilege because the defendant had no duty to inform the wife of these allegations. The test for such a duty was laid down in the following terms in *Stuart* v *Bell* [1891] 2 QB 341:

> 'Would the great mass of right-minded men in the position of the defendant have considered it their duty under the circumstances to make the communication?'

Common interest

Where the statement is made pursuant to a common interest between the parties then the statement may enjoy qualified privilege. An employer and an employee have a common interest in the conduct of the employee which is capable of leading to dismissal or other disciplinary sanction (*Watt* v *Longsden* (above) and *Bryanston Finance Ltd* v *De Vries* [1975] QB 703). However, if a claimant makes a valid criticism of the defendant's business, the defendant cannot defame the claimant and claim qualified privilege as a defence: see *Fraser-Armstrong* v *Haddow* (1994) The Times 21 January.

Horrocks v *Lowe* [1975] AC 135 was applied by the Court of Appeal in *Kearns* v *General Council of the Bar* [2003] 2 All ER 534. Responding to a request for guidance from a member of the Bar, the Bar Council sent a letter to all heads of chambers and senior clerks/practice managers stating – incorrectly – that the claimants were not solicitors. Two days later the Bar Council sent a letter of correction and apology to those who had received their original letter, a letter of apology having been faxed to the claimants the previous day. Nevertheless, without alleging malice, the claimants sued for libel and the Bar Council sought the summary dismissal of those proceedings on the grounds of qualified privilege. Eady J granted the application (see [2002] 4 All ER 1075) but, on appeal, the claimants contended that the Bar Council's original letter had not been protected by qualified privilege since it had not investigated or verified the position before it was written. The appeal was dismissed. Keene LJ said:

> 'The question of whether the existing relationship in any particular case gives rise to a common interest or to a duty-interest situation will often produce a somewhat sterile dispute, and certainly in the present appeal it is not the crucial issue. Whichever of those two categories is said to apply, the fact remains that each of them normally presupposes an existing relationship between the person who made the statement sued on and the recipient of it. In such a case, so long as the statement is fairly warranted by the occasion, and is made in the absence of malice, it will be protected by qualified privilege, irrespective of the degree of investigation or verification carried out by the maker of the statement and irrespective of whether one categorises the situation as one of common interest or of duty and corresponding interest.'

Protection of an interest

A defendant may make a statement in his own defence or the defence of his property and still claim the benefit of qualified privilege. This can be seen in *Osborne* v *Boulter* [1930] 2 KB 226. The claimant alleged that the defendant's beer was of poor quality. The defendant dictated a letter to his typist defending his beer and stating that the beer was of poor quality only because the claimant watered it down. It was held that the latter statement was privileged because it was made as part of company business in protection of their interests. Qualified privilege also extends to statements made to the proper authorities for the redress of a public grievance.

Freedom of information

Section 1(1) of the Freedom of Information Act 2000 provides, subject to certain exemptions, that any person making a request for information to a public authority is entitled to be informed in writing by the public authority whether it holds information of the description specified in the request, and if that is the case, to have that information communicated to him. Where any information communicated by a public authority to a person ('the applicant') under s1 was supplied to the public authority by a third person, the publication to the applicant of any defamatory matter contained in the information is privileged unless the publication is shown to have been made with malice: s79 of the 2000 Act.

23.15 Fair comment

The defence of fair comment is frequently invoked in the courts, especially by the press, and it is one of the defences which is important in setting the limits of free speech in this country. Nevertheless it is a defence which can only be invoked within certain rather rigid confines. In *Branson* v *Bower* (2001) The Times 23 July Eady J suggested that whether comment in a libel case could be shown to be fair depended only on whether a defendant had expressed his opinions honestly and on facts accurately stated. A defendant who invokes the defence of fair comment must plead the comment which is relied upon as constituting the defence with sufficient precision to enable the claimant to know the case which he has to meet (*Control Risks Ltd* v *New English Library Ltd* [1990] 1 WLR 183). The defendant must show that the matter to which his statement referred was one of public interest, that his comment was an opinion based upon true facts, that the comment was fair and that it was made without malice. We shall consider these four elements separately.

Public interest

The defendant's comment must relate to a matter of public interest. The question whether a matter is one of public interest is a question to be decided by the judge, but the courts have chosen to define public interest fairly widely. In *London Artists Ltd* v *Littler* [1969] 2 QB 375 Lord Denning stated that:

> 'Whenever a matter is such as to affect people at large, so that they may be legitimately interested in, or concerned at, what is going on; or what may happen to them or others; then it is a matter of public interest on which everyone is entitled to make fair comment.'

The case itself concerned a letter published by the defendant which alleged that the claimants had plotted to bring a successful play to an end by enticing the four principal performers to terminate their contracts. The defendant pleaded fair comment as a defence on the ground that the closure of a successful play was a matter of public interest. It was held, applying the test noted above, that people were legitimately interested in what went on in the theatre and that people in the show business industry welcomed publicity and so the matter was one of public interest. Lord Denning said that the test could also be satisfied where people had a legitimate concern in what was going on, rather than a legitimate interest. He gave as an example of legitimate concern the case of *South Hetton Coal Co Ltd* v *North-Eastern News Association Ltd* [1894] 1 QB 133. It was alleged that cottages, which were owned by the claimants and which constituted the majority of housing in a village, were in an insanitary condition. It was held that this was a matter of public interest because it was one in which people were legitimately concerned. Public interest would also include comments concerning public figures and politicians, theatres and plays, and the reviews of books etc.

If a judge in a defamation case has to rule on whether a defendant had a duty to report allegations about a person in public life, taking into account the nature, status and source of the material, he would not be assisted by a jury's conclusions on meaning: *Galloway* v *Telegraph Group Ltd* (2005) The Times 13 January.

Statement of opinion

The defendant's statement must be a statement of opinion and not one of fact. It is, however, very difficult in many cases to distinguish between a statement of fact and one of opinion. This is so for two principal reasons. The first is the inherent difficulty involved in drawing the distinction. One case in which it was difficult to draw the line was *Dakhyl* v *Labouchere* [1908] 2 KB 325. The claimant described himself as a 'specialist for the treatment of deafness, ear, nose and throat diseases'. The defendant, however, referred to him as a 'quack of the rankest species'. It was held that this was a statement of opinion and not one of fact. Winfield and Jolowicz pose the question (*The Law of Torts* (13th ed) p325) whether calling a person 'immoral' or a 'sinner' is a statement of opinion or a statement of fact? No clear answer can be given to this question.

The second difficulty lies in the extent to which the court should have regard to the wider context of the statement in deciding whether it is one of fact or of opinion. This was one of the issues which was before the House of Lords in *Telnikoff* v *Matusevitch* [1992] 2 AC 343. The claimant, a Russian emigre, wrote an article in the *Daily Telegraph* in which he argued, inter alia, that the BBC Russian Service failed to distinguish between Russia on the one hand and Communism on the other and that the service was staffed almost entirely from Russian speaking minorities of the Soviet Union. The defendant, who was also a Russian emigre, responded by writing a letter to the same newspaper which imputed racialist and anti-semitic opinions to the claimant. The claimant brought a claim for damages for libel and the defendant invoked the defence of fair comment. The point which separated the parties (and the House of Lords) was not whether the court should have regard to the wider context of the defendant's statement in deciding whether it was a statement of fact or opinion, but whether that context included the original article written by the claimant. The claimant argued that, in deciding whether or not the statements in the defendant's letter were fact or comment, the jury should have regard only to the words of the defendant and not to the original article written by the claimant. The majority of the House of Lords agreed and held that the context did not include the contents of the original article written by the claimant because many of the readers of the defendant's letter would not have read the article or, even if they had read it, its contents would not have been fully to their minds. This provoked a vigorous dissent from Lord Ackner. He argued that the freedom to comment on matters of public interest was vital to the functioning of a democratic society and that the defence was available to a defendant who had done no more than express an honest opinion on publications put before the public. He stated that it was sufficient for the defendant to have identified the publication on which he was commenting without having to set out such extracts from it as would enable his readers to judge for themselves whether they agreed with his opinion or not. This argument was, however, refuted by the majority. Lord Keith stated that the writer of a letter to a newspaper had a duty to take reasonable care to make clear that he was writing comment and not making misrepresentations about the content of the original article and Lord Templeman asserted that a critic must in future simply make clear that he is not quoting the claimant but is commenting on the words which the claimant had uttered (see further Sutherland (1992) 55 MLR 278).

Although the defendant's statement must be one of opinion and not one of fact, the opinion must be stated upon the basis of facts which are true. In *London Artists Ltd* v *Littler* (above) Lord Denning said that the commentator must get his 'basic facts right', by which he meant those facts which go to the 'pith and substance of the matter'. The defendant in *Littler* failed to establish one of these basic facts because he could not prove that the claimants had plotted to close the play (see too *Merivale* v *Carson* (1887) 20 QBD 275). This must be read subject to s6 of the Defamation Act 1952 which provides that:

> 'A defence of fair comment shall not fail by reason only that the truth of every allegation of fact is not proved if the expression of opinion is fair comment having regard to such of the facts alleged or referred to in the words complained of as are proved.'

Although the facts upon which the defendant made his comment must be true there is no requirement that all the facts be contained in the alleged libellous statement. It is sufficient that the facts are stated in such a way as to make clear the facts upon which the comment is based. In *Kemsley* v *Foot* [1952] AC 345 the defendant, Michael Foot, attacked the Beaverbrook Press and said that it was 'lower than Kemsley'. Kemsley, who was the owner of another newspaper, brought a libel action against the defendant on the ground that his statement implied that his newspapers were of low character. It was held that the article had sufficient factual content about the conduct of the claimant's newspaper for the defendant to be entitled to plead the defence of fair comment.

Fairness

Thirdly it must be shown that the comment was, in all the circumstances fair. In considering the fairness of the comment it has been held that the honesty of the defendant is the 'cardinal test' (per Lord Denning in *Slim* v *Daily Telegraph Ltd* [1968] 2 QB 157). Where the comment is based upon improper motives then the comment will be unfair. The test of fairness is an objective one and, once a defendant shows that his comment is objectively fair, the court will presume that his statement of opinion is honest unless the claimant can plead and prove express malice (*Telnikoff* v *Matusevitch* [1992] 2 AC 343). In *Reynolds* v *Times Newspapers Ltd* [1999] 4 All ER 609 Lord Nicholls of Birkenhead said:

> 'Traditionally one of the ingredients of [the defence of honest comment on a matter of public interest] is that the comment must be fair, fairness being judged by the objective standard of whether any fair-minded person could honestly express the opinion in question. Judges have emphasised the latitude to be applied in interpreting this standard. So much so, that the time has come to recognise that in this context the epithet "fair" is now meaningless and misleading. Comment must be relevant to the facts to which it is addressed. It cannot be used as a cloak for mere invective. But the basis of our public life is that the crank, the enthusiast, may say what he honestly thinks as much as the reasonable person who sits on a jury. The true test is whether the opinion, however exaggerated, obstinate or prejudiced, was honestly held by the person expressing it: see Diplock J in *Silkin* v *Beaverbrook Newspapers Ltd* [1958] 2 All ER 516 at 518.'

Where the defendant's comment consists of an allegation that the claimant is actuated by some corrupt or dishonest motive then it is much more difficult for the defendant to rely on this defence. This point can be seen in the case of *Campbell* v *Spottiswoode* (1863) 3 B & S 769. The defendant alleged that the claimant's purpose behind starting a scheme to spread Christianity among the Chinese was to promote the sale of his own newspaper. It was held that, although the defendant honestly believed that what he had said was true, he was not entitled to rely on the defence of fair comment because there was no reasonable basis of fact for his allegations. In such cases it is not the case that the defence is not available to the defendant, it is simply the case that he must show the existence of reasonable grounds for his belief.

Absence of malice

The defendant's comment must not be inspired by malice, which for this purpose consists of spite, ill-will or any other improper motive. It is for the claimant to show that the defendant was actuated by malice. Malice was successfully shown in the case of *Thomas* v *Bradbury Agnew* [1906] 2 KB 627. The Court of Appeal held that the hostility of the book review written by the defendant, combined with the hostility which he displayed in the witness box, showed that he was actuated by malice and so was not entitled to rely on the defence of fair comment. It appears to be the case that where the writer of the statement acted maliciously but the publisher did not, then the publisher will not be tainted with the malice of the writer and will remain entitled to rely on the defence of fair comment (*Lyon* v *Daily Telegraph Ltd* [1943] KB 746).

23.16 Limitation

Section 5 of the Defamation Act 1996 modifies s4A of the Limitation Act 1980 to reduce the limitation period for defamation to one year, and it also modifies s32A of the 1980 Act to allow the court the discretion to disapply this section. In libel cases, applications under s32A are treated with particular caution. The court will not, without satisfactory explanation for the delay, exercise its discretion to disregard the one-year limitation period, even in a case where (as here) the defendants had admitted that the delay had not affected their ability to defend: *Steedman* v *British Broadcasting Corporation* (2001) The Times 13 December.

23.17 Apology and amends

Where the defendant apologises for a defamatory statement which he has made, it is not a complete defence to the defamation action but it will have the effect of mitigating the damages for which he is liable. Section 2 of the Libel Act 1843 provides that where a statement was inserted in a newspaper without actual malice or gross negligence and the defendant has inserted a full apology for the libel either before or at the earliest possible moment after the commencement of the action then the defendant is entitled to rely on the defence of apology. The apology must be accompanied by a payment into court of a sum of money by way of amends.

23.18 Remedies

Damages

The primary remedy for defamation is damages and the principles upon which damages are awarded is discussed in Chapter 30. It should be noted that it is for the jury to assess the damages payable except where the summary procedure is used (see section 23.7). It should also be noted that exemplary damages may be available in a suitable case (see Chapter 30). At common law the ability of the appellate courts to review the award of juries is strictly limited (see *Cassell* v *Broome* [1972] AC 1027) and the unpredictability and lack of reality in many jury awards has been a major cause of concern. These issues were classically illustrated by the case of *Sutcliffe* v *Pressdram Ltd* [1991] 1 QB 153. The claimant, Sonia Sutcliffe, who was the wife of the 'Yorkshire Ripper', was awarded damages of £600,000 by a jury in respect of a libel published by the defendants, Private Eye. The defendants appealed to the Court of Appeal on a number of grounds, one of which was that the damages awarded by the jury was excessive. The Court of Appeal agreed. While being careful to affirm that the assessment of damages was the province of the jury and that the courts should not interfere unless the sum awarded was substantially in excess of any sum which the jury could reasonably have awarded, they held that the sum was, indeed, excessive and should be set aside. The Court of Appeal suggested that juries could properly be invited to consider the weekly or monthly sum which would be yielded by investing the capital sum or, in the case of smaller sums of money, to consider what they could buy with the sum of money. Nourse LJ added that the judge should in appropriate cases warn the jury of the possible consequences of awarding an excessive sum, in the sense that any appeal would expose the claimant to more delay, expense and anxiety. The hope was that, in doing so, juries would be more 'realistic' in their assessment of damages. But, despite these guidelines, juries in certain well publicised cases continued to set damage awards at spectacular levels and Parliament was forced to intervene. Section 8(2) of the Courts and Legal Services Act 1990 states that:

> '... rules of court may provide for the Court of Appeal, in such classes of case as may be specified in the rules, to have power, in place of ordering a new trial, to substitute for the sum awarded by the jury such sum as appears to the court to be proper.'

For this purpose 'case' means 'any case where the Court of Appeal has power to order a new trial on the ground that damages awarded by a jury are excessive or inadequate' (s8(1)). The scope of s8(1) and 8(2) was considered by the Court of Appeal in *Rantzen* v *Mirror Group Newspapers* [1993] 3 WLR 953 (discussed by Milmo [1993] NLJ 550). Prior to the enactment of the 1990 Act, the Court of Appeal could only interfere where the award of the jury was so excessive as to be 'divorced from reality' (*McCarey* v *Associated Newspapers Ltd* [1964] 1 WLR 855). However, it was held that this barrier against intervention should be lowered because the grant of an almost 'limitless discretion to a jury' did not satisfy the requirements of art 10 of the European Convention for the Protection of Human Rights and Fundamental Freedoms, which exists to protect the right to freedom of expression. So the court held that the critical question to be asked in considering the scope of the jurisdiction of the Court of Appeal was: 'could a reasonable jury have thought that this award was necessary to compensate the claimant and to re-establish his reputation?'. On the facts the court held that the sum awarded (£250,000) was excessive and exercised its power to substitute the sum of £110,000. The court also held that, in giving guidance to a jury on the assessment of damages in a defamation claim, the judge may direct the jury to consider awards made by the Court of Appeal under s8(1) in the hope that 'in the course of time a series of decisions of the Court of Appeal will establish some standards as to what are ... "proper" awards.'

In *Rantzen* the court held that juries should not be told of awards in personal injury cases. However, in *John* v *Mirror Group Newspapers Ltd* [1996] 2 All ER 35 the Court of Appeal realised that it would take some time to establish a framework of its awards. In the meantime it stated that it was rightly offensive to public opinion that a claimant in defamation should recover damages which were greater by a significant factor than if that same claimant had been rendered a helpless cripple or an insensate vegetable. The Court therefore held that both judges and counsel should be free to draw the attention of juries to these figures. This is not intended to promote equality of damages in both actions, but to enable a jury to compare a serious libel with (say) a serious brain injury. Thus, counsel for both sides and the judge should address the jury on the level of damages they consider appropriate. See also *Thompson* v *Commissioner of Police of the Metropolis* [1997] 2 All ER 762 where the Court of Appeal followed the *John* approach and *Grobbelaar* v *News Group Newspapers Ltd* [2002] 4 All ER 732 (section 23.12).

In *Kiam* v *MGN Ltd* [2002] 2 All ER 219, in proceedings for libel, the trial judge indicated that an award of damages within the range of £40,000–£80,000 might be appropriate. The jury awarded £105,000. The defendant appealed against this award, asking the Court of Appeal to exercise its power under s8 Courts and Legal Services Act 1990 to reduce it. Sedley LJ dissenting, the appeal was dismissed. Simon Brown LJ said:

'This court can only interfere with a jury's award if it is "excessive". (We are not here concerned with the other limb of the power, to vary an "inadequate" award.) The question for the court is whether a reasonable jury could have thought the award necessary to compensate the claimant and to re-establish his reputation. If the answer is "No", the award is to be regarded as excessive and the court will substitute for it a "proper" award. But what is a "proper" award? Is it whatever sum the court thinks appropriate, wholly uninfluenced by the jury's view? Or is it rather the highest award which the jury could reasonably have thought necessary? I take it to be the latter. In *Gorman* v *Mudd* [1992] CA Transcript 1076, for example, where the court substituted an award of £50,000 for the jury's award of £150,000, Neill LJ concluded that "on no possible view could the award of damages exceed £50,000", Rose LJ agreeing "that a proper award cannot exceed £50,000". The Court of Appeal should surely take as much account as it properly can of the jury's attitude to the case and only on this approach would it be doing so. To my mind, therefore, this court should not interfere with the jury's award unless it regards it as substantially exceeding the most that any jury could reasonably have thought appropriate ... the present award ... is not so far removed from my own (or evidently, the trial judge's) view of the true value of the claim as to justify the exercise of the s8 power.'

In *Galloway* v *Telegraph Group Ltd* (2005) The Times 13 January the claimant was awarded £150,000 by way of damages for libel in the defendant's newspaper. As Eady J explained, the allegations had been very serious, there had been no apology or plea of justification and there had undoubtably been aggravating features.

Note that where a case is settled out of court rather than allowed to proceed to trial, the defendants are not entitled to say in a statement made on behalf of the claimant that the payment into court of a substantial sum of money was done for commercial reasons. The inclusion of such an explanation detracts from the value of the payment in as being in itself a vindication: *Charlton* v *EMAP plc* (1993) The Times 11 June.

Interlocutory injunctions

An interlocutory injunction may also be granted in an appropriate case to restrain the publication of a defamatory statement (but only where there is some reasonable certainty as to the words of the publication: *British Data Management plc* v *Boxer Commercial Removals plc* [1996] 3 All ER 707), but the courts are very reluctant to grant such an injunction where the defence of qualified privilege, justification or fair comment is pleaded by the defendant, unless the claimant can show that the defendant dishonestly and maliciously proposes to publish the statement when he knows that it is untrue: see, eg, *Holley* v *Smyth* [1998] 1 All ER 853 (interlocutory injunction discharged since, on the present evidence, could not be concluded threatened publication plainly untrue).

In *Gulf Oil (GB) Ltd* v *Page* [1987] Ch 327 the Court of Appeal held that the rule that a claimant is not entitled to an interlocutory injunction to restrain the publication of defamatory material when the defendant pleads the defence of justification is not an absolute rule, but that it does admit of an exception. That exception arises where the defamatory material is published in the course of a conspiracy by the defendants which has as its sole or dominant purpose the infliction of injury upon the claimant (although even in such a case a court may refuse an application for an interlocutory injunction where to accede to the application would be to interfere to an unacceptable extent with freedom of speech, see *Femis-Bank (Anguilla) Ltd* v *Lazer* [1991] Ch 391). The court did not think that such a ruling had undesirable implications for freedom of speech. Parker LJ thought that it would only be in the 'rarest of cases' that the evidence would establish that the sole or dominant purpose behind the publication of, for example, a newspaper article was the infliction of injury upon the claimant. Thus where the claimant alleges that the defendants have conspired to cause him injury he need only satisfy the court that there is a serious question to be tried and the intent to injure to obtain his interlocutory injunction.

The Human Rights Act 1998 has not changed the rule that in an action for defamation a court will not impost a prior restraint on publication unless it is clear that no defence will succeed at the trial: *Greene* v *Associated Newspapers Ltd* [2005] 1 All ER 30.

23.19 Conclusion

As mentioned earlier, the Defamation Act 1996 has attempted to modernise the law of defamation. In particular, the summary, or 'fast track', procedure is designed to provide a rapid route to dispose of clear cut cases.

For claimants, however, the major problem is that legal aid is not available for defamation (or malicious falsehood) actions: see now s6 of, and Sch 2 to, the Access to Justice Act 1999.

It should be noted, though, that in *Steel and Morris* v *United Kingdom* (Application No 6841/01) (2005) The Times 16 February the European Court of Human Rights found this position unacceptable. In the mid-1980s London Greenpeace began an anti-McDonald's campaign. In 1986 a six-page leaflet entitled 'What's wrong with McDonald's?' was produced and distributed as part of that campaign. In 1990 McDonald's Corporation and McDonald's Restaurants Ltd issued a writ against the applicants claiming damages for libel allegedly caused by the alleged publication of the leaflet. The applicants were refused legal aid and so represented themselves throughout the trial and their subsequent largely unsuccessful appeal, with only some help from volunteer lawyers. The European Court held unanimously that the denial of legal aid to the applicants had deprived them of the opportunity to present their case effectively before the court and contributed to an unacceptable inequality of arms with McDonald's. There had, therefore, been a violation of art 6(1) of the European Convention for the Protection of Human Rights and Fundamental Freedoms 1950.

23.20 Breach of confidence

Although it is not part of the law of defamation, it is appropriate to note here recent developments in the law of confidentiality. In *Campbell* v *MGN Ltd* [2004] 2 All ER 995 the House of Lords heard that the claimant, a famous fashion model, had stated publicly that she did not take drugs. The defendant newspaper published articles revealing that she was a drug addict, giving details of the treatment she was receiving and photographs of her leaving Narcotics Anonymous meetings. In view of her public denial, the claimant accepted that the defendant had been entitled, in the public interest, to disclose the information that she was a drug addict and was receiving treatment for her addiction. However, she brought proceedings for breach of confidence and compensation under the Data Protection Act 1998 with respect to the additional information and photographs published relating to her attendance at Narcotics Anonymous meetings. She succeeded at first instance, but the Court of Appeal reversed this decision. On appeal to the House of Lords, the primary issue was the way in which a balance was to be struck between the right to respect for private and family life and the right to freedom of expression, in accordance with arts 8 and 10 of the European Convention for the Protection of Human Rights and Fundamental Freedoms 1950.

By a majority, their Lordships allowed the appeal and restored the trial judge's award of damages. Details of the claimant's therapy were private information which imported a duty of confidence. As to arts 8 and 10 of the Convention, here there were no political or democratic values at stake, nor was any pressing social need identified. The potential for disclosure of the information to cause harm was an important factor. In all the circumstances, there had been an infringement of the claimant's right to privacy.

In *Douglas* v *Hello! Ltd* [2001] 2 All ER 289 Sedley LJ thought that we – like some other jurisdictions – had reached the point at which it could be said with confidence that the law recognises and will appropriately protect a right of personal privacy, subject to a defence based on the public interest. Following this lead, in *Douglas* v *Hello! Ltd (No 3)* [2003] 3 All ER 996 Lindsay J found that there had been an unjustified intrusion into individuals' private lives without their consent and held that their claims, under the law of confidence, would be successful.

See also Chapter 30, section 30.24, *Interim injunctions*.

24

Trespass to the Person

24.1 Introduction

24.2 Battery

24.3 Assault

24.4 False imprisonment

24.5 The rule in *Wilkinson* v *Downton*

24.6 Harassment

24.1 Introduction

Trespass to the person comprehends the torts of battery, assault and false imprisonment as well as what is sometimes referred to as the rule in *Wilkinson* v *Downton*. These torts provide us with some further evidence of the role of the law of tort in protecting a person's interest in his personal security. They also demonstrate an overlap with the criminal law as the acts which give rise to the tortious liability of the defendant may also give rise to criminal sanctions. On the other hand, civil proceedings for trespass to the person cannot be brought without the permission of the court where the claimant has been convicted of an imprisonable offence committed on the same occasion as the alleged trespass: s329 Criminal Justice Act 2003.

24.2 Battery

The tort of battery has been defined by Trindade ((1982) 2 OJLS 211,216) in the following terms:

> 'A battery is a direct act of the defendant which has the effect of causing contact with the body of the claimant without the latter's consent.'

This definition of the tort is a helpful one because it highlights most of the essential ingredients of the tort. There are five ingredients of the tort and these ingredients are as follows.

Direct act

The act of the defendant must be the direct cause of the damage to the claimant. The most famous example of this principle is the case of *Scott* v *Shepherd* (1773) 2 W Bl 892. The defendant threw a lighted squib into a market place. The first 'recipient' of this squib instinctively threw the squib to the next stall where it was once again picked up and thrown to another part of the market where it exploded and injured the claimant. It was held that the defendant was liable for the injuries suffered by the claimant because they were a direct result of the act of the defendant. The acts of the stall holders in passing on the squib were instinctive and did not break the direct link between the act of the defendant and the injury to the claimant. This requirement of directness serves the function of marking off the limits of liability in a way done by the rules relating to remoteness of damage in negligence.

Intentional act

The act of coming into contact with the person of the claimant must be an intentional act. At one time it was probably the case that trespass to the person was actionable even where the contact with the claimant was accidental, in the sense that it was not negligent, but this view was rejected by Denman J in *Stanley* v *Powell* [1891] 1 QB 86 when he held that trespass to the person was not actionable in the absence of either intent or negligence. The view of Denman J may now be too wide because it is not clear whether trespass to the person may be committed negligently. It is clear from cases such as *Stanley* v *Powell* and *NCB* v *Evans* [1951] 2 KB 861 that it was once the case that it could be committed negligently.

However, this traditional view was challenged by Lord Denning in the case of *Letang* v *Cooper* [1965] 1 QB 232. The claimant was sunbathing on an area of grass which was also used as a car park. While she was sunbathing, the defendant negligently drove his car over the claimant's legs and injured her. She brought an action against the defendant more than three years after the incident. The defendant argued that her claim was time barred because, under the Limitation Act 1939, an action in 'negligence, nuisance or breach of duty' had to be brought within three years of the cause of action arising. The claimant argued that her cause of action did not lie in 'negligence' or 'breach of duty' but in battery and that in battery the limitation period was six years. The Court of Appeal, however, disagreed and held that the claimant's action was statute barred because it was based upon the defendant's failure to take reasonable care and so it was, for the purposes of the Limitation Act, an action in 'negligence' even though it could also be called an action in trespass to the person.

Lord Denning, with whom Danckwerts LJ concurred, took a broader view and held that, where the act causing the damage was intentional, then the cause of action lay in trespass to the person but that, where the act causing the damage was a negligent one, then the cause of action lay in negligence. Thus he was of the opinion that there was no overlap between the tort of negligence and trespass to the person. He repeated this view in *Miller* v *Jackson* [1977] QB 966 where he said that where the damage-causing act was unintentional then no cause of action lay in trespass to the person but only in negligence. This view that trespass to the person cannot be committed negligently was apparently accepted by the Court of Appeal in *Wilson* v *Pringle* [1987] QB 237.

See also *Blake* v *Galloway* [2004] 3 All ER 315, Chapter 9, section 9.9.

Hostility?

In the recent case of *Wilson* v *Pringle* (above) it was held that it was the act of touching the claimant which had to be intentional and that that touching had to be proved to be a 'hostile touching'. The aim behind this requirement is clearly to exclude from the ambit of the tort the ordinary everyday contact which is part of life. Such contact had previously been thought not to be a battery because the claimant consented to such contact (see further paragraph on *Defences* below). The Court of Appeal rejected such an approach and held that it was the element of hostility which was missing from such contact. However they held that hostility was not the same thing as ill-will or malevolence and that in each case the question of the existence of hostility was an issue of fact for the court to decide. Where the act of touching which gave rise to the action did not, of itself, display hostility then the Court of Appeal held that the claimant must plead the facts which he claims demonstrate that the touching was a hostile one.

But the authority of *Wilson* must now be viewed with some suspicion. In *Re F (Mental Patient: Sterilisation)* [1990] 2 AC 1, 72–73 Lord Goff doubted, obiter, whether *Wilson* was correct. He argued that the requirement that the touching be a 'hostile' one was difficult to reconcile with the principle that any touching of another's body is, in the absence of lawful excuse, capable of amounting to a battery. He stated that a prank which gets out of hand, an over-friendly slap on the back or surgical treatment by a surgeon who mistakenly thinks that the patient has consented to it may all constitute a battery, without the touching being characterised as hostile. Due regard must also be paid, in cases of medical treatment, to the libertarian principle that 'every human being of adult years and sound mind has a right to determine what shall be done with his own body' (*Schloendorff* v *Society of New York Hospital* (1914) 211 NY 125, 126 per Cardozo J). The requirement that the touching be a hostile one failed to give sufficient weight to this libertarian principle. It is suggested that the approach adopted by Lord Goff is, in fact, the correct one and that *Wilson* should be overruled. The requirement that the touching be a 'hostile' one threatened to deflect the inquiry from the real issue, which is whether the touching was consented to by the claimant, into irrelevant inquiries into the motives of the defendant.

Contact with the claimant

There must be contact with the person of the claimant before there can be an action in the tort of battery. In *Cole* v *Turner* (1704) 6 Mod 149 it was said that the 'least touching of another in anger is a battery'. The reference to touching in 'anger' should be noted because it was one of the authorities relied upon by the court in *Wilson* v *Pringle* [1987] QB 237 in holding that the claimant had to show that the touching was 'hostile'. The contact with the person of the claimant must be an active contact. So, for example, the person who blocks a doorway so that the claimant cannot get through does not commit the tort of battery when the claimant bumps into him in his effort to get through the doorway. The simple requirement that the contact be an active one means that something which is relatively trivial, such as an unwanted kiss, may be a battery. It is not necessary that the claimant be aware that contact has been made with his or her person. It is therefore a battery to kiss a person while he or she is asleep, but evidence would have to be led that, had the claimant been awake, he or she would not have consented to the kiss.

Defences

There are a number of defences to the tort of battery. One of the principal defences is that the claimant consented to the contact with his person. Thus the doctor or dentist who makes contact with the person of the claimant during an operation or other examination does not commit the tort of battery because the claimant will have signed a form under which he consents to the operation being performed. In *Chatterton* v *Gerson* [1981] QB 432 the claimant suffered a trapped nerve after a hernia operation. She went to see the defendant, who was a specialist, about her trapped nerve. He performed an operation to free the trapped nerve but, as a result of the operation, the claimant lost all sensation in her right leg. She sued the defendant in battery on the ground that she had not truly consented to the operation because its effect had not been properly explained to her. Her claim was rejected because it was held that an action in battery could only succeed where her consent to the operation was not real and that provided the doctor had informed her in general terms of the nature of the operation, which he had, she had no cause of action. The House of Lords in *Sidaway* v *Bethlem Royal Hospital Governors* [1985] AC 871 held that English law did not recognise the existence of the doctrine of informed consent. They held that the question to be asked in each case was not whether sufficient information had been disclosed to the claimant to enable her to make an informed choice about whether or not to undergo the operation but whether a reasonable doctor would have acted as the defendant had done in only releasing a certain amount of information.

The defence of consent may also be applied to participants in sports which involve physical contact. As long as the contact takes place in accordance with the rules of the game, then no action in battery will lie. But where the contact is not in accordance with the rules of the game, as when a person who does not have the ball is punched during a game of rugby, then an action in battery will lie (*R* v *Billinghurst* [1978] Crim LR 553).

It was once thought that the defence of consent explained why no action in battery lay when two people bumped into each other in the street. In *Cole* v *Turner* (above) Holt CJ said that 'if two or more meet in a narrow passage, and without any violence or design of harm, the one touches the other gently, it will be no battery'. In *Collins* v *Wilcock* [1984] 3 All ER 374 Robert Goff LJ sought to rationalise the defences on the ground that they are all part of the 'physical contact which was generally acceptable in the ordinary conduct of daily life'. This rationalisation was, however, rejected by the Court of Appeal in the case of *Wilson* v *Pringle* (above). Croom Johnson LJ said that it was not 'practicable' to define the tort of battery in terms of 'physical contact which is not generally acceptable in the ordinary conduct of daily life'. Instead it was held that it was the hostility of the touching which determined the existence of a contact which amounted to a battery. So, according to the Court of Appeal in *Wilson*, where two people bump into each other in the street or in a supermarket no action in battery arises unless it can be shown that one party had a hostile intent in bumping into the other. But, as was noted above, Lord Goff in *F* v *West Berkshire Health Authority* cast doubt upon the authority of *Wilson* and sought to restore the test which he had adopted in *Collins* v *Wilcock*; namely that the touching is not actionable when it is 'generally acceptable in the ordinary conduct of everyday life'.

Self defence also constitutes a defence to the tort of battery. Reasonable force may be used to resist an unlawful attack. The defence is only available where the steps taken in self-defence are not out of all proportion to the threatened harm (see *Lane* v *Holloway* [1968] 1 QB 379).

It is not entirely clear whether the claimant's damages can be reduced on the ground that he was guilty of contributory negligence. Some authority can be found for the proposition that damages are not reducible (see *Fontin* v *Katapodis* (1962) 108 CLR 177), but a contrary view may be gleaned from the cases of *Lane* v *Holloway* [1968] 1 QB 379 and *Murphy* v *Culhane* [1977] QB 94. However, this issue was recently considered by the Court of Appeal in *Barnes* v *Nayer* (1986) The Times 19 December. The defendant killed the claimant's wife with a machete, almost severing her head from her body. He was convicted of manslaughter by reason of diminished responsibility. His defence to the claimant's civil law claim was that he had been provoked by the deceased who had 'goaded' their respective sons into fighting each other and had then threatened the defendant's son with further violence. The defendant argued that the claimant's claim was barred on three grounds. The first was that it was barred by the maxim ex turpi causa non oritur actio (that no cause of action arises out of the wrong of the claimant). May LJ held that ex turpi causa could apply in an appropriate case to battery and that it would afford a complete defence to the claimant's action when it was applicable. But he held that the defence was not made out on the facts. The second ground was that the defence of volenti (see Chapter 13) was applicable because the claimant willingly accepted the risk of injury. Once again May LJ held that the defence could apply to battery and that where it did apply it would afford a complete defence. But he held that the defence was not made out on the facts. The third ground relied upon by the defendant was that the claimant had been guilty of contributory negligence. May LJ established the important point that, in his opinion, the claimant's contributory negligence could constitute 'fault' under s1 of the Law Reform (Contributory Negligence) Act 1945 so as to reduce the damages awardable by an appropriate degree (compare Hudson (1984) 4 Legal Studies 332 where, after much fuller consideration of the authorities, he concluded that contributory negligence is not a defence to battery). May LJ held that the defence was not applicable on the facts of the case because the defendant's response was out of all proportion to any act of the claimant so that no judge or jury could conclude that the claimant was guilty of contributory negligence. The claimant was therefore held to be entitled to recover in full from the defendant. Finally May LJ held that the defence of provocation could apply to battery but that the 'better view' was that its only effect was to reduce the exemplary damages payable and that it did not affect the compensatory damages payable.

At common law, a parent, or person with parental authority, is allowed to use reasonable punishment to correct a child. However, by virtue of s58(3) of the Children Act 2004, battery of a child causing actual bodily harm to the child cannot be justified in any civil proceedings on the ground that it constituted reasonable punishment. 'Actual bodily harm' here has the same meaning as it has for the purposes of s47 of the Offences against the Person Act 1861. Corporal punishment in schools was abolished by s548 of the Education Act 1996, as substituted.

24.3 Assault

The tort of assault may be defined as a direct threat made by the defendant to the claimant which has the effect of putting the claimant in reasonable apprehension of immediate physical contact with his person. It is important that the distinction between assault and battery be borne in mind. If I clench my fist in such a way as to put someone in reasonable apprehension of imminent contact with their person then I commit the tort of assault, but, if I actually punch that person, then I commit the tort of battery.

There is no requirement that the fear of imminent physical contact be produced by the words of the defendant. Indeed, in the example which we considered above, the fear of physical contact was produced by the clenching of the fist and not by any spoken words (for an example of the tort being committed without any words being spoken see *Mortin* v *Shoppee* (1828) 3 C & P 373). There is more controversy over whether the tort can be committed by words alone. The difficulty can be traced back to dicta of Holroyd J in *R* v *Meade and Belt* (1823) 1 Lew CC 184 when he said that 'no words or singing are equivalent to an assault'. The absurdity of this view has been demonstrated by commentators (see Trindade (1982) 2 OJLS 211, 231–2 and Handford (1976) 54 Can Bar Rev 563). For example, it means that the tort of assault cannot be committed in darkness where the claimant is put in fear of a battery by words which he hears but which are uttered by a person whom he cannot see. The better view, it is submitted, is that, where the words are sufficient of themselves to put the claimant in reasonable apprehension of a battery, then the tort of assault has been committed. Support for such a proposition can be found in the case of *R* v *Wilson* [1955] 1 WLR 493, and *R* v *Ireland* [1997] 4 All ER 225 (silent telephone calls capable of amounting to a criminal assault).

While it is unclear whether words alone can constitute an assault, words can negative what would otherwise be an assault. Such was the case in *Tuberville* v *Savage* (1669) 1 Mod Rep 3. The claimant and the defendant were involved in a heated argument. The defendant, while placing his hand on his sword, said that 'if it were not assize time, I would not take such language from you'. It was held that no assault had been committed by the defendant because his words negatived the apprehension of immediate contact which was aroused by him placing his hand on his sword. The statement made in *Tuberville* must be distinguished from a conditional threat because the latter may be actionable as an assault. For example if I said 'I'll break your neck unless you give me ten pounds' that could constitute an assault because it is a conditional threat and one which could give rise to reasonable apprehension of a battery (see *Read* v *Coker* (1853) 13 CB 850).

Although the claimant must be in reasonable apprehension of physical contact there is no requirement that he actually be afraid of the defendant. It is sufficient that he expects physical contact to take place. The apprehension of physical contact must be a reasonable one and it must be one of imminent contact. Thus the tort is not committed where the defendant does not have the capacity to carry out the battery. So, where the defendant threatens the claimant as the former's train leaves the station, the claimant cannot sue the defendant for assault because the fact that the train is leaving the station removes the defendant's present capability of carrying out a battery.

It is clearly an assault to place a loaded gun at the head of another, but what is the position where the pistol is unloaded? In *Blake* v *Barnard* (1840) 9 C & P 626 Lord Abinger CB was of the opinion that if the pistol was unloaded then no assault was committed. However in the criminal case of *R* v *St George* (1840) 9 C & P 483 Parke B stated that it was his opinion that to point an unloaded gun at another could constitute an assault at common law. It is submitted that the latter view is the preferable one and that provided that the claimant reasonably believes that the gun is loaded and that he is in danger of being shot then the tort has been committed.

In *Stephens* v *Myers* (1830) 4 C & P 349 it was held that the tort of assault had been committed when the defendant sought to punch the claimant but was physically restrained by a third party. It was held that, although the defendant was unsuccessful in his attempted battery, the tort of assault had been committed because the claimant was put in fear of a battery and, but for the intervention of the third party, the defendant had the means to carry out the battery.

24.4 False imprisonment

This tort is committed when the defendant intentionally causes the claimant's freedom to be totally restrained or causes the claimant to be confined within a particular limited area. The tort can be committed by making a wrongful arrest, by detaining someone for longer than is justifiable (see, eg, *R* v *Governor of Brockhill Prison, ex parte Evans (No 2)* [2000] 4 All ER 15 (prisoner detained beyond release date)) or simply by preventing someone from leaving a room.

In *ex parte Evans (No 2)*, above, it appeared that the prison governor, applying certain judicial decisions, had calculated that the respondent would be released from prison on 18 November 1996. On 15 November the Divisional Court ruled that those earlier decisions had been incorrect: the respondent should have been released on 17 September. Having been released on 15 November, the respondent claimed damages for false imprisonment during the period 17 September to 15 November. Affirming the decision of the Court of Appeal, the House of Lords said that the respondent's claim would be successful. False imprisonment was a tort of strict liability and the governor's reliance upon the earlier decisions was not sufficient to absolve him from liability. Their Lordships believed that art 5 of the European Convention for the Protection of Human Rights and Fundamental Freedoms supported their conclusion.

For many years there has been some controversy as to whether or not the claimant must be aware of the restriction upon his freedom. There were two conflicting cases on the point. The first case was *Herring* v *Boyle* (1834) 1 Cr M & R 377. A headmaster refused to allow a mother to take her son home for the school holidays because she had not paid his fees for the term. It was held that the tort of false imprisonment was not committed because there was no evidence that the boy was aware of any restriction upon his freedom.

On the other hand a different result was reached in the case of *Meering* v *Graham-White Aviation Co* (1919) 122 LT 44. The claimant was suspected of stealing some varnish from the defendants' factory. He was taken to the defendant company's offices and two of the works policemen remained close to him while he was questioned. In an action for false imprisonment the defendants argued that the claimant was unaware that he had been imprisoned and so it was impossible for the tort to have been committed. This argument was rejected by the Court of Appeal. Atkin LJ stated that:

> 'A person could be imprisoned without his knowing it. I think that a person can be imprisoned while he is asleep, while he is in a state of drunkenness, while he is unconscious, and while he is a lunatic ... Of course, the damages might be diminished and would be affected by the question whether he was conscious of it or not.'

This conflict of authority was, however, finally resolved (albeit obiter) by the House of Lords in *Murray* v *Ministry of Defence* [1988] 2 All ER 521. Lord Griffiths said that *Herring* was an 'extraordinary' case and that he could not believe that the case would be decided the same way today. He expressly approved of the judgment of Atkin LJ in *Meering,* stating that it was not difficult to envisage circumstances in which a claimant would suffer harm from false imprisonment even though he was unaware of the fact that he had been imprisoned (for example the case of a two-day-old baby locked in a bank vault). The knowledge of the claimant is therefore not relevant to the existence of the cause of action but to the recoverability of damages. Where the claimant is unaware of the fact that he has been falsely imprisoned and has suffered no harm he will normally only recover nominal damages.

This approach was adopted by the Court of Appeal in *Roberts* v *Chief Constable of the Cheshire Constabulary* [1999] 2 All ER 326. Having been arrested on suspicion of conspiracy to burgle, the claimant's detention was authorised, in accordance with the requirements of the Police and Criminal Evidence Act 1984, at 11.25 pm. In accordance with those requirements, his detention should have been reviewed no later than 5.25 am (ie, within six hours), but the review did not take place until 7.45 am when a further period of detention was authorised. The Court held that the claimant had been falsely imprisoned between 5.25 and 7.45 am and that he was entitled to compensatory (as opposed to nominal) damages for his detention during that period. Clarke LJ said:

> 'A person who was falsely imprisoned but who was unaware of his imprisonment and who suffered no harn would be entitled to only nominal damages. The [claimant] was not, however in that position here. He was no doubt aware of his imprisonment and, as I see it, he was entitled to be compensated for being unlawfully detained in a police cell for 2 hours 20 minutes when, in the absence of a review, he should have been released.'

The tort is only committed where the claimant's liberty is totally restrained. In *Bird* v *Jones* (1845) 7 QB 742 the defendant wrongfully roped off a section of the public footpath at Hammersmith Bridge. The claimant was stopped by the defendant and told that he could not climb over the ropes as he made his way along the footpath. He brought an action for false imprisonment. His action was unsuccessful because his liberty had not been completely restrained. Only part of the footpath was roped off and the claimant was free to go back the way he had come, cross the road and then proceed in the direction in which he was travelling.

Although the tort is not committed when the claimant has an avenue of escape open to him, that means of escape must be a reasonable one. The means of escape will not be reasonable if it involves danger to the claimant.

However, in *Pritchard* v *Ministry of Defence* (1995) The Times 27 January, the High Court held that in lawfully reguiring a person to serve in the armed forces could constitute false imprisonment since although limited liberty was granted to a serviceman, eg when not on duty, nevertheless a soldier was at all other times subject to restriction as to what he could do and that restriction could be enforced by military law. The position of the soldier in *Pritchard* seems close to the situation of the prisoner in *Weldon* (below); thus in appropriate circumstances total restraint of the claimant's liberty is necessary.

The restriction upon the liberty of the claimant must be unlawful before the tort can be committed. This requirement has given rise to difficulty in cases where prisoners have been confined in their cells in breach of prison rules. The Court of Appeal in *Weldon* v *Home Office* [1990] 3 WLR 465 held that, although it is true to say that a prisoner has been, to a large extent, deprived of his liberty upon imprisonment, he does retain a residual liberty which is to be exercised in accordance with prison rules and he can therefore bring an action for false imprisonment when that residual liberty is intentionally and without justification denied to him. But on appeal the House of Lords rejected the approach adopted by the Court of Appeal and held ([1992] 1 AC 58) that a prisoner does not have a residual liberty because his whole life is regulated by the prison regime. Although the conditions under which he is detained may be changed this does not deprive the prisoner of any liberty which he had not already lost when initially confined. This principle may, however, be the subject of two exceptions. The first is that both Lord Ackner and Lord Bridge held that a prisoner may have a residual liberty as against a fellow prisoner so that he can bring a claim for false imprisonment if he is locked in a confined space by a fellow prisoner (Lord Jauncey left this particular point open). Secondly, Lord Bridge stated that a prison officer who acted in bad faith by deliberately subjecting a prisoner to restraint which he knew he had no authority to impose may render himself personally liable to an action for false imprisonment because he lacks the authority of the governor and does not have the protection of s12 of the Prison Act 1952. The Home Office would not, however, be vicariously liable for such deliberate wrongdoing of the officer. The House of Lords also held that an otherwise lawful imprisonment could not be rendered unlawful because of the intolerable conditions of detention (thus disapproving of the dictum of Ackner LJ in *Middleweek* v *Chief Constable of Merseyside* [1992] 1 AC 179 which was to the contrary). But they held that, where the conditions of life were intolerable, the claimant would have available to him a public law remedy in the form of judicial review and may also have private law remedies in the form of an action in negligence (although see *H* v *Home Office* (1992) The Independent 5 May where the claimant's negligence claim failed), assault or misfeasance in the exercise of a public office (provided the requirements of these torts are satisfied). But no action will lie in false imprisonment.

The requirement that the restriction upon the liberty of the claimant be unlawful has given rise to difficulty in cases where occupiers purport to place restrictions upon the terms on which people can leave their premises. The law does, however, allow an occupier of premises lawfully to impose certain restrictions upon persons leaving his premises. Thus, in *Robinson* v *Balmain Ferry Co Ltd* [1910] AC 295 the defendants charged one penny on entry to their ferry and one penny on exit. The claimant paid his penny to enter the ferry but changed his mind about travelling on the ferry. But he refused to pay the penny to get off the ferry and so the defendants refused to allow him to leave. It was held that this refusal to allow the claimant to leave without paying the penny was not false imprisonment because the condition that a penny be paid was a reasonable one to impose. It should not be thought, however, that occupiers have carte blanche to lay down any conditions they please as to the terms on which a visitor may leave the premises. In *Sunbolf* v *Alford* (1838) 3 M & W 248 an innkeeper was held to have committed the tort of false imprisonment when he locked the claimant in when he refused to pay his bill.

A similar issue was at stake in the case of *Herd* v *Wearsdale Steel, Coal and Coke Co Ltd* [1915] AC 67. The claimant, who was a coal miner, refused, in breach of contract, to continue with his work and he demanded that he be taken up to the surface immediately. The defendants, who were his employers, refused to do this until it was time for the cage to come back to the surface at the end of the shift. As a result the claimant had to wait some time to get back to the surface and he alleged that this constituted false imprisonment. It was held that there was no false imprisonment as the claimant had voluntarily gone down the mine and the defendants were under no obligation to bring him back up until the end of the shift. This case could also be explained on the ground that it was sought to make the defendants liable for an omission and this could not be done in the absence of a positive duty on the defendants to come to the aid of the claimant. But both this case and the *Robinson* case have been criticised on the ground that they allow claimants to be imprisoned on the ground of a mere breach of contract (see Dias and Markesinis *Tort Law* (2nd ed) pp242–3).

There are a number of defences to the tort of false imprisonment. It is a defence to show that the claimant consented to his confinement (see on consent the discussion at section 24.2). The major defence is, however, that the claimant was lawfully arrested. The powers of arrest are contained within the Police and Criminal Evidence Act 1984. By s24(4) anyone may arrest without warrant anyone who is in the act of committing an arrestable offence, or anyone he reasonably suspects to be committing such an offence. This power does not extend to the situation where the offence has actually been committed, but s24(5) allows any person to arrest without warrant anyone who has committed the offence or anyone he reasonably believes committed the offence. Thus s24(5) provides a defence where the arrester arrests the wrong person, provided that an arrestable offence has actually been committed. Sub-sections 24(4) and 24(5) apply to any person, but by s24(6) a police officer has wider powers in that he may arrest without warrant anyone he reasonably suspects of committing an arrestable offence, even though no offence has been committed. Thus PACE preserves the trap in *Walters* v *W H Smith Ltd* [1914] 1 KB 595 in that a private person who arrests another after the offence has been committed must prove not only reasonable suspicion but that someone (not necessarily the person arrested) committed the offence. So, for example, a store detective may be liable in false imprisonment if he arrests a person on reasonable suspicion of theft and that person is subsequently acquitted in the criminal trial. *R* v *Self* [1992] 1 WLR 657 is an example of the trap in action.

The reasonableness of suspicion of an arresting constable, in the context of s24(6) of the 1984 Act, was central to the decision of the Court of Appeal in *Hough* v *Chief Constable of Staffordshire Police* (2001) The Times 14 February. The claimant was a passenger in a car stopped by a police patrol on a motorway because of a damaged windscreen. A routine check on the police computer revealed an entry concerning the owner of the car, warning officers that the occupant might be armed with a firearm. An armed response team was summoned and the claimant was arrested, handcuffed, searched and taken to a police station. No weapon was found on his person or in the vehicle. Later the claimant was released from custody. He brought an action for damages for wrongful arrest and false imprisonment.

In allowing the defendant's appeal, their Lordships were much influenced by the decision of the House of Lords in *O'Hara* v *Chief Constable of the Royal Ulster Constabulary* [1997] AC 286 which had not been brought to the attention of the judge at first instance. *O'Hara* established that the only relevant matters were those present in the mind of an arresting officer. Here, it was sufficient that the arresting officer's suspicion was formed on the basis of the entry on the police national computer. Simon Brown LJ made two further points:

1. It did not follow that any computer entry would of itself necessarily justify an arrest. If there was no urgency in the situation and if, in the light of the whole surrounding circumstances, some further inquiry was clearly called for before suspicion could properly crystallise, the entry alone would not suffice.
2. Should it subsequently appear that there had been no proper basis for making the computer entry, a claim in negligence might lie against the officer who had made it.

In principle, necessity may be a defence to false imprisonment, arising from a threat to commit a breach of the peace by a third party: *Austin* v *Commissioner of Police of the Metropolis* (2005) The Times 14 April (demonstrators and passers-by held within a police cordon for seven hours: containment was imprisonment but justified under doctrine of necessity).

Note that a person is not liable for false imprisonment when he merely gives information to the police, and does not himself instigate or procure it. Thus in *Davidson* v *Chief Constable of North Wales Police* [1994] 2 All ER 597 a store detective who incorrectly informed police that the claimant had been involved in shoplifting was not liable where the officers, in the exercise of their own discretion, had arrested and detained the claimant.

24.5 The rule in *Wilkinson* v *Downton*

In the case of *Wilkinson* v *Downton* [1897] 2 QB 57 the defendant, in pursuance of a practical joke, falsely told the claimant that her husband had been in an accident and that both his legs had been broken. The claimant believed that this story was true and was greatly upset and, in consequence, suffered nervous shock. The defendant was held liable for this nervous shock. In finding the defendant liable Wright J made the following statement of principle:

> 'The defendant has ... wilfully done an act calculated to cause physical damage to the female claimant, ie, to infringe her legal right to personal safety, and has thereby in fact caused physical harm to her. That proposition, without more, appears to me to state a good cause of action, there being no justification alleged for the act.'

This principle was applied in *Janvier v Sweeney* [1919] 2 KB 316. The claimant, a Frenchwoman, was engaged to a German who was interned on the Isle of Man. One of the defendants called at her house and falsely told her that he was representing the military authorities and that she was the woman they wanted as she had been corresponding with a German spy. In consequence the claimant suffered severe nervous shock. The Court of Appeal held that she was entitled to damages.

In *Wong* v *Parkside Health NHS Trust* [2003] 3 All ER 932 the claimant wheelchair administrator was employed by the first defendant from January 1995 to August 1996 when she was diagnosed as suffering physical and psychiatric injuries due to harassment and stress at her place of work. In March 1998 she brought proceedings against the first defendant employers based on negligence and their vicarious liability for the torts of their employees. The claim against the second defendant, also an employee, was based upon the 'tort of intentional harassment'. Questions arose as to: (1) the precise scope of the tort of intentionally causing harm under the principle in Wilkinson v Downton [1897] 2 QB 57; and (2) whether there was a tort of harassment at common law before the Protection from Harassment Act 1997 came into force. In answer to these questions, Hale LJ said:

> (1) 'For the tort to be committed ... there has to be actual damage. The damage is physical harm or recognised psychiatric illness. The defendant must have intended to violate the claimant's interest in his freedom from such harm. The conduct complained of has to be such that that degree of harm is sufficiently likely to result that the defendant cannot be heard to say that he did not "mean" it to do so. He is taken to have meant it to do so by the combination of the likelihood of such harm being suffered as the result of his behaviour and his deliberately engaging in that behaviour.'

> (2) 'Until [the 1997] Act came into force, there was power to restrain by injunction conduct which might result in the tort of intentional infliction of harm or otherwise threaten the claimant's right of access to the courts, but there was no right to damages for conduct falling short of an actual tort.'

These questions arose in the context of an unsuccessful appeal against the striking out of the claim against the second defendant. The Court of Appeal said that the trial judge had been correct in leaving out of account allegations made by the claimant of an assault (because it had been the subject of a successful private prosecution brought by the claimant and further proceedings were therefore barred by s45 of the Offences against the Person Act 1861) and a threat (because the claimant conceded that it had not caused her illness).

See, too, *Wainwright* v *Home Office* [2003] 4 All ER 969 where the claimants submitted that damages for distress falling short of psychiatric injury could be recovered if there was an intention to cause it. As Lord Hoffmann recalled, that submission was squarely put to the Court of Appeal in *Wong* v *Parkside Health NHS Trust* and rejected. Their Lordships affirmed that there was no general common law tort of invasion of privacy.

24.6 Harassment

Section 1(1) of the Protection from Harassment Act 1997 stipulates that (subject to certain exclusions: see s1(3)) a person must not pursue a course of conduct which amounts to harassment of another, and which he knows or ought to know amounts to harassment of the other. For these purposes, the person whose course of conduct is in question ought to know that it amounts to harassment of another if a reasonable person in possession of the same information would think the course of conduct amounted to harassment of the other: s1(2).

An actual or apprehended breach of s1 of this Act may be the subject of a claim in civil proceedings by the person who is or may be the victim of the course of conduct in question: s3(1). On such a claim, damages may be awarded for (among other things) any anxiety caused by the harassment and any financial loss resulting from the harassment: s3(2). If an injunction is granted in the proceedings, and the defendant appears to have broken it, the claimant may apply for the issue of a warrant for his arrest: s3(3). The civil standard of proof applies to injunction applications under s3 of the 1997 Act: *Hipgrave* v *Jones* (2005) The Times 11 January.

Where a campaign of harassment and intimidation had been pursued against breeders of guinea pigs for medical research, an order excluding protestors from an exclusion zone would not be imposed until an injunction under s3 of the 1997 Act had been put to the test and that injunctive relief would be no wider than was necessary: *Hall* v *Save Newchurch Guinea Pigs (Campaign)* (2005) The Times 7 April.

In this context, references to harassing a person include alarming the person or causing the person distress, a 'course of conduct' must involve conduct on at least two occasions and 'conduct' includes speech: s7(2).

In *Thomas* v *News Group Newspapers Ltd* (2001) The Times 25 July the claimant sought damages for what she alleged was harassment through articles published in the defendant's newspaper. The county court judge refused to strike out the claim on the ground that it disclosed no reasonable grounds for bringing it. The Court of Appeal concluded that this decision had been correct: the publication of press articles calculated to incite racial hatred of an individual was a course of conduct capable of amounting to harassment under the Protection from Harassment Act 1997. The Master of the Rolls said he was satisfied that the claimant had pleaded an arguable case that the newspaper harassed her by publishing racist criticism of her which was foreseeably likely to stimulate a racist reaction on the part of its readers and to cause her distress.

Emails threatening in tone, intimidatory or likely to cause fear, distress or alarm may constitute harassment: see, eg, *Potter* v *Price* [2004] EWHC 781 (QB) (business debt: stream of threatening emails sent to debtor: permanent injunction granted).

It should also be noted that in *R* v *Colohan* (2001) The Times 14 June the Court of Appeal decided that, under s1(2) of the 1997 Act, the test as to whether a course of conduct was one which a reasonable person would think amounted to harassment was objective. The mental illness of an offender, therefore, was not a defence; it was relevant only to sentence.

Vicarious liability

An employer will be held to be vicariously liable under s3 of the 1997 Act for harassment in breach of s1 committed by one of its employees in the course of his or her employment provided, in all the circumstances, it would be just and reasonable to do so: *Majorowski* v *Guy's and St Thomas's NHS Trust* (2005) The Times 21 March. However, misconduct on one occasion does not suffice: the same person should be the victim on each occasion when harassment was alleged to have occurred. Further, proof that the defendant employer foresaw or ought to have foreseen the particular type of injury suffered by the claimant as a possible consequence of the conduct complained of is a pre-requisite to a finding of liability: *Banks* v *Ablex Ltd* (2005) The Times 21 March.

25

Trespass to Land

25.1 Introduction

Trespass to land is a tort which has existed in England for many centuries. It is often thought of as a crime rather than as a tort, but its primary significance is, in fact, as a tort. It is only exceptionally that a trespass to land constitutes a criminal offence (see ss6–10 of the Criminal Law Act 1977 and ss61–80 of the Criminal Justice and Public Order Act 1994.

Trespass to land has been defined by Winfield and Jolowicz (*Winfield and Jolowicz on Tort* (14th ed) p383) as the 'unjustifiable interference with the possession of land'. It is a tort which is actionable per se, which means that it is not dependent upon the claimant showing that he has suffered damage as the result of the trespass of the defendant. In protecting the claimant's interest in the peaceful enjoyment of his property, trespass performs a function similar to that of the tort of nuisance (see Chapters 18 and 19). The two torts differ in that damage is normally an essential element in nuisance, whereas it is not in trespass and trespass is concerned with direct interference with the claimant's enjoyment of his property, whereas nuisance is concerned with indirect or consequential damage to his property.

25.2 Possession

Trespass to land is founded upon interference with the claimant's possession of his property. It should be noted that it is not ownership which gives rise to a cause of action in trespass, but possession. One consequence of the requirement that the claimant be in possession of the land is that, where the claimant is a lessor of land who has given up possession both in fact and at law, he can only bring an action in trespass where the damage which is done to the property does permanent damage to the property with the result that damage is done to his reversionary interest in the property (*Jones v Llanrwst UDC* [1911] 1 Ch 393). However, where the owner brings an action in trespass against a wrongdoer who claims to be in possession, the courts are willing to hold that the slightest action by the owner which evinces an intention to take possession is sufficient to maintain an action in trespass (see *Ocean Estates Ltd* v *Pinder* [1969] 2 AC 19).

The fact that a right of action is based upon possession means that use of the land is not sufficient of itself to constitute possession. The person who has a licence to occupy the land does not possess the land for the purposes of the tort of trespass, he simply has the use of the property (*Hill* v *Tupper* (1863) 2 H & C 121). Nor does it appear that a lodger or a guest in a hotel has possession for this purpose (*Allan* v *Liverpool Overseers* (1874) LR 9 QB 180).

The claimant's possession of the land need not amount to possession at law, it can be satisfied by possession in fact. Possession in fact does not require that the claimant be in possession of the property for 24 hours of every day. So, for example, the claimant who leaves the property to go out on an errand or to go to work still remains in possession in fact. Possession in fact covers cases where the claimant has no actual property interest in the land affected but does actually have possession of the land or is otherwise in control of it. Thus a claimant who had possession under a lease which was wholly void by statute was held to have possession for the purpose of the tort of trespass (see *Graham* v *Peat* (1861) 1 East 244).

Where the true owner does not have possession of the land then the owner cannot bring an action in trespass, subject to the rule laid down in *Ocean Estates Ltd* v *Pinder* (above). However, once the person who has the immediate right to possess actually takes possession of the property then, by virtue of the doctrine of trespass by relation, his possession is back-dated to the date at which he acquired the right to possess, so as to give him the right to sue in respect of trespasses which were actually committed while he was out of possession (*Dunlop* v *Macedo* (1891) 8 TLR 43).

25.3 Interference with possession

There must be some interference with the claimant's possession of the property. This interference can occur in many ways. However, the interference must cause direct and immediate interference with the claimant's possession of the property. The most common way of committing the tort is for the defendant to enter on to the land of the claimant without the claimant's permission. The tort can even be committed by placing something on the claimant's land; for example the placing of a ladder against the claimant's wall without his permission has been held to be a trespass (*Westripp* v *Baldock* [1938] 2 All ER 799, see also *Gregory* v *Piper* (1829) 9

B & C 591). It is not necessary that the defendant's initial entry be without the permission of the claimant; the tort can be committed by a person who abuses his permission to be on the land or who refuses to leave the land when asked to do so (see *Robson* v *Hallett* [1967] 2 QB 393, discussed further at section 25.5).

The interference which constitutes the trespass need not be of a 'one-off' nature; it can be of a continuing nature. Where the trespass is of a continuing nature, then it gives rise to a new cause of action from day to day for as long as the trespass lasts. This can be seen in the case of *Holmes* v *Wilson* (1839) 10 Ad & El 503. The defendants installed buttresses to prop up a road which they had noticed was sinking, but to install the buttresses they had to trespass on the claimant's land and the buttresses were actually installed on the claimant's land. The claimant sued the defendants in trespass and obtained £25 damages. He then brought a further action when the defendants failed to remove the buttresses but was met with the claim that his action was time barred. This argument was rejected by the court. It was held that this was a case of continuing trespass, which continued for as long as the buttresses were on the land, and so the claimant could bring an action in trespass until the buttresses were removed. It is also a continuing trespass to fail to remove something which was initially on the land lawfully but has ceased to be there lawfully, for example, because the permission to keep it there had expired (see *Konskier* v *Goodman Ltd* [1928] 1 KB 421).

These are the general principles to be applied in considering whether an interference with possession constitutes a trespass. However, it is necessary to give separate consideration to some particular forms of interference which have given rise to difficulty.

Trespass on the highway

A person can use the highway for the purpose of passage and for travelling from one point to another. However, where the highway is used for some purpose which is not reasonably incidental to the purpose of passage, the user of the highway may commit the tort of trespass against the person who is in possession of the highway. This can be seen in the case of *Hickman* v *Maisey* [1900] 1 QB 752. The defendant, who was a 'racing tout', was in the habit of walking up and down a short stretch of the highway and watching trials of racehorses taking place on the claimant's land so that he could see the form of the horses. It was held that the defendant was abusing his right of passage on the highway and that, as the claimant was the owner of the subsoil under the highway, he could maintain an action in trespass against the defendant. In *Harrison* v *Duke of Rutland* [1893] 1 QB 142 the defendant stood on the highway close to the claimant's pheasant shoot and opened and shut his umbrella and waved his handkerchief so as to scare the pheasants away. It was held that the defendant was liable to the claimant for trespass because his activities were not reasonably incidental to the purpose of passage and the claimant was the possessor of the highway.

Trespass to the subsoil

The trespass need not be committed against the surface of the land itself; it can also be committed against the subsoil. This can be seen in the case of *Cox v Moulsey* (1848) 5 CB 533, where the defendant was held to be liable in trespass to the claimant when he drove a stake into the subsoil which was owned by the claimant. So where the possession of the surface and the subsoil is in the hands of different persons it is only the owner of the subsoil who can maintain an action in respect of trespass to the subsoil and vice versa.

Trespass to airspace

It was once thought to be the case that trespass could not be committed in the airspace above a person's land unless there was contact with the claimant's land (see *Pickering v Rudd* (1815) 4 Camp 219). This view was, however, rejected in the case of *Kelsen v Imperial Tobacco Co Ltd* [1957] 2 QB 334. The defendant erected an advertising sign over his own property but the sign also overhung the claimant's property by some eight inches. It was held that a trespass had been committed and the defendant was therefore ordered to remove the sign.

However, it is not every intrusion into the claimant's airspace that will give rise to an action in trespass. It must be shown that the intrusion was at such a height that it interfered with the ordinary use and enjoyment of the property and the structures erected on the property. In *Lord Bernstein of Leigh v Skyviews & General Ltd* [1978] QB 479 the claimant, who was the owner of a country house in Kent, brought an action in trespass against the defendants, who were in the business of taking aerial pictures of property and who had taken an aerial photograph of the claimant's property. The claimant asserted that he was the owner of the airspace above his property and that he had not given the defendants permission to enter that airspace. The claimant relied upon the Latin maxim cujus est solum ejus est usque ad coelum et ad infernos, which means that the owner of the land owns the space above it up to heaven and the space below it down to hell. However, Griffiths J was unable to find authority for the proposition that a landowner's rights in respect of the airspace above his property extended to an unlimited height. He said that the Latin maxim, if applied literally, would lead to the 'absurdity of a trespass being committed by a satellite every time it passes over a suburban garden'. So it was held that the claimant's rights only extended to such a height as was necessary for the ordinary use and enjoyment of his property and that it did not extend to the flight of an aeroplane many hundreds of feet above his property.

In *Anchor Brewhouse Developments Ltd v Berkley House (Docklands Developments) Ltd* [1987] 2 EGLR 173 Scott J gave further consideration to the judgment of Griffiths J in *Bernstein*. The defendants, while developing a prestigious site in London, hired some cranes, the booms of which hung over into the claimants' airspace. The defendants argued that it was 'virtually essential' for the commercial development of the site for such cranes to be used. Nevertheless the claimants sought an injunction to restrain the instrusion of these booms into their airspace. Scott J held that the invasion of these booms did indeed constitute a trespass and that the claimants were entitled to their injunction. The defendants had argued that, as in *Bernstein*, the claimants' rights only extended to such a height as was necessary for the enjoyment of their property and that on the facts the intrusion of the cranes did not interfere with the claimants' ordinary use and enjoyment of their property. However, Scott J held that *Bernstein* was confined to the particular issue of overflying aircraft and that it could not be applied to the case where a static structure on the defendants' land hung over on to the land of the claimants. In the latter case Scott J held that the extent of proprietary rights enjoyed by landowners ought to be clear and that this could best be achieved by holding that, apart from the special case of overflying aircraft, every unauthorised intrusion into the airspace of another constitutes a trespass (see further McKendrick [1988] NLJ 23).

It should, however, be noted in this context that s76(1) of the Civil Aviation Act 1982 provides that no action in trespass or nuisance shall lie:

' ... by reason only of the flight of an aircraft over any property at a height above the ground which, having regard to wind, weather and all the circumstances of the case is reasonable, or the ordinary incidents of such flight ...'

However s76(1) must be read in the light of s76(2) which provides that:

'Where material loss or damage is caused to any person or property on land or water by, or by a person in, or an article, animal or person falling from, an aircraft while in flight, taking off or landing, then unless loss or damage was caused or contributed to by the negligence of the person by whom it was suffered, damages in respect of the loss or damage shall be recoverable without proof of negligence or intention or other cause of action, as if the loss or damage had been caused by the wilful act, neglect, or default of the owner of the aircraft.'

Section 76(2) of the 1982 Act was considered by the High Court in *Glen* v *Korean Airlines Co Ltd* (2003) The Times 18 April. The defendant's Boeing 747 crashed shortly after taking off from Stansted. Relying on the statutory tort created by s76(2) of the Civil Aviation Act 1982, persons living near the crash site claimed damages for psychiatric injury. Preliminary issues arose as follows: (1) whether 'material loss or damage', referred to in s76(2), is limited to 'physical loss or damage'; (2) whether 'personal injury', in s105 of the 1982 Act, includes mental injury where the mental injury is evidence of structural changes to the brain and/or central nervous system; and (3) whether, if damages are otherwise recoverable under s76(2), such recovery is subject to the common law rules as to categories of people who may recover damages? For these purposes it was assumed that the crash occurred, that all the claimants witnessed the crash and the events following the crash either seeing them or hearing them and that, as a result of such experiences, the claimants suffered sustained psychiatric injury. Simon J answered the three questions as follows:

1. No – as interpreted by s105 of the 1982 Act, the words 'loss or damage' were wide enough to permit recovery for psychiatric or mental loss or damage.
2. Yes – in any event, the defendant accepted that, in the light of the majority opinion in *Morris* v *KLM Royal Dutch Airlines* [2002] 2 All ER 565, a person can recover on the basis of a bodily injury if that person can establish that the mental injury is evidence of structural change to the brain or central nervous system.
3. Yes – the normal rules as to foreseeability and remoteness apply.

Trespass ab initio

Where the defendant's entry on to the claimant's land is with the authority of the law (rather than with the authority of the claimant) and the defendant subsequently abuses that right, there is an old rule of the common law which states that he becomes a trespasser ab initio, that is from the moment he enters on to the claimant's land. The rule is well established in the older authorities and only applies to wrongful acts and does not apply to non-feasance (see *The Six Carpenters' Case* (1610) 8 Co Rep 146a and *Elias* v *Pasmore* [1934] 2 KB 164). However this rule was recently considered by the Court of Appeal in *Chic Fashions (West Wales) Ltd* v *Jones* [1968] 2 QB 299. The police entered the claimants' shop with a warrant to look for particular merchandise which was believed to be stolen. They did not find these goods but they did find other goods which they erroneously believed to have been stolen. The claimants brought an action in trespass against the police officers in removing the goods not covered by the warrant. The action was unsuccessful on the ground that it was held that the police had the authority, when entering premises with a warrant, to remove anything which they believed to have been stolen. Lord Denning went further and criticised the doctrine of trespass ab initio on the ground that it rendered unlawful an act which was lawful at the time at which it was done. So the doctrine has been subjected to some criticism recently but it is unlikely to be abandoned and, indeed, Lord Denning himself applied the doctrine in the later case of *Cinnamond* v *British Airports Authority* [1980] 2 All ER 368.

25.4 Nature of the interference

Trespass is a tort of intention in the sense that the defendant must have intended to enter upon the land where the trespass was committed; it is not a tort of intention in the sense that the defendant must have intended to commit the tort of trespass. Therefore it is no defence to show that the defendant was unaware that the land on to which he had entered was land which belonged to someone else (*Conway* v *George Wimpey & Co Ltd* [1951] 2 KB 266).

However where the defendant can show that he had no intention of entering upon the land then he has not committed the tort. Thus the tort was not committed in *Smith* v *Stone* (1647) Style 65 where the defendant was dumped on the claimant's land by a gang of men. It was held that he had not committed the tort because there was no voluntary act on his part. Where the defendant enters the claimant's land under duress the tort can still be committed because his act in going on to the claimant's land remains a voluntary one (*Gilbert* v *Stone* (1647) Style 72).

It remains unclear whether trespass to land can be committed negligently, but, as was the case in trespass to the person (see Chapter 24, section 24.2), there is a trend in favour of holding that such actions must be brought in negligence and that an action in trespass may only be brought where the defendant's act was an intentional one (*Letang* v *Cooper* [1965] 1 QB 232). However, in *League Against Cruel Sports Ltd* v *Scott* [1985] 2 All ER 489, Park J appeared to be of the opinion that trespass could be committed negligently. The claimants, who were opposed to blood sports, owned a sanctuary for wild deer and refused the defendant permission to come on to their land during a local hunt. Despite this fact the hunt strayed on to the claimants' land on seven occasions and so the claimants sought an injunction to restrain this trespass. It was held that the master of the hunt was liable in trespass if he knew that there was a real risk of hounds entering on to the claimants' land and if he intentionally or negligently permitted the hounds to enter the claimants' land. If this decision is correct then it means that trespass to land can be committed negligently and that the approach of Lord Denning in *Letang* does not apply to all forms of trespass.

25.5 Defences

There are a number of defences to the tort of trespass. The principal defences are as follows.

Licence

There is no trespass committed where the defendant enters on to the claimant's land with the claimant's express or implied permission. Such a person is deemed to have a licence to enter upon the land of the claimant and it is only where that licence is exceeded by the defendant or the licence is lawfully revoked by the claimant that trespass can be committed. Even where the defendant's licence has been lawfully revoked by the claimant, the defendant has a reasonable time in which to leave the premises before he becomes a trespasser (see *Robson* v *Hallett* (above)).

The extent to which the defendant's licence can be lawfully revoked depends on the type of licence which the defendant has. Where his licence is a gratuitous one then it is clear that it may be revoked at any time on the giving of reasonable notice. The position is less clear where the defendant has a contractual right to be on the premises because the contractual licence may or may not be revocable. A licence may be irrevocable where a breach of the licence by the grantor would be restrained by granting an equitable remedy to the licensee. Where the licence is revocable the licensee will be confined to an action for breach of contract, but where the licence is held to be irrevocable any attempt to remove the licensee may give rise to an action in battery and the possibility of substantial damages. Where the defendant's licence is for a limited period of time and for a specific purpose, such as watching a film, then the licence is likely to be irrevocable for that limited period or particular purpose. Such was the case in *Hurst* v *Picture Theatres Ltd* [1915] 1 KB 1. The claimant paid to enter the defendant's cinema. When he sat down in the seat which he had paid for he was asked to leave the premises by one of the defendant's employees, who believed that he had not paid for his seat. The claimant refused to leave and was eventually ejected by the defendant's doorman. It was held that the defendant had no right to eject the claimant in this manner. The contract between the parties gave the claimant an irrevocable licence to be in the cinema for the duration of the performance and the defendant could not revoke the claimant's licence unless the claimant had exceeded the terms of the licence, which he had not. A licence will also be irrevocable where it is combined with an interest in the land (*Thomas* v *Sorrell* (1672) Vaughan 330).

Lawful authority

Where the defendant has lawful authority to enter upon the land of the claimant then the defendant does not commit a trespass. For example the police have powers under the Police and Criminal Evidence Act 1984 to enter premises and to search them. Another example of a person having lawful authority to enter upon the land of the claimant arises where the defendant enters the land pursuant to a public right of way. The defendant may also have a right at common law to enter upon the claimant's land, for example, to abate a nuisance or the power of a landlord to enter premises to distrain for rent.

Necessity

It is a defence to show that it was necessary for the defendant to enter upon the claimant's land. The scope of this defence was considered by Taylor J in *Rigby* v *Chief Constable of Northamptonshire* [1985] 2 All ER 985. The police fired a canister of CS gas into a building in order to force a dangerous psychopath to come out of the building so that he could be arrested. As the result of the use of the CS gas the claimant's shop was burnt out. It was held that the defence of necessity was available in an action in trespass provided that there was no negligence on the part of the defendant in contributing to the state of necessity. The defendant was, therefore, entitled to rely on the defence of necessity because of the need to arrest the psychopath. However, the claimant was held to be entitled to recover damages on the ground that the defendant had been negligent in firing the CS gas canister without any fire-fighting equipment being present.

25.6 Remedies

The claimant has available to him a number of remedies against a defendant who has committed a trespass. The principal remedies are as follows.

Damages

The claimant may seek a remedy in damages but, where the trespass is a trivial one, then damages will be nominal. Where damage is done to the claimant's land then the measure of damages is the diminution in value of the claimant's land and not the cost of restoring the land to the state it was in before the trespass. There is a possibility that the claimant may be able to recover aggravated or exemplary damages where the case is an appropriate one for the grant of such a remedy. Such was the case in *Drane* v *Evangelou* [1978] 1 WLR 455 where the claimant was thrown out of his lodgings after obtaining a reduction in his rent through the Rent Officer and the defendant calculated that it was cheaper to refuse to comply with any injunction than to take the claimant back. It was held that this was an appropriate case for the granting of £10,000 exemplary damages to teach the defendant a lesson.

Injunction

Where the trespass is of a continuing nature or the trespass has been threatened but not yet committed then the claimant may seek an injunction to restrain the trespass or to restrain any further trespasses. The general rule is that the claimant is prima facie entitled to an injunction in the case of a continuing trespass. This gives rise to difficulty in a case such as *Anchor Brewhouse Developments Ltd* v *Berkley House (Docklands Developments) Ltd* (above) where the present rules enable a claimant whose airspace has been invaded to hold a property developer to ransom. Scott J was clearly worried about the practical implications of his judgment, and he concluded by saying that it would be 'convenient if the Court had power, in order to enable property developments to be expeditiously and economically completed, to allow, on proper commercial terms, some use to be made by the developers of the land of neighbours'. However, he did not think that such a reform was within the competence of the courts, and he was of the opinion that resort would have to be had to Parliament to implement such a reform. On the other hand, it is arguable such a reform is within the competence of the courts, and that it could be achieved by the courts demonstrating a greater willingness to exercise their discretion to award damages in lieu of an injunction (see further McKendrick [1988] NLJ 23 and Chapter 30, section 30.24).

Re-entry

A person who is entitled to possession may re-enter the land either personally or through an employee or agent and will not incur liability in tort where reasonable force is used to remove the other party or his property (*Hemmings* v *Stoke Poges Golf Club* [1920] 1 KB 720). However, where the claimant forcibly obtains re-entry to his land then a criminal offence may be committed under s6 of the Criminal Law Act 1977. In *Burton* v *Winters* [1993] 1 WLR 1077 the Court of Appeal held that self-redress for trespass to land by encroachment was a summary remedy that was only justified in clear and simple cases or in an emergency.

Mesne profits

The claimant who has been wrongfully dispossessed of his land may claim in an action for mesne profits for the profits which the defendant has obtained from his occupation of the claimant's property, for damages for the deterioration of the property and for the reasonable costs of obtaining possession. The claimant need not show that he would have profited by renting the land out to someone else during the period of the defendant's occupation (*Swordheath Properties Ltd* v *Tabet* [1979] 1 All ER 240). The claimant can bring an action for possession and mesne profits in the same action (RSC O.15 r1), or he can sue for mesne profits after obtaining possession of the land or he can claim for mesne profits alone where his interest in the land has since been terminated.

Ejection

A person who has been dispossessed may bring an action for ejectment. A claimant is only entitled to such an order where he can establish that he has an immediate right to possession (see further *Winfield and Jolowicz on Tort* (13th ed) pp371–2).

Distress damage feasant

If a chattel is unlawfully on the claimant's land and has done actual damage to the claimant's property, the claimant may retain the property until the owner pays, or offers to pay, compensation for the damage which was done. This action has been abolished in relation to animals by the Animals Act 1971 (see further Chapter 22). This remedy does not give the claimant the right to sell the property, nor does it give him the right to use the property. When the defendant tenders a reasonable sum by way of compensation then the claimant must accept the sum and return the chattel to the defendant.

26

Deceit

26.1 Introduction

In *Pasley* v *Freeman* (1789) 3 TR 51 it was established that a defendant who wilfully or recklessly makes a false statement to another with the intention that the other shall act in reliance upon the statement, and the person does so rely upon the statement to his injury, the defendant is liable to the claimant in the tort of deceit. The imposition of liability in the tort of deceit is separate from the liability which is imposed for negligent mis-statement (on which see Chapter 7, section 7.6). The latter is a liability which is truly based upon negligence, whereas deceit is concerned with the imposition of liability for misrepresentation which is made fraudulently.

There are five separate elements to the tort of deceit, which will be discussed in the remainder of this Chapter.

26.2 False statement of fact

The claimant must show that the defendant made a false representation of fact. There are two separate elements to this requirement.

False representation

The first is that the representation must be false. This element can be split into two parts. The first is that the representation must be false, which is a question of fact. The second is that there must be a representation. The representation may be by speech or by conduct. Thus in *R* v *Barnard* (1837) 7 C & P 784 the defendant went into a shop in Oxford wearing a gown and mortar board and by his appearance obtained credit. It was held that the defendant had, by conduct, represented that he was a member of the University. He was therefore held to be guilty of obtaining credit by false pretences when it was discovered that he was not a member of the University.

The requirement that there must be a representation underlines the fact that there is generally no duty of disclosure in English law and that liability is not imposed for failing to speak (see *Wales* v *Wadham* [1977] 1 WLR 199). However a duty of disclosure may arise in certain exceptional cases and liability imposed in deceit for a failure to speak.

The first situation where a duty of disclosure may exist is where a representation, which was initially true, later becomes false to the knowledge of the maker of the original statement. Such was the case in *With* v *O'Flanagan* [1936] Ch 575. The parties were involved in negotiations for the sale by the defendant to the claimant of the defendant's medical practice. When the negotiations commenced in January the practice was said to be worth £2,000. However, by the time that the contract was signed in May, the practice was virtually worthless because of the illness of the defendant in the intervening period. The defendant did not disclose this fact to the claimant at the time of signing the contract. The contract of sale was set aside on the ground that the vendor was under an obligation to disclose the change of circumstances to the claimant. It is unclear why there should be an obligation to disclose a change of circumstances when there is no general duty of disclosure. One justification may be that, once the defendant has started to speak, he must tell the whole story. This, however, does not work where the defendant makes the initial representation by conduct rather than by words. The only justification which can be offered for the principle laid down in *With* is that the representation, once made, is deemed to be a continuing representation, so that it becomes a misrepresentation when the defendant fails to correct the representation when it becomes false.

The second situation where a person may become under a duty of disclosure arises where the defendant's statement was literally true but was, in fact, misleading. Such was the case in *Notts Patent Brick and Tile Co* v *Butler* (1886) 16 QBD 778. The defendant's solicitor, in response to a question from the claimant purchaser, said that he did not know of any restrictive covenant which affected the land. Although it was true that he did not know of any restrictive covenant, this was because he had not bothered to look. It was held that this was a misrepresentation which entitled the claimant to rescind the contract because the statement was so misleading that it amounted to a misrepresentation.

The third situation where a person may come under a duty of disclosure arises in contracts uberrimae fidei. These contracts are contracts of the utmost good faith, such as insurance contracts, and there is imposed an obligation to disclose all material facts. The final case arises where there is a fiduciary relationship between the parties which is sufficient to impose a duty of disclosure upon the defendant.

In *P* v *B (Paternity: Damages for Deceit)* [2001] 1 FLR 1041 a question arose as to whether the tort of deceit applied between a cohabiting couple where P contended that he had been deceived by his cohabitee, B, into believing that he was the father of her child. Stanley Burton J held that actionable deceit could arise between cohabitees. However, his Lordship added that the law should promote honesty between couples and actions for deceit could only be commenced when a relationship had already broken down.

Representation of existing fact

The second element is that the representation must be one of existing fact. Generally it can be assumed that a representation is one of existing fact unless it falls within one of the four following categories. The first is where the statement is a mere puff, such as slogan used by an advertiser to sell his products. It is a difficult question to determine whether such a statement is a statement of fact or whether it is a mere puff. In the case of *Dimmock* v *Hallett* (1866) LR 2 Ch App 21, the statement that land was 'fertile and improveable' was held to be a mere puff which could not constitute a statement of fact unless the circumstances of the case were extreme and a considerable part of the land was irredeemable. The second category is where the statement is one of opinion. Once again it can be difficult to distinguish between a statement of fact and a statement of opinion. In *Bisset* v *Wilkinson* [1927] AC 177 the statement by the vendor of land that he believed that the land which he was selling would support 2,000 sheep was subsequently found to be erroneous and the purchaser sought to rescind the agreement to sell the land on the ground that the defendant had misrepresented the carrying capacity of the land. It was held that he could not do so because the vendor's statement was one of opinion and not one of fact. The land had never been used for sheep farming before and the defendant's statement had simply been his opinion as to the number of sheep which the land could support. However, where the maker of the statement has special knowledge of the situation, then the court is likely to hold that the defendant must know of reasonable grounds to support his opinion and that a failure to possess such grounds may constitute a misstatement of fact. Thus in *Brown* v *Raphael* [1958] Ch 636 the defendant's solicitors stated that the annuitant was 'believed to have no aggregable estate', but they had no reasonable grounds for this statement. It was held that this statement was one of fact and not one of opinion because the statement was an extremely important one and also because the defendant's solicitors could have found out the true state of affairs themselves, whereas the claimant, who was the purchaser of the trust fund, was in no position to discover this information for himself. Where the defendant misrepresents what his true opinion is then this constitutes a misstatement of existing fact (see *Smith* v *Land and House Property Corporation* (1884) 28 Ch D 7).

Thirdly, a statement of intention does not constitute a statement of existing fact. However, if the defendant misrepresents his present intention then he makes a misrepresentation of existing fact. This can be seen in the case of *Edgington* v *Fitzmaurice* (1885) 29 Ch D 459. The defendants, who were company directors, stated in a company prospectus that their purpose behind issuing a subscription for debentures was to improve the company buildings and to expand the company business. The money was, in fact, required to pay off some of the company's debts. It was held that the defendants had misstated their purpose in issuing the debentures and that this constituted a misrepresentation of fact and so the defendants were held to be liable in deceit.

Fourthly, a statement of law does not constitute a statement of fact and so does not give rise to liability in deceit. However, it is not altogether clear in many cases whether the defendant has misstated the law or whether he has misstated a fact and the courts are likely to lean in favour of construing the misstatement as a misstatement of fact (see *West London Commercial Bank Ltd* v *Kitson* (1884) 13 QBD 360).

26.3 Knowledge of the falsity of the statement

The defendant must know that the statement is false or be reckless whether it be true or false. This was established in the famous decision of the House of Lords in *Derry* v *Peek* (1889) 14 App Cas 337, where it was held that a distinction must be drawn between unreasonableness of belief as a ground of action and unreasonableness of belief as evidence of dishonesty. The directors of a company issued a prospectus which stated that they had the right to run their trams on steam power. At that time it was necessary to get Board of Trade approval before it was possible to use steam power. The directors honestly believed that Board of Trade approval would be given as a matter of course. But the Board of Trade refused to give its approval and, as a consequence, the company was wound up. The claimant, who had bought shares in the company on the faith of the prospectus, brought an action against the directors in deceit. It was held by the House of Lords that the claimant did not have a cause of action in deceit. Lord Herschell stated that, in order to bring an action in deceit, fraud must be proved and nothing short of fraud would do. He then went on to say that fraud is proved when it is shown that a false statement has been made (i) knowingly, (ii) without belief in its truth, or (iii) recklessly, careless whether it be true or false.

The House in *Derry* took a very restrictive approach to the definition of fraud and made deceit a tort which it is very difficult to prove. In many cases it is easier for a claimant to bring an action in negligent misrepresentation at common law or to bring an action under s2 of the Misrepresentation Act 1967 than it is to bring an action in deceit. To bring an action in deceit it must therefore be shown that the defendant did not believe that his statement was true or was reckless whether it was true or false. Two points should be noted here. The first is that, in considering whether the defendant believed that his statement was true, the unreasonableness of his belief is only evidence that he did not believe that his statement was true; it is not a ground of action in itself. The second point relates to the meaning of the phrase 'reckless, careless whether it be true or false'. This phrase was considered by the Court of Appeal in *Angus* v *Clifford* [1891] 2 Ch 449. The defendants were company directors who purchased a gold mine and then issued a prospectus in which they stated that a report on the mine had been prepared by an engineer for the directors when, in fact, it had been prepared for the vendors of the mine. The defendants were held not to be liable to the claimant because they did not appreciate the importance of the words 'prepared for the directors'. Bowen LJ stated that 'careless whether it be true or false' did not mean careless in the duty of care sense. He said careless meant indifference to the truth or wilful disregard of the importance of the truth. Here the Court of Appeal can be seen to be attempting to draw a clear distinction between negligence and fraud and holding that carelessness, in the sense of a breach of the duty of care, does not give rise to a cause of action in deceit.

The last point which should be noted about the definition of fraud adopted by the House of Lords in *Derry* is that, once fraud is proved, the motive of the person who made the statement is irrelevant. This can be seen in the case of *Polhill* v *Walter* (1832) 3 B & Ad 114. The defendant purported to accept a bill of exchange on behalf of his principal, although he knew that he had no authority so to do. So the defendant knew that his statement was false but he had no intention of making a profit for himself; he simply believed that his principal would ratify his act. It was held that the defendant was liable in deceit because he had made a knowingly false representation and it did not matter that his motive in making that statement was an innocent one.

26.4 Intention that the statement be acted upon

The defendant must have made the false statement with the intention that it be acted upon. The only persons entitled to act on the statement are those persons or the class of persons whom the maker of the statement intended would act upon the statement. It is not, however, necessary to show that the defendant personally knew of the claimant. The easiest way of satisfying this requirement is to show that the statement was made to the claimant directly. This may, however, give rise to difficulty where the statement was made to a class of persons. This can be seen by contrasting the following two cases. The first one is *Peek* v *Gurney* (1873) LR 6 HL 377. The defendants issued a prospectus which misstated the true condition of the company. The claimant purchased shares in the company, but he did not purchase any shares in the first allotment made as the result of the issue of the prospectus. Instead he bought the shares at a later date on the Stock Exchange. It was held that the claimant was not entitled to succeed because the misstatement in the company prospectus was exhausted by the time that the claimant purchased his shares. The misstatement was only made to those persons who purchased shares in the initial allotment because it was to them, and only to them, that the prospectus was directed. A different approach was, however, taken in the second case of *Andrews* v *Mockford* [1896] 1 QB 372. The defendants made a false statement in a company prospectus and repeated that statement in a newspaper advertisement. The claimant bought the shares on the faith of the advertisement which, he believed, confirmed what was contained in the prospectus. When the company turned out to be a sham he brought an action in deceit against the defendants. It was held that the claimant was entitled to succeed because the statements contained in the prospectus were continuing ones which sought to impress upon the public that this company was a real one and not a sham. It was held that *Peek* was distinguishable on the ground that the statements there served a much more limited purpose than the prospectus in *Andrews*. So in this area much turns upon the court's interpretation of the defendant's purpose in making the statement.

In considering whether the defendant made the statement with the intention that it be acted upon, there is no need to show that the statement was made directly to the claimant. It can be satisfied by showing that the statement was made with the intention that it be passed on to the claimant (see *Commercial Banking Co of Sydney* v *RH Brown & Co* [1972] 2 Lloyd's Rep 360).

26.5 The claimant must act on the statement

It must be shown that the claimant acted on the false statement of fact made by the defendant. In other words the defendant's false statement must have been relied upon by the claimant. The defendant's false statement need not be the sole factor or even the decisive factor in persuading the claimant to act as he did. This can be seen in the case of *Edgington* v *Fitzmaurice* (above). The defendants' misstatement was said by the claimant to have been an influence upon him in deciding to invest in the company but he also said that he would not have advanced the money had he not believed, erroneously as it turned out, that the money was advanced on the basis of a charge upon the property of the company. It was held by the court that the claimant was still entitled to succeed with his action. It was held that the statement need not have been the sole inducement, it is sufficient that it was a material one, and that it was a material one if it was actively present to the claimant's mind when he invested the money. In *McCullagh* v *Lane Fox & Partners* (1994) The Times 25 January the High Court held that in the tort of deceit it was not necessary for the statement to be the only factor which caused the claimant to act as he did; it was enough that his judgment was influenced. Although the Court of Appeal upheld *McCullagh* on different grounds (see (1995) The Times 22 December) the first instance point on inducement was not disturbed.

In *Standard Chartered Bank* v *Pakistan National Shipping Corp* [2003] 1 All ER

173, a case which Lord Hoffmann felt was very like *Edgington* v *Fitzmaurice*, above, his Lordship said:

> 'It is said here that although [the claimant bank] would not have paid if they had known the bill of lading to be falsely dated, they would also not have paid if they had not mistakenly and negligently thought that they could obtain reimbursement. In my opinion, the law takes no account of these other reasons for payment. This rules seem to me based upon sound policy. It would not seem just that a fraudulent defendant's liability should be reduced on the grounds that, for whatever reason, the victim should not have made the payment which the defendant successfully induced him to make.'

His Lordship added that the rule in *Redgrave* v *Hurd* (see below) applies to both innocent and fraudulent misrepresentations, whereas the wider rule in *Edgington* v *Fitzmaurice* probably applies only to fraudulent misrepresentations.

The claimant will be unable to show that he relied upon the misstatement of the defendant when he was unaware of the existence of the representation (*Horsfall* v *Thomas* (1862) 1 H & C 90), where he regarded the representation as being unimportant (*Smith* v *Chadwick* (1884) 9 App Cas 187) or where he relied upon his own judgment (*Atwood* v *Small* (1838) 6 Cl & Fin 232). However, the mere fact that the claimant had the opportunity to discover that the defendant's statement was false does not mean that the claimant did not rely, or was not entitled to rely, upon the statement of the defendant. This can be seen in the case of *Redgrave* v *Hurd* (1881) 20 Ch D 1. The defendant was induced to purchase the claimant's practice and house on the basis of a misrepresentation made by the claimant as to the value of the practice. The defendant had asked the claimant about the value of the practice and the claimant had shown him some papers which he claimed evidenced the value of the practice. Had the defendant examined these papers he would have discovered that the business was worthless. He did not examine the papers. When he discovered the true condition of the business the defendant refused to go through with the contract and the claimant sought an order of specific performance. The defendant argued that such an order should be refused on the ground of the claimant's misrepresentation. The court refused to grant the claimant such an order, saying that it was no defence to a fraudulent misrepresentation to show that the defendant might, with reasonable diligence, have discovered the truth.

26.6 Damage to the claimant

Finally the claimant must show that he suffered damage as the result of the defendant's false statement. It was established in *Doyle* v *Olby* [1969] 2 QB 158 (noted by Treitel (1969) 32 MLR 526) that the proper measure of damages is reparation for all the loss that was directly caused by the transaction, whether it was foreseeable or not, and this measure includes consequential loss. See *Smith New Court Securities Ltd* v *Citibank NA* [1996] 3 WLR 1051 for an up-to-date discussion of this measure, and also *East* v *Maurer* [1991] 1 WLR 461 for consequential loss. Where the deceit has the consequence that the claimant is deprived of his goods, the court will generally award damages by reference to the market value of these goods, without reference to their cost of production (*Smith Kline & French Laboratories Ltd* v *Long* [1989] 1 WLR 1). It remains unclear whether or not exemplary damages can be recovered for the tort of deceit. In *Archer* v *Brown* [1985] 1 QB 401 Peter Pain J noted that there was a conflict of authority on this point, but he refused to attempt to resolve the conflict and held that the claimant was not entitled to exemplary damages on the facts. He did, however, award the claimant aggravated damages (see further Chapter 30).

27

Malicious Falsehood

27.1 Introduction

27.2 Falsehood

27.3 Malice

27.4 Damage

27.1 Introduction

This tort is called malicious falsehood by some commentators and judges, while others refer to it as injurious falsehood (in this Chapter it will be referred to as malicious falsehood). This tort is a tort of respectable antiquity and it consists of the making of a false statement, with malice, to a person other than the claimant, with the result that the claimant suffers damage.

The tort which we now call malicious falsehood was originally referred to as 'slander of title' because the first cases in which it was recognised were cases which involved one person making a false statement about the claimant's title to land with the result that the claimant was unable to sell the land or only able to sell it with greater difficulty than would otherwise have been the case (*Bliss* v *Stafford* (1573) Owen 37 and *Banister* v *Banister* (1583) 4 Co Rep 17a). However the scope of the tort has gradually expanded. It was also applied to cases of 'slander of goods', which was similar to 'slander of title' except that the defendant made an attack on the claimant's goods (*Kerr* v *Shedden* (1831) 4 C & P 528). The tort was also applied in cases of 'passing off' (discussed in Chapter 28). By the time of the decision of the Court of Appeal in *Ratcliffe* v *Evans* [1892] 2 QB 524 it was clear that the tort was not confined to cases of slander of title, slander of goods and passing off, but was a principle of general application. In *Ratcliffe* the defendant, who was a newspaper proprietor, maliciously and falsely implied in an article published in his newspaper that the claimant's firm had gone out of business. As a result of this publication the claimant suffered a considerable loss of business and he sought to recover from the defendant. It was held that the claimant was entitled to recover damages in respect of the defendant's malicious falsehood. Bowen LJ stated that an action would lie for written or oral falsehoods:

'... not actionable per se nor even defamatory, where they are maliciously published, where they are calculated in the ordinary course of things to produce, and where they do produce, actual damage.'

So by 1892 it was established that this tort was a tort of general application. Before examining the constituent elements of this tort it is necessary to distinguish this tort from the torts of deceit and defamation. Malicious falsehood can be distinguished from deceit on the ground that deceit is concerned with a false statement made by the defendant to the claimant which causes loss to the claimant, whereas malicious falsehood is concerned with a false statement about the claimant made to a third party as a result of which the claimant suffers damage. Malicious falsehood can be distinguished from defamation on the ground that defamation is concerned with attacks on the claimant's reputation, whereas malicious falsehood is not so confined and is generally concerned with attacks on the claimant's business or property (although a claimant who would otherwise have brought a claim in defamation may elect to bring a claim for malicious falsehood in order to get round the fact that legal aid is unavailable in defamation cases, see *Joyce* v *Sengupta* [1993] 1 WLR 337).

There are three basic elements to the tort of malicious falsehood. The first is that the defendant must have made a false statement to someone other than the claimant (section 27.2). The second is that the defendant must have made that statement with malice (section 27.3) and the third element is that the statement must have caused damage to the claimant (section 27.4).

27.2 Falsehood

As was the case in the tort of deceit, the falsehood must be a false statement of fact. It cannot be a false statement of opinion, nor can it be a mere puff. The same difficulties are experienced in this tort as are experienced in the tort of deceit in distinguishing between a statement of fact and a statement of opinion.

Particular difficulties have been experienced here in distinguishing between a trade puff and an actionable misrepresentation. This can be seen in the following cases. In *White* v *Mellin* [1895] AC 154 the defendant, who was the owner of a shop, stuck labels on the food produced by the claimant to the effect that the defendant's food was better in a number of respects than the food produced by the claimant. It was held that this was not actionable because the defendant was merely seeking to boost up his own product. Where, however, the defendant makes disparaging remarks about the claimant's goods, rather than contenting himself with boosting his own goods, then it is much more likely that the defendant's statement will be held to be actionable. This can be seen in the following two cases. In *Lyne* v *Nichols* (1906) 23 TLR 86 the defendant newspaper proprietor stated that the circulation of his paper was 'twenty to one of any other weekly paper in the district'. It was held that this statement was not a mere puff but was intended to be taken seriously and so was actionable upon proof of actual damage. The second case is *De Beers Products v Electric Co of New York* [1975] 1 WLR 972. The parties were both manufacturers of diamond abrasives for cutting concrete. As part of a sales drive the defendants published a pamphlet which incorporated a supposed laboratory report which had been conducted to compare the performance of the goods manufactured by the claimants and the defendants. The pamphlet contained adverse statements about the standard of the product produced by the claimants and stated that the defendants' product was superior. The claimants brought an action for slander of goods but the defendants claimed that the statement contained in the pamphlet was a mere puff. It was held by Walton J that the test to apply was whether the reasonable man would interpret the defendants' statement as being a serious one. It was held that the reasonable man would take the defendants' statement seriously because it was supposed to be a properly conducted scientific report. Walton J held that a trader was entitled to puff his own goods. He thought that the defendants were entitled to make a statement such as 'our goods are better than those which are produced by the claimants' even though that statement may be seen as denigrating the goods of the claimants. He held that the defendants were not, however, entitled to say that 'our goods are better than those of the claimants because the claimants' goods are rubbish', unless of course he can establish that the claimants' goods are indeed rubbish.

However, in *Vodafone Group plc v Orange Personal Communications Services Ltd* (1996) The Times 31 August the High Court held that the public were used to the ways of advertisers and expected a certain amount of hyperbole and comparisons, and that the statement 'on average Orange users save £20 every month' would not be understood by the public to mean that on average users of other mobile phones would save £20 a month if they transferred to Orange. This seems to be a strange decision, but the report of the case is rather brief.

27.3 Malice

The claimant must prove that the defendant's statement was made maliciously; that is, that the defendant acted out of some improper motive such as spite or a desire to injure the claimant. The burden of proving malice lies on the claimant. The test of what constitutes malice in the tort of malicious falsehood is the same as the test in relation to the torts of libel and slander (*Spring v Guardian Assurance plc* [1993] 2 All ER 273, 288 in the Court of Appeal. This decision was overturned by the House of Lords without considering this point). Where the defendant makes the statement knowing that it is false or reckless whether it be true or false then he has acted out of malice. In *Greers Ltd v Pearman & Corder Ltd* (1922) 39 RPC 406 the defendants falsely alleged that the claimant had infringed their trade mark for chocolates, which included the words 'Bouquet Brand'. However, the defendants had frequently stated in the past that they had no right to the exclusive use of these words. It was held that the fact that the defendants had made these allegations that the claimant had infringed their trade mark when they knew that this was untrue was sufficient to establish that they had acted out of malice. If it is proved that the defendants had acted out of malice it is irrelevant that the reason for their action was an attempt to further their business interests rather than an attempt to denigrate the business of the claimants. Thus in *Joyce* v *Motor Surveys Ltd* [1948] Ch 252 the defendants were held to have acted maliciously in telling the Post Office that the claimant, who was their tenant, had moved out of their premises and in telling the claimant's trade association that he had gone out of business so that they (the defendants) could sell the business with vacant possession.

However, where the defendant honestly believes a statement is true but in fact it is false the defendant has not acted out of malice. This is also the case where the defendant makes the statement carelessly but without any intention of injuring the claimant (*Balden* v *Shorter* [1933] Ch 247).

27.4 Damage

The claimant must show that he suffered pecuniary damage as a result of the defendant's statement: see *Allason* v *Campbell* (1996) The Times 8 May. The claimant must prove that he has suffered special damage, but where the defendant intended to cause harm to the claimant this is usually easily established by showing that the claimant suffered a general loss of business as a result of the defendant's false statement (see *Ratcliffe* v *Evans* (above)). The need to prove special damage has been dispensed with in certain cases by s3 of the Defamation Act 1952 which provides that:

> '... it shall not be necessary to allege or prove special damage –
> (a) if the words upon which the action is founded are calculated to cause pecuniary damage to the [claimant] and are published in writing or other permanent form; or
> (b) if the said words are calculated to cause pecuniary damage to the [claimant] in respect of any office, profession, calling, trade or business held or carried on by him at the time of publication.'

The purpose of s3 has been held to be one of giving 'the claimant a remedy in malicious falsehood despite the difficulty of proving actual loss' and so it cannot be the case that an award of damages under s3 must necessarily be nominal (*Joyce* v *Sengupta* [1993] 1 WLR 337, 347). Indeed, once a claimant is entitled to sue for malicious falsehood, whether on proof of special damage or by reason of s3 of the 1952 Act, there is no reason why, in an appropriate case, she should not receive aggravated damages for injury to her feelings caused by the defendant's insulting behaviour, in accordance with the dicta of Nicholls V-C and Sir Michael Kerr in *Joyce* v *Sengupta*: *Khodaparast* v *Shad* [2000] 1 All ER 545.

28

Passing Off

28.1 Introduction

28.2 Methods of passing off

28.3 Made by a trader in the course of a trade

28.4 Remedies

28.1 Introduction

The tort of passing off is committed where the claimant's goods are passed off by the defendant as being his own (that is, the defendant's) goods. The person whose goods have been passed off in this manner may have an action in tort in respect of any losses which he has incurred. Although this tort has been recognised for a number of years now, commentators continue to disagree on its classification. We noted in Chapter 27 that there is a link between passing off and the tort of malicious or injurious falsehood and that some have argued that passing off is part of malicious falsehood. There is also a link between passing off and the tort of deceit as the person who passes off his goods as belonging to another deceives the public. But it should be noted that the claimant in the passing off action is not the member of the public who has been deceived but the person whose goods have been passed off and he has not been deceived. On the other hand, as we shall note in Chapter 29, passing off could be classified as part of the economic torts because the subject matter of the tort of passing off is the protection of the claimant's financial interest in his property. It could also be classified as part of the law relating to intellectual property and ranked alongside copyright, trademarks and patents.

Despite this confusion as to the classification of the tort of passing off, it is included in a textbook on tort because it has been consistently recognised as part of the law of tort and because it differs from other types of intellectual property on the ground that the basis of the law lies in the common law and not in statute law.

The classic definition of the tort of passing off can be found in the judgment of Lord Diplock in *Erven Warnink BV* v *J Townend & Sons (Hull) Ltd* [1979] AC 731. Lord Diplock identified the five essential elements of the tort when he said that it is:

'... possible to identify five characteristics which must be present in order to create a valid cause of action for passing off: (1) a misrepresentation, (2) made by a trader in the course of trade, (3) to prospective customers of his or ultimate consumers of goods or services supplied by him, (4) which is calculated to injure the business or goodwill of another trader (in the sense that this is a reasonably foreseeable consequence) and (5) which causes actual damage to a business or goodwill of the trader by whom the action is brought or (in a quia timet action) will probably do so.'

These five elements must be proved to exist in any passing off action. Most of these elements are self-explanatory and require no further comment, so attention will be focused instead on the different ways in which this tort can be committed.

The crucial point of reference is the point of sale. Hence an identical appearance, revealed only after a purchaser had removed opaque wrapping, does not even furnish an arguable case: see *Bostik Ltd* v *Sellotape GB Ltd* (1993) The Times 11 January. The relevant date is the date of the commencement of the conduct of which complaint is made: *Inter Lotto (UK) Ltd* v *Camelot Group plc* [2003] 4 All ER 575.

28.2 Methods of passing off

The passing off of the claimant's goods as if they were the defendant's goods can take place in a number of different ways. The principal ways in which goods may be passed off are.

A direct statement that the goods belonging to the claimant in fact belong to the defendant

In *Lord Byron* v *Johnson* (1816) 2 Mer 29 the defendant, who was a publisher, advertised some poems which he had published as being written by Lord Byron when, in fact, they were written by someone else. It was held that the defendant had committed the tort of passing off.

Imitating the appearance of the claimant's goods

In *White Hudson & Co Ltd* v *Asian Organisation Ltd* [1964] 1 WLR 1466, the claimants manufactured 'Hacks' cough sweets in Singapore, which they sold in red cellophane wrappers and which came to be known as 'red paper cough sweets'. The claimants were, at that time, the only persons who sold cough sweets in such form in Singapore. The defendants then started to import into Singapore cough sweets called 'Peckos' which were also sold in red paper wrappers. The claimants proved that most of the customers in Singapore could not read English and simply asked for red paper cough sweets. It was held that the court would protect the claimants' interest in the appearance of their product and that the claimants would be granted an injunction to restrain the defendants from passing off their sweets as if they were the goods of the claimants. Innocence is no defence to a passing-off action: *Gillette UK Ltd* v *Edenwest Ltd* (1994) The Times 9 March.

In *Cadbury-Schweppes Pty Ltd* v *Pub Squash Co Pty Ltd* [1981] 1 WLR 193 the Privy Council held that a cause of action could lie, not only in respect of the physical appearance of the goods, but also in respect of the way in which they are advertised. Here the claimants had launched an advertising campaign which sought to associate their drink with a virile, sporting image. Shortly afterwards the defendants launched a similar advertising campaign. It was held that the claimants were not entitled to an injunction because they had not established that a virile, sporting image was associated by the public exclusively with their product. However, the Privy Council held that, had the claimants been able to establish this association, then an action in passing off could have succeeded in respect of the passing off of their advertising campaign.

Using a name similar to the claimant's goods

In *Reddaway* v *Banham* [1896] AC 199, the claimants were manufacturers of camel hair belting which they sold abroad. The belting contained a design with a camel and the words 'Camel Hair Belting' on it. The defendants also made camel hair belting with the words 'Camel Hair Belting' on it, but without the camel. The defendants argued that these words were simply a description of the goods which they were selling and not a passing off. It was held that the defendants had committed the tort of passing off because when the claimants' goods were sold abroad the words 'Camel Hair Belting' were not simply a description of the goods but were a trade mark of the claimants.

The description of the goods was also in issue in four further cases. The first is *J Bollinger* v *Costa Brava Wine Co Ltd* [1960] Ch 262. The claimants, who were champagne producers from the Champagne district of France, sought an injunction to restrain the defendants, who were wine merchants from Spain, from manufacturing a wine which was not produced in Champagne under the title of 'Spanish Champagne'. It was held that the word 'champagne' referred to the particular area where the wine was produced and that the producers from that area were entitled to protect the goodwill of the word 'champagne' and an injunction was granted accordingly. Similarly, in *Taittinger* v *Allbev Ltd* [1994] 4 All ER 75 it was held by the Court of Appeal that a non-alcoholic sparkling fruit drink marketed under the name 'Elderflower Champagne' which was neither champagne nor had any connection with its producers eroded the goodwill in the distinctiveness and exclusivity of the name 'champagne' and a similar injunction was granted. However, in *Harrods Ltd* v *Harrodian School* (1996) The Times 3 April the Court of Appeal were most concerned not to extend the decision in *Taittinger* to protect the claimants' goodwill. This decision, and this particular aspect of it, as been strongly citicised by S Lai in a recent article ([1996] NLJ 874). The third case is *Erven Warnink BV* v *J Townend and Sons (Hull) Ltd* (above). The claimants were manufacturers of a drink called 'advocaat', which was made from eggs and spirits. They had sold the drink for a number of years in England and the name 'advocaat' had acquired a considerable reputation and goodwill. The defendants then began to manufacture a drink made from sherry and eggs which they called 'Old English Advocaat'. The claimants sought an injunction to restrain the defendants from using the name advocaat. It was held that the name which was used by the claimants was a name which distinguished the claimants' product from the products of others and it was held that the claimants were entitled to an injunction to protect that name. Where, however, the name which the claimant is seeking to protect is a name which does not distinguish his goods but is given to a class of goods then an injunction will not be granted (see *British Vacuum Cleaner Co Ltd* v *New Vacuum Cleaner Co Ltd* [1907] 2 Ch 312).

The final case is *Mothercare UK Ltd* v *Penguin Books Ltd* (1987) The Times 8 July. The claimants sought an injunction to restrain the defendants from using the words 'Mother Care' in a book which they had published called 'Mother Care/Other Care'. The book was written by two academics and was somewhat polemical and the claimants said that it was their policy to avoid all such matters of controversy and to confine themselves to useful and practical advice to mothers. However, Dillon LJ was unable to see how the book, taken as a whole, indicated in any way that the claimants were associated with it. So he found that the claimants had not overcome the first of Lord Diplock's hurdles in *Erven Warnink* in showing that the defendants had misrepresented that the claimants were in any way involved in the production of the book and so the injunction was refused.

Using the claimant's name

Where the defendant uses the claimant's name, as opposed to the name of the claimant's products, the tort may be committed. This can be seen in the case of *Maxim's Ltd* v *Dye* [1977] 1 WLR 1155. The claimant was the owner of a famous restaurant called Maxim's in Paris and he sought an injunction to restrain the defendant from opening a French restaurant in Norwich with the same name. The restaurant in Norwich did not operate to the same standard as the restaurant in Paris and so the claimant was granted an injunction, even though he did not have any business in this country, because the conduct of the defendant was injuring the goodwill of the claimant's restaurant in Paris (contrast *Bernadin et Cie* v *Pavilion Properties Ltd* [1967] RPC 581).

Using the defendant's name

As a general rule the defendant is entitled to use his own name to advertise his products but this is subject to the qualification that the defendant cannot do so where that would be to mislead the public. This can be seen in the case of *Parker-Knoll Ltd* v *Knoll International Ltd* [1962] RPC 265. Both parties were furniture manufacturers, the claimants being a well-known company which traded in Great Britain, while the defendants traded in America. When the defendants started to trade in this country, the claimants sought an injunction to restrain the defendants from using their name on their furniture without distinguishing it from the products of the claimants. It was held by a majority of the House of Lords that the claimants were entitled to their injunction because they had established that their name had come to be associated with goods made by themselves alone and that the use by the defendants of their own name was likely to cause confusion among the public. It was not necessary for the claimants to show that the defendants intended to deceive the public, it was sufficient if it was likely that the public would be deceived by the defendants' use of their own name.

False attribution of authorship

In *Clark* v *Associated Newspapers Ltd* [1998] 1 All ER 959 it appeared that the defendant's newspaper, the *Evening Standard*, was publishing articles written by a Mr Peter Bradshaw which were parodies of the diaries of the claimant, then a Member of Parliament, which were still enjoying substantial sales. The claimant contended that the articles were in such a form that a substantial number of the newspaper's readers attributed them to his authorship. He brought an action under s84 of the Copyright, Designs and Patents Act 1988 (false attribution of work) and in passing off, seeking an injunction to restrain publication of the articles. The injunction was granted and two specific points made by Lightman J are worthy of note. First, for the common law tort of passing off to be established, a complainant must establish either actual damage or the likelihood of damage. False attribution of authorship (the statutory tort), most particularly to an author with an established reputation, is calculated to place his reputation and goodwill at risk of substantial damage and indeed to cause damage and damage may be presumed. Second, his Lordship's judgment should not be seen as a bar to the publication of parodies. Where the line is to be drawn between what does and what does not constitute false attribution of authorship is a question of judgment, and often a difficult question on which minds may differ. In this case in respect of the format which it adopted in the fully understandable aim of achieving the maximum impact on readers, the defendant made an honest and understandable error of judgment: the articles fell on the wrong side of the line. The vice lay in the format of the articles. The defendant could however continue to publish parodies of the diaries so long as there was no attribution of authorship to the claimant and it was made sufficiently clear that Mr Bradshaw, and not the claimant, was the author.

False endorsement

The law of passing off can apply to false endorsement: *Irvine* v *Talksport Ltd* [2003] 2 All ER 881. In that case Laddie J heard that, having obtained the rights to broadcast live the Formula One Grand Prix World Championship, the defendant radio station had sent a brochure to potential advertisers. On the front cover of the brochure was a photograph of the claimant, a prominent British racing driver, which had been purchased from a photograph agency. As purchased, the photograph showed the claimant holding a mobile telephone: as it appeared in the brochure, he was holding a portable radio bearing the defendant's name. In an action for damages for passing off, the court had to decide whether (1) the law of passing off applied to cases of false endorsement, and (2) it was necessary to show that the claimant and the defendant shared a 'common field of activity'. His Lordship held that passing off could apply to false endorsement and that it was not necessary to show that the parties shared a common field of activity: he awarded the claimant £2,000 by way of damages. The defendant appealed as to liability, contending that the image on the leaflet had been intended as a joke and that recipients were unlikely to believe that the claimant had endorsed the radio station. The claimant appealed against the assessment of damages. The Court of Appeal dismissed the defendant's appeal but the claimant's appeal was allowed, increasing the damages awarded to £25,000, the amount which, on a balance of probabilities, the defendant would have had to pay in order to obtain lawfully that which it had obtained unlawfully. Jonathan Parker LJ said:

> 'To my eye, the image on the front of the leaflet is the clearest representation that Mr Irvine has endorsed Talk Radio. The fact that the whole Formula One pack may have been intended as a joke, and may well have been perceived as such by recipients of it, seems to me to be nothing to the point. ... I find it difficult to conceive of a clearer way of conveying, by way of a quasi-photographic image, the message that a celebrity has endorsed a particular radio station than by depicting the celebrity listening intently to a radio bearing the station's logo.'

The 'common field of activity' requirement was enunciated by Wynn-Parry J in *McCulloch* v *May* [1947] 2 All ER 845. In *Harrods Ltd* v *Harrodian School Ltd* [1996] RPC 697, Millett LJ had observed that this approach was contrary to numerous previous authorities.

28.3 Made by a trader in the course of a trade

Where the parties are not in the same trade, it is much harder for the claimant to show that the public is likely to be confused by the defendant's alleged passing off of the property of the claimant. This can be seen in the case of *Granada Group Ltd* v *Ford Motor Co Ltd* [1972] FSR 103. The claimants, who were a major entertainment organisation, sought to restrain the defendants from calling their new car 'Granada'. It was held that they were not entitled to an injunction because there was no risk of confusion in the minds of the public between the defendants' car and the claimants' entertainment company. Similarly the claimant was unsuccessful in

McCullough v *May* [1947] 2 All ER 845. The claimant, who was a well-known children's broadcaster called 'Uncle Mac', sought to prevent the defendants from calling their breakfast cereal 'Uncle Mac's Puffed Wheat'. He failed on the ground that there was no common trading activity between the parties and so there was no risk of confusion in the minds of the public (cf *Henderson* v *Radio Corporation Pty Ltd* [1960] NSWR 576). Additionally, in *Hodgkinson & Corby Ltd* v *Wards Mobility Services Ltd* [1994] 1 WLR 1564, where the defendants copied the claimants' design for wheelchair cushions which were marketed under a different name, the claimant failed in a passing off action as the evidence showed that the only purchasers of the defendant's products were healthcare professionals who would not be deceived into thinking that they were buying the claimants' goods.

28.4 Remedies

In many cases the remedy which the claimant will seek is an injunction to restrain the defendant from continuing to pass off his goods as if they were the claimant's. The injunction may be granted on terms, such as where the defendant is permitted to continue to manufacture the goods as long as he distinguishes his goods from those of the claimant. In deciding to grant an injunction a judge may take into account the behaviour of the parties and refuse to grant an injunction if the claimant has failed to respond to reasonable enquiries and the defendants have, as a result, expended much time and expense in marketing their product: see *Dalgety Spillers Foods Ltd* v *Food Brokers Ltd* (1993) The Times 2 December.

The availability of injunctive relief was considered by the Court of Appeal in *British Telecommunications plc* v *One In A Million Ltd* [1998] 4 All ER 476. The defendant dealers registered and sold Internet domain names: in each case they registered domain names comprising the name or trade mark of the claimant. The claimants sought injunctive relief on the ground, inter alia, of passing off. Their Lordships concluded that such relief was appropriate and that the judge's decision to grant final injunctions quia timet would not be disturbed. Aldous LJ explained the position as follows:

> 'In my view there can be discerned from the cases a jurisdiction to grant injunctive relief where a defendant is equipped with or is intending to equip another with an instrument of fraud. Whether any name is an instrument of fraud will depend upon all the circumstances. A name which will, by reason of its similarity to the name of another, inherently lead to passing off is such an instrument. If it would not inherently lead to passing off, it does not follow that it is not an instrument of fraud. The court should consider the similarity of the names, the intention of the defendant, the type of trade and all the surrounding circumstances. If it be the intention of the defendant to appropriate the goodwill of another or enable others to do so, I can see no reason why the court should not infer that it will happen, even if there is a possibility that such an appropriation would not take place. If, taking all the circumstances into account the court should conclude that the name was produced to enable passing off, is adapted to be used

for passing off and, if used, is likely to be fraudulently used, an injunction will be appropriate.'

The claimant may also seek a remedy in damages for the loss which he has suffered as a result of the defendant's activities, or he may seek from the defendant an account of the profits which he has made as a result of the passing off.

An unincorporated association (here, of furniture manufacturing companies) may, through its members, own goodwill sufficient to found an action in passing off: *Artistic Upholstery Ltd* v *Art Forma (Furniture) Ltd* [1999] 4 All ER 277. In such a case, one of the members should sue in a representative capacity.

29

The Economic Torts

29.1 Introduction

The economic torts are concerned with the intentional, rather than the negligent, infliction of economic harm on another. In fact many of the cases which we shall discuss are concerned with the legal consequences of industrial action, although some are concerned with alleged unlawful competition. The common law has never developed a principle that commercial parties must trade fairly (see *Associated Newspapers Group plc* v *Insert Media Ltd* [1988] 1 WLR 509 where Hoffmann J rejected the proposition that 'any intentional act which is calculated to cause damage to the claimants' business or goodwill is actionable per se' and, while he accepted that the law in relation to unfair trading is not static, he refused to recognise the existence of a tort of 'unfair trading') and so, until the intervention of statutes such as the Fair Trading Act 1973, the common law regulation of trade and competition was left to the economic torts.

It is possible to divide the economic torts into four different nominate torts, but the adoption of such an approach has the consequence of ignoring the threads which are common to all the economic torts. So we shall discuss the economic torts in one Chapter and compare and contrast them. There has also been some debate recently as to whether or not the torts are in fact all part of the one innominate tort, called interference with trade or business by unlawful means. This issue is one to which we shall return after discussing the ground rules.

29.2 The ground rules

The foundation rules which are applicable to the economic torts were laid down at the end of last century and the beginning of this century. Through a trilogy of cases the House of Lords was given the opportunity to put the law on a coherent basis. Unfortunately they failed to set out any clear or principled approach and the consequences of this failure can still be seen in our law today.

The first of the three cases was *Mogul Steamship Co Ltd* v *McGregor, Gow & Co* [1892] AC 25. In this case the defendants sought to obtain a monopoly in the tea trade, which was at that time extremely profitable. They sought to obtain a monopoly by, amongst other things, cutting the price of tea so as to drive the claimants, who were shipowners involved in the tea trade, out of business. The defendants were successful in driving the claimants out of the trade and so the claimants brought an action against the defendants alleging that the defendants had conspired to injure them. The House of Lords held that the claimants had no cause of action against the defendants. They held that such a cause of action would only arise where the defendants had committed an unlawful act against the claimants. No such unlawful act had been committed. Competition, however vigorous or unfair, was not, of itself, an unlawful act.

In electing to impose liability when the defendant committed an unlawful act the House of Lords made an important choice. There were, in fact, two avenues open to the House. The first, and the one which the House chose, was to impose liability when the defendant commits an unlawful act. The second avenue open to them was to impose liability when one person, without justification, intentionally inflicts harm upon another. The adoption of such an approach might have achieved a different result on the facts of *Mogul*. It was at least arguable that the defendants had acted unfairly vis-a-vis the claimants. But the adoption of this approach would have led the courts into troubled waters. Let us take an example to illustrate the point. Suppose that several small traders have traded on a housing estate for a number of years and provided the residents with a satisfactory service. However, the owners of a large chain of supermarkets think that they can provide a better and cheaper service for the residents of the housing estate and for residents of nearby estates. They open up a large new store nearby and offer their products at a significantly lower price than those in the local stores, in an effort to attract the residents of the estate who previously were customers of the small traders. The traders lose money and some are forced out of business. Can these traders bring an action against the supermarket owners on the ground that the supermarket owners have intentionally inflicted economic loss upon them without justification? Had the House of Lords based liability in *Mogul* upon the fact that the defendants had acted without justification, then the traders could have argued that they had a case. This would have involved the courts in adjudicating upon what are acceptable and what are unacceptable forms of competition. Such an approach would have required the courts to make difficult policy choices, which could be dubbed as being 'political' choices. It is perhaps for this reason that the courts refused to adopt this approach. The line between what is lawful and what is unlawful does not require the courts to make such explicit choices of policy and provides a more certain guideline for subsequent courts and for legal advisers. However, as we shall note at different points in this Chapter, the line between what is lawful and what is unlawful is, to some extent, an arbitrary one and it has produced some rather strange results in the cases.

The second case in the trilogy is *Allen* v *Flood* [1898] AC 1. The case centred around a dispute between two trade unions. The ironworkers' union objected to members of the woodworkers' union doing certain work which they claimed had always been done by members of the ironworkers' union. An official of the ironworkers' union informed the employers of the woodworkers that they would stop work unless the woodworkers were dismissed. The employers gave in to this threat and dismissed the woodworkers, who brought an action against the official of the ironworkers' union who had threatened the strike unless the claimants were dismissed. This time the House of Lords was divided, but the majority held that the claimants had no cause of action against the defendant because the defendant had not done an unlawful act. The act of informing the employers that his members would go on strike unless the claimants were dismissed did not constitute an unlawful act because the members of the ironworkers' union were employed under contracts which were determinable at will and so, in threatening to bring them out on strike, there was no threat of the commission of an unlawful act. Nor had the contracts of the claimants been unlawfully interfered with because the employers had lawfully determined their contracts. So the principle laid down in *Mogul* was applied and the claimants were held to have no cause of action. The fact that the defendant was alleged to have acted out of spite was irrelevant because spite or malice could not, of itself, turn what was otherwise a lawful act into an unlawful act.

The final case in the trilogy is *Quinn* v *Leatham* [1901] AC 495. This case has given rise to considerable difficulty because it obscures the clear principle which was established in *Mogul* and *Allen*. The claimant was the owner of a fleshing business. He employed non-union men. The defendants, who were trade union officials, sought to persuade the claimant not to employ non-union men. The claimant was prepared to permit his employees to join the union but he was not prepared to require them to join the union as a condition of continued employment. So the defendants instructed their members who worked for a butcher, who was the claimant's principal customer, not to handle the claimant's meat. As a result of this action the claimant suffered loss and he brought an action against the defendants, alleging that they had conspired to injure him. The defendants had not committed an unlawful act against the claimant because, in instructing their members not to handle the claimant's meat, they had not instructed their members to breach their contracts. So an application of the principle laid down in *Mogul* required that the claimant's action be dismissed. But this was not the approach adopted by the House of Lords. The House held that the defendants had conspired unjustifiably to inflict loss on the claimant and so the defendants were liable. The jury had found that the defendants had acted out of malice and that they had no justification for their action and this finding was upheld by the House of Lords.

The obvious difficulty to which this case gives rise is how to reconcile it with the reasoning adopted in *Mogul* and *Allen*. On the face of it they appear to adopt totally inconsistent approaches. In *Mogul* and *Allen* the House of Lords held that a cause of action lay in respect of the unlawful infliction of harm and not in respect of simply unjustified infliction of harm, while in *Quinn* the House held that a cause of action does lie in respect of the unjustified infliction of harm. The accepted, if unprincipled, distinction between the cases is that in *Allen* there was only one defendant, whereas in *Quinn* there was more than one. So, where defendants conspire together to inflict harm on another, without having any justification for so doing, their lack of justification may turn an otherwise lawful act into one which is actionable in tort. The supposed rationale behind this distinction is that collective pressure is greater than the pressure which can be exerted by a single individual. The absurdity inherent in this approach was demonstrated by Lord Diplock in *Lonrho* v *Shell Petroleum Co Ltd (No 2)* [1982] AC 173. He pointed out that the fact that the law regards a limited company as a legal person destroys the argument that collective pressure is inevitably greater than the pressure exerted by a single individual. In the example which we considered above, involving the supermarket and the small traders, it is obvious that the supermarket can exert greater pressure than the small traders and to suggest otherwise and to treat the supermarket more favourably than the small traders is ludicrous.

So the principle established in *Quinn*, that the motive of a group of persons acting together can render an otherwise lawful act actionable, is an anomalous one and one which the House of Lords held in *Lonrho* was not to be extended. It is a rule which is confined to cases of conspiracy to injure and it does not undermine the general principle in English law that liability is based upon the unlawfulness of the defendant's actions.

Having examined the general principle which runs through the cases we shall now consider the separate nominate torts which have been recognised in English law and then we shall conclude by considering whether there is, in fact, one innominate tort which unifies these nominate torts. We shall commence by considering the anomalous tort of conspiracy.

29.3 Conspiracy

The tort of conspiracy is a tort of respectable antiquity. A useful definition of the tort was provided by Willes J in *Mulcahy* v *R* (1868) LR 3 HL 306, 317 in the following terms:

> 'A conspiracy consists not merely in the intention of two or more, but in the agreement of two or more to do an unlawful act, or to do a lawful act by unlawful means.'

It is clear from this definition that there are, in fact, two different types of conspiracy. The first type consists of a conspiracy to commit an unlawful act. This type of conspiracy conforms to the general principle which requires that the defendant commit an unlawful act. The second type of conspiracy consists of a conspiracy to do acts which, if done by an individual would be lawful, but which, by virtue of the fact that they are done in combination, become unlawful and actionable. This is the anomalous tort and the one which does not conform to the general principle requiring that the defendant commit an unlawful act. Although the tort of conspiracy has these two distinct branches there are some factors common to both branches and we shall consider these common elements before analysing the two branches of the tort.

There are three elements common to both branches of the tort. The first is that there must be two or more persons involved in the conspiracy. This requirement generally gives rise to no difficulties. However it should be noted that a company is treated as a legal person for this purpose and so a company can conspire with its directors (*Belmont Finance Corpn* v *Williams Furniture Ltd (No 2)* [1980] 1 All ER 393). This may need qualification in the case where it is alleged that the conspiracy is between a 'one man' company and the controller of that company because of the difficulty of showing that there were two minds involved in the conspiracy (*R* v *McDonnell* [1966] 1 QB 233, although it should be noted that this was a criminal case). There is an old rule of criminal law that a husband and wife cannot conspire together, but this rule has been held to be inapplicable to the tort of conspiracy (see *Midland Bank Trust Co Ltd* v *Green (No 3)* [1982] Ch 529 where it was held that the fictional unity of husband and wife did not apply to liability in the tort of conspiracy).

The second common element is that there must be a combination between the parties. The word combination has been preferred to agreement on the ground that the latter may be thought to require an agreement of a contractual kind when, in fact, all that is required is that the parties combine together with a common purpose (see *Belmont Finance Corpn* v *Williams Furniture Ltd* (above) p404). There is no requirement that the conspirators all join the conspiracy at the same time. It is sufficient that at some stage they combined together. Nor need the conspirators have exactly the same aim in joining the conspiracy but, the wider the difference in aim, the less likely it is that there will be a combination.

The third common element is that there must be damage to the claimant because damage is of the very essence of the tort. Once these three common elements are established, it must be considered which of the two branches of the tort has been committed. We shall consider unlawful means conspiracy first and then consider conspiracy to injure by lawful means.

Unlawful means conspiracy

This branch of the tort is consistent with the general principle which requires that the defendant commit an unlawful act. The only problem which arises here concerns what constitutes unlawful means. It is clear that conspiracy to commit a crime constitutes unlawful means and a conspiracy to commit a tort can constitute unlawful means (see the judgment of Lord Dunedin in *Sorrell* v *Smith* [1925] AC 700, 729–30). It is not, however, clear whether a breach of contract constitutes unlawful means for this purpose. In *Rookes* v *Barnard* [1964] AC 1129 Lord Devlin expressly left this particular point open, but the majority view amongst commentators is that it may constitute unlawful means (see *Clerk and Lindsell on Torts* (16th ed) para 15–23).

The most important recent case on unlawful means conspiracy is *Lonrho Ltd* v *Shell Petroleum Co Ltd (No 2)* [1982] AC 173. Shell, the defendants, built an oil refinery in Southern Rhodesia. Lonrho built the pipe-line to the refinery from a port in Mozambique and the expectation of the parties involved in the enterprise was that the pipe-line would be used to get the oil to the refinery. However, in 1965 the government of Rhodesia unilaterally declared independence (UDI) and the response of the British government was to pass the Southern Rhodesia (Petroleum) Order 1965 which made it a criminal offence to supply oil to Southern Rhodesia. Thus the pipe-line ceased to be used. But the claimants alleged that the defendants secretly conspired to maintain the supply of oil to Southern Rhodesia, without using the pipe-line, and that this continued the illegal declaration of independence and so increased the claimants' loss because it increased the length of time for which the pipe-line was out of use. It was held that the claimants did not have an action in tort in respect of the defendants' breach of the sanctions order because the mere prohibition upon members of the public doing what was otherwise lawful in trading with Southern Rhodesia was not enough, of itself, to found a cause of action for breach of statutory duty. More significantly, perhaps, the judgment of Lord Diplock was subsequently interpreted as authority for the proposition that, to establish a cause of action in unlawful means conspiracy, it must be shown not only that the defendants intended to injure the claimant but that, as in the case of conspiracy to injure by lawful means, the predominant purpose of the conspirators must have been to injure the claimant rather than further their own interests (see, for example, *Metall und Rohstoff AG* v *Donaldson Lufkin & Jenrette Inc* [1990] 1 QB 391). But the House of Lords in *Lonrho plc* v *Fayed* [1992] 1 AC 448 overruled the decision of the Court of Appeal in *Metall und Rohstoff* and held that, in cases of unlawful means conspiracy, it is not necessary to show that the defendants had as their predominant purpose an intention to injure the claimant; it suffices that they had intent to injure the claimant. The predominant purpose to injure test is therefore confined to the anomalous tort of conspiracy to injure by lawful means (see below). In *Lonrho plc* v *Fayed (No 5)* [1993] 1 WLR 1489 the Court of Appeal held that actual pecuniary loss could be recovered in an action for conspiracy, but that damages for injury to reputation and injury to feeling could only be recovered in defamation.

Where wrongful and damaging acts committed by a defendant alone do not give rise to a cause of action, the commission of those acts by two or more defendants in concert does not give rise to a cause of action, save in exceptional circumstances of which conspiracies to injure are possibly the only example: *Michaels* v *Taylor Woodrow Developments Ltd* [2000] 4 All ER 645.

Conspiracy to injure by lawful means

This is the anomalous form of the tort which is derived from *Quinn* v *Leatham* (above). Since it is a highly anomalous tort its ambit has been severely restricted. The most famous case concerned with this branch of the tort is *Crofter Hand Woven Harris Tweed Co Ltd* v *Veitch* [1942] AC 435. The case concerned the production of Harris tweed on the Isle of Lewis. Originally the tweed was made from hand spun yarn produced on Lewis. But, by 1930, many mill owners on Lewis were importing machine spun yarn from the mainland as it was much cheaper to do this. Some mill owners, however, persisted in using the local hand spun yarn. When the trade unions which represented the employees at the latter's mills sought a pay rise they were told that the mill owners could not afford it because of the competition provided by the importation of machine spun yarn from the mainland. So the trade union officials ordered the dockers, who were also members of the union, not to handle imported yarn, with the object of driving out the competition and enabling the mill owners to raise the wages. The dockers did this without breaking their contracts of employment. The claimants, who suffered loss as a result of this embargo upon the importation of machine spun yarn, brought an action against the defendant trade union officials alleging that they had conspired to injure them without justification.

It was held that the claimants had no cause of action against the defendants because the predominant purpose behind the defendants' actions was to defend the interests of their members and not to inflict loss on the claimants. This case established the important point that the pursuit of self-interest constitutes a justification for the tort of conspiracy to injure by lawful means. Although the pursuit of self-interest or selfish goals constitutes a justification, the defendant may not be able to rely on the defence when his actions are motivated by spite or vindictiveness. Such was the case in *Huntley* v *Thornton* [1957] 1 WLR 321. The defendant trade union officials hounded the claimant out of every job which he obtained in their district. It was held that their purpose in driving the claimant out of a job was not to defend the interests of the union but to uphold 'their own ruffled dignity'. This was held to be an unjustified purpose and the claimant was able to recover damages from the defendants (contrast *Scala Ballroom (Wolverhampton) Ltd v Ratcliffe* [1958] 1 WLR 1057 where the refusal of union members to play at a ballroom which operated a colour bar was held to be justified).

29.4 Inducing breach of contract

This is the major economic tort and the one which is most commonly committed in the course of industrial disputes. The tort has its origins in the case of *Lumley* v *Gye* (1853) 2 El & Bl 216. The claimant was a theatre owner and he claimed that he had entered into a contract with a famous opera singer, Miss Wagner, under which she was to sing only at his theatre for a period of time. The defendant, who was the owner of a rival theatre, procured Miss Wagner to break her contract with the claimant by promising to pay her more than she was receiving from the claimant. When Miss Wagner, in breach of contract, refused to continue to perform at the claimant's theatre, he brought an action against the defendant alleging that the defendant had induced Miss Wagner to break her contract with him and that this had caused him loss. It was held that the claimant was entitled to maintain an action for damages in respect of the wrong done to him by the defendant inducing Miss Wagner to break her contract with him. This tort has since given rise to a considerable body of case law and it can be analysed in the following five stages.

The forms of the tort

In the case of *DC Thomson & Co Ltd v Deakin* [1952] Ch 646 Jenkins LJ described the three different ways in which this tort can be committed. The first way is by directly persuading one of the contracting parties to break his contract. *Lumley* is a case within this category. The courts formally distinguish between persuasion to break the contract and the mere giving of advice that the contract will be broken, the latter not being actionable. However, the courts have been willing to find that the defendant has persuaded the party to break his contractual obligations. This willingness can be seen in the case of *Square Grip Reinforcement Co Ltd* v *MacDonald* 1968 SLT 65 where Lord Milligan said that, where the defendant was 'desperately anxious' to achieve a particular result, then a court was likely to construe a 'suggestion' made by the defendant as being persuasion but that, where the defendant was not 'really interested' in the result, then a court was not likely to construe a 'suggestion' as amounting to persuasion. This test is hardly a difficult one for the claimant to satisfy. It appears that the only person who can sue in respect of such direct persuasion is the contracting party who is harmed by the other party's breach of contract. The duty of the party who receives the inducement is to resist the inducements and so he cannot bring an action in tort in respect of any loss which he incurs as a result of the breach of contract (per Upjohn LJ in *Boulting* v *Association of Cinematograph, Television and Allied Technicians* [1963] 2 QB 606, 639–40).

The second way in which this tort may be committed arises where the defendant prevents performance of the contract taking place by some other direct and wrongful means. An example given by Jenkins LJ in *Thomson* was of a defendant wrongfully taking the contracting party's tools so that he could not carry out his contractual obligations. The intervention of the defendant here must be wrongful in itself.

The third way in which this tort can be committed is where the defendant (referred to as 'A') induces a third party, such as an employee of a customer of the claimant, to break his contract with his employer (referred to as 'B') with the result that his employer (B) is unable to perform his contractual obligations with the claimant (referred to as 'C'). The four requirements of this limb of the tort were laid down by Jenkins LJ in *Thomson* v *Deakin* (above). The first was that the defendant (A) must have known of the contract between the claimant (C) and the other contracting party (B). The second was that the defendant (A) must have intended to breach the contract between C and B by inducing the employees of B to break their contracts of employment. The third requirement is that the employees so induced must have broken their contracts of employment and finally the breach of the contract between B and C must have ensued as a necessary consequence of the breach by the employees of B of their contracts of employment. This form of the tort was the form which was in issue in *Thomson* v *Deakin* (above). The claimants were newspaper publishers who only employed non-union labour. The defendant trade union officials tried to compel the claimants to stop employing non-union labour and, in seeking to do this, they told their members to boycott the claimants' supplies. Bowaters, who supplied the claimants with paper, refused to carry out their contracts with the claimants because of the fear of a dispute with their own employees if they continued to supply the claimants with paper. The claimants sought an injunction to restrain what they believed to be the unlawful acts of the defendants. The Court of Appeal refused to grant an injunction on the ground that there was no evidence that the employees of Bowaters had breached their contracts of employment. This failure to show such a breach was fatal to the claimants' action because unlawful means is of the essence of the tort. The indirect procurement of a breach of contract by means which are not in themselves unlawful is not actionable.

Although these three forms of the tort are separate and distinct it can be difficult in a particular case to say whether it is the direct or the indirect form of the tort which has been committed. Thus in *Thomson* it was also argued that the defendants had committed the direct form of the tort. This claim failed because there was no evidence that the defendants had sought to induce Bowaters not to perform their contract with the claimants; the inducement had been an indirect one via the employees of Bowaters. The difficulty of distinguishing between the different forms of the tort can also be seen in the judgments of the House of Lords in *JT Stratford & Sons Ltd* v *Lindley* [1965] AC 269. The claimants (P) hired out barges to a third party (C). The defendant trade union officials wished to exert pressure on P to settle a dispute and they instructed employees of C not to handle any of the barges belonging to P. This action soon had a serious effect on P's business and so they sought an injunction against the defendants to restrain the industrial action. The House of Lords held that the defendants had committed the tort of inducing breach of contract and granted the injunctions. It was not entirely clear, however, which form of the tort had been committed. The majority treated it as a case of indirect procurement because they thought that the defendants had persuaded the employees of C to break their contracts, whereas the minority treated it as a case of direct procurement because they thought that the defendants had persuaded C not to perform their contract with P. Although in *Stratford* it did not really matter which form of the tort had been committed, it may be important to know which was committed in some cases because unlawful means is essential to the indirect form of the tort but, in the case of the direct form of the tort, it need only be shown that the defendant persuaded a contracting party to break his contract with the claimant.

Since the tort of wrongful interference with contractual relations is not committed unless the alleged tortfeasor intended to procure a breach of, or the non-performance of an obligation in a contract, an invalidly appointed receiver who assumes control of a party's contractual rights does not commit the tort. *OBG Ltd* v *Allan* (2005) The Times 24 February.

Knowledge and intention

Once it is established which form of the tort was committed, it must be shown that the defendant acted with the requisite knowledge and intention. This tort is a tort of intention and so does not encompass the negligent invasion of contractual rights. The defendant must be shown to have knowledge of the contract which has been broken and must have acted with the intention of bringing about a breach of that contract.

Although it must be shown that the defendant knew of the contract which was broken, it need not be shown that the defendant knew the exact term of the contract which was broken. In many cases it will be inferred that the defendant knew that the industrial action was likely to lead to a breach of contract. In *Merkur Island Shipping Corp* v *Laughton* [1983] 2 AC 570 both the Court of Appeal and the House of Lords were prepared to hold that the defendant trade union officials, by virtue of their work in the trade, must be deemed to know that the industrial action would lead to a breach of contract.

While it must be shown that the defendant intended to procure a breach of contract, this requirement can be satisfied by demonstrating that the defendant was reckless as to whether a contract was breached or not. In *Emerald Construction Co Ltd* v *Lowthian* [1966] 1 WLR 691 Lord Denning said that:

'Even if [the defendants] did not know of the actual contract, but had the means of knowledge – which they deliberately disregarded – that would be enough. Like the man who turns a blind eye. So here, if the officers deliberately sought to get this contract terminated, heedless of its terms, regardless whether it was terminated by breach or not, they would do wrong. For it is unlawful for a third party to procure a breach of contract knowingly, or recklessly, indifferent whether it is a breach or not.'

Breach

As the tort is entitled inducing breach of contract it would be reasonable to assume that the claimant must show that the defendant induced a breach of contract. But this is not necessarily so. At first instance Hoffmann J in *Law Debenture Trust Corporation* v *Ural Caspian Oil Corporation Ltd* [1993] 1 WLR 138, 151 stated that it was sufficient that 'the right which has been violated is a *secondary* right to a remedy arising out of the tortious inducement of a breach by a third party of its primary obligation under a contract.' Thus where the defendant induces a third party to break his contract with the claimant with the result that the claimant is deprived of a remedy which he would otherwise have had against the third party, the conduct of the defendant may be tortious. This view, however, was rejected by the Court of Appeal ([1994] 3 WLR 1221 which held that the defendant had acted legally and hence was not liable to the claimant.

However, it may be sufficient to show that the performance of the contract was interfered with. The origins of this development can be traced back to the case of *Torquay Hotels Co Ltd* v *Cousins* [1969] 2 Ch 106. The defendants, during the course of an industrial dispute, persuaded various petrol companies not to deliver oil to the claimants' hotel. Esso, the claimants' principal suppliers, did not deliver any oil because their drivers were members of the defendant union and so would not cross the picket line. The claimants managed to procure some alternative supplies for a short period of time but the alternative suppliers were soon warned off by the defendant union. The claimants brought an action against the defendants seeking an injunction restraining them from inducing a breach of contract between Esso and themselves. The difficulty was that their contract with Esso contained an exclusion clause or a force majeure clause which absolved Esso from the obligation to deliver oil when their failure to deliver was caused by events outside their control, including industrial action. So it appeared that there was, in fact, no breach of contract. Nevertheless the defendants were held to have committed a tort and the claimants were granted their injunctions. There are two ways in which this finding that the defendants were liable can be analysed.

The first way is to adopt the narrower approach based upon the reasoning of the majority in *Torquay Hotels*. This approach focused upon the existence of the exclusion clause. The majority perceived the exclusion clause in defensive rather than definitional terms; that is, they saw the exclusion clause as providing a defence to a breach of contract. On this view of the nature of the exclusion clause there was a breach of contract and, while the exclusion clause provided Esso with a defence to any action brought on the contract against them by the claimants, it could not be relied upon by the defendants who were not party to the contract. This interpretation does not conflict with the requirement that there must be a breach of contract because it holds that there was, in fact, a breach of contract and that the reason the defendants were held to be liable was that they could not rely on an exclusion clause which had been drafted for the benefit of someone else. The difficulty with this view is that it misrepresents the true nature of an exclusion clause, which is to define the obligations which the parties have accepted and not to act as a defence to a breach of an obligation (see Yates *Exclusion Clauses in Contracts* (2nd ed) Chapter 1 and the judgment of Lord Diplock in *Photo Production Ltd* v *Securicor Transport Ltd* [1980] AC 827). The perception of the exclusion clause in definitional terms would have required the majority to give a direct answer to the question whether a breach of contract was a necessary ingredient of the tort.

The second way of analysing the case is to adopt the wider principle laid down by Lord Denning in the following terms:

> 'Interference is not confined to the procurement of a breach of contract. It extends to a case where a third person prevents or hinders one party from performing his contract, even though it be not a breach.'

This statement appears to be a much broader statement of principle than that adopted by the majority. However it is unclear whether Lord Denning was referring to the direct form of the tort or the indirect form. The better view is that he was referring to the direct form of the tort (see *Clerk and Lindsell on Torts* (16th ed) para 15–05). If this view is correct it creates a tort of rather uncertain limits. Presumably it would not apply to the case where a defendant induced a contracting party to exercise an option to terminate a contract because in terminating the contract no unlawful act was committed. The difficulty is that, where there is interference with performance short of a breach, no unlawful act is committed by the defendant and it is virtually impossible to mark out the limits of liability with any degree of certainty.

However, in *Merkur Island Shipping Corp* v *Laughton* (above) Lord Diplock interpreted Lord Denning's judgment as relating to the indirect form of the tort (for criticism see Wedderburn (1983) 46 MLR 632). In *Merkur* the House of Lords held that there was a tort of interfering with contractual rights by unlawful means. Lord Diplock held that the four-stage approach to the tort of indirectly inducing a breach of contract adopted by Jenkins LJ in *Thomson* v *Deakin* (above) was not confined to cases of breach of contract but that it also extended to cases where there was interference with the performance of the contract short of breach. The same four-stage approach is to be adopted in cases of interference with performance by unlawful means except that at stages one and four the reference is to interference with performance rather than breach. So it is now clear that in the case of the indirect form of the tort it is not necessary to show that there has been a breach of contract but the position is wholly unclear in relation to the direct form of the tort. Much depends on the interpretation placed upon Lord Denning's judgment in

Torquay Hotels (see too the decision of the House of Lords in *Dimbleby and Sons Ltd v National Union of Journalists* [1984] 1 WLR 427, noted by Carty (1984) 100 LQR 342).

The Court of Appeal has, however, recently stated that it is most important not to extend the principle of *Lumley* v *Gye* outside its proper limits. In *Middlebrook Mushrooms Ltd* v *Transport and General Workers Union* (1993) The Times 18 January a trade union's campaign of distributing leaflets outside supermarkets urging members of the public to support dismissal of employees of a mushroom producer by refusing to buy the producer's mushrooms was not tortious. If the case was to fall within the *Lumley* v *Gye* category the persuasion had to be directed to one of the parties to the contract; the union's leaflet was directed to the customer, not the management of the supermarkets who were neither encouraged nor discouraged to take any action. Where direct pressure was brought to bear on strangers to the contract and the effect on the contracting party was indirect it was necessary to show that some unlawful means had been used if the conduct was to be actionable.

Damage

Damage is the very gist of this tort but the courts are willing to infer that the defendant's inducement of the breach of contract has caused loss to the claimant.

Justification

The scope of the defence of justification as a defence to the tort of inducing breach of contract was helpfully discussed by the Court of Appeal in *Edwin Hill & Partners* v *First National Finance Corporation* [1989] 1 WLR 225. Stuart-Smith LJ identified two circumstances where the defence has succeeded. The first was 'where the contract interfered with is inconsistent with a previous contract with the interferer' (*Smithies* v *National Association of Operative Plasterers* [1909] 1 KB 310). The second was where there was a 'moral duty to intervene'. Such was the case in *Brimelow* v *Casson* [1924] 1 Ch 302. The defendant trade union official induced actresses working for the claimant theatre manager to break their contracts of employment. His justification for inducing them to break their contracts was that their wages were so low that they were compelled to resort to prostitution to supplement their wages. It was held that this was sufficient to justify the defendant's actions. On the other hand, Stuart-Smith LJ noted that the following factors have been held not to constitute justification: 'absence of malice or illwill or intention to injure the person whose contract is broken' (*South Wales Miners' Federation* v *Glamorgan Coal Co* [1905] AC 239), 'the commercial or other best interests of the interferer or the contract breaker' (*South Wales Miners' Federation* v *Glamorgan Coal Co* (above)) and the 'fact that A has broken his contract with X does not of itself justify X in revenge procuring a breach of an independent contract between A and B' (*Smithies* v *National Association of Operative Plasterers* (above)).

29.5 Intimidation

The tort of intimidation was resurrected from obscurity by the House of Lords in the important case of *Rookes* v *Barnard* [1964] AC 1129 The claimant was an employee of BOAC. The three defendants were trade unions officials, two of whom were employed by BOAC. Despite an informal agreement between the union and BOAC that all employees at the claimant's place of work would be union members, the claimant resigned from the union. The defendants then notified BOAC that there would be a strike unless the claimant was dismissed. BOAC gave in to this threat and lawfully determined the claimant's contract. The claimant, having no cause of action against BOAC, brought an action for damages against the defendants. It was held that the defendants had committed the tort of intimidation and that there was no statutory immunity for this tort and so the claimant was entitled to succeed. There are five basic ingredients of this tort. The tort consists of a threat by the defendant against a third party that the defendant will use some unlawful means against the third party unless the third party does or refrains from doing some act which he is entitled to do and as a result the claimant suffers loss. The five ingredients of the tort are as follows.

Threat

The defendant must threaten the third party or put pressure upon him to adopt a particular course of action. This was satisfied in *Rookes* by the defendants' threat that there would be a strike unless the claimant was dismissed. The courts formally distinguish between a threat and a warning, the latter being insufficient to ground an action in the tort of intimidation. A threat must be of the 'or else' kind, although there is no requirement that the warning be express rather than implied.

Unlawful act or means

The defendant's threat to the third party must be a threat of some unlawful act. If the defendant simply threatens to do that which he has a legal right to do the tort is not committed. The difficulty here concerns what constitutes unlawful means. It is clear that it encompasses threats of a criminal nature or threats to commit a tort. The important point which *Rookes* established was that, for this purpose, a breach of contract counts as unlawful means. Lord Devlin said that there was nothing to distinguish a threat to breach a contract from a threat of violence; the one could be as coercive as the other (for full consideration of *Rookes* and the finding that a breach of contract can constitute unlawful means see Wedderburn (1964) 27 MLR 257 and Hoffman (1965) 81 LQR 116).

Submission to the threat

Thirdly the third party must submit to the threat of the defendant. This was satisfied in *Rookes* because BOAC gave in to the threat and dismissed the claimant. This requirement is, in many ways, an obvious one because it is only through the third party submitting to the threat that damage is caused to the claimant. Had BOAC in *Rookes* not submitted to the threat, the claimant would not have lost his job and he would not have suffered any damage.

Damage

The fourth element of the tort is that the claimant must suffer damage as a result of the third party submitting to the defendant's threat. Once again damage is the very essence of the tort.

Justification

It is unclear whether or not there is a defence of justification to the tort of intimidation. A good argument can be made out that there should be no such defence because the tort is only committed where there has been the use of some unlawful means and a defendant should not be able to justify an unlawful act. In *Rookes* Lord Devlin expressly left the point open as it did not arise for consideration on the facts of the case. However, in the case of *Morgan* v *Fry* [1968] 2 QB 710 Lord Denning suggested that the defence may be available to trade union officials who commit the tort when intimidating an employer to dismiss people who are 'really troublemakers' (see to similar effect his judgment in *Cory Lighterage Ltd* v *TGWU* [1973] ICR 339). The exact status of these dicta remains uncertain.

So far we have been considering three-party intimidation, where the threat is made against a third party with the intention that damage be done to the claimant. But does the tort exist in the two-party form? This could arise where A threatens B with an unlawful act unless B does or refrains from doing some act which he is entitled to do and thereby loss is intentionally caused to B. There is a dearth of authority on this particular point. In *Rookes* v *Barnard* Lord Evershed was of the opinion that the tort could be committed in the two-party form, as were Lord Denning and Lord Pearce in *Stratford* v *Lindley* (above). However, in *Stratford* Lord Reid said that he was not convinced that two- and three-party intimidation were truly comparable. The main difference is that, in the case of two-party intimidation, the claimant has an alternative remedy open to him (for example, if he is threatened with a breach of contract he has a remedy in contract) whereas, in the case of three-party intimidation, the only possible remedy available to the claimant is in tort. A strong argument can be made that the claimant should be confined to his remedy in contract, especially since the development of the doctrine of economic duress in contract, but the balance of the authorities suggests that the claimant will also have an action in the tort of intimidation.

29.6 Economic duress?

In *Universe Tankships of Monrovia* v *International Transport Workers Federation* [1983] 1 AC 366 Lord Scarman suggested that there was a tort of economic duress. He said that it was established law that:

> 'Duress, if proved, not only renders voidable a transaction into which a person has entered under its compulsion but is actionable as a tort, if it causes damage or loss.'

Lord Scarman cited two authorities in support of this proposition, *Barton* v *Armstrong* [1976] AC 104 and *Pau On* v *Lau Yiu Long* [1980] AC 614, but neither of them make any mention of there being such a tort. The recognition of such a tort would have serious implications for the general rule that liability in the economic torts rests upon the unlawfulness of the defendant's acts. The reason for this is that the boundary of economic duress lies in the distinction between legitimate and illegitimate pressure and not between lawful and unlawful pressure. So, if Lord Scarman's view was to be accepted, it would mean that liability could exist in the absence of unlawful means, something which is not countenanced by *Allen* v *Flood*. It is therefore submitted that Lord Scarman is wrong and there is no tort of economic duress (see too Carty and Evans [1983] JBL 218).

29.7 Interference with trade by unlawful means

We have already noted that unlawful means is an essential ingredient in three of the nominate torts which we have discussed so far. It is an essential element in conspiracy to injure by unlawful means, the indirect form of the tort of inducing breach of contract and in intimidation. Unlawful means is also an essential component in the tort of interference with contractual rights which was recognised by the House of Lords in *Merkur Island Shipping Corpn* v *Laughton* (above). This leaves out the anomalous tort of conspiracy to injure by lawful means and it also does not take account of the direct form of the tort of inducing breach of contract. It could be argued that in the latter form of the tort there is a breach of contract which is induced and that that could be called unlawful means. However, it is submitted that this is the wrong way of looking at the direct form of the tort because it is really concerned with the protection of contractual rights rather than the prohibition of the use of unlawful means. Thus the direct form of the tort really lies in a separate category from the other economic torts because of its purpose of protecting contractual rights.

Nevertheless, direct inducement of a breach of contract apart, unlawful means plays a crucial role within the economic torts and there have been suggestions that the nominate torts be drawn together into one innominate tort entitled interference with trade or business by unlawful means (see generally Carty 'Intentional Violations of Economic Interests: The Limits of Common Law Liability' (1988) 104 LQR 250).

There has also been some judicial recognition of the existence of such a tort. Lord Reid said in *Stratford* v *Lindley* (above) that the defendants' industrial action made it 'practically impossible' for the claimants to continue with their business and that 'it was not disputed that such interference with business is tortious if any unlawful means are used'. The leading proponent of this tort has, however, been Lord Denning. He referred to the existence of the tort in *Daily Mirror Newspapers Ltd* v *Gardiner* [1968] 2 QB 762, *Acrow* v *Rex Chainbelt* [1971] 1 WLR 1676 and, in *Torquay Hotels* v *Cousins*, he said:

> 'I have always understood that if one person deliberately interferes with the trade or business of another, and does so by unlawful means, that is, by an act which he is not at liberty to commit, then he is acting unlawfully, even though he does not procure or induce any actual breach of contract.'

The existence of the tort was also recognised by the House of Lords in *Merkur Island Shipping*, although there Lord Diplock talked mainly about the tort of interference with the performance of a contract by unlawful means and only gave passing approval to the wider tort of interference with trade by unlawful means. The tort was also recognised by the Court of Appeal and the House of Lords in *Hadmor Productions* v *Hamilton* [1982] 2 WLR 322 and by the Court of Appeal in *Lonrho plc* v *Fayed* [1990] 2 QB 479) and in *Department of Transport* v *Williams* (1993) The Times 7 December where it was held that the criminal offence established by s303 of the Highways Act 1980 of wilfully obstructing any person carrying out his duties under the Act also constituted the tort of wrongful interference with business..

Given that there is now a substantial body of authority which recognises the existence of this tort, the vital question now becomes: what are its limits? In *Lonrho plc* v *Fayed* (above) the Court of Appeal held that it was not necessary to establish that it was the predominant purpose of the defendant to injure the claimant. On the other hand, it was held that the claimant must prove that the unlawful act of the defendant was directed against the claimant or was intended to harm the claimant. The crucial question, however, is: what constitutes unlawful means? It is reasonably clear that a crime, a tort and a breach of contract may constitute unlawful means. But it is not yet clear that English law has reached the stage where it is ready to recognise that a wide range of wrongs may constitute unlawful means. For example, in *Lonrho* v *Shell Petroleum* (above) the defendants did breach a penal statute and that breach did interfere with the claimants' business, but the claimants were unable to recover from the defendants in tort. It may be that this was because the action was held not to be aimed at the claimants or it may be that it was because there are certain types of breaches of penal statutes which do not count as unlawful means. On the other hand, the Court of Appeal in *Associated British Ports* v *Transport and General Workers' Union* [1989] 1 WLR 939 envisaged a much wider role for unlawful means, holding that a non-actionable contravention of a statute could count as unlawful means provided that there was a sufficient intention to injure the claimant. Although the decision of the Court of Appeal was subsequently reversed by the House of Lords on the construction of the particular regulations which were the subject-matter of the dispute, the House of Lords did not comment upon the wider dicta of the Court of Appeal and it remains to be seen how far, if at all, the reasoning of the Court of Appeal remains authoritative.

This doubt about the generality of unlawful means can also be seen in the case of *Chapman* v *Honig* [1963] 2 QB 502. The defendant landlord gave the claimant notice to quit because the tenant had given evidence in an action brought by other tenants against the landlord. In taking this action against the claimant the defendant was guilty of a criminal contempt of court. Yet the majority of the Court of Appeal held that the commission of this criminal offence did not give the claimant a cause of action in tort. On the other hand in *Acrow* v *Rex Chainbelt Inc* (above) a different result was reached. This time the defendants inflicted loss upon the claimant's business through ignoring a High Court injunction, thereby committing a contempt of court. It was held that unlawful means included a contempt of court and that, provided the defendants' actions were done with the intention of harming the claimants' business, that was sufficient to establish liability in tort. However the *Chapman* case was not discussed and so it is difficult to know how to attempt to reconcile the two cases (see too the conflict between the two 'bootlegging' cases *Ex parte Island Records* [1978] Ch 122 and *RCA* v *Pollard* [1982] 3 WLR 1007).

So, although it is possible to argue that English law does recognise the existence of a tort of interference with trade by unlawful means, the tort is still at a very early stage in its development. Thus conflicts arise as to what constitutes unlawful means and the courts appear to give inconsistent answers to this particular question. It is only as the courts build up a body of case law that principles will begin to emerge which will help us to understand exactly what constitutes unlawful means for the purpose of this tort.

29.8 The statutory immunities

Many of the cases which we have discussed are cases concerned with industrial action. It is important to note that many of these cases were decided against the backdrop of a statute which provided persons engaged in industrial action with certain immunities from suit in tort provided that they were acting in 'contemplation or furtherance of a trade dispute'. This is not the place for an in-depth analysis of the trade dispute immunities, but the statutory foundation of the present law is noted in Chapter 2, section 2.2, *Trade unions*.

29.9 Conclusion

English law recognises that there are distinct nominate economic torts, but the major issue for the courts today concerns the existence of the innominate tort of interference with trade by unlawful means. This issue is likely to arise in trade dispute cases in the future. It is less likely to arise in the context of alleged unlawful competition because the legal regulation of competition is now heavily dominated by statute and the common law has little role to play. The difficulty with the heavy influence of trade dispute cases on the development of the economic torts is that most of these cases are heard on interlocutory proceedings where the discussion of the case law and of legal principles is, of necessity, very brief. This is not the best way for the development of the law to occur and it may take some years for the courts to put this area of law on a coherent basis and to decide what exactly constitutes unlawful means.

30

Remedies

30.1 Introduction

The remedies available to a litigant in a tort action tell us a great deal about the interests which the law of tort seeks to protect. For example, one of the issues which was discussed in Chapter 1 was whether the aim of tort law is to compensate the victims of torts or whether it is to punish those who commit torts. It is in the area of remedies that we are able to find an answer to that question.

The principal remedies which may be available to a claimant in a tort action are damages, an injunction and self-help. In this Chapter we shall confine ourselves to a discussion of the general principles which are applicable to the granting of a remedy in tort. Where there are particular rules applicable to particular torts these have been discussed when dealing with the substantive law of that tort.

As damages is the most important remedy in tort law we shall concentrate upon the general principles applicable to the grant of an award of damages.

30.2 Types of damages

The general principle which lies behind the award of damages in a tort action is that damages are awarded to put the claimant in the position which he would have been in had the tort not been committed, in so far as this can be done by an award of damages. Tort law therefore aims to protect the reliance interest rather than the expectation interest (see further the discussion at Chapter 1, section 1.4). Since the aim of tort law is to protect the reliance interest of the claimant it is clear that the primary aim of damages is compensatory, rather than punitive (see *Cassell v Broome* [1972] AC 1027 and the discussion of this issue at Chapter 1, section 1.2). Although this is the general purpose behind a damages award there are, in fact, a number of different types of damages which may be awarded in a tort action. The principal ones are as follows.

Nominal and contemptuous damages

Nominal damages are awarded where some right of the claimant's has been infringed but the claimant has suffered no loss. The claimant receives a very small sum of money by way of damages, which has the effect of vindicating the right that has been infringed. Such was the case in *Constantine v Imperial Hotels Ltd* [1944] KB 693 where the claimant, who was a famous West Indian cricketer, was refused accommodation in one of the defendants' hotels but was given accommodation elsewhere. It was held that the defendants were in breach of their duty as common innkeepers because their refusal to give the claimant accommodation was unjustified. The claimant was therefore awarded five guineas damages.

Contemptuous damages are awarded where the court awards a derisory sum, which is the smallest coin of the realm, and which indicates that, while the claimant's action was technically justified, it was without any merit and should not have been brought. Such awards are most commonly made in libel actions. Where the court awards contemptuous damages the claimant also runs a considerable risk that the court will also express its disapproval of him having brought his action by refusing him costs or even ordering him to pay the defendant's costs.

General and special damages

General damage need not be specifically pleaded because it is the damage which is presumed to be caused by torts, such as libel, which are actionable per se. Special damage, on the other hand, must be specifically pleaded because, as in the tort of negligence, damage is part of the cause of action and so must be proved to have been suffered.

The terms general and special damages may, however, be used in another sense. In personal injuries cases losses which are capable of reasonably precise calculation, such as loss of earnings to the date of trial, are known as special damages and must be specifically pleaded. General damages are damages which are not capable of reasonably precise calculation, such as future loss of earnings and loss of amenity.

Aggravated and exemplary damages

Aggravated damages are said to be a species of compensatory damages in the sense that they are awarded to compensate the claimant rather than to punish the defendant. Aggravated damages may be awarded where the conduct of the defendant in committing the tort was such as to cause injury to the feelings or pride of the claimant. Where aggravated damages are awarded they should be 'moderate' (see *Archer* v *Brown* [1985] QB 401 and *W* v *Meah* and *D* v *Meah* [1986] 1 All ER 935). However the court may be reluctant to award aggravated damages in a negligence action. This can be seen in the case of *Kralj* v *McGrath* [1986] 1 All ER 54. The claimant suffered excruciating pain as a result of the negligence of the defendant obstetrician in delivering her twins. The defendant's negligence caused one of the twins to be born with severe disabilities and it died shortly after it was born. Woolf J stated that the conduct of the defendant was 'wholly unacceptable' and that he had put the claimant through the most dreadful agony. However, he held that medical negligence cases were not appropriate for the grant of aggravated damages because of the conflict with the general principle that damages in a negligence action were to be compensatory. Instead the proper approach was to increase the compensatory element of the damages recoverable to take account of the fact that the defendant's conduct had made it more difficult for the claimant to recover.

The effect of *Kralj* may be to make it more difficult to distinguish between cases where the appropriate course of action is to award aggravated damages and cases where the proper course is simply to increase the compensatory damages recoverable. At the other end of the scale it can also be difficult to distinguish between aggravated damages and exemplary damages (on which see Lord Wilberforce in *Cassell* v *Broome* (above)). The difference between the two is that the function of exemplary damages is to punish the defendant, whereas the function of aggravated damages is to compensate the claimant but, as Lord Wilberforce pointed out in *Cassell*, in practice it can be very difficult to say where compensation ends and punishment begins.

In *Rookes* v *Barnard* [1964] AC 1129 Lord Devlin set out the circumstances in which exemplary damages can be recovered in English tort law and this approach was applied by the House of Lords in the later case of *Cassell* v *Broome* (above). Exemplary damages are an exceptional remedy in English tort law because they are not consistent with the compensatory function of tort law. In *Rookes* v *Barnard* Lord Devlin held that, apart from the case where the grant of exemplary damages is authorised by statute, there are only two cases in which exemplary damages are available in English tort law. In *Cassell* it was held that exemplary damages are not available in any other case, no matter how illogical the present state of the law is, on the ground that exemplary damages are an anomaly and that their availability is not to be extended beyond these two cases.

The first case where exemplary damages are available is the case of oppressive, arbitrary or unconstitutional action by a servant of the government. 'Servants of the government' is not confined to central government but includes servants of local government and the police. In *Cassell* Lord Reid said that this category did not extend to oppressive action by a private corporation, however illogical such a distinction may be. In *Holden* v *Chief Constable of Lancashire* [1987] QB 380 it was held by the Court of Appeal that exemplary damages could be awarded in cases of unlawful arrest irrespective of the lack of oppressive behaviour by the arresting officer. This was because the requirement was that there be 'oppressive, arbitrary *or* unconstitutional action' by a servant of the government and not that there be 'oppressive, arbitrary *and* unconstitutional' action. This seems a rather literal approach to the interpretation of the judgment of Lord Devlin and it fails to follow the tenor of his judgment which was that exemplary damages are an exceptional remedy and not to be widely awarded. However, it was held that, although the issue of whether or not to grant exemplary damages should not have been withdrawn from the jury, the jury should have been directed to take account of the lack of aggravating circumstances in making their award of exemplary damages.

In *Kuddus* v *Chief Constable of Leicestershire Constabulary* [2001] 3 All ER 193 a police constable having forged the appellant's signature on a written statement withdrawing the appellant's complaint of theft of his property, the respondent Chief Constable admitted that the forgery and the constable's conduct amounted to the tort of misfeasance in public office. The respondent accepted that the appellant had a viable claim for aggravated damages, but the appellant's claim for exemplary damages had been struck out. The House of Lords said that the claim for exemplary damages should not have been struck out. Lord Mackay of Clashfern:

'I consider that the question whether the tort of misfeasance in public office carries the power to award exemplary damages should be answered by saying that the mere fact that the tort sued upon is of misfeasance in public office does not determine the issue. The issue is determined by whether the factual situation is covered by either of Lord Devlin's formulations [in *Rookes* v *Barnard* [1964] 1 All ER 367]. In the present case it is accepted that the factual situation does come within Lord Devlin's first category ['oppressive, arbitary or unconstitutional action by the servants of the government'] and although on the facts so far as pleaded I regard this as extremely doubtful, for the purposes of this appeal I would be prepared to accept it and accordingly I am of the opinion that the appeal should be allowed and that the claim for exemplary damages should proceed without in any way restricting the judge in his consideration of this issue.'

It should be mentioned that in *Three Rivers District Council* v *Bank of England (No 3)* [2000] 3 All ER 1 the House of Lords found that the tort of misfeasance in public office has two forms; (i) cases where a public power is exercised for an improper purpose with the specific intention of injuring a person or persons, and (ii) where a public officer acts in the knowledge that he had no power to do the act complained of and that it would probably injure the claimant. In the second category, an act performed in reckless indifference as to the outcome is sufficient to ground the tort.

The question of damages for misfeasance in public office received further consideration in *Watkins* v *Secretary of State for the Home Department* [2004] 4 All ER 1158. Alleging that certain prison officers had broken statutory prison rules in relation to his correspondence with his legal adviser, the claimant prisoner sought damages for misfeasance in public office. The trial judge found that the officers had acted in bad faith in connection with their breaches of the rules, but he dismissed the claim because there had been no resulting damage to the claimant in the form of financial loss or physical or mental injury which, in his (the judge's) view, was a necessary ingredient of the tort. The Court of Appeal allowed the claimant's appeal against this decision, a nominal award of general damages was made against the officers and the case was remitted to the county court for determination of whether exemplary damages should be awarded and, if so, in what amount. Laws LJ said:

'Now I may explain the two kinds of case which I have in mind. Where a claimant is exposed to economic or material injury by virtue of the public officer's wrongful and malicious act, it will be inherent in his claim that he has suffered quantifiable loss; and he does not have to prove that in causing such loss the public officer has violated some free-standing right which the claimant enjoys. That is one class of case. But the claimant may be adversely affected in a different sense. The wrongful act may have interfered with a right of a kind which the law protects without proof of any loss. In that case, the public officer's interference with the right will complete the tort and no actual damage needs to be shown. This is the second class of case. Its paradigm is the instance where the public officer's unlawful conduct has interfered with a constitutional right.

Three Rivers District Council v *Bank of England (No 3)* [2003] 3 All ER 1 was an instance of the first class of case (assuming, after the second hearing before their Lordships' House, that the claimants succeed on the facts). *Ashby* v *White* (1703) 1 Sm LC (13th edn) 253 was an instance of the second class of case ... this present case also falls into the second category. Just as in *Ashby* v *White*, the public officers' unlawful and malicious acts interfered with a constitutional right enjoyed by the claimant. In *Ashby* v *White* it was the right to vote. Here it is access to the Queen's courts.'

In *AB* v *South West Water Services Ltd* [1993] 1 All ER 609 the Court of Appeal said that the combined effect of *Rookes* v *Barnard* [1964] AC 1129 and *Cassell & Co Ltd* v *Broome* [1972] 1 All ER 801 was that a claim for exemplary damages must be 'in respect of a cause of action for which prior to 1964 such an award had been made'. In *Kuddus*, their Lordships rejected that approach and overruled that decision. See also *Costello* v *Chief Constable of Derbyshire Constabulary* [2001] 3 All ER 150 (claim to exemplary damages for conversion had no basis in law or fact).

The second case in which exemplary damages may be available is where the defendant has calculated that he will make a profit for himself by committing the tort, even after paying compensatory damages, and in the case of defamation the publisher had no genuine belief in the truth of what he published: *John* v *Mirror Group Newspapers Ltd* [1996] 2 All ER 35. *Cassell* itself came into this category. The defendants published a book which made defamatory statements about the claimant. The book was published in the face of threats by the claimant that he would bring a libel action against the defendants. The jury awarded the claimant £15,000 compensatory damages and £25,000 exemplary damages. The defendants appealed on the ground that the damages which the jury had awarded were excessive. It was held that this was a case in which the jury was entitled to award exemplary damages because the defendants had calculated that it was worth running the risk of the book being held to be libellous because of the profits which they thought they would make from the sales of the book. It should be noted that the mere fact that a publication is published with the intention of making a profit is not sufficient, of itself, to bring the case within this category; there must be some evidence that the defendant decided that there was a profit to be made out of his wrongdoing. In other words the courts are saying to potential tortfeasors that tort does not pay.

See, too, *Borders (UK) Ltd* v *Commissioner of Police of the Metropolis* (2005) The Times 15 April (exemplary damages fill moral gap: may be awarded even if capable of quantification).

Child abuse

In *Coxon* v *Flintshire County Council* (2001) The Times 13 March the Court of Appeal said that physical, emotional and sexual abuse of children in care by those who were supposed to provide that care falls into a wholly different category from psychiatric damage that follows other personal injuries. The injury is of a different character. The essential element of the damage is the extent to which the injury compounded and multiplied the effect of the pre-existing condition. In that case, their Lordships dismissed the defendant council's appeal against an award of £70,000 damages, including £35,000 for pain, suffering and loss of amenity, in respect of physical, emotional and sexual abuse suffered by the claimant whilst in its care in 1979 to 1980.

Assault and battery

In *Richardson* v *Howie* (2004) The Times 10 September the county court judge awarded the claimant £10,000 by way of damages for assault and battery: the award included £5,000 for aggravated damages. The Court of Appeal substituted an award of £4,500 by way of general damages. Thomas LJ said that it was accepted that, at least in cases of assault and similar torts, it was appropriate to compensate for injury to feelings, including the indignity, mental suffering, humiliation or distress that might be caused by such an attack, as well as anger or indignation arising from the circumstances of the attack. It was also now clearly accepted that aggravated damages were in essence compensatory in cases of assault. Therefore, a court should not characterise the award of damages for injury to feelings, including any indignity, mental suffering, distress, humiliation or anger and indignation that might be caused by such an attack, as aggravated damages; a court should bring that element of compensatory damages for injured feelings into account as part of the general damages awarded.

30.3 The protection of the reliance interest

So the general principle is that the object of damages in tort is to restore the claimant to the position which he was in before the tort was committed, as far as this can be done by an award of damages. The law of tort is therefore, in theory, fully committed to the protection of the reliance interest. We shall examine the principles which the courts have applied in personal injury cases and in cases of damage to property and then consider the commitment of the law of tort to the principle of full compensation and to the protection of the reliance interest (see section 30.22).

We shall start our analysis by considering the general principles applicable in personal injury cases (sections 30.4–30.18) and then consider the principles applicable to damage to property (section 30.20). In seeking to compensate the claimant in a personal injuries case the damages which may be awarded by the courts can be divided into two categories: pecuniary loss (see section 30.4–30.12) and non-pecuniary loss (see sections 30.13–30.17). We shall now consider the approach which the courts adopt in awarding damages in each of these two categories.

30.4 Pecuniary loss

Where the claimant suffers serious injury as a result of the defendant's negligence then pecuniary loss is likely to constitute the major element of the claimant's claim. Loss of earnings is likely to constitute the principal component of a claim for pecuniary loss, although it may include a wide variety of other losses such as the cost of medical treatment or the loss of pension rights.

In a personal injury action, a claimant is not entitled to damages in respect of gratuitous services performed by his wife for his business as a result of his injury: *Hardwick* v *Hudson* [1999] 3 All ER 426. In makings this decision, the Court of Appeal distinguished the voluntary provision of caring services. There, damages may include recompense for the carer, provided that part of the damages is held on trust by the claimant for him or her. See also section 30.10.

In *Patel* v *Hooper & Jackson* [1999] 1 All ER 992 the Court of Appeal considered the measure of damages to be paid where a surveyor had negligently overvalued a house which the claimants proceeded to purchase and afterwards believed to be uninhabitable. Distinguishing *South Australia Asset Management Corp* v *York Montague Ltd* [1996] 3 All ER 365, their Lordships said that there should be a once and for all award and that it should comprise only the difference between the defendant's valuation and the property's true value plus stamp duty (£25,000 plus £250), general damages of £2,000 each for living in 'relative discomfort' and the cost of alternative accommodation between the date of purchasing the property and the date on which, in mitigation of their loss, the claimants ought to have sold it.

30.5 Loss of earnings: actual and prospective

The claimant can recover for his loss of earnings to the date of trial. This is so no matter what the claimant was earning; he is entitled to have his earnings maintained by the tortfeasor. This is consistent with the aim of a damages award in returning the claimant to his pre-accident position. The effect of this principle is that it is cheaper negligently to run over a tramp than it is negligently to run over a millionaire.

The greatest problems arise, however, with loss of future earnings because the courts have to engage in what is no more than educated guesswork. It requires the court to consider such imponderables as how long the claimant would have lived, how long he would have continued to work, what his prospects of promotion were and the rate of inflation in the future.

Basically what the courts do is to calculate the claimant's net annual loss (which the courts call the multiplicand) and then multiply that loss by a figure based upon the number of years for which the disability is likely to last (which the courts call the multiplier). We shall consider separately how the courts calculate the multiplicand and the multiplier.

In assessing the claimant's net annual loss the courts start by calculating the claimant's gross earnings which he would have earned but for the accident. The starting point for this calculation is the claimant's earnings at the date of the accident but allowance is then made for the possibility of an increase in pay or for promotion (see *Ratnasingam* v *Kow Ah Dek* [1983] 1 WLR 1235). Once this sum is calculated then a deduction must be made for the tax which the claimant would have paid on his earnings (*British Transport Commission* v *Gourley* [1956] AC 185) and for social security contributions which he would have paid.

Once the net annual loss is calculated then an appropriate multiplier must be selected. However it is not simply the case that a calculation is made of the likely duration of the disability. In practice the multiplier tends to be lower than that, with the maximum multiplier being in the range of 16–18. There are two main reasons behind the courts' refusal to award the full number of years purchase. The first is that the courts discount for what is known as the 'general vicissitudes of life'. For example, in *Jobling* v *Associated Dairies* [1982] AC 794 Lord Bridge said that the vicissitudes principle flowed from the fundamental principle that the object of an award of damages is to put the claimant, so far as this can be done, in the position which he would have been in had it not been for the defendant's wrong. The assumption that the claimant would, in every case, continue to work for the rest of his life would result in the over-compensation of claimants. So the courts discount at a rate of approximately 10 per cent for the vicissitudes of life (see Atiyah *Accidents, Compensation and the Law* (4th ed) p176).

The second reason why the courts do not award the full number of years purchase is that the claimant has received the money in a lump sum and so discount must be made for his accelerated receipt of the money. The sum is calculated on the basis that the lump sum paid will be exhausted at the end of the period of disability and that the lump sum, plus the interest which that sum has earned, will be sufficient to maintain the claimant at his pre-accident position. The difficulty with this method of calculation is that there is a danger that high levels of inflation will erode the value of the claimant's award.

The courts have refused to increase the multiplier to take account of the fact that the income likely to be produced by the award may attract tax at the higher rates (*Hodgson* v *Trapp* [1989] AC 807). The incidence of taxation may be a factor to be taken into account in selecting a multiplier towards the top of the conventional scale but, once having selected a multiplier on the conventional basis, extra years should not be added on to take account of possible higher rates of taxation.

The whole question was considered by the House of Lords in *Wells* v *Wells; Thomas* v *Brighton Health Authority; Page* v *Sheerness Steel Co plc* [1998] 3 All ER 481. In all three cases the claimant had suffered severe injuries as a result of the defendant's admitted negligence. What was the correct method of calculating lump sum damages for the loss of future earnings and the cost of future care? Lord Hutton explained the position – and their Lordships' decision – as follows:

'Under our present system of law the compensation to which each claimant is entitled must, unless the parties agree otherwise, be paid in a lump sum and there is no power for the courts to award periodical payments. Therefore each claimant must receive a lump sum to provide compensation for the annual cost of lifetime nursing care and for the loss of future earning capacity. The method adopted by the courts to calculate such compensation was described by Lord Oliver of Aylmerton in *Hodgson* v *Trapp* [1988] 3 All ER 870 at 879, [1989] AC 807 at 826:

> "Essentially what the court has to do is to calculate as best it can the sum of money which will on the one hand be adequate, by its capital and income, to provide annually for the injured person a sum equal to his estimated annual loss over the whole of the period during which that loss is likely to continue, but which, on the other hand, will not, at the end of that period, leave him in a better financial position than he would have been apart from the accident. Hence the conventional approach is to assess the amount notionally required to be laid out in the purchase of an annuity which will provide the annual amount needed for the whole period of loss."

The multiplier which the courts could apply to the annual cost of nursing care and the annual loss of earning capacity to produce the lump sum of compensation is determined by reference to the respective periods in the future for which the cost will be incurred and the loss will be sustained, but discounted to allow for the immediate receipt of the lump sum rather than the receipt of periodical payments over a number of years. The discount is assessed by reference to the assumed rate of return on the lump sum when invested, so that the higher the rate of interest assumed the smaller the multiplier. ...

I have reached the conclusion that under the present principles which govern the assessment of compensation and having regard to the availability of [index-linked government securities (ILGS)], the [claimants] are entitled to compensation assessed by taking a discount rate based on the return on ILGS. The return on ILGS fluctuates but the schedules of the month end returns during the past three years show a net average return of about 3 per cent. Therefore I consider that this rate should be adopted as the rate to arrive at the multiplier in the present cases in place of the conventional discount rate of 4.5 per cent applied by the Court of Appeal.'

Lord Hutton acknowledged that the consequence of their Lordships' decision would be a substantial rise in awards and insurance premiums, but any change in the approach could only be made by Parliament which, unlike the judges, was in a position to balance the many social, financial and economic factors which would have to be considered if such a change were to be contemplated. See generally *Herring* v *Ministry of Defence* [2004] 1 All ER 44 (supremely fit young man contemplating career in police: suffers severe spinal injuries as a result of defendant's negligence: assessment of damages for loss of future earnings).

A claimant cannot recover, as part of his damages, the predicted costs of investment advice and fund management charges incurred in the management of a prospective award: *Page* v *Plymouth Hospitals NHS Trust* [2004] 3 All ER 367. See, too, *Eagle* v *Chambers* [2005] 1 All ER 136 (panel brokers' fees not recoverable).

Further developments should be noted as follows:

1. A court awarding damages (including an interim payment) in an action for personal injury could, with the consent of the parties, make an order under which the damages are wholly or partly to take the form of periodical payments: Damages Act 1996, s2(1), (2). The 1996 Act provides enhanced protection for structured settlement annuitants: see ss4–6. For the substitution of ss2, 4 and 5,

and the amendment of s6(1), of the 1996 Act, with effect from 1 April 2005, see the Courts Act 2003, ss100, 101. In particular, the new s2 gives courts the power to order, without the consent of the parties, that damages for future pecuniary loss (ie loss of future earnings and care costs) in personal injury cases are wholly or partly to take the form of periodical payments, linked to the retail price index, and requires the court to consider in all cases whether periodical payments are appropriate. The new s2A enables Civil Procedure Rules to specify matters which the court is required to take into account when considering whether to order a periodical payment or approve an assignment, and when considering the security of the payment, while the new section 2B gives the Lord Chancellor an order-making power to enable the court to vary periodical payments under specified circumstances. For the court's power to vary orders and agreements in personal injury cases under which all or part of the damages take the form of periodical payments, see the Damages (Variation of Periodical Payments) Order 2005.

The new s4 replaces ss4 and 5 of the 1996 Act. The purpose of this substitution is to ensure that protection under the Financial Services Compensation Scheme can apply to a wider range of options for funding periodical payments. It replaces the term 'structured settlement' which is no longer apt given the court's power to order periodical payments. The section also makes provision for the treatment of periodical payments in the event of the recipient's bankruptcy.

2. Section 32A of the Supreme Court Act 1981 (inserted by s6 of the Administration of Justice Act 1982) applies to personal injuries cases in which there is:

> '... proved or admitted to be a chance that at some definite or indefinite time in the future the injured person will, as a result of the act or omission which gave rise to the cause of action, develop some serious disease or suffer some serious deterioration in his physical or mental condition.'

In such a case the court has power to make a provisional award (see also section 30.19), in which damages will be awarded on the basis that the disease or deterioration will not materialise but where, if it does, the claimant can come back to court for a further award of damages in respect of the disease.

3. In determining the return to be expected from the investment of a sum awarded as damages for future pecuniary loss in an action for personal injury, the court must, subject to and in accordance with rules of court, take into account such rate of return (if any) as may from time to time be prescribed by an order made by the Lord Chancellor, although this does not prevent the court taking a different rate of return into account if any party to the proceedings shows that it is more appropriate in the case in question: Damages Act 1996, s1(1), (2) and see, eg, *Cooke* v *United Bristol Healthcare NHS Trust* [2004] 1 All ER 797. The Damages (Personal Injury) Order 2001, made under s1, prescribes 2.5 per cent as

the rate of return which courts are required to take into account when calculating damages for future pecuniary loss in an action for personal injury.

4. As to the recovery of National Health Service charges, see Part 3 (ss150–169) of the Health and Social Care (Community Health and Standards) Act 2003.

30.6 The lost years

The claimant may, as a result of the tort of the defendant, have a reduced expectation of life. The effect of this is that the claimant suffers a loss of earnings in the period in which he would have worked had it not been for the tort of the defendant. It had been held by the Court of Appeal in *Oliver* v *Ashman* [1962] 2 QB 210 that the claimant could not recover for such a loss. The Court of Appeal interpreted the decision of the House of Lords in *Benham* v *Gambling* [1941] AC 157 as denying the existence of such a claim.

However, a different approach was adopted by the House of Lords in *Pickett* v *British Railways Engineering Ltd* [1980] AC 136. As a result of the negligence of the defendants, the claimant, who was 52, only had an expectation of life of one year. He claimed for the loss of earnings in respect of the years which he would have worked had it not been for the negligence of the defendants. The House held that he was entitled to recover for his earnings in the lost years and so overruled *Oliver*.

The defendants had argued that the true loss was not the loss of the claimant but the loss of his dependants and that the correct way of proceeding was to change the law so as to enable them to sue for such losses (they were unable to sue because a claim could not be brought under the Fatal Accidents Act 1976 where the deceased, while he was still alive, had sued the tortfeasor to judgment or had settled the claim). Lord Wilberforce saw the force of this argument but he held that it did not correspond with the expectations of the victim because his future earnings were of value to him. So he held that a rule which entitled the victim to recover in respect of his earnings in the lost years came closest to the expectations of the ordinary man.

The defendants also argued that the assessment of damages was too speculative and so the courts should not award damages in respect of the lost years. This argument was dismissed on the ground that chances and hypotheses are part of the system of personal injury litigation and that the judges were capable of dealing with this. In cases of very young claimants the court is extremely unlikely to award the claimant damages in respect of the lost years because the process is so speculative (*Croke* v *Wiseman* [1981] 3 All ER 852). However, where the claimant is a five-year-old superstar he or she may be able to recover something for the lost years because the process then ceases to be entirely speculative (see *Gammell* v *Wilson* [1982] AC 27, 78).

Although the right to claim damages for loss of expectation of life has been abolished (see section 30.16), such abolition does not extend to damages in respect of loss of income: Administration of Justice Act 1982, s1(2).

30.7 Loss of earning capacity

The claimant may, in cases of continuing disability, remain in his pre-accident employment but subject to the risk that, should he lose that job, he will be placed at a disadvantage in the labour market. Such was the case in *Moeliker* v *A Reyrolle Ltd* [1977] 1 All ER 9. The claimant lost part of his thumb at work due to the negligence of the defendants. He was able to continue in his pre-accident job but he claimed that he would be at a disadvantage were he to lose that job and be thrown into the open labour market because his disability made it more difficult for him to do his job. It was held that an award of damages in respect of loss of earnings capacity should only be made where there is a real or substantial risk that the claimant will lose his job before the end of his working life. Where there is such a risk then damages should be awarded. Where the risk of him losing his job is low then an award measured in hundreds of pounds should be given, but where the risk is serious then the damages should be measured in thousands of pounds. On the facts the risk was low and the claimant was awarded £750.

However in the case of *Foster* v *Tyne and Wear CC* [1986] 1 All ER 567 Lloyd LJ doubted whether there was a separate head of damages called loss of earning capacity, which was separate from loss of future earnings. He noted the decision of the Court of Appeal in *Moeliker* but said that, while it was not necessary to decide the point, he preferred the view of the Pearson Commission and the Law Commission that there was no difference between the two except the degree of precision with which it was possible to quantify the loss.

30.8 Loss of pension rights

Where the claimant suffers a loss of future earnings he may also suffer a loss of pension rights. He is entitled to be compensated for such a loss, although the calculation of his pension had he continued to work may give rise to considerable practical difficulties (see *Auty* v *National Coal Board* [1985] 1 All ER 930).

It should also be noted in this context that in *Dews* v *National Coal Board* [1988] AC 1 the House of Lords held that the claimant could not recover, as part of his loss of earnings, the contributions which would have been made to a compulsory pension scheme had he not been absent from work when he was injured by the negligence of the defendants. It was held that the claimant was not entitled to recover these unpaid contributions because the failure to pay these contributions did not result in any loss of pension rights and so he had not suffered any loss.

Mention should also be made of *Needler Financial Services Ltd* v *Taber* [2002] 3

All ER 501. Acting on the assumed negligent advice of the claimant financial services company, Mr Taber transferred his deferred benefits under an occupational pension scheme to the Norwich Union. Having retired and found that his Norwich Union pension was less than he would have received under his original scheme, Mr Taber sought compensation. When Norwich Union was demutualised Mr Taber received an appropriate number of shares: should the value of these shares be taken into account when determining the amount that he should receive? The answer was 'No': the demutualisation benefit by way of shares had not been caused by the pension misselling. As Sir Andrew Morritt V-C explained:

> '... the relevant question is whether the negligence which caused the loss also caused the profit in the sense that the latter was part of a continuous transaction of which the former was the inception ... the demutualisation benefit was not caused by and did not flow, as part of a continuous transaction, from the negligence. In causation terms the breach of duty gave rise to the opportunity to receive the profit, but did not cause it (see ... *Galoo Ltd* v *Bright Grahame Murray* [1994] 1 WLR 1360 at 1375).'

30.9 Loss of housekeeping capacity

It may be that the claimant does not work in paid employment but that he or she plays an important part in the running of the household. In *Daly* v *General Steam Navigation Co Ltd* [1980] 3 All ER 696 the claimant was injured as a result of the negligence of the defendants and suffered a partial disability to perform her housekeeping duties. It was held that the losses caused by this disability pre-trial were recoverable as part of the damages for pain and suffering (contrast *Roberts* v *Johnstone* [1989] QB 878) but that the claimant could recover for future loss of housekeeping ability and that the proper measure of damages was the cost of employing domestic help for eight hours per week. The claimant was not, however, under any obligation to employ a domestic help. It was up to her how she wished to spend the damages awarded and if she wished to struggle through the housekeeping on her own and spend the damages on something else then she was perfectly free and entitled to do so.

In *Lowe* v *Guise* [2002] 3 All ER 454 the Court of Appeal heard that the claimant had been injured as a result of the negligent driving of the defendant. The claimant lived with his mother and his severely disabled brother. Prior to the accident the claimant had provided gratuitous carer services for his brother, estimated at some 77 hours per week. For two months following the accident he had been unable to provide any care to his brother at all. Thereafter he had resumed looking after his brother, but he had been limited by his injuries to providing only 35 hours per week, the shortfall being made up by his mother. Could he recover damages for the carer services that he was no longer able to provide? The court answered this question in the affirmative and Rix LJ said:

'... the disabled brother is part of the household and one whose care had, prior to the accident, been the [claimant's] prime responsibility. That care was not a mere gratuitous favour bestowed on a third party, but was a responsibility of his own, adopted by him and owed to his brother, but also to his mother with whom he shared the household. When he lost the ability to care for his brother for more than 35 hours per week, he lost something of real value to himself (as well as to his brother) which was his contribution to his family's welfare, and his loss imposed a corresponding obligation on his mother to make good by her own care what he was no longer able to provide. In my judgment the [claimant] is entitled to claim in respect of the loss of his ability to look after his brother. Since he will maintain his state [invalid care] allowance, he has suffered no loss so far as that allowance is itself concerned. But he has suffered a loss nevertheless because, even though his care was provided gratuitously, it can and ought as a matter of policy to be measured in money's worth. To the extent that his mother has by her own additional care mitigated the [claimant's] loss, it may be that the [claimant] would hold that recovery in trust for his mother ... The common law should not, and need not, leave the question "am I my brother's keeper?" with the wrong answer.'

This decision should be compared with the decision of the House of Lords in *Hunt v Severs* [1994] 2 All ER 385 (see below) where the defendant tortfeasor was himself the voluntary carer.

A dependency claim by infants under the Fatal Accidents Act 1976 should not include damages related to the value of services provided by their father and step-mother, in place of their deceased mother, if the damages would not reach the service providers because they did not wish to be paid for their service: *H v S* (2002) The Times 3 July.

30.10 Medical expenses

The claimant may incur substantial expense in obtaining medical treatment and the general principle is that the claimant is entitled to the cost of medical expenses which he reasonably incurs as a result of his injury (*Cunningham v Harrison* [1973] QB 942). Section 2(4) of the Law Reform (Personal Injuries) Act 1948 provides that in determining the reasonableness of any expenses the possibility of obtaining them on the National Health Service is to be ignored. Given that we have had a National Health Service for over 50 years, the wisdom of such a provision is far from obvious (see Atiyah *Accidents, Compensation and the Law* (4th ed) pp181–3). Even the Pearson Commission recommended that the cost of private medical care should only be recoverable where it was reasonable on medical grounds for the claimant to obtain private medical care.

Damages under this head include the cost of transport to and from hospital and the cost of going on a special diet. But s5 of the Administration of Justice Act 1982 provides that 'any saving to the injured person which is attributable to his maintenance wholly or partly at public expense in a hospital, nursing home or other institution shall be set off against any income lost by him as a result of his injuries'.

One other interesting problem which arises under this head concerns the case where the injured party is cared for by a member of the family. Can the defendant be required to pay for the cost of this care? Two possibilities arise. The first is that the volunteer could proceed directly against the tortfeasor. The difficulty here is that the volunteer has no action in tort against the tortfeasor nor does he have a contract with him. So the only possibility is a restitutionary action against the tortfeasor on the ground that the tortfeasor has been unjustly enriched at the expense of the volunteer. However the courts have preferred to hold that the loss is truly the loss of the injured party because, as the result of the negligence of the defendant, he has a need of medical care and should be compensated for that need. In *Housecroft* v *Burnett* [1986] 1 All ER 332 it was affirmed that the loss was truly that of the injured person and that the purpose of the award was to provide for the reasonable and proper cost of the care (see also *Roberts* v *Johnstone* [1987] QB 878). It was held that where a relative (but not the defendant: *Hunt* v *Severs* [1994] 2 All ER 385) gives up work to look after the claimant the court will award a reasonable recompense to the claimant, but that the ceiling on such an award is the commercial rate for providing such care (see too *Donnelly* v *Joyce* [1974] QB 454). This solution works well unless the claimant refuses to hand over any money to the volunteer. In *Cunningham* v *Harrison* (above) Lord Denning said that the damages recovered were held on trust by the claimant for the volunteer, and such a solution was approved by the House of Lords in *Hunt* (above).

Awards for gratuitous care are not reserved for very serious cases: *Giambrone* v *JMC Holidays Ltd (No 2)* [2004] 2 All ER 891 (defendant's customers developed gastro-enteritis on holiday in Majorca: after return home, care given by family beyond part of ordinary family life: awards of damages correctly made for value of that gratuitous care).

30.11 Deductions

In an effort to ensure that a claimant is not over-compensated as the result of an award of damages, deductions may be made from the award to reflect benefits which the claimant has received as a result of his injuries. The theme which has been clear in recent developments is this desire to ensure that claimants are not over-compensated as a result of an award of damages.

The present statutory scheme is to be found in the Social Security (Recovery of Benefits) Act 1997 which applies where a person makes a compensation payment (whether on his own behalf or not) to or in respect of any other person in consequence of any accident, injury or disease suffered by the other, and, any listed – recoverable – benefits have been, or are likely to be, paid to or for the other during the relevant period in respect of the accident, injury or disease: s1(1). Before a person makes a compensation payment he must apply to the Secretary of State for a certificate of recoverable benefits (s4(1)) and he must pay the amount so certified to the Secretary of State before making the compensation payment: s6(1), (2). The amount of compensation payable is reduced by the amount of recoverable benefit (s8, Sch 2, as amended) according to the following table:

(1) *Head of compensation*	(2) *Benefit*
1. Compensation for earnings lost during the relevant period	Disablement pension payable under s103 of the Social Security Contributions and Benefits Act 1992 Incapacity benefit Income support Invalidity pension and allowance Jobseeker's allowance Reduced earnings allowance Severe disablement allowance Sickness benefit Statutory sick pay Unemployability supplement Unemployment benefit
2. Compensation for cost of care incurred during the relevant period	Attendance allowance Care component of disability living allowance Disablement pension increase payable under ss104 or 105 of the 1992 Act
3. Compensation for loss of mobility during the relevant period	Mobility allowance Mobility component of disability living allowance

In assessing damages in respect of any accident, injury or disease, the amount of any listed benefits paid or likely to be paid is to be disregarded: s17 of the 1997 Act. An award of interest on damages for past losses of earnings falls within the expression 'compensation for earnings lost' in Sch 2 to the 1997 Act and is therefore subject to reduction on account of payments by the tortfeasor to the Secretary of State to reimburse benefits paid to the claimant as a result of the tortfeasor's wrong: *Griffiths* v *British Coal Corporation* (2001) The Times 13 March.

In calculating the amount of a compensation payment certain payments are left out of account and these are set out in Sch 1, Pt I, to the 1997 Act as including the following:

1. Any small payment as defined in regulations.
2. Any payment made to or for the injured person under s130 of the Powers of Criminal Courts (Sentencing) Act 2000 (compensation orders against convicted persons). ...

5. Any payment made to the injured person by an insurer under the terms of any contract of insurance entered into between the injured person and the insurer before –

a) the date on which the injured person first claims a listed benefit in consequence of the disease in question, or
b) the occurrence of the accident or injury in question.

6. Any redundancy payment falling to be taken into account in the assessment of damages in respect of an accident, injury or disease.
7. So much of any payment as is referable to costs.
8. Any prescribed payment.

In two appeals to the House of Lords, *Wisely* v *John Fulton (Plumbers) Ltd, Wadey* v *Surrey County Council* [2000] 2 All ER 545, the question arose as to whether, in an action for damages for personal injuries, social security benefits received by the injured person that are disregarded in the assessment of special damages by virtue of s17 of the Social Security (Recovery of Benefits) Act 1997 must be disregarded when interest is being calculated on those damages. Their Lordships decided that the benefits received should be disregarded in calculating interest. As Lord Hope of Craighead explained:

> 'The effect of s17 of the 1997 Act, in the context of the scheme which the Act lays down, is that the amount of any listed benefits paid or likely to be paid during the relevant period must be disregarded in the assessment of interest on the damages which are to be assessed without taking account of those benefits.'

Assuming a rule as to mitigation can be said to be a rule relating to the assessment of damages, on its language s17 precludes an insistence that any of the benefits set out in Sch 2 to the 1997 Act should be used in any way to mitigate loss: *Eagle* v *Chambers* [2005] 1 All ER 136.

As far as other benefits and other sources of income are concerned resort must be had to the common law. In *Parry* v *Cleaver* [1970] AC 1 the general principle was stated that a benefit was only to be deducted where the benefit truly reduced the loss which the claimant had suffered. Thus wages or sick pay paid by the employer as a matter of contractual obligation are deductible in full because they reduce the claimant's loss but it appears to be the case that ex gratia payments made by employers are not deductible (see *Dennis* v *London Passenger Transport Board* [1949] 1 All ER 779). Money received under a disablement pension scheme is not deductible, even where the tortfeasor is the claimant's employer and therefore the 'provider' of the pension scheme, because the pension is the fruit of the employee's work and is attributable to his work in the past; it is not a replacement for his loss of earnings (*Smoker* v *London Fire and Civil Defence Authority* [1991] 2 AC 502).

In *Longden* v *British Coal Corp* [1998] 1 All ER 289 Lord Hope of Craighead explained that the effect of *Parry* v *Cleaver* and *Smoker* v *London Fire and Civil*

Defence Authority is that incapacity and disability pensions fall outside the general rule that prima facie all receipts due to the accident must be set against losses claimed to have arisen because of the accident. The only reason why incapacity and disability pension payments received after the normal retirement age must be brought into account in computing the claim for loss of pension after that age is that the claim at this stage is for loss of pension, so one cannot properly calculate the loss of pension arising in this period without taking into account receipts of the same character arising in the same period. Therefore, in the case which was then before their Lordships, the claimant was required to set against his claim for the loss of the retirement pension an appropriate portion of the lump sum which he had received on his retirement on the ground of incapacity.

Unemployment benefit received before the trial is deductible in full (*Nabi v British Leyland (UK) Ltd* [1980] 1 All ER 667), as is supplementary benefit received before the trial (*Lincoln v Hayman* [1982] 1 WLR 488). However the proceeds of an insurance policy are not deductible (*Bradburn v Great Western Railway* (1874) LR 10 Ex 1), nor are charitable donations (unless, perhaps, the charitable donation is provided by the tortfeasor, see *Hussain v New Taplow Paper Mills Ltd* [1988] 2 WLR 266). Lord Reid said in *Cleaver* that in the case of charitable donations it would be unjust if the only person who benefited from the receipt of charitable donations was the tortfeasor because his obligation to the claimant would thereby be reduced.

In *Hussain v New Taplow Paper Mills Ltd* [1988] AC 514 the defendant employers took out insurance against their contractual obligation to their employees to maintain them at a rate of 50 per cent of their pre-accident earnings under a long-term sickness benefit scheme, which was payable where the employee had been incapacitated for work as the result of an accident in the course of his employment and after the employee had been off work for 13 weeks (during which period he received his full pay). The insurance scheme was funded entirely by the employers and there was no evidence that the claimant's wages would have been higher if the defendants had not operated such a scheme. The defendants argued that the proceeds of this long term sickness benefit scheme were deductible because they were in the nature of earnings. The claimant argued that they were not deductible because they were in the nature of payments from an insurance policy and so were not deductible under the principle laid down in *Parry v Cleaver* (above). It was held that the sums were deductible because they were in the nature of earnings as the scheme was stated to be a continuation of salary and there was no policy reason why these payments should be left out of account because they went directly to reduce the claimant's loss. Lord Bridge stated that to hold that the claimant, who had paid no insurance premiums, should receive his full wages from two different sources (the employer and the tortfeasor) positively offended his sense of justice, and this sense of injustice was even more acute where, as here, the employer and the tortfeasor were one and the same person. It should be noted, however, that the House of Lords did not consider the situation where the claimant is able to show that the payments are part of his wage structure in the sense that his wages would be higher if the insurance scheme were not in operation (although in the Court of Appeal, [1987] 1 All ER 417, Kerr LJ stated that in such a case the conclusion may be that the sums are not deductible).

In *Colledge* v *Bass Mitchells & Butlers Ltd* [1988] 1 All ER 536 the Court of Appeal held that a redundancy payment which had been paid by the defendants should be deducted from the damages payable to the claimant. The claimant, who was an employee of the defendants, was injured at work due to the negligence of the defendants. Before the action was heard the claimant was offered voluntary redundancy by the defendants. The claimant accepted this offer and was given a redundancy payment of £9,000. The defendants argued that the redundancy payment should be deducted from the damages award. However, the trial judge held that the redundancy payment was not to be deducted because it was a reflection of past service and was not attributable to the accident. On appeal the Court of Appeal held that, as it was unlikely that the claimant would have been made redundant apart from the injury, the money fell to be deducted. In the words of Lord Reid in *Parry* v *Cleaver* (above), the redundancy payment had been received as a result of the accident and therefore it fell to be deducted.

Reference must also be made to the judgment of Lord Bridge in *Hodgson* v *Trapp* (above). More important than the narrow point of law at stake in this case (whether attendance and mobility allowances were deductible) was the *manner* in which Lord Bridge dismissed the claimant's argument. He rejected the argument that such state benefits were analogous to charitable payments, stating that he found the concept of public benevolence a 'difficult one to comprehend'. Significantly, he added that to refuse to make a deduction would only:

> '… add to the enormous disparity, to which the advocates of a 'no-fault' system of compensation constantly draw attention, between the position of those who are able to establish a third party's fault as the cause of their injury and the position of those who are not.'

It is clear that the courts wish, as far as possible, to avoid the conclusion that a claimant can be compensated twice for the same loss. The point can be neatly illustrated by reference to the case of *Berriello* v *Felixstowe Dock & Railway Co* [1989] 1 WLR 695. The claimant, who was an Italian seaman, was injured as a result of the negligence of the defendants. The Cassa Marrittima Meridionale (administered by the Italian State) paid him a sum of money on account of his injuries and notified him that a further sum would be paid. Crucially, the money was recoverable by the CMM if the claimant recovered damages in respect of the loss for which the payments had been made. The Court of Appeal held that the payments made by CMM were not deductible because here, unlike *Hussain* and *Hodgson*, there was no fear of double compensation; the claimant was required to repay the money received to CMM. Dillon LJ stated that, if an English statute were to provide that a welfare benefit was to be recoverable from the recipient if he recovered damages from a third party in respect of the loss in relation to which the welfare benefit had been paid, then he could not 'conceive that the English courts would require the welfare benefits to be deducted in the assessment of the amount of damages payable to the injured person'.

It should also be noted that one case sits rather uneasily with the policy of prevention of double compensation. That case is *McCamley* v *Cammell-Laird Shipbuilders Ltd* [1990] 1 All ER 854. The claimant suffered serious injury in an accident caused by the negligence of the defendants, his employers. The defendants' holding company had taken out a policy of insurance under which the defendants were described as the insured and the employees as insured persons. Payments were made independently of fault and were calculated by a multiplication of the claimant's earnings and were paid in the form of a lump sum. The claimant was unaware of the existence of this policy until after his accident when he received the sum of £45,000 which had been paid to the defendants under the policy. The Court of Appeal, distinguishing *Hussain*, held that the £45,000 was not to be deducted because it was an act of benevolence. The critical features of *McCamley* appear to be that the money was paid in the form of a lump sum (and not in the form of a replacement for wages), the money was payable regardless of fault and the money was not attributable to any particular recognised head of damage.

However, in *Gaca* v *Pirelli General plc* [2004] 3 All ER 348 Dyson LJ said that *McCamley* was wrongly decided and should no longer be followed for two principal reasons. First, the payment in that case manifestly was not analogous to a payment within the classic benevolence exception: it is unreal to treat the payment of benefits under an insurance policy as equivalent, or even analogous, to payments made by third parties out of sympathy. Second, ex gratia payments made to employees by their employer tortfeasors do not normally fall within the benevolence exception, even if it can be shown that they are made from motives of benevolence. His Lordship explained that he had used the word 'normally' because it would be possible, in theory at least, and so long as there is nothing in his insurance policy to put his cover at risk if he takes such a course, for the tortfeasor to make an ex gratia payment, and to spell out explicitly that the payment is a gift made on the basis that it should not be deducted from any damages that may be awarded to the employee if litigation ensues. In that exceptional situation, the position may be different.

In *Gaca* the claimant suffered serious injury in an accident at work and the defendant employer admitted liability. Under a personal accident insurance policy held by the defendant, the claimant was paid £34,167.18 for temporary total disablement and, following the termination of his employment on grounds of ill health, a further £88,620 for permanent total disability. The defendant contended that these sums should be deducted from the damages awarded to the claimant. While the provision of health insurance may not have been a contractual entitlement, the claimant knew that it was part of his employment package. The Court of Appeal decided that the payments under the insurance policy were indeed deductible from the claimant's damages. As Dyson LJ explained:

'It has ... been stated on a number of occasions that there are two classes of payment to a claimant as a result of an accident which are not required to be brought into account in the assessment of damages. These are often referred to as the two exceptions against the rule against double recovery of damages. They are: (i) payments made gratuitously to the claimant by others as a mark of sympathy ("the benevolence exception"); and (ii) insurance moneys ("the insurance exception"). ... I would hold that this case does not come within the benevolence exception because: (a) the payments were made by the tortfeasor, and (b) the payment of benefits under the insurance policy was not equivalent, or analogous, to payments made by third parties out of sympathy. ... [As to the insurance exception, the] insurance moneys must be deducted unless it is shown that the claimant paid or contributed to the insurance premium directly or indirectly. Payment or contribution will not be inferred simply from the fact that the claimant is an employee for whose benefit the insurance has been arranged. ... [Counsel for the claimant] cannot identify any evidence which shows that the claimant paid or contributed to the cost of the insurance policy. All he can point to is the fact that the fruits of the claimant's labour enabled the defendants to pay for the insurance. But ... that is not enough to avoid the deduction of the benefits from his damages.

Where an employee lied in completing a medical questionnaire, enabling him to continue in his work, but is subsequently injured as a result of his employer's negligence, public policy requires that he is not entitled to recover any loss of future earnings: *Hewison* v *Meridian Shipping PTE* (2003) Solicitors Journal 10 January.

30.12 Other pecuniary losses

The claimant may suffer other types of pecuniary loss, such as the loss of ability to carry out a profitable hobby. Another example was provided by the Court of Appeal in *Jones* v *Jones* [1985] QB 704 where the claimant's injuries resulted in the breakdown of his marriage. It was held that he was entitled to recover from the defendant the cost of maintaining two homes, instead of one (see too *Meah* v *McCreamer* [1985] 1 All ER 367, a decision doubted by the Court of Appeal in *Clunis* v *Camden and Islington Health Authority* [1998] 3 All ER 180). However, in *Pritchard* v *J H Cobden Ltd* [1988] Fam 22 a differently constituted Court of Appeal held that the financial consequences of a divorce were not recoverable on the grounds that divorce was not a loss but was a redistribution of the parties' assets; it was too remote and as a matter of policy it was not recoverable. So the Court of Appeal refused to follow *Jones* v *Jones* and it is unclear which decision will now be followed. See also Chapter 31, section 31.3.

30.13 Non-pecuniary loss

The difficulties in assessing damages become even more acute when we consider non-pecuniary losses. The whole question was reviewed by the Court of Appeal in

Heil v *Rankin* [2000] 3 All ER 138 and all that follows under this head must be read in the light of their Lordships' decision. The Law Commission had recommended that the level of damages for non-pecuniary loss for personal injury should be increased and made specific recommendations in that regard. In the absence of intervention by Parliament, their Lordships felt that it was appropriate for the court to review the level of awards in this area and to consider, inter alia, the commission's recommendations. As to damages for pain, suffering and loss of amenity, their Lordships were unable to accept the commission's recommendations that increases should be substantial, but they agreed that modest increases were required. Their Lordships concluded that it was in the case of the most catastrophic injuries that the awards were most in need of adjustment and that the scale of adjustment which was required reduced as the level of existing awards decreased. At the highest level, awards should be increased by a sum in the region of one-third: there was no need for an increase in awards which were at present below £10,000. Between those awards at the highest level, which required an upwards adjustment of one-third, and those awards where no adjustment was required, the extent of the adjustment should taper downwards.

In the event, their Lordships applied this new approach to *Heil* v *Rankin* (an award of £6,000 by way of general damages was not disturbed) and the seven other appeals which were heard at the same time.

Non-pecuniary losses can be divided into four categories, which we shall now discuss.

30.14 Pain and suffering

The claimant is entitled to recover for the pain and suffering which he has endured and which he will endure as a result of the negligence of the defendant. Where the claimant is unaware that he has suffered any pain and suffering because, for example, he has remained unconscious throughout, then he cannot recover any damages under this head (*Wise* v *Kaye* [1962] 1 QB 638). A claimant cannot recover for pain and suffering which takes the form of sorrow and grief; it must be shown that the claimant has suffered recognised nervous shock (*Kralj* v *McGrath* [1986] 1 All ER 54). In *Hicks* v *Chief Constable of the South Yorkshire Police* [1992] 2 All ER 65 the claimants died of traumatic asphyxia at the Hillsborough tragedy. The medical evidence established that, once asphyxia had set in, unconsciousness would have followed within a few seconds and death would have occurred shortly afterwards. It was held that damages were only recoverable for the pain and suffering, including the knowledge of impending death, which the claimants had suffered in the few seconds between the onset of asphyxia and the ensuing unconsciousness and death. On the facts it was held that no damages were recoverable at all because these last few seconds were, in reality, part of death itself and 'fear of impending death felt by the victim of a fatal injury before that injury is inflicted cannot by itself give rise to a cause of action which survives for the benefit of the victim's estate' (per Lord Bridge, for criticism see Unger (1992) 142 NLJ 394).

Where the claimant has suffered a loss of expectation of life as a result of the negligence of the defendant, the court is required under s1(1)(b) of the Administration of Justice Act 1982 to take into account in assessing damages for the claimant's pain and suffering 'any suffering caused or likely to be caused to him by awareness that his expectation of life has been so reduced'.

30.15 Loss of amenity

The claimant is entitled to be compensated for his loss of capacity to engage in activities which he enjoyed before his injury. The difficulty which has arisen here is whether the claimant must be aware of his loss of enjoyment. The issue was considered by the House of Lords in *H West and Son Ltd* v *Shepherd* [1964] AC 326. The claimant was a 41-year-old married woman who suffered severe head injuries in an accident which resulted in cerebral atrophy and paralysis of all four limbs. There was some evidence that she might be aware to some extent of the condition which she was in. The majority of the House of Lords upheld an award of £17,500 to the claimant for loss of amenities. There was a strong dissent from Lords Reid and Morris. They argued that one can no more compensate an unconscious person than one can compensate a dead person and that the purpose of an award of damages under this head was to compensate the claimant for his loss of happiness and that nothing could therefore be awarded where the claimant was unaware of his loss of happiness. The majority replied that a living person should not be treated as though he were dead and that a person who is alive is entitled to recover damages in his own right.

The minority also argued that the approach of the majority would give rise to serious anomalies because the claimant who was unconscious but who survived until after the trial would recover damages under this head whereas the person who died shortly before the action would not be able to recover damages. The majority countered this reasoning by pointing out that the only logical stopping point for the minority was to say that the recoverability of damages depended upon the claimant's awareness of his loss of amenity and the unhappiness which that loss caused him. Lord Pearce said that it would be 'lamentable' if the recoverability of damages were to depend on protestations of misery by the claimant.

In *Lim Poh Choo* v *Camden and Islington AHA* [1980] AC 174 Lord Scarman said that he did not underestimate the 'formidable logic and good sense' of the minority opinions in *West*, but he said that the case had stood as an authority since 1963 and that its reversal would cause widespread injustice unless it was part of a widespread legislative reform of the law. So it is highly unlikely that *West* will ever be overruled. The only point which suggests that the minority approach in *West* has found some favour is that the damages which were awarded in *West* amounted to £17,500, whereas only £20,000 was awarded in 1977 in *Lim Poh Choo*, which, when inflation is taken into account, constitutes a considerably smaller sum than that awarded in *West*. So the only prospect for change is that the damages awarded under this head may decline rather than disappear altogether.

30.16 Loss of expectation of life

In *Flint* v *Lovell* [1935] 1 KB 354 it was held that there was an independent head of damages called loss of expectation of life. However in *Benham* v *Gambling* [1941] AC 157 it was held that damages awarded under this head should be a modest conventional figure, which was fixed at £200. This claim was, however, abolished by s1(1)(a) of the Administration of Justice Act 1982 and has been replaced by a claim for bereavement (see s1A of the Fatal Accidents Act 1976, as inserted by s3(1) of the 1982 Act), which is a fixed sum which may be awarded to a spouse for the loss of a spouse and to parents for the loss of a child who at the time of death (not the time of the accident, see *Doleman* v *Deakin* (1990) The Times 30 January) had not attained the age of 18. The level of bereavement damages was raised to £10,000 for causes of action accruing on or after 1 April 2002.

30.17 The injury itself

Where the claimant loses an arm or a hand as a result of the defendant's negligence then damages may be claimed in respect of that injury. In many cases it will not be easy to distinguish between the injury and the consequences of the injury and the court will award a sum which covers both losses. But in respect of the injury itself the judges set a tariff for the loss of various limbs or faculties. The value placed upon such losses is, to some extent, arbitrary, as there is no market for the replacement of limbs (regard should be had to Kemp and Kemp *The Quantum of Damages*, or to Current Law, to see the sums currently awarded by the courts for the loss of limbs or faculties). But at least the effect of the operation of the tariff system is to ensure a measure of consistency in the awarding of damages.

30.18 Interest

In times of inflation it is obvious that interest must be claimed on damages because there will usually be a considerable lapse of time between the date of the accident and the date of the trial. In cases of damages for personal injuries or death exceeding £200 the court must, under s35A of the Supreme Court Act 1981, award interest unless there are special reasons for not doing so. Interest can only be claimed on losses from the date on which the cause of action arose (see, eg, *Nykredit Mortgage Bank plc* v *Edward Erdman Group Ltd (No 2)* [1998] 1 All ER 305; see also *IM Properties plc* v *Cape & Dalgleish* [1998] 3 All ER 203) to the date of the trial because in respect of future pecuniary losses no loss has been sustained at the date of trial and so no interest can be awarded for such losses.

Pecuniary loss carries interest at the rate of half of the short term interest rate from the date of the accident to the date of the trial (*Jefford* v *Gee* [1970] 2 QB 130 and *Cookson* v *Knowles* [1979] AC 556). Interest on non-pecuniary loss is only recoverable from the date of the service of the writ to the date of trial because such loss is assessed at the date of the trial and so the claimant is not affected by the loss of value of the money and need only be compensated for his loss of use of the money (*Wright* v *British Railways Board* [1983] 2 AC 773). Judgment debts carry interest at the rate of 8 per cent: s17 of the Judgments Act 1838, as amended.

30.19 Death in relation to tort

Where the negligence of the defendant results in the death of another then special rules have been evolved to deal with this issue. At common law the rule was that death extinguished a cause of action which the deceased may have had against the defendant. At the same time no cause of action accrued for the benefit of the dependants of the deceased. Both these rules have now been abolished so that now two actions are normally available arising out of the death of the deceased.

The first is that under s1(1) of the Law Reform (Miscellaneous Provisions) Act 1934 all causes of action 'subsisting against or vested in [the deceased] shall survive against, or, as the case may be, for the benefit of, his estate'. Thus the effect of this section is to enable the claimant's estate to bring an action where the claimant was killed by the negligence of the defendant. The principles applicable in assessing damages are generally the same as in a personal injuries case, except that exemplary damages are not recoverable, a claim for bereavement does not survive for the benefit of the deceased's estate and a claim for loss of earnings in the lost years can only be brought by a living claimant (s4(2) of the Administration of Justice Act 1982, for criticism see Cane and Harris (1983) 46 MLR 478).

The second action which may be brought is that under the Fatal Accidents Act 1976 the dependants of a deceased person who was wrongfully killed may bring an action in damages under the provisions of that Act. The dependants may only bring an action under the Act if the deceased person would have been able to bring an action against the defendant (s1(1) of the Fatal Accidents Act 1976). Thus any defence which the defendant would have been able to rely on against the deceased is also available against the dependants. See, eg, *Jameson* v *Central Electricity Generating Board* [1999] 1 All ER 193 (deceased's claim settled before his death therefore defendant would not have been liable if death had not ensued).

'Dependants' are defined in ss1(2) and 1(4) of the 1976 Act as the deceased's spouse, former spouse or cohabitee, parents, children, grandparents and grandchildren and any brother, sister, uncle or aunt, or their issue. A relationship by affinity (that is, by marriage) is treated as if it were a relationship of consanguinity (blood) and a relationship of half blood is treated as if it were a relationship of the whole blood.

The dependants can maintain an action for damages for bereavement (see section 30.16), any funeral expenses which have been incurred and claims for actual and future pecuniary loss. The main problem here lies in assessing damages for pecuniary loss. The purpose behind the award of damages here is to maintain the dependants in the position which they would have been in had the deceased still been alive. The courts start by calculating the deceased's earnings and then deduct a sum to represent the deceased's personal and living expenses. Where the deceased is the mother of a small child who is not in paid employment then the damages are assessed on the basis of the wages which would be payable to a notional nanny and not on the cost of fostering the child (although for criticism of the 'notional nanny' approach see the judgment of Sir David Croom-Johnson in *Hayden* v *Hayden* [1992] 4 All ER 681, 693). In assessing the wages which would be payable to a notional nanny discount must be made for the fact that the extent of the services required by a child decreases as the child gets older (see *Spittle* v *Bunney* [1988] 3 All ER 1031). In *Cresswell* v *Eaton* [1991] 1 All ER 484 the claimants' mother was killed in an accident caused by the negligence of the defendant. For a short while the claimants lived with their grandmother but she died some two years later. In the circumstances the claimants' aunt gave up her job as a traffic warden to look after and care for the claimants. Simon Brown J held that the claimants' losses were of two types. The first was what he called the 'disbursement dependency', by which he meant the claimants' loss of their mother's financial support. The second loss was the 'services dependency', by which he meant the loss of their mother's care. The difficulty here was that their mother had been in employment prior to her death and so was a 'part-time carer', whereas the aunt gave up her employment to become a 'full-time carer'. Simon Brown J held that:

> 'Where a claim is based in large part on a relative's actual loss of earnings reasonably incurred, modest discount only should be made to reflect the part-time nature of the deceased mother's care. And that is so even if it is as much the emotional as the physical needs of the children which make it reasonable for the relative to give up work.'

But he held that there is 'room for a somewhat larger discount' in relation to relatives who do not actually lose any earnings as a result of providing the care. On the facts Simon Brown J made a deduction of 15 per cent for the aunt's care but 30 per cent for the grandmother's care (she did not suffer any loss of earnings).

Once this has been done then the court will calculate the likely duration of the dependants' dependency, which is a process similar to that adopted in calculating the multiplier in a personal injuries action. In assessing damages and the length of dependency the prospects that the deceased's widow will remarry are to be ignored (s3(3) of the 1976 Act), but not the possibility that the parties would have divorced where the evidence reveals that possibility: *Martin* v *Owen* (1992) The Times 21 May.

Any benefits which have accrued or will accrue or may accrue to the dependants from the estate of the deceased or otherwise as a result of the death of the deceased are to be disregarded (s4 of the 1976 Act). Thus in *Wood* v *Bentall Simplex Ltd* (1992) The Times 3 March the Court of Appeal held that in assessing damages it is irrelevant that a loss from one source might be balanced by a benefit since s4 required benefits to be disregarded. This section produces an odd contrast with the rules relating to deductions in a claim brought by an injured claimant because s4 clearly sanctions double compensation. The courts have, however, experienced great difficulty in interpreting s4, as can be seen in the following three cases. The first case is *Pidduck* v *Eastern Scottish Omnibuses Ltd* [1990] 2 All ER 69. The deceased was killed as a result of the negligence of the defendants. At the time of his death the deceased was in receipt of a non-contributory pension from his employers and, after his death, his widow continued to receive an allowance based upon her husband's pension entitlement. The defendants argued that the sums paid to the widow under the pension scheme were to be taken into account in quantifying the damages payable to the widow. But it was held that the allowance was a 'benefit' which accrued to the widow 'as a result of' her husband's death and it was therefore to be disregarded under s4. Purchas LJ held that the purpose behind s4 was:

'... to produce an exception to the common law rules for calculating quantum of damages, namely to prevent the deduction of a benefit which would otherwise have to be deducted in order to arrive at the true loss on a common law basis.'

The second case is *Stanley* v *Saddique* [1992] 1 QB 1. The claimant's mother was killed in a road accident caused by the negligence of the defendant. After her death the claimant's father met another woman who subsequently became the claimant's stepmother and the 'motherly services' which the stepmother provided were of a 'higher quality than could foreseeably be expected to have been provided by the [claimant's] mother'. The defendant argued that account should be taken of this benefit to the claimant and that s4 only excluded from consideration direct pecuniary benefits. But the Court of Appeal held, after a careful examination of the legislative history of what is now s4, that they were required by the Act to disregard this benefit in calculating the damages payable.

The third and most difficult case is the decision in the Court of Appeal in *Hayden* v *Hayden* [1992] 4 All ER 681 (criticised by Kemp (1993) 109 LQR 173). The claimant brought a claim against the defendant, her father, whose negligence had resulted in the death of her mother. The claimant was four at the date of the accident. After the accident the defendant gave up work and provided significant services for the claimant in caring for her in place of her mother (although there was some controversy as to the quality of the care so provided). The trial judge found that the mother had been an excellent mother and probably would have bestowed on her daughter more attention than her father had been able to do. One of the issues which arose before the Court of Appeal was whether the care provided by the father fell to be disregarded under s4. By a majority, the Court of Appeal held that it was not to be disregarded. McCowan LJ dissented. He relied on *Stanley* v *Saddique* (above) for the proposition that there is to be no reduction in the damages payable to take account of the care voluntarily provided in substitution for the mother's services and that, for this purpose, it was irrelevant that the care had been provided by the tortfeasor himself. The majority disagreed. Parker LJ chose to follow the reasoning of the Court of Appeal in *Hay* v *Hughes* [1975] QB 790 rather than *Stanley*. He and Sir David Croom-Johnson stated that the father was simply discharging his parental duties and it could not be said that the services were provided 'as a result of' the mother's death. Although Sir David Croom-Johnson emphasised that the question of what is a 'benefit' must be regarded as a question of fact, there is clearly a division of opinion as to the proper interpretation of s4 and the matter is in need of urgent consideration by the House of Lords so that the inconsistencies which have arisen can be removed.

In *Cox* v *Huckenhull* [1999] 3 All ER 577 the point in issue concerned the assessment of damages under the Fatal Accidents Act 1976 where the financial dependency of the claimant is based upon state benefits paid to or in respect of the deceased. When Mr and Mrs Cox were both 58 they were involved in a car accident which was entirely the defendant's fault. Mrs Cox was killed and Mr Cox sustained severe injuries. All claims were settled except Mr Cox's claims for loss of financial dependency and loss of his wife's services. Mrs Cox had been severely disabled all her life and, since being made redundant six years before the accident, Mr Cox had been his wife's full time carer. Since that time, the couple's income consisted entirely of state benefits. In assessing Mr Cox's entitlement for loss of financial dependency, the Court of Appeal said that the couple's total income from benefits would be calculated, omitting housing benefit, council tax benefit and the invalid care allowance. Mr Cox was entitled to 50 per cent of the resulting figure, subject to a pre-trial multiplier of 2.6 and a post-trial multiplier of 10.5. As to his claim for loss of his wife's services, although Mrs Cox had been able to make a significant contribution to the running of the home, because of her disabilities and deteriorating health this was not a case where it was possible to quantify the loss of services on the basis of employing a housekeeper or even a part-time home help. Instead, their Lordships decided that Mr Cox would be awarded a lump sum of £7,500. In the event, the total amount awarded, including interest, was £61,673.82

Finally, in *Watson* v *Wilmott* [1991] 1 QB 140 the court considered the impact of adoption on the claimant's claim for damages. The claimant's mother was killed in an accident caused by the negligence of the defendant and, some months later, his father committed suicide as a result of the depression caused by the death of his wife. The claimant was looked after by his aunt and uncle who later adopted him. Garland J held that the adoption had to be taken into account in the quantification of the dependency. In the case of the loss of the claimant's father, the loss of dependency was to be calculated by comparing the claimant in the position he would have been in had his father lived with his position with his adoptive father; therefore the sum to be awarded was the claimant's loss of dependency on his father less his dependency on his adoptive father. But, in so far as his dependency on his mother was concerned, Garland J held that the adoption replaced his non-pecuniary dependency on his deceased mother and that therefore the non-pecuniary dependency on his mother was to be assessed only up to the date of his adoption.

Where a person is awarded provisional damages (see section 30.5) and subsequently dies as a result of the act or omission which gave rise to the cause of action for which the damages were awarded, the award of the provisional damages does not bar an action in respect of that person's death under the Fatal Accidents Act 1976. However, such part (if any) of the provisional damages, and any further damages awarded to the person in question before his death, as was intended to compensate him for pecuniary loss in a period which in the event falls after his death is taken into account in assessing the amount of any loss of support suffered by the person or person's for whose benefit the action under the 1976 Act is brought. No award of further damages made in respect of that person after his death may include any amount for loss of income in respect of any period after his death: Damages Act 1996, s3(1)–(4). In this context 'provisional damages' means damages awarded by virtue of s32A(2)(a) of the Supreme Court Act 1981 and 'further damages' means damages awarded by virtue of s32A(2)(b) of that Act: s3(5) of the 1996 Act.

30.20 Damage to property

Where it is the claimant's property rather than his person which suffers damage the same principle is applicable, which is that the claimant must be returned to the position which he was in before the damage was done. If the property is completely damaged then the proper measure of damages is the market value of the goods at the date they were destroyed (*Liesbosch Dredger* v *SS Edison* [1933] AC 449). In *Southampton Container Terminals Ltd* v *Hansa Schiffahrts GmbH* (2001) The Times 13 June the Court of Appeal held that, in assessing damages for the tortious loss of a chattel such as a working crane, the court was entitled to award only the current resale value of the chattel and not the cost of replacing it if the benefit would be wholly disproportionate to the claimant's loss. The principle in *Ruxley Electronics and Construction Ltd* v *Forsyth* [1996] AC 344, that reinstatement should not be ordered where the benefit to the claimant would be out of all proportion to his loss, applied equally to the tortious destruction of a chattel in use as to a breach of contract. The overriding principle was that damages should be reasonable as between the parties. Here, the crane's loss caused inconvenience but not loss of capacity and no serious financial loss.

If the goods were used for a profit-making purpose then the claimant may recover for the profit which he has lost or he may recover the cost of hiring a substitute if it was reasonable to do so (*Martindale* v *Duncan* [1973] 1 WLR 574).

Where the goods are damaged rather than completely destroyed the measure of recovery is generally the diminution in value of the goods (*The London Corporation* [1935] P 70). In many cases this will be equivalent to the cost of repair but where the cost of repair exceeds the diminution in value the claimant will be confined to the latter sum unless the property is unique (*O'Grady* v *Westminster Scaffolding* [1962] 2 Lloyd's Rep 238) or, perhaps, where it is the claimant's land which has been damaged (*Dodd Properties Ltd* v *Canterbury City Council* [1980] 1 WLR 433).

30.21 Damage to reputation

The situation may arise where the claimant has suffered no damage to his person or property, but due to the negligence of the defendant the claimant has suffered distress, anxiety and injury to his reputation. Thus in *McLeish* v *Amoo-Gottfried & Co* (1993) The Times 13 October, where the claimant was wrongly convicted of a criminal offence due to the admitted negligence of his solicitor, the High Court held that the claimant could recover damages for distress and mental anxiety. The Court also held that although damages for loss of reputation could not be recovered in this case as a separate head of damage, it could enhance his award for distress and mental anxiety.

Damages for injury to feelings was one of the areas considered by the Technology and Construction Court in *R* v *Secretary of State for Transport, ex parte Factortame (No 7)* (2001) The Times 10 January and Judge Toulmin QC's observations included the following:

1. damages for injury to feelings can only be awarded in relation to those torts where the claimant's self-esteem is an important and integral part of the damage for which compensation is awarded;
2. such damages can only be awarded in respect of torts committed by private persons, or by government officials acting in circumstances where the claimant could recover damages if the act was done by a private person.

30.22 The commitment to the protection of the reliance interest

The law of tort is theoretically committed to the principle of full compensation and to the complete protection of the reliance interest. In practice it comes close to the complete protection of the reliance interest. There are, however, certain limitations on the recoverability of compensation. For example a loss which is too remote cannot be recovered (see Chapter 11) nor, of course, a loss which was not caused by the defendant's negligence (*South Australia Asset Management Corporation* v *York*

Montague Ltd [1996] 3 WLR 87; see also *Platform Home Loans Ltd* v *Oyston Shipways Ltd* [1999] 1 All ER 833 (negligent valuation: damages limited to amount of overvaluation)), and discount is made for contingencies and vicissitudes. We have also noted that there is a risk that inflation will erode the value of the claimant's award. The claimant is also under a duty to mitigate his loss. Thus he cannot recover in respect of any part of his loss which he could have avoided by the taking of reasonable steps (*Darbishire* v *Warran* [1963] 1 WLR 1067; see also *Walker* v *Geo H Medlicott & Son* [1999] 1 All ER 685 (see Chapter 7, section 7.9) and *Patel* v *Hooper & Jackson* [1999] 1 All ER 992 (section 30.4)). This doctrine is based on the need to avoid the waste of resources in society. The claimant need only take reasonable steps to mitigate his loss and what is reasonable depends on all the facts and circumstances of the case. All that can be said is that the standard of reasonableness is not high because a tortfeasor is not entitled to require that his victim take great steps to mitigate his loss. For example in *Selvanayagam* v *University of the West Indies* [1983] 1 All ER 824 it was held that, in the case of personal injuries requiring surgery, the test to apply is whether 'in all the circumstances including particularly the medical advice received, the claimant acted reasonably in refusing surgery'. Thus where the surgery involves considerable risk to the claimant or its outcome is uncertain it will not generally be unreasonable for the claimant to refuse to undergo surgery.

In *Geest plc* v *Lansiquot* [2003] 1 All ER 383, like *Selvanayagam* a decision of the Privy Council, it seems to have been accepted that the onus of proof on the issue of mitigation is on the defendant. Indeed, the Board appears to have approved the statement of Donaldson MR in *Sotiros Shipping Inc* v *Sameiet Solholt, The Solholt* [1983] 1 Lloyd's Rep 60 at 608, where he said:

> 'A [claimant] is a under no duty to mitigate his loss, despite the habitual use by the lawyers of the phrase "duty to mitigate". He is completely free to act as he judges to be in his best interests. On the other hand, a defendant is not liable for all loss suffered by the [claimant] in consequence of his so acting. A defendant is only liable for such part of the [claimant's] loss as is properly to be regarded as caused by the defendants' breach of duty.'

30.23 Tort and the expectation interest

Although tort is committed to the protection of the reliance interest we have also noted cases in which tort law has intervened to protect the expectation interest, that is the damages award has had the effect of enforcing a promise by putting the claimant in the position which he would have been in had the promise been carried out according to its terms and not in the position which he was in before the promise was made. Cases in which the expectation interest has been protected include *Junior Books Ltd* v *The Veitchi Co Ltd* [1983] 1 AC 520 and *Ross* v *Caunters* [1980] Ch 297. These cases have already been discussed (see Chapter 1, secton 1.4, Chapter 7, sections 7.7 and 7.9) and the same ground will not be traversed again;

suffice it to emphasise the point that these cases create difficulties in ascertaining the relationship between tort and contract.

30.24 Injunctions

An injunction is an equitable remedy which is available in the discretion of the court. The general principle which guides the court in considering whether or not to grant an injunction is stated in s37 of the Supreme Court Act 1981 to be that it must appear to the court to be 'just and convenient' to make such an order. Injunctions are particularly significant as a remedy in certain torts and of little or no relevance in other torts. For example they are of little or no interest in negligence, but are of great significance in nuisance, trespass and the economic torts. Once again we will confine ourselves to a consideration of the general principles governing the granting of injunctions. Where there are special rules applicable to a particular tort these have been discussed when dealing with the substantive law of that tort. Injunctions can come in different shapes and sizes and there are, in fact, a number of different types of injunctions. The principal types are as follows.

Prohibitory injunction

A prohibitory injunction is an injunction which orders the defendant to refrain from continuing with his tortious activity. This is the form of injunction which is most commonly sought (for example in nuisance cases or cases involving the economic torts). The general principle which the courts apply in considering whether to exercise their discretion and grant an injunction is whether damages would be an appropriate remedy. Where damages are appropriate an injunction will generally not be issued. In many cases of a continuing tort damages will not be an adequate remedy and so this hurdle will be relatively easy to overcome. The court will also have regard to the conduct of the parties who are seeking the injunction, any delay in seeking the remedy and the effect of the grant of an injunction on innocent third parties.

Mandatory injunction

A mandatory injunction is of considerably less significance than a prohibitory injunction. A mandatory injunction is an injunction which requires the defendant to take some positive step, for example to remove something which constitutes a trespass on the claimant's land. Such an injunction will not be granted where damages would be an appropriate remedy, but there are other restrictions upon the availability of this type of injunction. In *Morris* v *Redland Bricks Ltd* [1970] AC 652 the House of Lords held that a mandatory injunction will only be granted where the claimant shows that there is a very strong probability that grave danger will accrue to him in the future if the injunction is not granted and the injunction must be sufficiently specific for the defendant to be able to know exactly what he has to do to comply with the terms of the injunction.

Quia timet injunction

Where the tort has not yet been committed, but the claimant apprehends that he will suffer imminent substantial damage from the commission of the tort, the court has jurisdiction to grant a quia timet injunction which has the effect of restraining the defendant from committing the tort. To obtain such an injunction the claimant must show that damage is almost certain to occur and that the damage is imminent.

Interim injunction

The claimant may not wish to wait for the full trial of his action to obtain his injunction. So he may attempt to obtain an interim injunction. Such an injunction is granted quickly pending the full trial of the action. This type of injunction is particularly important in trade dispute cases. In considering whether or not to grant such an injunction the court does not inquire into the substantive merits of the case; instead the claimant must show that there is a serious issue to be tried and that the balance of convenience lies in his favour (see *American Cyanamid Co v Ethicon Ltd* [1975] AC 396 and Gray (1981) 40 CLJ 307). Where the court does grant an injunction the court will require an undertaking from the claimant that he will compensate the defendant for the damage that the interim injunction has caused him if the defendant succeeds at the full trial of the action.

In libel proceedings, where a defendant puts a short statement before the court, verified as true, in which he maintains that he can and will justify the alleged libel, the rule had always been, and remains, that the claimant is unable to obtain an interim injunction to restrain publication of an allegedly defamatory statement unless it is plain that the plea of justification is bound to fail: *Greene v Associated Newspapers Ltd* [2005] 1 All ER 30. The Court of Appeal said that the less stringent test in *Cream Holdings* (see below) did not apply to defamation proceedings.

In cases where an interim injunction might affect the exercise of the right to freedom of expression, s12(3) of the Human Rights Act 1998 introduced a marginally higher threshold test for the grant of an order than that previously applied by the court: *Imutran Ltd v Uncaged Campaigns Ltd* [2001] 2 All ER 385. As Sir Andrew Morritt V-C there explained, theoretically and as a matter of language 'likelihood' was slightly higher in the scale of probability than 'a real prospect' of success. However, his Lordship added that the difference between the two was so small that he could not believe that there would be many, if any, cases which would have succeeded under the *American Cyanamid* test but would now fail because of the terms of s12(3) of the 1998 Act.

In *A v B* [2002] 2 All ER 545 the Court of Appeal took the opportunity to issue guidelines to assist the judiciary and the parties where an application for an interim injunction involves a conflict between personal privacy and press freedom. Amongst many other things, their Lordships said that the fact that if the injunction is granted it will interfere with the freedom of expression of others and in particular the freedom of the press is a matter of particular importance. This well-established common law principle is underlined by s12(4) of the 1998 Act. Any interference with the press has to be justified because it inevitably has some effect on the ability of the press to perform its role in society. This is the position irrespective of whether a particular publication is desirable in the public interest. The existence of a free press is in itself desirable and so any interference with it has to be justified. Above all, before granting an interim injunction, a judge should be satisfied that, after the trial, it is likely that an injunction would be granted. Frequently what is required is not a technical approach to the law but a balancing of the facts. The weight which should be attached to each relevant consideration will vary depending on the precise circumstances. In many situations the balance may not point clearly in either direction. If this is the position, interim relief should be refused.

In *A* v *B* it appeared that A, a footballer with a Premier league club, was married and that he and his wife had two children. There was no dispute that A had had adulterous relationships with both C and D and, by bringing these proceedings and obtaining the injunction, A hoped to prevent his wife learning of his adultery since, if she were to learn of this, it could prejudice his marriage and his long-standing relationship with his wife and also indirectly harm his children. C and D sold their stories to the defendant B, a national newspaper, and A hoped to restrain publication of them. His application failed since it was most unlikely that, after a trial, a permanent injunction would be granted. In these circumstances the grant of an interim injunction would be an unjustified interference with the freedom of the press. See also Chapter 23, section 23.20.

In the context of a dispute as to the right of a newspaper to publish confidential information concerning alleged corruption within a group of companies, in *Cream Holdings Ltd* v *Banerjee* [2004] 4 All ER 617 the House of Lords was called upon to determine the correct approach to the application of s12(3) of the Human Rights Act 1998. Their Lordships concluded that the court could not make an interim restraint order unless it was satisfied that the applicant's prospects of success at the trial were sufficiently favourable to justify such an order being made in the particular circumstances of the case. As to what degree of likelihood made the prospects of success 'sufficiently favourable', the general approach should be that courts would be exceedingly slow to make interim restraint orders where the applicant had not satisfied the court that he would probably ('more likely than not') succeed at trial. Nevertheless, there would be cases where it was necessary for a court to depart from that general approach, and a lesser degree of likelihood would suffice as a prerequisite, eg, where the potential adverse consequences of disclosure were particularly grave or where a short-lived injunction was needed to enable the court to hear and give proper consideration to an application for interim relief pending the trial or any relevant appeal.

Damages in lieu of an injunction

The court has a discretion to grant an award of damages in lieu of an injunction. The courts are, however, extremely reluctant to exercise their discretion and award damages in lieu of an injunction (for consideration of the rules applied by the courts see Chapter 18, section 18.13 and Jolowicz [1975] CLJ 224).

30.25 Self-help

Lastly, the claimant may be able to take steps himself to alleviate his position without having resort to the courts. However, the courts are extremely reluctant to allow a claimant to take the law into his own hands in this way; see, for example, the restrictions placed on the self-help remedy in *Burton* v *Winters* [1993] 1 WLR 1077 for trespass to land as discussed on Chapter 25, section 25.6 above. But we have noted that there are certain cases where the claimant can take steps to protect himself. For example steps can be taken to abate a nuisance, distress damage feasant may be relied upon, a person who is falsely imprisoned may escape, a person who is being attacked can use self defence and a trespasser may be ejected provided that only reasonable force is used. These remedies are all exceptional and can only be exercised within rigid confines and are unlikely to be extended.

31

Miscellaneous Defences and Limitation

31.1 Introduction

31.2 Mistake

31.3 Illegality

31.4 Necessity

31.5 Limitation

31.1 Introduction

In this Chapter we shall be concerned with various defences which may be invoked by a defendant in a tort action. Two of the principal defences, contributory negligence and volenti, have already been dealt with (see Chapters 12 and 13) and so will not be dealt with in this Chapter. Similarly where a defence is peculiar to a tort then it has been discussed in relation to that tort (as is the case with defences such as justification and fair comment in defamation) and will not be discussed further here. Attention in this Chapter will therefore be confined to a miscellany of general defences such as mistake, ex turpi causa, necessity and limitation.

31.2 Mistake

Mistake is not a general defence in a tort action. For example a defendant cannot plead that it was a mistake that he ran the claimant down, although if the mistake was such that a reasonable man could have made it then it may indicate that the defendant was not negligent. Similarly, mistake is not a defence to a defamation action. However, there are cases where mistake can operate as a defence. For example an honest but mistaken belief in the truth of a statement will negative liability in deceit.

31.3 Illegality

On grounds of public policy a cause of action may be denied to a claimant who suffers damage as a result of the tort of the defendant while participating in criminal activity. This defence is sometimes described in the maxim ex turpi causa non oritur actio. Thus in *National Coal Board* v *England* [1954] AC 403 Lord Asquith stated:

> 'If two burglars, A and B, agree to open a safe by means of explosives, and A so negligently handles the explosive charge as to injure B, B might find some difficulty in maintaining an action for negligence against A.'

The operation of this defence was classically illustrated in the case of *Ashton* v *Turner* [1981] QB 137. The claimant suffered injury due to the negligence of the defendant in driving a getaway car from the scene of burglary in which they had both participated. Ewbank J held that, on grounds of public policy, the defendant did not owe to the claimant a duty of care (see also *Smith* v *Jenkins* (1970) 119 CLR 397).

There must be a causal connection between the damage which the claimant suffered and the crime in which he was participating. This is clearly satisfied in the example given by Lord Asquith in *National Coal Board* v *England* (above). However, another example given by Lord Asquith illustrates the limits of the defence: he said that if B stole A's watch while they were on their way to carry out the burglary then A could bring an action in tort against B because the theft was totally unconnected with the burglary.

The scope of the defence is difficult to define. It has been held that the defence is not confined to cases in which the claimant is engaged in criminal conduct (*Kirkham* v *Chief Constable of Greater Manchester Police* [1990] 2 QB 283). In *Euro-Diam Ltd* v *Bathurst* [1990] 1 QB 1 Kerr LJ stated that the ex turpi causa defence rests ultimately:

> '... on a principle of public policy that the courts will not assist a [claimant] who has been guilty of illegal (or immoral) conduct of which the courts should take notice. It applies if in all the circumstances it would be an affront to the public conscience to grant the [claimant] the relief which he seeks because the court would thereby appear to assist or encourage the [claimant] in his illegal conduct or to encourage others in similar acts.'

A similar approach was taken in *Thackwell* v *Barclays Bank plc* [1986] 1 All ER 676, 687, *Saunders* v *Edwards* [1987] 1 WLR 1186. This 'affront to public conscience test' was also adopted by Beldam LJ in *Pitts* v *Hunt* [1991] 1 QB 24 (discussed in more detail at Chapter 13, section 13.5). There the claimant was a pillion passenger who encouraged the first defendant, whom he knew was drunk, had no licence and was uninsured, to drive in a reckless and foolhardy manner which resulted in the death of the first defendant and serious injury to the claimant. Beldam LJ held that, if someone had been killed as a result of the activities of the claimant and the first defendant, the death would have amounted to manslaughter. He therefore held that it would be an 'affront to public conscience' to permit the claimant to bring a claim for damages for the injury which he suffered as a result of his participation in such criminal activity. Dillon LJ, on the other hand said that he found the 'affront to public conscience test very difficult to apply' because 'the public conscience may well be affected by factors of an emotional nature'. He held that the claimant's claim was barred because his claim was based directly upon the illegality. This was not a case in which the claimant had 'suffered a genuine wrong' to which the allegedly unlawful conduct was 'incidental'. Balcombe LJ adopted an approach similar to that adopted by Dillon LJ. He held that the claimant's claim must fail because the joint illegality in which he and the first defendant were engaged was such that the court could not determine the standard of care to be observed.

The defence was considered in some detail by the House of Lords in *Tinsley* v *Milligan* [1993] 3 WLR 126 where it was held that it did not apply to an arrangement which was undertaken to assist in the perpetration of fraud on the Department of Social Security over a number of years. The defendant succeeded on the grounds that her claim was based on an equitable title to property and she was not forced to plead or rely on an illegality, even though the title was acquired in the course of an illegal transaction. See also the case of *Tribe* v *Tribe* [1995] 3 WLR 913 where the Court of Appeal followed *Tinsley*.

After a full review of the authorities, Lord Goff rejected the public conscience test as constituting a 'revolution' in the law and this view, although expressed in a dissenting judgment, was agreed with by a majority of the Court (Lords Goff, Keith and Browne-Wilkinson). The defendant succeeded on the narrow ground that she was merely seeking to enforce a resulting trust, and the test applied by the House seems to require some reliance on the illegality, at least in contractual situations.

The defence was also considered in *Revill* v *Newberry* [1996] 2 WLR 239 where an occupier shot a trespasser who was involved in criminal activities on his land. The court held that the occupier was liable for injuries suffered by the trespasser from the use of force which exceeded reasonable limits. The court held that there was no room for the ex turpi causa doctrine to apply, or that any claim by a trespasser would be barred no matter how excessive or unreasonable the force used. See too *Meah* v *McCreamer (No 2)* [1986] 1 All ER 943 (claimant not entitled to damages for compensation ordered to be paid to rape victims) and *Clunis* v *Camden and Islington Health Authority* [1998] 3 All ER 180 (claim struck out since based on claimant's own illegal act).

31.4 Necessity

Necessity can operate as a complete defence to negative liability in tort. In such a case the defendant argues that his course of action was the lesser of two evils and that he has intervened to prevent greater damage being occasioned. To be able to rely on the defence the defendant must show that he has acted as a reasonable man would have done. However, the courts are extremely reluctant to rely upon this defence. This can be seen in the case of *Southwark LBC* v *Williams* [1971] Ch 734 where squatters sought to invoke the defence of necessity as a defence to the claimant's action. Lord Denning stated that the plea of necessity:

> '... would be an excuse for all sorts of wrongdoing. So the courts must, for the sake of law and order, take a firm stand. They must refuse to admit the plea of necessity to the hungry and the homeless; and trust that their distress will be relieved by the charitable and the good.'

A similar approach was adopted by the House of Lords in *Burmah Oil Co* v *Lord Advocate* [1965] AC 75 when Lord Upjohn stated:

> 'No man now, without risking an action against him in the courts, could pull down his neighbour's house to prevent the fire spreading to his own; he would be told that he ought to have dialled 999 and summoned the local fire brigade.'

Again, campaigners against genetically modified crops and plants who enter upon property where field trials are being conducted and pull up a proportion of the genetically modified crops in order to obtain publicity for their campaign are not entitled to rely upon the defence of necessity or public interest in an action against them for trespass: *Monsanto plc* v *Tilly* (1999) The Times 30 November. Indeed, Mummery LJ there said that the defence was only available to the individual in cases of emergency where it was necessary for the private citizen to act in the face of immediate and serious danger to life or property and the citizen acted reasonably in all the circumstances. Even in cases of emergency, trespass by the individual, in the absence of very exceptional circumstances, could not be justified as necessary or reasonable if there existed (as in the case which was then before him) a public authority responsible for the protection of the relevant interests of the public.

The defence may be invoked by a surgeon who operates in an emergency without obtaining the claimant's consent.

31.5 Limitation

Statute has intervened to impose time limits within which an action in tort must be brought against a defendant. The general rule contained in s2 of the Limitation Act 1980 (referred to as the 1980 Act) is that an action in tort cannot be brought more than six years from the date on which the claimant's cause of action accrued. The crucial issue is to identify when the cause of action accrues because it is from that date that time begins to run. In the case of torts which are actionable per se time begins to run from the date of the defendant's act which constituted the tort. But in the case of torts which are dependent upon proof of damage time begins to run from the date of damage: see, eg, *Byrne* v *Hall Pain & Foster* [1999] 2 All ER 400 (negligence action relating to surveyor's report statute-barred since action commenced more than six years after exchange of contracts for property's purchase, even though within six years of completion).

A combination of breaches of art 43 (ex art 52) of the EC Treaty and s2(1) of the European Communities Act 1972 amounts to a breach of statutory duty which is a tort governed by s2 of the 1980 Act: *R* v *Secretary of State for Transport, ex parte Factortame (No 7)* (2001) The Times 10 January.

However, this general rule is the subject of a number of exceptions. The first arises in the case of actions for damages for negligence, nuisance or breach of duty (whether the duty exists by virtue of a contract or of provision made by or under a statute or independently of any contract or any such provision) where the damages claimed by the claimant consist of or include damages in respect of personal injuries to the claimant or to any other person (Limitation Act 1980, s11(1) and note that, for this purpose, 'breach of duty' does not encompass intentional trespass to the person, *Stubbings* v *Webb* [1993] 2 WLR 120, discussed by Rogers [1993] NLJ 258). In such a case s11(4) of the 1980 Act states that the limitation period is three years from the date on which the cause of action accrued. The cause of action accrues when the claimant suffers actionable damage. This causes unfairness to the claimant in a case such as *Cartledge* v *E Jopling & Sons Ltd* [1963] AC 758, where the claimant was unaware of the fact that he had suffered damage for more than three years. To remedy this s11(4) provides the alternative that time begins to run from the date of the claimant's knowledge of the damage (see further the complex provisions which have been enacted dealing with the issue of the knowledge of the claimant in s14 of the 1980 Act). It should be noted that all that is necessary for time to run is that the claimant is aware of the injury and that it was caused by the defendant; there is no need for the claimant to be aware that the injury results from a tort on the part of the defendant: *Broadley* v *Guy Clapham & Co* [1994] 4 All ER 439; *Dobbie* v *Medway Health Authority* [1994] 1 WLR 1234. However, in *Hallam-Eames* v *Merret* (1995) The Times 25 January both these cases were considered by the Court of Appeal who warned against over-simplification of the reasoning in these two authorities. Although the plaintiff did not have to know that he had a cause of action, or that the defendant's acts could be negligent, the claimant did have to have knowledge of facts which were causally relevant to the issue of negligence: see *Forbes* v *Wandsworth Health Authority* [1996] 4 All ER 881 for a discussion of this point. So, for example, a patient whose condition deteriorates following an operation and who infers that the operation has not been a success but who has nothing to alert him to the fact that he had been injured during the operation has been found not to be fixed with knowledge by s14 of the 1980 Act: *James* v *East Dorset Health Authority* (1999) The Times 7 December. But see *Henderson* v *Temple Pier Co Ltd* [1998] 3 All ER 324 (claimant fixed with her solicitors' deficiencies).

In *Adams* v *Bracknell Forest Borough Council* [2004] 3 All ER 897 it appeared that the claimant left the defendant's school in 1988 at the age of sixteen. In November 1999 the claimant met by chance an educational psychologist who suggested to him that he might be suffering from dyslexia. In June 2002 the claimant issued proceedings alleging that the defendant had failed to provide him with a suitable education since it had neglected properly to assess his educational difficulties and to provide him with appropriate treatment. The defendant pleaded that the claim was barred under s11 Limitation Act 1980. As a preliminary issue, the county court judge decided that the claimant's date of knowledge of his condition, within s14 of the 1980 Act, was not before November 1999 and the Court of Appeal dismissed the defendant's appeal against this decision. However, the House of Lords allowed the defendant's appeal and dismissed the action. Lord Hoffmann said:

> 'In the absence of some special inhibiting factor, I should have thought that Mr Adams could reasonably have been expected to seek expert advice years ago. The congeries of symptoms ... which he said had been making his life miserable for years, which he knew to be rooted in his inability to read and write and about which had sought medical advice, would have made it almost irrational not to disclose what he felt to be the root cause. If he had done so, he would no doubt have been referred to someone with expertise in dyslexia and would have discovered that it was something which might have been treated earlier.'

Their Lordships also decided that:

1. the lack of ability to read and write could be a personal injury for the purposes of s11 of the 1980 Act;
2. there were no special reasons for exercising the discretion under s33 of the 1980 Act (see below) to disapply the limitation period.

See, too, *McDonnell* v *Congregation of Christian Brothers Trustees* [2004] 1 All ER 641 (claim for physical, emotional and sexual abuse subject to six-year time limit) and *KR* v *Bryn Alyn Community (Holdings) Ltd* [2004] 2 All ER 716 where the Court of Appeal said, amongst other things, that claims for personal injuries in respect of deliberate conduct, whether considered in the context of vicarious responsibility or not, were not caught by the provisions of s11 of the 1980 Act. It followed in that case that, in the absence of some provable allegation of systematic negligence on the part of the first defendant (the owner of the children's homes in question), its employees' deliberate abuse of children did not fall within s11 and was therefore governed by the non-extendable six-year period of limitation rather than the extendable three-year period.

The court has a discretion to allow the action to proceed even if it is commenced outside the three-year period, but the discretion must be exercised in the light of the guidelines contained in s33 of the 1980 Act. In deciding how to exercise its discretion, the court should apply the balance of prejudice test: *McGhie* v *British Telecommunications plc* (2005) 149 SJ 114. The only actions excluded from the s33 discretion are those involving the same defendant and the same cause of action as was the subject of earlier, timeous proceedings which, for whatever reason (eg, failure to serve), have ceased to exist: *Shapland* v *Palmer* [1999] 3 All ER 50.

The second exception arises where the claimant dies as a result of the tort of the defendant. In such a case, where the death occurs within three years of the accrual of the cause of action, then a fresh three-year period commences in favour of the personal representative or the dependants, running from the date of death or the date of knowledge of the death (s11(5) of the 1980 Act).

The third exception relates to a tortious act which causes latent damage to property. Here the position is governed by the Latent Damage Act 1986. Before considering this Act it is necessary to have regard to the law as it existed prior to the Act. The law prior to the Act was discussed in the case of *Pirelli General Cable Works Ltd* v *Oscar Faber & Partners* [1983] 2 AC 1. The House of Lords held that in the case of damage to property time begins to run from the date when damage occurs to the property, whether or not that damage is reasonably discoverable (for the present standing of *Pirelli* see McKendrick in '*Pirelli* Re-examined' (1991) 11 Legal Studies 326). This ruling had serious implications, particularly for purchasers of buildings, because the six-year limitation period could have elapsed before the damage was actually discovered or was even discoverable (although the problem was not confined to building cases; see, for example, *D W Moore & Co* v *Ferrier* [1988] 1 All ER 400, where it related to the negligent drafting of a restraint of trade clause by a solicitor). The Latent Damage Act 1986 essentially provides that in the case of latent damage (other than in the case of personal injury) the normal six-year period operates, with the addition of a three year period which begins to run from the date on which the claimant discovered, or ought to have discovered the damage, subject to a longstop which has the effect of barring all claims brought more than fifteen years from the date of the defendant's negligence (see further on this complex piece of legislation Stanton (1986) PN 75).

Finally, where the action is based on fraud, or the defendant has deliberately concealed any relevent fact, time does not begin to run until the claimant has or could have discovered the fraud or concealment: s32 Limitation Act 1980. It does not matter whether the concealment occurred at the time of accrual of the cause of action or subsequently; in either case time does not run until discovery or imputed discovery of the facts by the claimant: *Sheldon* v *Outhwaite (Underwriting Agencies) Ltd* [1995] 2 WLR 570.

For the purpose of extending the limitation period pursuant to s32(1)(b) of the 1980 Act, it is not necessary for the claimant to demonstrate that the fact relevant to his right of action had been deliberately concealed in any sense greater than that the commission of the act was deliberate in the sense of being intentional and that that act or omission, as the case may be, did involve a breach of duty whether or not the actor appreciated that legal consequence: *Brocklesby* v *Armitage & Guest* [2001] 1 All ER 172. This Court of Appeal decision was applied by Laddie J in *Liverpool Roman Catholic Archdiocese Trustees Incorporated* v *Goldberg* [2001] 1 All ER 182 (even if facts known to the claimant, intentional commission of breach of duty, unlikely to be discovered, creates legal fiction that they were not).

In *Cave* v *Robinson Jarvis and Rolf* [2002] 2 All ER 641 the House of Lords disapproved of the Court of Appeal's decision in *Brocklesby* v *Armitage & Guest* and overruled Laddie J's decision in *Liverpool Roman Catholic Archdiocese Trustees Incorporated* v *Goldberg*. In *Cave* the claimant alleged that the defendant solicitors had been negligent in preparing a document conferring upon him mooring rights. The defendants pleaded, inter alia, that the action was time-barred and the claimant contended that s32(2) Limitation Act 1980 applied since the allegedly negligent drafting was an intentional act and any breach of duty was unlikely to be discovered for some time. The claimant's contention was accepted at first instance and by the Court of Appeal: time had not begun to run until the alleged drafting flaw had come to light. Did s32(2) apply even where (as here) the defendant had not been aware that he had been committing a breach of duty? It did not, said their Lordships: the defendants' appeal would be allowed. As Lord Millett explained:

> 'Section 32(2) was ... enacted to cover cases where active concealment should not be required. But such cases were limited in two respects: first, the defendant must have been guilty of a deliberate commission of a breach of duty; and secondly, the circumstances must make it unlikely that the breach of duty will be discovered for some time. Given that s32(2) is (or at least may be) required to cover cases of non-disclosure rather than active concealment, the reason for limiting it to the deliberate commission of a breach of duty becomes clear. It is only where the defendant is aware of his own deliberate wrongdoing that it is appropriate to penalise him for failing to disclose it. In my opinion, s32 of the 1980 Act deprives a defendant of a limitation defence in two situations: (i) where he takes active steps to conceal his own breach of duty after he has become aware of it; and (ii) where he is guilty of deliberate wrongdoing and conceals or fails to disclose it in circumstances where it is unlikely to be discovered for some time. But it does not deprive a defendant of a limitation defence where he is charged with negligence if, being unaware of his error or that he has failed to take proper care, there has been nothing for him to disclose.'

See, too, *Williams* v *Fanshaw Porter and Hazelhurst* [2004] 2 All ER 616 (defendant solicitors made bad mistake: fact of that negligence concealed from claimant client: claimant entitled to invoke s32(1)(b) of 1980 Act).

Other provisions of the 1980 Act which are of particular relevance include s10 (special time limit for claiming contributions under s1 of the Civil Liability (Contribution) Act 1978), s11A (actions under the Consumer Protection Act 1987 in respect of defective products), ss12 and 13 (special time limit for actions under Fatal Accidents legislation), s14A (special time limit for negligence actions where facts relevant to cause of action are not known at date of accrual), s14B (overriding time limit for negligence actions not involving personal injuries), s28 (extension of limitation period in case of disability) and s28A (extension for cases where the limitation period is the period under s14A(4)(b)).

32

Torts to Chattels

32.1 Introduction

In this Chapter we shall discuss certain specific torts which exist to protect an owner of goods, or some other person having an interest in goods, from unlawful interferences with those goods. It must be remembered that, quite apart from these specific torts, a wrongful act towards goods can produce liability under one of the more general torts, such as negligence or nuisance. In what follows, however, only those torts which are peculiar to goods will be examined.

All of these specific torts have a long history, and by the mid-twentieth century it had become clear that they stood in urgent need of reform. In 1971 the Law Reform Committee (*Conversion and Detinue*, Cmnd 4774) reported, recommending

463

radical modernisation and clarification of the law. But the legislation which followed – the Torts (Interference with Goods) Act 1977 – fell short of the Committee's proposals and has some unsatisfactory aspects. The result is a continuing state of doubt in several areas.

Despite their antiquity, the chattel torts have proved readily adaptable to modern circumstances. In recent case law, they have been invoked (with varying success) as a means of recovering commercial commodities detained by industrial action (*Howard E Perry Ltd* v *British Railways Board* [1980] 1 WLR 1375; *Harold Stephen Ltd* v *Post Office* [1977] 1 WLR 1172) or pornographic literature from the police (*Roandale* v *Metropolitan Police Commissioner* [1979] Crim LR 254 CA. The remedies provided by the 1977 Act were even invoked by the Secretary of State for Defence in his action against the *Guardian* newspaper to recover photocopied documents 'leaked' by Sarah Tisdall (*Secretary of State for Defence* v *Guardian Newspapers* [1985] AC 339, affirming [1984] Ch 156).

32.2 Common law ingredients of the chattel torts

Until 1978, the law recognised four main torts which could be committed against the personal property of another. These were:

1. Trespass to goods
2. Conversion
3. Detinue
4. The special action on the case for damage to a reversionary interest.

Each tort had its individual sphere of operation, although in practice categories (1) to (3) would substantially overlap. With the exception of detinue – which, as we shall see, was abolished by the 1977 Act – all of these torts survive unaltered today.

32.3 Trespass

Trespass to goods consists of any unauthorised interference with the personal property of another, provided that the act constituting the interference is immediate and direct. Thus, to deliberately damage or destroy a chattel (for example by setting fire to it, or hitting it with a hammer) would be a trespass. The classic illustration is given in *Fouldes* v *Willoughby* (1841) 8 M & W 540 where it was held that scratching the panel of a coach would be a trespass. Trespass does not lie for indirectly caused damage, such as the laying of bait for animals (*Hutchins* v *Maughan* [1947] VLR 131) and for this reason it has occasionally been doubted whether there can be vicarious liability for trespass, although on balance it seems likely that there may.

To use goods without the owner's permission, even without harming them, seems to constitute a trespass (*Penfolds Wines Pty Ltd* v *Elliott* (1946) 74 CLR 204);

so does any unauthorised removal of goods, again whether this produces any harm or permanent deprivation or not (*Kirk* v *Gregory* (1876) 1 Ex D 55). If the taking is deliberate, it is no defence to show that the taker honestly believed the goods to be his (*Wilson* v *Lombank Ltd* [1963] 1 WLR 1294), nor is it a defence to show that one removed the goods for their own safety, unless this was actually reasonably necessary for their protection (*Kirk* v *Gregory* (above)). There is, nevertheless, some doubt as to whether all trespass is actionable per se, or whether certain types of trespass to goods, at least, require proof of special damage. It seems clear that a deliberate taking, touching or misuse can give rise to an action in trespass without proof of damage (see *Penfolds Wines Pty Ltd* v *Elliott* (above); *Kirk* v *Gregory* (above) and *Leitch & Co* v *Leydon* 1931 SC (HL) 1). On the other hand, New Zealand authority suggests that, if the trespass is merely inadvertent, actual damage must be proved (*Everitt* v *Martin* [1953] NZLR 298). In England, the question may no longer be significant because after *Letang* v *Cooper* [1965] 1 QB 232 it is possible that trespass to goods, like trespass to the person, is confined to deliberate, intentional interference. *Wilson* v *Pringle* [1987] QB 237, in indicating that, while there need be no actual intent to harm the victim, the touching must be intentional and 'hostile' could have been understood as suggesting that actual harm is not necessary to an action for trespass to the person (and, if so, the same rule may apply to trespass to goods) but *Wilson* must now be seen in the light of the doubt cast upon its correctness by Lord Goff in *Re F (Mental Patient: Sterilisation)* [1990] 2 AC 1, 73 (see Chapter 24, section 24.2).

Certainly a defendant who acts neither deliberately nor negligently cannot be sued for trespass to goods (*National Coal Board* v *Evans* [1951] 2 KB 861). Contributory negligence is no defence in proceedings founded on intentional trespass to goods (s11(1) Torts (Interference with Goods) Act 1977). The use of the word 'intentional' in this section suggests that the law may still recognise other forms of trespass to goods, such as inadvertent trespass.

Generally speaking, co-ownership is no defence to any action founded on trespass to goods (s10 Torts (Interference with Goods) Act 1977).

The tort was considered by the Court of Appeal in a modern setting in *Vine* v *Waltham Forest London Borough Council* [2000] 4 All ER 169. Feeling unwell and distressed, the claimant parked her car in one of two bays on privately owned land. From her driving seat, her view of a warning notice ('No parking … vehicle left unattended … liable to be clamped …') was obscured by a Range Rover in the other bay. She left her car for a few minutes without seeing the notice and on her return she found that it had been clamped, in effect by the defendants. In order to recover her car the claimant paid the fine specified in the notice (£105). She brought an action alleging that the defendants had wrongfully immobilised and detained her vehicle. Her appeal against the recorder's (trial judge's) dismissal of her claim was successful and, by way of damages, she was awarded the amount of the fine plus the credit card charge and interest and £5 for loss of use of the car. Roch LJ said:

'The act of clamping the wheel of another person's car, even when that car is trespassing, is an act of trespass to that other person's property unless it can be shown that the owner of the car has consented to, or willingly assumed, the risk of his car being clamped. To show that the car owner consented or willingly assumed the risk of his car being clamped, it has to be established that the car owner was aware of the consequences of his parking his car so that it trespassed on the land of another. That will be done by establishing that the car owner saw and understood the significance of a warning notice or notices that cars in that place without permission were liable to be clamped. ... The recorder made a clear finding of fact that the appellant did not see the sign.'

32.4 Conversion

Conversion was defined by Atkin J in *Lancashire & Yorkshire Ry* v *MacNicoll* (1919) 88 LJKB 601 as:

'... dealing with goods in a manner inconsistent with the rights of the true owner ... provided ... there is an intention on the part of the defendant in so doing to deny the owner's right or to assert a right which is inconsistent with the owner's right.'

A more modern, but similar, definition was given by Lord Templeman in the Privy Council case of *Maynegrain Pty Ltd* v *Campafina Bank* [1984] 1 NSWLR 258, when he said that '... conversion is committed whenever one person performs a positive wrongful act of dealing with goods in a manner inconsistent with the rights of the owner'.

In one sense, conversion is a tort of strict liability: provided the defendant actually intends to deal with the goods in a manner which in fact interferes with (or is inconsistent with) the owner's rights, the mere fact that the defendant does not intend to violate these rights is no defence. Indeed, the defendant may be totally and blamelessly ignorant of the owner's interest in the goods, or even of his existence, and still be liable for conversion. Thus the innocent purchaser of goods from a thief, who has stolen them from the owner without the purchaser's knowledge, commits a conversion against the true owner by taking delivery of it (*Jerome* v *Bentley* [1952] 2 All ER 114; *Moorgate Mercantile Co* v *Twitchings* [1977] AC 890). Other examples of conversion include deliberate destruction (but probably not mere deliberate damage); the wrongful taking of goods if accompanied by an exercise of the rights of ownership; wrongful detention of goods, likewise if contradicting the rights of the owner (see *Howard E Perry Ltd* v *British Railways Board* (above)); misuse of goods if severe enough to amount to a denial or violation of the owner's title; and the unauthorised sale of another's goods, as in *Willis* v *British Car Auctions* [1978] 1 WLR 438 (where an auctioneer who sold a car at the request of a person whom he honestly believed to be the owner was held liable in conversion to the real owner). The receipt of goods under an unauthorised pledge is also a conversion (s11(2) Torts (Interference with Goods) Act 1977) but by s11(3) of the 1977 Act the mere verbal denial of an owner's title, unaccompanied by some positive conduct actually interfering with that title, is not (cf the position before the Act, as discussed in *Oakley v Lyster* [1931] 1 KB 148). There cannot be converstion of a chose in action: *OBG Ltd v Allan* (2005) The Times 24 February.

Conversion may even be committed by a defendant who is acting honestly in what he conceives to be the owner's best interests. In *Hiort v Bott* (1874) LR 9 Ex 86 the defendant (to whom the claimant's goods had been mistakenly delivered) indorsed the delivery order over to X (the claimant's supposed agent), who used it to misappropriate the goods to his advantage. It was held that, although the defendant acted solely in order to facilitate the return of the goods to the claimant, he was guilty of conversion. The result might have been otherwise, however, if the defendant had actually been put in possession of the goods against his will as an involuntary bailee: in such a case, the mere handing of them over to a third party whom the defendant believes to be the owner's agent will not be conversion unless, in delivering the goods, the defendant has acted without reasonable care (*Elvin and Powell Ltd v Plummer Roddis Ltd* (1933) 50 TLR 158).

Conversion can also be committed by the deliberate exposure of the goods to the risk of loss or destruction. In *Moorgate Mercantile Co v Finch* [1962] 1 QB 701 the use of a hired car for smuggling led to the confiscation of the car by the customs authorities. It was held that the smugglers were guilty of conversion. In *Garnham, Harris & Elton v Ellis* [1967] 2 All ER 940 a haulage company engaged to carry a load of copper wire wrongfully subcontracted the job to a second firm without checking their credentials, and the wire was stolen. It was held that the first carriers were guilty of conversion. Conversion can also be committed by a defendant who candidly acknowledges the true owner's title but refuses to surrender up his goods on the ground that he fears undesirable industrial or other consequences if he does so *(Howard E Perry Ltd v British Railways Board* (above) and see *Redler Grain Silos Ltd v BICC Ltd* [1982] 1 Lloyds Rep 435). Conversion may also be committed, in appropriate circumstances, by a defendant who was not in possession of the goods at the material time (*Bryanston Leasings v Principality Finance* [1977] RTR 45).

As with trespass to goods, contributory negligence is no defence to proceedings founded on conversion (s11(1) Torts (Interference with Goods) Act 1977). No action for conversion will lie, however, where the claimant or his agent actually consented to the performance of the acts in question *(Maynegrain Pty Ltd v Campafina Bank* (above)).

Generally speaking, co-ownership is no defence to an action founded on conversion (s10 Torts (Interference with Goods) Act 1977).

Successive conversion

In *Kuwait Airways Corp v Iraqi Airways Co (No 3)* [2002] 3 All ER 209 the House of Lords heard that during the invasion and occupation of Kuwait, the Iraqi forces seized ten of the claimant's (KAC's) aircraft and flew them to Iraq. The Iraq Revolutionary Command Council (RCC) dissolved the claimant and transferred all its property to the state-owned defendant (IAC). Before military action began, the claimant sued for the return of the aircraft, or payment of their value, and damages. In the course of the war, four aircraft ('the Mosul Four') were destroyed by coalition bombing. The other six ('the Iran Six') were evacuated to Iran and eventually returned to Kuwait on payment of a substantial sum by the claimant to the Iran Government for their safekeeping. Their Lordships held (Lord Scott of Foscote dissenting) that the claim in respect of the Mosul Four would fail since, on the facts, the claimant had been unable to satisfy the Iraqi law 'but for' test as to loss or damage. However, as to the Iran Six, where the aircraft were recovered largely undamaged, the Iraqi test was no more stringent than the requirements of English law. Accordingly, in principle, the damages awarded should include the amount paid to the Government of Iran, the reasonable costs of overhauling and repairing the aircraft on their return and the reasonable costs of chartering substitute aircraft and making good any loss of profits. Lord Nicholls of Birkenhead said:

'... in the present proceedings the court has to apply the so-called double actionability rule, as generally understood since the decision of the House in *Chaplin* v *Boys* [1969] 2 All ER 1085. The rule is that, in order to be actionable here, the acts done abroad must satisfy both limbs of a dual test. The acts must be such that, if done in England, they would be tortious. Additionally, the acts must be civilly actionable under the law of the country where they occurred ... In general, the basic features of the tort [of conversion] are threefold. First, the defendant's conduct was inconsistent with the rights of the owner (or other person entitled to possession). Second, the conduct was deliberate, not accidental. Third, the conduct was so extensive an encroachment on the rights of the owner as to exclude him from use and possession of the goods. The contrast is with lesser acts of interference. If these cause damage they may give rise to claims for trespass or in negligence, but they do not constitute conversion ... Here, on and after [RCC's dissolution of KAC], IAC was in possession and control of the ten aircraft. This possession was adverse to KAC. IAC believed the aircraft were now its property, just as much as the other aircraft in its fleet, and it acted accordingly. It intended to keep the goods as its own. It treated them as its own. It made such use of them as it could in the prevailing circumstances, although this was very limited because of the hostilities. In so conducting itself IAC was asserting rights inconsistent with KAC's rights as owner ... IAC's acts would have been tortious if done in this country.'

In *Marcq* v *Christie Manson & Woods Ltd* [2003] 3 All ER 561 it appeared that the claimant's painting by a Dutch master was stolen in 1997: its theft was reported to the police and entered on the Art Loss Register. In 1997 a Mr Schünemann gave the painting to the defendant auctioneer to sell at auction. The painting did not sell: the defendant returned it to Mr Schünemann. The trial judge struck out the claimant's proceedings against the defendant for conversion and breach of duty as bailee: see [2002] 4 All ER 1005. The claimant appealed unsuccessfully against this decision. Tuckey LJ said:

'I agree that an auctioneer who receives goods from their apparent owner and simply redelivers them to him when they are unsold is not liable in conversion provided he has acted in good faith and without knowledge of any adverse claim to them. ... The auctioneer intends to sell and if he does so will incur liability if he delivers the goods to the buyer. But his intention does not make him liable; it is what he does in relation to the goods which determines liability. Mere receipt of the goods does not amount to conversion. In receiving the goods from and redelivering them to their apparent owner the auctioneer in such a case has only acted ministerially. He has in the event merely changed the position of the goods and not the property in them. This I think is a just conclusion … If of course there are circumstances which should put the agent on inquiry then a positive case of negligence on conventional grounds can be alleged. But no such case is or, on the assumed facts, could be made here. I do not accept that the law of bailment or something akin to it can be stretched so as to found a duty of the kind alleged. Quite apart from anything else the law of conversion, which attaches strict liability in certain circumstances, has been developed over the years to provide the remedy, if any, in cases such as these. Now to invoke different principles from the law of bailment is not justified. Auctioneers … must of course take care to avoid dealing with works of doubtful title since they will be strictly liable if they sell on behalf of anyone other than the true owner, but that is not a policy reason for making them liable when they do not sell and simply return the goods to their client in good faith and without notice of the true owner's interest.'

32.5 Detinue

Detinue could be committed in two ways. First, by wrongfully refusing to deliver goods to the person entitled to them *(Alicia Hosiery Ltd* v *Brown Shipley & Co Ltd* [1970] 1 QB 195). Secondly, detinue could be committed by a bailee's negligently losing the goods in breach of his duty of care under the bailment (*Goodman* v *Boycott* (1862) 2 B & S 1; *Houghland* v *R R Low (Luxury Coaches) Ltd* [1962] 1 QB 694). In the second case, once the goods were shown to have been lost, the burden of proving that he had taken reasonable care rested on the bailee (*Houghland* v *R R Low (Luxury Coaches) Ltd* (above)). The tort of detinue is now abolished in England (see further section 32.7).

32.6 The reversionary action

As will be seen later (see section 32.8), none of the foregoing actions will lie if the claimant had, at the time of the wrongful interference, neither possession of the goods nor the immediate right to their possession. Such a right would be lacking, for example, if A had bailed goods to B for a finite period during which a third party – C – wrongfully damaged, destroyed or misappropriated those goods. To repair this deficiency and to allow the owner with merely a postponed right of possession to sue, the courts devised a special action on the case. The leading authority is *Mears* v *LSW Ry* (1862) 11 CB (NS) 850, where the lessor of a barge which was damaged by a third party during the term of the hirer's possession was held entitled to recover damages from that third party, even though his own right of possession was deferred, and not immediate, at the time of the damage. In order to invoke this special action, however, the claimant must prove some lasting impairment of his reversionary interest: either enduring damage or, in the case of loss of the goods, the absence of any reasonable prospect of their being recovered (*Moukataff* v *BOAC* [1967] 1 Lloyd's Rep 396). Further, the claimant's loss must be suffered in his capacity as reversionary owner and not in some other capacity *(Candlewood Navigation Corp* v *Mitsui OSK Lines, The Mineral Transporter* [1986] AC 1).

32.7 Redistribution of tort liability by statute

The Torts (Interference with Goods) Act 1977 made certain radical changes to the substantive content of the chattel torts. The most important was the abolition of detinue (s2(1)). In order to preserve that aspect of detinue which arose from the negligent loss of a bailor's goods, s2(2) of the 1977 Act now provides that an action in *conversion* lies against a bailee for the loss or destruction of goods which the bailee had allowed to happen in breach of his duty to his bailor. Conversion is therefore expanded to include a form of wrong which it did not include at common law. No statutory provision is made to accommodate within the tort of conversion the other species of detinue discussed above, concerning the wrongful withholding or detention of goods. In *Howard E Perry* v *British Railways Board* (above) Megarry VC held, however, that all cases of detinue were in any event also cases of conversion at common law; and therefore that the abolition of detinue has not reduced the area of wrongful conduct to goods because such detention, formerly actionable in detinue, always gives rise to an action in conversion. Some authors (see Palmer (1981) 44 MLR 87) regard this equation as questionable, however, and point to the statement of Mansfield CJ in *Morris* v *Pugh* (1761) 4 Burr 1241, 1243 that a wrongful detention was merely *evidence* of conversion.

Conversion and trespass survive largely unimpaired as independent torts, conversion being (as we have seen) substantially expanded by s2(1) of the 1977 Act. These torts are, nevertheless, affected by the 1977 Act in three main ways, as follows.

General collective notion of 'wrongful interference with goods'

The first impact of the Act is that conversion and trespass are grouped, along with all the other torts to chattels, within the general, collective concept of 'wrongful interference' or 'wrongful interference with goods'. In creating this new collective concept, the Act does not create a new substantive tort, nor – apart from detinue – does it abolish the old torts. Rather, the Act merely creates a 'hold-all' phrase in order to group the pre-existing torts together for the purpose of certain general, mainly procedural, reforms. These include the statutory definition of the remedies which a court can order in cases of wrongful interference (ss3, 4), the principles whereby a claimant's title to goods may be extinguished upon his/her being awarded damages in a wrongful interference action based on the goods' full value (s5), the rules against double liability (s7), the statutory reversal of the old principle which prevented certain defendants in wrongful interference actions from pleading a superior title in a third party (s8) and special rules for concurrent actions (s9) (most of these procedural reforms will be discussed later in the Chapter). By s1 of the 1977 Act 'wrongful interference' as used elsewhere in the Act means conversion, trespass, negligence so far as it results in damage to goods or to an interest in goods, and any other tort (except for detinue, which is abolished) so far as it results in such damage. This definition would include the special action on the case for damage to a reversionary interest (see section 32.6).

Specific rules affecting individual chattel torts

Certain individual torts are also made subject to specialised substantive reforms by the Act. Examples are the ban on contributory negligence as a defence in conversion or intentional trespass actions (s11(1)), the special provisions whereby an improver of goods might be awarded an allowance based on the extent of his improvement (s6) and the new section which deals with actions as between co-owners of goods (s10).

New rules on disposal of uncollected goods

Finally, the Act introduces new rules as to the disposal of uncollected goods (ss12, 13 and Sch 1). These will not be separately discussed.

32.8 Title to sue

Before proceeding to a detailed examination of the 1977 Act, however, we shall look at the qualification which a claimant must demonstrate, in his relationship with the goods, in order to sue for trespass or conversion. What precise type of interest entitles an aggrieved party to bring these actions?

Trespass

Anyone who was in possession of the goods at the time when the tort was committed can sue in trespass, whether or not he is the owner and even though he may have come by his possession illegally: the law appears to consider it best to protect all possession, however obtained, from the incursions of unauthorised intruders (*Parker* v *British Airways Board* [1982] 1 QB 1004, per Donaldson MR, but cf *Thackwell* v *Barclays Bank plc* [1986] 3 All ER 676, 689, per Hutchinson J).

A person may also sue in trespass if he lacks possession but has an immediate right of possession to the goods at the time of the wrong, provided in this case that the act complained of is also a trespass against the party actually in possession, and thus occurs without that party's consent *(Penfolds Wines Pty Ltd v Elliott* (above)). Occasionally, the latter rule is artificially avoided by holding that a claimant who is not in actual custody of the goods nevertheless has legal possession of them for the purpose of enabling him to sustain an action in trespass against a third party who unjustifiably seizes the goods without his consent (see, for example, *Wilson v Lombank Ltd* (above)).

A person who lacks both possession and an immediate right of possession cannot sue in trespass. Thus even an owner of goods may be debarred from suing in trespass if he lacks any immediate possessory entitlement to the goods.

Conversion

As with trespass, the mere fact of ownership of goods will not necessarily qualify their owner to sue in conversion. The claimant must show either that he had possession of the goods at the material time, or that he had an immediate right of possession *(Marquis of Bute v Barclays Bank* [1955] 1 QB 202; see also *Surrey Asset Finance Ltd v National Westminster Bank plc* (2000) The Times 30 November (conversion claim failed since claimant unable to establish immediate right to possession of cheque prior to presentation)).

The crucial significance of possession may also be see in *Costello v Chief Constable of Derbyshire Constabulary* [2001] 3 All ER 150. Believing that it had been stolen, a police officer seized a car while it was in the claimant's possession. The Police and Criminal Evidence Act 1984 enabled the police to retain the car for certain purposes but, after those purposes had been exhausted, they continued to keep it. Mr Costello claimed the return of the car and damages for wrong detention. The trial judge found that the claimant knew that the car had been stolen and, for this reason, he dismissed the claim. No criminal proceedings were brought against the claimant. The Court of Appeal allowed the claimant's appeal since, subject to any statutory provision to the contrary, the claimant had a possessory title to the car which was good against the world except anyone who could establish a better title. Here, the true owner of the car was unknown. Lightman J said:

> 'In my view on a review of the authorities, (save so far as legislation otherwise provides) as a matter of principle and authority possession ... is entitled to the same legal protection whether or not it has been obtained lawfully or by theft or by other unlawful means. It vests in the possessor a possessory title which is good against the world save as against anyone setting up or claiming under a better title. In the case of a theft the title is frail, and of likely limited value (see eg *Rowland v Divall* [1923] 2 KB 500), but none the less remains a title to which the law affords protection.'

Possession

The concept of possession is largely self-explanatory. Possession of the goods is the interest most commonly relied upon by finders of lost property, who wish to enforce their right to retain it against some other person who is not the real owner (see, for example, *Parker* v *British Airways Board* [1982] QB 1004, discussed at section 32.14). It should be noted, however, that in cases where the defendant in a wrongful interference action can actually identify a specific third party as having a better right to the goods than the claimant who is relying on his mere possession, that defendant is entitled to have the third party joined as a party to the proceedings (see s8 of the 1977 Act, discussed at section 32.9).

The immediate right to possession

Even if he is the owner, a claimant whose right to possession of the goods is suspended at the time of the alleged wrong cannot sue in conversion. This has been recognised since *Gordon* v *Harper* (1796) 7 Term Rep 9, where a landlord of premises was held unable to sue a third party in conversion for the third party's wrongful seizure of the furniture during the lease, because it was the tenant, not the landlord, who was in possession and had the continuing right to possession at the material time: the landlord's right to assume possession was merely deferred or suspended, and thus the tenant was the proper claimant in this case.

It does not necessarily follow, however, that a bailor of goods can never sue in conversion. First, the bailment may be 'at will', entitling the bailor to repossess the goods from the bailee whenever he wishes. In such a case, the bailor clearly enjoys an immediate right to possession, and thus has the necessary qualification to sue in conversion (see, for example, *Manders* v *Williams* (1849) 4 Ex 339). Secondly, a bailee with an initially secure period of possession (such as a hirer for a 12-month term) may break the terms of the bailment in some particularly fundamental manner (called a 'deviation'). By so doing, the bailee will forfeit his continued right of possession of the goods and will cause the bailor's immediate right of possession to revive, thereby entitling the bailor to bring conversion proceedings not only against the bailee himself but against any third party who thereafter converts the goods. Further, the mere fact that the terms of the bailment set out certain specific events upon which the bailor's right of possession is to revive does not mean that that statement of events is necessarily exhaustive: there may still be other, unspecified forms of fundamental breach which can resurrect the bailor's immediate right to possession (*Union Transport Finance* v *British Car Auctions Ltd* [1978] 2 All ER 385).

According to a majority of the Court of Appeal in *International Factors* v *Rodriguez* [1979] 1 QB 351, a claimant whose action in conversion is based on a mere immediate right to possession must show that this springs from some *proprietary* right in the goods: a purely *contractual* right of possession would be insufficient. Whereas this was undoubtedly the rule for actions in detinue (*Jarvis* v *Williams* [1955] 1 WLR 71), however, there is some doubt as to whether it is an accurate expression of the law in relation to conversion (cf *Winkworth* v *Christie, Manson & Woods* [1980] Ch 496, 499, per Slade J and the New Zealand case of *Harris* v *Lombard (New Zealand) Ltd* [1974] 2 NZLR 161).

More recently, Lord Brandon has stated that a purely equitable interest in goods would not be sufficient to ground an action in negligence for loss of or damage to those goods (*The Aliakmon* [1986] AC 785, 812). In his Lordship's view, the equitable owner would have to join the legal owner as a party to the action in order to be able to sue. If that is the rule for actions in negligence, it is likely that a similar principle would be held to apply to an action for conversion. This may, in turn, suggest that a purely equitable interest would not qualify as the necessary 'proprietary right' for the purposes of the principle stated in *International Factors Ltd* v *Rodriguez* (above). However, it should be noted that *International Factors Ltd* v *Rodriguez* itself was a case where the claimant had an equitable interest grounding an immediate right to possession and there the claim was successful; moreover, the Privy Council appeared willing to countenance an action in conversion in *Maynegrain Pty Ltd* v *Campafina Bank* (above), where the claimant's interest in the relevant goods was solely that of an equitable pledgee. From these decisions it seems relatively clear that, if it *is* necessary for a claimant's immediate right of possession to arise from some proprietary right in the goods before he/she can sue in conversion, a purely equitable right would suffice. A statement by Lord Brandon elsewhere in his judgment in *The Aliakmon* (above) appears to support this view and to indicate that when Lord Brandon spoke earlier of the insufficiency of a mere equitable property interest he was assuming a case where the claimant had no current possessory right to the goods. Lord Brandon said that:

> 'There may be cases where a person who is the equitable owner of certain goods has also a possessory title to them. In such a case he is entitled, by virtue of his possessory title rather than his equitable ownership, to sue in tort for negligence ...'

In *MCC Proceeds Inc* v *Lehman Bros International (Europe)* [1998] 4 All ER 675 the Court of Appeal said that an equitable owner has no title at common law to sue in conversion unless he can show that he had actual possession or an immediate right to possession of the goods claimed. Mummery LJ distinguished *Healey* v *Healey* [1915] 1 KB 938 and *International Factors Ltd* v *Rodriguez*, above, since there the respective claimants had been in actual possession of the chattels or had an immediate right to possession of the cheques.

32.9 Pleading jus tertii

At common law there were certain situations where a defendant in an action for wrongful interference with goods was precluded by law from asserting that someone other than the claimant had a better right to the goods. This meant in turn that the claimant was able to recover the full value of the goods – or the full cost of repairing the damage to them – even though he/she was not the owner.

The first such situation arose when a bailor was suing his/her bailee; the original delivery of possession to the bailee was deemed to give rise to an implied undertaking on the bailee's part not to deny the bailor's title. This obligation was sometimes described as an estoppel on the bailee's part, precluding him/her from pleading 'jus tertii' (the right of a third party *Biddle* v *Bond* (1865) 6 B & S 225). It did not apply when the bailee had been authorised by the real owner to defend the action on his behalf or where the real owner had actually demanded the return of the goods; moreover, in difficult cases the bailee could invoke the interpleader process and drop out of the dispute, but only when an actual demand by a third party had been made on him. If the bailor was not in fact the owner and recovered the full value of the goods from the bailee under this principle, he/she held the residue of that value on trust for the true owner after deduction of the value of the bailor's own interest.

The second situation arose when goods were damaged, destroyed or misappropriated, while in the possession of a bailee or other possessor, as a result of the wrongdoing of a third party. The classic case was *The Winkfield* [1902] P 42, where the Postmaster-General of Natal was held entitled to recover the full value of letters and mail packets destroyed through the negligent sinking of one of his vessels, even though he did not own those letters and packets and suffered no financial loss by virtue of their destruction. The view adopted by the Court of Appeal was that, in the absence of the true owners, possession counted as title. Of course, the possessor in a case like *The Winkfield* held the residue of the proceeds on trust for the real owner after deduction of his/her own limited interest.

These common law examples of 'extra-compensatory' damages proved unsatisfactory and s8 of the 1977 Act appears to have been designed to abolish them. Section 8(1) now provides that a defendant in proceedings for wrongful interference *shall*, contrary to the former position, be entitled to show that someone other than the claimant has a better right to the goods than the claimant, and that the old 'jus tertii' rule is therefore abolished. The remainder of s8 is directed towards enabling the defendant in such a case to have the real owner (or other third party enjoying a superior interest in the goods) involved in the proceedings, so that the court can share out all the respective interests in one single piece of litigation. It has recently been held in *De Franco* v *Commissioner of Police of the Metropolis* (1987) The Times 8 May that s8(1) entitles the defendant to have joined in the proceedings a third party who did have an interest in the goods at the time of the wrongful interference with the goods, but has ceased to enjoy any such interest by the time of the litigation.

32.10 Double liability

Section 8 (above) is designed to operate in conjunction with s7 of the 1977 Act. By this, the court is obliged to give such relief as will avoid double liability on the part of the wrongdoer in any proceedings to which two or more claimants are parties (s7(2)). The court will achieve this result by apportioning the overall value of the goods (or the cost of their repair in a case of damage) among the various claimants according to their respective interests. 'Double liability' is defined for this purpose in s7(1). Special provision is needed, however, when only *one* claimant has appeared in the original proceedings. An example would be the case of a defendant who has paid full damages in conversion to the current possessor of the goods, having been unable at the time of those proceedings to identify any third party as being the true proprietor thereof. In certain circumstances, the true owner might subsequently appear and recover a second set of full damages from the defendant, who would then be doubly liable. Sections 7(3) and (4) attempt to deal with such situations. By s7(3), upon satisfaction, in whole or in part, of any claim for an amount exceeding that which would be recoverable if the rule against double liability applied, the claimant is liable to account over to the other person who has a right to claim, to such an extent as will avoid double liability. By s7(4) where, as the result of enforcement of a double liability, any claimant is unjustly enriched to any extent, he shall be liable to reimburse the wrongdoer to that extent. An illustration of the interaction of those provisions is provided by the special statutory example attached to s7(4):

> 'For example, if a converter of goods pays damages first to a finder of the goods, and then to the true owner, the finder is unjustly enriched unless he accounts over to the true owner under subsection (3); and then the true owner is unjustly enriched and becomes liable to reimburse the converter of the goods.'

32.11 Improvement to goods

Although it is now well established that the claimant in an action for trespass or conversion can normally recover as damages no more than his actual loss (*Bryanston Leasings Ltd* v *Principality Finance* [1977] RTR 45; *Butler* v *The Egg Board* (1966) 114 CLR 185), in cases of conversion this measure would often be equivalent to the full value of the goods. Assessment of their value could, however, give rise to difficulty if the defendant had expended money in improving the goods before the action for conversion was commenced against him. The difficulty could be avoided if the act of improvement occurred after the defendant had converted the goods because normally the value for the purposes of liability in conversion was the value at the date of conversion. Even when the improvement preceded the conversion, however, the courts began to allow the defendant to deduct from the value of the goods at the date of conversion an allowance to represent the extent to which he had improved them. The classic illustration of this common law development is *Munro* v *Willmott* [1949] 1 KB 295). The claimant was given a temporary licence by the defendant to leave her car in his yard. The claimant then disappeared and, some years later, the defendant decided that he wished to convert his yard into a garage. Being unable to get in touch with the claimant, he decided that the best thing to do was to do the car up and sell it. This is what he did and he spent £85 doing the car up. Before the defendant did the car up it was worth £20, but he sold it for £100. The claimant eventually turned up and sued the defendant for conversion of her car.

The defendant was held liable. The car was worth £120 at the date of judgment, but Lynskey J only awarded the claimant damages of £35, because he granted the defendant an allowance of £85 for the cost of the improvements which he had made to the car (see too *Greenwood* v *Bennett* [1973] QB 195).

An attempt to clarify the common law position has now been made by statute. Unfortunately, the statute is confined to those improvers who have improved the goods 'in the mistaken but honest belief' that the goods belonged to them, which would exclude a defendant in a position like that of the improver in *Munro* v *Willmott*. According to s6(1) of the 1977 Act, if proceedings for wrongful interference are brought against an innocent improver as described above, an allowance shall be made in the resultant award of damages 'for the extent to which, at the time as at which the goods fall to be valued in assessing damages, the value of the goods is attributable to the improvement'. Similar provisions exist to deal with the consequential problems which can arise when a defendant has bought improved goods in good faith from an innocent improver, or as part of a chain of purchasers which includes an innocent improver (ss6(2)–(4)).

Academic opinion is divided as to whether s6 of the 1977 Act abolishes the somewhat wider common law power to award an allowance to an improver, as acknowledged in cases like *Munro* v *Willmott* (above). A recent decision has now indicated that the old common law allowance (which was not limited to 'innocent' improvers) has survived s6 and now co-exists alongside the narrower statutory allowance (*Highland Leasing* v *Paul Field* [1985] CLY 3224).

32.12 Forms of judgment

Section 3(2) of the 1977 Act sets out the various forms of relief which a court may award, in proceedings for wrongful interference with goods, against a person who is in possession or control of those goods. These categories are an order for delivery of the goods and for payment of any consequential damages; or an order for delivery of the goods but giving the defendant the alternative of paying damages by reference to the value of the goods, together, in either alternative, with payment of any consequential damages; or damages.

A court may award damages under the last of these provisions even though the defendant has returned the goods to the claimant or disposed of them to a third party at the time of the judgment, so long as the defendant had actually been in possession or control of the goods at the time when the proceedings were commenced *(Hillesden Securities* v *Ryjack* [1983] 1 WLR 959). Relief can, however, be given only under one of the three foregoing categories of relief. Relief under the first category is at the discretion of the court (s3(3)(b)), whereas it is a matter for the claimant to choose between the second and third categories (s3(3)(b)). Consequential provisions are contained in s3(4)–3(8) of the 1977 Act, and s4 of the Act makes broadly equivalent provision as to the forms of relief available in interlocutory proceedings for wrongful interference.

32.13 Effect of judgment on title to goods

In any case of wrongful interference in which the damages awarded to the claimant are (or would fall to be) assessed according to the whole of his interest in the goods, once the defendant pays those damages or settles the claim (as defined by s5(2)) the claimant's title to these goods is extinguished (s5(1)). In other words, the payment of damages based on the value of the goods makes the defendant the owner and expunges the claimant's ownership. A relatively unimportant exception to this principle is created by s5(3), while s5(4) extends broadly the same general rule to cases where a claimant accounts over to a third party under s7(3) of the Act (see section 32.10). The extinction of the claimant's title on payment of full damages can be displaced by any agreement between the parties, and must take effect subject to any relevant court order (s5(5)).

32.14 Title to lost goods

An owner of goods who loses them remains, of course, their owner and can always (subject to the Limitation Act) recover them from a finder or an occupier on whose land the goods were lost (*Moffatt* v *Kazana* [1969] 2 WLR 71). In cases where the true owner does not reappear to claim his property, however, the normal principle is that a finder who has reduced the goods into his possession has a right to them against the whole world except the real owner. Thus in *Armory* v *Delamirie* (1721) 1 Stra 505 a chimney sweep's boy who had found a jewel was held entitled to recover it (or damages for its value) from a jeweller to whom he handed it for valuation, and who had refused to return it to him.

This principle is, however, based upon the assumption that the finder has been the first person to reduce the goods into his possession. If that is so, the old rule enunciated in *The Winkfield* (above) – that possession counts as title – operates in his favour, allowing him to defend his possession against any third party interloper. Nor will the interloper be entitled to avail himself/herself of s8 of the 1977 Act (see section 32.9) in this situation because we are assuming that the real owner remains unidentified. In certain cases, however, someone other than the finder will already have obtained an earlier or 'supervening' possession of the goods when the finder assumes control of them. In such a case, it is that other party, and not the finder, who has the right to retain the goods against everyone but the true owner.

There are two main situations in which supervening possession of this type can arise. The first is where an employee finds goods in the course of his employment, that is where his employment is the cause and not merely the occasion of his finding of the goods. In such a case, the finder's possession is deemed to be that of his employer and the finder gets no possessory right to the goods against his employer (see *Parker* v *British Airways Board* (above) per Donaldson MR and cf *Byrne* v *Hoare* [1965] Qd R 135 (FC), where a policeman on point duty who found a gold ingot on land adjoining the road was held entitled to keep it as against his employer authority).

The second situation arises when goods are found upon land which is occupied by someone other than the finder (or, of course, the goods' owner). In certain circumstances, the occupier's occupation of the land or premises will have conferred upon him an earlier possession over lost goods situated thereon than that of the finder who eventually comes on to the land and picks the goods up. Such prior possession can exist even though the occupier was unaware of the presence of the goods on his land. Certainly the occupier will have acquired such earlier possession when the goods are buried on the land, or attached to it in a manner which suggests that he is asserting exclusive control over the place in question: *Waverley Borough Council* v *Fletcher* [1995] 3 WLR 772 and see, for example, *South Staffordshire Water Co* v *Sharman* [1896] 2 QB 44, where workmen who found gold rings as a result of carrying out instructions to clean out a pool on the water company's land were held not entitled to retain the rings as against the water company, their employer. Where the goods have been found merely lying on the premises, and the premises are of a kind to which the public are permitted access, the occupier does not obtain a superior possessory right by virtue of the fact of his occupation alone unless he has 'manifested an intention to exercise control over the building and the things which may be in or on it' (*Parker* v *British Airways Board* (above) per Donaldson MR); see also *Waverley Borough Council* v *Fletcher* (above). Such an intention may be difficult to establish, as the *Parker* case itself demonstrates. There a traveller who found a gold bracelet on the floor of an executive lounge at Heathrow Airport was held entitled to retain it as against the defendants, who were the occupiers of the lounge. The nature of the premises, the degree of public access and the quality of the control over the area exerted by the occupiers were such that the Court of Appeal felt unable to conclude that the occupiers had asserted any superior possession over the lost article, prior in time to that of the finder himself. In so holding, the court followed the decision in *Bridges* v *Hawkesworth* (1851) 21 LJQB 75 (see also the Canadian case of *Kowal* v *Ellis* (1977) 76 DLR (3d) 546).

Of course, if the owner of the relevant premises has never occupied them personally before the finder discovers lost goods on or in these premises, the landowner cannot be said to have acquired a superior possession of the article (*Hannah* v *Peel* [1945] KB 509). It has also been stated obiter that a finder who was trespassing on the premises at the time of the find does not acquire any enforceable possessory right against the occupier (*Parker* v *British Airways Board* (above)), and in *Waverley Borough Council* the Court of Appeal declined to disapply the principle regarding goods found in land because the finder in excavating soil had committed a trespass.

33

Malicious Prosecution

33.1 Introduction

The tort of malicious prosecution is the commonest form of the group of torts concerned with the abuse of legal procedure. It is a tort of considerable antiquity. It dates back to the reign of Edward I. As such, the tort was developed at a time when there was no police force so it was important that the courts did not develop rules of tort law which would have the effect of discouraging people from bringing prosecutions. On the other hand the courts had to try to ensure that people were not unjustly accused of something which they had not done and then left without means of redress. The courts have tended to give greater weight to the first of these policies rather than to the second. The consequence has been that there have been very few successful actions brought in respect of alleged malicious prosecutions. Winfield and Jolowicz (*Winfield and Jolowicz on Tort* (14th ed) pp572–3) question whether this restrictive approach is still justified today. They point out that prosecutions are brought today by the police and so there is little likelihood of the police being put in fear of bringing such prosecutions by civil actions for alleged malicious prosecutions.

The limits of the tort were considered by the House of Lords in *Gregory* v *Portsmouth City Council* [2000] 1 All ER 560. While a member of the defendant council, the claimant was suspected of having abused his position by using confidential information for personal advantage. Following hearings in accordance with the council's disciplinary procedures the claimant was removed from various of

480

the council's committees, but he applied for judicial review and the decision was quashed. He sued for malicious prosecution but their Lordships decided that his action could not succeed. As Lord Steyn explained:

'In English law the tort of malicious prosecution has never been held to be available beyond the limits of criminal proceedings and special instances of abuse of civil legal process. Specifically, it has never been extended to disciplinary proceedings of any kind. On the contrary, it has been stated by the House of Lords that this tort does not extend to disciplinary proceedings. The point arose in *Calveley* v *Chief Constable of the Merseyside Police* [1989] 1 All ER 1025. The House held that there was no common law duty of care owed by a chief constable to a police officer who was the subject of disciplinary proceedings. Lord Bridge of Harwich, speaking for a unanimous House, observed: "Where no action for malicious prosecution would lie, it would be strange indeed if an acquitted defendant could recover damages for negligent investigation." … In other words, Lord Bridge observed that since the tort of malicious prosecution is unavailable it follows a fortiori that an action in negligence does not lie.'

It should be noted that there is a strong connection between this tort and the tort of false imprisonment (on which see Chapter 24, section 24.4). Where X arrests Y on a false accusation X may be liable for the tort of false imprisonment, but when Y is taken into police custody X ceases to be liable for the tort of false imprisonment. However he may be liable for the tort of malicious prosecution.

There are a number of elements to the tort of malicious prosecution and we shall now give consideration to these separate elements.

33.2 Prosecution

The claimant must show that he was prosecuted by the defendant. It is not necessary that the defendant conduct the prosecution in person, although it must be shown that the defendant took some steps to initiate the prosecution. Thus in *Martin* v *Watson* [1995] 3 WLR 318, a complainant falsely and maliciously gave a police officer information and the facts relating to the alleged offence were solely within the complaint's knowledge. As the officer could not have exercised any independent discretion as to whether to prosecute, and the false information was the reason for the prosecution, the House of Lords held that the complainant was the person responsible for the prosecution and could be sued for malicious prosecution.

Martin v *Watson* was distinguished by the Court of Appeal in *Mahon* v *Rahn (No 2)* [2000] 4 All ER 41. In the later case, when the Securities Association (SA), predecessor of the Securities and Futures Authority, was conducting inquiries into the claimants' firm of stockbrokers, it sought information from the defendant bankers. The defendants supplied certain information to the SA and sent a copy of their letter to the Serious Fraud Office (SFO). The SFO brought criminal charges against the claimants, but the prosecutions collapsed. The claimants sought damages for, inter alia, malicious prosecution. The claim failed since there was no real prospect that the claimants could prove that the defendants should properly be regarded as prosecutors.

An expert who prepares a report for the police, on the basis of which the police decide to prosecute, does not commit the tort (see *Evans* v *London Hospital Medical College* [1981] 1 WLR 184). But, if the defendant actually signs the charge sheet and states that he is prepared to give evidence, that has been held to be sufficient to constitute the initiation of a prosecution (*Malz* v *Rosen* [1966] 1 WLR 1008). The courts draw a distinction between the giving of information and the making of a charge. Where the defendant gives false information at a prosecution brought by another person, the defendant has not brought the prosecution so he has not committed the tort of malicious prosecution.

33.3 Prosecution ended in the claimant's favour

It is essential that the claimant show that the prosecution brought against him by the defendant was unsuccessful. The courts do not permit this tort to be used as a means of retrying the criminal action. Even if the conviction is obtained by fraud and there is no appeal against that conviction the claimant cannot bring an action for malicious prosecution (*Basebe* v *Matthews* (1867) LR 2 CP 684). The reason for this is that the courts are afraid that the claimant will use the civil action to retry the criminal action on the merits. In *Reynolds* v *Kennedy* (1784) 1 Wils 232 it was held that the claimant was not entitled to bring an action for malicious prosecution where he was convicted but the conviction was reversed on appeal. However, it is unlikely that this case would be followed today.

The claimant need not show that he was acquitted; all that need be shown is that the prosecution was not successful. This can be done by showing that the prosecution was discontinued with the leave of the court (*Watkins* v *Lee* (1830) 5 M & W 270), that the prosecution was non-suited (*Goddard* v *Smith* (1704) 1 Salk 21) or that the indictment was quashed because of a defect (*Jones* v *Gwyn* (1712) 10 Mod 148). It is unclear what is the effect of a nolle prosequi (which is the staying by the Attorney-General of proceedings on an indictment). In *Goddard* v *Smith* (above) it was held that the claimant could not bring such an action after a nolle prosequi, but it is unclear whether that decision will be followed today.

33.4 Without reasonable and probable cause

The claimant must show that the defendant had no reasonable and probable cause for bringing the prosecution. This is difficult for the claimant to do because the burden of proof is on him and he is required to prove a negative. There is no distinction between what is reasonable and what is probable (*Herniman* v *Smith* [1938] AC 305). In *Glinski* v *McIver* [1962] AC 726 Lord Devlin stated that it need not be shown that the defendant thought that it was probable that the claimant would be convicted; instead it must be shown that the defendant did not have reasonable grounds for thinking that there was a case to be tried.

The requirement that there was no reasonable and probable cause for the prosecution involves the consideration of two distinct questions. The first is: did the defendant actually believe that there was a case for the initiation of a prosecution? This is a subjective test and is a question to be answered by the jury on the basis of the facts known to the defendant at the time which he initiated the prosecution. The burden of proving lack of honest belief is on the claimant. The second question is: did the defendant reasonably believe that there were grounds for a prosecution? This time the test is an objective one and it is a question to be answered by the judge. Where the defendant has received legal advice as to whether or not to prosecute and has acted on that advice it will be very difficult for the claimant to show that the defendant did not have reasonable and probable cause (see *Abbott* v *Refuge Assurance Co Ltd* [1962] 1 QB 432).

33.5 Malice

The claimant must prove that the defendant brought the unsuccessful prosecution maliciously. This is a question of fact for the jury to decide and it is for the claimant to show that the defendant was motivated by malice. In *Glinski* v *McIver* (above) Lord Devlin said that malice 'covers not only spite and ill-will but also any motive other than a desire to bring a criminal to justice'. The fact that the defendant had no honest belief in the guilt of the claimant is evidence, but not conclusive evidence, that the defendant was actuated by malice. The issue of malice must be kept separate from the issue whether the defendant had reasonable and probable cause. The defendant may be motivated by malice yet have reasonable and probable cause.

33.6 Damage

The claimant must show that he has suffered damage as the result of the malicious prosecution brought by the defendant. In *Savile* v *Roberts* (1698) 1 Ld Raym 374 Holt CJ identified the following three types of damage which are recoverable under this tort.

Damage to reputation

Here the claimant must prove that the defendant's accusation was defamatory of him. Where the accusation is not defamatory, such as where the claimant was falsely accused of pulling the communication cord on a train (*Berry* v *British Transport*

Commission [1961] 1 QB 149), the claimant cannot recover damages for malicious prosecution.

Damage in respect of the personal security of the claimant

Such damage could consist of, for example, detention of the claimant.

Pecuniary loss

Such loss could consist of pecuniary loss such as the cost of defending the prosecution (*Berry* v *British Transport Commission* (above)).

Finally, it should be noted that where a claimant in a case of malicious prosecution seeks exemplary damages the jury is entitled to take into account the conduct of the claimant, so that, where the claimant has provoked the defendant or otherwise acted in a manner which is not acceptable, that conduct can be taken into account in the assessment of damages (*Bishop* v *Commissioner of Police of the Metropolis* (1989) The Times 30 November).

33.7 Search warrants

In *Keegan* v *Chief Constable of Merseyside Police* (2003) The Times 17 July Court the claimant alleged, inter alia, malicious procurement of a search warrant which had been executed at his home in October 1999. The judge cited from *Gibbs* v *Rea* [1998] AC 786 the four ingredients of the tort, namely: (1) a successful application for a search warrant; (2) lack of reasonable and probable cause to make the application; (3) malice; and (4) resultant damage arising from the issue or execution of the warrant. On the facts of the case ingredients (1), (2) and (4) were made out, (3) was not satisfied. The claim was dismissed as was the appeal against this decision since the law still required that where it was alleged that a warrant had been maliciously procured the claimant could succeed only if he showed that the application for the warrant was made for an improper motive. Incompetence or negligence would not suffice. Kennedy LJ added that if the present case had related to events occurring after the implementation of the Human Rights Act 1998 it would have been necessary to consider the impact of the right to respect for privacy enshrined in art 8 of the European Convention for the Protection of Human Rights and Fundamental Freedoms 1950, and the requirement of proportionality.

Index

Internet Law

Dr Charles Wild, BSc (London), LLM, PhD (Sheffield), Pg Cert HE, CPE, LPC,
Head of the University of Hertfordshire School of Law,
Head of the Centre for International Law,
Mr Stuart Weinstein, BA (Williams), JD (Columbia), Attorney-at-Law
(California, District of Columbia and New York), Solicitor
and Mr Neil MacEwan, LLB, LLM, LPC

This new text offers, for the first time, a complete review of the area of Internet law. The discussion commences with an analysis of e-contracts, ranging from details of their formation, on-line terms and conditions through to a consideration of associated jurisdictional and choice of law issues. In addition, e-finance is considered, focusing on the use and regulation of credit cards on the Internet together with an evaluation of other methods of payment, including Smart Cards and electronic money. The text also covers intellectual property and data protection issues which specifically arise from the transfer and subsequent utilisation of data on the Internet, including responses in the form of cryptography, privacy enhanced technology and regional legislative responses. Finally, more specific topics such as domain names and spam will be included so as to provide the student with comprehensive coverage of this dynamic and challenging area of law. Whilst the legal content is UK based, the combination of UK, US and EU authors ensures that every aspect of this global subject is dealt with from a cross-jurisdictional perspective. An essential text for any student studying this subject or anyone interested in issues surrounding the Internet.

For further information on contents or to place an order, please contact:

Customer Services
Old Bailey Press
at Holborn College
Woolwich Road
Charlton
London
SE7 8LN

Telephone: 020 8317 6039
Fax: 020 8317 6004
Website: www.oldbaileypress.co.uk
E-Mail: customerservices@oldbaileypress.co.uk

ISBN 1 85836 573 2
Soft cover 246 x 175 mm
400 pages approx
£15.95
Due September 2005

Revision Aids

Designed for the undergraduate, the 101 Questions & Answers series and the Suggested Solutions series are for all those who have a positive commitment to passing their law examinations. Each series covers a different examinable topic and comprises a selection of answers to examination questions and, in the case of the 101 Questions and Answers, interrograms. The majority of questions represent examination 'bankers' and are supported by full-length essay solutions. These titles will undoubtedly assist you with your research and further your understanding of the subject in question.

101 Questions & Answers Series

Only £7.95 Published December 2003

Constitutional Law
ISBN: 1 85836 522 8

Criminal Law
ISBN: 1 85836 432 9

Land Law
ISBN: 1 85836 515 5

Law of Contract
ISBN: 1 85836 517 1

Law of Tort
ISBN: 1 85836 516 3

Suggested Solutions to Past Examination Questions 2001–2002 Series

Only £6.95 Published December 2003

Company Law
ISBN: 1 85836 519 8

Employment Law
ISBN: 1 85836 520 1

European Union Law
ISBN: 1 85836 524 4

Evidence
ISBN: 1 85836 521 X

Family Law
ISBN: 1 85836 525 2

For further information or to place an order, please contact:

Mail Order
Old Bailey Press at Holborn College
Woolwich Road
Charlton
London
SE7 8LN

Telephone: 020 8317 6039
Fax: 020 8317 6004
Website: www.oldbaileypress.co.uk
E-Mail: mailorder@oldbaileypress.co.uk

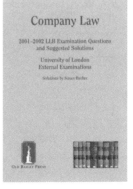

Unannotated Cracknell's Statutes for Use in Examinations

New Editions of Cracknell's Statutes

Only £11.95   Due 2005

Cracknell's Statutes provide a comprehensive series of essential statutory provisions for each subject. Amendments are consolidated, avoiding the need to cross-refer to amending legislation. Unannotated, they are suitable for use in examinations, and provide the precise wording of vital Acts of Parliament for the diligent student.

Company Law
ISBN: 1 85836 563 5

Equity and Trusts
ISBN: 1 85836 589 9

Constitutional & Administrative Law
ISBN: 1 85836 584 8

European Union Legislation
ISBN: 1 85836 590 2

Contract, Tort and Remedies
ISBN: 1 85836 583 X

Family Law
ISBN: 1 85836 566 X

Criminal Law
ISBN: 1 85836 586 4

Land: The Law of Real Property
ISBN: 1 85836 585 6

Employment Law
ISBN: 1 85836 587 2

Law of International Trade
ISBN: 1 85836 582 1

English Legal System
ISBN: 1 85836 588 0

Medical Law
ISBN: 1 85836 567 8

Revenue Law
ISBN: 1 85836 569 4

For further information or to place an order, please contact:

Customer Services
Old Bailey Press at Holborn College
Woolwich Road, Charlton
London, SE7 8LN
Telephone: 020 8317 6039
Fax: 020 8317 6004
Website: www.oldbaileypress.co.uk
E-Mail: customerservices@oldbaileypress.co.uk

Old Bailey Press

The Old Bailey Press Integrated Student Law Library is tailor-made to help you at every stage of your studies, from the preliminaries of each subject through to the final examination. The series of Textbooks, Revision WorkBooks, 150 Leading Cases and Cracknell's Statutes are interrelated to provide you with a comprehensive set of study materials.

You can buy Old Bailey Press books from your University Bookshop, your local Bookshop, directly using this form, or you can order a free catalogue of our titles from the address shown overleaf.

The following subjects each have a Textbook, 150 Leading Cases, Revision WorkBook and Cracknell's Statutes unless otherwise stated.

Administrative Law
Commercial Law
Company Law
Conflict of Laws
Constitutional Law
Conveyancing (Textbook and 150 Leading Cases)
Criminal Law
Criminology (Textbook and Sourcebook)
Employment Law (Textbook and Cracknell's Statutes)
English and European Legal Systems
Equity and Trusts
Evidence
Family Law
Jurisprudence: The Philosophy of Law (Textbook, Sourcebook and
    Revision WorkBook)
Land: The Law of Real Property
Law of International Trade
Law of the European Union
Legal Skills and System
    (Textbook)
Obligations: Contract Law
Obligations: The Law of Tort
Public International Law
Revenue Law (Textbook,
    Revision WorkBook and
    Cracknell's Statutes)
Succession (Textbook, Revision
    WorkBook and Cracknell's
    Statutes)

Mail order prices:	
Textbook	£15.95
150 Leading Cases	£12.95
Revision WorkBook	£10.95
Cracknell's Statutes	£11.95
Suggested Solutions 1999–2000	£6.95
Suggested Solutions 2000–2001	£6.95
Suggested Solutions 2001–2002	£6.95
101 Questions and Answers	£7.95
Law Update 2004	£10.95
Law Update 2005	£10.95

Please note details and prices are subject to alteration.

To complete your order, please fill in the form below:

Module	Books required	Quantity	Price	Cost
		Postage		
		TOTAL		

For the UK and Europe, add £4.95 for the first book ordered, then add £1.00 for each subsequent book ordered for postage and packing.

For the rest of the world, add 50% for airmail.

ORDERING

By telephone to Customer Services at 020 8317 6039, with your credit card to hand.

By fax to 020 8317 6004 (giving your credit card details).

Website: www.oldbaileypress.co.uk

E-Mail: customerservices@oldbaileypress.co.uk

By post to: Customer Services, Old Bailey Press at Holborn College, Woolwich Road, Charlton, London, SE7 8LN.

When ordering by post, please enclose full payment by cheque or banker's draft, or complete the credit card details below. You may also order a free catalogue of our complete range of titles from this address.

We aim to despatch your books within 3 working days of receiving your order. All parts of the form must be completed.

Name

Address

E-Mail

Postcode

Telephone

Total value of order, including postage: £

I enclose a cheque/banker's draft for the above sum, or

charge my   ☐ Access/Mastercard   ☐ Visa   ☐ American Express

Cardholder: ....

Card number

☐☐☐☐ ☐☐☐☐ ☐☐☐☐ ☐☐☐☐

Expiry date   ☐☐☐☐

Signature: ....Date: ....